ISBN 978-1-330-03210-7
PIBN 10008675

For support please visit www.forgottenbooks.com

# 1 MONTH OF
# FREE
## READING

at

## www.ForgottenBooks.com

By purchasing this book you are eligible for one month membership to ForgottenBooks.com, giving you unlimited access to our entire collection of over 700,000 titles via our web site and mobile apps.

To claim your free month visit:

www.forgottenbooks.com/free8675

# Similar Books Are Available from
# www.forgottenbooks.com

# Poet Lore

## A Magazine of Letters

EDITED BY

CHARLOTTE PORTER
HELEN A. CLARKE

COMPILED BY

FRANK R. HOLMES

## Volume 5

## 1893

AMS REPRINT COMPANY
NEW YORK, N. Y. 10003

Δ
11453.5 (5)

**AMS REPRINT COMPANY**
**New York, N. Y. 10003**

*Printed in U.S.A.*

# INDEX.

POET-LORE

Vol. V.

————wilt thou not haply ſaie,
Truth needs no colloure with his cullour fixt;
Beautie no penſell, beauties truth to lay:
But beſt is beſt if neuer intermixt.
Becauſe he needs no praiſe, wilt thou be dumb?
Excuſe not ſilence ſo, for't lies in thee,
To make him much outliue a gilded tombe:
And to be praiſed of ages yet to be.
Then do thy office ————

No. 1.

# JOHN RUSKIN AS LETTER-WRITER:

## WITH EXTRACTS FROM HITHERTO UNPUBLISHED LETTERS.

ALIKE by the splendor of his genius and the greatness of his achievement, John Ruskin occupies chief place among the ethical writers of the Victorian era. Long years since, the 'Seven Lamps of Architecture' came as a new revelation to many young and inquiring spirits; while those who had, some sixteen years previously, responded to the passionate note of 'Sartor Resartus,' found themselves prepared for this new voice, — none the less, perhaps, in that its tones rippled more peacefully to their ears. Timorous mortals were roused into unwonted activity at the daring audacity of the new teacher; but young and enthusiastic readers felt that a prophet had arisen in Israel, who would once again lead them out of the bondage of routine and formalism into wider and ampler lands of promise. Years passed; and the author of 'Modern Painters' and the 'Seven Lamps' surpassed even the dazzling promise of his youth, becoming, in the fulness of the days, a kind of spiritual guide to many a soul wandering in the labyrinth of contending opinions, or almost lost in "sunless seas of Doubt." With the death of Carlyle, it was tacitly acknowledged that the mantle of Elijah had fallen upon Elisha ; and Ruskin naturally, as by a sort of divine right, stepped into the place vacated by the master-mind of the century.

In his day Ruskin has played many parts. Wayward and capricious, he at times reaches the verge of eccentricity ; yet the strange beauty of his diction, and his noble and fearless advocacy of Truth and Justice, appeal even to those who have not failed to note many seeming contradictions and intolerances. Yet there is one aspect of his work in which he is not perhaps fully known, and that is as " letter-writer." Possibly few men of the century, save and excepting Carlyle, have been more voluminous letter-writers ; and what is more to the point, Ruskin's letters are a distinct addition to our human experience, are more or less of a self-revelation, and are an essential part of his life-history. That he himself feels this to be so is evident from some words of his own, where, in addressing a correspondent so recently as 1890, he says : "You may print this beginning (and the *end* I shall print myself if you do not) when and wherever you like ; as anybody else may, whatever I write, at any time, or say — *if only they don't leave out the bits they don't like.*"

Concerning this aspect of Mr. Ruskin's work, I have now before me a beautifully got-up little book (the rarity of which will be evident when I say that only half-a-dozen copies have been privately printed, and that these are marked at the bottom of the title-page " not for sale "), entitled " Letters upon Subjects of General Interest from John Ruskin to Various Correspondents." These letters — six-and-thirty in all — are but a tithe of the number their author must have written in the course of his long career ; but they are full of suppressed fire, and luminous with genius. Some four of them only have as yet been made public, — one of these four appearing in POET-LORE for July, 1891 (vol. iii. pp. 361, 362). I purpose, therefore, giving the readers of this magazine some account of them, making full extracts from such of the letters as have not hitherto been published.

Looking over these letters, one notes at once how Mr. Ruskin is ever revealing himself. Here we can trace his likes and dislikes, dashed off at a white heat, in apparent carelessness as to result, so long only as the Truth is made visible. We note, too, the generous nature of the man, as revealed in many side-lights of his character; while none the less apparent are the little prejudices and idiosyncrasies that make up the lives of great as of small. It is good, also, in these days, to find out — what, indeed, never wanted finding out — that Mr. Ruskin practised what he preached, as witness the following : —

" I hear that my people have been practising it on the plates, by beating down the printers. Would you kindly send me word what the printers ought to have, for good and careful printing, and I will see about it. . . . I believe —— must have kept some of their men at home to finish this. I am very much obliged to them, and should like the printers who stayed in to do it to have half-a-crown each, from me, for a holiday present. Will you kindly give orders to that effect ? "

Some of these letters, as may be anticipated, deal with his own work. Here is one such, dated June, 1849, which will be acceptable to all possessors of the original edition of the ' Seven Lamps of Architecture.'

" I have seen, with much pleasure, the favourable notice of the ' Lamps ' in the London journals ; for considering the way in which the book clashes with many wide interests and received opinions, I had not hoped for so kind a reception of it ; but as none of the reviewers appear to have understood the purpose and value of the illustrations, I think it right that you at least should have it in your power to give some answer to any verbal objections that may be made to their apparent rudeness.

" I have been a little too modest in the preface — and had calculated too much on the reader's discovery of what I ought to have told him : namely, that though indeed many portions of the plates on which I had spent considerable time, have, owing to the softness of the steel, ended in a ' blot,' yet, such as they are, they are by far the most sternly faithful records of the portions of architecture they represent which have ever yet been published ; and I am persuaded that, in course of time, this severe truth will give them a value far higher than that which is at present set upon plates of more delicate execution. . . . The degree of fidelity of the drawing, in Plate VI. of the 'Seven Lamps,' of a single arch of this church [San Michele of Lucca] I can only relate to you by a particular instance. Just above the head of the strange long-eared quadruped at the top of the arch, the sloping border of the block of stone out of which he is cut is seen to become thicker, and to be divided by a line which looks like a mistake. In that place, the block of serpentine above did not fit exactly into its place, and the builder has fitted in a thin wedge-shaped bit of marble to fill up the gap; which is marked by the double line. In like manner, it will be noticed that the partition between this quadruped and the horseman in front of him is double, while all the other partitions are single bars of marble — this also is *fact*. Such a degree of accuracy as this may perhaps at first appear ludicrous — but I have always held it for a great principle that there are no *degrees* of *truth;* and from habit I have made it just as easy to myself to draw a thing truly as falsely. The accuracy of the other plates, excepting those specified as taken from somewhat obscure Daguerreotypes, is not less; and I believe a time will come when even their execution will be thought better of than it is at present. That, however, I contentedly leave to public judgment. One point, by the bye, should be noticed, that, as the plates were all of fragments, I did not think it necessary to risk losing some of their accuracy by reversing them on the steel — and they are therefore reversed in the impression.

Very truly yours,

J. RUSKIN.

In some of these letters we get delightful glimpses of the great art critic's attitude toward questions then stirring the public mind; and many quaint touches and quiet strokes of humor come into play. Take the following, for example: —

THUN, SWITZERLAND, Aug. 18th [1859].

MY DEAR ——: I am very much helped in all ways when I find anybody cares for me at all. . . . I must say in writing first, I did not say that political economy of mine was 200 (did I say *two?* perhaps *one*—allowing for steam—would have been enough) years in advance of the age, because I thought it either my own best work, or a good book absolutely: but simply because, as far as it goes, it is founded on principles which it will take the world still another one hundred years to understand the eternity of. If you look at the *Galignani* of to-day, you will see it gravely stated as a great and recent discovery, in a Russian journal, that the interests of a nation are not to be sacrificed to those of an individual. In another one hundred years England may discover that human beings have got souls, which are the eminently Motive part of the Animal ; and that to get as much Material result as you can out of the animal, his soul or Heart must be in a healthy state — also his stomach (including liver and intestines) ; and his brains not in a state of congestion. Political Economists of this age fancy they can reason about men without their souls as mathematicians do about lines — as length without breadth. But they are slightly wrong in this matter, for the mathematician reasons on his line in Ideal perfection : and they on humanity in Ideal and even more impossible Truncation. They have founded a vast series of abstruse calculations, made with profound skill and accuracy, on the original hypothesis that a triangle has only two sides. I would have taken up these subjects more seriously, were it not still in question with me how far certain truths connected with them *can* be spoken in the present state of the public mind. It is often impossible, often dangerous, to inform people of great truths before their own time has come for approaching them ; and there is much which people will one day know as well as their alphabets, which I should be sorry to tell my class at the Working Men's College at present. Meanwhile it will be very naughty of you to growl at me and my book, while I am thus muzzled. But you may have your go at it (for I shall write nothing more on such matters for some time to come), till I can paint a little better at all events. I'm very busy with clouds and colours, and in a state of disgust with my and everybody else's country which makes me perforce dumb.

And we have been all* well on this journey. I was nearly made seriously ill by the German frescoes, it was as bad as living in Bedlam or a hospital for cretins — to look at Cornelius's† things long : but I got little consolatory peeps at Titians and such things, which the Germans hang out of the way in corners, and so got over it.

Nice sensible discussions you're having in England there about Gothic and Italian, are n't you ? And the best of the jest is that besides nobody knowing which is which, — there is not a man living who can build either. What a goose poor Scott ‡ (who will

---

* " All ; " that is, himself and parents. See ' Præterita,' vol iii. p 26.

† Cornelius, — a celebrated German painter (born 1784), who executed a number of frescos at Munich.

‡ Referring to Mr. Gilbert Scott, and his design for the Foreign Office. (See ' Arrows of the Chace,' vol. i pp. 144, 145 )

get his liver fit for *pâté de Strasbourg* with vexation) must be, not to say at once he 'll build anything.

Always affectionately yours,

J. RUSKIN.

This collection of letters would hardly be complete without a word to that remarkable man, Mr. Rawdon Brown, — so great a student of Venetian archives, and historian of Venice, where indeed he lived for the best part of his life.   Here it is : —

DENMARK HILL, May 10, 1862.

DEAR MR. BROWN, — I can't write letters just now.   I am always tired, somehow, but I mean to take your advice, and hope to get round a little, yet.   I have no house of my own, not even rooms ; and living with two old people, however good, is not good for a man.   I should have tried to get abroad again before this, but found they had let all the Turner drawings get mildewed at the National Gallery during its repairs.   So I stayed to get the mildew off as well as I could, and henceforward I've done with the whole business ; and have told them they must take it off themselves, next time, or leave it on — if they like.   I shall not enter the Exhibition ; it is merely a donkey-race among the shopkeepers of the world. . . . I do not care the least about people's religious opinions.   What I meant to say was, that for a man who has once at any time had any hope of life in another world, the arrival at conviction that he has nothing to look for but the worn-out candle end of life in this, is not at first cheerful. . . . This letter was begun, with a better pen, three weeks ago.   Since then, my discomforts have come to a climax and, I think, to an end (one way or another, for I feel so languid that I'm not sure I'm not dying), but to an end of better comfort, if I live.   For the only people whom I at all seriously care for, in this British group of islands * and who, in any happy degree of reciprocity, seriously care for me (there are many who care for me without my caring — and *vice versa*) — wrote three days ago to offer me a little cottage dwelling house, and garden, and field, just beside their own river, and outside their park wall : — and the river being clear and brown, and rocky ; the windows within sight of blue hills ; the park wall having no broken glass on the top ; and the people, husband and wife, and two girls and one boy, being all in their various ways good and gracious ; I've written to say I'll come, when I please ; which will, I suppose, be when I want rest and quiet, and get the sense of some kindness near me.   Mean-

* This is the family referred to in ' Præterita,' vol. iii. pp. 103, 113, 178, 179, etc.

time, I am coming, if it may be as far towards *you* as Milan, to see the spring in Italy once more. But I don't think I can come to Venice, even to see *you*. I should be too sad in thinking — not of ten — but of twenty — no, sixteen years ago — when I was working there from six in the morning till ten at night, in all the joy of youth.

Ever affectionately yours,

J. Ruskin.

Eminently characteristic this — but oh, the pity of it! Thirty years have passed since these words were written; yet happily the master is still with us, albeit the burden of life now is lying heavily upon him.

*William G. Kingsland.*

London, England.

(To be continued.)

---

# GENTLE WILL, OUR FELLOW.

Writ in 1626 a. d. by John Heminge, Servant of His Gracious Majesty King Charles I.; edited in 1892 a. d. as "All, though feigned, is true" by F. G. Fleay, Servant of all Shakespearian Students in America, England, Germany, or elsewhere.

---

### To the General Reader.

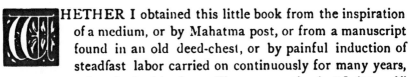

HETHER I obtained this little book from the inspiration of a medium, or by Mahatma post, or from a manuscript found in an old deed-chest, or by painful induction of steadfast labor carried on continuously for many years, matters not to inquire in this place. The one question is, "Is it true?" to which I answer it is truer than most histories, and wellnigh as true as the most truthful of fictions; truer than Macaulay, and wellnigh as true as 'Robinson Crusoe;' though not nearly so true as 'Tom Jones,' 'Don Quixote,' or 'King Lear.' There is not a statement in it for which there is not evidence enough to gain admission into the most accurate of biographies, were it written of any man other than Shakespeare, with regard to whom alone is it the fashion to require the same amount of logical evidence, if the date of a play is in question, as if some physical law in Nature had to be demonstrated. Nevertheless, I put it forth as a fiction in form, however true in substance, — no other method being open to me to avoid thorny paths of controversy, which would lead me astray from my main object, which is to place in your hands the results of long and wearisome investigation, apart from the arguments which serve as their foundation, which may be found by whosoever cares to track them in the four volumes of my larger work. I need hardly say that no other such book already exists : had there been one, I should have been the last to add to the ever-growing cairn which hides, while it glorifies, the fame of our ever-living poet. Nor have I any pretence to the position of a creative maker of fiction ; the motto of the book is, if not " all is true," at any rate " all would be true."

*F. G. F*

LONDON, May, 1892.

---

TO THE MOST NOBLE

WILLIAM EARL OF PEMBROKE,

Lord Chamberlain to the King's most excellent Majesty.

RIGHT HONORABLE,

*Whilst I study to be thankful for the indulgence you have used to the late issue of the Remains of your servant Shakespeare,* I have also studied how I might best fulfil your gracious command to set down such particulars concerning his life, and especially his plays, while with us here in London, as might enable the general reader to peruse the same in that order in which they were presented on our stage, and at the same time to distinguish what portions of the plays as issued by us were not wholly from his own hand. That we could not do this while printing the plays themselves was irksome to us, but unavoidable. For in the first place we had to put out the copy, being of such magnitude, unto divers printers, in order that the book might be completed within a reasonable time ; and these men, having miscalculated their copy, made a sad confusion in their paging, as may be seen at the ends of the plays of ' Romeo and Juliet ' and of '2 Henry IV.' in the printed copies, moreover, some plays did not come to our hands in time for insertion in their proper places, they having been entered to other men, and we having to buy of them the right to insert them in our book.   For some indeed, ' Pericles ' and ' The Yorkshire Tragedy,' their possessor, Pavier, would not come to our terms by any means and we had to leave them out altogether.   Then again the separation into Comedies, Histories, and Tragedies stood in the way of such an order of arrangement by way of time as Ben Jonson had given us in his Folio; and yet the division we used, making three exact volumes, was in many ways a convenient one.   So it came to pass that two of these parts were put forth without any order, while in the third we placed the plays in the order of the events narrated. Now as to the matter of authorship we thought it good to include, as far as we could, every play in which our friend and fellow had had a hand at all; for we thought it pity that anything of his should be lost, and we thought it matter of public notoriety that he had been in his earlier time a coadjutor of other men and a cobbler of other men's plays for new performance.   This indeed is more to his credit than otherwise: no man works in his trade so well as he that hath served his apprenticeship thereto ; and we never dreamed that any could be so obtuse or dull as to suppose that such a play as the first part of ' Henry VI.,' in which the very groundlings know the difference between the opening scene by Marlowe and the Talbot death-scene by Shakespeare, could be by us intended to be set out as by Shakespeare alone.   In one thing I own we were ill-advised: we ought to have informed the reader that some of the later plays were not in all parts as Shakespeare left them, but had been reformed by Beaumont, Middleton, and others.   Yet we could not put them forth as in their original copies; for these had been burned in the unfortunate fire at the Globe, and we were driven perforce to use such copies as we had at the Blackfriars, — which, being suited to a more worthy audience, had been somewhat abridged to make room for masks and dances and songs.   Moreover, the songs in ' Macbeth,' being taken from such a well-known play as Middleton's ' Witch,' and the extreme likeness of the ' Tempest ' mask to Beaumont's other mask, told the story for us to those that know in such matters: and what matter for the others ?   We looked for an audience fit but few. But all this will more fully appear in the slight work which I have now the honor to submit to your Lordship's kindly indulgence ; and which, if it come to the press now, I beseech your honorable Lordship to allow to be dedicated to you: if it do not, I hope it may hereafter meet with as favorable a patron to your late servant, but I know not where such is to be found.

Your Lordship's most bounden

*John Heminge.*

At my house in ALDERMANBURY, Christmas.

[It appears from the contents of the following book that this letter was written in 1626, when Jonson was paralyzed and not expected to recover: on his restoration to health the work was probably thrown aside and meant to be published at his death; but Heminge died first by some years. I must add that much of the language and all the punctuation and dates have been accommodated to our modern method by me. — *F. G. F.*]

I. SHAKESPEARE IN THE SERVICE OF THE EARL OF LEICESTER AND OF LORD STRANGE.

NIGH twenty years since, in the autumn of 1587, I with my fellows, then servants to the noble Earl of Leicester, was playing at the town of Stratford upon Avon. We had in the year before this travelled through many parts of Europe, having followed the noble Earl to the Low Countries; after that been commended by him to the King of Denmark, Frederick the Second; and from that gracious King to Christian the first, the elector of Saxony. This was in 1586; we were at Dresden in October. We then returned to London, where we acted in January of the next year; but we could get no great number of spectators: the two great companies, Her gracious Majesty's and the Lord High Admiral's, with their new poets, Master Greene and Master Marlowe, were so run after that any other company had but poor picking after they were served. We had no poet who could raise his vein on the stilts of 'Tamberlaine,' or utter such brave words as the furious Orlando: and so, as the weakest must needs go to the wall, we thought it better to travel than play at a loss in London; and in our travel we came, as I have said, to Stratford upon Avon: and then for the first time I saw William Shakespeare.

He was then some three and twenty years of age, having been, as I afterwards learned, baptized 26 April, 1564; but, although so young, had a wife and three children: his wife was some eight years older than he was, and, though I saw little by her, methought she was inclined to be shrewish. Maybe untoward circumstances had soured her temper: for they were but poorly off when Shakespeare (or gentle Will as we were wont to call him) offered to join our company. Indeed, a man must have been very poor or very wretched to take up with such a band of stragglers as we were then, little better than the Earl of Essex' men or L. Chandos', and noway to be compared to Her Majesty's or the Admiral's. Little did we think that one who came to London with us so poor should become a wealthy burgess of his native place, the friend and poet of my Lord Southampton, one of the chief sharers in the finest theatres in London, and, as Master Jonson hath said, a "Star of poets," who deserves the homage of all the stages in Europe.

For about two years we led this wandering life, acting in London when we could, but in the country for the most part, when the death of our noble patron, the Earl of Leicester, in September, 1588, left us to seek for a new lord. Just in the nick Master Edward Alleyn, the famous founder of the College of God's Gift, at Dulwich, was seeking how to make up a company for my Lord Strange. Ned Alleyn, as we always called him, was a shrewd man with a quick eye to business, and what does he do but straight buys me up all the playbooks and apparel and properties, which had belonged to the Earl of Worcester's men, whose lord died in February, 1589, and with these he sets us up in London; acting one while at the Curtain which was then one of the two great theatres, at another while at the Cross Keys innyard. After a short time we began to prosper under Ned's management, to which his unparalleled acting contributed not a little : moreover he got Master Wilson to write plays for us, to the no slight annoyance of Master Robert Greene, who was still the chief writer for the Queen's men, and also Master George Peele. But neither the witty jests of the one nor the humorous characters of the other could have sufficed to bombast out the blank verse, of which Kit Marlowe had set the fashion, had they not had a coadjutor in gentle Will. It were useless to give a list of the many plays in

which he aided these poets, seeing that in our late issue of his
plays we have thought fit not to preserve them: indeed many of
them were lost, and in some of those that remained he had replaced
the lines of his early tutors by better of his own, as you will see
hereafter.   But if you are curious in this matter you may find in
the stolen copies of his ' Romeo' and his ' Merry Wives of Windsor '
some of the lines he thus replaced, and enough is as good as a feast
in this matter.   I say not this in disparagement of the worthies of
those times, but since gentle Will and rare Ben, to say nothing of
Beaumont, Fletcher, Massinger, Webster and the rest, who have
since graced our stage with their rare productions, it were mere
folly to expect a reader to spend his time on these infants of our
scarce-grown theatre.   The only poet of that time worthy to be
named with the giants of later growth was Kit Marlowe the " dead
shepherd," so dear to our Will, as those who have read his comedies well know; and to his joining with our company, we are
not yet come.

There is only one matter connected with this time that I need
notice here: in November, 1589, our company, together with my
Lord Admiral's, were inhibited by the Lord Mayor for " handling
in our plays certain matters of Divinity and State."   My Lord
Admiral's men thereon left playing; but, seeing that neither the
Paul's boys nor the Queen's men, who had brought Divinity and
Master Marprelate on the stage, were included in the inhibition,
we did not think fit to obey an order so manifestly partial and
unjust; and accordingly we played at the Cross Keys that same
afternoon.   The Lord Mayor pretended that he could not hear of
those other players; but as immediately after our " contempt," as
he was pleased to call it, he prohibited " all playing " till Lord
Burghley's pleasure should be further known ; and as the orders
for the licensing of plays, made within a week from the time of his
committing two of our fellows to the Comptor, applied to all the
companies alike ; it is certain that the Council did not regard the
matter with the same eyes as my Lord Mayor.   The whole stir
was originated by that pestilent reprobate Parson Robert Greene,
who was jealous of our growing advancement and in one of his

later libellous paperbucklers, — as he was wont to call his pamphlet, accused Master Wilson of " simple abusing of Scripture." This he did just a year afterwards, in November, 1590. The play which was thus set forth as offensive against Divinity was ' Fair Em; ' but the real offence was that in it Wilson, who had till then been acting in the adulterous parson's plays for the Queen's men, and who indeed had brought this scurrilous knave to that company, had brought him in this play on the stage as Manvile. The other play which meddled with state matters was, if I remember aright, ' David and Bethsaba,' by Master George Peele, in which the matter of the late Queen of Scots was supposed to have been travestied by my Lord Admiral's men. And in truth it is not easy to read now, — much less was it to speak then, — the lament of David over Absalom, whom he had allowed to be slain by Joab, without thinking of our own Queen's sorrowing over the execution of Queen Mary.

Nothing of note do I remember that happed during the next two years; but in the Christmas of 1592 a great change ensued in the position of our company. On St. John's Day we for the first time were honored by our gracious Queen's acceptance of our service in the presentation of a play at Court for her delectation ; her own company having acted before Her Majesty on St. Stephen's Day preceding for the last time. From that day until this present our fellows have always held the chief place in all Court presentations during the reigns as well of Her late Majesty Queen Elizabeth as of her lamented successor the father of our present sovereign, whom God defend. We trust to maintain by our industry no lower room in the favor of His Majesty for the time to come.

You may be sure that the sudden change in Her Majesty's favor had no small effect on her own men, who had till then been our most fortunate rivals. They never held up their heads again, but went into the country, scarce ever showing in London after this. Nay, the chiefest of them straightway left their company and joined our own ; among them Dick Burbadge, Harry Condell, Will Sly, and Harry Cordy. To this success, which stayed always in the remembrance of our fellow Shakespeare as our battle of Agincourt, he makes allusion in the witty play of 'The Taming of the Shrew,' as he last presented it, when he makes one Sly say, "Look in the chronicles: the Slys are no rogues: we came in with Richard Conqueror;" meaning thereby that Will Sly came in with Dick Burbadge who played the part of Richard the Conqueror in that strange old half-German play of 'Alphonsus the Emperor of Germany.' These men brought with them many old plays written by Greene, Marlowe, Peele, Lodge, and other men; and Ned Allen, who was then courting Joan Woodward, stepdaughter of Philip Henslow, being the leader and a chief sharer in our company, thought it would be for our advantage, seeing that we stood so well in Court favor and had now a goodly number of plays in our possession, if we could have a theatre of our own, and not be driven to play in innyards, such as the Cross Keys, as we had often had to do; for there were at that time but two theatres about London, the Theater and the Curtain, both in Shoreditch; and four companies, the Admiral's, my Lord of Pembroke's, my Lord of Sussex', and our own: two or more of whom ofttimes desired to play on the same day at one of these theatres. So after some wrangling we determined that we would join with the aforesaid Philip Henslow and set up our rest at the Rose on the Bankside, which he had then in hand a building as a theatre. The place was convenient for us, being easy to get to by water; while the other theatres for the better sort were only to be reached on horse-back, the ways to them being miry and heavy; and it was handier to call for a sculler, when the play was over, than to hire a boy to care for one's horse, while the play was performing. Nor could we choose a nearer place, no playing being then allowed within the walls as now it is.

*F. G. Fleay.*

(To be continued.)

# SHAKESPEARE'S MIRANDA AND TENNYSON'S ELAINE.

EORGE ELIOT, speaking of Dessoir, the actor, tells us that she was very much pleased by the simplicity with which he one day said, " Shakespeare ist mein Gott ; ich habe keinen anderen Gott."

We have here an unmistakable case of "acute Shakespeare-olatry." But whether we call it simplicity or gross impiety, such praise, or indeed any praise, of Shakespeare, is superfluous and even wearisome to the ears of English-speaking people. We all believe in his supreme excellence both as a dramatic artist and as a deep-sighted interpreter of human nature ; and if we have learned to regard him as the standard by which all other competitors are to be measured, and their shortcomings ascertained, we can still conceive the possibility of a Poet-Pantheon in which more than one Immortal has a place.

Tennyson, while perhaps the best-known and most popular of contemporary English poets, has his limitations, like all the rest ; whereas the genius of Shakespeare is said to be universal.* Any comparison, therefore, between two such widely differing characters, being a comparison between the infinite and the finite, would be illogical and meaningless.

Tennyson has been accused of numerous plagiarisms which, it is supposed, constitute no inconsiderable offset against his claim to originality. Mr. Collins is not the first or only one who has observed that his poetry is constantly re-echoing the tones and thoughts of others, unconsciously to himself, it may be, but none

---

* Indeed, extravagance has gone so far as to call him the *most* universal genius ; Gervinus, following Hazlitt, says: " Es kann wenig Zweifel sein dass Shakespeare der universellste Genius war, der je lebte." This is quite as bad as Colonel Bath's eulogy in ' Amelia,' " That Shakespeare was a fine fellow. He was a very pretty poet indeed." Thackeray says: " I should like to have been Shakespeare's shoe-black, just to have lived in his house, just to have worshipped him, to have run on his errands, and seen that sweet, serene face."

the less audibly to the world.  And it would seem that nothing
is too small for him to bring home from the remotest corner of
the realm of letters ; for instance, " the tiny trumpeting gnat " is
a Tennysonian expression, but the association of gnat and trumpet
is by no means a new idea, for in the pseudo-Homeric 'Battle of
the Frogs and Mice ' we read of " gnats having large trumpets and
sounding the dreadful signal of battle."  Even 'The Princess' recalls
the story of Rasselas, for there we are told that " The Princess
thought that of all sublunary things knowledge was the best.  She
desired first to learn all sciences, and then purposed to found a
college of learned women in which she would preside."

Still, this tendency to imitation, whether intentional or not, is
no very grievous fault in Tennyson, for he has an original splendor
of his own that needs no borrowed light.  It has been said that
his reputation might rest on ' In Memoriam,' like that of Petrarch
on his ' Sonnets ; ' but the foundation of the Laureate's fame is
not so circumscribed.  In the epic grandeur of 'The Passing of
Arthur ' we almost hear " the mighty thunder-roll of Homer's
verse ; " and wherever we read in ' The Idyls of the King,' we
cannot help wondering how the Spirit of Romance could so inspire the minstrel of to-day.

When I consider the almost ethereal characteristics of my
comparison, I am reminded of Dr. Hudson's language: " It may
well be doubted whether criticism has any fingers delicate enough
to grasp them."  However, notwithstanding what has been said,
I desire to suggest a comparison, the subjects being purely
psychological and the time of action hardly more than a moment ;
in short, I am attempting, as it were, to apply the process of
instantaneous photography to the phases of the heart.

How a young woman left to her natural disposition will be-
have when she has just fallen in love, is a secret which both
Shakespeare and Tennyson have ventured to reveal, — the former
in the character of Miranda, the latter in that of Elaine ; and
the question is. which of the two artists represents the typical
woman ?

When we compare two craftsmen with a view of determining

their relative superiority, it is only right that each should be judged by his best work ; and we know that 'The Tempest' was the product of Shakespeare's maturer years, while the fifth 'Idyl of the King' belongs rather to the middle period of Tennyson's poetic life ; but taking it as a fair sample of his skill in that particular style of composition, I suppose the matter of time will not affect the merits of the question.

To begin, then, both Miranda and Elaine were reared to womanhood in total seclusion from the society of men ; that is, of men who could by any possibility have inspired them with the tender passion. And we are now to study, comparatively, the external symptoms of the process by which two susceptible young feminine hearts were made to pulsate with that curiously accelerated rhythm which flows from what Mr. Grant Allen calls "the divinest and deepest of human intuitions, — love at first sight."

Marlowe says : —

> " Where both deliberate, the love is slight ,
> Who ever loved that loved not at first sight ? "

There was no deliberation here on the part of the maidens, at least. Eros drew on them at sight, and the drafts were duly honored in both cases. It must be noted also that each was a case of *first* love at first sight, for neither had ever had an opportunity of loving before.

Lord Byron once said : " I cannot conceive why people will always mix up my own character and opinions with those of the imaginary beings which, as a poet, I have the right and liberty to draw. They do me great injustice." It is true that this mode of criticism is extremely liable to error; but it is not altogether unreasonable to look for indications of an author's feelings toward the offspring of his own imagination. However that may be, I make the point, because commentators often speak of Shakespeare's characters as if they were veritable human beings with dispositions, experiences, feelings, purposes, and even secrets wholly independent of the mind that created them. This may be called the scientific method, and proceeds upon the theory that the ideal world to which the poet translates us is fashioned on the same

3

general plan as the actual one in which we live ; that its person
ages are endowed with the same faculties and passions that w
ourselves possess, and so we have the right, and are expected t
judge them by the same standards that we apply to real men an
women. But that is losing sight of Shakespeare himself, — missin
him where he might be found ; for with all his habitual sel
suppression, he will at times betray his sympathy or antipath y
for some particular form of wisdom or folly, virtue or vice, as
exemplified in his own creations. And thus it might not be
wholly impossible to discover much of his moral and æsthetic
διάθεσις by studying the manner in which he deals, personally and
not artistically, with his different characters. For instance, it is
generally agreed that he despised Falstaff and admired Henry V.;
and why not add Miranda to the list of his favorites ?

Moreover, some commentators go the length of assuming facts
from a purely arbitrary combination of circumstances entirely outside the ostensible design of the author; for example, Mr. Paton
has argued with much earnestness and ingenuity that Macbeth was
the third murderer at the assassination of Banquo. But why
should this be a matter of argument ? Does Shakespeare ever
keep secret or leave to conjecture what is important to be known ?
On this principle of interpretation, it might be argued that inasmuch as the castle of Astolat was situated near a river, Elaine's
wakefulness after her first meeting with Lancelot was probably
caused by a sudden attack of malarial fever. Ingenuity sometimes
mistakes itself for genius, and therefore goes astray. Whether
Rosalind's voice was soft or sharp, whether Lady Macbeth's eyes
were blue or brown, whether Desdemona snored or "slept in
peace," are questions for which we have no answer, nor is it at all
likely that critical or even antiquarian research will ever throw
any light upon the subject. We must be satisfied with what the
poet chooses to give us. The ideal world of fiction has no more
to do with probabilities than a picture has. We may imagine
what lies hidden behind a painted cloud or mountain ; but the artist
can claim no credit, nor be held responsible for our imaginings.

We must conclude, then, that Miranda and Elaine felt and

acted differently, because their temperaments were different ; and these were different, because, in the wisdom of their respective creators, they were constituted differently.   This is quite obvious. Shakespeare could have made Miranda somewhat less demonstrative, or Tennyson could have represented Elaine as a little less reserved, if he had so desired ; but Miranda was purposely created outspoken yet thoroughly self-poised, while Elaine was purposely created reticent and utterly helpless in the faculty of self-control. And so the difference is at last between the poets themselves, which is no very recondite truth, after all.

Hence, according to Tennyson's conception, a maiden falling in love, under the peculiar circumstances which surrounded Elaine, is very much like a sick child ; for even when married, he tells us, she must not "lose the childlike in the larger mind."   With her, it was the first trial of a heart that had never had so much as the experience of a transient fancy ; and when the passion came, it overwhelmed her with its strange and potent influence.   The conception, as elaborated, is highly sentimental and full of tender pathos, but it is incomplete, because it fails to foretoken the nobler possibilities of developed womanhood.   And yet it may be asked, how could this be done in an undeveloped woman ?   I answer, By at least forbearing to represent her as "a form in wax" to melt and perish in the fervor of incipient passion.   Womanhood naturally begins with love ; and to have it consumed by that which should only quicken and unfold it, is at best "a great perturbation in nature."   When Elaine said to Lancelot, "I have gone mad, I love you, let me die," she ceased to be rational and became a pathological rather than a poetical subject.

> " ' Ah, sister,' answer'd Lancelot ; ' what is this ? '
> And innocently extending her white arms,
> ' Your love,' she said, ' your love, to be your wife.'
> And Lancelot answer'd, ' Had I chos'n to wed,
> I had been wedded earlier, sweet Elaine ;
> But now there never will be wife of mine.'
> ' No, no,' she cried ; ' I care not to be wife,
> But to be with you still, to see your face,
> To serve you and to follow you thro' the world.' "

There is something very pitiful in the almost frantic tone o supplication with which the girl here urges her suit; and yet w cannot exactly *sympathize* with her, because we cannot identif ourselves with one who has "gone mad."

Miranda, on the contrary, never "loses her head" in order t serve her heart. Along with plenty of common-sense and a well balanced nervous system, there is a certain dignity of mann about her which, in her intercourse with Ferdinand, she nev lays aside, nor does she ever declare her love to him until tells her, —

> "Hear my soul speak :
> The very instant that I saw you, did
> My heart fly to your service."

Then she asks, "Do you love me?" and he answers,

> "Oh Heaven, oh earth, bear witness to this sound
> And crown what I profess with kind event,
> If I speak true! If hollowly, invert
> What best is boded me, to mischief. I
> Beyond all limit of what else i' the world
> Do love, prize, honor you.

*Mir.*                    I am a fool
> To weep at what I 'm glad of.

*Ferd.*                    Wherefore weep you?

*Mir.*     At mine unworthiness that dare not offer
> What I desire to give and much less take
> What I shall die to want. But this is trifling :
> And all the more it seeks to hide itself,
> The bigger bulk it shows. Hence, bashful cunning!
> And prompt me, plain and holy innocence!
> I am your wife, if you will marry me ;
> If not, I 'll die your maid!"

She speaks of dying, but unlike Elaine, is in no hurry for t event.

But I have wandered out of my course, and must go back the beginning.

Miranda had lived from infancy on the enchanted island wi Prospero, her father ; and he was the only man she had ever see so far as her remembrance went, except the hideous Caliban, w was " not honored with a human shape." Accordingly, when Ferdinand, led on by the bewildering song of Ariel, approaches, and she lifts her eyes, at Prospero's bidding, to look upon the stranger, young and princely as he was, a sudden emotion prompts her to express herself first in a transport of amazement, and then of admiration. " What is 't ? " she asks ; "a spirit ?  I might call him a thing divine, for nothing natural I ever saw so noble." She had been accustomed all her life to hear of spirits, and as she knew nothing of men, she at once regards him as something supernatural; but wonder soon gives way to pity, and she says, —

> " Why speaks my father so ungently ?  This
> Is the third man that e'er I saw, the first
> That e'er I sighed for."

She is not addressing these words to Ferdinand, but rather speaks them unconsciously to herself.  They are not intended as a declaration of love, — that calls for a response, — but are simply the spontaneous, irrepressible utterance of deep, compassionate emotion.  Sight had awakened her good-will, because Ferdinand was endowed with all the beauty of early manhood ; the seeming unkindness of Prospero moved her sympathy, because the stranger was in great and visible distress ; and so both her fancy and her heart were ready to respond with all the quickness of a sound and sensitive nature.  In a word, she was full of life and sensibility, and could no more conceal her inner consciousness than a lily can withhold its fragrance or a star its light.  She had fallen in love without knowing it, although she made it plain enough to Prospero, if not to Ferdinand.

Is this natural or unnatural behavior for a woman in love ? According to our notions of decorum, a maiden should not be demonstrative, but should keep her love, and even her admiration, secret from all the world, until she has been formally solicited to confess it ; but possibly these notions of ours are not according to nature, and may impose undue restraint upon the natural liberty of women.  Queens and goddesses, like Dido and Kalupso, who hold themselves exempt from such restraint, enjoy a prerogative in this matter which ordinary women do not share ; and

it may have been Shakespeare's conception that the nearer a wor
approaches that exceptional state of freedom, the nearer she coi
to the true ideal of womanhood.   Miranda, as has often been
served, knew nothing of the artificial rules and customs of so
intercourse, because she had never lived in society, and coi
quently her nature must have developed to its full proportions,
biassed by the social lies that warp us from the living truth.
reveal her love was therefore as easy and natural to her as the
pression of any other feeling or emotion; and withal, there is
much sweetness and modesty and candor in her words and cond
that, allowing her, as we must do, a proportionate share of persc
beauty, we are constrained to adjudge her " the divine perfecl
of a woman," the most lovable of Shakespeare's women.

Elaine had passed her whole life at Astolat with her father ;
two brothers.

> " What know I ?
> My brethren have been all my fellowship,"

is the account she gave of herself to Gawaine ; and so she knew
little of the outside world as did Miranda.

But the great Sir Lancelot, travelling in disguise to
" Diamond Jousts" at Camelot,

> " Lost his way,
> Till as he traced a faintly-shadow'd track,
> That, all in loops and links, among the dales,
> Ran to the Castle of Astolat, he saw,
> Fired from the west, far on a hill, the towers.
> Thither he made and blew the gateway horn."

Admitted within the court, he is met by the lord of the castle ;
his two sons, Torre and Lavaine, and close behind them stept
lily maid Elaine, his daughter.   In the course of the conversat
which immediately ensues, Lancelot accepts Lavaine as his gu
for the morrow's journey, promises him the diamond, should
win it in the lists, and then suggests that he bestow it on Elai
The appropriateness of such a gift to such a maiden being go
humoredly questioned by her brother, she flushes " slightly at

slight disparagement Before the stranger knight," who thereupon takes occasion to pay a graceful compliment to her beauty.

> " He spoke and ceased : the lily maid Elaine,
> Won by the mellow voice before she look'd,
> Lifted her eyes, and read the lineaments.
>
> .    .    .    .    .    .    .    .
>
> Marr'd as he was, he seem'd the goodliest man,
> That ever among ladies ate in Hall,
> And noblest, when she lifted up her eyes.
> However marr'd, of more than twice her years,
> Seam'd with an ancient sword-cut on the cheek,
> And bruised and bronzed, she lifted up her eyes
> And loved him, with that love which was her doom."

But why so suddenly ?  Lancelot was more than twice her age. We are not told that she specially admired his character or achievements, or that she was even acquainted with them ; nor was there anything in his marred and battered face to attract, but much to repel, the favorable regard of a pure and tender-souled maiden. For whatever of nobleness his features might once have worn, they were now defiled by the traces of an unholy passion and darkened by the shadow of a guilty conscience, — blemishes which even his honorable battle-scars could not atone for.  Still she loved him at first sight.  And later in the evening, when she heard him discourse of ": court and table round," and say of Arthur, " there lives no greater leader,"

> " Low to her own heart said the lily maid,
> ' Save your great self, fair lord.' "

The fool " said in his heart," and so did Elaine, but not for foolishness.  Her childlike bashfulness was out of all proportion to her womanly instinct, and she could not help herself.  Notwithstanding the rare force and intensity of her passion, she taxed her will to smother it and kept the burden pressing on her heart.  In fact, love made her ill; and that is only saying that she was love-sick, for "all that night long his face before her lived and held her from her sleep."

We know not how Miranda slept the first night after meeting

with the Prince ; but we are well assured that her rest was undis
turbed by fever or by vision. Not so, however, with Elaine. Bu
what was she thinking about through all those sleepless hours
She was not thinking at all, but contemplating the fancied se
blance of Lancelot's face, that persistently haunted her ima
nation and "held her from her sleep." Now, this was certair
a very high compliment to Lancelot's face, if not to Elaine's go
taste.

But as I intended at the outset to do little more than sugge
the comparison here partially presented, I shall not attempt to ca
it out in all its details, for they are numerous.

The subsequent history of the two heroines reflects instructiv
light on the beginning. Miranda was destined for happiness,
Elaine for misery ; and, after all, the difference between the two
characters is probably to be sought in the different motives of
the poets. It was the difference between "a tree planted by the
water side," and the tree of which it was said, "Cut it down ; why
cumbereth it the ground ?" One artist sets out to exhibit the picture of a sweet young life unfolding into the full bloom of health
and happiness ; the other shows us a tender bud, whose promise is
soon to be overtaken by the blight and bitterness of adverse fate.
And so love was joyous emancipation to Miranda, but oppressive
bondage to Elaine.

According to Mrs. E. Lynn Linton, whose feeling and taste en-
title her to rank as an authority, "The Greek ideal of Womanhood
stands as the most beautiful in the world." And yet neither Miranda nor Elaine would ever have been "married to immortal verse"
by any Greek poet of the classic age, whether lyric, epic, or dramatic. In the Greek tragedy, and presumably in actual Greek life,
woman's love had only three serious phases ; namely, that of the
wife for her husband, that of the daughter for her father, and that
of the sister for her brother. Medea and Alkestis illustrate the
first, Antigone and Electra, the second and third, of these phases.
The sentimental attachments of young men and maidens seemed
hardly worthy of poetic treatment ; and consequently such love-
stories as 'Hero and Leander' or 'Pyramus and Thisbe' were

utterly ignored by the tragedians. But we all remember that Shakespeare made 'Pyramus and Thisbe' ridiculous, while Ovid, Marlowe, and Schiller found in 'Hero and Leander' a subject of true poetic value.

*Samuel D. Davies.*

## THE WHEEL OF FORTUNE.

MORTE ARTHURE, ll. 3250-3273; 3349-3393.

[The Thornton *Morte Arthure* is an Early English alliterative Arthurian poem, the manuscript of which dates from about 1440 A. D. The poem itself was probably composed before 1400. In the passage quoted, King Arthur has had a strange dream, and has summoned his philosophers to explain it. His dream is of the Wheel of Fortune, and of the Nine Worthies who have once been seated in honor upon it, and afterward cast down. Eight of these worthies are Hector, Alexander, Julius Cæsar, David, Joshua, Judas Maccabæus, Charlemagne, and Godfrey of Bouillon. Arthur himself is the ninth, and the dream foretells his own downfall.]

*King Arthur speaks : —*

    "THEN descends in the dale, adown from the clouds,
A duchess preciously dight in diapered weeds ;
In a surcoat of silk full wondrously hued,
With embroidery o'erlaid low to the hem,
With ladylike folds the length of a yard,
And all curiously trimmed with ribands of gold ;
With brooches and bezants, and other bright stones,
Her back and her breast were adornèd all over.
With caul and with coronal *she was* queenly arrayed,
That so comely in color were ne'er before known !
    " She whirled a wheel about with her white hands :
Revolved she all quaintly* the wheel as she would.
The rowel was red gold, with royal stones,
Covered with richness and rubies enow ;

---

* That is, cunningly.

4

The spokes were all splinted with slivers of silver,
The space of a spear-length, springing full fairly.
  " Thereon was a chair of chalk-white silver,
All checkered with carbuncles, changing of hue.
Upon the circumference, there clave kings in row,
With crowns of clear gold, that cracked in sunder.
Six were from that settle full suddenly fallen ;
Each one sate by himself, and murmured these words :
' That ever I reigned in this rout, rue I it ever ! ' "

  [A description follows of eight of the nine worthies, then King
Arthur speaks again : ]

  " She lifted me up lightly with her lean hands,
And set me softly in the see ; — the sceptre she reached me ; —
Skillfully with a comb she combed then my head,
*So* that the crisping crook reached to my crown ;
Dressed on me a diadem that full fairly was dight,
And syne proffered me a globe pight full of fair stones,
Enamelled with azure, — the earth thereon depicted, —
Circled with the salt sea on every side,
In sign that I truly was sovereign on earth.
  "Then she brought me a brand with full bright hilt,
And bade me brandish the blade : ' The sword is mine own :
Life has left many a man at its swing ;
The while thou shalt swink with the sword, it shall never fail thee !
  "Then went she with peace, — and rested when she liked, —
To the trees of the wood : richer were never !
Was no pomarie so pight by princes on earth,
Nor apparel so proud, save *in* Paradise only !
She bade the boughs bow down, and bring to my hand
Of the best that they bare on their branches so high.
They inclined at her hest, all wholly at once,
The highest of every wood, I assure you, forsooth.
She bade me spare not the fruit, but try where I liked :
' Take of the finest, thou free man,
And reach to the ripest, and riot thyself !

Rest, thou royal king, for Rome is thine own,
And I shall readily grant * thee peace at the nearest,
And pass thee the rich wine in rinsèd cups !'
   " Then she went to the well by the wood passes,
That welled all with wine, and wondrously ran ;
Caught up a cupful, and covered it fairly, —
She bade me dearly draw, and drink to herself, —
With all liking and love, that any lady should.
   " But at the mid-day, full suddenly her mood changed,
And made much menace, with marvellous words.
When I cried upon her, she cast down her brows :
' King, thou criest for naught, by Christ who made me !
For thou shalt lose this war † and all thy life after.
Thou hast lived in delight and lordship enow !'
   " She turned the wheel about, and whirled me under,
Till all my quarters the while were crushèd to pieces,
And with that chair my chin was chopped in sunder ;
And I have shivered with cold, since this chance happened me.
Then awakened I forsooth, all aweary with dreams ;
And now knowest thou my woe : explain as thou likest."

*Translated by Anna Robertson Brown.*

---

## THE DEMOCRACY OF APRILE.‡

BOTH subject and title have been assigned me by our Committee of Arrangements, and I confess that the title has been suggested by an insight more penetrating than my own; for "democracy" had not struck me as a prominent trait in this subordinate character. But I will be loyal to the quest. I will seek and find the required quality, even if it be only germinally present, and no larger than a grain of mustard-seed.

The dramatic value of Aprile in the poem is very great; for Browning uses him as a most effective foil and contrast to Para-

---

* Lit., enroll.                    † Lit., game.
‡ Read before the Browning Society of Boston, Oct. 25, 1892, by Charles G Ames.

celsus. Still greater is his value as a factor in the spiritual development of Paracelsus; for at sight and hearing of this new man, so different from himself and so phantomlike, Paracelsus becomes aware of a fatal defect in his own theory of life and in his line of conduct. He is shaken wide awake; his moral horizon is suddenly and vastly widened; best of all, a contagious impulse sets his heart beating to a new measure, yet rather wildly, and not rhythmically, because not at all adjusted to his mental habits. Thus, in this "Bohemian" Italian poet, half-mad and already dying, chance-met at the house of a Greek conjurer in Constantinople, Paracelsus encounters a good angel, — a messenger of his own higher destiny.

Let us follow the movement. Aprile himself is a weak character, — a hyperæsthetic artist, a passionate dreamer, whose sky-vaulting genius, as he too late discovers, has only landed him in a ditch. He has failed to bring anything to pass, because his active sensibility is not matched with a working will, or a habit of industry.

As he feels himself sinking into the Under-world, he seems to hear a mournful song of welcome, — a chorus of low, faint voices. but "fatal-clear," "as if," he says, —

> "As if all Poets, God ever meant,
>  Should save the world, and therefore lent
>  Great gifts to, but who, proud, refused
>  To do His work, or lightly used
>  Those gifts, or failed thro' weak endeavor,
>  So, mourn, cast off by Him forever, —
>  As if these leaned in airy ring
>  To take me ; this the song they sing :
>
>> "Lost, lost! yet come,
>>  With our wan troop make thy home.
>>  Come, come! for we
>>  Will not breathe, so much as breathe
>>  Reproach to thee!
>>  Knowing what thou sink'st beneath.
>>  So sank we in those old years.
>>  　.　　.　　.　　.　　.
>> "Must one more recreant to his race
>>  Die with unexerted powers,

And join us, leaving as he found
The world, he was to loosen, bound?

. . . . . .

" How should we clothe how arm the spirit
Shall next thy post of life inherit —
How guard him from thy ruin ?
Tell us of thy sad undoing
Here, where we sit, ever pursuing
Our weary task, ever renewing
Sharp sorrow, far from God, who gave
Our powers, and man they could not save."

Then, for the first time, Aprile discovers Paracelsus : —

" Ha, ha ! our king that wouldst be, here at last ?
Art thou the Poet who shall save the world ? "

He begs Paracelsus to sing some of the songs that are destined
to sound down the ages.

Paracelsus is still so full of himself and his own great schemes
that he not only accepts this praise as a matter of course, but takes
Aprile for one of those who is to follow in his track and reap his
sowing, or be a learner of the lore he is to leave behind. So he
proudly announces himself : —

" I am he that aspired to KNOW! And thou?
*Apr.* I would love infinitely, and be loved !
*Par.* [In scornful pity.] Poor slave ! I am thy king indeed."

Then Aprile drops into confession of his own failure and the
reasons : —

" Born a spirit, dowered even as thou,
Born for thy fate — because I could not curb
My yearnings to possess at once the full
Enjoyment, but neglected all the means
Of realizing even the frailest joy.
Gathering no fragments to appease my want,
Yet nursing up that want till thus I die."

As Aprile breaks out bewailing,

" I would love infinitely. . . . Ah, lost, lost ! "

Paracelsus betrays, through his contempt, a startled conscience : —

" Ah ! 't is some moonstruck creature, after all.
. . . Yet he seemed
To echo one foreboding of my heart."

Further on, Aprile returns to this mood of self-reproachful moralizing : —

> "Knowing ourselves, our world, our task so great,
> Our time so brief, 't is clear if we refuse
> The means so limited, the tools so rude
> To execute our purpose, life will fleet,
> And we shall fade, and leave our task undone."

The next passage from which we quote gives us Browning at his best. In answer to the challenge of Paracelsus, "Tell me what thou wouldst be," the spirit of Aprile revives and expands, and he launches into a rich and eloquent description of his artist-ambition, and the sources and subjects of his inspiration, — all saturated with his twofold passion of loving and being loved. He tells in glowing lines how he had hoped, as sculptor, to carve and cast all the fair forms of human life ; next, as painter, to give to these forms their equally fair setting in nature, as the Creator has done ; then, as poet, to pour into language all the thoughts and passions that have stirred the souls of men ; meanwhile supplying all chasms with music, —

> "Music, breathing
> Mysterious motions of the soul, no way
> To be defined, save in strange melodies."
>
> .     .     .     .     .     .
> "Last, having thus revealed all I could love,
> And having received all love bestowed on it,
> I would die: preserving so throughout my course
> God full on me, as I was full on men:
> He would approve my prayer.  'I have gone through
> The loveliness of life : create for me,
> If not for men, or take me to Thyself,
> Eternal, infinite love!'"

At the heart of this is there nothing but self-love, or self-seeking, after all?  Yet see how the altruistic principle breaks out like a fire : —

> "Could I retain one strain of all the psalm
> Of the angels, one word of the fiat of God,
> To let my followers know what such things are.
> I would adventure nobly for their sakes.

> Not these alone
> Should claim my care ; for common life, its wants
> And ways, would I set forth in beauteous hues :
> The lowest hind should not possess a hope,
> A fear, but I 'd be by him, saying, better
> Than he, his own heart's language."

In a passage full of heart-break, he asks if Paracelsus has not also felt the force of the temptations that have proved fatal to himself (that is, to Aprile), — the bewildering multitude of dazzling shapes of beauty ; the seduction of " memories, regrets, and passionate loves ; " and even the absorbing interest in " man's applause or welfare " which makes one neglect his work.

> " Say, though I fell, I had excuse to fall ;
> Say, I was tempted sorely ! "

Then comes a burst of magnanimity and disinterestedness which carries all before it : —

> " Lo, I forget my ruin, and rejoice
> In thy success, as thou ! Let our God's praise
> Go bravely through the world at last ! What care
> Through me or thee ? I feel thy breath. Why ! tears ?
> Tears in the darkness, and from thee to me ? "

So as the death-mists gather over Aprile, a fountain of tenderness opens in the heart of Paracelsus, and a new light enters his mind.

> " Love me henceforth, Aprile, while I learn
> To love ; and, merciful God, forgive us both !
> We wake, at length, from weary dreams.
> . . . . . . . .
> I too have sought to KNOW, as thou to LOVE —
> Excluding love, as thou refusedst knowledge.
> Still, thou hast beauty, and I, power. We wake :
> . . . . . . . .
> Die not, Aprile ! We must never part.
> Are we not halves of one dissevered world ?
>                   Part ? Never !
> Till thou the lover, know ; and I, the knower,
> Love — until both are saved !

It is time to ask, What is the secret or nature of the subtle spell which Aprile, all unconsciously, casts over Paracelsus? What penetrating spirit-power is this, which, even in the half-delirious speech of the dying poet, checks the contemptuous arrogance of the power-loving philosopher, and makes him docile as a child? It is the touch of human nature that makes them kin. I think that while Paracelsus at first takes his own superiority for granted, and is proudly willing that Aprile should salute him as the coming King of Men, he is soon deeply humbled by the discovery that Aprile, despite his illusions, possesses, in his very childlikeness, a quality of life and an element of wisdom which puts to shame the stronger man, convicts him of defect and folly, and compels him to change the direction of his search for light and power. In short, Paracelsus is now first brought to realize that there is, and must be, a principle more central and vital than belongs to the scientific or intellectual faculty alone.

The burning interest which Aprile feels in humanity — the democratic interest which makes him look out on the world of men as a product and reflection of the love of God — is in sharp contrast with the cold grandeur and proud isolation of spirit which have made Paracelsus contemptuous toward history, unwilling to avail himself of other men's learning, unsympathetic toward the struggles of mankind, and indifferent even to their applause. But now that he has felt the throbbing and the breaking of a human heart, his own heart thrills to the memory of one early friendship; he has been powerfully drawn toward one who loved mankind, and he too feels the need of "a world of men." Aware that the fruit of the Tree of Knowledge has turned to ashes on his own lips, he cannot help suspecting, from the new hunger of his heart, that there is also a Tree of Life, which he has yet to seek.

Turning from the dead Aprile, he now goes forth to seek the world of the living. Yet he is already spoiled for a career in such a world; he is too old, as well as too cold, to open affectionate relations with humanity. He tries to become a teacher, but he can neither be patient with stupidity nor forgiving to ill-tempered rivals. Not his deeper spirit, not the new and tender life that is slowly maturing in the inner cells of his being, but the harsh and hard crust, or rough and prickly burr, which has formed over his exterior, is what other men chiefly feel when they are in contact with him.

When at last he gasps away his breath in the hospital at Salzburg, poor, neglected, and scorned by all save Festus, the one faithful friend of his youth, it is by the ray of light which fell on his spirit twenty years before, when he wept over the dead Italian poet, that he not only reads aright the record of his own errors, but sees also that the most imperfect form of human love is a revelation of the Love which is all-perfect and eternal.

In the final colloquy with Festus, Paracelsus tells the story of his life as he sees it in the light of afterthought. "Too soon," he says, " I left the instincts of that happy time." " What happy time?" asks Festus; and Paracelsus answers, " When but the time I vowed myself to man." Then he goes on to recite how he failed, how the passion for service was weakened in him by a growing lust of power. So there grew in him a contempt for man's past, and for all methods of gradual development, — an impatience to accomplish by "power" an instantaneous or magical transformation of the world. The interview with Aprile — " the poor melodious wretch " — had made him aware of his own deep error ; as he says, —

> " Made me know One Sin
> Had spotted my career from its uprise.
> . . . . . .
> In my own heart, love had not been made wise
> To trace love's faint beginnings in mankind,
> To know even hate is but a mask of love's,
> To see a good in evil, and a hope
> In ill success; to sympathize, be proud
> Of their half-reasons, faint aspirings, dim
> Struggles for truth, their poorest fallacies,
> Their prejudice and fears and cares and doubts;
> All with a touch of nobleness, despite
> Their error, tending upward, although weak ;
> Like plants in mines, which never saw the sun,
> But dream of him, and guess where he may be,
> And do their best to climb and get to him.
> All this I knew not, and I failed."

5

Paracelsus thus owns his debt to Aprile, who had reawakened in him the altruistic instinct of his youth, — that instinct which feeds faith in the common people, and so nourishes the root of all true democracy.

When Aprile came to him, he was ready to die of despair ; and now that he is really dying, the vision of the future is darkened by a sense of error, weakness, and failure, yet in that darkness he holds fast to his restored faith in the divine destiny of humanity, and feels the support of a deathless hope.

As the strong-willed, self-sufficing, and imperious man feels himself poised above the abyss of mystery which mortals dread, the heart of a little child returns to him. Power and knowledge fail ; love and trust remain. Through Festus he is in touch with this world of dissolving phantoms, and knows that it is a human world ; through Aprile, he is in touch with a realm of higher reality, and knows that this too is a human world.

> " Festus, let my hand —
> This hand, lie in your own, my own true friend.
> Aprile!   Hand in hand with you, Aprile ! "

*Charles G. Ames.*

## A STUDY OF TENNYSON'S 'LOCKSLEY HALL' AND 'SIXTY YEARS AFTER.'

THE following study, outlined in the shape of Questions and Answers, was prepared in order to be used by a teacher in class work. As it proved successful, it may be of use and interest to others. The "answers" are not meant to be exhaustive, but explanatory and suggestive; how much help from them is desirable is left to the judgment of the teacher.

I. In what manner is the story told? Under what circumstances is it continued in 'Locksley Hall Sixty Years After'?

By the hero himself in the course of a long soliloquy, narrative, meditative, and fanciful.

In the later poem a second character is introduced, the hero's grandson, who has evidently just told him of a similar love-experience, calling his own afresh to the mind of the elder.

*Query for Discussion:* Does this added person of the drama make the later poem more dramatic than the earlier, or is there more dramatic power shown in the imagined presence of Amy and of her husband in the first ' Locksley Hall' ?

II.   Was Locksley Hall an inland seat ?   Describe the setting of the story as far as possible from the indications given in the poems, and show the relation of the scenic background to the poem itself.

See stanzas 2 (" the curlews call," flying about the " moorland," and glancing through the air like " dreary gleams "), 3 (the " sandy tracts," " ocean ridges," etc.), 6 (" the beach "), 19 (" by the waters " and " the stately ships "), 20 (" barren shore," etc.), and also the last stanza.   Notice, in the same way, all such references in ' Locksley Hall Sixty Years After ;' and in both earlier and later poems trace the probable connection of many of the images and fancies of the speaker with the seashore scenery before his eyes. For example, in stanza 7, " the centuries behind me like a fruitful land reposed," as if spoken by one facing the sea ; in stanzas 8 and 60, " dipt into the future far as human eye can see," in stanzas 61 and 62, " the heavens fill with commerce," " argosies," etc., " pilots of the purple twilight," " airy navies," and all such allusions, in both poems ; in ' Sixty Years After,' also notice in stanza 97, " Forward, backward," etc., " in the immeasurable sea," and so on, and see how all these passages are naturally suggested by the seaside situation of Locksley Hall, and how valuable they are too, in giving the reader a picture of the scene, and putting him unconsciously in sympathy with it.*

III.   What is the story of the poem ?   Sum up from the meditations of the hero what they tell of himself and his love-story, and also what light they throw on the heroines, Amy and Edith.   What is meant by the " Fairy tales of Science "?   Can you explain the symbolism of these lines near the close of the poem ? —

---

* If this study is to be used in class work, give to one member of the class the task of finding out and showing the probable poetic value of all such allusions ; to another the next question, and so on.

" Thro' the shadow of the globe we sweep into the younger day :
Better fifty years of Europe than a cycle of Cathay.
Mother-Age (for mine I knew not) help me as when life begun :
Rift the hills, and roll the waters, flash the lightnings, weigh the Sun."

In the stanzas 4–9 he reveals to us plainly his intellectual tendencies. He has a wide range of sympathies, and takes a poet's
delight in the beauties of Nature, watching many a night the constellations as they sink into the west. Notice, also, his imagery
drawn from astronomy in ' Sixty Years After,' in the stanzas referring to the dead moon, of Venus "closer on the sun," of Hesper
and Mars, and the alternate chaos and cosmos of world-systems.
His poetical temperament is also illustrated in his use of the expression, " Fairy tales of Science." It indicates that it was the
wonders and mysteries of the discoveries of science which fascinated
him, so astonishing as to be like marvellous fairy tales. He delights also to view the progress of humanity from the remotest times
to the present, — " The long result of time," — and he pictures to
himself the glorious possibilities in the future.

In the passages that follow we are introduced to his emotional
nature, as affected by his cousin Amy's acknowledgment of her
love, and her marriage. Reading his account of it through to " And
our spirits rushed together at the touching of the lips," the impression he seems to convey is that he was drawn into his love-affair
partly because it is in the course of nature to fall in love (for " In
the Spring a fuller crimson comes upon the Robin's breast," etc.),
and partly because he perceives his cousin is in love with him, —
" her eyes on all my motions with a mute observance hung."

When his disappointment comes, he is mortified by it, as if it
were a slight to his superiority, and in the following stanzas he
tries to thrust the pain of it aside. He has known the delight of
moments made golden by love, and of selfishness lost in concord of
two minds ; but his selfishness returns in full force at the first discord in the song. His outbursts are now directed against Amy, her
husband, society, peace, civilization, the temperate climate, and
womanhood in general. He calls Amy shallow, and her husband
coarse, and tortures himself with pictures of her unhappy relations

with this country clown, who, after the first gust of his passion is over, will be engrossed in the pleasures of drinking; he tells her ironically to soothe him then with her finer fancies, which will be quite lost on his stupidity, and to which the young man satirically supposes " he will answer to the purpose, easy things to understand." Then, not being able to bear the image of the two together, which his jealous imagination has brought before him, he bursts out, Othello-like, with the wish to kill her if so they may die in an embrace, and then lashes out against the artificial bonds of such marriages, pretending love where there is none, against all unnatural conventionalities and the regard for money that makes a rich fool important (" Cursed be the social wants that sin against the strength of youth," etc.).

Still consolation for himself is his desire ; and he wonders if he can divide his pleasant from his tormenting memories of Amy, fancy her dead, and love her for the love she used to bear him (his love for her not seeming to amount to much as comfort) ; but he concludes that remembering past happiness is the worst of his pangs, and so turns on Amy again, telling her to drug her memories, lest when she is awakened at night by a start of her hunting-loving husband, she may be tormented with the idea of the different life she might have had with him.   He seems to derive comfort from prophesying unpleasant things of Amy, angry that she will probably have a baby to solace her, — " a lip to drain thy troubles dry," — and make her love the father better, and forget him ; he supposes she will counsel her daughter against love-matches, and even hint at trials of her own borne by her for duty's sake.   This so irritates him that he jeers at her hypocrisy with his "Perish in thy self-contempt !" and determines to care for her no longer ; but he must do something, and he knows not what, in a day when gold is more than honor.   He would have been a warrior, — "I had been content to perish," etc., — but the days are too tame for fighting.   At the sound of his comrades' bugle-horn, the idea that they would laugh at him for being jilted rouses his scorn of Amy again, and also of womanhood in general.   Here in this temperate climate — " Here at least where Nature sickens," etc. — a woman's passion is too cool ; in the East, where suns are hotter and women more passionate, he will marry and live a life of nature, and not waste himself on books. But he likes books evidently, and he cannot deceive himself, after all ; he prefers the work of intellect, — civilization to the pleasures of the body merely. Such rest as he has pictured allures him, but does not hold him ; and he acknowledges that as from the half of the globe wrapped in night we pass to the half bathed in daylight, so we pass from the Old World to the New, and fifty years of civilized European life are better than centuries of sheltered, motionless Chinese existence. He invokes, then, the Mother Age of the world, since his own mother he knew not, to help him with her potency ; and as when in the formative period of the world she wrought upon the earth, to "rift the hills and roll the waters," etc., so may she make his paths straight, and enlighten the eyes of his imagination. Thereupon this beautiful image of his own fancy entrances him, and he congratulates himself that he has not yet lost the promise of poetic inspiration. Comforted with himself, he can now leave Locksley Hall, taking meanwhile a sombre delight in the storm that is rising, as if to avenge him, and already "roaring seaward."

As to the love-story and its consequences, we learn from the earlier poem that two cousins who have been brought up together at Locksley Hall fell in love with each other. The hero was born in the East Indies ; he never knew his mother ; and his father dying in battle, he was left an orphan to the careless guardianship of a selfish uncle. His cousin Amy's father is, we guess, lord of Locksley Hall, and the squire whom Amy's parents force her to marry is the next heir, — Amy apparently being an only child, whom her parents wish to connect in marriage with the male heir.

From the second 'Locksley Hall' we learn that upon the squire's death, sixty years later, the hero and his grandson revisit the Hall to attend the squire's funeral, and to be present as his successors at Locksley Hall, for Amy died a year after her marriage, and her husband has never married again ; while the hero has married, and having lost his son Leonard in a naval battle, it happens that Leonard's son will be the next lord of Locksley Hall.

As to the heroines of the two poems, in person and in character, we have only a few glimpses. The color of Amy's eyes, her complexion and disposition, are glanced at in stanzas 13 and 14, and in stanza 10 of the second poem. That Edith's was a stronger nature appears in stanzas 25–27 of ' Sixty Years After.'

*Queries for Discussion:* Is the emotional side of the hero as finely balanced as the intellectual side? Is his love of progress and mankind inconsistent with his regard for the past and for himself? And does this inconsistency foreshadow the doubt and discontent of ' Sixty Years After'? What light is thrown on the character of his love by his outbursts against Amy? Would it be fair to judge of Amy and her husband by what he says of them in his first anguish? In ' Sixty Years After' he says he judged them harshly. Do you agree with him altogether? Was it well for Amy to marry as she did? When obedience to parental wishes and love are in conflict, which should be followed? How would Desdemona's view of filial duty agree with Amy's? Did Cordelia believe her love and duty were altogether her father's? (See ' Othello ' and ' Lear.') But the end of the story shows that none of the hero's evil prophecies came true ; and as for the " clown," it appears that he remained constant to Amy's memory, while the hero found an Edith to console him. Whose love do you think was the greatest — Amy's, or his, or the squire's ?

*P. A. C.*

# THE CHRISTMAS MAGAZINES AND LITERARY DECAY.

FROM THE CORRESPONDENCE OF —— —— AND *

THE seasonable idea, — Christmas is being translated into all languages in the shops now, including gibberish. How strikingly is it expressed in the magazine tongue! I have been amusing myself of late, dear * * *, during this merry tide of time, in looking within the gilt and colored covers whose various pretty and unusual decorations shout " Holiday trade " at you, for the queenly, indefinable, yet unmistakable presence of Literature.

Lo! my table is spread before me with fresh and attractive wares. Here, for shining example, is the prosperous, omnipresent *Century*, prominent with timely Madonnas. Brand-new revivals these, yet they are, after all, and necessarily, but affected reflections of an art-form that is past. In such art, subject-matter and inspiration are historic, you will say, — in a sense, literary. Yes; but the word-painting which goes with these pictures throws no ray of light upon their deep-rooted sources, or on the import of the French Neo-Christian movement in art and literature. It is mere pretty letterpress for the gallery; it is not even a *catalogue raisonné*, although it wears an air of being written for the pictures, — an artificiality which makes its own proper prettiness as suspicious as rouged beauty. Verse comment on pictures, and prose comment on picturesqueness, is foremost; and what else there is may be summed up as Geography, Biography, and Philanthropy. Of course I find no fault with all this, I am hunting up the literary phenomena incident to Christmas, and more or less characteristic of all the year round. There is literary material here, a chaos of it, ready to the touch of the literary artist; but Literature herself, goddess of whom I am fain, nowhere do my eyes descry her in this favored haunt of the magazine-world, save in one of the short stories. Can she be found in the photographed inanities of " smart society," which crowd into every corner of 'Sweet Bells out of Tune' ? It is unjust to say she lurks nowhere in a serial story of which only a part is open to my quest. Her apparition may glow behind the fog of frivolous talk, and the sunsetting of the story be more radiant for them in the end; but surely her shining front does not peer forth as yet. Miss Wilkins's delicate workmanship in her " prose poem " looks somewhat like an experiment. What of Literature here? One glimpse of an averted pose, let us say. Wherein lies the difference I feel in ' My Cousin Fanny' ? Pathos, humor, delicately implied significance, the unobtrusive morality of an original yet thoroughly realistic and modern theme, moreover, — best of all, — dramatic quality. It is a prose monologue in which the speaker, who is not the writer, is as thoroughly characterized as " Cousin Fanny."

In the Christmas *Harper's* Art has first innings too, but not quite so much at Literature's expense as in *The Century*. The timely Virgin is here also ; but the consideration is of art types, a subject of intrinsic rational interest, and the article has the effect of being illustrated rather than the illustrations *articled*. Miss Wilkins again, in her ' Pastels,' heightens the literary flavor of the number, and in her witch-drama, too, although it is not as unerring a bit of work as the story form of the same theme which appeared in *Harper's* nearly a year ago. Brander Matthews's twin pieces, — ' Cameo and Pastel,' — of the dancing girls of effete Rome, and the studio dancer of effete New York, give evidence of a criticism of contemporary life which is hopeful, to say the least, of the happy discovery of those manifold varieties of American literature we yearn to find some day, says ' The Editor's Study' of the same number, in the magical ' Islands of Bimini.'

*Scribner's* and *The Cosmopolitan* yield no different literary aroma. Completely separable from the rest of *The Cosmopolitan* is Howells' ' Traveller from Altruria ; ' and other constituents of both magazines are, as in *The Century*, Art, Biography, Geography, and Philanthropy. Literature appears in the toothsome guise of Fiction ; but only here and there does the Fiction reveal Realities alive from within. There is just enough cleverness and promising workmanship to make one wish the writers' habitual or assumed fetters would fall, and untrammelled exercise make their wit at once broader and deeper-reaching, more constructive and more earnest. For Literature loves freedom better than prudence, and is likelier to descend in the reckless glory of her genius upon revolutionary ideals that are pushing their new paths into souls, than upon such carefully curbed Sunday-school bookishness as, in ' Apples of Gold,' in *Scribner's*, commends advice which tutors a wife to a life of dissimulation, and finds truth impossible in marriage because it might disturb the husband's vanity.

Ah ! but *The Atlantic* remains. Shall I not find there the goddess, — Literature ?

> Heart fear nothing, for Heart thou shalt find her
> This time herself, not the trouble behind her."

6

*The Atlantic*, like *The Forum*, makes no grab at the holiday purse by flaunting a bedizened outside, and inside it does not slave under the yoke of "timeliness" as to Madonnas; yet here, too, biography and geography bear sway in the shape of memoir and travel. Lettered and most readable is Miss Repplier's 'Wit and Humor;' still it is reminiscent bookishness, not present-day thoughtfulness. The table-talk of 'The Contributors' Club' is, let us confess, a deal better than the admired *Spectator*, but upon its plan. What there is of Literature does not possess herself of the Present; the Past is still master, and not yet father of things to be.

Gathering up my impalpable facts derived all along the ranks, from the always contemporaneous and creditable *Forum*, the ethical *Arena*, and the well-bred *Atlantic*, to the sensational department-store periodicalism of the *Ladies' Home Journal*, I thereupon rashly theorize, not that Literature is decaying, not that Utilitarianism and Frivolity have met together and parted the earth between them, not that Conservatism or Despair is the sole refuge of poor souls who love Literature, but that Literature is evolving with many a devious turn back and sidewise, modifying its whole nature the better to press forward into closer relation with life.

So biography, geography, and philanthropy, politics and sheer business, slum waifs, venal voting, and the tariff, sanitary plumbing and pedagogics, are the once undiscovered countries which democracy has annexed to the old narrow boundaries of public interest; and the unsolved inviting question is, Who shall subdue these stubborn fields for Literature and make them bring her forth new fruit and an abounding harvest.

Wordsworth spoke once of "inevitableness" as a necessary element of a great and true literature. But I feel the editor and his feeling for the publisher, the publisher and his feeling for the advertiser, the advertiser and his feeling for "circulation" behind these fine Christmas magazines. Such subservience is death to spontaneity. Literature of talent may be manufactured, and made to agree with the established order; the literature of Genius grows and makes its own order. Respect to the powers within man! Yea, verily, " it is not in our stars, but in ourselves, that we are underlings ; " and in the sad case of poor literature, it may appear that its degeneracies and market-bidding obsequiousness, though they are all ours, justly enough, need only the breath of our own moral energy to re-shape them into new forms of power and beauty. Force, constructive, idealizing force,

"Cleave thou thy way with fathering desire
Of fire to reach to fire ! "

Walking down through muddy streets palled in mist, and thronged with electrics, drays, and the rude clatter of commerce; overhead, for all the sky that I could see, horizontal layers after layers of trolley, telegraph, and telephone wires ; tall warehouses and offices to the left of me, and a world of railroad-tracks to the right, — all at once from this unlovely prospect darted forth the morning express ; clouds of smoke in ineffably feathery puffs of various grays rose into sudden sunlight. The motion, the beauty, the energy and significance filled me with delight. Starting from such crowded marts of trade, let Literature show its inborn force and live in the dawning sunlight.

—— ——.

## POETIC CRITICISM : HORACE TO STEDMAN.*

A sceptical French school-master whose pupil challenged him to say what he did believe in, anyway, seemed to lay bare the eternal verities with a butcher's hand when he replied, " I believe just zis, zat good *bœuf* make good *bouillon*."

* The Art of Poetry. The Poetical Treatises of Horace, Vida, and Boileau, with the Translations by Howes, Pitt, and Soame. Edited, with introduction and notes, by Albert S. Cook. Boston : Ginn & Co., 1892. — Sidney. The Defense of Poesy, otherwise known as an Apology for Poetry. Edited, with introduction and notes, by Albert S. Cook. Boston : Ginn & Co., 1890. — Shelley. A Defense of Poetry. Edited, with introduction and notes, by Albert S. Cook. Boston : Ginn & Co., 1891. — John Henry Newman. Poetry with reference to Aristotle's Poetics. Edited, with introduction and notes, by Albert S. Cook. Boston : Ginn & Co., 1891.
The Nature and Elements of Poetry, by Edmund Clarence Stedman. Boston & New York : Houghton, Mifflin, & Co., 1892.

In all the valuable series of poetic criticism that Professor Cook has done the public the substantial service of bringing together, there is no trace, up to Shelley's ' Defense,' of inquiry into the anterior causes conditioning the growth of the poets whose characteristics differentiate the poetic broth of nations and ages. It was reserved for the latter-day French criticism resulting from Romanticism, — criticism made popular by Taine, — and for the later comparative criticism not yet arisen, but clearly rising into prominence, and of which Posnett's book is the first manual, — it was reserved for this new school of criticism to inquire into the nature of the pasturage where the poetic species browsed, and to distinguish and classify varieties, all of which it can find good if each be genuinely of its own kind.

Horace, Vida, Boileau, and their English adapters, Pope, Byron, and the rest, busied themselves with recipes for making the traditional poetic *bouillon* without imagining that different material required different treatment ; and Addison judged Miltonic flavors according to the poetic formulæ prescribed by past masters in the art of literary confection.

What they all have to say, however, is of great interest in spite of the archaic air it wears ; and because of its old-world fashion it is to the student of literature of the greatest possible interest. He will delight in noticing the curious correspondences with which, for example, all these critics deprecate originality and commend judicious stealing.

Says Horace : " Safer shall the bard his pen employ " to " dramatize the tale of Troy, Than venturing trackless regions to explore, Delineate characters untouched before ; " and " these old fields," he intimates gently, will yield the poet his private product if he copy skilfully.

Vida advises the bard " to beat the track the glorious ancients trod," their " bright inventions " to his " use convey," cautioning him, however, to " Steal with due care and meditate the prey."

Boileau warns the poet that a perfect poem is not the work of fantasy, but of care and time, therefore he must not choose a modern rough-named Childebrand for his hero, but the smooth-named Ulysses, Agamemnon, or Æneas, who seem "born for poetry." Neither must he write without the "ancient ornaments of verse," such as "Jove's thunder," "Neptune's wrath," and "Pan's whistle."

Many other such traits of criticism that throw their light upon the path of poesy through the centuries, the reader may have the pleasure of finding for himself in these well-printed, valuable little books, whose editing, moreover, is so thoroughly done, the notes at the end of each treatise elucidating so exhaustively references and obscure allusions, that no other editions will so well serve the purpose.

Addison's praise of 'Paradise Lost,' which Matthew Arnold found inefficient, is well defended by Professor Cook in his Introduction. He certainly shows that Milton would have accepted Addison's main canons of taste, and that Arnold gave only lame reasons for his disparagement of Addison. Yet the modern reader will scarcely fail to feel, as Arnold seems to have felt, that the pleasure he himself draws from Milton is not satisfied by Addison's account of its excellences. Why should it be? The difference in feeling marks the movement of the race as unerringly as the clock-hand points the hour. Arnold did not seem to see that it would better be the critic's pleasurable task to learn from Addison what Milton's epic was to him — and to all the people of his day who showed their agreement by buying out so many copies of the *Spectator* — than to find fault blindly. That Arnold did not find it in him to take such a view shows his limitations, or rather it reveals, in turn, another step forward in time.

Newman's essay is notable as a criticism of critical authority. By the tragedies themselves of Æschylus and Euripides, which transcend the Aristotelian rules as to plot, he finds Aristotle's criticism insufficient; but when he also attempts to define, the works he sets aside as faulty — 'Romeo and Juliet,' for example — show the limitations of his prescription. And again when his religious bias comes in to determine his own criteria, and he draws certain parallels of Poetry with Revealed Religion, it leads him to find the Christian virtues poetical, — meekness, gentleness, compassion, contentment, modesty; and to call ruder feelings — anger, emulation, martial spirit, and love of independence — rhetorical rather than poetical. Here again "the villany he has taught us" confutes him; the 'Iliad,' for example, which his distinction would certainly condemn as rhetorical rather than poetical, condemns him, — a condemnation which his admiration for Homer converts into stultification.

Sidney's Defense of Poesy, and Shelley's, alike produced to silence rude voices that were raised against the Muse, show differences that reveal the steps of her progress. Sidney begins with the plea that poetry was the earliest branch of literature and is, therefore, to be honored. This argument, weighty for poetry in his day, is strong against it in a later age. It is, indeed, implied to its discredit in Peacock's 'Four Ages of Poetry,' against which Shelley wrote. His first task, therefore, is to speak against the idea that poetry was superannuated. If it early marked "the unapprehended relations of things," and first gave man words to use which through use became dead signs, it was the more necessary that poesy should arise anew "to create afresh the associations which have been thus disorganized." Its utterances, then, were not mere echoes from the past, but prophecies of the future. The poet's office was closely knit with life.

In its cursory review of a wide range of poetic work (Greek, Roman, Hebrew, Italian, French, English) Shelley's book is the link that connects us with the modern work of criticism which we may take as the climax of this poetic progression, — Stedman's 'Nature and Elements of Poetry.'

The catholicity of taste and wise forbearance in definition which mark this book above others give us subtle proof that its author has wandered in many woods of various leafage, catching songsecrets from the bird-choirs of many a golden summer. What Poetry does, rather than how she does it, is his inquiry. What charm she works within the soul is the secret he would track, rather than what must be her proper guise and garment. Accordingly, body and life appear together in the first postulate of his definition, that poetry is rhythmical and imaginative language; and its service — to express " the invention, taste, thought, passion, and insight of the human soul " — is the subject-matter of the volume.

Upon the old contention between the two sides of art — creation and self-expression — Mr. Stedman's umpireship is admirably impartial. " Its degree of objectivity is not the test of poetry. The true question is how good is each in its kind."

In another famous battle of words, the debate between truth and beauty, a ruling is given, from which we venture to infer an application of the first principle of modern criticism — the relativity of ideas — to only one side of the question. A truth which is half a lie, says Mr. Stedman, is intolerable. The expression of truth is necessarily incomplete, so it is necessarily false, and therefore didactic verse is detestable. This would be an equally good argument against beauty; for the expression of beauty that is all a beauty is as impossible to grasp and stay as a truth that is all a truth ; it is necessarily incomplete, necessarily false, and — detestable ? The very quality fastened upon as the test of the enduring beauty of the lyric — Evanescence — is but a sign of that relative apprehension of the Eternal Absolute which is ever incomplete, fleeting, changing, but not detestable ; and surely it does not constitute the only lyric charm. Its opposite note, the note of permanence, is struck with as great and more original effect in Browning's ' Magical Nature,' or, for a late example, in Mr. Aldrich's poem, ' Seeming Failure,' in the last *Century.*

Mr. Stedman's persuasiveness of style and imagery and tolerant sweetness of thought leave us with little wish to dissent from his generally well-qualified conclusions. Yet we are not ready to agree with an epigram which says of Browning's drama that it is not so much life as biology. The distinction between Elizabethan characters and those Browning has drawn, on which this phrase is based, may disclose instead, just the free and instant spirit of the modern genius in the act of holding itself true to an evolving complexity of human character and experience, fusing into one potency the self-expressing and the creative elements of art, and finding increasing recognition of its beauty as it already has of its penetration and vigòr. "The conquests of poetry, in fine," for we will use no poorer words than Mr. Stedman's, to conclude, "are those of pure intelligence and of emotion that is unfettered."

*P*

# NOTES AND NEWS.

## A BROWNING MUSICAL QUERY.

In the 'Parleying' with Charles Avison we read : —

> "Praise 'Radaminta' — love attains therein
> To perfect utterance. Pity — what shall win
> Thy secret like 'Rinaldo'?"

Should not 'Radaminta' be 'Radamisto'? Handel wrote an opera with this latter name (first performed in 1720), and he seems to be the composer meant, as 'Rinaldo' was also his work.

Farther on in the same 'Parleying' we find this passage : —

> "I sprinkle my reactives, pitch broadcast
> Discords and resolutions, turn aghast
> Melody's easy-going, jostle law
> With license, modulate (no Bach in awe),
> Change enharmonically (Hudl to thank),
> And lo, upstart the flamelets, — what was blank
> Turns purple, scarlet, crimson!"

Who was "Hudl"? I am told that the name is not to be found in any biographical dictionary, nor in Grove's 'Dictionary of Music.' Is it possibly a corruption of "Handel," as 'Radaminta' probably is of 'Radamisto'? The *ductus litterarum* would favor this emendation, if a more plausible one is not suggested by somebody better acquainted with musical matters than I can pretend to be. Whether "the Largo" in the next sentence is the famous one by Handel I do not know ; but if it is, this may tend to confirm the conjecture that he is the mysterious "Hudl."

One thing is certain, — that there are many misprints and corruptions in the latest standard edition of Browning (the sixteen-volume one of 1888–89), the author's "revision" having been careless and incomplete. It is sufficient proof of this statement that he neglected to correct misprints in earlier editions which I pointed out to him, and which he admitted to be misprints, before this edition was published, — like "Yon golden creature," for "You," etc., in 'A Blot in the 'Scutcheon' (i. 2); "crowding" for "crowning," in 'Colombe's Birthday' (act i.) ; "conjecture" for "conjuncture," in the same play (act v.), etc. Errors in punctuation, many of which materially affect the sense, are very frequent.

Critics and commentators might well give more attention than they have done to detecting and pointing out these corruptions of Browning's text. *W. J. R.*

Cambridge, Nov. 4, 1892.

## THE QUERY ANSWERED.

That Dr. Rolfe is right in his conjecture as to ' Radaminta,' is made still more probable by the fact that ' Radamisto' was for a time one of Handel's most popular operas, and would thus suggest itself to the poet along with ' Rinaldo' as a pertinent illustration of his thought. We are told that at its first performance at the Haymarket, under the auspices of the Royal Academy of Music, there was an audience such as had never been seen in London. For the first time, the royal family appeared at the Haymarket. The applause was extravagant and the excitement intense, if an anonymous writer, quoted by Hawkins, is to be credited.

"In so splendid and fashionable an assembly of ladies to the excellence of their taste we must impute it there was no shadow of form or ceremony, scarce indeed any appearance of order or regularity, politeness or decency. Many who had forced their way into the house with an impetuosity but ill suited to their rank and sex actually fainted through the excessive heat. Several gentlemen were turned back who had offered forty shillings for a seat in the Gallery after having despaired of getting any in the pit or boxes."

The final link in this chain of probability, transforming it into a certainty almost, is the existence in this opera of the favorite air "Ombra cara di mia sposa," in which a husband weeps for his wife whom he supposes dead, and to which Browning evidently referred in the line, " Love attains therein to perfect utterance." Contemporaries of Handel consider this "one of the most beautiful airs that exist," and Handel himself thought it one of the best he had ever written.

That "Hudl" might be a misprint for "Handel" seems very plausible, especially when it is remembered that Handel was at least *among* the first to use the species of modulation called enharmonic. However, Hudl does not owe his existence to the omnipresent printer's error; he was a veritable man of flesh and blood, who lived, nobody knows exactly when, in Germany, who rejoiced in the initials J. J., and who no doubt made the world richer by his pains in writing a ' Tabular View of Modulation from any one Key to all other Keys, Major or Minor.' This, then, is the cause of the poet's gratitude to him, for by his aid he might modulate to any key and quite liven up old Avison's meagre modulation from "Tonic down to Dominant."

The "Largo" in the next sentence can hardly be Handel's famous one, for that was not a love-song, but a song sung in praise of a plane-tree, being the first aria for tenor in the opera of ' Xerxes.' It seems rather to refer to the generally yearning air of that movement, just as "Hatred rages in the Rubato" refers to the character of that movement which is used "for expressing the ebb and flow of feeling within narrow limits of time." *C.*

—— EVER since Shakespeare distilled the poetry there is in a moon-lit night as he did in the ever-famous scene in ' The Merchant of Venice,' the world has had a forcible example of the inspiring beauty of "the lesser light;" and readers of POET-LORE will not be insensible to the poetry that attaches to the lunar annual novelty to which Mr. Porter has ingeniously joined both use and information. Concerning this new calendar, — ' The Columbian Annual for the First Year of the New American Century,' — this letter from its author, which appeared in a recent number of the New York *Tribune*, will be of interest : —

Those who remember the discussion concerning the true commencement of the year, begun in *The Tribune* and continued in other papers a year ago, may be interested to know that this year, which marks the beginning of a new American century, the moon will do her best to rectify the mistake for which she was made responsible when the Julian calendar was proclaimed, nineteen hundred years ago. She will make her next appearance as new moon in the western sky, on the very day of the winter solstice, or possibly, to careful observers favorably situated, on the eve of the solstice, thus indicating as nearly as possible the true commencement of the year and the true New Year's Day.

It was the custom among ancient nations who used the lunar calendar to keep a sharp lookout for each reappearance of the moon as marking the beginning of a new month. At Rome a pontifex was set to watch for the first appearance of the slender curve, and as soon as he descried it a sacrifice was offered and a proclamation was made. The fact that sacrifices were offered on these occasions shows that the impression produced by each renewed appearance of this celestial indicator of the progress of time amounted almost to a religious feeling. Cæsar seems to have deferred to this feeling in proclaiming the new calendar, and in order that the people might adopt it the more readily, and without scruple, he made the year commence with the first new moon after the winter solstice, instead of on the day of the solstice ; and this, it seems, is what makes our New Year's Day come ten days too late.

If any one is disposed to try the lunar calendar according to the suggestion of one of *The Tribune's* correspondents of last year, the coming somewhat remarkable coincidence of the first appearance of the new moon with the winter solstice will be a good time to begin ; and any one making this experiment will doubtless be surprised to find how good a calendar the Almighty hung in the sky when " He appointed the moon for seasons " and made the " sun know his going down." He will discover the origin of weeks in the moon's quarters, and also of the Roman nones, ides, and calends, and probably he will find himself counting forward as the Romans did, so many days to the first quarter, to the full, to the new. He will also be able to tell with much certainty the day of the month (moonth) by the shape of the moon and her position in the sky. And altogether he will understand how the nations and tribes of

the earth were able to get on tolerably well without almana
other artificial calendar, before the moon was deposed by imp
edict from the position she anciently held as the measure
time.

*D. G. P(*

WATERBURY, CONN., December 5.

---

# THE NORWEGIAN PEASANT LAD AND HIS DRE₄ TUNE.

### By Bjórnstjerne Bjórnson.

---

HE walked in the forest the whole day long —
    The whole day long;
For there he had heard such a wonderful song —
    Wonderful song:

He fashioned a flute from a willow spray —
    A willow spray,
To see if within it the sweet tune lay —
    The sweet tune lay:

It whispered and told him its name at last
    Its name at last;
But, e'en as he listened, away it passed —
    Away it passed.

Yet oft, while he slumbered, again it stole
    Again it stole,
With touches of love upon his soul —
    Upon his soul.

Then he tried to catch it, and hold it fast —
    And hold it fast;
But he woke, and into black Night it passed
    Black Night it passed!

" Lord God, take me into Night, I pray —
Into Night, I pray ;
For the Tune has taken my heart away
My heart away ! "

Then answered the Lord : " It is thy friend —
It is thy friend ;
Though not for an hour shall thy longing end —
Thy longing end.

" Naught in the world will thy heart suffice —
Thy heart suffice,
Save this, which in vain thy spells entice —
Thy spells entice ! "

*Translated by E. D. Girdlestone.*

—— ALTHOUGH *the* Browning Society is now defunct, many of the local societies have once more resumed their work. Among these I may mention the Islington and Clerkenwell Browning Union. This little society holds its monthly meetings in a very busy centre of our great metropolis, and has been the means of gathering together many who had not hitherto read their Browning. It asks but a nominal subscription for membership, issues no transactions, and makes little public profession of faith ; but it has nevertheless done a real work, and afforded much pleasure and instruction to many busy workers. Some interesting papers have been read during the present year, — notably by the Rev. J. S. Jones on ' Browning and Christianity ;' Mr. F. T. Parsons on ' Colombe's Birthday ;' Mr. H. Beamish on ' Pathos and Humor in Browning ;' and Miss C. G. Barnard on ' Saul.' Other evenings have been devoted to readings from the poet's works ; while not the least satisfactory portion of the society's work was a dramatic reading of ' Colombe's Birthday ' by several of the members. This was done without any extraneous professional aid, and was a genuine success, — so much so that it was repeated on a subsequent occasion. It is increasingly felt by many workers that small societies in various localities are the best means whereby it can be hoped to make Browning "understanded of the people ;" and the success of the above union would seem to prove this. *W. G. K.*

# SOCIETIES.

The Clifton Shakspere Society, Bristol, England. —The programme prepared by this Society for its eighteenth session, 1892–93, includes the following plays with propositions for debate : —

TITUS ANDRONICUS. Oct. 22, 1892. — 1. 'Titus Andronicus' and some of the so-called doubtful plays were written by Shakespeare between 1584 and 1590. 2. The savage atrocities of the story are distinct proof that Shakespeare did not write 'Titus Andronicus.' 3. 'Titus Andronicus' was an ironical censure on Marlowe's style.

CAMPASPE. Nov. 26, 1892. — 1. Lyly's work is marred by the way in which he used his superficial learning to curry favor with Queen and Court. 2. Dramatic literature is indebted to Lyly for the introduction of vivacious prose-dialogue. 3. In 'Midas,' Lyly replied to the attack made upon him in the early draft of 'Love's Labour's Lost.'

1 HENRY VI. Dec. 17, 1892. — 1. The extraordinary popularity of '1 Henry VI.' upon its first production is a true measure of Shakespeare's early genius. 2. The display of book-learning in '1 Henry VI.' is not uncharacteristic of a beginner, and is to be found in some of Shakespeare's undoubted plays. 3. The travesty of the noble character of Joan of Arc is proof that Shakespeare did not write '1 Henry VI.'

2 HENRY VI. Jan. 28, 1893. — 1. The 'Contention' was a garbled and spurious version of Shakespeare's '2 Henry VI.' 2. The striking excellence of many passages in '2 Henry VI.,' and its obvious connection with the other historical plays, prove Shakespeare to be the only possible author. 3. The misrepresentation of the motive of Cade's insurrection is not at all in Shakespeare's manner.

FAUSTUS. Feb. 25, 1893. — 1. Marlowe took the plot of 'Faustus' from Spies' 'Historia,' brought from Germany by one of the English actors. 2. Of the additions to 'Faustus' by Dekker, Bird, and Rowley, those by Dekker are indistinguishable from Marlowe's own writing. 3. 'Faustus' is a dramatic failure.

3 HENRY VI. March 25, 1893. — 1. 'The True Tragedy' was a surreptitious and tinkered version of Shakespeare's '3 Henry VI.' 2. Shakespeare's wonderful power of differentiating his characters comes out very strongly in '3 Henry VI.' 3. The treatment of the character of Margaret of Anjou in '2 and 3 Henry VI.' is conclusive evidence against the Shakespearian authorship.

THE COMEDY OF ERRORS. April 22, 1893. — 1. The brevity of 'The Comedy of Errors' is accounted for by the fact that the play as we have it is an abridged acting edition. 2. The description of 'The Comedy of Errors' as a mere farce is, considering the tragic background of the play, singularly inappropriate. 3. The portraiture of Adriana represents a phase in Shakespeare's home-life.

FRIAR BACON. May 27, 1893. — 1. Of the Elizabethan dramatists Greene alone had the literary characteristics of Shakespeare. 2. Margaret in ' Friar Bacon ' is the finest delineation of woman-character in the pre-Shakespearian drama. 3. Greene's reference to Shakespeare shows no more than a protest against the admission of an uneducated man amongst University playwrights.

**Browning Society of the New Century Club of Philadelphia.** — The first general meeting of this Society was held on Nov. 10, 1892. The President, Miss Helen Bell, in her speech ot welcome, announced that after the regular programme there would be some Tennyson memorial numbers added in honor of the poet whose loss is so deeply deplored by all English-speaking peoples.

Under the general head of Romanticism, the evening's discussion was directed to a comparative study of Browning's and Keats's Ideals of the Beautiful, and their Development of the Theories of Art. After appropriate readings by Mrs. S. B. Stitt and Dr. Mackuen, the paper of the evening, entitled, ' Ideals of Beauty as illustrated in Keats and Browning,' was read by Miss Alice Groff (to be printed in POET-LORE). After an interesting discussion on the question " Is Browning Consistent in developing his Theories of Art ? " participated in by Professor Willis, affirmatively, and by Miss Wharton, negatively, the Tennyson programme was opened by Mr. Francis Howard Williams. He said, —

" We speak so glibly and easily about genius that we forget how exceedingly rare the thing itself is, and we undervalue it accordingly. Dr. Henry Van Dyke, after assigning the first place to Shakespeare and the second to Milton, asks, ' Who so worthy as Tennyson to complete the glorious triumvirate ? ' So far as this I do not venture to go. A resemblance to Milton, however, is evident because in Tennyson's work is that prevailing faith without which no great poetry ever has been written. By this I do not mean to indicate adherence to any creed or school of religious thought, much less the verbal expression of a dogmatic theology; but I mean that underlying sense of spiritual existence which renders the poet susceptible to immaterial influences, — the only inspiration out of which true poetic utterance ever has sprung. We hear through all the organ tones of the ' In Memoriam' the unerring music of another world. It is the prevailing faith in things unseen, the recognition of the truth that the spiritual is the only real, which makes ' In Memoriam ' a beacon to the eyes of men forever. But Tennyson departs from Milton where a didactic motive yields to a sense of Beauty. Tennyson, in delicacy and artistic perfection, is the legitimate heir of Keats ; though Keats was the better Pagan ; there was in him more of the first fine careless rapture. Shelley is of too rare and ethereal stuff to be compared with aught that lies below the skies. Byron is insincere and cynical. Wordsworth was lacking in passion and utterly devoid of humor, two qualifications of the first importance, which Tennyson possessed in a marked degree.

"Here in the twilights Tennyson wrought but by suggestion ; may we not rejoice that that form of Beauty which glimmered like a star before his seeking eyes has now yielded to him the rapture of fulfilment?"

A paper from the pen of Miss Stockton, read by Miss Egner, followed, and a reading of ' Sir Galahad ' by Miss Boyer. Miss Marie Kunkel, an accomplished vocalist, rendered a number of Mr. Leefson's songs to his accompaniment, and the evening closed with the singing of Tennysonian songs by the highly trained Ziska Quartette.

The First Study Meeting was held November 23, at which the chief feature was the discussion on the question, stated by Mr. Harrison S. Morris, "Are the Poets of the Pre-Raphaelite School indebted more to Keats than to Browning ?" Dr. Woods, Miss Agnes Repplier, Professor Brooks, and others took part. *J. Sulzberger.*

**The Boston Browning Society** held its fifty-sixth regular meeting at the Brunswick, Dec. 27, 1892, President F. B. Hornbrooke in the chair. The subject under discussion was Browning's Expressions of General Poetic Principles. After a reading from ' The Two Poets of Croisic,' by Miss Emily J. Ladd, Prof. Daniel Dorchester, Jr., read his paper on ' The Nature of Poetic Expression ' (which will be given in full in POET-LORE for February). Mrs. Celia P. Woolley, Mrs. C. G. Ames, and Mrs. Louise Chandler Moulton followed, all giving extemporaneous addresses bearing upon different phases of the general subject. Mrs. Woolley discussed ' The Poet's Personal Relation to his Poetry ;' Mrs. Ames considered the core of truth, which, after some questioning, she found in Browning's *dictum* in ' The Two Poets of Croisic ' that between "bards none gainsay as good," " there's a simple test Would serve, when people take on them to weigh The worth of poets," to ask "Which one led a happy life." Mrs. Moulton dissented from this at first, but, in giving many personal reminiscences of Browning's cheery humor, finally seemed to show to lovers of Browning, at least, that his poetry reflects the sunniest genius.

# POET-LORE

Vol. V.    No. 2.

——wilt thou not haply saie,
Truth needs no collour with his collour fixt,
Beautie no pensell, beauties truth to lay:
But best is best if neuer intermixt.
Because he needs no praise, wilt thou be dumb?
Excuse not silence so, for't lies in thee,
To make him much outliue a gilded tombe:
And to be praised of ages yet to be.
Then do thy office ——

## THE OLDEST ENGLISH LYRIC.

HE day is fast arriving when attention will be paid to the treasures of our older English poetry as such. It is natural enough that the study of the language in its philological aspects should be precedent to an appreciation of the literary side of the subject. This has, in fact, been he case. But as special students of English have been long familiarizing themselves with the linguistic problems in connection with ld English work, the ground has been prepared for those whose chief interest is in the humanities and who would use the acquired land as a field for the cultivation of the flowers of song. Signs are not lacking that what has been regarded as the private preserves of specialists will soon be the legitimate property of all lovers of literature. It is significant that an attempt to offer a literary translation of 'Beowulf,' our first great English epic, by an American scholar, Professor Hall of William and Mary College, is to be followed hard on by another from English hands, — that of Professor Earle. Dr. Gummere's recent admirable work on 'Germanic Origins,' with its copious and spirited renderings from 'Beowulf' and other Old English poems, is, again, a book pointing the same way.

8

It is high time, then, to approach the hoary remains of English
song, not so much in the spirit of comparative philology as in
that of æsthetic appreciation. In this mood I write of what is in
the opinion of most scholars the oldest English lyric which has
been transmitted to us as flotsam from the wreck of the centuries. A foreword as to nomenclature. I use the term *Old English* as synonymous with *Anglo-Saxon* and as preferable thereto ; it
is the designation applied by progressive students to all our literary
remains in England from the earliest monuments extant to about
the middle of the twelfth century ; thence to the year 1500, say, we
may speak of Middle English ; the remaining literature being de-
nominated, of course, Modern English. Perhaps the strongest
argument for thus naming our earlier literature is the emphasis it
puts on the fact that we are dealing with but one tongue, seen in
its varying stages of growth. An idea of the vital connection between ' Beowulf ' and Browning is thus inculcated ; whereas, if we say
*Anglo-Saxon*, a feeling of something foreign in kind as well as distant in time is begotten. It is this oneness, this organic relation
of the English language and literature through all stadia of its development which is now being accented by scholars, and hence
those terms are best which are in conformity with that conception.

In spite of this assertion that our older poetry should be regarded
as of a piece with what is more modern, it must be confessed
frankly that at the first approach to it the student is likely to be
repelled, or, at any rate, given pause. On the threshold he is met
with a rude setting aside of verse canons and conventions of to-day
while he is bidden to breathe an atmosphere which substitutes a
sharp and bracing keenness for the soft languors and southland
allurements to which he may have been more accustomed. This
poetry, forsooth ! This is barbaric, inchoate, an outrage on the
æsthetic, and unworthy even of the nether slopes of Parnassus
Somewhat so runs his thought. But persisting in the will to get at
one with this strange product, the same student in due time begins
to feel the tonic of the air ; to habituate himself to the rough, bold
grandeur of the scenery ; to enjoy the natural cadences of the wind
that harps in his ear. In other words, what seemed irregularity o

rhythm is seen to be a looser-moving but law-abiding metre; harshnesses of word-use reveal their fitness and vigor ; and a deep, rich music, a fuller-mouthed tone-color is heard, such as modern words and melodies are more miserly in offering; while uncouth inversions and sentence-gyrations resolve themselves into the fit and felicitous way wherethrough those gleemen of long ago vented the song and sentiment that was in them.   And so there comes a real delight in the virile strength and grave sub-tones of music germane to Old English verse.

As is now pretty well understood, alliteration, employed with regularity and artistic consciousness, is to Old English poetry what rhyme is to modern, the latter being unknown.   In offering a translation, then, of such verse, its alliterative character, as well as its rhythmic character, should be reproduced when possible.   As to the law of the use of alliteration, it is enough to say here that every normal Old English line has four accents, divided by a cæsura, and that three of these — the first, second, and third — take the alliteration on the rhythmically accented word.   Add to this that the lilt or measure is prevailingly trochaic with such intermixture of dactyls as to give a freer and less monotonous effect, and an intelligent notion of the mechanics of Old English poetry may be had.   Thus it will be seen that the oldest verse-type in English is opposed in its movement to what may be called the modern verse-type, *par excellence;* namely, the iambic pentameter as seen in blank verse.   This fact suggests psychologic causes and offers a fascinating line of inquiry.   How different the swing of the tripping trochees or leaping dactyls from the stately march of the line of Marlowe or Shakespeare!   I subjoin a single Old English line with the stresses marked, by way of illustration : —

"Hále hílde-deor Hróthgar grêtan."
(" The hale hero, Hrothgar to greet.")

Two other characteristics of Old English verse remain to be mentioned, — the metaphor, and parallelism. The metaphor is to our primary poetry what the simile is to its later development; it is a stylistic feature permeating all Old English writing, and it imparts an effect of vividness and force that give the literary product a distinct complexion of its own. Readers of the Elizabethan dramatists are aware what a leading *rôle* is there played by the metaphor — or *kenning*, as it is known in Old Norse poetry — when compared with its modern use. But with Shakespeare and his contemporaries the simile (which is really the metaphor expanded) is also made much of, sharing the rhetorical honors with its older fellow-figure. But in the Old English days, the simile was practically undeveloped; it was for a later and more self-conscious age to cultivate it. Thus, in the epic of 'Beowulf,' a composition of about 3,200 lines, there is but one simile in the modern expanded sense, while metaphors star every page. The gain in strength by this close-packed, terse figuration is immense.

Again, Old English shares with Hebrew poetry the characteristic of parallelism or repetition of the thought in slightly altered phrasing. The Hebrew Scriptures offer hundreds of familiar and well-loved illustrations : " For a thousand years in thy sight are but as yesterday when it is past, and as a watch in the night." Similar constructions continually meet the student of Old English verse, or indeed of Germanic verse in general, whether English, Low or High German, or Scandinavian. At bottom this so-called parallelism is, in all probability, the creature of the emotional impulse which by the law of its being demands a wave-like repetend of the thought expressed by clauses of parallel formation. The impulse, too, being emotional, is also rhythmical, and here is another reason for repetition. In Old English, however, what was in its genesis impulsive and of the emotions, became a formal mark of verse, and a most effective rhetorical device, when skilfully managed.

With these brief comments now upon some of the most obvious phenomena of Old English poetry on its subjective and objective sides, let us come at our oldest English lyric.

An exact date cannot be given to the poem variously known as 'Deor's Lament,' 'The Minstrel's Consolation,' or 'Deor the Scald's Complaint,' according to the names prefixed to it by English or German scholars ; but it is safe to say that nothing of lyric song that has survived the centuries antedates it, and that its subject-matter points plainly to a time before the

Anglo-Saxon occupancy of England in the fifth century. This lyric, then, is a poem of forty-two lines, with a natural division into six strophes by a recurrent refrain. In this feature of the refrain it is unique in Old English song. Like almost all the poetry of this first period, it is profoundly melancholy in tone. Says Dr. Bright, speaking of another lyric of this earliest Anglian epoch, 'The Wanderer,' "the dominant note is that of sadness;" and this remark applies with equal force to the poem under consideration, and to like lyric utterances. Explain it as we may, the old harpers and song-makers felt the mystery and mournfulness of life far more than they did its flitting gleams of joy. That they hailed from a land where the bright summer was brief, and the main season the nipping and dark winter, doubtless enters into the explanation. A fair title for the piece is, I think, 'The Minstrel's Consolation,' since the mood voiced is one of sturdy defiance and heartening against trouble, although it is true that Deor the singer is unco' sad over his ill-fortune. The setting of the poem is as follows: Deor is a court minstrel who has fallen on evil days. He is an exile, and has been supplanted in the favor of his liege lord by another scald. In his poverty and loneliness he soothes his wretched state by casting over in his mind the heavy haps of other men and women, and then commenting on them with this philosophic repetend, having its tinge of grim fatalism: They lived through that hard luck; I can get through this. He starts by mentioning Weland, the famed smith of Germanic legend and literature, appearing in the German poem 'Gudrun' as Wîeland. The trade of a smith, it should be remembered, was the most honorable of early employments. I translate the first stanza, preserving alliteration and accent as far as I am able: —

> "Exile to Weland was wondrous familiar,*
> The one-minded earl, he irkings endured;
> He had to companion him longing and care,
> Winter-cold wretchedness; woes did he wot of,

---

* The word *brownrman* in the original is a *crux* with scholars, and half a dozen readings have been suggested by as many editors. But since the general sense of the line is that Weland has experienced exile, — that is, is a man acquainted with grief, — I have given the gist of the passage without trying to solve the particular problem.

> After that Nithad had him in durance,
> Weakening sinew-wounds gave the good wight.
> That ill passed over, and so may this one!"

It does not appear plainly here what the trouble is about. But very soon it is divulged that woman was a source of woe with our Germanic forebears, albeit highly and deservedly esteemed, as we know from the testimony of Tacitus and from internal evidence. The story seems to be that Weland begot a child with Beadhild, and was then attacked by her father, Nithad, and driven into exile because of his amour; thus much we may more or less dimly divine. Exile was the *pis aller* of the Anglo-Saxon and his Germanic brothers, — a condition far worse than death, especially a brave spear-death on the battle-field, which last was judged an end fit and fair. Exile (it is well to recall that the word *wretch* is derived therefrom) meant being hunted from home and fire, from kindred and kindly king, to wander in strange places with every man's hand against you, and your hand against every man. There is, therefore, great pathos always in its mention in Old English verse, coming out in its finest, most moving expression in 'The Wanderer' already referred to. Line 6, with its implication, in "good wight," that Weland did not act like a common, heartless seducer, lends romance to the tale. The hint is that it was a matter of love on both sides. This comes out clearer in the next stanza : —

> "The death of her brothers was not to Beadhild
> So sore in her mind as her own matter:
> That she full plainly had to perceive
> How she was eaning;* ne'er was she able
> To counsel with confidence what she should do.
> That ill passed over, and so may this one!"

Here we have an all too-familiar picture, — the maiden brooding over her sin, and dreading the day of her delivery. The strong statement, verging on heartlessness, it would almost seem, that her own plight grieved her far worse than the death of her blood-kin, is justified when we recall what store the Germanic peoples set by

---

* Pregnant, about to bring forth a child. The same as yeaning; the form is used here, as it is the exact word used in the original.

female chastity, — wifely infidelity, for example, being punished often with death by hanging, or whipping to death at the hands of sister women. We must not let sentiment blind us to the true values here. "There was a total absence of sentiment in Germanic life," says Professor Gummere; and the bold remark is better understood when we realize that marriage with folk of this stock was originally a barter and sale. "It's not man that marries maid, but field marries field," is a peasant saying in the old days ; and the infinite change and uplift in the conception of the relation of the sexes, with its chivalry, worshipful atmosphere, and romantic episodes, all of which begins to show in the mediæval *milieu*, is likely to cheat us into a false modernization of the events in reading older literature, unless we are on guard. To go on with stanza three, a short one : —

> " We know of murder in many a battle;
> The Geats' princes were left possessionless,
> So that a sad love stole all their sleep.
> That ill passed over, and so may this one ! "

The reference is a more general one this time. The scald recalls one of many feuds he knows of in which one side was utterly discomfited, so that the fighting men lost their *heimath* and became exiles, — again an allusion to that sorriest of endings! The "sad love" of line 4 would seem to have in mind the homesick yearning of the men-at-arms for their native burgs. A more personal note is again struck in the next stanza, which is still shorter : —

> "Thirty of winters Theodoric possessed
> The Maering's burg; 't was known to many.
> That ill passed over, and so may this one ! "

Theodoric is, of course, the famous king of the East Goths, and the " burg " mentioned is a castle belonging to Atli, the Hun, of bloody memory. The former is represented as having occupied the latter's stronghold for a generation ; and the poet's remark that this fact was of common knowledge adds to the disgrace, for with the Old English, as with the Germanics in general, what fame blows about the world, that is the man. The idea of subjective, spiritual satisfaction in the face of public contumely is a much

later, indeed, a Christian one.   A longer stanza now treats of another early leader : —

> " I have heard also all about Ermanaric's
> Wolfish mind ;  he ruled a wide folk
> In the realm Gothic; he was a grim king.
> Many a man sat wrapped round with sorrows,
> Weening on woes, wishing right sorely
> That such a kingdom were overcome.
> That ill passed over, and so may this one ! "

The characterization of the Gothic ruler Ermanaric as a " grim
king " is a laconic way of hitting off a stern and truculent reign
in the stormy days when the barbarian tribes were making the old
imperialism of Rome tremble at its gates.   Whether a particular
deed of wolfishness is here alluded to is food for conjecture.
Evidently the Gothic rule was a thing of the past when the song
was made;  this the refrain shows.   The fact that Ermanaric died
at the hands of subject princes because of his cruelties, lends wings
to the imagination in deciding what warlike sleight he was here
master of.

The sixth and final strophe is not only the longest, but by far the
most interesting in the lyric;  and this because it is very subjective,
revealing the personality of the bard in a way so rare in Old English poetry as to make it noteworthy and precious.   As a rule, the
verse is epic in its cast, with an epical objectivity and impersonality;  and in the scant lyrical remains, where the subjective element
would be found if anywhere, the song-maker is seldom obtruded,
and, with one or two exceptions, never named.   There is a vibrant
and deep sound of grief, moreover, in this summing up and application of the woful instances he has been levying history for.

> " The care-full one sitteth, severed from joys,
> Mourning in his mind : to himself thinketh
> How that a share of sorrow is endless.
> Let him remember that thro' the world
> The wise Lord full often showeth favor
> To many an earl, shapeth honor for him,
> The surest joy, — to one a deal of woe.
> Now of myself I will be saying :

How I was whilom the Heodening's scald,
Dear to my lord, Deor was my name.
Many years had I a happy lot,
A lenient lord, until that Heorenda,
Song-ready man, won the land-right
That the earl-protector erewhile gave me.
That ill passed over, and so may this one!"

It is an effective and affecting scene that is conjured up. The poet's days of prosperity seem over with, yet he tries to look on his lot with philosophy, and we have a brave acceptance of fate as he reminds himself that it is God's way to deal out good to some, evil to others ; and another twist of Fortune's wheel may bring sunnier things again. The mention of Providence here, by the bye, may be regarded as Christian interpolation, the gist of the poem being heathen in feeling, fatalistic rather than piously resigned. Our oldest treasures of poetry — the 'Beowulf' notably — show this warp of heathen structure and substance shot with golden threads of the brighter faith to lighten up its sombre hue. The feudal relation of singer and sovereign, too, is here evoked. In fancy we may conjure up the great drinking-hall, with its high seats facing east and west ; upon one of them sits the chief in war armor, his arm begirt with golden rings, which he breaks when he would reward his liegemen. The other is vacant until some neighbor chief shall come as guest to toss off cups of mead, and drink wassail to his host. The yellow-haired queen moves among the crowded rows of warriors who are ranged at benches along the sides of the hall, tendering them ale out of gem-ornamented beakers, or bowing in seemly fashion a welcome to the strangers ere she take her place beside her lord on the high seat. How her gold armlets twinkle in the ruddy glare of the roaring fires ablaze on the mighty hearth in the midst of the hall! What a clatter of spears and clang of shields, as the men lean their weapons against the wall and fall to carousing with frank gluttony. Shame to him who, putting the round-bottomed bowl to his bearded lip, drains it not to the last drop, and fails to throw it empty on the bench! For it will roll over on its side and bewray such a weakling by letting the brown liquor wet the boards. Poor candidate he for the joys of Walhalla, for the

9

mead that the great goat gives down instead of milk when its teats
are squeezed each evening for the immortally thirsty warriors of
Odin! But let the revelry be hushed. For a clear-eyed minstrel,
at bidding from the king, steps out in front of the grouped spear-
men, so picturesque in the glancing firelight, and, harp at breast,
sings his wild strain and wins sure meed of applause and gift of
gold. His song will be of some hero of a bygone day who grap-
pled with and overcame dire giants and uncouth monsters by sea
and land; or of a brother singer who, once the favored follower,
sitting at his lord's feet and feeling the kind though kingly hand
stroking his blond hair, is now adrift upon dark waters, chanting
an exile's melodious despair between the sea and star-filled sky.
Or again, the song-man will call to mind some border trouble be-
twixt unfriendly tribes, in which the prowess of one strong-armed
leader gained for his kinsmen victory and honor over the wide
earth.

In this story, with its small sub-structure of fact, history, folk-
lore, legend, and mythology will mingle to make a monument of
poetry, a sure stimulation to the fancies of those fierce but imaginative ale-quaffers beneath the rafters of the gabled beer-hall. It is in
some such setting as this that we must place the Deor of our lyric,
representing a race of professional rhapsodists and poets, the last
surviving flicker of whom is seen in such modern representatives
as the Devonshire song-men described by Baring-Gould in the
March number of the *English Illustrated Magazine* last year.
The *comitatus* is the institution lying behind this sketch of the
primitive singer, — the *comitatus*, with its root in personal loyalty
between man and master. As the fighting man owed friendship
and fealty to his liege lord, so the minstrel, too, living on the favor
of the ring-dispenser (as the lord is so often called in Old English),
owed him service of song, and became attached to his house and
his fortune. Hence, therefore, the soreness of his reverse as pictured for us in this lyric. This unknown, though not nameless,
bard stands for the Germanic race in being high-mooded and deep-
hearted, bound to endure what the Norns might send, yet very
sorrowful over what had been and was not, — the warmth and light

of the feast-hall, the hands and voices of trusty friends and kins-men. Our oldest English lyric, then, is seen to be a poem with a true personal note, yet with epic features, as in its marshalling of past events and personages. Professor ten Brink notes that it is the only lyric of the time having any connection in this way with the hero-saga, or epic. But not only is it of historic interest, it has, I think, intrinsic poetic charm — but lamely indicated in my handling — and a pathos that makes the past of our forefathers gleam of a sudden with life and a homely human meaning.

*Richard Burton.*

# JOHN RUSKIN AS LETTER-WRITER:

### WITH EXTRACTS FROM HITHERTO UNPUBLISHED LETTERS.

*(Continued from January Number.)*

WITH Ruskin, as with Carlyle, the "condition of England question" is ever a favorite topic. Less fierce in his expression than was his great master, he is yet at one with him in his denunciation of many of our modern ideas, and of so-called panaceas for the amelioration of the work-ers. In several of these letters the social question crops up, and has for him apparently a more absorbing interest than the work immediately to hand. He is especially interested in the *workmen*, — those who live, as it were, from hand to mouth, and whom he duly recognizes as the motive-force which impels the industrial machinery of the world. On the question — so often discussed, so rarely looked at dispassionately — of the organization of labor he has a word to say ; and if it is not a last word, it is an eminently wise one. For Ruskin possesses in a pre-eminent degree the *see-ing* power, intuitively recognizes the right thing to do — even though it be in advance of the time. Here is a letter which, after the lapse of three and thirty years, is well worthy of careful perusal : —

BONNEVILLE (SAVOY), SWITZERLAND, Sept. 1859.

MY DEAR ——: By some fatality it seems to happen just now that I can't get on with my own business without being perpetually distracted by something more interesting in other people's. Everybody is so absurd that it's like trying to paint in the midst of a pantomime, and I never can write a serious word about anything for the public, without feeling as if I were talking sentiment to the Pantaloon.

Here now, are those ineffably rich letters which people are writing every day to the *Times*, about this Builders' strike — and the delightfully moral and intellectual efforts of your political economists to persuade the men that labour can't be organised, when the half of the labour of the country of all kinds (from your cabman's sixpennorth of oaths and flogging, up to your Premier's five thousand pounds worth — or how much has he? — of architectural * and other useful knowledge) is organised already. Your soldiers kill people : your Bishops preach to them : your lawyers advise them : and your physicians purge them : for a shilling — or six-and-eightpence — or a guinea — according to the stated value of murder or physic ; and you never think of offering your Bishoprics to the people who will confirm cheapest, or getting yourself cured of the gout by contract. And it seems to me, bricklaying (though it is not easy, and susceptible of many degrees of fineness in the art) is rather a more organisable kind of labour than sermon-making, or diagnosis.

I hav'n't any patience left to write ; but if you have any, you might do a great deal of good just now by examining this subject of the organisation of labour thoroughly, and putting, as far as you can make it, an exhaustive article in the *Times* about it. And if you cannot do this, at least point out (*àpropos* of this unhappy strike of the poor builders) that whatever the rights or wrongs of the strike question may be, they will probably suffer more than they gain by their present way of dealing with it ; and that the true way of carrying out their views is to acquiesce, so long as they are workmen, in the present state of things ; but to strain every nerve to become masters ; and then, when they *are* masters, to carry out the principle of the organisation of labour among their own workmen — and to die for it, if need be ; it being a principle quite worth dying for, if it be true. And there is some likelihood of its being so, ever since a great master-workman went into his market to hire his labourers at their penny a day — and

* The reference is again to the Foreign Office.

had a roughish quarrel with some of them, on this very matter of the organisation of labour, before night.

You may think that's a fair day's work enough that I propose to *you*, — the "examination of the organisation of labour thoroughly." But you would find it easier and simpler than it looks, if, among the innumerable examples of good, and evil, apparently arising sometimes from organised and sometimes from free labour, you keep hold of this main clue — that organisation which is intended for the advantage of either separately, injures *both;* but chiefly those for whose advantage it was intended. There is another still surer clue, but one which, though you may use it yourself, you can't at present suggest with hope of toleration to the British public — namely, that what is Justest, is also Wisest.

There is no way in which that verse — "The Fool hath said in his heart, No God" — was ever so completely fulfilled, as in the modern idea that Political Economy depends on Iniquity instead of Equity; and on ἀνομία instead of δικαιοσύνη.

We keep to our plan of being home in early October (just in time for dead leaves and fogs). I resolved six years ago never to pass another October out of a mountain country — and have never been in a mountain country in October since. Few people have seen this part of the world in October, and it is perhaps more wonderful then than at any time, the mountains being literally clothed with gold and purple. The worst of it is that in cold weather one likes one's dinner — and the cookery hereabouts is free labour, and done cheap. So is the guiding at Zermatt — and they have just dropped a traveller into a crevasse — and left him there.

Affectionately yours,

J. RUSKIN.

Now and again, in these letters, we come across some exquisite human touches, — something that reveals to us that deep down in this man's heart lie thoughts that are oftentimes "too deep for tears." In 'Præterita' (vol. i. p. 33) we read : "The one I practically and truly miss most, next to father and mother, is this Anne, my father's nurse and mine." Concerning this same Anne, here is a letter, under date 1871 : —

"Our poor old Anne died yesterday, I think painlessly — so ending a life of very good work, in the service of other people ; and, as far as I know, without having in the whole course of it done me any harm to a human creature ; or received much benefit, be-

yond bread and meat, from any one.  She died, I suppose, in a
minute or two, all by herself; and I hope dreamily — else she would
be pained by not having me to say goodbye to."

Ruskin is nothing if not the vehement censor of our modern
customs and ways.  Very scathing in his denunciations is he at
times, and, above all, terribly in earnest.  Grim thoughts seethe in
his soul — burning there in inextricable confusion, till, in some
great moment they have birth, in a white heat of passion, not un-
mixed with pain.  Here is one, dated 1875 : —

"In the strongest conviction, I would assert that the father
should never provide for the children.  He is to educate them and
maintain them to the very best of his power, till they are of mature
age — *never live upon them* in their youth (damned modernism eats
its own children young, and excuses its own avarice by them when
they are old!).  When they are strong, throw them out of the nest,
as the bird does.  But let the nest be always open to them.  No
guilt should ever stand between child and parent.  Doors always
open to daughter harlot, or son thief, if they come!  But no fortunes left to them.  Father's house open, nothing more.

"Honourable children will have their own houses ; and, if need
be, provide for their parents — not the parents for them."

Truly a word in season, this, sternly Draconic, yet surely full
of a sublime pathos, and not far from the Kingdom of Heaven.
It is a word that need be uttered ; for after nineteen centuries
from the utterance of the New Commandment, it has come to this :
that parents *do* live on their children, sending them out into the
world inadequately equipped, for the sake of a few shillings weekly
being added to the common exchequer, — which few shillings, could,
in the majority of cases, by parental sacrifice, be dispensed with until the child's physical and intellectual equipment was complete.

On occasion, too, the lion could be roused, — and roused very
effectually.  Here is his scathing reply to a certain correspondent
who had written him to the effect that since he disparaged so much
iron and its manufacture, might it be asked how his books were
printed, and how their paper made, adding, "Probably you are
aware that both printing and paper-making machines are made of
that material" : —

SIR,—I am indeed aware that printing and paper-making machines are made of iron. I am aware also, which you perhaps are not, that ploughshares and knives and forks are. And I am aware, which you certainly are not, that I am writing with an iron pen. And you will find in 'Fors Clavigera,' and in all my other writings, which you may have done me the honour to read, that my statement is that things which have to do the work of iron should be made of iron — and things which have to do the work of wood should be made of wood ; — but that, (for instance) hearts should not be made of iron, nor heads of wood ; and this last statement you may wisely consider, when next it enters into yours to ask questions.

　　　　　　Your obedient servant,　　　　　J. RUSKIN.

Some of the letters in this volume are addressed to one who for many years was Mr. Ruskin's confidential servant and personal attendant ; and these letters emphasize the beautiful relationship existing in Mr. Ruskin's mind toward all who in any way served him. They invariably conclude, " Ever your affectionate Master, J. Ruskin," and amid the " orders " given we find interpolated brief descriptions of scenery or more personal reminiscences ; as, for instance, under date November, 1882, — " I think you will be interested in hearing that I am just settled by my wood-fireside, in my own room here, after getting through the Mont Cenis from Lucca. I came from Annecy to-day in time for a climb to the great waterfall before dinner, and feel very much like — twenty years ago. Somehow, I never fancy that *you* can be older — or anybody but myself — than we all were then."

Knotty questions, too, would seem to have been solved by the Master at times. Here is his reply to a young lady who evidently had something on her mind : —

DEAR MISS,—The law of England is absolutely one with the moral law in all its enactments respecting parental authority. It certainly would not sanction a compulsory marriage. Obedience, both to God and our parents, means essentially *Love*. Love and honour your Father and Mother, — obey them, in all their just pleasure. But you are yourself wholly responsible for the charge of your body and soul.

　　　　　　Ever your faithful servant,　　　　　J. RUSKIN.

Here is a word to the modern educationalist : —

"I feel strongly that a boy's *likings* ought to be consulted in every way. Teach a duck always to swim — but don't allow it to swim inelegantly. Put its whole strength and self-command into its swimming. People are always trying now-a-days to teach ducks to fly and swallows to swim."

One more extract may be permitted here. Writing after his recovery from his first serious mind-illness, he says : —

"Though I hope to be able for quiet work in the future, I must never again risk the grief and passion of writing on policy or charity; and scarcely permit myself the excitement of correspondence, much less that of society. But I would not have it thought that I have grown sullen, or that I regret anything that I have said or intended. I merely miscounted my days, and overrated my strength."

That was all, — "miscounted his days, and overrated his strength." But alas ! it was enough ; and the most optimistic of us can hardly look for any new work from the master's pen. We can but hope that the evening of his life may be cheered by the love and gratitude of many thousands of the English-speaking people, to whom he has been not alone prophet and teacher, but a right-human friend and brother.

*William G. Kingsland.*

LONDON, ENGLAND.

# GENTLE WILL, OUR FELLOW.

WRIT IN 1626 A. D. BY JOHN HEMINGE, SERVANT OF HIS GRACIOUS MAJESTY KING CHARLES I. ; EDITED IN 1892 A. D. AS "ALL, THOUGH FEIGNED, IS TRUE" BY F. G. FLEAY, SERVANT OF ALL SHAKESPEARIAN STUDENTS IN AMERICA, ENGLAND, GERMANY, OR ELSEWHERE.

*(Continued.)*

T the Rose, then, we began to play, Feb. 19, 1592, and on March 3, we acted our first *new* play; this was the first part of 'Henry VI.' It was in great part the same as when it was written for the Queen's men by Marlowe, Greene, Peele, and Lodge ; but it was the new scenes, in which Talbot's last battle and death were enacted, that stirred the whole town. Thirteen times did we present this play at the Rose within four months, and scarce any other play brought us in so much money. Ten thousand spectators, as Master Nash bears witness, embalmed the bones of Talbot with their tears during this time. These scenes were added by Shakespeare ; and it must, no doubt, have irked Greene that a play which had scarce been noticed when he and his coadjutors wrote it for the Queen's men should now be in all men's mouths as the best play of the year. Moreover, Greene had lost his occupation ; for the Queen's men had broken, and the other companies would not employ him. The Admiral's men he had cheated by selling his ' Orlando ' twice over, once to them and once to the Queen's ; Lord Pembroke's men he had grievously abused in his ' Menaphon,' and he had hired Master Nash to abuse them also, which was harder to bear, for Tom Nash had a bitterly witty tongue, and he had stigmatized Marlowe as a Canterbury cobbler, Kyd as an English Seneca, and Wilson as a parrot-teaching Roscius.

Finding, then, that the stage entirely failed him, Greene made his last effort at the writing of pamphlets, and botched up his ' Groat's worth of Wit,' in which he addresses Marlowe as an atheist, Lodge as a satirist, and Peele as a shifting companion, but all as his fellow-writers ; and begs them not to company with the puppets that speak, from the poets' mouths, the antics garnished with their colors. Then his enmity to one of these puppet antics bursts out ; he calls our gentle Will a Johannes factotum, the only Shakescene in a country, in his own conceit. But it is not as a player that he is specially angered against him ; it is as a play-writer, who thinks he can bombast out a blank verse as well as the best of the three poets he addresses, and he shows the cause of his virulent passion to be the new scenes in ' Henry VI.' by a travesty of a line in the second part of the play written by these same men and acted by the same players — namely, Her Majesty's — a few years before.

This precious piece of a deformed nature was not imprinted till after Greene's death in the autumn, when Master Chettle gave it to the press, to the displeasure, both of Peele, who was then writing for us, and of Marlowe, who incontinently joined us and wrote for us the play of 'The Guise,' which Master Alleyn, who played the Guise's part so famously, enacted in the winter of the same year. Master Lodge, who was then abroad, also wrote for our company afterwards ; and Nash, who was thought by some to have had a hand in this scurrilous address to Greene's three quondam companions, vehemently denied it, so that it did us much good instead of the harm intended, as such malice overleaping itself often does. As for Shakespeare, he took no note of the matter ; he was hard to move by any personal attack ; but had it been Ben Jonson, the case had been altered indeed.

Other new plays were acted by us in the spring of 1592. 'Titus and Vespasian,' which was on the same plot as 'Titus Andronicus,' was, with many other of our plays, afterwards acted in Germany by Brown and his fellows, — the same Brown from whom Alleyn bought the properties, when he first formed us into a company for my Lord Strange. Another of our new plays was 'The Knack to know a Knave.' In this, Will Kempe — who had the same gift of tickling the groundlings by his extemporal merriments that Dick Tarleton had — inserted the receiving the King by the men of Gotham, himself acting the Miller, and uttering on the stage much more than is set down in the printed book. I mention this here because it was a thing that Shakespeare could not away with, he always holding that the poet alone ought to judge what necessary business of the play should be considered. But he hath told you this himself in his 'Hamlet,' when this pitiful ambition of Will Kempe and such fools is marked as needing reformation. It hath, however, outlived Shakespeare's time, and I fear me will last as long as the stage itself.

One other play I ought to notice on account of its strange quality. This was 'The Seven Deadly Sins,' plotted by Tarleton for the Queen's men in 1585. In this there were seven separate plots, one for each sin, all bound together by speeches made by Lydgate as presenter to King Henry VI. We got this play at the same time as the other plays of these men ; and as it was too long to present in one afternoon, we played half of it under its other title of ' Four Plays in One,' Shakespeare, as his wont was, taking the King's part, and I taking Lydgate's. This was in March, 1592. Tarleton had called it 'Three Plays in One,' not reckoning the Induction as a play. When we left the Rose, Alleyn kept the plot and the copy, and I believe still holds them. The method of Beaumont and Fletcher's ' Four Plays in One ' was taken from this outdated play, which also, it would seem, gave the hint for the Induction to the play of ' Pericles ; ' nor is it altogether unlike that to the Robin Hood plays by Monday and Chettle. But although even within the last few years we have had such inductions on our stage, they are in my mind but clumsy contrivances, and show merely the dryness of the poet's brain.

In the latter part of June, the plague began to prevail in Southwark, and the Rose was closed by authority for fear of infection, and we were ordered to play for three days in the week only at Newington Butts, where plays had not been used on working-days for a long time. It was a bad time, and we did nothing of special note in it. We petitioned the Council for our own sakes and those of the poor watermen, who fell into great straits by reason of their loss of their customary fares to the Bankside ; and the watermen themselves likewise petitioned, so that by the grace of my Lords, when the plague fell below forty deaths in the week, in December, we were allowed to play again at the Rose. But if our stage lost in one way, it gained in another ; for it was during this time that Shakespeare wrote his first poem, ' Venus and Adonis,' which hath been so largely read that it hath been at this present time nine several times imprinted, and, being dedicated to my Lord of Southampton, procured for us His Lordship's especial patronage, and through him that of my Lord of Essex, which was of great advantage to us for many years. I have always thought that our Will, had he been as blessed with worldly goods at that time as he was afterwards, would have left the stage altogether and turned sonnets or writ nothing for the rest of his life ; how great a loss this would have been to the stage, we, and all who have read our late collection of his plays in Folio, know full well. Whether it would have been better for himself is known only to Him who, as Will says, " shapes our ends, rough hew them how we will."

In December, then, we opened again at the Rose, and then acted the jealous comedy out of which Shakespeare afterwards made his ' Merry Wives of Windsor,' which so pleased our gracious Queen ; as well it might, having been written by Her Majesty's own command within the space of two weeks ; and we also acted ' The Guise,' afore-mentioned, by Marlowe. But this was the only play which he wrote for us especially, he having been killed in the next May by one Archer in a tavern at Deptford. Shakespeare loved him, and although at that time Marlowe was surely the greater of these two great play-makers in Tragedy (for Comedy he never attempted), no word of jealousy ever occurred between them. Indeed, it was not till Marlowe was dead that Shakespeare began to carry on the work of the dear dead shepherd, as he was wont to call him, whose ' Edward II. ' was the precursor of the ' Richard II.' of his friend, and whose ' Doctor Faustus ' (in the part that was wholly his) first fathomed on the stage those vague, mysterious depths which are sounded with a deeper plummet in the ' Hamlet ' of his successor.

In February, 1593, the plague so increased that the playhouses were again closed, and so they remained till Christmas. During this time we travelled in the country and played such plays as we had by us, but Shakespeare bestowed the most of his leisure in writing his poem of ' The Rape of Lucrece,' which he published in May of the next year, with a dedication to my Lord of Southampton, with whom, after his first poem, he had become intimate. Shakespeare dedicated to His Lordship therewith his love without end ; all he had done, and all he had to do, were, he said, devoted to him ; and he wished him long life and happiness. Neither did he say this without cause, for never thereafter did he dedicate to any man any work of his, poem or play. In this he far differed from the most part of the poets of these times who wellnigh all have sought to gain a new patron by a new dedication to every work of theirs that they have given to the printer's hand, if it were no more than a fourpenny pamphlet. But he could not abide such doings. He served one patron in this world, even as he would serve one Master in the next. Had my Lord been so minded, *he* might have had our fellow's plays, so far as they were printed, also dedicated to him, which he would not, because after he married with Mistress Elizabeth Vernon, he cared not to have his name staled in public with aught connected with the stage, which was then thought to be a base and degrading occupation, yet, my Lord's consent being withheld, our Will would never bestow them on any other. Neither would he consent to the fashion of printing commendatory verses before his plays, as many have practised, nor would he write such for the plays of others. By their own worth such things should stand or fall, and not by private friendship or purchased flattery.

At this same time he also began to make those sugared sonnets to my Lord Southampton, which he read among his private friends, but which were afterwards published, not by him, but by Mr. W. H., my Lord's stepfather, Mr. William Harvey, I suppose, though other men think otherwise. The printer of these, one Thorpe, took such diligence to be obscure in his dedication that of late absurd interpretations have been made of it ; one of which, that by " Mr. W. H." he intended my Lord William Herbert, the Earl of Pembroke, is the most ridiculous. Any one who will care to look at the books printed by this Thorpe before as well as after these sonnets will find dedications by him to this Earl, with all his titles fully and deservedly displayed. I might say much more on this matter, but all who knew Shakespeare are so fully aware that the "love" of which he speaks in his sonnets is the same as the "love" in the ' Lucrece ' dedication, and that he never divided it unto a second patron, that I care not to waste my time and labor in fighting the air. Rather will I set down plainly all I know of this matter.

In the year 1593, shortly after Shakespeare became an intimate of my Lord Southampton, at the instance of Mr. William Harvey, the "only begetter" of these sonnets, he wrote the first of them, in which he adjured my Lord to marry, for at that time he was entirely averse to matrimony, and his friends were afeared that this noble family might become extinct. In these the understanding reader will find more than one allusion to our travel of that year. Now, during this travel in the western parts of England, some of us stayed for a while at an inn, which had Saint George for its sign. The town I will not name, as it might rip up old scandals to the annoyance of persons of good repute, who are still alive. At this inn the innkeeper had a pretty daughter, who, in spite of the temptations incident to her calling, had alway preserved her good repute. Between this damsel and our fellow Shakespeare there ensued divers love-passages which caused us great amusement, for she was free of speech and no way misliking anything that savored of honest mirth, and he accosted her in the vein of a lover on the stage, calling her English Lucrece (belike because he was writing of Roman Lucrece at that time), chaste Susanna (he and I being the wicked elders), and the like. But that anything beyond jesting words passed between them, or that anything dishonorable was intended by the lady, that I utterly deny. My Lord of Southampton, hearing of this at one of our meetings among our private friends, must needs go to see this phœnix himself, and maintained the jest, saying that he had come to take possession in the name of William Conqueror, whose ambassador he was. In the like merry manner was he answered by the maid. Many a sonnet did Shakespeare indite on this argument in mockery of the tedious strings of such Italianate subtilties as Masters Constable, Daniel, Drayton, and others then wrote to their noble patronesses under feigned names, as if they had been, forsooth, their mistresses, and were like to marry their poor poets. But to say sooth, all this mockery was but Paul's work, matter for the printers, a playing of puppets under an earnest guise, whereas these sonnets of our Shakespeare, made on a feigned rivalry, are full of life-blood. All that he wrote, even to the babble of a tapster or a waiting-maid, was made according to the saying of the dead Philisides, " Look in thy heart and write."

This story got talked about at Oxford, and one of the University pens there, who called himself Hadrian Dorrell (Heaven only knows what his true name was), published in September, 1594, a slanderous book called 'Willoby, his Avisa' in which he makes W. S., "the old player," seriously advise Henry Willoby to seduce the lady. He tells her christened name, Avice, describes the place where she lived, near Austin's Oak, in Worcestershire, gives the sign of the inn, and so forth. This was so scandalous that some men cried out against it, — not Shakespeare, to be sure; all the notice he took was to write another sonnet, in which he plays upon the three Wills, — the Will of the lady, Will for Willoby, and himself, Will Shakespeare. This Dorrell, in June, 1596, sends forth another imprint of his libel, in which he feigns that he never meant any real person by Avisa, and declares that Willoby had written it five and thirty years since, although in his first edition he had said that this Willoby was a very young man, "a scholar" at a university. This apology was too glaringly false to be seriously taken. It was plain to every eye that "W. S.," the old player, was meant for William Shakespeare; and if so, "H. W." could only mean Henry Wriothesley, his friend and patron, as openly acknowledged in his dedications, however this *Dor* might bodge up his slander by pretending that Harry Willoby was a real person. Thus his libel was evident, and so thought my Lord Grace of Canterbury, and the Bishop of London; for under their commandment the book was stayed, June, 1599, and not printed again during Her late Majesty's reign.

Shakespeare did not leave writing of these sonnets till my Lord of Southampton's marriage, in 1598, and in one of the last of these he alludes to the peace of Vervins in April of that year. "Peace proclaims olives of endless age."

Master Drayton and Master Gervase Markham, who both took to themselves the mention of the "alien pen" who had dedicated books to the Lord Southampton, were mightily offended. Drayton withdrew his sugared lines from his 'Matilda,' in which he had mentioned Lucrece as "acting her passions on our stately stage," and Markham ridiculed the 'Venus and Adonis,' in his plays of 'The Fair Maid of the Exchange,' and 'The Dumb Knight.' Neither of these men could endure a sarcasm in jest, and both of them were ready to inflict one in earnest.

II. SHAKESPEARE IN THE SERVICE OF MY LORDS HUNSDON.

ON the 16 April, 1594, our patron Ferdinand, Earl of Derby,
died. We had acted under his name as the Earl of Derby's men
in our travels from the 25 September in the year before, when he
succeeded to the earldom at the death of his father Henry, the
former Earl. I am thus particular in noting a matter of seemingly
small import, because in later years some confusion has arisen in
men's minds between our company and that known afterwards as
the Earl of Derby's, whose patron was the Earl William; and some
have supposed that Shakespeare was a servant of that Earl, as also
of my Lord of Pembroke. This was not so. He never left our
company even for a year; but in those times of plague, the theatres being shut, and we on our travels, the memories of men were
easy to mistake in matters of no great public import. On our
travels, in 1593, in the summer, to Chelmsford, Bristol, Shrewsbury,
Chester, York, we were my Lord Strange's servants; but it was as
Lord Derby's men that in February, 1594, we bought up the plays
that had been presented by the Earl of Pembroke's players, when
these men, after being reduced to great straits by the plague, and
not having means to travel, were driven by their poverty to pawn
even their apparel, and ceased to act in London at all for three or
four years.

Shakespeare was especially desirous to have these plays, because
there were among them several of Marlowe's, who died some six
months before this; also some of Master Kyd's, and others. Of
Marlowe's there were 'Edward III,' and 'Richard, Duke of York;'
of Kyd's, 'Hamlet,' and 'The Taming of a Shrew;' there was
also an old play of 'Hester,' and one on 'Titus Andronicus.'
Most of these were refashioned by Shakespeare for our own stage.
In that of 'Edward III.' he inserted the story of the Countess of
Salisbury, and we acted it incontinently. 'Titus Andronicus' he
likewise corrected for immediate presentation; and one unfinished
play by Marlowe on 'Richard III.' he completed and perfected.
This was the play in which Burbadge was so famous, especially for

the manner in which he said the words, "My kingdom for a horse."
We did not, however, enact it at that time, but we did a few months
after, when we had become my Lord of Hunsdon's men.

*F. G. Fleay.*

(To be continued.)

## SHAKESPEARE.

MASTER, what veil of flesh thy spirit wore
   The too brief hour it sojourned here on Earth,
   To me is question of such little worth
My soul is wroth to hear men number o'er
   Their *pros* and *cons :* " The baffling mask he bore,
   Hid — Raleigh ? " " Nay, 't was Bacon ! note the girth,
   This champion belt none else could fill." Our mirth
Grows with each guess. "What ! " (hear them !) " is such lore
   For poacher ? — player ? For World's poet choose
A hind ? " Ay ! If God's breath could change red clay
   To soul, by breath of genius 't is His use
Further to puff the spirit's dross away.
   Babblers, enough ! Who cons the wondrous whole,
   Finds meshed therein a rounded human soul.

*Alice Williams Brotherton.*

## THE NATURE OF POETIC EXPRESSION.*

THE question, What is poetry? like the questions, What is life?
What is truth? will ever be asked, but will never be answered satisfactorily. As Augustine said of one of these, " If not asked, I
know ; if you ask me, I know not."

The various attempts to define poetry have resulted in its dis-
section ; its " disjecta membra " have been presented, but not its
living form. Shelley, for example, styles it " the language of the
imagination," but he states simply its chief characteristic, and not

---

* Read before the Boston Browning Society, Nov. 27, 1892.

its distinguishing one. Byron calls it "the feeling of past worlds and future," but he thus indicates that with which poetry is largely but not wholly employed. "It is an imitative art," says Aristotle, "imitative of the passions and manners of men;" but such also are painting and sculpture and music. In the language of Wordsworth, "Poetry takes its origin from emotion recollected in tranquillity;" "it is the impassioned expression in the countenance of science;" "it is the breath and finer spirit of all knowledge;" but this is mystical eulogy. We need all these definitions and more, to compass our conception of poetry.

The difference between what is poetry and what is not poetry is fundamental and can be determined. Let us seek to know this difference rather than to criticise those who have misapplied the word "poetry" and given it imperfect definition; let us clear up our own conceptions, and make more distinct and definite the vague feelings and ideas with which we regard it.

Poetry in its broadest acceptation is something which may exist in that which does not even require the instrument of words, but can speak through the audible symbols called musical sounds, and even through the visible ones that are the language of sculpture, painting, and architecture. Nature is poetical; Lord Byron calls the stars "the poetry of heaven," and tells us that to him "high mountains were a feeling," and that mountain and wood and sky spake : —

> "A mutual language clearer than the tones
> Of his land's tongue, which he would oft forsake
> For Nature's pages glassed by sunbeams on the lake."

In early times poetry was much less restricted in its meaning than it is to-day; it was identified with dancing, singing, and pantomime, the symbolic action making more clear the feeling or thought, and the gesture or act being emblematical of what was sung. In this early poetry, the magic symbolism of dance and gesture predominated, and poetry, as we understand it, existed only in the refrain of a few simple words. Choral song of all kinds, the war song, the marriage hymn, the dirge, the chants to the ancestral gods the songs of the spring and autumn festivals, were accompanied by march and dance, and frequently by pantomime.

The proverb, the riddle, the fairy tale, the charm, and even the forms of primitive law originated in poetic feeling desiring an artistic form for its expression. For a thousand years at least, man knew poetry only as an animated song or a vivacious speech. Even as late as Aristotle, the musical and the scenic were regarded as poetic elements.

The consideration of the nature of poetic expression involves a comprehension of the nature of artistic expression in general. Of this I can give only a bare outline.

It is a characteristic of man, considered as a spiritual being, that he is not satisfied with mere sense impressions and sensations; he compares these with others whose images memory recalls; between these objects of his comparison and the train of ideas passing in his consciousness, there is also reciprocal action; separations and combinations of ideas follow, and thus his sense apprehension of things is reinforced and transformed by his critical energy of mind. Thus concepts are formed and fixed images of particular objects, which arouse certain feelings.

Now, expression is a necessary consequence of excitation. " By a naturally predetermined physiological necessity the soul is compelled to express, in tones at least, the general character of its inner states; the organic unity and connection of the thought-forming phantasy and the sound-forming voice," as Lotze puts it, " are manifest. . . . Language begins with the meaning attached to these sounds and the peculiar form of thought into which that meaning is thrown."

"While many," says John Henry Newman, " use language as they find it, the man of genius uses it indeed, but subjects it withal to his own purposes, and moulds it according to his own peculiarities. The throng and succession of ideas, thoughts, feelings, imaginations, and aspirations which pass within him; the abstractions, juxtapositions, the comparisons, the discriminations, the conceptions, which are so original in him; his views of external things — his judgments upon life, manners, and history;

the exercises of his wit, of his humour, of his depth, of his sagacity
— he images forth all these innumerable and incessant creations,
the very pulsation and throbbing of his intellect, he gives utterance
to them all in a corresponding language, which is as multiform as
this inward action itself, and analogous to it, — the faithful expression of his own personality attending on his own inward world of
thought, as its very shadow."

But sounds, gestures, and language are not the only means of
expression. "Art is a language," says Millet; and how eloquently
he used it! The artist requires a form, be it a painting, a statue, a
symphony, a cathedral, or a poem, that shall so far correspond to
what he desires to express that the beholder or hearer shall par-
take of the artist's thought and feeling. It may not be possible to
trace the precise connection between the artistic form and the idea
or feeling behind it.

What is there in Thorwaldsen's group of a mother flying in her
sleep bearing two babes and followed by an owl, that is like night?
Nothing in the things themselves; that is, there is no phenomenal
likeness. Yet when looking upon that marble group, we feel restful, just as Thorwaldsen did when imbued with the stillness of
night. When Alfred Sensier, a French critic and collector, saw
Millet's famous picture for the first time, it was almost finished.
Millet said to him, "What do you think of it?" "It is the
Angelus!" Sensier cried. "It is indeed. You can hear the
bells," joyfully responded the artist. "I am contented; you understand it. It is all I ask." There is no phenomenal likeness
between the sound of bells and that picture. Yet Millet was able
to transmit that sound with all its holy associations to the soul of
Sensier.

If we are curious to know how an artist does this, we may
derive some satisfaction from the thought that behind the phenomenal world, behind the shapes and colors and sounds of things,
there is an ideal world of which they are but the appearances, the
sensible representations; the artist by his imaginative combinations seeks to image forth the ideas that are immanent alike in the
soul of man and in Nature; he thus expresses that which is uni-

versally intelligible and which may be recognized in different forms.
But this explanation does not fully explain; it is enough, however,
for our present purpose that we establish the fact so grandly stated
by Wordsworth · —

> " My voice proclaims
> How exquisitely the individual mind
> . . . to the external world
> Is fitted ; and how exquisitely too
> The external world is fitted to the mind
> And the creation (for by no lower name
> Can it be called) which they with blended might
> Accomplish."

In poetic expression, as in every kind of artistic expression,
content and form are as essential to each other as soul and body
are, and by their "blended might" accomplish more than any mere
addition of the two. A poem in a language that we do not know
may please us by its rhythm or melody, but how much greater the
effect when we understand the meaning! On the other hand, a
trivial thought may be dressed in such fair ornament, may be so
rhythmically expressed, that it may pass for something of great
excellence, but a careful examination detects "the counterfeit
presentment" and reduces it to its true value. There are as many
gradations in depth and clearness of apprehension among poets as
among philosophers.

There is, however, this difference between the thought of the
philosopher and that of the poet : in philosophy, thought is abstract, and expressed in the form of concepts and judgments; in
poetry, the thought is concrete, even sensuous, and glistening with
images. In philosophy, the appeal is to the pure intellect, and the
sensible is ignored for the sake of the pure idea; in poetry, the
sensible is courted, that the idea may be married to a beautiful form
and stir the feelings. The thought of the poet, like that of the
philosopher, must be elevated and self-consistent, but does not, like
his, become satisfied with the truth alone ; it seeks the true, but it
covets the beautiful and finds its end in sensuous manifestation.

Browning recognizes the necessity for this sensuous expression
of thought in his criticism of a metaphysical poet, in ' Transcendentalism ' : —

> " Stop playing, poet !  May a brother speak ?
> 'T is you speak, that 's your error.  Song 's our art :
> Whereas you please to speak these naked thoughts
> Instead of draping them in sights and sounds.
> True thoughts, good thoughts, thoughts fit to treasure up !
> But why such long prolusion and display,
> Such turning and adjustment of the harp,
> And taking it upon your breast, at length,
> Only to speak dry words across its strings ? "

The question has been asked, Was this poem Browning's mockery of his critics or self-criticism?  Neither.  This poem is only Browning's way of saying that the results of philosophic work can never become generally current, or " dear and genuine inmates of the household of man " until they are put into sensuous form and vitalized by emotion, which is the peculiar work of art.

The poet gets his material from two worlds, an outer and an inner.  By the outer world is meant the external world with its myriad forms of organic and inorganic life.  As the poet contemplates the forces of Nature, ever manifesting themselves in beautiful forms, he has inklings of the inward life that moulds the outward forms, and his own energies of thought and feeling are stimulated to similar creative action.  Burns was very sensitive to such inspiration.  " I have," he says, " some favorite flowers in spring, among which are the mountain daisy, the hare-bell, the fox-glove, the wild briar-rose, the budding birch, and the hoary hawthorn, that I view and hang over with particular delight.  I never hear the loud solitary whistle of the curlew in a summer noon, or the wild mixing cadence of a troop of gray plover, without feeling an elevation of soul like the enthusiasm of devotion or poetry."  And Byron, looking upon " clear, placid Lake Leman " in the hush of night, was similarly moved.

More important than the outer world to the poet is the inner, the world that includes the whole life of the human soul, — all its slumbering potencies, " whatever is most profound and mysterious in the heart and thought of man, with all contrasts, oppositions and contradictions of his nature, his grandeurs and his miseries, his pains and his sufferings, all his sentiments and all his passions."

The poet forages in both worlds, and out of his garnered sub-stance creates that which blends Nature and the soul in a beautiful form.

An elementary part or unit of a poetic substance may be termed the motive, the idea, the theme. A poem may have only one mo-tive, or it may have a ruling motive with subordinate ones. The latter may be unfoldings, parts of the former, but still different. Certain German poets have understood by the idea a universal statement or tenet, and have made their characters the bearers of this principle. But poets generally, certainly the great world-poets, have comprehended in their motives a certain survey of human thought, feeling, and action.

Browning has attempted a kind of poetic expression in which he says no one has been successful. He has attempted to reveal truth "with an immediate reference to the common eye and appre-hension of his fellowmen." This, of course, requires a mode of expression that is objective and sensuous.

He has also sought to embody "the thing he perceives not so much with reference to the many below, as to the One above him, the Supreme Intelligence which apprehends all things in their ab-solute truth. Not what man sees, but what God sees — the Ideas of Plato, seeds of creation lying burningly on the Divine hand — it is toward these that he struggles." Here the treatment must be subjective and sublimely abstract. Browning says that there "is no reason why these two modes of poetic faculty may not issue hereafter from the same poet in successive perfect works, ex-amples of which, according to what are now considered the exigen-cies of art, we have hitherto possessed in distinct individuals only. A mere running in of the one faculty upon the other is, of course, the ordinary circumstance. Far more rarely it happens that either is found so distinctly prominent and superior as to be pronounced comparatively pure; while of the perfect shield, with the gold and silver side set up for all comers to challenge, there has yet been no instance." If Browning has not always succeeded in becoming sublimely abstract and beautifully sensuous, he has significantly pointed out the path for the poetry of the future to follow. His shortcomings may be regarded as an advance upon the brilliant achievements of those who have followed a lower and a narrow idea for the very same reason that the art of the old painters of Florence, as he has shown, was greater and grander than Greek art.

> " ' T is a life-long toil till this lump be leaven —
> The better! What's come to perfection, perishes.
> Things learned on earth, we shall practise in heaven:
> Works done least rapidly, Art most cherishes."

I pass to consider, briefly, certain elements of poetic expression.

The whole process of poetic activity, from the first outflashing of the poetic motive to its expression in language, is determined by imagination and emotion. By these powers of the soul thought is concentrated, strengthened, and colored in its expression, the poetic substance becomes incarnate, and " bodies forth the forms of things unknown."

There is a close relationship between the imagination and the memory. The Greeks most appropriately called the Muses the daughters of Zeus and Mnemosyne; that is, the freely creating power of the god and the recollection or remembrance. Both the imagination and the memory have the capacity to reproduce impressions in the form of images. Probably no impression is reproduced by the memory exactly as it first affected the mind, but is only more or less perfectly recalled. In the activity of memory, the mind seeks to recall its impressions as exactly as possible, but in its imaginative activity the mind is free, it seeks to refashion the memory-image, to magnify and embellish it after some ideal; thus other images are called up, selection is made, and an imaginative product is formed.

There is also a strong resemblance between an imaginative activity and dream activity. The study of the dream, "that stifled poet in us," is a help to the understanding of poetic imagination.

In our waking hours, in revery, certainly, and in those moments when we are more fully conscious, imagination seems to work of its own free will. A series of fancies seems to run out of a single impression; a single form calls up a history, and a story or history brings before us the characters that figure in it.

The poetic imagination is confined to that activity of mind

which, discovering some definite whole hovering before it consciously, seeks to make something in verse after the likeness of this ideal. Such creative activity may be completed so swiftly that the mind may be hardly conscious of any effort, but it knows its end and the readiest course to reach it.

Imagination presents the universal, not by means of generalizations as reason does, but by means of particular characters and events, or by some accompaniment or manner of appearance. " When the Sun went down to unyoke his steeds " is Homer's way of saying "it was the hour of sunset." "When the sickle went to the field " is another poet's manner of telling us that it was harvest-time. "Thus doth she," Coleridge says,

> " when from individual states
> She doth abstract the universal kinds,
> Which then reclothed in divers names and fates
> Steal access thro' our senses to our minds."

No poet has more beautifully than Browning made great truths flash in apparently trifling incidents and episodes. Indeed, it seems as if the humbler the character, the more trifling the incident, the more " heaven " he has sought to pour into that "shut house of life."

I have separated imagination and emotion as elements of poetic expression for purposes of treatment merely. The soul of the poet is one ; no separation is possible except in an accommodated sense. No activity of the mind is possible without feeling, least of all the imaginative; indeed, imagination at its highest has been defined as " the intellect winged by emotion to go forth and gather honey from the bloom of creation." In the exercises of imagination the mind experiences its tensest action, and feeling imparts the tension. What heat is to the physical world, passion is to the poet ; it fuses and crystallizes the commonplace and thus makes the jewels of expression.

The philosopher and the scientist must keep their feelings under control, lest they intrude upon their researches, and color " the dry light" in which alone the objects of thought and investigation should be viewed. But as George Eliot says in ' Middlemarch,'

"To be a poet is to have a soul so quick to discern that no shade of quality escapes it, and so quick to feel that discernment is but a hand playing with finely ordered variety on the chords of emotion — a soul in which knowledge passes instantaneously into feeling and feeling flashes back as a new organ of knowledge."

I now come to the last element of poetic expression, — that which differentiates poetry from every other form of expression in language, the metrical. Language attains its highest artistic expressiveness by means of something added to it. Poetry makes such an addition; in early times she added dance, and music, and pantomime; "the three musical arts — dance, music, poetry — were one. Thus in the earliest Greek dithyrambs the measured music of the voice was aided not only by the flute or lyre, but by harmonious movements also of the body during recitation. . . . So it was, also, that the earliest Teutonic poetry — of which First-English is a part — united the three forms of movement. The Anglo-Saxon, Scop or Gleeman added to his rhythmic chant the emphasis of chords struck on a rude harp — the gleebeam ; and this had for its successor the rustic fiddle, to which, in the days of Elizabeth, a poor after-comer of the gleemen might sing 'Chevy Chace' with rough untutored voice, and stir the heart of Philip Sidney like a trumpet ;" in modern times, poetry seeks by a series of sounds, by such co-ordinations as rhythm, tone-color, melody, and harmony, together with the associations that these excite, to give to language its fullest expressiveness, and to the soul the greatest pleasure.

All poets deserving the name have "felt music's pulse in all her arteries," and carried the throbbing life of melody into their verses.

*D. Dorchester, Jr.*

## STAGE TYPES OF LADY MACBETH.

Of the acting of Lady Macbeth there are at least three conceptions : one makes her terrible, the other fascinating ; the third both fascinating and terrible ; and a fourth might be added, — appealing, in which the femininity pleads rather than fascinates, entreats and never commands.

Mrs. Pritchard, the annals of the stage tell us, made her terrible. Her composure was marble-like, and in contrast to Garrick's superagitated manner in 'Macbeth' produced a profound impression of terror. She must indeed have embodied the fateful ideal of the character with much completeness and to the exclusion of other phases. This ideal is doubtless the popular one, and with it doubtless the notion of a physical counterpart after the manner of Maclise's famous painting of the banquet scene, in which the Lady Macbeth is a Gaelic giantess whose little finger suggests a thickness greater than a man's loins; a woman of brawn and muscle to scuttle a ship or cut a throat. Thus ever the vulgar ideal; thus never the vulgar fact. The vivid passion to do and dare never wastes its strength on bulk, nor hangs out signs and banners in countenance or carriage, that all may know its habitation. It is the delicate frame instinct with nerve-force that embodies spirits like these, as Shakespeare with his consummate art indicated by having Lady Macbeth speak of her " little hand."

Mrs. Siddons, who has largely fixed the stage tradition, made Lady Macbeth both fascinating and terrible, or rather she thought her both; she made her chiefly terrible, always imperious, — her raven hair and piercing eyes, her queenly form and stately mien, lending themselves with vast effect to the purpose. In the sleep-walking scene, for example, her manner was wide-awake, her movements alert. She stepped quickly, poured imperceptible water from an imaginary ewer, bent her body to listen to imaginary sounds, and hurried to retake the light where she had left it, that she might with all speed drag Macbeth to their chamber. There is no more instructive passage in the literature of the theatre than that in Hazlitt (or is it Dr. Doran's 'Annals'?) which tells of Mrs. Siddons' first study of the part, alone in her home at night. The terror of the character so overcame her as to sweep aside, not only her sense of its fascination and womanly pathos, but herself; and that she was never able to dominate it, her acting of it as well as her confession testified. She was wont to declare that her embodiment was not consistent with the feminine and fascinating creature whom she believed Lady Macbeth to be.

Charlotte Cushman's Lady Macbeth was wholly terrible, with a
side-light here and there of human weakness.   Macbeth she held
to be "the grandfather of all the Bowery ruffians," and she scorned
him in kind and mightily.   Fanny Kemble made of her Lady Macbeth a fiend, unrelieved.

Modjeska's Lady Macbeth was set forth with acuteness and
discrimination by the writer in the January number of POET-LORE
(1892), who said, to quote briefly, —

"The first impression of Modjeska's Lady Macbeth, by its contrast with more usual renderings, is one of almost too much feminine quickness, feminine strength, and feminine weakness mixed,
and an over-subtlety of the dependence of her *rôle* on that of her
husband ; but whatever may be thought of the elaborate insight
and delicacy of her conception of the part, the idea being granted,
admiration for the poignant sensibility, the grace, and intelligence
of the impersonation must follow."

Whether the femininity of Modjeska's portrayal be too great may
be questioned.   Like the "value" of some one color in a painting,
it may be too great in proportion to the other colors in the picture.
Certain it is that this temper of the character is the key to its
pathos, though in danger constantly, of course, of opening to the
whole a sense of weakness.   In the sleep-walking scene Modjeska
presents a sheer wreck of womanhood, the depths, not of divine, but
devilish despair, — despair in which there is no hope, — a picture
touching and true to the key to which she sets the character.   The
gliding step and sleep-drugged, shrinking motions are consonant
with the somewhat persuasive rather than peremptory temper in
which she reads the part, — the temper which Siddons was sensible
to, but the converse of that which she portrayed.   Though it can
hardly be said that Modjeska's conception of the character is its
fascination, — rather that other attribute of femininity, appeal,
this at least is dominant.   It inspires pity, not awe, never terror ;
pleads rather than constrains.   In the great passage beginning,
"I have given milk," in which Macbeth is spurred to the act, the
force of Modjeska's rendition is the picture of woman's weakness
she makes, as if to say, "You being a man should therefore do this,

if I a weak woman could do so." And throughout the urgency to "screw his courage to the sticking place," the exhortation never hardens and flashes like a flaming sword barring the way back, but is ever ductile, flowing, entreating, the weakness of the woman and her subjection to the man pleading constantly, and so following.

As essentially feminine as this portrayal, but wholly fascinating as this is entreating, is Ellen Terry's Lady Macbeth, if the consensus of newspaper criticism may be accepted. She makes her an exquisite, fragile, feminine creature with golden hair; and by this she so affronted that instinct in man which does love to sweep on in a pack full cry after a woman, hounding her to death, that the critics declared she was simply a Guinevere or some other exquisite being out of Arthurian legend. Yet Lady Macbeth is surely all that Ellen Terry made her. A woman, to excite continually the love of a sensitive, imaginative, selfish, exacting man like Macbeth, has all need of loveliness.

But Lady Macbeth has more than this. Though a woman, she was a queen, and she was a Fate; but she was this because she was so much a woman. It is the wholly feminine nature, and it only, that can subordinate all life into a passionate resolve so unreckoning in every consequence that before her the man stands in awe as something more than human; and so man has ever pictured Fate — personified the resistless forces not ourselves, moving on life — as a woman.

In Lady Macbeth this incarnation is supreme. When Macbeth has invoked her to the great purpose of their lives, he has aroused pure fate, unconscious force, that in human conception can stop nothing short of accomplishment.

*Morris Ross.*

## A PROPHECY OF AMERICA.

FROM THE CORRESPONDENCE OF —— —— AND *

Dear —— ——: Just one hundred years ago, William Blake, whom Swinburne calls "the one single Englishman of superior and simple poetic genius born before the closing years of the eighteenth century, the one man of that date fit to rank with the old great names," sat in his humble little back room, which served as bedroom, kitchen, dining-room, and work-room, — sat with his face toward the light, and created that wonderful poem in his series of prophecies called 'America.' I happened to notice this fact the other day; and this being the year of what might be called the posthumous celebration of the anniversary of our being discovered, I suppose I caught the anniversary fever, and felt that at any hazard I must remove one grain more from the appalling desert of my ignorance by reading this prophecy at once, — not an easy thing to accomplish, as you know, for the complete series of his prophecies exists only in a limited *facsimile* edition of one hundred copies of Blake's own original engravings.

Happily, I found a copy of this edition at the library, — a starred book, so precious that the direst necessity of the most gifted genius could not prevail upon the stern powers who guard the legions of books to allow it to be taken out. I myself heard one whom I conclude was one of these same geniuses irately demanding if the three stars on a book he wanted stood for " purgatory, pandemonium, and hell."

When I get hold of a book of which only one hundred copies exist, I like metaphorically to roll it about on my tongue as a delicious morsel before swallowing it. I like to ponder over the titlepage, and study the printer's imprint, and get myself generally into the proper frame of mind for the fullest enjoyment of it.

But the stars forbade, and I had to content myself with reading it then and there, with an obnoxious poster leering at me, bearing on its horrid front the legend, " No one on pain of death [I think it said] must make any tracing whatever of any drawing or design thereof, with any manner of pencil, tracing paper, or drawing implements whatsoever." As if I had any intention of attempting so sacrilegious an act as to trace the wondrous designs of William Blake, where every the smallest leaf and stem is almost palpitating with life, and seems to possess, one might venture to say, the " subtle thing called spirit."

The man who could bravely wear a *bonnet rouge* in England

during the French Revolution should give voice to wise words on the subject of liberty. Wise they are, without a doubt ; but like the oracles of old, they need interpreters. He is, I profoundly believe, the only man that ever lived who absolutely invented a mythology. All myths with which we are familiar, like the old story of the foundation of the world that rests upon an egg, which rests upon a turtle's back, which rests upon something else, vanish along with man himself among pre-antediluvian, anthropoid chatterings. No wonder, then, when an absolutely new mythology is presented to ordinary beings, whose minds know no law of knowledge but the addition and subtraction of inherited concepts, they stand appalled and cry out, "This man was mad." From this charge, Gilchrist and Swinburne have nobly defended him ; and the last has certainly thrown much light on the tortuous paths of the Prophecies.

The principal mythologic being who figures in 'America' is Orc, — a creature whose flesh is fire, who, amidst chaotic turmoil of the elements, rises from the Atlantic and announces to Albion's wrathful and terrified angel in thundering tones the gospel of liberty. The passage is so fine that I copy it for you to read :—

"The morning comes, the night decays the watchmen leave their stations
The grave is burst, the spices shed, the linen wrapped up :
The bones of death, the cov'ring clay, the sinews shrunk and dried,
Reviving shake, inspiring move, breathing, awaking
Spring like redeemed captives when their bonds and bars are burst :
Let the slave grinding at the mill, run out into the field :
Let him look up into the heavens and laugh in the bright air
Let the enchained soul shut up in darkness and in sighing
Whose face has never seen a smile in thirty weary years
Rise and look out, his chains are loose, his dungeon doors are open
And let his wife and children return from the oppressors scourge :
They look behind at every step and believe it is a dream
Singing. The Sun has left his blackness and has found a fresher morning
And the fair moon rejoices in the clear and cloudless night
For Empire is no more, and now the Lion and wolf shall cease."

Orc seems to be the symbol of eternal progress, to whom are joined all the terrible attributes of rebellion, — war and carnage and disregard of law, which are the ruthless aids in the attainment

of higher levels. Not all good, we should think, but Blake, like
Whitman, believes that "Everything that lives is holy, life delights in life; Because the soul of sweet delights can never be
defiled."

Opposed to this scourging, redeeming god of fire, is the jealous
god Urizen, the conserver of the past, who weeps his frosty tears
into the fiery depths. From Orc, long in fetters, and the shadowy
daughter of the Western Continent is born the American Revolution. The thirteen angels of the thirteen provinces sat perturbed
upon their magic seats, aroused by the terrible blasts of trumpets
blowing a loud alarm across the Atlantic. The Boston angel takes
the lead in throwing off the yoke; all the other angels follow, rend
off their robes, throw down their sceptres, and burning with the
fire of Orc, they descend headlong from the heights and stand by
Washington, Paine, and Warren. But I can give you no adequate
idea of the gigantic force and awe-inspiring effect of this poem;
though it is prophecy after the fact, the principles developed are
of universal application, the American Revolution becomes a tremendous symbol of liberty in the abstract, and there are vague
suggestions of prophetic import to the effect that the fires of
revolution shall not only bring political liberty for the whole world,

for the gates of the thrones of Italy, Spain, and France shall be
consumed by Orc, — but religious and personal liberty, and liberty
for women, for he also sees —

> "The female spirits of the dead, pining in bonds of religion
> Run from their fetters."

Time alone will show whether he is right, and whether the beneficent designs of the spirit of evolution can only be carried out
by the purging fires of revolution, the direful Orc.

                    Yours,

# A REVIEW OF THREE DRAMAS BY AMERICAN WRITERS.*

In the opinion of Mr. Edmund Clarence Stedman, the coming poetical manifestation in America, to appear in the near future, is to be dramatic, and those who entertain a sincere regard for Mr. Stedman's critical acumen are eagerly watching for the premonitory signs of the fulfilment of this prophecy, so consoling to the lover of poetry at its highest.

The establishment of the Theatre of Arts and Letters in New York is a good omen, though the sceptical might doubt the ability of even the cultured audience to appreciate drama of the highest order, more than they doubt the possibility of an American poet to produce it, so vitiated has taste become through its unresisting acceptance of drama with no literary merit whatever. It may even be doubted whether literature can ever be brought back to the stage. Although it is a favorite dictum of the critics that a drama which does not act is no drama, I sometimes suspect that, owing to the differentiating process always going on, we shall soon be obliged to recognize two legitimate species of drama, — one to be acted and one to be read : the first a reflex of the external localized life of the time, mirror-like in its faithful representation of talk as it is (which is certainly neither prose nor poetry); the second, a reflex of human character in its far-reaching universal relations, the language, not a representative of talk as it is, but lifted into the ideal realm of literary prose or poetry.

Three recent dramas by American writers are especially worthy of attention, — Amélie Rives's 'Athelwold,' Richard Hovey's 'Launcelot and Guenevere,' and Harriet Monroe's ' Valeria.'

---

* Athelwold, by Amélie Rives, *Harper's*, February, 1892. New York : Harper and Bros. — Launcelot and Guenevere : A Poem in Dramas, by Richard Hovey. New York : United States Book Co., 1891. — Valeria and Other Poems, by Harriet Monroe. Chicago : A. C. McClurg and Co., 1892.

All of them indicate ability of a high order, but are they true evangels of what the American poet may in the future attain to in dramatic writing, or only the accomplished work of talent with its gaze resting upon the glories of a departing sun, unaroused by any fresh harmonies which might be caught from the lyre of a newly risen Apollo?

Some analysis of the dramas may serve to answer this query in part.

In the first place, the dramatic motive of all three dramas is identical, — the old, old story which extends back to Aryan times, of the conflict between two men, a lover and a husband, for one woman, which has become most familiar to us as it is found in the Arthurian legends of Launcelot and Guenevere. This plot, old as it is, admits of innumerable variations, because the individuality of the beings so grouped may run the whole gamut of human possibilities in character.

Amélie Rives has succeeded in combining the elements of the plot in such a way that our sympathies do not go out to any of the chief actors in it.

King Edgar, though he cares not to have his kingship recognized in his personal intercourse with his friend Athelwold, abates not one jot of his kingly prerogative as it was recognized in those embryonic times, when it comes to the point of claiming as his, by right, the wife of his friend.

Athelwold, sent to do the king's wooing for him, himself loves, as such messengers are wont to do, and love in him conquers honor, as he understands it, from the first. He deceives the king as to Elfreda's beauty, declares that the report of it is a myth, and the king, with the touching magnanimity of the great, proposes that his beloved thane shall marry the ugly heiress for her gold.

Neither is the heroine, Elfreda, a lovable being, though she is certainly interesting. So full is she of ambition and the love of admiration that even while she is swearing her undying love for Athelwold, one is conscious of an under-current of faithlessness, a feeling evidently shared by Athelwold himself. At last, when the test comes, she fails him.

The latent fineness of Athelwold's character comes out at this point. His fealty to his king is lost in his greater fealty to the sanctity of the marriage relation. When Athelwold lies slain, and it is too late, Elfreda tears off the jewels with which she had bedecked herself to captivate the king, and makes a great plaint, declaring she will follow her husband; but there is no certainty left in the reader's mind that her ambition will not get the better of her grief, and that shortly she will marry the king, whose last speech in regard to her is significant: " Call thy Lady's women, she hath but swooned, I think." Though the characters do not any of them act in a way to rouse the emotions, the delineation of them is managed so artistically as to make it a positive pleasure to read the drama. We feel that Edgar, Athelwold, and Elfreda are true representatives of the age where the author has put them. A modern Athelwold would risk all by confessing to the king; but the king must needs be strong who would recognize the paramount right of love over royal prerogative, and the woman must needs be strong — as Colombe in Browning's drama was strong — to withstand the glitter of royalty, if she were given the choice.

Had they, therefore, been actuated by any higher ethical principles, the drama would have lost the antique flavor which is one of its charms, and which Amélie Rives knows so well how to enhance with her quaint English.

When all is said, however, in praise of the clever construction of the plot, the consistency of the character-drawing, the smoothness and vigor of much of the blank verse, the charming touches of naturalness in such scenes as that between Elfreda and her nurse, the fact remains that the drama is retrospective. It contains no reflection of the great thoughts which stir the heart of this century.

In his 'Launcelot and Guenevere' Mr. Hovey has certainly fulfilled Milton's famous saying that poetry should be sensuous and passionate. He has portrayed the love of these two so that no doubt is left in the mind but that it is love indeed, — love bounded only by eternity, not a passion limited by the exigencies of time and space. Indeed, if he had not succeeded in conveying this impression, there are certain passages in this drama which would come dangerously near descending into the shadows of sensuality. The knights and ladies of Arthur's court, including Arthur himself, do not appear clothed in all the beauty of purity; and even Launcelot and Guenevere, stricken by fate with immortal love though they were, might have exercised a little more reserve to advantage.

Comparisons with Tennyson's 'Idyls' naturally suggest themselves; but Mr. Hovey's musical and often impassioned verse bears the juxtaposition well, while the version he gives of the story serves to place Launcelot and Guenevere in a better light than Tennyson does. Like Amélie Rives, he has not been at all times able to steer quite clear of imitations of Shakespeare. Who will not think of the cloud-capped palaces when he reads,

> " Let Britain sink
> Beneath the Atlantic and the solid base
> And universal dome of things dissolve
> And like the architecture of a cloud
> Melt in the blue inane " ?

The scenes in which the watchmen figure are such palpable imitations of similar scenes in Shakespeare as to shake for the moment one's faith in Mr. Hovey's creative faculty. Could he not have invented a newer species of humor than that which makes the watchman declare that he is set there to " apprehend benefactors "? He even carries his imitation to the extent of introducing an anachronism, for the first watchman, trying to be wise, refers to Mark Antony as " An oracle, he that killed Cæsar in the play. He killed him oracularly." These, however, are small matters in comparison with the real beauty to be found in the greater part of his poetry.

The first drama, ' The Quest of Merlin,' a sort of mystical prologue to the second, ' The Marriage of Guenevere,' is full of subtile suggestions. In his quest to discover the fate of the marriage between Arthur and Guenevere, the earth-born Merlin, with all his magic, gets a glimpse of much of which he can scarcely grasp the meaning.

He is shown that through all the evil and turmoil of life, Good holds the sceptre, and will at last reign supreme, and that perfect love is the goal toward which all human efforts tend, and that all humanity contributes its share toward the final completion.

But all this is presented to him through successive scenes in which all manner of mythologic beings and angels figure, from the mysterious Norns to the fairies of mediæval lore and the fauns and satyrs of Greece.

There is an especially striking scene between Aphrodite and the Valkyrs, who recognize the need of each other's qualities to produce rounded womanhood.

Guenevere in the drama following is probably, in the author's opinion, the human manifestation of this compact between the goddesses of the South and the North, though it might seem that her Valkyr qualities are rather swallowed up in her Aphrodite qualities, at least after she meets Launcelot. Before that event, in one of the finest passages in the poem, she rails against the bondage of woman; and though she does not show herself quite on a plane with self-respecting modern womanhood, she indicates that spirit of rebellion which has made the modern woman possible.

Though the subject is old, there is much poetic thought displayed in Mr. Hovey's handling of it, which makes of it not a drama of any special time or place, but a world-drama approaching the ideal of Goethe's ' Faust,' and which all American lovers of poetry should be glad to welcome as an earnest of future possibilities in the drama of American poets.

Nor should they be less interested in Miss Harriet Monroe's 'Valeria,' in which her powers, become so justly famed in her Columbian Ode, are shown at their height.

Her dramatic motive is more complex than that of the preceding dramas. Mixed up with the love, there is political treachery to the Prince on the part of the lover Florimond.

Valeria, the poor singing-girl who, through the interest of the Prince, has become court minstrel, though she has declared her love for Florimond, cannot resist the gratification to her ambition when the Prince, who is capable of constant devotion, asks her to be his wife. But her free "Artist Soul" soon finds the bondage of marriage intolerable. She conspires with Florimond, whom the Prince thinks his friend, against the life of her husband.

The poisoned wine stands on the table when the Prince rushes into the room, exclaiming that he has killed the man who dared to warn him that his friend Florimond and his wife are conspiring to poison him ; and to show his perfect trust in them, he drinks the wine down. In his faith in his wife and friend, he is the exact counterpart of King Arthur in Hovey's drama. It would be difficult to imagine more tragic situations than these, though in the case of Arthur it is more heart-rending, for the love of Launcelot and Guenevere is a fatality not to be changed, while in Miss Monroe's drama, true love is for the first time born in Valeria for the Prince who has so fatally defended her. Though externally a tragedy, ending in the death of the hero and heroine, the goal — the achievement of a perfect love — is reached.

There is a strength and originality about Miss Monroe's lines which proclaim her to be a poet of unusual promise ; it is to be hoped that the general indifference of the public to dramatic writing will not deter her from attempting more in this line, for which she seems especially endowed. Why should not the complexities of character and social life in the America of to-day furnish material even more worthy to be moulded by her poetic touch than those of Florence in the fourteenth century ?

*C.*

## BOOK INKLINGS.

—— " GREAT poets ask the people for bread," says Schumann, "and the people give them, after they are dead, a stone!" Sometimes not for a long time after they are dead is there any recognition of their transcendent value to mankind. Not the slightest memorial to John Keats had there ever been in England until now, when it is proposed to place one in Hampstead Church, by Americans, and through the efforts of Americans, — Professor Norton, Miss Guiney, and Mr. Day.

The Shelley Memorial in Horsham is another belated token of appreciation ; and none the less a memorial of Shelley's increasing value to the plodding earth his wings of thought and ardor took him so far in advance of, is the American Centenary Edition of Shelley, brought out in such perfect typographical shape and style by Houghton, Mifflin, & Co., in such judicious editorial fashion by George Edward Woodberry. Through these comely volumes, the poet of the ' Ode to Liberty' should find a thronging audience in this New World. That he is enabled thus fitly to appeal, at last, " To the eternal years enthroned before us In the dim West" is the more stirring thought when we remember certain pathetic lines he once wrote. Mr. Woodberry gives these words of his, not in the Memoir, where he sums up for us what is most valuable to know of the facts of Shelley's life, but in the Notes, where he gives letters and all information that can throw a light on the poet's creative work. There may be found these lines, which show us the disappointment of the " heart of hearts" over the deafness of his people : —

" Nothing is more difficult and unwelcome than to write without a confidence of finding readers ; and if my Play of ' The Cenci ' found none or few, I despair of ever producing anything that shall merit them."

Is there any one who is dull to the splendor of ' The Cenci ' now ? (The Complete Works of Percy Bysshe Shelley. The text newly collated and revised and edited, with a memoir and notes, by George Edward Woodberry, Centenary Edition in four volumes. Boston & New York : Houghton, Mifflin, & Co., 1892.)

—— ALL lovers of literature who like to see their idols fitly housed will view with delight the new edition of Landor's Works now issuing from the press of J. M. Dent & Co., of London. It would be hard to find more satisfactory examples of book-making. The binding is dark green, with handsome design in gold covering the back, while on the front cover is a crest or seal in gold with the motto, " Shadows we are and like shadows depart." Nor is the inside, with its heavy paper and uncut leaves, less attractive. The volumes so far received include two containing his ' Poems and

Dialogues in Verse' and the first of two containing his ' Longer Prose Works.' They are edited by Chas. S. Crump, whose introduction gives, it seems to us, a very fair estimate of Landor's powers as a poet. He has also supplied many interesting notes, and a valuable bibliography of Landor's works. The volumes are further enriched by frontispiece illustrations. In Vol. I. is a dainty etching of Llanthony Abbey ; in Vol. II. a *facsimile* of a letter of Landor's ; and from Vol. III. gazes out upon us the serious, intellectual face of Aspasia. Of the soul that inhabits this beautiful house there is no need to speak here. (New York: Macmillan & Co.)

# NOTES AND NEWS.

## LONDON LITERARIA.

THE Laureateship would still seem to be an open question. There has been no whisper of its having been offered to Mr. Swinburne; indeed, under existing conditions, one can hardly imagine the most democratic of premiers crowning with the laurel the author of ' Songs before Sunrise ; ' and albeit the Swinburne of to-day is apparently not the sterling Radical and out-and-out Republican of twenty years ago, the verse then written is as imperishable as it is exquisite, and the sentiments therein enunciated remain. Is the post of Laureate, however, to be kept open pending a fresh volume of verse from the pen of Mr. William Watson ? It would almost appear to be so in the light of Mr. Gladstone's offer to the poet of a literary " pension " of £200 for *one year only.* That it should for the present be kept open is in every way preferable to any premature appointment; but unfortunately the recent mental illness of Mr. Watson may militate against his proving, for some time to come, the full strength of his poetic gifts. That he has poetic genius of a very high order, his ' Lachrymæ Musarum ' bears ample testimony ; and greater work than this may be expected from him. Given length of years, one may safely prophesy that he will become in due time Laureate, if not the immediate successor of Tennyson. Concerning Mr. Watson's present condition, readers of POET-LORE will be glad to learn that his health has greatly improved; and it is hoped a month or two spent quietly abroad will fully restore his mental balance.

An interesting Tennysonian episode was the recent sale at Sotheby's of the original autograph manuscript of the ' Poems of Two Bruthers,' entirely in the handwriting of Alfred and Charles Tennyson, — mostly in that of the former. It forms a book of eighty-eight leaves, exclusive of covers, — on which are written part of the poems and other matter ; also, apart from the volume, the title, advertisement, errata, and an introductory poem, ' 'T is sweet to lead from stage to stage.' On the reverse of the title appears an autograph letter to the publishers, Messrs. Jackson, referring to a poem being omitted from the portion of the volume in type. The contents is on a separate sheet, in the body of an interesting letter in the handwriting of Alfred Tennyson, respecting copyright, etc. There was also the original receipt given to the publisher for £20, the sum agreed upon for copyright of the volume ' Poems by Two Brothers,' signed by Alfred and Charles. On the reverse of the leaf, with the errata, is a note signed " C. and A. T.," referring to the publication of the authors' signatures. Three of the autograph poems seem to have been cancelled, as they do not appear in the published work. Accompanying the above was the publisher's reserved copy of the book, — perfectly clean, in the original boards. After a short fight between Mr. B. F. Stevens (the Anglo-American bookseller) and Messrs. Macmillan (of Cambridge), the " lot " was secured by the latter for £480!

Mr. William Morris has evidently a " large order " on hand at his Kelmscott Press. Chief of the many important works announced for early issue is the poet's new romance, ' The Well at the World's End.' This will form a large quarto volume, printed in double columns, and will contain four woodcuts by C. F. Murray. For this work, what Mr. Morris terms the " Chaucer " type will be

14

used. It appears that the poet has three descriptions of type, — the "Golden," the "Troy," and the "Chaucer," his earlier productions being printed in "Golden" type, while the "Troy" type has hitherto been reserved for Caxton reprints. Another book on hand at the Kelmscott Press is 'Shakespeare's Poems and Sonnets,' reprinted from the first editions; while three other works are in preparation: a new edition of the 'Story of the Glittering Plain,' with twenty-three illustrations by Walter Crane; 'Cavendish's Life of Wolsey,' reprinted from the original manuscript; and the works of Geoffrey Chaucer, with some sixty designs by Burne-Jones. Yet another work on hand is Caxton's 'Order of Chivalry,' which will be accompanied by a translation, by Mr. Morris, of 'L'Ordère de Chevalerie,' — a French poem of the thirteenth century.            *William G. Kingsland.*

LONDON, ENGLAND, Jan. 7, 1893.

———

—— ON the last-discovered Shakespearian relic, *The Twentieth Century* furnishes note and comment as follows : —

"Evanston, Ill., possesses a relic of inestimable value, — a hair and a half (or perhaps a hair and two halves) of an eyebrow of Shakespeare. Evanston is the seat of an institution of Higher Learning, the Northwestern University, and it is proposed to purchase the relic for the university museum. The usual question of genuineness arises with regard to this as to all relics, whether sacred or secular, and though the documentary evidence is not absolutely conclusive on the affirmative side, it is pretty strong. The present owner, Sarah W. Gillette, inherited the relic from her father, Dr. H. C. Gillette, who died in Evanston, 1878. He obtained it by purchase from R. G. Oaks, an English wood-carver, who gave to the doctor a memorandum of its history as far as his relation to it extended. Oaks first saw the relic in 1851, when he had in his hand the original Kesselstadt plaster death-mask of Shakespeare, intrusted to him by the Duke of Devonshire for the purpose of carving a laurel wreath to encircle the brow. In examining the mask 'for the pores in the plaster to decide whether the cast was original or not,' Oaks found two hairs of the eyebrow sticking in the cast. 'I extracted one,' he writes, 'the other broke.' There is the history of that hair and a half (or other vulgar fraction of a hair) back to 1851, and from 1851 back to its starting point it is presumably borne on the wings of the voluminous Shakespeare lore. I am willing to admit its genuineness, but I should like very much if somebody would illumine my crass ignorance and tell me what earthly, or unearthly or superterrestial, use the relic can serve. If it could, like a bone of St. Ann or St. Antony, make the blind see, the deaf hear, the paralytic walk and dance, there would be reason for its cult; as it does none of these things nor anything like or else, except perhaps to make fatuity more fatuous, I wonder much why it should be treasured, and above all why it should be thought of as an object to be enshrined in the museum of a university."

## A NOTE ON 'LOCKSLEY HALL.'

" 'T is the place, and all around it, as of old, the curlews call,
  Dreary gleams about the moorland flying over Locksley Hall."

In the interesting study of ' Locksley Hall' in the January number of POET-LORE (p. 35), a portion of this stanza is paraphrased thus : "' the curlews call,' flying about the ' moorland,' and glancing through the air like ' dreary gleams.'"

The construction and meaning of the passage have been much discussed in the English *Notes and Queries* and other periodicals. Some critics have assumed that " curlews call" is a misprint for " curlews' call," — the possessive with another noun, instead of the nominative and verb ; and they quote, in illustration of the bold metaphor, certain passages in the Greek poets in which a voice or sound is said to shine forth or " gleam," — as, for instance : —

ἔλαμψε ἀρτίως φανεῖσα φάμα (Sophocles) ;
βοὰ πρέπει (Pindar).

For myself, I always took "gleams" to be in apposition with "curlews," as the writer in POET-LORE does ; and in the first edition of my ' Select Poems of Tennyson' (1884) I so explained the construction, adding : " The birds, as they fly over the hall, seem like *dreary gleams* in the sky." I felt very sure that this was the right interpretation ; but I was none the less gratified when it was confirmed and aptly illustrated by Dr. Horace Howard Furness, who, in a letter acknowledging the receipt of a copy of the book, congratulated me on having explained the passage correctly, and added: " The curlews have dusky backs, indistinguishable at twilight, but white breasts, and as they fly in coveys are not noticed until on wheeling they show for a moment these ' gleaming' breasts. I saw them first when I was riding at sunset across the dreary plain of La Mancha in Spain, and I could n't imagine what these momentary flashes of light were until I happened to see a flock near at hand, when I involuntarily exclaimed, ' Locksley Hall !' and the line which had long puzzled me was explained."

Not long afterward I received a letter from Lord Tennyson, in which he informed me that the *gleams* are not curlews at all, and that " *dreary gleams flying* is put absolutely — while dreary gleams are flying."

I quoted both letters in the next edition of my little book, but I could not refrain from adding : " There is no appeal from this, of course ; but we almost feel like saying that if the poet did not mean what our friend and we took him to mean, he *ought* to have done so ! " It still seems to me the more natural and the better interpretation. If I remember right, the other and authoritative one was not suggested by any of the critics who took part in the discussions of the passage to which I have referred above. The *flying* naturally connects itself with the birds, and the change of subject is awkward and perplexing. It introduces the only reference in the poem to the clouded sky ; and even after we know that it *is* such a reference, it is at first no clearer than the sky. What *are* these " dreary gleams " flying overhead ? Mr. F. T. Palgrave, in his ' Lyric Poems of Lord Tennyson,' which to me bears internal evidence of having passed under the poet's eye, has the brief note, " of flying light," in explanation of *gleams*. Does he mean light seen through rifts in the flying clouds, or flying patches of cloud in the lower strata of the atmosphere seen against the darker general background of clouded sky? I suspect it is the latter, but I am not sure of it. No doubt the picture was clear in the poet's imagination, but it is not so to mine. I prefer to see the *gleams* as the white-breasted curlews, as I had seen them from the time I first read the poem fifty years ago until I got Lord Tennyson's correction of my note upon it in 1884.

While on the subject of 'Locksley Hall' let me add that, in the second edition of my 'Select Poems of Tennyson,' I printed two unpublished stanzas of the poem which Mrs. Frances Kemble transcribed into Dr. Furness's copy of the edition of 1842. They read as follows : —

> "In the hall there is a picture, Amy's arms are round my neck,
> Happy children, in a sunbeam, sitting on the ribs of wreck.

> "In my life there is a picture, she who clasp'd my neck is flown.
> I am left within the shadow, sitting on the wreck alone."

They were inserted after the nineteenth stanza, and come in aptly after the allusion to the seashore and the "stately ships." They were subsequently put, with a change of tense, into the second 'Locksley Hall.'

Mr. Arthur Waugh, in his 'Alfred Lord Tennyson,' just published, says that Mr. Edmund Gosse has a copy of the edition of 1842 which belonged to B. W. Procter ("Barry Cornwall"), and in which he had inserted these same stanzas. The reading of the first line in this copy is, "In the hall there hangs a painting," etc., which agrees with the later 'Locksley Hall,' and is probably as the poet wrote it. I presume that Mrs. Kemble transcribed the lines from memory.

It will doubtless be news to the readers of POET-LORE that the original manuscript of 'Locksley Hall' (or *one* of the original manuscripts) is in the possession of a gentleman in Massachusetts, to whose father it was presented by the author many years ago. It has some interesting variations from the published poem, but the owner is pledged, as his father was, not to allow these to get into print, though he occasionally shows them in confidence to his intimate friends. I shall not tell who he is, for obvious reasons. When at Aldworth this past summer I asked Mr. Hallam Tennyson if he was aware of the existence of this manuscript. He replied that he was, and gave me some particulars concerning it which I had not learned on this side of the ocean.

*W. J. Rolfe.*

CAMBRIDGE, Jan. 17, 1893.

# SOCIETIES.

**The Boston Browning Society** held its fifty-seventh regular meeting on Tuesday, December 27, Rev. Philip S. Moxom in the chair. The minutes of the previous meeting were read and approved. The programme was opened according to announcement by the reading of 'Pambo' and 'Popularity' by Prof. S. S. Curry. Rev. Francis B. Hornbrooke was introduced as the first essayist of the afternoon, and read a paper entitled 'The Poet's Attitude toward his Critics.' This attitude should depend on the kind of criticism he meets. About that which judges the judge more severely than the poet, he need not concern himself at all. Criticisms touching form and method, whose writers have not looked through these to find the poet's message, are equally of little value, and the poet should simply go on educating his readers, making his appeal to those who will appreciate him in due time. It is less easy to define the attitude a poet should take toward those critics who accept him for what he is and try to judge how far he has accomplished what he tried to do. Mr. Hornbrooke reviewed the positions of Wordsworth, Byron, Tennyson, and Browning toward such criticism, and concluded by believing that while a poet might indeed learn something from it, yet in general he must sing his own song in his own way, and believe in his message too deeply to be overmuch concerned regarding its first reception. (This paper will appear in full in POET-LORE.)

Miss Helen A. Clarke read a paper entitled 'The Value of Contemporary Judgment.' She looked back to the times of the Elizabethan writers to discover the opinions of their contemporaries concerning them, and quoted also from early reviews of Wordsworth, Keats, Shelley, and Coleridge. When a poet appears in an age of literary growth and enthusiasm, contemporary judgment is likely to be appreciative; in an artificial age it is likely to be exaggerated in its appreciation; while criticism of the poet who is also a prophet is generally of little value. Contemporary judgment ranges now through all degrees of worth, since we judge no longer by schools, but by individuals. The relativity of all art is fast becoming the chief principle of criticism. (This paper will appear in full in POET-LORE.)

Discussion on the question 'Should the True Poet sing to the Masses, not to the Few?' was opened by Miss Heloise E. Hersey.

In answering this question it is necessary to take a midway position, since neither a definite "Yes" nor a definite "No" can cover the ground. We must ask first "To whom *have* they sung in the past?" From the folk-singers *par excellence*, like Longfellow, Burns, Cowper, and Chaucer, one learns that the prime requisite of a song for the many is musical quality, — a term implying also simplicity. Next it must be an expression of universal passion, and such poems are usually deeply religious, deeply patriotic, or humorous. Secondly, there are the poets whose words never reach the masses, but whose message, by some mysterious process, percolates through all society. This is true of Bacon's essays, and it is becoming true of Emerson's writings in prose, and of Shelley's in poetry. It is a great thing to write a poem which shall touch the many, like 'The Psalm of Life,' but it is also a great thing to write one like 'The Statue and the Bust,' which shall reach with the same lesson a man the other could not affect. There is still a third class of poets, — those who never by any chance or transformation touch the popular heart, but these are all for the day only.

If we compare the work of the kindergarten teacher, educating the half-forsaken little ones in a great city, with the work of the college professor, instructing young men who are to go out and test in actual experience theories of social relations, we feel that no one can tell which is the more important, since we must have different criterions for judging worth than those which are based on numbers. There is little need of grading poets at all, but if we must do it, let it be by the procreation of ideas.

The chairman summed up briefly certain points of the afternoon's study. The true poet sings at last for all, but there are spheres of art and poetry into which one cannot enter who has not striven and overcome. We must grow up to the prophet, if we would understand him.

Professor Curry then said that the word of the modern critic was coming to be appreciation, and that criticism stood no longer as the expression of a narrow, exclusive set. The new critic will try to apprehend the vision that has stirred the poet. All art is democratic, and unless the poet speak to the soul of the race, he is forgotten.

Rev. Julius H. Ward spoke of the influence certain criticism had had in preparing the way for Tennyson at a turning-point in his career. He turned aside from discussion to propose that the papers of the Society should be published in some permanent form.

Rev. H. G. Spaulding was introduced as one who had lately been unable to attend the meetings of the Society. He thought the true poet would care little for either praise or blame as such, but that he would care greatly for appreciation, and he quoted from a letter Browning had written him to show how honestly welcome such appreciation had been to him. The great poet would sing to nobody, but shoot his arrow in the air, sure to find his song at last in the heart of a friend.

Mr. Estes announced that the Browning Society papers would be printed in POET-LORE, and that henceforth, according to vote of the council, official reports of the proceedings of the Society would likewise appear in its pages.                                         *E. E. Marean.*

The Browning Society of the New Century Club of Philadelphia held its Second General Meeting on December 8. Under the head of 'Song in Youth,' selections were read from Browning's 'Pauline,' Tennyson's 'Nothing Will Die,' and Chatterton's 'Ane Excelent Poem of Charitie.' A paper dealing with 'Public Indifference to the Early Utterances of Poets' was read by Mrs. Richard P. White. This was followed by a discussion of the question, 'Was the Tragedy of Chatterton's Life due to the Lack of Public Appreciation?'

On December 22d, the Second Study Meeting was held. The readings were 'A Toccata of Galuppi's,' and selections from Tennyson's 'The Voyage of Maeldune' and Keats's 'The Eve of St. Agnes.'

As the subject of discussion for the evening had been assigned to Dr. D. G. Brinton, whose absence in Europe prevented him from stating the regular question, 'Do Poets exhibit any Constant Relation between Certain Colors and Certain States of Mind?' another subject was substituted, dealing with the 'Poetic Treatment of External Influences on the Passions.' Mr. Francis Howard Williams stated the question, and a lively and interesting discussion followed, which continued until the time of adjournment. Mr. Gilchrist, the biographer of Blake, was present and joined in the discussion.                              *J. Sulzberger.*

The Scarborough Literary Society, England, has prepared the following programme on Ruskin for its present session, 1892–93:

RUSKIN IN INDUSTRY: A PRACTICAL DEMONSTRATION. October. Lecture by Mr. GEO. THOMSON, of Huddersfield. (Books suggested for reading, — 'Fors Clavigera;' 'Unto This Last.')

JOHN RUSKIN: HIS HOME AND HIS ECONOMICS. November. Lecture by J. W. GRAHAM, M. A., of Manchester. ('The Crown of Wild Olive;' 'Munera Pulveris.')

THE SOCIAL TEACHINGS OF RUSKIN. December. Lecture by Mr. E. S. PICKARD, of Leeds. (Books as above, also, 'Time and Tide.')

RUSKIN'S STYLE. January. Paper by Mr. E. R. CROSS.

PAINTING AND PAINTERS. February. Paper by E. A. COOPER, M. A. February. ('Modern Painters;' 'Lectures on Architecture and Painting.')

ART AND MORALS. March. Paper by MISS ALICE THOMPSON. (Books as above, also, 'Stones of Venice;' 'Seven Lamps of Architecture.')

Vol. V.      No. 3.

——wilt thou not haply saie,
Truth needs no collour with his collour fixt;
Beautie no penſell, beauties truth to lay:
But beſt is beſt if never intermixt.
Becauſe he needs no praiſe, wilt thou be dumb?
Excuſe not ſilence ſo, for't lies in thee,
To make him much outliue a gilded tombe,
And to be praiſed of ages yet to be.
Then do thy office ——

# THE SOCIALISTIC THREAD IN THE LIFE
# AND WORKS OF WILLIAM MORRIS.

THE socialists of Hammersmith are accustomed to meet weekly at Kelmscott House, the London home of Mr. Morris on the Upper Mall, — socialists they are called, neighbors they appear to be as they come together in families for an evening's conference. Frequently Mr. Morris will act as chairman. Sometimes he will speak. One night he had spoken with more than usual sadness upon the hope of his life, and in closing he uttered these words: " Neighbors, it is Peace that we need that we may live and work in hope and joy." Leaving the hall, the writer stood with a friend for a half-hour beneath the elm-trees, looking out over the river. The tide was flowing quietly to the sea. A light mist obscured the opposite shore. The river, the passing boats, the bridge, the city beyond, were all toned down to a common grayness. Neither of us spoke a word. The peace of the evening seemed to mingle with the words we had heard and to give direction to our thoughts. Then, near at hand, we heard the same voice of the poet saying, —

"So with this Earthly Paradise it is,
   If ye will read aright, and pardon me,
   Who strive to build a shadowy isle of bliss,
   Midmost the beating of the steely sea,
   Where tossed about all hearts of men must be."

William Morris, master-workman, poet, and socialist, was born
March 24, 1834, at Walthamstow, a village in Essex not far from
London.  He was the eldest-born of a family of nine.  His father
was an enterprising business man of the city.  At Walthamstow
William went to a school kept by Dr. Greig, a Scotchman, who
describes his pupil as a rollicking boy, full of the vigor of life.
After the death of Mr. Morris, in 1848, the family moved to Marlborough, where William attended the College and began to take
interest in art and archæology.  He went "steeple-chasing," and
was fond of memorial brasses.  In 1852 he entered Oxford at
Exeter College.  At that time the University was in the midst of
a mediæval revival which was fostered on the one hand by the
Tractarian College of Newman, and on the other by the artistic
guild of the pre-Raphaelite Brothers.  Under the influence of Rossetti, Holman Hunt, and other painters of the mediæval school,
Morris, with his college chum, E. Burne Jones, became a student
of the Middle Ages.  He passed his college days in comparative
idleness and in dreams.

In 1856 Morris and a few other idealists started a monthly magazine, called *The Oxford and Cambridge Magazine.*  Like its proto-
type, *The Germ* of 1850, the organ of the pre-Raphaelites, it had
an existence of a year.  To this magazine Rossetti contributed
some of his finest poems, including ' The Burden of Nineveh ' and
' The Blessed Damozel.'  Morris wrote for successive numbers a
series of mediæval romances, having such titles as ' A Dream,'
' Gertha's Lovers,' ' The Hollow Land,' and ' Golden Wings.'  Each
story is depicted with an artist's love of color and with a poet's
imagery, and all are steeped in the spirit of a time " long ago."

" Long ago there was a land, never mind where or when, a fair
country and good to live in, rich with wealth of golden corn, beautiful with many woods, watered by great rivers and pleasant trick-

ling streams; moreover one extremity of it was bounded by the washing of the purple waves, and the other by the solemn watchfulness of the purple mountains " ('Gertha's Lovers').

There are a few poems in the volume also by Morris. 'Summer Dawn' is as beautiful as anything he has since written, and is touched by a characteristic grayness.

> "Pray but one prayer for me 'twixt thy closed lips,
>   Think but one thought of me up in the stars,
>   The summer night waneth, the morning light slips,
>   Faint and grey, 'twixt the leaves of the aspen, betwixt the closed bars
>   That are patiently waiting there for the morn —
>   Patient and colorless, though Heaven's gold
>   Waits to float through them along with the sun.
>   Far out in the meadows, above the young corn,
>   The heavy elms wait, and restless and cold
>   The uneasy wind rises; the roses are dun;
>   Through the long twilight they pray for the morn
>   Round the lone house in the midst of the corn.
>     Speak but one word to me over the corn,
>     Over the tender bow'd locks of the corn."

The poet's next step after leaving Oxford was to enter the office of Mr. G. E. Street, a London architect, who is best known as the builder of the Law Courts in the Strand. Here he worked for nearly a year. Then he began to study painting and artistic decoration. In 1857 he was associated with Jones, Rossetti, Hunt, Prinsep, and others in painting upon the walls of the Oxford Union Debating Hall the frescoes, now but dimly visible, illustrating the Arthurian Romance. The subjects treated by Morris were Sir Palonides and the jealousy of Sir Tristram and the Fair Isulte. His first volume of poems, 'The Defence of Guenevere, and Other Poems,' was published in 1858, under the interest awakened by Tennyson's and Southey's studies of the Arthurian Period. In comparison with Tennyson, Morris is seen to be a veritable child of the Middle Ages. He writes of Arthur as a contemporary; Tennyson is essentially modern. The influence of Rossetti and of Browning is distinctly marked in this early volume. The general effect is that of the painter, but 'The Judgment of God' reads quite like one of Browning's dramatic lyrics.

In a review in *The Literary Gazette* of March 6, 1859, written by Mr. Richard Garnett, Morris is referred to as Rossetti plus Browning. The prophecy is there made that Morris will prove a " poet whom poets will love."

In 1861 Morris joined with Madox Brown, E. Burne Jones, Rossetti, and Philip Webb, in forming an art firm with the intent of designing and manufacturing stained-glass windows, mosaics, wall-papers, artistic furniture, and general household decorations. A guild of idealists, one exclaims, like a Brook Farm Commune! But the distinguishing mark of these artists was their conviction of the honor of labor and the glory of thoroughness. Each was gifted with a love of order and splendor, and filled with a deep sense of the need of beauty in human life. To join art to labor, to add pleasure to the things of common use, was the purpose of the company.

The work of the manufactory is carried on at Merton Abbey, a village on the Thames, far enough from London that Nature still lingers in its environs, and the birds find room for joyful song. The very name of the place is suggestive of a mediæval workshop. In the twelfth century Gilbert Norman, Sheriff of Surrey, built here a monastery for canons of the order of Saint Austin. It was patronized by Stephen and Matilda, and endowed with rich gifts. In 1236 there was held within its walls a Parliament which enacted the "Statutes of Merton," wherein the English nobles reply to the prelates : " We will not change the laws of England."

An old mansion, half-draped with trees and hidden in shrubbery, stands by the roadside at the edge of the village. Behind the house, under the great elms, are grouped the low and unpretentious buildings of the factory. From the neighboring gardens comes an odor of grass and roses. The air is tumultuous with the songs of blackbirds and thrushes. Crows caw in the far elms. At one side, the slow waters of the Wandel, gathered here into a lily-covered pond, are coaxing a mill-wheel, green with moss, lazily to turn. Willows grow along the banks of the stream and bend down over it ; willows and sky are reflected from the surface of the water. Over all there is a sense of sunny summer. The scene tells of sympathy and loving harmony with Nature. There is no air of the factory, no clang of machinery, no dust, no haste or distraction. Within the buildings men and women are at work weaving at looms, dyeing and printing cloths, and putting together the windows.

In the designing-room is Mr. Morris himself. Half-finished sketches, some bold cartoons evidently by the hand of E. Burne Jones, are scattered about the room. Morris is dressed as usual in a plain suit of blue serge and flannel. He is short of stature, but robust, and full of the most restless energy. The features of his face are large and rugged, but full-blooded, luminous, and well modelled. A kindly poet's expression is given by the eye, and the mouth beneath the gray beard. His head is covered with curly gray hair, which he brushes back over his forehead with his hand, as he leans to his work. One feels in the presence of a vital personality who is in love with labor and all the life of the world.

In speech, when aroused by his theme, Morris is rapid and nervous. For thirty years he has claimed for art a place in common labor. He pleads first of all for simplicity of life. From simplicity of life would rise up a longing for beauty and artistic creation, which can only be satisfied by making beauty and art a very part of the labor of every man who produces. Labor, he argues, is not a preparation for living, it is our very life. And the rewards of labor? The reward of creation, the wages which God gets. Art comes back most to the artist. Everything made by man has a form, and that form is either beautiful or ugly. The one gives pleasure; the other is a weariness. Decoration is simply the expression of man's pleasure in successful labor. And the price of pleasure? Simply permission to the workman to put his own intelligence and enthusiasm into what he is fashioning; simply permission to make his hands set forth his mind and soul. Only then is labor sanctified, because then it is in the direction of a man's life. A structure should rise out of the soul. Order, or meaning, is the moral quality of structure. Make matter express a meaning, and the worker becomes a moral master. We must, therefore, travel back from the machine to the human. For men

must "prove their living souls against the notion that they live
in you or under you, O wheels." The machine, the great achievement of the nineteenth century, which promised to relieve our
drudgery, has instead increased our burdens. The wonderful inventions which in the hands of far-seeing men might be used to
minimize the labor of the many are only used for the enrichment
of their owners.

Morris reverts, therefore, in his conception of an ideal future,
to the traditions of labor in operation in the Middle Ages, when
the human meaning wrapped up in the term "hand-made" was
well known, when the handicraftsman took pride in his work;
and it is by the truest instinct that the poet turns thus: —

"Let us think of the mighty and lovely architecture of mediæval Europe, of the buildings raised before Commerce had put the
coping stone on the edifice of tyranny by the discovery that fancy,
imagination, sentiment, the joy of creation and the hope of fair
fame are marketable articles too precious to be allowed to men
who have not the money to buy them, to mere handicraftsmen and
day laborers. Let us remember there was a time when men had
pleasure in their daily work, but yet as to other matters hoped for
light and freedom even as they do now" ('Art and Socialism').

When to-day the traveller, by some happy chance, comes upon
the work of that early day, — some homely cottage or richer abbey-
church, which seem to grow out of the familiar nature amid which
they stand, — he is touched by their human happy significance.
All men shared then in art. However unequal men were in their
social relations as king and common folk, the art of that day was
free and democratic. By his labor many a man, a slave in body,
was free in soul. And art grew and grew great until the material
world seemed bound beneath the spirit's rule. Then the Gothic
ages came to their end. The life of the Renaissance made all
things new. And strangely, while the difference between king
and subject has been destroyed, art has become the birthright of
the few.

For himself, Morris repeats the conditions out of which pure
art alone can spring. He is a man before he is a poet. He has

cultivated body, heart, and brain, choosing to live before he wrote. Out of his life springs pure art. All his work is done with evident ease and pleasure. By his own example Morris calls us back to the human, back to that labor which is highest life.

Meanwhile Morris has been writing rapidly and well. 'The Earthly Paradise' appeared ten years after 'The Defence of Guenevere.' 'The Life and Death of Jason' was begun as one of the series of the epic, but was published separately in 1867. During one of his holiday rambles in company with E. Magnússon, of Cambridge, he had visited Iceland, and together the two translated several Icelandic sagas in r868 and 1869. In 1875 appeared 'The Story of Sigurd the Volsung' and some Northern love-stories. Translations of the Æneids and Odyssey, some Northern stories, lectures on art and socialism, a volume of 'Poems by the Way,' ' The Dream of John Ball,' and ' News from Nowhere' constitute his later writings.

With his works before us we ask, What is the key to the poet's life? What is the mainspring of his action?

There are two dominant words in Morris's works, — death and life.

The first volumes from the poet's pen were wrought in the spirit of the Middle Ages. They reflect all that was most vital in the ediæval period, its romance and splendor, its gold and glittering steel, its fantastic passions and unreality, likewise its wonders, its doubts, its desires, its haunting sadness.

'The Defence of Guenevere' was dedicated "To my Friend, Dante Gabriel Rossetti." The genius of the poet and the painter is very much akin. Both were appointed from youth to the service of art and song. Their genius was alike nurtured in a mediæval household where romantic themes were familiar, and heroic fancies welcome. Early the two became stanch and sympathetic friends. It is an Oxford tradition that both were enamoured of the beautiful lady, the "Beata mea Domina!" of 'The Defence of Guenevere.'

> "All men that see her any time,
> I charge you straightly in this rhyme
> What and wherever you may be —

> "To kneel before her; as for me,
> I choke and grow quite faint to see
> My lady moving graciously,
>         Beata mea Domina!"

This is the wife to whom 'The Earthly Paradise' is dedicated, but who, with her daughter May, appears again and again in Rossetti's paintings, angel and child. Then for a number of years Rossetti was a constant guest of the Morris family at the Kelmscott Manor House on the upper Thames. Their interests were nearly identical. Their outlook upon life was quite the same. Each had withdrawn to a world of lovely forms and sweet sounds and dreams apart from modern thought and struggle. Each drew his inspiration from the beauty of old-world story. They are both sensuous, both colorists of a high order. Rossetti is excelled by none since Titian in the peculiar triumph of his touch in color. Morris is gifted with the painter's vision; he is moved to delight by the color and form of outward things. Rossetti's lavish greens and golds and scarlets are reflected from the other's poems, which seem ever bathed in light as from painted abbey-windows. In the work of each there is an element of sadness. Those pathetic half-dream faces so characteristic of the paintings look out from the pages of the poems. Even the colors of the decorative fabrics of the Morris manufactory, those harmonies in olive and saffron and bronze, gray-green and blue, are conceived for the most part in a mood of sadness.

What is it, indeed, that touches the brush of all these brother painters? The Four Seasons of E. Burne Jones might be used to illustrate the several months of 'The Earthly Paradise.' Beautiful and sad are Spring and Summer. Autumn stands wearily by the side of a lake, looking pensively across the lilies. Chill Winter, in life's November, is saddest of all; clad in hooded cloak, she is warming her hands by the fire, bending down over a book of prayer, waiting for the end: "Who shall say if I were dead, What should be rememberèd?"

Death is the haunting presence in all. Morris dwells constantly upon the theme of death, the lapse of time, the approach of age. To the carriers of the Golden Fleece the sirens sing,

".Come to the land where none grows old." The mariners of 'The Earthly Paradise' sail to the west for a paradise of rest and immortality where age cannot enter or death destroy. Death accompanies the young men and maidens, even though they sing the carols of the morn. Death whispers in the wind that showers down the blossoms in the orchard. On the very dawn of May, the merry month when the Lord of Love goes by, the poet holds his breath and shudders at the sight of Eld and Death. He cannot make death a little thing. His heart is oft too weary to struggle against doubt and thought. Seldom for his words can we forget our tears.

Morris has often been compared with Chaucer. 'The Earthly Paradise' was confessedly conceived under the inspiration of " my master Chaucer." And earlier, in ' Jason,' he yearns for

> " Some portion of that mastery
> That from the rose-hung lanes of woody Kent
> Through these five hundred years such songs have sent
> To us, who, meshed within this smoky net
> Of unrejoicing labor, love them yet."

And truly with the master the pupil may be matched in faculty of portraiture and story-telling, and in melody of perfect verse. For Morris has use of every poetic means at Chaucer's command, and does " bring before men's eyes the image of the thing my heart is filled with." But again they differ as sunshine and shadow. There was for Chaucer no month but May. His pages are steeped in light and dew. He has the candor of the morning, is jovial, sane, and strong. Morris chooses rather to string his lyre on some sad evening of the autumn tide. He lacks the elder poet's serenity of soul. He can sing the woe of Psyche, but her joy on entering her immortality of bliss he cannot sing : —

> " My lyre is but attuned to tears and pain
> How shall I sing the never ending day ? "

While Morris is supreme as an epic narrator, objective and impersonal, and tells a story, unlike Spenser and Tennyson, but like Boccaccio, Chaucer, and Walter Scott, for the story's sake, he is yet, in a manner, subjective, and his works are permeated by the modern social lament that the world is "out of joint." 'The

Earthly Paradise' is not merely a collection of tales; it is Morris's solution of the problem of our human life. Each tale ends the same, — " needs must end the same and we men call it death."

> " So if I tell the story of the past
> Let it be worth some little rest, I pray
> A little slumber ere the end of day."

His socialistic purpose is still more manifest in the story of Sigurd and the Niblungs, which occupies a medial place between the early poems and the later prose works. The epic narrative is here determined by a central thread of purpose. From the many loosely related and unmeaning incidents of the traditional saga our bard has selected those only which should complete the one essential tale of greed and wrong and redemptive love. Richard Wagner, whose definite ideal intent none can gainsay, out of the same materials constructed a cycle of dramas of similar significance. By reason of the requirement of a dramatic form, the one is led to culminate the play with the death of Siegfried and the consuming flames on Valhalla. Morris, as is consistent with an epic narrator, continues the story to the fall of the Niblung kings, but beyond this he cannot go ; the work of fate is ended. Sigurd, faring forth to do battle with the foes of the gods, thinks the time is long "till the dawning of love's summer from the cloudy days of wrong." So John Ball complains, and the writer of ' News from Nowhere' thinks the same.

Probably Chaucer had less reason for complaint than has Morris. Things were not well in England, as Langland and the Kentish preacher said, but Chaucer and his folk could still be " merrie." To-day who can be merry ? Not Morris at least : —

" Think of the spreading sore of London swallowing up with its loathsomeness field and wood and heath without mercy and without hope, mocking our feeble efforts to deal even with its minor evils of smoke-laden sky and befouled river: the black horror and reckless squalor of our manufacturing districts, so dreadful to the senses which are unused to them that it is ominous for the future of the race that any man can live among it in tolerable cheerfulness " (' Art and Socialism').

(To be continued.)

*Oscar L. Triggs.*

# UNPUBLISHED LETTERS OF JOHN RUSKIN.

O far these Ruskin letters have shown the master as critic, censor, or preacher, and have portrayed the many-sidedness of his genius. We now come to a series of letters which, if of a more cursory nature, are none the less important, revealing as they do what may be termed the more playful side of his nature. A second volume of Ruskin letters * has recently been privately printed, under the editorial supervision of Mr. Thomas J. Wise, who merits the heartiest thanks of all Ruskin students, for the careful and loving manner in which he has fulfilled his task, various "notes," etc., adding to the interest and utility of the work. Mr. Wise has, I believe, received the express permission of Mr. Ruskin to print any letters that have emanated from his pen; and we cannot be too grateful for the freedom with which he has used this permission. In printing but a very few copies (not one of which is for sale) Mr. Wise has probably exercised a sound judgment; but whenever the time arrives for a final and complete biography of Mr. Ruskin, these letters, with those printed in the preceding volume, will prove simply invaluable. Those in the present volume cover a period of some sixteen years, and were addressed to a well-known London bibliopole. Slight as some of them are, they are none the less interesting; and even the most seemingly unimportant of them tend to show the manner of man the writer is. The gentleman to whom they were addressed was for some years in frequent business relations with Mr. Ruskin; so that in the main they deal with the writer's needs of the moment concerning old or new books. At the same time, however, these notes are by no means mere business effusions, — for it is not in Mr. Ruskin's nature to avoid side issues that crop up; on the contrary, we con-

---

* Stray Letters from Professor Ruskin to a London Bibliopole. London : privately printed (not for sale). 1892.

stantly find him weaving interpolations on divers matters into letters concerning what he may desire to purchase, or what he no
longer needs, and therefore wishes to sell.

For example, in a business note of but half a dozen lines in
extent we come across the following: "Will you send me the best
recent edition of Vasari, and the best translation also. *I am terribly nervous about chance of misreading anything.*" In a note
dated February, 1870, we read: "Tennyson is quite fallen, he
must be ill." Again, "It is a lovely district to-day; cloudless, and
the lake an expanse of boiling blue like the blue of ground ivy."
Under date Aug. 3, 1878, we find the following pithy sentence:
"I want to assure you how pleased I was with Jones's work [Mr.
Burne Jones's 'Golden Stairs'], and much else derivate from it, in
the Grosvenor. I shall be compelled to disturb my peace among
the hills here by giving Master Mallock his pickle in next *Nineteenth Century.*"

Scattered among these seemingly business communications are
glimpses of the outside world, — touches which reveal to us the
hand of the master in the fulness of its power. Writing from
Aylesbury in May, 1875, he says: —

"I am very glad to have been brought here at this moment; —
the hawthorn, and buttercups and clover, purple and gold, being
beyond anything I have ever yet dreamed of in England; and the
walks through it all so heavenly. . . . I think 'Fors' for June, though
delayed for a day or two, won't be a bad one; for the biography,
simple though it be, amuses me myself as it comes into my head;
and the correspondence tickles me."

Here is a self-revelation eminently characteristic: —

"Your letter, as far as I can guess, lets me hope you really can
come down *just now;* and I am in a state of disquiet with myself
from having nobody else to speak to, which will make it a special
charity to me if you will, — the rather that there are very few people that I would ask, many of my best friends having angles, which
get into my ribs and hurt me, when we are living together."

Some *few* of these letters, too, possess an interest of a more
personal nature, and have a touch of pathos all their own. One

can well imagine that the life of the professor — altogether apart from his work — has been saddened in many ways; and yet he seems ever to rise above all the environments by which he is hampered or surrounded, and to find in his own special work the one antidote to the sorrow that sways his soul. Here is one such letter, dated Brantwood, May 7, 1878 : —

MY DEAR —— : I do not doubt your being pleased to hear, from myself, that I have once more dodged the doctors ; and hope, henceforward, with Heaven's help, to keep them out of the house — at least, till I lose my wits again. I'm picking them up at present, here and there, like the cock with the pomegranate grains in the 'Arabian Nights ;' which I find just now my best "entertainments " — after the spring flowers. These last have had no "doctoring," in my wood ; and grow — and do — as they like exactly; which I perceive to be the intention of Providence that they — and I — *should*, and propose to follow their good example as I best can. Above all, never to write any business letters, — except when I want to buy books, or missals ! You have n't anything in that way, have you, to tell me of ?

At any rate, will you please at once set your Paris agents to look out for all the copies that come up, at any sale, of Rousseau's 'Botanique' with coloured plates, 1805 — and buy all they can get ; which on receiving (if ever a kind Fors sends some) you will please forward to —— forthwith, to be kept in store for a St. George's Guild school-book.

I'm not allowed to write letters by Joan * yet ! — but shall coax her to let this one go, now it's written; and am ever
Affectionately yours,        J. RUSKIN.

Mind, this order for Rousseau is quite serious. I am working on 'Proserpina' steadily, and that edition is out and out the best elementary botany existing.

Serious though this "order" may have been, the bibliopole was, I believe, unable to obtain any copies of Rousseau's 'Botanique.'

An earlier letter (Rome, 1874) lets us into the secret of Mr. Ruskin's "reading" at this time, and is, indeed, interesting enough in itself to bear extracting : —

---

* Mrs. Arthur Severn.

"I have been taking a course of Emile Gaboriau to acquaint myself with modern Paris: he seems to me to have a wonderful knowledge of the town and its evils. As specimens of its average middle class literature, these novels — generally beginning with a murder, and having some form of theft, or delicate form of adultery, for principal subject — all through are highly curious. But from all I see and read we are advancing faster to revolutions, and miseries of the horriblest kind, than I ever dreamed ; and I have not taken a cheerful view of matters this many a day."

It is to be feared, though, that Mr. Ruskin rarely did take a cheerful view of "men and things," — albeit he took an eminently sane view.

About the beginning of 1875, the bibliopole forwarded for the inspection of the master a collection of seventeenth-century broadside ballads, together with a collection of Hogarth's prints in various states, which called forth the following letter: —

KIRBY LONSDALE, Jan. 25th, 1875.

MY DEAR ——: You never did me a greater kindness than in sending me these books to look at. I suppose they are far beyond my power in price, — and for that matter the songs I should not care to have, and even the Hogarth would be a horror in the house. But yet I could n't part with them before I had to come away, they were full of such intense interest to me. I never had seriously studied Hogarth before, — and he and Fielding pull so splendidly together, stroke and bow. The songs entirely justify what you said; but you see they have one quality — to me a very redeeming one — perfect naturalness and *openness*, while in modern literature every fine passage of sentiment is liable to have a lurking taint in it. At least these ballads would do *me* not the least harm, while Tennyson's 'Vivien' would do me much. — However, I feel rather knocked down, on the whole, by them. . . .
Always faithfully and gratefully yours,

J. RUSKIN.

Here, again, is an interesting excerpt *re* the *Academy Notes* of 1875 : —

"*Such* a bother the thing has been to me, — one can't see the pictures for the crowd, and I miss some, and over-rate others, again and again. But there's a nice spicy flavour in it now, I think — as a whole — quite a ' loving cup ' for the Academy."

Mr. Ruskin had been very anxious to purchase some of Sir Walter Scott's manuscripts, then in the market ; but on their running up beyond what was considered a legitimate price, the bibliopole did not buy. Thereupon the professor remonstrated in the following playful strain : —

BRANTWOOD, CONISTON, LANCASHIRE, February, 1881.

DEAR PAPA —— : Why, am not I a " boy " ? — and should n't I like to be more of one than I am ? And I wish your old head was on my young shoulders.

What on Earth do you go missing chance after chance like that for ! I 'd rather have lost a catch at cricket than that ' St. Ronan's.' Do *please* get it anyhow for me this once. I can't telegraph — the nasty people won't let me send a man — and — there 's the bell ringing for dinner !

Seriously, my dear ——, I do want you to secure every Scott manuscript that comes into the market. *Carte blanche* as to price — *I* can trust *your* honour ; and you may trust, believe me, *my* solvency. But I am deeply grateful for the more than kind feeling which checks you in your bids. Go calmly, but unflinchingly, in next time — and never fear, for

Ever your loving son GEORGE.

A month later he again writes : —

" A nasty attack of that overwork illness I had three years ago came on again. I 'm well through it I hope ; but the ' St. Ronan's Well ' MS. will be a wonderful balsam to my wounded soul. Send it on instantly, if you 've got it. . . . Hand shaky a little, *just yet,* nothing wrong really with head or heart, thank God ! "

Why he was so eager concerning ' St. Ronan's Well ' appears from a letter dated March 24, 1881 : —

" In my Essays on Fiction in the *Nineteenth Century*, you will see that ' St. Ronan's Well ' is marked as pre-eminently characteristic of the condition of clouded and perverted intellect under which Scott suffered, at intervals, ever since his first attack of gout in the stomach. These two attacks of *mine* have been wholly on the brain — and, I believe, conditions merely of passing inflammation. But the phenomena of the two forms of disease are intensely important to me, in relation to my future treatment of myself."

He adds that he is now buying Scott's and other manuscripts for his future museum. One more extract on this subject. Three days later he writes : —

" I am more grateful than you could at all believe for your thought of me. I am so desolate in this world, that the sense of any one's really watching over me, and caring about me in a useful way, is like balm and honey. But you need n't be anxious. These books are really bought for the Sheffield or other St. George's museums ; and I, with one foot — and perhaps one knee — in the grave, have only to catalogue and describe them. But, I daresay, I shall be able to stand on one leg, and keep my head above ground yet awhile; — only you really need n't care how much I'm worth at the bank — where the wild thyme does *not* blow."

Playful and humorous as many of these letters are, we note, toward the close of the correspondence, a certain softness of tone and touch of added pathos, though at times the old asperities appear ; as this, for instance, sometime in 1881 : —

"Please send me these Carlyle 'Reminiscences.' I'm up to reading them now, and that rascally article of Mrs. —— has put my bristle up, —and I must give her a hiding — somewhere — short and sweet. The comic thing is, that the three sentences of Carlyle's she quotes above are the only ones worth printing in the entire article."

Five years later he writes: —

" Your pathetic note has lain beside me. I could not at first answer, for I was very ill, — but this sweet spring sunlight on the moor cheers me, and makes me feel as if we both might rejoice in spring days again. But I am recovering very slowly from the depression of this last illness, and can only say, that I am ashamed of having been sad."

The following may fittingly form our last excerpt from this most entertaining volume : —

" I know that my illnesses have greatly weakened the physical grasp of the brain, so that I can never more write things rich in thought like the preface to ' Grimm ;' but I believe the general balance and truth of thought are still safe — or even safer than before the strain. Yes, there *is* a new world coming ·— God knows what ! But there 's a handful of good seed coming up, every here and there."

The handful of seed has been sown, and in dipping into these letters we seem to have come in at the gleaning ; for the harvest, long since gathered in, was golden in very deed. Who shall measure the result of this man's sowing? One thing at least we can say : the result has been for good — not evil. Here and there, as in these letters, some petulant word, some harsh judgment, has cropped up amid the " good seed ; " but the " flaws " have been few indeed, the " measure " has been " good," nay, overflowing ; while the whole, founded as it is on the ethics of the Sermon on the Mount, stands almost alone in splendor of achievement and beneficence of result.

*William G. Kingsland.*

LONDON, ENGLAND, February, 1893.

# GENTLE WILL, OUR FELLOW.

WRIT IN 1626 A. D. BY JOHN HEMINGE, SERVANT OF HIS GRACIOUS MAJESTY KING CHARLES I. ; EDITED IN 1892 A. D. AS " ALL, THOUGH FEIGNED, IS TRUE " BY F. G. FLEAY, SERVANT OF ALL SHAKESPEARIAN STUDENTS IN AMERICA, ENGLAND, GERMANY, OR ELSEWHERE.

T hath been questioned of certain plays by what right my fellow Condell and I have given them room in our late collection of Shakespeare's plays, seeing that scarce a line in some of them can with confidence be alleged to be written by him, and in more he had only, as Master Heywood would say, a main finger ; while other plays, such as ' Pericles,' we have left out altogether, yet are they well known to be partly his. Now this being the first mention I have made of any of the plays in question, it seems to be a fitting place to defend ourselves concerning them ; and, firstly, for our omissions ; it is well known that about half of Shakespeare's plays had been printed by other men, and belonged to them, with whom we had to make some agreement before we could ourselves again print them. With most of

these men, — Law, Smethwicke, Heyes, Johnson, — we made terms
fairly and without much trouble ; but one man, T. Pavier, who had,
Heaven knows how, become possessed of certain of these plays,
gave us much vexation. Some plays, indeed, of which we had true
and perfect copies, such as ' Henry V.,' and the second and third
parts of 'Henry VI.,' — of which his imperfect copy was called, ' The
Whole Contention of York and Lancaster,' — we obtained a right to
publish, although they were entered to him in the stationers' books,
he being afraid of a suit at law thereby ; but others, ' Pericles,' ' The
Yorkshire Tragedy,' and the old play of ' Titus Andronicus,'
— it was first called ' Titus and Vespasian,' — he would by no
means be induced to part from on any reasonable terms, and so
remained their sole possessor. We did not print these because
we could not. Pity it was that Master Shakespeare was so careless of the children of his brain ; but when he lost all hope of having any heir of his body, he left these other children to the care of
strangers to shift for themselves. As for the play of ' Edward
III.,' it belonged to one Snodham, who followed Pavier in his dealing with us.

As to the printing of plays not entirely written by Shakespeare,
our rule was this : to leave out no play which came to our hands
from him ; we thought it better to include many weaker lines by
other men than to leave out one that bore the stamp of his merit.
I shall note all these in their proper places. Suffice it here to say
that although his ' Titus Andronicus ' was kept from us by Pavier,
the play we printed was corrected by him, and by him brought on
the stage, after it had been less perfectly acted by the players of
my Lord of Sussex in February, and when they broke, by my Lord
of Pembroke's men.

In April of this same year, my Lord of Derby died, and in May
we entered the service of Henry Carey, Lord Hunsdon, then Lord
Chamberlain. Ned Alleyn then left us, preferring the Lord Admiral's service, as was natural. The Admiral's men acted at the
Rose, the house of his father-in-law, Henslow, whose step-daugh-
ter, Jean Woodward, Alleyn had married in October, 1592 ; but
after three days' performance they were inhibited on account of

the plague, and during the first fortnight in June they played at Newington Butts with us, — one company on one day, one on another; but we played no new play at that time. In the middle of June the Admiral's men went back to the Rose, and we to the Theater in Shoreditch. Burbadge had become our chief actor, now that Alleyn had left us; and the Theater, which was the first built of all the theatres in London, was built by his father. As the Queen's men, who used to act there, had now completely broken, and my Lord of Sussex's men, who had succeeded them, had broken also, it was natural that Burbadge should wish to act in his father's theatre, which was likely soon to become his own by inheritance. The Queen's and the Sussex men, such as were left of them, had patched up a company, who — after acting to wellnigh empty benches at the Rose, in the winter of 1593 — went into the country. We heard no more of them in London, where there were now three companies left, — the Admiral's at the Rose, the Earl of Pembroke's at the Curtain, and ourselves at the Theater. But for four years we were the only men who were called to the Court for the delectation of Her Majesty in the Christmas festivities.

From this time forward Master Shakespeare was not merely one of our chief sharers and principal actors, — such he had already been under Mr. Alleyn, — but was also our one provider of plays for presentation. His seven years' apprenticeship as coadjutor of other men had expired, and his coadjutors were no longer with us. Marlowe and Wilson had died in the plague year, and Peele now left us for the Admiral's men.

Henceforth he was always our main support and sometimes our only stay; nor was any new play acted by us without its passing through his hands. He usually wrote for us two plays a year entirely of his own making, and in some years these were the only new plays we presented. In this our policy was far different from that of our chief rivals, the Admiral's men; for they, trusting to the longing for novelty which is so constant in the common multitude, would set up their bills for new plays once, nay, ofttimes twice, in the month, and would employ some dozen poets at the least in making their plays, at one time three or four of these poets writing in one play. But to say sooth, many of these so-called new plays were but old ones furbished up and new named; and the payment for them being but small — some six or eight pounds a play at the most — the authors felt it not against their consciences to get paid over and over again for some old friend with a new face. Henslow, who arranged their accounts, was a usurious pawnbroker who would rather keep a poet, as he thought, in his debt, and so in his power, than bind him by gratitude for friendly offices; and so such men as Dekker and Peele, who were shifting companions, cared not how they cheated him. He had neither wit nor learning enough to know an old play from a new one. Heywood and Chapman, who also wrote for him at this time, had not yet grown to their full strength, and were not thought of by the better sort. So it was that our Shakespeare's two plays a year, which were so full of philosophic thought as well as poetic beauty that a man might read them over every year which he lived and yet find new food for his mind in them, brought us more gain in our public action, to say nothing of our Court presentations, than these men's twenty, in which the speeches neither fitted the character nor were the scenes orderly digested.

At the Theater we acted during the summer; but in the autumn, when the rains made access to that place hard for them who could not pay for horse hire, we asked the Lord Mayor for allowance to play at the Cross Keys in Gracious Street, according to our old wont; but although we promised that we would come to an end before four in the afternoon, that we would use no drums nor trumpets, and be contributory to the parish poor, no permission could we obtain, and had perforce to be content with the house outside the liberties.

At this time Shakespeare's career as chief poet to our company begins; and from this time till he left us, a friend of sixteen years, he was not only the Shake-scene of our company, as Green malignantly called him, but the Shake-sphere of the London stage, then the greatest in the whole world; and so of that little world in which, as he truly said, the mirror is held up to that greater one in which all men and women are merely players. I shall therefore be more precise than I have been in setting down particularly the occasions of the productions of those plays, which, as I have said elsewhere, those who like not are in manifest danger not to understand. The earliest of these was the play of ' Errors.' This was played before Her Majesty at Greenwich, where the Court then was, on the day after Christmas Day, in the daytime ; and again before the worshipful Society of Gray's Inn, at night, on the same day. As then presented, it was entirely Shakespeare's, although, as was his wont, he made no scruple of retaining, especially in the first scene, any lines of the older play which he thought good. If he found a rough diamond, he made it his own by his polishing and his new setting. The first form of this play, some four years earlier, had much in it that was not his. Neither was the plot his ; it was much like the ' Menæchmi ' of Plautus, and somewhat like his ' Amphytrio.' But scarcely ever did he trouble about his plot ; he took it as he found it in older plays by other men, in pamphlets by Greene or Lodge, in the English Chronicles or the Lives of Plutarch. He left the reputation of being the best plotter to Monday or others of the like low vein ; any story sufficed him if the personages of the story were veritable men and women.

This play was closely followed by the ' Midsummer Night's Dream,' which, being originally written for the marriage of a great lord whose name I think it not fitting to set down here, had to be altered at the end when we presented it at Court ; but both endings are printed in our Folio for the further delectation of the reader.

The next comedy from Shakespeare's hand was ' The Two Gentlemen of Verona,' which, like the ' Errors,' was refashioned from an earlier play in which another pen had good share.

Then came ' The Merchant of Venice,' which was the last comedy of his which we acted at the Theater. These comedies we presented, one new one in each year, during the four years that we played in that house, — from 1594 to 1597.

I must now speak of the tragedies which he wrote for us during these same four years. The first of these was ' Richard II.' In this play the scene of Richard's deposition by Bolingbroke gave great offence to Her Majesty, and we were forbidden either to play or print the same. I shall have to speak of this again hereafter; but I may note here that scarce one of our plays of which the plots were taken from the English Chronicles escaped the serpent's tongue of Envy or the castigation of the Master of the Revels. We were at this time regarded as of the faction of my Lord of Essex (I doubt not because my Lord of Southampton bestowed on us his especial favor and commendation); and we were often, without good reason or any reason at all, suspected of meddling with State matters. Just after this we enacted the play of 'Sir Thomas More,' which, because it had a rising of 'prentices in it, and some of the characters, as befitted their parts in the play, spoke contemptuously of the French, which things were well known to be matters of history, was severely handled by the Revels Master, who expunged whole scenes, so that great part had to be written over again. He particularly objected to one scene in which Sir Thomas was confined for contempt. The imprisonment of the Earl of Hertford for the like reason, and the 'prentice broils of 1595, gave some color to the objections to this play; but the mutilation of Shakespeare's 'Richard II.' merely because the Queen would not hear of a deposition, and still more that of his next historical tragedy of 'King John,' in which well-nigh a whole act was expunged, was, methinks, far-fetched, and, as I shall show, dear-bought.

After the play of 'John,' Shakespeare wrote for us the tragedy of 'Romeo and Juliet,' as it hath been acted from that time. The old form of this play, as it was presented in 1591, had many scenes from another pen, some of which may be still seen in the miserable stolen quarto edition as first printed. In the old play of 'The Troublesome Reign of John,' which some dishonest printers have endeavored to pass off as his, he had no share whatever; neither did we act it, but the Queen's men. Nathless, he, as his wont was, used it for the plot, keeping a few of its lines when they fitted with his own.

I must now leave the stage for a while to say a few words as to Shakespeare's private life, with which at this time I became better acquainted than I had been. From the time that he first joined us, for nine years, he had not, so far as we knew, visited his birthplace ; but in the year 1596 he heard of the extreme sickness of his only son, Hamnet, and went there, but only in time to see him die and attend his burial in August. From what I knew afterwards, I judged that his main hope had been to found a family. He was always frugal, and had already saved a considerable sum of money ; but now this hope being disappointed, his love seemed to be centred in his daughters. In this I judge him not by his words, for he was not, like Jonson, given to speak much of his family, but by his actions.

In the next October he obtained arms for his father: "In a field gold upon a bend sables, a spear, the point upward, headed argent; and for his crest or cognizance a falcon, with his wings displayed, standing on a wreath of his colors, supporting a spear, armed, headed, or steeled silver, fixed upon a helmet, with mantle and tassels."

In Easter the next year he purchased the freehold of New Place, its mansion and its grounds, in Stratford, for £60 ; and yet William Shakespeare, of New Place, Stratford, Gentleman, when in London had but mean lodgings in Southwark, near the Bear Garden.

*F. G. Fleay.*

## WHAT SHOULD BE THE POET'S ATTITUDE TOWARD HIS CRITICS?*

WHAT should be the attitude of the poet toward his critics ? That is a question hard to answer. If we know the poet himself, if we fully comprehend the thickness or thinness of his skin; the state of his nerves, and the way in which he views his work, then we may easily enough tell what his attitude toward his critics will be. Or again, if we study the experiences of poets and their conduct under criticism, we may learn what their attitudes toward

* Read before the Browning Society of Boston, Dec. 27, 1892.

their critics have been. But the trouble is that these experiences are never quite the same, and so from them we are unable to derive any absolute rule. Here, as in ethics, what ought to be cannot be formed out of what is.

What the poet's attitude toward his critics should be must depend upon the critics. All critics are not the same critics. There are critics whom the poet should not honor with the consideration of a moment. Most of what is said, is no more than the snap judgments of men or women, who write, not out of the insight of minds that have " leisure to be wise," but out of the hurried glimpses of those who are always on the run. These are the critics who write out of the abundant fulness of their ignorance, who pass confident judgments on systems of philosophy to which they have perhaps read the preface, or on poems with whose titles they are perhaps acquainted. Their criticisms often create what is called public opinion. Many people read them and accept them as infallible utterances. But they are only for the day, and with the day they pass out of mind. The poet might as well vex his soul about the insects that buzz around him on his daily walk as with those so-called opinions of the press. Schopenhauer somewhere compares the daily paper with the second-hand of a clock, — like that, he says, it moves fastest, and, also like that, it is usually wrong. All criticism from that source the poet will wisely ignore. Its praise or blame is but " a snow flake on the river, a moment seen, then gone forever."

There is much criticism that reveals nothing so much as the incapacity of the critic. Its special value lies in the knowledge it gives us of his own limitations. When Dr. Samuel Johnson was urged to answer Bishop Berkeley's philosophy, which denies the substantial existence of matter, he stamped on the ground and said, " Thus I refute it." But he did nothing of the kind. He only showed that he was capable of experiencing sensations, and that he was incompetent to appreciate a thinker like Berkeley. So, many of the judgments of critics on poems judge the critics more than the poets. The unfavorable comments of Voltaire and Goethe on the ' Divine Comedy ' of Dante show how even great men may sometimes miss the mark in their criticism, when for some reason they are unable to sympathize with his spirit. So long as the poet feels sure that the critics have misapprehended his work, and have condemned it only in the light of their prejudices and constitutional limitations, his attitude toward them should be one of perfect indifference. He should feel, " I know what I have done, as yet; you do not." He must quietly wait until they learn the secret of his aim and purpose.

There are critics who blame the poet because he is not clear. Now, clearness is a literary virtue, but it is not the only one. The clearness of a writer must always be relative and dependent upon certain conditions. The subject may be one which cannot be considered in such a way as to make it clear at once, or without any mental effort on the part of the reader. Where this is profound, and so demands subtlety of thought and closeness of reasoning and delicacy of expression, it is impertinent for the critic to say it is not clear. If it is as clear as the theme to be discussed will allow, that is all he has the right to demand. If it be true that the writer has failed to state his thought in the best possible way, and that more pains on his part would have required less on the part of his readers, then he is to be blamed, and he will do well to heed the judgments of his critics. But the lack of clearness need not all be in the poet. It takes two minds to make anything clear. The poem may be luminous, its reader opaque. When the pupil described an acute angle as obtuse, the teacher felt called upon to observe that the obtuseness was somewhere else than in the angle. He has the right to demand some labor of mind and heart from his readers. What is not clear to one who reads as he runs may be, and very often is, clear as sunlight to him who will stop to ponder. There is a kind of poetry capable of being understood on the first reading. In some cases this may be necessary, since no one will ever care to read this easy poetry a second time. Nor does a poet like Robert Browning profess to write for those to whom it is painful to gird up the loins of their minds. Poetry must sometimes be simple ; but poems which have nothing but their simplicity to commend them are not the ones of which the bread of life is made.

Then there is poetry which we think we readily understand because we have heard it repeated so often, because it has become an organic part of our speech and thought. The new poet is often condemned because he is not so easily understood, as people feel Shakespeare and Milton are. They complain of him just as some people complain of the town to which they have recently come, because it is not so sociable as the town where they were born and reared, and where their kinsmen have lived for generations. To this the poet can only say that when his lines have been read for two or three hundred years it will seem clear and simple and obvious enough. The poet need not heed those who blame him for his obscurity. He must feel that he has the right to ask that the judgment of his poetry should be based upon some capacity for poetic insight, and upon patient thought and study. With critics who have no gift of discernment, or who will take no pains to enter into the significance of his work, he has simply nothing whatever to do. When they urge that they cannot see any vision in his poetry, he may properly retort, as Turner did to the person who could not see in the landscape what he did, "Don't you wish you could?"

The poet is sometimes condemned by his critics because of the form of his poetry. He may have seen fit to embody his vision in shape unusual and uncustomary. Some old form is held up to him as the proper one, and he is blamed for his failure to conform himself to it. When a poet like Wordsworth appears, the literary world, reared on Dryden and Pope, imbued with the idea that what is called classical is the only true form for verse, protests, and cries out with Jeffrey in the 'Edinburgh Review,' "This will never do." But the true poet should know that there is something of more worth and significance than mere form, — even the eternal spirit of poetry which he is bound to sing. It should be enough for him that some vision is given him to set to celestial music. With Wordsworth he may say, "The manner depends upon the matter." The same truth and beauty may be brought in many ways, one as good as the other, each one good in so far as it serves to bring the glad tidings to the mind and heart. The poet may well apply to himself what Browning in Christmas Eve says of the preacher : —

> " It were to be wished the flaws were fewer
> In the earthen vessel, holding treasure,
> Which lies as safe in a golden ewer :
> But the main thing is, does it hold good measure."

Conscious that he is bringing to weary hearts some drops of the water of life, the poet may well dismiss all criticism of his method as something which concerns only the mechanism of poetry. There are critics who blame the poet because he treats his themes in an unusual manner. They have become accustomed to poetry which describes events, the appearances and deeds of persons, or the completed results of their thought. Now, however, they are summoned to a very different task. A poet, like Browning, for example, appears, who brings characters before them as they unfold their innermost selves and brings to light what lies hidden in the depths of their souls. Such a poet expects his reader to put himself in the place of his characters, to use imagination enough to apprehend their situation and state of mind without any formal description. He expects his reader to do something for himself, to exercise his imagination, which is often the last thing he wants to do. Then our poet, it may be, is not content with telling what his persons thought, but endeavors to make his readers see why they thought as they did. He tries to reveal the soul in the formation of its judgments, and to enable the reader to see the nature of a man or woman as God sees it. Now all that is painful, as is all unusual action of the mind. When Fichte gave his first lecture at Jena, he said to his hearers, " Think the wall." That was an easy task, soon accomplished. " Now," he continued, "think that which thinks the wall." This demand threw his audience into confusion, perplexity, despair. A task like that had never before been required of them. So a critic will begin to read a poet of the kind we have been describing, and he is puzzled to know what he is about. He does not know where to start with him ; he confuses the sentiments of the character in the poem with those of the poet himself, or he thinks the poet is stating a law of life, when, indeed, he is only describing the mood of one person under the stress of special circumstances.  He has never been called upon to see a soul in itself ; so it is no wonder he dislikes the poet who demands it of him.  Now, of course, the critic ought to blame himself, but he never does.  He declares it is all the fault of the poet.  He can find nothing in him, and he speedily concludes there is nothing in him to be found.  So he either abuses our poet, or deems him unworthy of his consideration.  The new method of poetry always has a hard time of it, and he who ventures upon it should not be surprised at the treatment he receives.  It is useless for him to complain, for no one will heed him, — useless, too, for him to waste his time in trying to prove that his critics are mistaken.  His true course is to go on, to do his best work in the way he has been moved to do it, to educate his readers so that at last they may be able to discern the truth and beauty and the intrinsic value of his poetry.  His appeal must be to those who in due time will learn to divine the meaning of his mission, and who will find in him the satisfaction of mind and heart they seek.  In the mean time the best he can do is to be silent and quietly to wait in the calm assurance that any word with truth and beauty in it will always find its audience, "fit though few."

There are critics, however, whose judgments are concerned neither with the form nor with the method of poetry. These, with real wisdom, see clearly that this is not their province.  They take the poet as he is, and ask how far he has been true to his own idea of his task.  They scan his verse; they examine his figures; they scrutinize the structure of his poem.  Critics of this kind may often be severe and unsympathetic, but they also often have keen eyes.  They may sometimes miss or ignore the real beauties in a poem, but they seldom fail to indicate actual defects.  What should be the attitude of the poet toward these critics ?  We know what, in some cases, it has been.  Wordsworth went on his way, serene and undisturbed, or if a little vexed, so calmly confident that he was above all criticism that it made no impression upon him.  Perhaps it would have been well if he had listened to this kind of criticism more than he did. It might have saved him from writing lines such as these : —

> " Once more the Ass with motion dull
> Upon the pivot of his skull
> Turned round his long left ear."

Lord Byron, in his rage at the review of his ' Hours of Idleness,' wrote his famous satire, ' English Bards and Scotch Reviewers.' We admire it when we are young ; as we grow older we are less satisfied with it. We still say, Well done, but we ask, Why have done it at all? — " Doest thou well to be angry ? " Tennyson showed himself at his best under this kind of criticism. Perhaps no poet ever received a more merciless castigation than he in the *Quarterly Review* of 1833. But he made no reply; and after years of silence he came forth again with new and better work, and much of the old recast, showing that he was willing to learn from his critics. Perhaps the criticism of others made him clearly see what he himself had vaguely felt were blemishes. If anything, he yielded almost too much to some criticisms. In his ' Dream of Fair Women ' he had made Iphigenia say, —

> " One drew a sharp knife through my tender throat
> Slowly — and nothing more."

Upon which the smart reviewer remarked, " What touching simplicity, what pathetic resignation ! — he cut my throat — nothing more." So Tennyson has changed the passage, but hardly for the better. As it first appeared, it was far more expressive and beautiful. Still, in spite of this and a few other exceptions, Tennyson has shown the true attitude in which the poet should stand toward his critics. He tried to learn from them, and in some measure he regarded them as an external literary conscience. The poet who does this may not find it necessary to change his former work at the bidding of even the shrewdest critic; but he may, by paying heed to him, learn how to do more faultless work in the future.

Of course, the blame or praise of nobodies should go for nothing with the poet, though Cervantes shows us in ' Don Quixote ' how even the praise of a lunatic may give him pleasure. But there are those whose praise should compensate him for the neglect and ridicule of all else besides. Recognition and commendation from those who stand on the heights to-day is a promise of the meed he will receive from all in days to come. He should rejoice in the appreciation of kindred souls, in the " consensus of the competent," in the praise of those whose mission it is to teach the world what to praise. And yet the poet should not write with the standards of critics, even the best, in his conscious view. He should not allow even the greatest critic to shape his phrases, to control the selection of his themes or the manner of their treatment; he must sing of what he sees in the way most congenial to himself. The essence of his poetry must ever lie in its spontaneousness. Like Shelley's skylark, he should pour forth his " full heart In profuse strains of unpremeditated art." The great poems of the world will always be the result, not of the definitions of the head, but of the abundance of the heart. When they are written, criticism at its best can only point out for us the gleams of glory that shine in and through them; it can never tell us the secret of their being. Nor should the poet pose for his critics. With Tennyson, let him say, —

> " I think not much of yours or of mine ;
> I hear the roll of the ages."

In what attitude Browning stood toward his critics it is perhaps impossible to say. We know so little of his inner life that we can only guess his feelings about them. He had to bear something worse of the most unsparing kind, and that was the bitter thought that for him there was no response. He sang, and there seemed no one who cared to heed his singing. A nature less cheery and sunny than his might well have become soured and embittered by this apparent conspiracy of silence. But he simply went on, and did what his nature prompted him to do. We know how he was pained by the conduct of those, like Carlyle, who knew his worth, and who praised him in their conversation with their friends, but who never uttered a word of praise in some public way, when such a word would have given him an early fame. We know that he was pleased when recognition came to him, "even at the eleventh hour," as in a letter to a friend he so pathetically says. It must have seemed as if fate were indeed against him when the favorable criticism of 'Pauline' by John Stuart Mill was kept out of one of the leading English reviews because some one who had not read it had already given it a single line of comment as contemptuous as it was ignorant. It kept him out of the place he actually deserved for years.

For the average opinion of the English public he cared nothing, as we learn from his allusion to it in 'The Ring and the Book.' He knew better than any one what average public opinion about anything is really worth. His larger and deeper subjects demanded another manner of treatment than that to which the world was accustomed. He was willing to work and wait until his message was heeded and welcomed. While he waited, he had all along the support and comfort of those to whom was given power to "discern the things that are excellent." Calmly and manfully he bore silence, neglect, blame, misunderstanding, and the frequent laughter of fools. None of these things moved him from his purpose to reveal the mysterious workings of the soul of man. He had that steadiness of purpose, that unflinching loyalty to his ideal, which neither praise nor blame can turn aside; for Browning was

> "One who never turned his back, but marched breast forward,
>   Never doubted clouds would break,
>   Never dreamed, though right were worsted, wrong would triumph,
>   Held, we fall to rise, are baffled to fight better,
>     Sleep to wake."

*Francis B. Hornbrooke.*

## WHERE SHAKESPEARIAN CRITICS DISAGREE.

"If I do not keep step with my companions, it is because I hear a different drummer. Let a man step to the music which he hears, however far away," exclaimed Thoreau.

We have all seen a long procession marching by, and have noticed that those some distance from the front were not keeping step with their leaders, nevertheless the swinging foot was in perfect unison with the music that struck loudest upon the ear. I have thought that maybe this might account for the great diversity of opinion among critics. Each one of them, and each one of us, think and see, keeping time to that God-given melody which is one's own individual inheritance. Some of us may hear the heavy, mournful notes of the Dead March in ' Saul,' some the light, tripping airs of Sullivan's operas, and others again, — a more favored few, — hear the strains that Mozart sent ringing down through all the corridors of time. If you hear the Dead March, and I hear the ' Gloria in Excelsis,' then by what right have you to say that my interpretation, though diametrically opposed to yours, is not a true one?

Upon the play of ' Henry IV.,' for example, what follows speaks for itself. This from Hazlitt: "The characters of Hotspur and Prince Henry are two of the most beautiful and dramatic, both in themselves and from contrast, that ever were drawn. . . . We like Hotspur the best upon the whole because he was unfortunate." On the other hand, Johnson, who, according to Hazlitt, does poetry by the rules of mathematics, says : " Percy is a rugged soldier, choleric and quarrelsome, and has only the soldier's virtues, generosity, and courage." Hudson sees "that he has a rough and passionate soul, great strength and elevation of mind, with little gentleness and less delicacy, and a force of will that rises into poetry by its own chafings."

In regard to Prince Hal and Falstaff, Hazlitt says : " The truth is, we never could forgive the Prince's treatment of Falstaff; though perhaps Shakespeare knew what was best, according to the history, the nature of the times, and the man. We speak only as dramatic critics. Whatever terror the French in those days might have of Henry V., yet to the readers of poetry at present, Falstaff is the better man of the two. We think of him and quote him oftener." Furnivall says : " When Hal becomes king, his treatment of his brothers, the Chief-justice, and Falstaff, is surely wise and right in all three cases. One does feel for Falstaff, but certainly what he ought to have had he got, — the chance of reformation." And according to Hudson: "The bad usage which Falstaff puts upon Shallow has the effect of justifying to us the usage which he at last receives from the Prince. . . And something of the kind was needful in order to bring the Prince's character off from such an act altogether bright and sweet in our regard. For after sharing so long in the man's prodigality of mental exhilaration, to shut down upon him so, was pretty hard."

A noted divine recently said, during one of his sermons, that there was nothing infallible but Euclid's Geometry; after such a sweeping assertion as this, people may be pardoned for failing to see the humor of Falstaff. I thought possibly that was a peculiarity of some of the members of the Shakespeare Club to which I belong; but here comes Coleridge, who denies that Falstaff has, properly speaking, any humor. Hudson, on the contrary, says of the same subject: "Falstaff is altogether the greatest triumph of the comic muse that the world has to show. . In this judgment I believe that all who have fairly conversed with the irresistible old sinner are agreed." And Charles Cowden Clarke remarks: "The character of Falstaff is, I think, the most witty and humorous combined that was ever portrayed."

This play of criticism would be 'Hamlet' with Hamlet left out, if I did not add a few opinions from different authors on the subject of the "melancholy Dane."

> "The time is out of joint : O cursed spite,
> That ever I was born to set it right !"

"In these words," said Goethe, "I imagine, is the key to Hamlet's whole procedure, and to me it is clear that Shakespeare sought to depict a great deed laid upon a soul unequal to the performance of it. The impossible is required of him, not the impossible in itself, but the impossible to him." Of this Dowden says: "Goethe told half the truth but only one half, that Hamlet is a man to whom the idea of persistent action, and in an especial degree, the duty of deliberate revenge is peculiarly antipathetic. Thus far was the German poet right, but, as in the case of 'Romeo and Juliet,' the tragic nodus was not wholly of a subjective character. The world

fought against the lovers, and they fell in the unequal strife.
Now Goethe failed to observe that this also was the case with
Hamlet." Whereupon here comes in Schlegel, who tells us that
he does not wholly agree with Goethe ; he thinks the opinion of
the latter entirely too favorable. He agrees with him in regard
to the weakness of Hamlet's character, but he goes further and
says : " The Dane is not solely impelled by necessity to artifice
and dissimulation, but he has a natural inclination for crooked
ways. He is a hypocrite towards himself. His far fetched
scruples are often mere pretexts to cover his want of determination." Coleridge agrees with Goethe in the main ; he thinks
Hamlet vacillates from sensibility, and procrastinates from thought,
and loses the power of action in the energy of resolve ; while Hudson, who seems to disagree with many other writers in this regard,
says : " I have never been able to see in Hamlet anything like the
mean and miserable lack of manhood or of executive force which
some critics charge him with. As for his holding back from killing Claudius, I do not, I can not, ascribe this to any fault or blam-
able weakness in himself or to any subjective causes whatsoever ;
it proceeds, and I think proceeds rightly and legitimately, from
objective causes, causes that are objectively valid and sufficient.
. . . The supreme desire of Hamlet is to think and do what is
right morally, socially, politically, and according to old English
ideas." The writer concludes : " I therefore hold it a matter of
high concernment to us, that we learn to regard him as a truly
heroic and honorable pattern of manhood."

Certain phases of character seen in Lear's Cordelia cause a
great deal of discussion in our Shakespeare Club. I am pleased to
see that the critics differ as widely as we. Richard Grant White
says : " Cordelia had one fault, that fault was pride, the passion that
led to the first recorded murder ; and with her pride went its too
often attendant, a propensity to satire, the unloveliest trait that
can mar a lovely woman's character. When in the first scene she
demurely says,

> ' The jewels of our father, with wash'd eyes
> Cordelia leaves you : I know you what you are,'

we feel that it is sharply said, but might better be left unsaid, and we sympathize a little with Regan in her retort." Hazlitt, while he speaks in the highest terms of praise of the love Cordelia bears to Lear, admits that "her love has a little of her father's obstinacy in it." But Hudson explains Cordelia's "foolish reserve," as White calls it. Partly from a conscious purpose, "but more from an instinct of dutiful affection, she tries to assuage and postpone his [Lear's] distemper, with the temperate speech of simple truth ; duty and love alike forbidding her to stimulate his disease with the strong waters of fleering and strained hyperbole. Then too a fine moral tact seems to warn her that the medicine of reason must be administered to the dear old man in very gentle doses, else it will but feed his evil. And her treatment is well adapted to keep her father in tune, but that her holy purpose is baffled by the fulsome volubility of her sisters."

Evidently Mrs. Jameson does not agree with the assertion of Mr. White that "satire is the unloveliest trait that can mar a lovely woman's character." She says, speaking of the same speech of Cordelia : "The irony here is so bitter and intense, and at the same time so feminine, so dignified, that who but Cordelia could have uttered it?" Mrs. Jameson discovers few flaws in Shakespeare's women. Even in Lady Macbeth she finds more nobility of soul than the poet ever dreamed of. She tides over the most glaring faults with a happy ease of expression, that argues a good heart if nothing else. Isabel, in 'Measure for Measure,' seems to call out a variety of opinions from the critics. Hazlitt admits that he is not greatly enamoured of Isabel's rigid chastity, though she could not act otherwise than she did. Andrew Lang, in his exceedingly interesting Shakespearian articles, says : "Can we admire her when she arranges the midnight meeting of the unconscious Angelo and his forsaken betrothed Mariana ? Isabel had no choice, to be sure ; it was for her brother's life that she dabbled in this intrigue, but she shows no dislike or disgust." Of the scene in which Claudio begs for his life at the expense of his sister's honor, and she repudiates him with the utmost scorn and loathing, this same writer exclaims : "Is this a natural mood? could a girl speak thus to a brother, degraded as he is? One can more easily imagine Isabel turning and departing in silence, crushed by sorrow and shame, but this is her last word — ' 'T is best that thou diest quickly.' " Coleridge, too, thinks she contrives to make herself unamiable. But Hudson considers that in this scene between the brother and sister, the conduct of Isabel is in every way creditable to her. He says: " The truth is she is in a very hard struggle between affection and principle; she needs and hopes to have the strain upon her womanly fortitude lightened, by the manly fortitude of her brother. And her harshness of reproof discovers the natural workings of a tender and deep affection in an agony of disappointment, at being urged by one for whom she would die to an act she shrinks from with holy horror, and justly considers worse than death. Her character appears to me among the finest, in some respects the very finest, in Shakespeare's matchless cabinet of female excellence."

Shall we read the Sonnets? Let us look up authority before we begin. Hazlitt says: " Our admiration of Shakespeare ceases with his plays. In a word, we do not like his poems because we like his plays. It has been the fashion of late to cry up our Author's poems as equal to his plays. This is the desperate cant of modern criticism." But Richard Grant White declares that " Whoever can read them once and not read them again, and again, borne on and up by their strong flow of feeling, lost in the fascinating mystery of their allusions, has not the root of the matter in him."

And so they go on, each one marching to the music that he hears, while the old poet sleeps calmly in his grave, oblivious that the children of his brain are presenting chameleon hues to the vision of mankind.

*L. Howard.*

# TO A BEAUTIFUL NUN.

FAIR Nun, that slowly wanderest
  Through byways of the town,
Tell me the thoughts thou ponderest,
  Demure, with eyes cast down!

The world around is beautiful;
  No joy to thee it brings,
Because thy spirit dutiful
  Is set on heavenly things.

The sunlight is not vanity,
  Nor pleasure sign of ill;
Bright greetings of urbanity
  May tender heart-strings thrill.

But all these things are naught to thee;
  Such visions thou must shun.
Another code is taught to thee,
  Thou solemn-vestured Nun!

Thy talents, — make no use of them
  To win the world's applause;
Such use were but abuse of them
  To hurt Religion's cause.

Thy voice, though rich and glorious,
  Must not in mirth take part;
Thy hands must be laborious
  In charity, not art.

Thy face would grace society,
  Thy hand be sought in love;
But all thy realm is piety;
  Thy heart is fixt above.

Yet calm and unregretfully
  Thou goest on thy way
As though desire were met, fully,
  In that one word "obey."

No thought of earthly joy disturbs,
  For earthly love must cease ;
No trivial annoy disturbs
  The current of thy peace.

Surrounded by thy purity
  As by an angel's arm,
Thou passest in security
  Amid all sin and harm.

Sweet bride of heaven, abidingly
  Thy thoughts all heavenward flow ;
And thus alone, confidingly,
  Thou walkest here below.

The sombre garb thou wearest here,
  The rosary, the cross, —
Symbol of what thou bearest here, —
  Make all things seem but dross.

Above, the wedding raiment waits,
  The crown, the promised spouse ;
For all the loss the payment waits,
  The answer to thy vows.

For this thou hast forsaken all
  Thy beauty might have won ;
For this alone hast taken all
  The sorrows of a Nun.

Fair Nun, my heart acknowledges
  A pang to see thy face.
I care not for theologies,
  I only care for grace.

And yet I would not change thy lot
  To that of mortal bride.
Let God alone arrange thy lot
  And in thy heart abide !

*Nathan Haskell Dole.*

## MAURICE MAETERLINCK: DRAMATIST OF A NEW METHOD.*

NEAR the close of Maeterlinck's last drama, 'Pelléas et Meli-sande,' there is a significant scene between the old king Arkël and the little princess Melisande. In his half-blind old age, says the king, he has acquired, he knows not at all why, "a trust in the good faith of events." He has always seen that "young and noble souls make young and noble and fortunate events." It is they, he believes, who shall "open the door to the new era" he foresees.

Maeterlinck's work — especially his latest work, in 'Les Aveugles' and 'Pelléas et Melisande' — stands with Arkël at the door-sill of that change in world insight and impulse which means a new era. It anticipates the opening of the door. Only "trust in the good faith of events" could have taken him so far on the new path he has struck out; only faith in the power within souls to shape happy events would suggest that souls can be relied upon to respond to intangible allusions born of the common experience and the universal vision.

The apprehension of the unknown future lying on the other side of the door, which is the motive of his recent dramas, finds fit expression in his treatment of the worn literary words of the past as symbols fresh-minted for new offices and strange effects. It is art that appeals not only, or mainly, to experience of facts and acts, but to experience of sophisticated thought upon such facts and acts. To make this new drama, the mind fruitage of antecedent literature is tributary.

---

* La Princesse Maleine. Maurice Maeterlinck. Bruxelles: Paul Lacomblez. 1890. — Les Aveugles [containing 'L'Intruse' and 'Les Aveugles']. Maurice Maeterlinck. Bruxelles: Paul Lacomblez. 1890. — Pelléas et Melisande. Maurice Maeterlinck. Bruxelles: Paul Lacomblez. 1892. — The Princess Maleine. Translated from the French by Gerard Harry, and The Intruder. By Maurice Maeterlinck. With an Introduction by Hall Caine. London: William Heinemann. 1892.

In ' La Princesse Maleine' delicate, fleeting, yet unmistakable reminders of Shakespearian situations are a part of the mechanism of the play ; for example, ' Romeo and Juliet ' lurks behind the scene between the father and mother, the nurse and Maleine ; ' Hamlet ' behind the scenes with Prince Hjalmer, and his Horatio, Angus; ' Lear ' behind the child-like break-down of the old king's grief and terror and remorse when Maleine lies dead.

In ' Pelléas et Melisande' the under-current of suggestion flows from Ibsen's strong revolt for a new order, for the freedom of woman, and for unfettered individual human action. There is no direct imitative use of either the great Englishman or the brave Norseman ; the clever artist works upon his readers' knowledge of them for his own purposes. He counts, too, upon his public's being aware of a long descent of romantic and dramatic traditions, which, standing thus ready in the background of human consciousness, may be trusted to respond whenever the familiar spring is touched.

How Maeterlinck plays upon this anterior consciousness, as surely as if it were real stuff instead of an immaterial association of ideas, may appear if I give here a bare brief of his last play. Shorn, as it must be, of the æsthetic and literary charm of the piece itself, it may yet serve to show something of the originality of his dramatic method.

The play opens at the gate of the castle; servants cry from inside, " Open the door ! Open the door ! "

The porter, from inside, grumbles, " Why do you wake me up ? Go out by the little doors ; there are enough of them ! " One servant answers, " We come to wash the sill; open, therefore, open ! " Others cry, " Great things are to happen ! " " There are to be famous feasts ! " " Open the great door wide, then ! " " Open ! "

The porter urges them to wait. He does not know whether it can open. " It never has opened. Wait till the light comes."

The servants declare that it is light enough already ; they see the sun.

The big keys croak and rasp in the locks. The porter fears it will wake everybody up.

Fearing and pulling, they slowly open the door, to find the sun

rising over the sea.   They pass in and out freely.   " I am going
to wash the sill," says the first servant; the second thinks it can
never be cleaned; others cry for water.   " Yes, yes," says the porter, sarcastically ; " sluice it with water.   Spill the deluge on it, and
you will never get it clean."

This strange scene is virtually a symbolic prologue.   It puts us
in key with the piece.   It has nothing to do externally with the
story of the play, and it introduces none of its characters, yet it
seems to have everything to do with the intent of the story, and to
introduce its motives under the images, — light, the sea, the open
door, the clandestine little doors, and the endless cleaning the great
exits and entrances upon life need.

Shakespeare puts us in possession of the key-note of his plays
with the opening words of often insignificant characters.   Maeterlinck is perhaps aware of this in framing thus differently yet correspondingly this prologue.

The plot proper begins in the second scene.   A man who has
had experience of life, a widower whose hair is beginning to grow
gray, meets a little maiden in a forest where both have lost their
way.

Evidently, like Shakespeare's forest of Arden or Prospero's isle,
this forest never grew outside the tale ; unlike any forest of Shakespeare's, it impresses one, though without any allegorical clumsi-
ness, as being more than a forest, —a forest-symbol of those old
growths of conventional life in which the human soul often loses its
way.

The little maiden weeps beside a fountain.   She has lost therein a crown that had been given her, — a beautiful crown, it seems to
the man, who sees it under the water ; but the little princess tells
him she would rather die than have him recover it for her.   Some
one gave it to her who frightened her, from whom she fled.
Golaud frightens her too.   She is afraid he will touch her.   But
he cannot leave her, he says, alone in the forest and at night;
she must come with him.   "Where are you going ? " she asks.
" I don't know," Golaud confesses ; " I too am lost."   They go
out of the wood together.

Neither an ordinary fountain is this nor an ordinary crown, yet it strikes one as more real, though in an ideal sense,— the sense in which Elizabeth Browning speaks of " the ideal," as " the only real." The incident of Golaud's saving Melisande from the harm that may come to her alone in the forest, by taking her to himself, of necessity rather than of her own will, also strikes the inward intelligence as glancing with grave irony at that chivalry of man which has protected woman by confiscating her to his own private behoof. But it is the inward intelligence that catches these innuendoes ; there are no carven inscriptions to that effect. If the art which insinuates them had been less delicate, some of Maeterlinck's not over-subtle English reviewers might not have missed him as they have ; but then, it would not be such good and original art.

Golaud and Melisande next appear together as man and wife. Golaud writes to his young step-brother, Pelléas, of his marriage and return to the court of his grandfather, King Arkël.

The reader is led to suspect that Pelléas is the one who darkly discovered to Melisande that crown of womanhood she wore for him, and which Golaud also thought so beautiful ; for no sooner does Pelléas read this letter than he begs leave to go away at once to visit a sick friend who must see him before he dies. Arkël himself is on the brink of the grave, however, and loath to let the young man leave him, so his proposed flight is deferred, and the fated meeting comes between Pelléas and Melisande. On the shore, in sight of the great ship which brought her, a monstrous tempest brewing, they meet. When the queen leaves them alone together, he offers her his hand. She excuses herself from taking it ; her hands are full. " I go to-morrow !" he adds. " Oh, why go ?" she asks ; and the first act ends. It is the spring of action through which the next acts follow. To an abandoned fountain in the park of the castle, another extraordinary fountain, said to open the eyes of the blind, Pelléas brings Melisande. There, fascinated, leaning far over the water, tossing her wedding-ring up and down, but thinking nothing less than that she would always catch it again, she loses it. " What shall we say to Golaud ?" " The truth," answers Pelléas ; but in the next scene, when Golaud misses the ring, the girl-wife is no stronger than Desdemona. She dropped it, she says, in a sea-cave, where she was playing with Yniold, Golaud's little son, and the tide chased them out before she could find it. Golaud sternly sends her out at once, with Pelléas, to find it.

The scene in the cavern, with the agitation of their fearful hearts, the necessity of deception, the beauty of the moonlit place, the alarm and flight of Melisande when they find three famine-stricken wretches asleep there, creates an unaccountable impression of the horror of forbidden love.

The third act finds Pelléas and Melisande drawn together still more intimately, and still more afraid of the intimacy they crave. Golaud's first fears of their relations are next developed. The act closes with two remarkably effective scenes. In the one Golaud leads Pelléas through the enormous caverns in the cellars of the castle whence, from a subterranean lake, arises a smell of death that poisons the air of the castle above. " The king will not believe that the smell comes from here," says Golaud. " There is hidden work going on here that no one suspects, and one of these nights the whole castle will be swallowed up if they don't take care." To the edge of the gulf Golaud leads him. Suddenly he saves him from its black waters. His guidance and his deliverance are equally threatening.

This scene in the castle vaults is as striking an example as could be given of the new use to which Maeterlinck has put the old stage properties as familiar to every modern reader as " hell's mouth " or " the devil " was to the mediæval public. Unactual as they seem here, they suffice to call up the revengeful atmosphere in which Golaud's suspicion and jealous rage may live appropriately. The idea, too, of the mephitic caverns that honeycomb the castle's foundations suggests the poisonous insecurity underlying many of the social structures the Past has bequeathed the world, and fits in with the dramatic use Maeterlinck seems to make of Golaud's assertion of marital rights.

As the brothers return to the upper air, Golaud warns the

young man to avoid Melisande without making his avoidance marked.

In the other scene, Golaud questions his son about mamma and Uncle Pelléas. They are often together, the boy tells him innocently. "I hear they don't get on well together, and quarrel," says Golaud.

The boy confounds him by answering, "Yes." He adds, "They quarrel about the door, because it cannot be open."

"Do they tell you to go play somewhere else?" asks the father again. "Oh, no, papa," the child answers; "they are afraid when I am not there."

Golaud holds the boy up to the window and forces him to report what they are doing. "They are doing nothing," says Yniold.

"Are they not near together? Do they not talk? What are they doing? They must be doing something," insists the father. "They are looking at the light," answers the child.

The fourth act closes with a last scene of the lovers by the fountain, in a transport of innocent passion. Golaud falls upon them there, sword in hand.

The gossip of the servants opens the last act. They talk about Pelléas's death, Golaud's own wound, big enough to kill, yet from which he is recovering, Melisande's little scratch too small to kill a pigeon; yet they are waiting for the moment which shall "tell them of themselves" to gather ceremoniously in her death-chamber.

In Melisande's room her husband harasses her to tell him the truth. "Is she culpable?" "No! no! Why do you ask?" she says. Is it the indifference of death which benumbs her to his imputations? Is it the purity of an unexpanded girlish soul imprisoned from the bud? Is Golaud gross as an Othello who never had any right but a forced one? These are questions the reader is impelled to ask.

Arkel brings to her bedside her baby girl, born too soon. "She does not laugh," says the mother. "She is tiny; she is going to weep, too. Oh, I pity her!"

This strange play of undeveloped femininity cut off by masculine dominance closes with Arkël's words, — "The child must live now in her place. It is the poor little one's turn!"

Melisande, like Maleine, falls a poor little victim to the big powers that be, but she is a fragile slave, with little of Maleine's spiritual force.

In the dialogue between Arkël and Melisande, already cited as especially significant in the light it throws upon the whole play, Arkël pities her bright and delicate youth immured in the gloom of the old castle, with all that it implies of unyielding law and custom, and when she insists that she is happy, he answers, "Maybe thou art one of those who are unhappy without knowing it."

Mr. Hall Caine, in his terse and clever introduction to the English translation of 'La Princesse Maleine' and 'L'Intruse,' cites two sayings of Maeterlinck concerning his work. These fragments of self-criticism Mr. Hall Caine thinks neither happy nor luminous; to me they are both. The first throws light upon the artistic purpose of that consciousness of Shakespeare one feels in 'Maleine,' hovering in the air, an undescried yet palpable presence, haunting and affecting the emotions. It hits off whimsically that feeling which Maeterlinck and many others seem to have had, that the robust days of large and primitive dramatic action are passed with the giants of their times. Imitation of such action *un*sicklied o'er with the pale cast of modern thought is lifeless; but to write with reference to that stout heritage of elder days, and to use it, not as it was, but as it lives to-day, condensed within the minds of ensuing generations, is to adapt it freshly to new uses, and to bring to our eyes again Shakespeare in little. Perhaps something of that sort is implied in Maeterlinck's figure of speech when he says, "I have tried to write Shakespeare for a theatre of marionettes."

The second piece of self-criticism refers to what Browning has well called "artistry." Maeterlinck says his prose is really loose verse, — "*des vers libres.*" Mr. Hall Caine finds this a condemnation of his style, for the established reason given in antiquated "rhetorics," that poetical prose is poor prose. But let us ask rather if it suits his work, and if this is not a new poetry never contemplated by that old definition, and therefore not amenable to its restriction. This garment of loose verse stretches itself to suit the various subtle purposes of modern dramatics as no limiting metre ever can; and I take Maeterlinck's explanation to be another sign of well-planned intention to let new work find its own tools.

In ' L'Intruse ' and ' Les Aveugles,' not only are the involutions of the symbolism poetic, the outward form is so too. The succession of the severely simple and natural speeches following a certain symmetry and arrangement, with frequent repetitions, having both the balanced force of a refrain and the emphasis of forthright everyday talk, make these short pieces dramatic poems.

Much has been said of the sombre fear with which ' L'Intruse ' strikes the heart, but nothing has been said of the humorous touches that lighten its gloom, characterize its figures, and show a capability that plans to use the terror of the main idea as part of a larger inference. I cite an example or two of this humor: —

" *The Father* [*speaking of the Grandfather*]. Once he was as rational as we are. He never said anything extraordinary."

" *The Father*. The silence is astonishing!
" *The Daughter*. One could hear an angel tread.
" *The Uncle*. That is why I do not like the country."

The first piece in that remarkable volume, ' Les Aveugles,' has been well described and well translated. It rivets the attention and thrills the marrow inevitably. The second piece, ' Les Aveugles,' has been somewhat neglected, although it should not be separated from its companion play, ' L'Intruse.' It is a necessary part of the whole, — which is, indeed, by Maeterlinck entitled as a whole, — ' Les Aveugles.'

In ' L'Intruse,' or ' The Intruder,' he makes us trace out the steps of Death's approach as shown in the ominous impressions they make on the watching family group. In ' Les Aveugles ' he takes the motive of ' L'Intruse,' which is Death, the physical fact, as a symbol of a deeper death, — none the less a fact, but stranger and of larger import, — the death of an old epoch, at the threshold of a new age, for a humanity yet blind to its meaning. The men and women are separated from each other. The beneficent priest and guide of the old order sits dead and helpless in their midst. They call in vain upon him ; they question the value of the women's moral insight ; " the rule of the old men " yet weighs upon them ; they babble inconsequently of their terror and their incapacity. Yet the weakest and youngest among them is the least blind ; and the implication of the strange and grewsome scene is that there is no hope for them unless they give up the idea of help from anywhere but from themselves.

As this strongly modelled piece has been passed over by the translators who introduced Maeterlinck to the English public, a translation of it will be given in POET-LORE, the first instalment of which here follows.

*P*

## THE SIGHTLESS.

### BY MAURICE MAETERLINCK.

*An ancient Southern forest, with a look of eternity, under a sky thick with stars. In the middle, deep within the shadows, is seated a very old priest enveloped in a large black mantle. His head and breast, slightly thrown back and deathly still, rest against the trunk of an enormous hollow oak. His face is frightfully pale with the fixed lividness of wax ; the purple lips are parted. His eyes, unspeaking and set, no longer see anything on this side of eternity, and are bloodshot as with the stress of immemorial tears and sorrows. His hair, of the purest white, falls in straight thin strands over a face whiter and more worn than anything around it in the listening silence of the sombre forest. His emaciated hands are clasped rigidly upon his knees. To the right, six blind old men are seated on stones, stumps, and dead leaves. To the left, in front of the old men, and separated from them by an uprooted tree and bowlders of rock, are seated six women, also blind. Three of them pray and bewail, in a dull voice, unceasingly. Another is extremely old. The fifth, in a posture of dumb idiocy, holds a little sleeping child on her lap. The sixth is strangely young, and her hair falls over her whole form. They are dressed, like the old men, in the same sombre flowing garments. Most of them lean their elbows on their knees, with their faces in their hands, and all seem to have lost their capacity to make any unnecessary motion. They no longer turn their heads at the stifled, disquieting noises of the island. Huge funereal trees, yews, weeping-willows, and cypresses, protect them with their faithful shade. Not far from the priest, a cluster of long sickly asphodels flower in the night. It is extraordinarily sombre, in spite of the moonlight, which, here and there, scatters for a moment the shadows cast by the foliage.*

*First Man, blind from birth.* He has not returned yet?

*Second Man, blind from birth.* You waked me up!

*First Man.* I was asleep too.

*Third Man, blind from birth.* I was asleep too.

*First Man.* He has not come yet?

*Second Man.* I hear nothing coming.

*Third Man.* It should be time to return to the hospital.

*First Man.* We ought to know where we are.

*Second Man.* It has grown cold since he went away.

*First Man.* We ought to know where we are!

*The Oldest Blind Man.* Is there any one who knows where we are?

*The Oldest Blind Woman.* We have been walking a long time; we must be very far from the hospital.

*First Man.* Ah! The women are in front of us?

*Oldest Woman.* We are sitting in front of you.

*First Man.* Wait; I am coming over to you. [*He gets up and feels his way.*] Speak! Let me hear where you are!

*Oldest Woman.* Here! We are sitting upon some stones.

*First Man.* [*He comes forward and hurts himself against the trunk of the tree and the bowlders.*] There is something between us —

*Second Man.* He would do better to stay in his place.

*Third Man.* Where are you sitting? Will you come over here by us?

*Oldest Woman.* We dare not get up.

*Third Man.* Why did he separate us?

*First Man.* I hear praying in the direction of the women.

*Second Man.* Yes; it is the three old women who are praying.

*First Man.* This is not the time to pray.

*Second Man.* You will pray by-and-by in the dormitory. [*The three old women continue their prayers.*]

*Third Man.* I should like to know by whose side I am sitting?

*Second Man.* I believe I am next to you. [*They feel around them.*]

*Third Man.* We cannot touch each other!

*First Man.* However, we are not far from one another. [*He gropes around him and strikes with his stick the fifth blind man, who groans heavily.*] The one who does not hear is beside us. I don't hear everybody. We were six before. I am going to call the roll. Let us ask the women too; we must know whom to count upon. I always hear the three old ones praying. Are they all together?

*Oldest Woman.* They are sitting beside me on a rock.

*First Man.* I am sitting on dead leaves.

*Third Man.* And the beautiful blind girl, where is she?

*Oldest Woman.* She is close by those who are praying.

*Second Man.* Where is the idiot and her child?

*The Blind Girl.* He is asleep; do not wake him.

*First Man.* Oh, how far you are from us! I thought you were in front of me.

*Third Man.* We know pretty well all we need to know; let us talk a little, while we await the priest's return.

*Oldest Woman.* He told us to wait for him in silence.

*Third Man.* We are not in church.

*Oldest Woman.* You don't know where we are.

*Third Man.* I am afraid when I am not talking.

*Second Man.* Do you know where the priest has gone?

*Third Man.* It seems to me that he has left us too long —

*First Man.* He is getting too old. It appears that he himself has not seen anything for some time. He dare not acknowledge it for fear some one else will take his place among us; but I suspect he sees scarcely anything. We must have another guide; he does n't listen to us any more, and we have become too many.

21

There are only the three sisters and he in the house who can see anything, and they are older than we are.    I am sure he has wandered away, and that he is looking for the road.    Where has he gone ?    He has no right to leave us here —

*Oldest Man.*  He has gone very far away ; I believe he told the women so.

*First Man.*  He only talks to the women now !   Don't we exist any more ?   We shall have to complain finally !

*Oldest Man.*  To whom will you complain ?

*First Man.*  I don't know yet ; we shall see, — we shall see.   But where can he have gone ?   I will ask the women.

*Oldest Woman.*  He was tired of walking so long ; I believe he is sitting this moment amongst us here.   He has been very sad and very weak for some days.   He is afraid since the physician died.   He is alone.   He says scarcely anything.   I don't know what has happened.   He positively would go out to-day.   He said that he would see the island for the last time, in the sunshine, before winter.   It seems the winter will be very long and very cold, and that the ice is already coming down from the North.   He was very restless too ; they say that the great storms of these last days have swollen the river, and that all the dikes are swept away. He said, too, that the sea frightened him.   It seems it is mounting up without any cause, and that the cliffs of the island are no longer high enough.   He was going to see, but he has not told us what he saw.   Now I believe that he has gone to fetch bread and water for the idiot.   He said that perhaps he would go a long way off.   We must wait.

*The Blind Girl.*  He took my hands when he went away, and his hands trembled as if he were afraid.   Then he embraced me —

*First Man.*  Oh ! oh !

*The Blind Girl.*  I asked him what had happened.   He told me that he did not know what was going to happen.   He told me that the reign of the old men was about to end, maybe —

*First Man.*  What did he mean by saying that ?

*The Blind Girl.*  I did not understand.   He told me he was going to the site of the great lighthouse.

*First Man.* Is there a lighthouse here?

*The Blind Girl.* Yes; at the north of the island. I think that we are not far from it. He said he could see the light from the lantern even here, through the leaves. He never seemed sadder to me than he was to-day. I think that he had been weeping for several days. I do not know why, but without seeing him, I also wept. I did not hear him go away; I did not question him any more. I heard him smile very gravely; I heard him close his eyes and wish to be silent.

*First Man.* He said nothing to us of all this.

*The Blind Girl.* You do not listen when he speaks!

*Oldest Woman.* You all murmur when he speaks!

*Second Man.* He simply said to us "good-night" as he went away.

*Third Man.* It must be very late.

*First Man.* He said "good-night" two or three times as he went away, as if he were going to sleep. I heard him look at me as he said "Good-night! good-night!" The voice changes when one looks at any one fixedly.

(To be continued.)

*Translated by the Editors.*

---

## BOOK INKLINGS.

—— To review works of fiction does not ordinarily come within the scope of POET-LORE; but, through the kindness of authors and publishers, having received several such works, we depart from our usual custom and take pleasure in setting forth for the consumption of our readers a few of the short stories so lavishly supplied by all manner of creative pens in the present literary dispensation. Among much of this sort of literary confection that is somewhat tasteless, it is pleasant to note the earnest purpose of a series of stories like Dr. Paul Carus's 'Truth in Fiction: Twelve Tales with a Moral.' The fables which he has invented to point his morals are in most cases clever and entertaining, particularly the first one in his book, 'The Chief's Daughter.' The drift of it is to show how the outward forms of all religions are merely the husks enclosing a kernel of truth. The Chief's daughter, recognizing this through the teaching of a Christian missionary, yet allows herself to be sacrificed according to the religious rites of her tribe, but, with her last breath, she preaches the higher form of Christianity. When the morals, however, are made to illustrate the superiority of monism, Dr. Carus's own peculiar "ism," over all other forms of philosophical belief, we are not ready to cry "Amen" from our hearts, though we appreciate the skill of the dialectics, which, without carrying conviction, makes his *appear* the better part. Those who, like Dr. Carus, are convinced of the untenableness of the doctrine of agnosticism or the ethical principle of the "greatest good to the greatest number" will derive much amusement from the story called, 'The Philosopher's Martyrdom,' in which a *reductio-ad-absurdum* argument is used. But what is there in heaven or earth which cannot be, if one has the mind to do it, reduced to an absurdity? (Truth in Fiction: Twelve Tales with a Moral. By Paul Carus. Chicago: Open Court Pub. Co. 1892.)

—— 'PERCHANCE TO DREAM' is the alluring title of a collection of short stories by Miss Margaret Sutton Briscoe. The stories have for the most part an original flavor, and are so well written as to augur marked success for Miss Briscoe in the future. The first story, which gives its name to the book, tells of the sensations of a man who retains his senses at the same time that he is to all intents and purposes drunk. He has the unenviable gift of seeing himself as "ithers see him" under such degrading circumstances; and the pain of his wife, the scorn of her brother and friend, serve him a wholesome lesson. The story is told with something of the grewsomeness of a tale of Edgar Allan Poe; and one can only wish that all intemperate men might have the same experience or, at least, read Miss Briscoe's powerful little story. Though this is doubtless the strongest piece of work in the book, we were especially attracted to the charming little sketch, 'Die Which I Won't,' which possesses a pathos and natural simplicity indicative of the truest art. (Perchance to Dream, and Other Stories. By Margaret

Sutton Briscoe. New York : Dodd, Mead, and Co. 1892.) —— MRS.
W. K. CLIFFORD's skill as a writer of short stories has been borne
witness to in high quarters. For ourselves we can only say that
we do not enjoy an acquaintance with such utterly soulless beings
as she has introduced us to in her volume entitled, 'The Last
Touches.' There is much striving to endow them with soulfulness,
but they seem to us little better than puppets draped in the rags
and tatters of passion, who take the name of love in vain. Doubtless, however, they are very true to life in some of its most disheart-
ening phases. —— WE have not the space adequately to review
Marion Crawford's brilliant novel, 'Don Orsino,' in which is drawn
with masterly skill the young man of the transition period, — a gently
nurtured youth, who chafes against the conventions of his caste,
who hates its idleness, and longs for some occupation in the world,
and finding nothing better to do in the Rome of the past decade
than to build houses to sell, soon finds himself hopelessly handicapped by the sharp practice of his banker; still, the experience
has developed his character and shown him to possess qualities
worthy of some better chance of exerting themselves. The love
portion of the story involves two sacrifices which one may doubt
the right of any human being to make, for rank injustice to oneself
brings little more good in its train than injustice to others, as is
proved in one of the cases in point. The consequences of the other
sacrifice do not come out in this story, but perhaps will be revealed
some day in another volume, which will portray the Don Orsino of
riper years. The reader will find in this book the same fascinating
qualities which have already made Marion Crawford one of the
most interesting novelists of the day. (The Last Touches, and
Other Stories. By Mrs. W. K. Clifford. Don Orsino. By F.
Marion Crawford. New York : Macmillan and Co.)

# NOTES AND NEWS.

——THAT was a taking Browning story which Mrs. Louise Chandler Moulton told the Boston Browning Society at one of its recent meetings. The story was Browning's own ; and he set off the little incident whimsically, and in high glee, for Mrs. Moulton's benefit, at a London dinner, *à propos* of a story in *The Atlantic* called 'A Browning Courtship.' "Perhaps it was founded on the real Browning Courtship," said Browning, "for there really was a Browning Courtship once."

At our request Mrs. Moulton has kindly written down for us this true story, which Browning told to her : —

"There was a girl in London, well-descended, well-bred, well-dowered, and born to charm. A suitor for her hand presented himself, — a man of title, of fortune, and of all sorts of personal gifts and graces. Above all, he was deeply and romantically in love with the girl. He proposed for her hand, and she told him that while she liked him very much, she felt that it would be absolutely fatal to her happiness to marry a man who could not sympathize fully with her intellectual tastes. 'Do you love the poetry of Robert Browning ?' she asked him, very seriously. Alas ! Prince Charming had never read it. He had fancied, somehow, that he was not up to it, and had not experimented. The lady's beautiful eyes looked at him with sad astonishment.

"' Ah, it is of no use to talk about our marriage,' she said. 'I adore Browning — simply adore him — and I could never be happy with a man who did not share the strongest intellectual interest of my life.'

"Prince Charming sighed, in despair. Then his face brightened. 'I see a hope,' he said. 'What if you should put me on probation ? I think I 'm not so dull but I could learn ; and surely no man ever had such strong reason for trying.'

"So it was settled, at last, that he should have three months in which to prove his power to understand Browning. 'The Death in the Desert' was the poem selected as the test of his ability. I wonder if anybody coached him. I half think Dr. Furnivall did.

"At any rate, after three months he came up for examination and passed triumphantly. He knew not only the poem, but all the side-lights that could be thrown upon it. He was penetrated with its grandeur and its beauty. In short, if he had belonged to a Browning Club he could not have understood it better.

" Up to this time Browning had never heard of the young lady ; but now she wrote to her adored poet, and told him of her happiness, of which she seemed to consider him the author, and begged him to be present at the wedding which was soon to take place. And Browning went. And he kissed the bride, too ; and as she was a very pretty bride, he did not mind this part of his duty."

—— It is with great pleasure that we learn of the projected literary weekly in Philadelphia. Since the dissolution of that excellent journal, *The American*, several years ago, Philadelphia has been without a representative in the choice American coterie of weekly and bi-monthly literary reviews. It stands to reason, therefore, that the children of her brain receive somewhat scant courtesy at times, since left to go forth into the world alone and unprotected by the approving and encouraging smiles of their own mother.

The names upon the editorial staff of *The Citizen* — for so the new weekly is christened — will be quite sufficient to insure it an immediate welcome among its *confrères*. We note among the purely literary names, Mr. Francis Howard Williams, Mr. Harrison S. Morris, Miss Agnes Repplier, Miss Anne H. Wharton, — a gentle band of apostles of beauty, whose influence will be exercised to foster a race of mellifluous and honey-tongued writers. And if at times the reader would fain hear something of other virtues than beauty, he will no doubt find it in the sturdy economic trend of Prof. Edmund J. James, whose editorial duties will be, we presume, to see that sociology is not neglected.

—— After some years spent in looking into the sources of the drama, Mr. F. M. Warren, of Adelbert College, expresses the opinion (see *Modern Language Notes*, January, 1893) that prose fiction has had nothing to do with the development of the drama. On the other hand, the drama has often been found at the birth of fiction, and has even presented certain kinds of novels with their plots. " As a general rule conceding the usual number of exceptions, I find that a period of novel writing follows a period of dramatic excellence, and repeats in manuscripts or in print the leading themes of the plays of the previous generation."

# SOCIETIES.

**The Boston Browning Society** held its fifty-eighth regular meeting on Tuesday, January 24. President Hornbrooke, in opening the meeting, dwelt on the thought uppermost in all minds, — the sudden death of Bishop Brooks on the day before, and referred to the fact that he had intended to be present with the Society at this time. Mrs. Richard Arnold read selections from 'Balaustion's Adventure.' Rev. Philip S. Moxom prefaced the reading of his paper on 'Balaustion's Opinion of Euripides' with further tribute of sorrow and affection for the leader who had passed away, and explained the necessarily unfinished condition of his essay, promising its completion at an early date. He related the story of this "beautiful dramatic poem, the centre of which is the 'Alkestis.'" Miss Helen Leah Reed read a paper on 'Aristophanes' Philosophy of Poetry.' (This paper will appear in full in POET-LORE.)

The question, "Is the Divergence between Aristophanes and Euripides more apparent than real?" was discussed by Mr. Thomas Sergeant Perry. He did not believe in the theory that these two dramatists were really in friendly relations with each other. All the evidence is against the supposition. Aristophanes never mentioned Euripides except to abuse him, and it is difficult to imagine all these diatribes to have been intended in a Pickwickian sense. With equally good reason might we believe him also a devoted ally of Cleon and the sophists. Nor is there anything novel in the supposition that he was really a good hater, since, although now a classic, Aristophanes was once a man. Comic writers are the most serious people in the world, and no one attempts to deny his sincerity of purpose. Hatred of what one considers contemporaneous error is not uncommon ; and why should the Athenian conservative not have distrusted the most brilliant representative of the new spirit ?

No discussion was held further on this subject, as Rev. Julius H. Ward rose to relate reminiscences of Bishop Brooks, and was followed by Mrs. Crosby on the event that filled all hearts.

*Emma Endicott Marean.*

POET-LORE

Vol. V.

———wilt thou not haply ſaie,
Truth needs no collour with his collour fixt?
Beautie no penſell, beauties truth to lay:
But beſt is beſt if neuer intermixt.
Becauſe he needs no praiſe, wilt thou be dumb?
Excuſe not ſilence ſo, for't lies in thee,
To make him much outliue a gilded tombe:
And to be praiſed of ages yet to be.
Then do thy office ———

No. 4.

# SHAKESPEARE'S 'JULIUS CÆSAR.'*

O portions of Roman history seem so real to us as those
which Shakespeare has made the subjects of his plays.
History merely calls up the ghost of the dead past, and
the impression it makes upon us is shadowy and insub-
stantial; poetry makes it live again before our eyes, and we feel
that we are looking upon men and women like ourselves, not their
misty semblances. It might seem at first that the poet, by giving
us fancies instead of facts, or fancies mingled with facts, only dis-
torts and confuses our conceptions of historical verities; but if he
be a true poet he sees the past with a clearer vision than other
men, and reproduces it more truthfully as well as more vividly.
He sees it indeed with the eye of imagination, not as it actually
was; but there are truths of the imagination no less than of the
senses and the reason. Two descriptions may be alike imaginative,
but one may be true and the other false. The one, though not a
statement of facts, is consistent with the facts and impresses us as

* It is ........ ..... rtions of this ...... rinted several ... ... ' ᴅ land with-

the reality would impress us ; the other is neither true nor in keeping with the truth, and can only deceive and mislead us. Ben Jonson wrote Roman plays which, in minute attention to the details of the manners and customs of the time, are far more scholarly than Shakespeare's. He accompanies them with copious notes giving classical quotations to illustrate the accuracy of the language and the action. The work evinces genuine poetic power as well as laborious research, and yet the effect is far inferior to that of Shakespeare's less pedantic treatment of Roman subjects. The latter does not know so much of classical history and archæology, but he has a deeper insight into human nature, which is the same in all ages. Jonson has given us skilfully modelled and admirably sculptured statues, but Shakespeare living men and women.

THE DATE OF THE PLAY. — Of the three Roman plays ‘ Julius Cæsar’ is the earliest in the order of composition, though second in the historical series. It is quite certain that it was written as early as 1601, while ‘ Antony and Cleopatra ’ was not produced until 1608, and ‘ Coriolanus,’ in all probability, not until 1609 or 1610. Malone believed that ‘ Julius Cæsar ’ “could not have appeared before 1607 ;” and Chalmers, Drake, and the early commentators generally, were unanimous in accepting his conclusions. Among the more recent editors, Knight is the only one worth mentioning who considers it “ one of the latest works of Shakespeare.” Halliwell-Phillipps, in his folio edition (1865), fixes the date as “ in or before the year 1601 ” by the following lines in Weever’s ‘ Mirror of Martyrs,’ printed in that year : —

> “ The many-headed multitude were drawne
> By Brutus’ speech, that Cæsar was ambitious ;
> When eloquent Mark Antonie had showne
> His virtues, who but Brutus then was vicious ? ”

No editor since 1865, so far as I am aware, has hesitated to agree with Halliwell-Phillipps that these lines “ unquestionably are to be traced to a recollection of Shakespeare’s drama, not to that of the history as given by Plutarch ; ” but the eminent critic himself subsequently modified his opinion on this point. In his ‘ Outlines of the Life of Shakespeare ’ (6th ed. 1886, vol. ii. p. 257), he says:

" There is supposed to be a possibility, derived from an apparent reference to it in Weever's ' Mirror for Martyrs ' that the tragedy of ' Julius Cæsar' was in existence as early as 1599 ; for although the former work was not published till 1601, the author distinctly tells his dedicatee that ' this poem . some two yeares agoe was made fit for print.' The subject was then, however, a favorite one for dramatic composition, and inferences from such premises must be cautiously received. Shakespeare's was not, perhaps, the only drama of the time to which the lines of Weever were applicable; and the more this species of evidence is studied, the more is one inclined to question its efficacy."

Sundry old plays on the history of Cæsar have come down to our day, but Weever's allusion does not fit any of them, while it does fit Shakespeare's play exactly. It does not follow that the latter must have been written as early as 1599, for the reference to it in the ' Mirror of Martyrs ' may have been inserted just before the book went to press two years later. The date 1599, however, is not inconsistent with the internal evidence of metre and style, which, in a case like this, is of more value than the external. Mr. Stokes (' Chronological Order of Shakespeare's Plays,' 1878, p. 88), after a careful discussion of all the evidence, sums up the matter thus : " The great similarity of style between this play and ' Hamlet ' and 'Henry V.' has been pointed out by Gervinus, Spedding, Dowden, Hales, and others, and, I suppose, must have been felt by nearly every reader. It is not only shown by the many allusions to Cæsar in these plays [allusions, by the by, which show a co-ordinate estimation of his character], but by the ' minor relations ' of these plays. This point is so strong that, taking into considera-tion some of the references mentioned above, there can scarcely be any doubt that the original production of this play must be placed in 1599–1600. It may have been revised afterwards, and the appearance of several works bearing similar titles in 1607 suggests, as Mr. Fleay says, its reproduction at that date."

Mr. Fleay, by the by, believes that the present play "has been greatly shortened," as " shown by the singularly large number of instances in which mute characters are on the stage — which is totally at variance with Shakespeare's usual practice ;" and also "by the large number of incomplete lines in every possible position, even in the middle of speeches." He believes, moreover, that the play was revised by Ben Jonson, who in his 'Discoveries' tells us that Shakespeare wrote (in iii. 1. 47), "Cæsar did never wrong but with just cause." Mr. Fleay adds : "That this original reading stood in the acting copies till not long before the 1623 folio was printed, is clear from the fact that Jonson, in the Induction to his 'Staple of News' (1625), alludes to it as a well-known line requiring no explanation — 'Cry you mercy,' says Prologue, 'you never did wrong but with just cause.' * This would imply that Shakespeare did not make the alterations himself ; a hypothesis confirmed by the spelling of *Antony* without an *h :* this name occurs in eight of Shakespeare's plays, and in every instance but this invariably is spelled *Anthony*. . . . The ' *et tu, Brute,*' about which so much has been written, was probably taken from Ben Jonson's ' Every Man out of his Humour' (i. 1)." This was well answered by Mr. J. W. Hales (in the discussion of Mr. Fleay's theory in the New Shakspere Society of London, June 26, 1874) : "If Ben Jonson had really revised Shakespeare's ' Julius Cæsar,' he would certainly have told us that he, the great Ben, had set his friend's ' ridiculous' passages all right. Jonson was not the man to hide his light under a bushel." It may be added that if the scholarly Ben had corrected the *Anthony* it is inconceivable that he should have permitted the impossible Latin form *Calphurnia* to stand, or that he should have retained the *Decius* Brutus for *Decimus* Brutus. It is as absurd to suppose that Jonson could have overlooked these things as that Bacon could have originated them. To the latter, as to the former, Decius Brutus would have been like Christopher Sly's " Richard Conqueror." †

---

* Whether Shakespeare actually wrote this (see the notes in my edition of 'Julius Cæsar,' pp 157, 191) is by no means certain ; but, if he did, there was no good reason for Jonson's ridicule of it. As Halliwell-Phillipps remarks, "if *wrong* be taken in the sense of *injury* or *harm*, as Shakespeare sometimes uses it, there is no absurdity in the line ; " or, as Miss Lucy Toulmin Smith suggests, the dramatist may have had in mind the well-known legal maxim, " The king can do no wrong."

† Yet Judge Holmes, in his ' Authorship of Shakespeare ' (3d ed. 1886, vol. i. p. 289), in quoting Bacon's ' Essay on Friendship' as a parallel to the second act of ' Julius Cæsar,' does not see that in the very passage quoted Bacon has " Decimus Brutus" and "Calpurnia ; " thus proving — if we needed any proof — that the philosopher knew what the author of the drama, whoever he may have been, evidently did *not* know !

THE HISTORICAL SOURCES OF THE PLAY. — Although, as mentioned above, there were several earlier plays on the same subject, we have no reason to believe that Shakespeare made any use of them. His material was drawn almost exclusively from Sir Thomas North's translation of Bishop Amyot's French version of Plutarch's ' Lives.' In no other historical play, English, Greek, or Roman, has he followed his authorities so closely and minutely. As more than one critic has pointed out, "much which one unacquainted with Plutarch would consider in form and manner to be quite Shakespearian, and which has not unfrequently been quoted as peculiarly his own," is taken bodily from the old Greek biographer. Gervinus remarks : " From the triumph over Pompey (or rather over his sons), the silencing of the two tribunes, and the crown offered at the Lupercalian feast, until Cæsar's murder, and from thence to the battle of Philippi and the closing words of Antony, which are in part exactly as they were delivered, all in this play is essentially Plutarch. The omens of Cæsar's death, the warnings of the augur and of Artemidorus, the absence of the heart in the animal sacrificed, Calphurnia's dream ; the peculiar traits of Cæsar's character, his superstition regarding the touch of barren women in the course, his remarks about thin people like Cassius ; all the circumstances about the conspiracy where no oath was taken, the character of Ligarius, the withdrawal of Cicero ; the whole relation of Portia to Brutus, her words, his reply, her subsequent anxiety and death ; the circumstances of Cæsar's death, the very arts and means of Decius Brutus to induce him to leave home, all the minutest particulars of his murder, the behavior of Antony and its result, the murder of the poet Cinna ; further on, the contention between the republican friends respecting Lucius Pella and the refusal of the money, the dissension of the two concerning the decisive battle, their conversation about suicide, the appearance of Brutus's evil genius, the mistakes in the battle, its double issue, its repetition, the suicide of both friends, and Cassius's death by the same sword with which he killed Cæsar — all is taken from Plutarch's narrative, from which the poet had only to omit whatever destroyed the unity of the action."

Even the blunders of Plutarch, or his copyists and editors (like the *Decius* Brutus, *Calphurnia*, etc.), are literally reproduced in the play.

THE LEADING CHARACTERS OF THE PLAY. — As Craik has remarked in his excellent commentary on this play, it is evident from the many allusions to Cæsar in the other plays, that his character and history had made a deep impression on the dramatist. After quoting these allusions, Craik says with truth that " they will probably be thought to afford a considerably more comprehensive representation of the mighty Julius than the play which bears his name," wherein " we have a distinct exhibition of little else beyond his vanity and arrogance, relieved and set off by his good-nature or affability." He adds : " It might almost be suspected that the complete and full-length Cæsar had been carefully reserved for another drama." Hazlitt, in a similar strain, says that the hero of the play " makes several vaporing and rather pedantic speeches, and does nothing ; indeed, he has nothing to do." Other critics have been equally puzzled by Shakespeare's delineation of Cæsar. Hudson, indeed, goes so far as to call it " little short of a downright caricature." He is in doubt whether to explain this by supposing that Cæsar was too great for the hero of a drama, " since his greatness, if brought forward in full measure, would leave no room for anything else," or whether it was not the dramatist's intention " to represent Cæsar, not as he was indeed, but as he must have appeared to the conspirators ; to make us see him as they saw him ; in order that they too might have fair and equal judgment at our hands." The critic is disposed to rest on the latter explanation, but to me it seems very clearly a wrong one. What the conspirators thought of Cæsar is evident enough from what they themselves say of him. It was not necessary to distort or belittle the character to make us see *how* they saw him ; and to have done it to make us see him *as* they saw him would have been a gross injustice to the foremost man of all this world, of which we cannot imagine Shakespeare guilty.

To my thinking, the explanation of the matter lies on the surface. The " complete and full-length Cæsar," to re-quote Craik's words, could not be fully and fairly presented in these closing scenes of his career. As Hazlitt has said, he *does* nothing, *has* nothing to do. It might be added that he has nothing even to *say*, in the way of heroic utterance. He is merely the " walking gentleman " of the stage in two or three scenes, before he has to stand up and be killed in the middle, or somewhat earlier than the middle, of the play. What opportunity has he to impress us as " great Cæsar " unless by directly telling us that he is ? A certain assumption of the god, a certain boastful insistence on his freedom from ordinary human weakness, — that he is *not* one of the cowards that die many times before their deaths, *not* one whom flattery or importunity can induce to bend from his fixed purpose, — this is all that is left him for asserting his pre-eminence over " ordinary men." It is Plutarch's Cæsar that the dramatist reproduces,— ambitious for kingly power, somewhat spoiled by victory, jealous and fearful of his enemies in the State, and superstitious withal, yet hiding his fears and misgivings under an arrogant and haughty demeanor. We see him, moreover, at a critical point in his career, hesitating between his ambition for the crown and his doubt whether the time had come for venturing to assume it. It may be a question whether even Cæsar himself, at such a crisis in his fortunes, might not show something of the weakness of inferior natures.

His boastful speeches after all are not so frequent as certain of the critics would have us believe, and some of them are directly suggested by Plutarch ; as, for instance, the one I have quoted about cowards. Plutarch says that when his friends " did counsel him to have a guard for the safety of his person," he would not consent to it, " but said it was better to die once than always to be afraid of death."

Shall we then say with certain other critics that Cæsar is in no sense the hero of the play, and that it should not have been named for him, but should have been called ' Marcus Brutus ' instead ? The important part that Brutus fills in the drama is obvious, as I shall have occasion to illustrate further on ; but Cæsar is nevertheless the mainspring of the action, and appropriately furnishes the title. He dies, to be sure, early in the third act ; and up to the hour of his death he has done nothing, said nothing, of special interest or importance. But his real share in the *action* of the play, paradoxical as it may seem at first, begins with his death. He is, so to speak, a "very lively corpse;" and Shakespeare has emphasized the fact by several significant utterances. Note Antony's graphic prophecy over the dead body of the Dictator, — the vision of the "Domestic fury and fierce civil strife" that are to follow the murder, —

> "And Cæsar's *spirit*, ranging for revenge,
> Shall in these confines, *with a monarch's voice*,
> Cry Havoc! and let slip the dogs of war."

And later how eloquently does Antony make "sweet Cæsar's wounds, poor, poor dumb mouths," speak for him to the crowd in the forum, who rush to fire the traitors' houses with the very brands from the funeral pile of Cæsar! And Cæsar is still the "evil spirit" of the conspirators, as his ghost warns Brutus on his first visit, and will "see him again" on the battlefield that is to settle his fate. And there at Philippi both Brutus and Cassius, as the poet takes pains to make them tell us with their own mouths, die by the very swords that had been turned against Cæsar. As Cassius falls, he cries : —

> "Cæsar, thou art revenged
> Even with the sword that killed thee!"

and Brutus, looking on the dead Cassius, exclaims : —

> "O Julius Cæsar, thou art mighty yet!
> Thy spirit walks abroad, and turns our swords
> In our own proper entrails."

It is not long before he verifies this by his own suicide; but again, in his last words, he pays tribute to the posthumous power of the murdered Julius : —

> "Cæsar, now be still :
> I killed not thee with half so good a will."

As I have said, these are significant utterances. Shakespeare meant that we should not fail to see that Cæsar, though dead, was "mighty yet," the ruling power, the Nemesis, of the latter half of the play, making good his right to the honor given him in the title, as he had in nowise had the opportunity of doing in the earlier half.                                                    *W. J. Rolfe.*

(To be continued.)

# SHAKESPEARE AND LYLY.

I N going over the plays of John Lyly, the reader notices many resemblances to Shakespeare. They are scattered and fragmentary,— sometimes a bit of plot, sometimes a character, sometimes an expression, as though the flavor of a thought stayed by him or the music of a line lingered in his ear, and he unconsciously borrowed it. These resemblances, taken from Lyly's plays alone, his ' Euphues ' not being included, have been grouped together in the following pages, not with a view of showing any influence which Lyly may have had upon Shakespeare, for they had little in common, but simply as a bit of Shakespeare's experience ; in the idea that everything is interesting that throws any light on his reading or his life.

Lyly's career preceded Shakespeare's, lapping over it about ten years ; so that the last half of Lyly's literary life corresponds roughly with the first half of Shakespeare's. He was a sentimental writer, stilted in style and affected in manner, but very popular with the court, where his plays were often performed. Minto describes them as " vessels filled to the brim with sparkling liquor which stands to Shakespeare's comedy in the relation of lemonade to champagne; the whole thing is a sort of ginger-pop intoxication."

We have eight dramas which are generally accepted as Lyly's, besides one bearing his name which is now rejected as spurious. The genuine plays are, — ' The Woman in the Moon,' ' Campaspe,' ' Sappho and Phao,' ' Endymion,' ' Galatea,' ' Midas,' ' Mother Bombie,' and ' Love's Metamorphosis.' The exact date of their production is uncertain, but the above order may be accepted as probably about right.

Let us now take them up successively, and note their points of contact with Shakespeare's works, many of which we shall find noted in Fairholt's Lyly and Malone's Variorum Shakespeare.

23

Beginning with 'The Woman in the Moon' (written perhaps 1580–82), the prologue says this play is "but the shadow of our author's dream."

> "If many faults escape in her discourse
> Remember all is but a poet's dream."

In the same way Puck, in the Epilogue to the 'Midsummer-Night's Dream,' declares the play to be but a "vision," and for that reason asks the pardon of the audience for the poet's shortcomings.

> "If we shadows have offended,
> Think but this and all is mended ;
> That you have but slumber'd here,
> While these visions did appear."

Next comes 'Campaspe' (printed 1584), containing the pretty song by Trico (Act V., Sc. i.) with these lines about "the lark so shrill and clear " : —

> "How at heaven's gate she claps her wings,
> The morn not waking till she sings."

Compare 'Cymbeline,' Act II., Sc. iii., lines 21–22, —

> "Hark, hark ! the lark at heaven's gate sings,
> And Phœbus 'gins arise," —

also Sonnet 29, lines 10–12 : —

> "and then my state,
> Like to the lark at break of day arising
> From sullen earth, sings hymns at heaven's gate."

In 'Sappho and Phao,' IV., ii. (printed 1584), Venus, in love with Phao and scorned by him, says, "Phao, I entreat where I may command." This resembles a passage in the forged letter, 'Twelfth Night,' II., v., where Olivia says to Malvolio, "I may command where I adore."

'Endymion' (printed 1591) shows us more positive points of contact. "Sir Tophas," one of the characters, is a bragging soldier, and he is accompanied by a diminutive page named Epitheton. The similarity between this combination and that of Don Armado and Moth in 'Love's Labour's Lost' can hardly be accidental. It is a curious coincidence that when Moth asks Armado, I., ii., why he calls him a "tender juvenal," Armado replies that it is a "congruent epitheton." The boastful soldier is repeated in Pistol and Parolles; but he was no novelty; he had afforded amusement to the stage ever since the days of the Greeks. The name "Sir Tophas" reappears in 'Twelfth Night,' IV., ii., as Sir Topas, the imaginary curate, who visits Malvolio in prison. Again, in 'Endymion,' IV.; iii., Cynthia compels Pythagoras to abjure his "ridiculous opinions;" and in 'Twelfth Night,' IV., ii., the clown as Sir Topas thrice mentions the "opinions of Pythagoras," calling on Malvolio to abjure them. The same scene in 'Endymion' contains the Pinching Song, which seems to have suggested the one in 'Merry Wives,' V., v. In 'Endymion' the fairies dance around Corsites, who is asleep under a tree, just as the make-believe fairies do around Falstaff under Herne's Oak, and pinch him while they sing: —

> "Pinch him, pinch him, black and blue.
>
> . . . . . . . .
>
> Pinch him blue,
> And pinch him black,
> Let him not lack
> Sharp nails to pinch him blue and red,
> Till sleep has rocked his addle head."

This play furnishes us still another illustration, for the conversation between the Constable, the Watch, and the Pages in 'Endymion,' IV., ii., calls to mind the Constable and the Watch in 'Much Ado.'

In 'Galatea' (printed 1592, but written before 1585), two girls, Galatea and Phyllida, each unacquainted with the other, are both disguised as boys, and each falls in love with the other as a boy. The embarrassments caused by this disguise recall to our minds Julia in 'Two Gentlemen of Verona,' Viola in 'Twelfth Night,' and Rosalind and Celia in 'As You Like It.' Galatea asks Phyllida, III., ii., "Have you ever a sister?" and the supposed boy replies, "My father had but one daughter, and therefore I could have no sister;" compare Viola's equivoque under similar circumstances in

'Twelfth Night,' II., iv., "I am all the daughters of my father's house," etc.

Once more, in 'Galatea,' IV., iv., Phyllida says to Galatea, "Seeing we are both boys, and both lovers, — that our affection may have some show and seem as it were love, — let me call thee mistress." Galatea replies, "I accept that name ;" compare with this 'As You Like It,' III., ii., and IV., i., where Rosalind, in boy's dress, agrees to pose as Orlando's mistress. So when Phyllida, 'Galatea,' III., ii., says to the admiring Galatea, "I have sworn never to love a woman," we are again reminded of 'As You Like It,' where Rosalind in similar terms rejects Phœbe's love : " And so am I for no woman."

In the refrain of the Nymphs' song, IV., ii., "Let her come hither," Fairholt notes a resemblance to that in Amiens' song, 'As You Like It,' II., v.: "Come hither, come hither, come hither."

The second scene of Act III., where Diana's nymphs come on the stage one by one, confessing that they have broken their vows by falling in love, recalls at once the similar scene in 'Love's Labour 's Lost,' IV., iii., where the King and his Lords appear in like order, each admitting that he has broken his oath to have nothing to do with the tender passion.

In 'Midas,' I., ii. (printed 1592), the banter between the servants on the qualities of Petulus's mistress must be the original of Launce's inventory of his mistress's charms in 'The Two Gentlemen of Verona,' III., i.

A further instance may be noted in 'Midas,' III., iii. ; the means here suggested to the Princess by her ladies for passing the time pleasantly are repeated in 'Richard II.,' III., iv., where the Queen asks her ladies, "What sport shall we devise to drive away the heavy thought of care?"

There are several passages common to Shakespeare and Lyly which were probably public property as proverbial expressions ; for example, 'Midas,' III., ii., alludes to the common saying that one was no number. Compare Sonnet 136, and 'Romeo and Juliet,' I., ii., 33. In 'Mother Bombie,' I., i. (printed 1594), Dromio says,

"I smell your device ; it will be excellent ;" compare 'Twelfth Night,' II., iii., 153 : "Excellent, I smell a device."

Again, in the third scene of the first act, Sperantus says, "Prisius, you wring me on the withers and yet winch [wince] yourself ; " *cf.* 'Hamlet,' III., ii., 232. Lyly's 'Euphues' also is quoted by Furness in illustration of this passage. In the second act, third scene, Silena says, "I think gentlemen had never less wit in a year," etc. Capell thinks the Fool in 'Lear,' I., iv., 160, has this line in mind when he says, "Fools had ne'er less grace in a year." So the speech of Silena in IV., ii., " I cry you mercy, I took you for a joint stool," is repeated *verbatim* by the Fool in ' Lear,' III., vi., 50.

In 'Love's Metamorphosis,' III., ii. (printed 1601, but written much earlier), occurs this line, " The sea which receiveth all things and cannot be filled." The same figure is found in Sonnet 135 ; indeed, we may trace it clear back to the Preacher in the Old Testament, who said, Ecclesiastes i. 7, " All the rivers run into the sea ; yet the sea is not full." The mechanical arrangement of some of the scenes in this play, especially Act III., Sc. i., and Act V., Sc. iii., where the characters come forward in regular set order, is like some scenes in Shakespeare's early plays, especially ' Love's Labour 's Lost.'

Besides the parallels noted above, we find more or less of the staple current jokes of the day common to both writers, such as the puns on *waste* and *waist, tongs* and *tongues,* and others like them, which may also be called public property.

Another similarity, one rather of sentiment than of language, may be spoken of before closing this list. If we may be allowed to consider the first series of Shakespeare's Sonnets as a chronicle of ardent friendship between men, we can find a remarkable parallel of sentiment in ' Endymion,' especially in III., iv., where Eumenides tells Geron, " The love of men to women is a thing common and of course ; the friendship of man to man infinite and immortal," and the old man answers " all things (friendship excepted) are subject to fortune. When adversities flow, then love ebbs ; but friendship standeth stiffly in storms." Or, as transmuted by the genius of Shakespeare (Sonnet 116) : —

> " It is an ever fixèd mark,
> That looks on tempests and is never shaken.
>
> .    .    .    .    .    .    .
>
> Love alters not with [Time's] brief hours and weeks,
> But bears it out even to the edge of doom."

The " love " sung in this sonnet is the " marriage of true minds," regardless of sex. The whole passage in Lyly is worth reading, as in it we find him at his best, forgetting for a moment his affectations and indulging in a little real sentiment.

The scenes in ' Love's Labour's Lost,' where Shakespeare satirizes Lyly's school in their " taffeta phrases" and " figures pedantical," are so familiar it has not been thought necessary to quote them. But in spite of his sense of their absurdity, once in a while in his earlier work the great master himself dropped into the Euphuistic vein, from which we may be thankful he soon delivered himself entirely.

The above list includes all the common points I have noted in reading Lyly's plays. The most striking resemblances between the two authors are taken from the songs and comic scenes ; in Lyly chiefly from ' Endymion ' and ' Galatea ;' in Shakespeare mainly from his comedies, especially ' Love's Labour's Lost ' and ' Twelfth Night.' It may be said that after all they amount to very little when we consider the total number of the plays and the prevailing carelessness among authors in those days about borrowing from one another. This is true enough, but the interest to us lies in the light it casts upon Shakespeare's literary life. It shows us that he was familiar with these plays of Lyly's, using scraps of them in the make-up of his comedies, just as he borrowed from Holinshed and Plutarch. He drew matter from every source at his command. Sidney's ' Arcadia ' gave him suggestions both for poem and plot ; we trace the power of " Marlowe's mighty line " in his early tragedies, and Lyly's gentler muse contributed its own quota to the lighter side of this great gallery of human life.

*Horace Davis.*

# GENTLE WILL, OUR FELLOW.

WRIT IN 1626 A. D. BY JOHN HEMINGE, SERVANT OF HIS GRACIOUS MAJESTY KING CHARLES I.; EDITED IN 1892 A. D. AS "ALL, THOUGH FEIGNED, IS TRUE" BY F. G. FLEAY, SERVANT OF ALL SHAKESPEARIAN STUDENTS IN AMERICA, ENGLAND, GERMANY, OR ELSEWHERE.

T this time another author began to write for us, and continued to do so for the space of three years. This was Thomas Lodge, afterward Dr. Lodge, now lately deceased, so that there is no longer any need to conceal his name. He was at that time in hiding, an arrest being out against him, which was furthered by my Lord Cobham. The plays he wrote for us were, first, 'Mucedorus,' — a slight thing, but much liked by the people, who never tired of the merry conceits of Mouse. It drew full houses, and since it was published in 1598, hath passed through many editions. I shall have to speak again of this play hereafter. The next was 'A Warning for Fair Women,' which told the story of a murder of one Browne, much like in plot to the old play of 'Arden of Feversham,' to which there was a Prologue which hath been much misunderstood. In it Tragedy is visited by Comedy for setting forth

"How some damned tyrant to obtain a crown
Stabs, hangs, imprisons, smothers, cutteth throats."

This has been interpreted as if the play of 'Richard III.,' by Shakespeare, were glanced at. This would make of us Saturns to devour our own offspring. The play really intended was that of 'Muley Mollocco,' or 'The Battle of Alcazar,' and the author, George Peele. For Lodge goes on to say how a filthy, whining ghost comes screaming like a pig, and cries, "Vindicta." Where is there any ghost in Shakespeare's plays who cries "Vindicta"? There are three in 'Muley Mollocco,' another in the old Queen's play of 'Richard III.,' and still another in 'Locrine,' all written by George Peele. Nor hath any other author that I wot of brought such a ghost upon the stage, though Marston has, in his 'Antonio and Mellida,' used the word "vindicta." Besides Lodge, Jonson, in his 'Poetaster,' and Fletcher, in his 'Fair Maid of the Inn,' have ridiculed these whining ghosts of Peele's.

The occasion of this satire was that Peele had left us when we went to the Theater; and Ned Alleyn had obtained this very play on 'Alcazar' from us, although we had acted in it at the Rose under him. In the Christmas time of 1596, Peele, Dekker, and some others had patched up a new play called 'Stukeley,' on part of the same plot; of which, who lists to know more may read it, as it is printed, and may understand the whole matter better by perusing what Ben hath writ in 'The Poetaster.' As the Admiral's men were ever girding at us in their plays, we thought no harm to answer them in this; and even Shakespeare, in his 'Henry IV.,' hits this same play of 'Alcazar,' where in the second part thereof he makes Pistol quote a line from it: "Feed and be fat, my fair Calipolis." But this was after 'Wily Beguiled' had been played, wherein the Admiral's men had handled us over roughly.

Peele died shortly after in no creditable manner. Strange it was that of three men, Marlowe, Peele, and Lodge, whom Greene had warned against us as "antics garnished with their feathers," every one thereafter wrote for our company at several times.

The third and last play which Lodge wrote for us was 'The Alarum for London,' or 'The Siege of Antwerp,' at the time when the fear of the Spaniards was so great all through the land. But in that same year, by the decision of my Lord Hunsdon, who had succeeded Lord Cobham, he was freed from fear of arrest, and left writing of plays altogether. Nor in any case would he have remained with us along with Jonson, with whom he was at enmity. He willed us to keep his play-writing a secret, because he thought it an unmeet occupation for a Doctor of Physic, and had, so long since as in 1589, forsworn it as "penny knaves' delight." We never divulged it; although his three plays for us were all published, as our custom in that matter was, each of them two years after it was acted, not one of them bore his name; but the University pen that wrote 'The Return from Parnassus' smelled it out, and introduced him, along with Drayton, in that play as hiring themselves to our fellows, Burbadge and Kempe, to act at our theatre.

Meanwhile our company had ups and downs in London. For from the time of the death of my Lord Henry of Hunsdon until that of William Brooke, my Lord of Cobham, who succeeded him as Lord Chamberlain, — that is, from July 23, 1596, until March 3, 1597, — we, who were by no means favored by the new chamberlain, were further harassed by the refusal of the landlord of the Theater to renew the lease, although Richard Burbadge, our fellow, and his brother Cuthbert, had offered him a higher rent. Seeing that we could not come to any agreement with this curmudgeon, it seemed good to the Burbadges, with the consent of their fellow-sharers, — Shakespeare, Condell, and the rest, — to remove, if we could, to the Curtain, which stood hard by. This we accordingly did in October, 1597, my Lord Pembroke's men, who then occupied the Curtain, joining with the Admiral's for a short time at the Rose, but soon after travelling in the country. We closed the Theater in July, and did not act in London during the summer heat. This was wittily brought upon the stage in the play of ' Wily Beguiled,' wherein Will Cricket — that is, Will Kempe, one of our sharers — is made to say, "to let my house, before my lease is out, is cut-throatery ; and to scrape for more rent is pole-penury." This play also merrily alludes oftentimes to Shakespeare's ' Romeo and Juliet,' and his ' Merchant of Venice.'

At this same time the private theatre at Blackfriars was opened with the children of the Chapel Royal under Nathaniel Giles. James Burbadge had bought the house of Sir William More and made it into a theatre, and when he died in the year after (1597), we had some talk of setting up in it ourselves, but for divers good reasons we preferred the Curtain. The small square room would have ill suited our actors, who were accustomed to speak in a large round with an open yard. The greater expense for lights and the smallness of the auditory would have necessitated a much larger payment for admission ; and even then, if the audience were at all full, we should have had to allow them on the stage itself, — which

24

thing indeed was afterward done by these boys, to the great discomfiture of the actors, — and we should have entirely foregone our chief frequenters, the understanders in the yard and the twopenny gallery men. True it is that thirteen years after we found it convenient to take this place for ourselves, at a time when the fashion of these children had quite died out. It was then needful for us to provide entertainment for the better sort in a place of their own, as one may say ; yet have we never, as some have and still do, confined ourselves to our private house, for we have ever held that a stage, on which the mirror is truly held up to nature, is one of those things which should be fostered by all good governments, and is not so much, as masks and the like with their gorgeous scenes and lavish expense are, a luxury for the rich as a thing to be desired for all, rich and poor alike.

Before we moved to the Curtain, another thing happened which I may not pass over, for that ill-minded men have so ofttimes scoffed at us, the grand possessors, as they call us, for not printing the plays of our fellow Shakespeare during his lifetime. It might suffice to say we did what we would with our own; but it is, methinks, better to set down the plain truth in the matter. While we were yet acting as Lord Hunsdon's men, in the Christmas time of 1596, one Danter printed a miserable, stolen copy of ' Romeo and Juliet,' nothing according to the true text, but patched up from the old play of 1591, as it was before Shakespeare reformed it for us five years after, and containing much that was not his, and the rest most imperfectly given, in no way by our license or through our means. Now, Shakespeare was not careful to be presented in print, but he would not be mispresented. Accordingly, in 1599, we allowed a true and perfect copy of this play to be imprinted ; it had then been on the stage two years, which was the time we generally required to elapse, before any play of ours was, as they say, made Paul's work. But before that, and immediately at the heels of the stolen ' Romeo,' we sent forth the ' Richard II.' — which was entirely a child of Shakespeare's brain — and ' Richard III.' (which was altogether fashioned by him, although the foundation thereof was not his) in their proper shape, saving that we were forbidden by authority to print the scene of Richard's deposition by Bolingbroke. To neither of these did Shakespeare prefix his name as author in the first editions ; nor was his name put on the title of any play till 1598; and then only, it was supposed, at the instance of Ben Jonson. To the ' Romeo' he never set his name at all. The man was too modest to set any store by such trifles as plays were then esteemed ; much less would he have collected them in Folio, as we have done recently, or have bestowed on them high-flown dedications to great ones, and sent them forth with verses commendatory from his fellows, whether poets or actors. Scarcely could we get him to allow them to appear at this time at all in print, and after four years we ceased to publish them altogether, unless we were driven to do so by some wrongful proceeding of other men.

Before we left the Theater Shakespeare had written for us yet another History, the first part of 'Henry IV.,' in which he had introduced certain "irregular humourists," Sir John Oldcastle, Harvey, and Russell. At the same time Drayton wrote for us, ' The Merry Devil of Edmonton,' in which Sir John Oldcastle and Smug the smith were brought in as great drinkers of ale. Now, this bringing Sir John Oldcastle on the stage gave mighty offence to Henry Brooke, my Lord Cobham, who was descended from Joan Cobham, wife to the true John Oldcastle, who had his title of Baron of Cobham in her right only. Some men would have it that we put this Oldcastle on the stage in the dress and manner of this Henry Brooke, who had just then missed the getting the appointment of Lord Chamberlain, our own patron and master, George Carey, Lord Hunsdon, having been preferred to him, as he ought indeed to have been preferred to his father, William Brooke, in the year before. But, I would ask any man, in reason, is it not more likely that Shakespeare, finding the character of Sir John Oldcastle in the old Queen's men's play, from which he took part of his plot, used the name, inadvertently, not thinking of Lord Cobham in any way ? However this may be, and thought is free, Her Majesty, in December, 1597, required the name to be altered, which was accordingly done, Falstaff, Peto, and Bardolph being put in the place of

Oldcastle, Harvey, and Russell. The christened name, " Sir John, was retained in both plays, Shakespeare's and Drayton's. Th Falstaff — who is the glory of the English comic stage, and hath at sundry times, been seen by more spectators to their infinit delight than any other character on any scene whatever, English or other, ancient or modern — comes in, as we shall see, in other plays, of which the second part of ' Henry IV.,' which was a-writing when the Queen ordered this alteration, was one. We acted it among the first after we moved to the Curtain. But however the name has been altered in the scene and in the editions, Falstaff is still known, and will be for many a year to come, among the people as the fat Sir John Oldcastle.

This matter did not, however, end with our theatre; for wha does Master Drayton do, when he finds this stir made, but leav us incontinently and go to the Admiral's men, just before Christmas 1597, and write for them ; and two years afterward he (with Mon day, Hathaway, and Wilson as his coadjutors) botches up two plays on Sir John Oldcastle, the first of which they printed in the next August, 1600, with a prologue setting forth that they presented no " aged counsellor and youthful scion," but " a valiant martyr and virtuous peer," and speaking of our " forged invention " the former time. Nor did they stop here; they had the incredible impudence to put on their title " by William Shakespeare," — a " forged inven- tion," which we soon took order to make them alter. They never reached to a second impression, nor could they dispose of all the first one for all their lying; it was " gross as a mountain, open, pal- pable," and deceived none. In this same play Drayton put in a Sir John, — a priest much like the Sir John who had once been Oldcastle in the ' Merry Devil.' We might have made the first copy of the ' Merry Devil ' public, and shown who it was that had caused the stir, but Shakespeare would not; he misliked these quarrels, and never entered on them further than justice and self-defence made necessary.

Another play by Shakespeare which we acted at the Curtain was ' Love's Labour 's Lost,' which we also presented at Court in the Christmas of 1597. This was an old play reformed with some of the characters changed and the whole play enlarged. It had been at first acted eight years before, being the first play in which Shakespeare wrote. It was wellnigh all in rhyme, — a fashion which he much followed at his beginning, but which he, as time wore on, forsook with good reason. Would that all our authors would do so ! such jigging lines hardly ever speak well, and do not, as Inigo would say, "conduce to the feasibility" of the scene.

This same Christmas the Admiral's men, after an interim of seven years, began again to be summoned to act for Her Majesty's pleasure, which ended the monopoly we had enjoyed of the Court Christmas festivities all such time as we had been acting at the Theater. This revival was followed by that of 'Love's Labour 's Won,' but it was so entirely rewritten that we thought fit to give it a new name. We now called it 'Much Ado About Nothing,' or 'Benedick and Betteris.' I think that the growing mislike to rhymed lines was one of the reasons for this play being so greatly altered. In its new shape it is in great part written in prose.

It was while we played at the Curtain that Shakespeare brought to us one who is now acknowledged by all to be our best stage author living. Now that Fletcher and Webster are dead, there is no one that can be named with him unless it may be Master Massinger; for Master Chapman hath long ceased to write for the stage, and Beaumont and Shakespeare, who were his only superiors, have now been dead these ten years. Need I say that I mean the rare Ben Jonson ? It was at the winter of 1598 that he came to us; he had in September fought with one Gabriel Spencer, one of the Admiral's men, for whom Jonson was at that time writing, and killed him in the duel. For this he was arraigned at the Old Bailey, convicted of felony, and branded in the thumb, having escaped the gallows by claiming his benefit of clergy. For us he wrote his 'Every Man in his Humour,' one of the best of his plays. He also acted himself, especially in the part of Jeronyimo in the old play by Kyd, which we revived at this time.

During this year we allowed to be printed the first part of 'Henry IV. ;' we thought it unfit that the false rumors concerning the Oldcastle matter should remain unchallenged, and the best contradiction we could offer was the making the play public. Shakespeare did not set his name to it; but since Her Majesty had approved of 'Love's Labour's Lost,' as presented to her at Christmas, we published that play also; and then for the first time Shakespeare's name was displayed on the title of a play. He also put his name to the new editions of 'Richard II.' and 'Richard III.' this same year; nor was anything of his printed after without his name, except 'Romeo and Juliet' and the stolen, imperfect copy of 'Henry V.'

(To be continued.)

*F. G. Fleay.*

# THE USE OF ALLITERATION IN SHAKESPEARE'S POEMS.

IN a previous paper* I pointed out what appears to me to be one of the greatest charms and excellencies of the English language, but one which is strangely ignored by philologists, — I mean the natural significance of elementary sounds. I propose now to say something of the manner in which this feature of our language is rendered most effective.

English, in common with other Gothic tongues, is markedly distinguished from French by the strong accentuation given to some particular syllable in each word or phrase. This accent will generally be observed to fall upon the radical letters, those which give its distinctive character to a word. There are often significant combinations, and by repetition of the significant sound, emphasis is always imparted to it. Hence the power and one of the charms of alliteration, or the recurrence after short intervals of the same accented letters.

It would be easy to show that the predominance of alliteration

---

* 'The Music of Language, as illustrated in Shakespeare's "Venus and Adonis."' POET-LORE, November, 1892, page 562

forms a part of the very genius of our language ; and while it gives force to the dialect of the rudest peasant, its artistic employment renders it capable — in the hand of the orator or poet — of marvels of expressiveness, infinitely various and often exquisitely delicate.

To begin with, alliteration is very common in simple Saxon phrases which we are using every hour. We speak of " making up our mind," "taking by turns," " waging war," " rallying round," " running riot," " running a risk," etc. The same artifice gives force to antithetical words : " make or mar," " peer and peasant," " grave and gay," " foul and fair," " sweet and sour," " friend and foe," and so on *ad infinitum.*

Proverbs, which have been said to embody the wisdom of many in the wit of one, abound in illustration of the same practice : " One swallow does not make a summer;" " Waste not, want not ; " " Time and tide wait for no man ; " " A cat may look at a king ; " " Every dog has his day," and so forth.

To see how important a place alliteration occupied in the estimation of our Anglo-Saxon forefathers, we have only to glance at their poetry. Their versification contained few rhymes, and depended neither on the length nor number of syllables in a line, but was based entirely on alliteration. After the middle of the sixteenth-century alliteration ceased to follow any rigid rules; but it has always played an important part in the rhythm of versification.

English prose is almost as much indebted as English verse for force and harmony to the skilful use of alliteration. Our authorized translations of the Bible, throughout the New Testament and in the poetical portions of the Old, is alliterative in almost every verse ; and to alliteration is due the specially rhythmical character of the Book of Common Prayer.

Yet the part played by alliteration in English literature is almost ignored in works on the English language, style, and kindred subjects. It is commonly alluded to as a "trick" which is rather to be avoided than otherwise. Charles Churchill's line on "apt alliteration's artful aid" is pretty sure to be quoted with two or three passages in Shakespeare in which its abuse is ridiculed, and then the matter is dropped. Now, if the use of marked alliteration in almost every sentence is a blemish in composition, then it is certain that Addison, Lord Lytton, George Eliot, Thomas Carlyle, Washington Irving, and, in fact, all our greatest masters of prose style, did not know how to write English.

In 'Love's Labour 's Lost,' its *abuse* is ridiculed when Holofernes says, "I will something affect the letter, for it argues facility. The preyful princess pierced and prick'd a pretty pleasing pricket." And so in 'A Midsummer-Night's Dream,' when Pyramus says : —

> "I thank thee, Moon, for shining now so bright;
> For, by thy gracious, golden, glittering gleams,
>   I trust to take of truest Thisby sight."

And yet in these very plays alliteration is perhaps more employed than in any other Shakespearian dramas.

Let me briefly illustrate, by means of a few Shakespearian stanzas and sonnets, the cunning with which alliteration is there employed. The approach of Venus to Adonis is thus described :

> "He sees her coming, and begins to glow,
> Even as a dying coal revives with wind,
> And with his bonnet hides his angry brow;
> Looks on the dull earth with disturbed mind,
>   Taking no notice that she is so nigh,
>   For all askance he holds her in his eye."

I would first of all remark that nearly every word in this stanza contains sonorous vowels or diphthongs. The assonance or repetition of the same vowel-sound with different consonants is very marked. The brilliant diphthong *i* is the keynote as heard in "dying," "revives," "wind," "hides," "mind," "nigh," and "eye." The consonantal alliterations occur in almost every other word, "coming," "coal," "'gins," "glow," "bonnet," "brow," "notice," "nigh." In "dying," "dull," emphasis is given to the *d*, which, it may be remembered, I maintain to be ominous of negation or evil. *H*, I say, indicates height, or covering, and here we have "hide" and "hold."

I pass on to the next stanza but one : —

> " Now was she just before him as he sat,
> And like a lowly lover down she kneels;
> With one fair hand she heaveth up his hat,
> Her other tender hand his fair cheek feels :
>   His tenderer cheek receives her soft hand's print,
>   As apt as new-fall'n snow takes any dint."

Notice how different in tone this is to the former stanza : the soft sound, *ee*, predominates here; accented *ee* occurs in this verse in " she " (three times), " kneels," " heaveth," " cheek " (twice), "feels," and " receives," — nine times in all.  Then we have " like a lowly lover," *l* signifying form, affection, or physical quality ; " with one fair hand she heaveth up his hat,"— *h* indicating height or covering.

Now for a stanza from 'Lucrece.'  When she determines to destroy herself, it is said : —

> " This plot of death when sadly she had laid.
> And wiped the brinish pearl from her bright eyes,
> With untuned tongue she hoarsely called her maid,
> Whose swift obedience to her mistress hies ;
>   For fleet-wing'd duty with thought's feathers flies.
>   Poor Lucrece' cheeks unto her maid seem so
>   As winter meads when sun doth melt their snow."

There is no dominant tone in this stanza, but it is very rich in expressive words and more alliterative than the others.  There is " plot," " pearl," " brinish," " bright," " timid tongue," " maid," " mistress," " fleet," " feather," " flies," " so," " sun," " snow," " maid," " mead," " melt."

Alliteration is useful in five ways.  There are illustrations of all of them here : first, it simply gives rhythm and emphasis, as here in " plot" and " pearl ; " second, it accentuates antithesis, as in " mistress " and " maid ; " third, it appreciates allied or related ideas, as " sun " and " snow ; " fourth, it emphasizes significant combinations of letters, as *fl* in " fleet " and " fly," equivalent to rapid motion ; fifth, it imparts effect to assonance, as in the line, " And wiped the brinish pearl from her bright eyes."

Allow me, in conclusion, to examine one of the sonnets, the 128th : —

"How oft, when thou, my music, music play'st,
Upon that blessed wood whose motion sounds
With thy sweet fingers, when thou gently sway'st
The wiry concord that mine ear confounds,
Do I envy those jacks that nimble leap
To kiss the tender inward of thy hand,
Whilst my poor lips, which should that harvest reap,
At the wood's boldness by thee blushing stand!
To be so tickled, they would change their state
And situation with those dancing chips,
O'er whom thy fingers walk with gentle gait,
Making dead wood more blest than living lips.
 Since saucy jacks so happy are in this,
 Give them thy fingers, me thy lips to kiss."

There are in this sonnet about twenty words, on which I might dilate, as naturally expressive according to my principles. "Sounds" is eminently sonorous, and answers to its meaning ; it runs with "sweet" and "sway," and the natural significance of "sweet" is best felt when compared with "sour ;" the pronunciation of the latter renders taste impossible. The *s* in "sway," as in "swerve," "switch," "swing," etc., adds effect to the motion-expressing *w*. "Lips," which occur three times, and are here associated with liking, point to *l* as indicative of physical sensation. *Le* final, in "tickle," expresses indistinct motion ; as *st*, in "stand" and "state," implies rest or resistance ; "kiss," the last word in the sonnet, is, I think, a very pleasantly significant onomatopæan with which to conclude.

*S. E. Bengough.*

## IAGO'S CONSCIENCE.

THE general characterization of Iago is apt to be a summing up of his attributes of keen wit, self-concentration, envy, hard-heartedness, cool, scheming villany ; in one word, he is called *conscienceless.* Is this a true summary? Granting him these qualities will not determine a lack of conscience. Is he without that "blushing shamefaced spirit that mutinies in a man's bosom"?

We say *is*, for Iago, being Shakespeare's creation, is a man of all time, therefore our interest in him is as great as if he were an historic man. Has Shakespeare, in this delineation, departed from his usual fidelity to nature? is an interesting query.

The most villanous man shows, at some time in his career, some trace of at least a rudimentary conscience. Is Iago given as an exception necessary to prove the rule? Or is he the type of an abnormal class lacking the distinctive mark of rational beings? If he is this sort of inhuman creation, never stirred or warned by an inward monitor, then he cannot be held guilty of moral transgression. He must be accepted as elder brother of Mephistopheles, created to work evil, and progenitor of the monster Frankenstein.

To have clearly before the mind's eye a somewhat exact outline of conscience will aid in determining Iago's moral responsibility. This definition should be sufficiently broad to embrace those features claimed as essential marks of conscience. If these are noted to be, the inward state of disturbance of a rational being when courses of action involving questions as to right and wrong are presented for his inspection and decision ; this decision followed by a feeling of approval of the right and disapproval of the wrong ; a succeeding state of impulsion toward a choice of the right ; of obligation to yield to this for no other reason than conformity with right ; of uneasiness, self-condemnation, even remorse, if this urging is disregarded, — we have a standard by which to test Iago's possession of a moral nature.

This outline assumes an antecedent knowledge of right and wrong. Like the gods, Othello's Ancient knew good from evil :

> " The Moor, howbeit that I endure him not,
> Is of a constant, loving, noble nature."

The familiar lines beginning, " Good name in man or woman, dear my lord, Is the immediate jewel of their souls," contain as elevated a bit of moral sentiment as Sir Philip Sidney, with his " high-erected thoughts," could have produced.

> " If Cassio do remain,
> He hath a daily beauty in his life
> That makes me ugly,"

shows an envious and reluctant admiration of the finer qualities of the lieutenant's character.

He also knew that some men choose the course of virtue, " You shall mark Many a duteous and knee-crooking knave," and, " Whip me such honest knaves " expresses his sarcastic contempt for them. In his transparently frank confession to Roderigo he evinces none of that inward disturbance which is the prelude to the entire act of spiritual worthiness. Calling on himself to decide which way he shall choose, he does it without hesitation,

> " Others there are
> Who, trimm'd in forms and visages of duty,
> Keep yet their hearts attending on themselves,
> . . . These fellows have some soul;
> And such a one do I profess myself.
>
> . . . . . . . .
>
> Heaven is my judge, not I for love or duty,
> But seeming so, for my peculiar end."

His intelligence and psychological insight enable him to trade upon the, to him, foolish fancy of men who actually hold evil in bad esteem. Like the devils who, when they "will their blackest sins put on," "do suggest at first with heavenly shows," he can put on the semblance of conscientious scruples to serve a particular purpose. To impress Othello with his uprightness as well as his devotion, he says, —

> " Yet do I hold it very stuff o' the conscience
> To do no contrived murder: I lack iniquity
> Sometimes, to do me service."

At the precise moment of uttering this, he was not wearing his heart on his sleeve.

The modest and courageous manner in which he expresses his reasons for not telling his thoughts in response to Othello's imperious demand is a fine touch of artfulness, —

> " Utter my thoughts ? Why, say they are vile and false ; . . .
> . . . Who has a breast so pure,
> But some uncleanly apprehensions
> . . . in session sit
> With meditations lawful ? "

Of the same specious nature is the confession of his faults to the credulous Moor, —

> " I confess, it is my nature's plague
> To spy into abuses, and oft my jealousy
> Shapes faults that are not,"

thus frankly dealing with the truth, as the Devil is reported to quote Scripture, " for his purpose." When Emilia's tongue lashes the unknown " insinuating rogue," the " cogging cozening slave," who, " to get some office," must have vilely slandered her innocent mistress, Iago, from the height of his seeming righteous indignation, protests, " Fie, there is no such man ; it is impossible."

So far appears an active exhibition of pure intellect with no conscientious delayings nor with any trace of conscientious direction or government of his actions. No design has been altered from its original evil purpose. No sign of pity or even of ironic commiseration for his unconscious victims, the puppets of his overmastering will, is evident.

Roderigo he calls " noble heart" in sheer mockery, not troubling to conceal his wickedness from this pliant tool, scoffing openly even at Roderigo's faint belief in good, " Virtue ! a fig ! 't is in ourselves we are thus or thus." Having thoroughly fooled him, the disappointed suitor is dismissed from the schemer's thoughts with the scornful, " Thus do I ever make my fool my purse." When, at the last, Iago plunges his dagger into the deluded assassin, his exclamations, " O murderous slave ! O villain ! " are not indications of any change in his mental attitude. They are uttered merely to conceal his villanous work and to advance his hellish stratagem.

His lack of humanity and morality show most emphatically in connection with the Moor. The general's trust and friendship are used as aids to bring the infernal scheme to a more rapid completion. The cold-blooded soliloquies in which, from time to time, he mirrors himself to himself, reviews the state of affairs, and debates as to the precise steps next in order, show no slightest feelings of compunction. In one of these monologues (Act I., Sc. iii.), after outlining his plot, he assures himself of his success, because Othello —

> " holds me well;
> The better shall my purpose work on him."

He sees perfectly the hideousness of the business on which he has
embarked, —

> " Hell and night
> Must bring this monstrous birth to the world's light."

Toward the close of II., iii., he again takes a comprehensive
view of the progress of the tragedy and his own moral attitude.
The lurid depths of his Satanic soul are revealed in the closing
words, —

> " So will I turn her virtue into pitch,
> And out of her own goodness make the net
> That shall enmesh them all."

Even when this " super-subtle Venetian " has drawn the strangling
cords of his cunningly contrived net about his unsuspecting victims,
and fate takes him in hand to undo him quite, no remorse for his
part in it is aroused on viewing his work.   Desdemona's most
damnable taking off, nor Othello's black despair, nor the knowledge of his own rapidly approaching retribution moves him to confession.   He says, —

> " Demand me nothing : what you know, you know :
> From this time forth I never will speak word."

Although a moment before, Ludovico says, " This wretch hath half
confessed his villany," it seems to have been for the purpose of
inculpating Othello in the attempted murder of Cassio.

Having reached the conclusion of this merely suggestive review,
what shall the verdict be ?   We see that Iago has the attributes of
a being responsible for his deeds, — power of forethought, of choice,
and of determination.   Could he so exist and yet lack conscience?

It is necessary to recall that our knowledge of his early life is
merely inferential.   The "four times seven years " in which he had
" look'd upon the world " had made him what we find him, — short
time for such a finished production.   What good promptings, if
any, he had scoffed at and scouted, what urgings, if any, toward

a higher plane of rationality, he had defied, Shakespeare does not set forth. Yet in this history, which we accept as real, veritable, and unbiassed, of a man's inner life, we feel that some pure intuitions toward righteousness must have had sway, and we expectantly seek for their traces even in this debased and blackened human soul. The master, whose knowledge of the human heart was sure, does not disappoint our expectations. " And what 's he then that says I play the villain ? When this advice is free I give and honest ? " might be taken as a strain of fiendish rejoicing over his own cleverness in working evil through righteous means, were it not that, a few lines farther on, he repeats the thought in a way that shows he is contrasting right with wrong, —

> " How am I then a villain,
> To counsel Cassio to this parallel course,
> Directly to his good ? "

So far he has done no irredeemable evil. Here he can stop his machinations and retain his good repute; the words certainly indicate uneasiness as to the world's opinion of him. Here is the point where he sets at naught gratitude, friendship, honor, and uprightness. Iago, knowing, according to his own words, that he is on the point of joining himself with devils in their blackest sins, settles the matter with most consummate ease when he closes one of his soliloquies with " As I do now."

In spite of his contempt for his wife, it is in connection with her that such uneasy promptings as may indicate stirrings of conscience arise. When, in the beginning of the drama, he determines to compass his revenge, the contemplated retaliation appears, even to his rancor, far in excess of the injury. To still his uneasy soul he seeks for some deeper wrong inflicted on him by the Moor as a more plausible motive, and the despised Emilia serves as a pretext.

On the exposure of his villany the ghost of his murdered conscience, stirring up his self-love, makes him wince under her adverse criticism. Shakespeare, with his fidelity to the law of the natural unfolding of events and his insight into the power of slight causes to produce great results, contrives that Iago's nearest approach to remorse is caused by the creature whom he has almost disregarded in his scheming, whom he calls " a common thing — a foolish wife." It is through her affection and devotion, — qualities unsuspected by her husband, spite of his astuteness, — that in him is aroused the fear of exposure. Her unexpected daring lays bare his evil course, and she stirs him by her bitter denunciations. His "Go to! charm your tongue," and, "What! are you mad? I charge you, get you home!" are not as effectual as his previous successful home rule had led him to expect. Goaded to frenzy by her revelations and reproaches, he at last commits the useless crime of murdering her, — useless, because already, as he could know if his usual cool effrontery had not been overthrown by the sting of her words, enough is revealed to send him to torture and ignominious death. And what has unsettled that well-established and practised effrontery? What leads him, case-hardened and defiant sinner, and certainly no coward, to run from Othello's sword? " Thus conscience doth make cowards of us all."

It thus appears that Iago feels some inward disturbance on forecasting his line of action; he can approve the right and condemn the wrong; and although he seems to have not the slightest impulsion toward right for right's sake, he shows decided uneasiness intensifying into remorse, not for his evil deeds, but for their disastrous recoil on his own head. And is not this a common development of remorse? Man sins and sins and marches on triumphantly, regardless of the facts; then suddenly retribution blocks his way; he has to pause, and that pause gives opportunity for remorse to enter in and gnaw the vitals.

Surely Iago's experience is a setting forth of the certainty with which the inward monitor avenges outrages against man's high attributes of rationality and spirituality.

*A. M. Spence.*

# THE VALUE OF CONTEMPORARY JUDGMENT.*

UPON first thoughts the intrinsic value of contemporary judgment seems to amount to almost nothing : " Few things," says Mr. Addington Symonds, "are more perplexing than the vicissitudes of taste, whereby the idols of past generations crumble suddenly to dust, while the despised and rejected are lifted to pinnacles of glory."

These words apply with especial force to the change wrought in the critical attitude toward those great torch-bearers who lit up so gloriously the first years of our own century. During these early years there came into existence *The Quarterly Review*, *Blackwood's*, *The Edinburgh*, *The Examiner*, — magazines which, like Milton's Satan, had " through their merit, been raised to a bad eminence," and "insatiate to pursue vain war with Heaven," discharged their critical office, as if all poets manifesting unusual genius were their natural enemies. All of us are, by hearsay, familiar with the awful terror of their weapons ; but it is doubtful whether imagination has ever clothed the tradition in a way at all approaching the fatuous reality of their printed words. Like many critics of the present day when dealing with poets of the calibre of William Blake, George Meredith, or Robert Browning, they found the poetry of the Lake and so-called Cockney schools " obscure." Wordsworth's ' Ode to Immortality' was considered by *Blackwood's* a most illegible and unintelligible poem. "We can pretend to give no analysis or explanation of it." So vicious an example of obscurity is it, that the reviewer has "every reason to hope that the lamentable consequences which have resulted from Mr. Wordsworth's open violation of the established laws of poetry will operate as a wholesome warning to those who might otherwise have been seduced by his example."

*The Quarterly* made superhuman efforts to get through with ' Endymion,' and concludes, "We are no better acquainted with

* Read before the Boston Browning Society, Dec. 27, 1892.

the meaning of the book through which we have so painfully
toiled than we are with that of the three which we have not looked
into." It wonders whether "Mr. Keats is his real name," for it
doubts that any man in his senses should put his "name to such a
rhapsody." 'Prometheus,' in the words of *The Literary Gazette* of
1820, is little else but "absolute raving. . . . A mélange of nonsense, cockneyism, poverty, and pedantry." And in the estimation of *The Edinburgh Review*, one of the most notable pieces of
impertinence of which the Press had lately been guilty was the publication of 'Christabel,' whose author had "the monstrous assurance to come forward coolly at that time of day and tell the reader
of English poetry, whose ear had been tuned to the lays of Spenser,
Milton, Dryden, and Pope, that he made his metre on a new
principle."

Such criticism as this makes one feel like exclaiming, as Childe
Roland did of the blind horse, "I never saw a tribe I hated so,"
and writing down all contemporary critics as a race specially
scorned of Providence in the matter of penetration. But it must
not be forgotten that the era marked by this extraordinarily vitu-
perative criticism occupies but a small portion of the whole body
of English criticism, and bearing in mind also the scientific
method of proceeding so much in vogue at present, with its deductions based upon facts, — always facts, — we are warned not to
come to too hasty conclusions. Only an eternity of Gradgrinds in
immortal conclave could definitely settle the question.

Though not able in the nature of the case to collect and sift all
the facts, we can glance at a few and make at least provisional
deductions.

Turning to the dawn of the Elizabethan Age, we find that criticism in our modern sense had not yet been developed, but there
then flourished a race of critics of verse forms, who, not occupied
with the individual merits of poets, were one and all bent on the
improvement of English poetic forms. Puffed up with a little Classical knowledge, they would take Horace or Virgil for their Apollo.
The general surceasing of bald rhymes was determined upon ; fixed
rules for quantitative metre were to be adopted ; hexameters were

to reign supreme. Even the poet Spenser was touched by this fever for artificial improvement; but his natural genius happily saved him from going too far, and in one of his famous letters to Harvey, after some praise of the hexameter, he winds up, "Why a God's name may not we, as else the Greeks, have the kingdom of our own language, and measure our accents by the sound, reserving quantity to the verse?" In spite of the fact, however, that these formulators of cast-iron rules for the construction of poetry were opposed to such poetical practice as that of Spenser, they were not unconscious of his genius. The most rabid of the Hexametrists says, when speaking of contemporary poets, " I confess and acknowledge that we have many excellent and singular good poets in this our age, as Master Spenser . . . and divers others whom I reverence in that kind of prose rhythm, wherein Spenser hath surpassed them all. I would to God they had done so well in trew Hexametres, for they had then beautified our language." This reminds one of Miss Jenkyn's criticism, in ' Cranford,' on the author of ' The Pickwick Papers,' "Doubtless, a young man, who might do very well if he would take Dr. Johnson for a model." Spenser was also mildly praised of Sir Philip Sidney: "' The Shepherd's Calendar' hath much poetry in his eclogues, indeed worthy the reading, if I be not deceived."

It was quite natural that the romantic drama then growing up should be scorned by this new-old school ; and every one is familiar with the wit and learning with which Sidney exposed its fallacies. Fortunately, however, for the poets of that day, their fame did not depend upon a scant word of praise uttered by the rhetoricians. We have a picture in that curious old play, ' The Return from Parnassus,' of the necessity devolving upon every poet of finding an aristocratic patron, who was generally to be bought at the expenditure of a little, or rather of a good deal, of judicious flattery. Once taken under the wing of a nobleman, the popular judgment did the rest, and the "scollers" found their grumbling of little avail. No doubt these same " scollers " flung their sneers at Shakespeare, — a fact also patent in ' The Return from Parnassus.' The University gentleman who wrote this play for a cultured audience might find it amusing to make his Gullio — an empty pretender to knowledge — the only one to "worship sweet Mr. Shakespeare;" but even while the cultured audience was laughing at the hit, the Universities (in the person of Francis Meres, who was Master of Arts of both Cambridge and Oxford, and Professor of Rhetoric in Oxford) had placed their approval upon Shakespeare. Sincerely appreciative is his quaintly worded praise, — "As the soul of Euphorbus was thought to live in Pythagoras, so the sweet, witty soul of Ovid lives in mellifluous and honey tongued Shakespeare. . . . As Epius Stolo said that the Muses would speak with Plautus tongue if they would speak Latin, so say I, that the Muses would speak with Shakespeare's fine-filèd phrase if they would speak English."

Such contemporary notices as have come down to us, with some few exceptions, such as Greene's famous ".Shake-scene" speech, go to prove the general estimation in which Shakespeare was held during his life. Though later Shakespeare idolaters have loved to enlarge on Ben Jonson's malignity toward Shakespeare, Gifford has shown pretty conclusively that the malignity was on the part of the idolaters toward Jonson, while the unbiassed reader will certainly find much more praise than blame in Ben Jonson's utterances upon Shakespeare. As he says of Shakespeare, we may say of his criticisms of Shakespeare, "There was ever more in him to be praised than pardoned."

By the time Milton appears on the scene, Classical models have had their due effect. Gabriel Harvey would no doubt have hailed with delight Milton's blank verse, but alas! "It is never the time and the place and the loved one altogether." The poet who excelled in blank verse came too late for the critics who would have appreciated it; and we find him obliged to preface the second edition of 'Paradise Lost' with an apology for blank verse. But he was not altogether without contemporary praise, and from a very high source. Dryden, the great Mogul of letters, said in the preface to his poem, 'The State of Innocence,' that 'Paradise Lost' was "undoubtedly one of the greatest, most noble, and most sublime poems which either this age or nation has produced." He admired it so much evidently that he thought it worthy of his own most august improvement. 'The State of Innocence' was the result, — a version of ' Paradise Lost,' which, as Milton expressed it, was "tagged with rhymes."

In Dryden and Pope we have the spectacle of poets who attained the widest recognition in their lifetime, — literary dictators, as some one has called them, poets who wrote in a school which was generally approved by the taste of the time, and which they may be said to have both reflected and led. Their successes, it is true, raised up against them a number of envious scribblers. But this was not an age when the poets died of criticism, as Keats is said by Byron to have done; the bitterest invective of a disappointed hack could not compete with the terrible shafts of sarcasm wielded by a Pope or a Dryden. Whenever the poets gave battle to the critics on their own ground, the critics were worsted, and dispersed like Penelope's suitors under the bow of Odysseus.

From this rapid glance at a few well-known facts, is it possible to draw any deductions ? I think we may at least conclude, even with this scant material, that before deciding as to the value of contemporary judgment, a great many factors must be taken into account. The general admiration for Shakespeare during his lifetime has been developed by succeeding generations into the profoundest reverence for his genius ; and no one would hesitate to say that when Meres wrote of him as he did, in 1596, he expressed a contemporary opinion of real and lasting value. On the other hand, it is doubtful whether the consensus of opinion at the present time would ratify the popular contemporary judgment in regard to Dryden and Pope. John Dennis's opinion that the precepts in the ' Essay on Criticism ' were false and trivial, the thoughts crude and abortive, might even find an echo in a modern mind.

In both these eras, however, the poets were decidedly in the ascendant; they did not make their *début* into the literary world under the chaperonage of the critics. Their appeal was direct to the public. But there is this difference between the two periods, — while the Elizabethan Age was not the forerunner of any school of criticism based upon it, by which the works of the succeeding era were judged, the Classical era furnished the foundation of the future criticism, whose superstructure towers into the present. With the growth of prose, criticism gradually usurped the place of poetry as guide in literary matters; and when a new race of poets with new ideals arose, they were in the position of rebels against the established order of things, and it was the duty of the critics, as the purveyors of taste, to warn all readers against these dangerous poetical anarchists.

Shakespeare in his day, and Pope and Dryden in theirs, depended, therefore, on the critical judgment of the " general " rather than upon that of a particular critic or school of critics, and that each prospered in his own day indicates that each was the legitimate offspring of his time.

I think, then, that from these illustrations we may venture as provisional deductions that when a poet is the outcome of a great age of spontaneous poetical activity, such as the Elizabethan Age, — when not only were the poets many and good, but the general public was largely receptive to poetical influences, — contemporary judgment is likely to be appreciative and therefore of intrinsic value ; when the poet is the outcome of an age of artificial poetical activity, such as that of Pope, when poets and public are alike busied with the form rather than the spirit of poetry, contemporary judgment is likely to be exaggerated in its approval, and of lesser value; but when the poet is not so much the outcome as the prophet of a coming great age, and with ideals opposed to the art conventions of his time, contemporary judgment is unequal to the task of appreciating him, and is consequently of little or no value.

Yet even in the most unappreciative age, there were voices crying in the wilderness to announce its poets. Shelley as critic saw that " in spite of the low-thoughted envy which would undervalue contemporary merit," his own age would be a memorable one in intellectual achievements. " We live," he says, " among such philosophers and poets as surpass beyond comparison any who have appeared since the last national struggle for civil and religious liberty."

There are numerous other factors which might be considered in a discussion of this subject, such as political bias, personal friend-ship or enmity, the individual penetration of the critic, and which would no doubt modify these general conclusions in many special instances, such, for example, as Queen Elizabeth's judgment upon 'Richard II.,' which she would not allow to be acted because a king was deposed in it.

The cases of valueless contemporary judgment which Brown-ing has poetized in ' The Two Poets of Croisic ' are especially inter-esting in this connection, as showing how unusual and fortuitous circumstances may bring about a meteor-like popularity for which there is no lasting foundation. It was not the poetic skill of René Gentilhomme which gained him his short-lived popularity, but a happy coincidence which revealed him in the light of a prophet. Popularity from such a cause could be gained only amid uncritical and superstitious surroundings.

The fictitious popularity of Des Forges through his sister Mal-crais can perhaps be best explained by reference to that vanity resident in the breast of man, which was flattered, in the case of La Roque, by having a feminine poet, whose rhymes reflected the charming weakness of her sex, throw herself upon his tender mercy. Perhaps France, in the age of Voltaire, is the only country where popularity founded on such a basis would be possible. Picture the stern rebuff she would probably have received at the hands of a man like Fitzgerald.

Toward the latter half of this century we see a curious combi-nation of conditions which admits of the culmination of the " Cock-ney School " in Tennyson, — for is he not the heir of Keats ? — and the beginning, and perhaps the culmination also, of a new school in Browning. Yet Tennyson, who had had the ground ploughed for him, to a certain extent, by his predecessors, did not escape the ill-natured censure of a " Rusty Crusty Christopher ;" and how is it with Browning?

It is a widely spread tradition, on the one hand, that Browning was never appreciated until the Browning Societies found him out; and on the other hand, there are Philistines who imagine that the amateurish idolaters of which Browning Societies are supposed to be composed have set themselves up against the authority of criticism. So much has been said of the criticism in a certain Review, which, when 'Pauline' first appeared, dismissed it in one line as "a piece of pure bewilderment," that it has come to be regarded as a sort of model of all early Browning criticism. But a survey of those criticisms which appeared before 1860 reveals the fact that there were a number which at once recognized in Browning a poet of extraordinary power, some even venturing to declare him the greatest genius since Shakespeare.* Of course there were those who grumbled, those who were silent; and as time has gone on and the poet's work has been more read, there has been an ever-increasing chorus of discordant voices, some appreciative, some the reverse. Neither upon Browning nor upon Tennyson does contemporary opinion approach to any degree of unanimity.

We are perhaps too close at hand to weigh the value of the judgment in regard to these two master-spirits of the Victorian Age ; but he who runs can see, illustrated by the criticism on these two poets alone, that, with the growing complexity of life, criticism has become more and more a matter of the individual insight and preferences of the critic. The almost autocratic authority of a school has given way to the somewhat precarious authority of the individual ; and as a natural consequence, contemporary judgment ranges through all degrees of value.

As the bulwarks of the old, authoritative criticism are crumbling to decay, there is arising a new order of criticism, to which Browning stands in the closest affinity. One of the fundamental principles of this criticism is the relativity of all art. Posnett points out how no art expression in any age can be more than an approach to a universal ideal, subject, as it always is and must be, to limitations of time and place. The old criticism weighed every new manifestation in art by past achievements, which in course of time came to be regarded almost as divine revelations in art, rather

---

* Among these appreciative reviews may be mentioned one of ' Pauline,' by Allan Cunningham, *Athenæum*, 1833 ; Review of ' Strafford,' *Literary Gazette*, 1837 ; Review of ' Paracelsus,' *The Theologian*, 1845 ; Review by James Russell Lowell, *North American Review*, 1848 ; Review in *Massachusetts Quarterly*, 1850 ; Review in *Christian Remembrancer*, 1857, and others.

than as imperfect human attempts to all-express beauty. This same principle of relativity is the touchstone by which Browning tries every realm of human endeavor, and the failure which he records everywhere is but a recognition of this all-pervading law of evolution.

A fine example of its application to art is to be found in the ' Parleying with Charles Avison,' where he says all arts endeavor to preserve hard and fast how we feel as what we know, yet none of them attain thereto, because the province of art is not in the true sense creative.

> " Arts arrange
> Dissociate, redistribute, interchange
> Part with part, lengthen, broaden, high or deep
> Construct their bravest, still such pains produce
> Change, not creation."

In short, the province of art is to use the materials of knowledge, of which the *mind* takes cognizance, in giving outward form and expression to the creative impulses born of the soul. Knowledge being limited, art must also be limited in its capacity to all-express these creative impulses. What, then, must be the attitude of the critic?

He certainly must not expect to find perfect creations in art which shall be a law unto all time. His duty will be, as Symonds defines it, " to judge, but not without understanding the natural and historical conditions of the product under examination, nor without making the allowances demanded by his sense of relativity," or as Browning, with the finer human touch of the poet, puts it, he must bring his " life to kindle theirs." The critic in this school cannot dogmatically dismiss some poets as beneath his notice and claim kingship for others. Every poet, great and small, must find a place in his scheme of human art development. Unbiassed, he must look down from the lofty summit of universal sympathy.

With the light of the new criticism in his eyes, who shall say to what heights of value the contemporary judgment of the future critic may not rise?

*Helen A. Clarke.*

# THE SOCIALISTIC THREAD IN THE LIFE AND WORKS OF WILLIAM MORRIS.

*(Continued from March Number.)*

MORRIS writes, in short, in the spirit of a man who recognizes life's tragic conditions. In all his sweet lines we feel that the writer's soul is filled with weariness. Woe seems to him inevitable and universal. The world of his vision is like the weary Titan of Arnold's poem, staggering on to the goal, bearing the too great load of her fate. He is essentially a Teuton with the pagan sense of fatalism. Fate is the key-word of 'Jason' and 'The Earthly Paradise.' Sigurd and the Volsung heroes are guided ever by the Norns: —

"And what the dawn has fated on the hour of noon shall fall."

"Yea, a man shall be
A wonder for his glorious chivalry
First in all wisdom, of a prudent mind,
Yet none the less him too his fate shall find."

Unique, indeed, among literatures in pathos of anticipated calamity is one of the 'Poems by the Way,' entitled the 'Burghers Battle,' where lamentation mingles with calm resignation, exampling the pathos of foreboded fate: —

"Look up! the arrows streak the sky,
The horns of battle roar;
The long spears lower and draw nigh,
*And we return no more.*"

Even the stories, 'The House of the Wolfings' and 'The Story of the Glittering Plain,' are touched with a light which is half sad, like the silver haze of the Indian summer presaging November snows.

The thought of love alone puts all doubts away. Yet love cannot escape the universal law.

> " Love while ye may; if twain grow into one
> 'T is for a little while; the time goes by,
> No hatred 'twixt the pair of friends doth lie,
> No troubles break their hearts — and yet and yet —
> How could it be ?   We strove not to forget ;
> Rather in vain to that old time we clung,
> Its hopes and wishes, round our hearts we hung.
> We played old parts, we used old names in vain,
> We go our ways, and twain once more are twain ;
> Let pass — at latest when we come to die
> Thus shall the fashion of the world go by."   (' Jason.')

Yet love while ye may.   The sufficiency of love is the subject of the morality play of ' Pharamond,' which showeth of a king whom nothing but love might satisfy.   Love sings, —

> " I am the Life of all that dieth not,
> Through me alone is sorrow unforgot."

And the poet concedes, —

> " LOVE IS ENOUGH : though the world be a-waning
> And the woods have no voice but the voice of complaining."

In sear October, midst the failing year, he cries, —

> " Look up love !  Ah cling close and never move !
> How can I have enough of life and love ? "

The reason !

> " Ah, what begetteth all this storm of bliss
> But Death himself, who, crying solemnly
> E'en from the heart of sweet Forgetfulness,
> Bids us ' Rejoice, lest pleasureless ye die,
> Within a little time must ye go by.
> Stretch forth your open hands and while ye live
> Take all the gifts that Death and Life may give.' "

Death and age and forgetfulness are so abhorrent that every minute is made more mindful as it passes by.   The poet has a feverish eagerness to enjoy whatever is beautiful, — every love and friendship, every fine creation of the artistic thought, every charm of Nature, every touch of sun and shadow, every note of the winds or the seas, — eagerness to take delight in life itself before the night cometh, when no man can enjoy.

> " Love is enough : cherish life that abideth,
> Lest ye die ere ye know him and curse and misname him."

The singer cannot know the meaning of death. He knows the meaning of life as little. Yet, as if in rebuke to those of us who hate life though we do not fear death, he cries, " What happiness to look upon the sun ! " So

> " In the white-flowered hawthorn brake,
> Love be merry for my sake ;
> Twine the blossoms in my hair,
> Kiss me where I am most fair —
> Kiss me love ! for who knoweth
> What thing cometh after death ? "

The poet's philosophy of fated life is, moreover, interwoven with a great faith in the consolation of art and labor. Art is his own passionate delight. As an artist he is content and calm. His poems are of unvarying sweetness and purity, with every superlative metrical excellence. The heart of the writer has been in his work. He bids farewell to his finished book as a lover; "I love thee whatso time or men may say of the poor singer of an empty day." What delight is taken in the telling of a story ! In the mediæval manner he dallies at whatever attracts his interest. His descriptions are true and perfect and absolutely free from all that is artificial. Greatest care is taken in depicting works of human handiwork. He loves to picture golden vessels and ivory thrones and webs of price and sculptured gate and pictured ceiling and painted palaces and marble halls. A city is described, —

> " Walled with white walls it was, and gardens green
> Were set between the houses every where ;
> And now and then rose up a tower foursquare
> Lessening in stage on stage ; with many a hue
> The house walls glowed, of red and green and blue,
> And some with gold were well adorned, and one
> From roofs of gold flashed back the noon-tide sun."

Entering the palace, we note the decorations and furniture : —

> " With hangings fresh as when they left the loom
> The walls were hung a space above the head,
> Slim ivory chairs were set about the room,
> And in one corner was a dainty bed,

That seemed for some fair queen apparellèd
And marble was the worst stone of the floor
That with rich Indian webs was covered o'er."

See the wonders of Æetes' marble house ! —

" The pillars, made the mighty roof to hold,
The one was silver and the next was gold,
All down the hall ; the roof, of some strange wood
Brought over sea, was dyed as red as blood,
Set thick with silver flowers, and delight
Of intertwining figures wrought aright.
*With richest webs the marble walls were hung,*
*Picturing sweet stories by the poets sung*
*From ancient days, so that no wall seemed there,*
*But rather forests black and meadows fair,*
*And streets of well-built towns, with tumbling seas*
*About their marble wharves and palaces,*
*And fearful crags and mountains ; and all trod*
*By changing feet of giant, nymph, and God,*
*Spear-shaking warrior and slim-ankled maid."*

But how give people eyes and soul for art and beauty ? How but by guarding the fairness of the earth and sky ? Must we not make the city as refreshing as the meadows, as exalting as the mountains ? Art and Nature are interdependent. Art is the expression of reverence for Nature. The spirit of the new days is to be delight in the life of the world, love of the very surface of the earth. Surely if the seasons are to arouse in us no other feelings than misery in winter and weariness in summer, then art too will fail, and we shall live amidst squalor and ugliness.

Morris is passionately fond of the sun and air. He loves the moist green meadows and silver streaming rivers of his England. To the fields and woods he is wont to go for sound and color and pure sensuous delight. " If I could but say or show how I love it, — the earth and the growth of it and the life of it ! " His every work is a witness to this loving sympathy. In the landscapes of ' The Earthly Paradise ' he notes the elements of delight, — sounds, sights, and odors, the songs of birds, the hues and tints of Nature, the winds orange-scented, or heavy with odors from thymy hills, or laden with the redolence of bean-flowers and clover and elder-blossoms. In some land long ago there was

> " A valley that beneath the haze
> Of that most fair of autumn days
> Shewed glorious ; fair with golden sheaves,
> Rich with the darkened autumn leaves.
> Gay with its water meadows green
> The bright blue streams that lay between —
> The miles of beauty stretched away."

In another country —

> " Now midst her wanderings, on a hot noon-tide
> Psyche passed down a road, where on each side,
> The yellow corn-fields lay, although as yet
> Unto the stalks no sickle had been set ;
> The lark sung over them, the butterfly
> Flickered from ear to ear distractedly,
> The kestrel hung above, the weasel peered
> From out the wheat-stalks on her unafeared,
> Along the road the trembling poppies shed
> On the burnt grass their crumbling leaves and red."

A different aspect of Nature is presented in the story of Sigurd, where Nature encompasses the heroes about with the likeness of a fate. In harmony with the Northern sense of fatalism, days and nights form the background of deeds. Morn falls to noon-tide, and the sun goeth down in the heavens, and the dusk and the dark draw over, and the stars to heaven come, and the white moon climbeth upward, and the dusk of the dawn begins, and day opens again, — 'mid light and darkness the heroes ever move. Follow Sigurd as he rides with Regin to the Glittering Heath : —

> " And the sun rose up at their backs and the grey world changed to red,
> And away to the west went Sigurd by the glory wreathed about.
> . . . . . . . . . .
> " So ever they wended upward, and the midnight hour was o'er
> And the stars grew pale and paler, and failed from the heavens' floor,
> And the moon was a long while dead, but where was the promise of day ?
> No change came over the darkness, no streak of the dawning grey ;
> No sound of the winds uprising adown the night there ran :
> It was blind as the Gaping Gulf ere the first of the worlds began.
> . . . . . . . . . .
> " But lo, at the last a glimmer, and a light from the west there came,
> And another and another, like points of far-off flame ;
> And they grew and brightened and gathered ; and whiles together they ran
> Like the moonwake over the waters ; and whiles they were scant and wan,

> Some greater and some lesser, like the boats of fishers laid
> About the sea of midnight; and a dusky dawn they made,
> A faint and glimmering twilight."

Then through the twilight Sigurd wends his way to meet the Foe of the Gods, and ere daylight is come the heart of the Serpent is cloven.

> " Then he leapt from the pit and the grave and the rushing river of blood,
> And fulfilled with the joy of the War-God in the face of earth he stood
> With red sword high uplifted, with wrathful glittering eyes;
> And he laughed at the heavens above him for he saw the sun arise,
> And Sigurd gleamed on the desert, and shone in the newborn light,
> And the wind in his raiment wavered, and all the world was bright."

After reading 'The Earthly Paradise,' it is not surprising to find in 'News from Nowhere' that the very essence of the new day of fellowship and rest is delight in the natural· beauty of the world. The poet is not now describing a land long ago, but his England new-created; and this is his picture of an old house on the upper Thames, and of the new joy:—

" On the right hand we could see a cluster of small houses and barns, new and old, and before us a grey stone barn and a wall partly overgrown with ivy, over which a few grey gables showed. We crossed the road, and again almost without my will my hand raised the latch of a door in the wall, and we stood presently on a stone path which led up to the old house. . . . My companion gave a sigh of pleased surprise and enjoyment; nor did I wonder, for the garden between the wall and the house was redolent of the June flowers, and the roses were rolling over one another with that delicious superabundance of small well-tended gardens which at first sight takes away all thought from the beholder save that of beauty. The blackbirds were singing their loudest, the doves were cooing on the roof-ridge, the rooks in the high elm-trees beyond were garrulous among the young leaves, and the swifts wheeled whirring about the gables. And the house itself was a fit guardian for all the beauty of this heart of summer.

" Once again Ellen echoed my thoughts as she said: 'Yes, friend, this is what I came out for to see; this many-gabled old house, built by the simple country-folk of the long-past times . . . is lovely still amidst all the beauty which these latter days have created. . . . It seems to me as if it had waited for these happy days, and held in it the gathered crumbs of happiness of the con-fused and turbulent past.'

"She led me up close to the house, and laid her shapely sun-browned hand and arm on the lichened wall as if to embrace it, and cried out, 'O me! O me! How I love the earth, and the seasons, and weather, and all things that deal with it, and all that grows out of it, — as this has done!'"

The development of Morris's life has been gradual. His genius was nurtured and matured in a dim, mediæval atmosphere. His early writings were suited to the fragile sense of some lady of an ancient bower whose eyes might wet when "heaven and earth on some fair eve had grown too fair for mirth." The poet confesses his verses have no power to bear the cares of the earners of bread. For himself and for those who could be lulled by his songs of an empty day he built a shadowy isle of bliss, "East of the Sun and west of the Moon," in the golden haze of the past. Each year, however, his work becomes more wide and sane. Each work advances upon the last in intensity of human feeling. The influence of Rossetti was not permanent. His own robust nature leads him into the arena of daily life. 'Sigurd,' while an epic of the past, is concerned with ideal human life. Said Sigurd to the King of the Niblungs : —

"And I would that the loving were loved, and I would that the weary should sleep
And that man should hearken to man, and that he that soweth should reap."

In 'The Dream of John Ball' and 'News from Nowhere,' Morris grasps at length the concrete problems of social existence. In 1884 he joined the London Socialistic League, to whose official organ, *The Commonweal*, the poet is a frequent contributor.

A sense of fate applied to life increased the worth of living. Life, he found, is worth living for its own sake, for love of friends, and joy and work and freedom. His philosophy of life is combined with a faith in the stimulating power of art. Early he had reached a profound conviction of the purpose of art as an indispensable element in human life.

"Beauty which is what is meant by art, using the word in its widest sense, is I contend, no mere accident of human life which people can take or leave as they choose, but a positive necessity of life, if we are to live as Nature meant us to, that is unless we are content to be less than men" ('Lectures').

In his combined claim for art and labor — the return of art, "that is to say, of the Pleasure of Life," to the people — he has reached by an elemental instinct a great truth of the world; for industrial liberty, to gain which we are now struggling, the best fight and the last, does not mean freedom *from* labor but *in* labor. Industrial liberty means the return of art and manhood to common work. "Life," says Ruskin, "without industry is guilt, and industry without art is brutality." The world to-day, in short, is under the necessity of gratifying the art instinct; that is, of humanizing labor, or of suffering the punishment of slavery. Economics, as well as humanity, requires that art and labor be once more united.

Thus the social burden of the times has been laid upon the poet's mind and heart. His passion for life and beauty inflames him with a desire to bring all men within the circle of their ministration. But before him perpetually is the city of London, huge and unsightly. He hears the murmur and moan from the hard-used race of men. From his home by the river he sees the workings of a selfish commercialism which has taken monetary profit and loss, and not the human kind, as its basis for calculation. With a heart laden with anger, he enters a protest against "man's inhumanity to man." With a heart laden with love he preaches the doctrines of brotherhood, — even if needs be by revolution. The key to his revolutionary position is contained in an address made before a Trades Guild assembly : —

"I do not want art for a few, any more than education for a few or freedom for a few. No, rather than that art should live this poor thin life among a few exceptional men despising those beneath them for an ignorance for which they themselves are responsible, for a brutality which they will not struggle with; rather than this, I would that the world should indeed sweep away all art for a while — rather than the wheat should rot in the miser's granary I would that the earth had it, that it might quicken in the dark."

The democratization of art is the social aim of William Morris. That civilization which does not carry with it the whole people is doomed to failure.

"Let me remind you how only the other day in the life-time of the youngest of us many thousand men of our own kindred gave their lives on the battle-field to bring to a happy ending a mere episode in the struggle for the abolition of slavery: they are blessed and happy for the opportunity came to them, and they seized it and did their best, and the world is the wealthier for it: and if such an opportunity is offered to us shall we thrust it from us that we may sit still in ease of body, in doubt, in disease of soul?" ('Art and Socialism.')

As a prophet of the new industrialism, William Morris is one of the most significant men of this century. He must command respect even from those who cannot share in his socialistic hope. No stunted capacity or sordid aims have ranged him on the side of socialism. It is a real burden that he is bearing. He has reverence for the life of man upon the earth. To the cause of humanity he has now subordinated his whole poetic genius. No longer by poetic melody does he seek to lull the workers into dreams. With a strenuous hope and with a sturdy strife at breast he turns to the future, and with that longing for rest that never leaves him, creates in the heroic age to come a romance of rest and peace and good-will. And if others can see it as he has seen it, then it may be called a vision rather than a dream.

*Oscar L. Triggs.*

## THE SIGHTLESS.

### BY MAURICE MAETERLINCK.

#### (*Continued.*)

*Fifth Man.* Have pity upon those who cannot see!

*First Man.* Who is this talking so unreasonably?

*Second Man.* I think it is the one who does n't hear.

*First Man.* Be quiet! This is not the time to beg!

*Third Man.* Where did he go to get the bread and water?

*Oldest Woman.* He went to the sea-shore.

*Third Man.* One does not venture toward the sea at his age.

*Second Man.* Are we near the sea?

*Oldest Woman.* Yes; be quiet a moment, — you will hear it. [*Murmuring of the sea near at hand and very calmly against the cliffs.*]

*Second Man.* I hear nothing but the three old women praying.

*Oldest Woman.* Listen well; you will hear it through their prayers.

*Second Man.* Yes; I hear something which is not far away from us.

*Oldest Man.* It was sleeping; they say that it awakes.

*First Man.* He was wrong to bring us here; I do not like to hear that noise.

*Oldest Man.* You know very well that the island is not large, and that it can be heard without leaving the hospital yard.

*Second Man.* I never listened to it.

*Third Man.* It seems as if it were beside us to-day; I do not like to hear it so near.

*Second Man.* Nor do I; besides, we did not ask to go out of the hospital.

*Third Man.* We have never before come as far as this; it was useless to bring us so far.

*Oldest Woman.* It was very fine this morning; he wished to have us enjoy the last sunny days before shutting us up for all winter in the hospital.

*First Man.* But I like to stay in the hospital better!

*Oldest Woman.* Besides, he said that we ought to know something of the little island where we are. He himself has never explored it entirely. There is a mountain which nobody has ever climbed, valleys into which no one likes to descend, and grottos where as yet none have penetrated. He said, in short, that we must not always wait for the sun in the vault-like dormitories. He would bring us to the sea-shore; he has gone there alone.

*Oldest Man.* He is right; one must think to live.

*First Man.* But there is nothing to see about here.

*Second Man.* Are we in the sunlight now?

*Third Man.* Is the sun up still?

*Sixth Man.* I think not; it seems to me that it is very late.

*Second Man.* What time is it?

*All the Others.* I don't know. No one knows.

*Second Man.* Is it light yet? [*To the sixth blind man.*] Where are you? Come now, you who see a little, let us see!

*Sixth Man.* I think it is very dark. When there is any sun, I see a blue line under my eyelids; some time ago I saw one, but now I see nothing at all.

*First Man.* As for me, I know that it is late when I am hungry, and I am hungry.

*Third Man.* But look up at the sky; maybe you will see something there!

[*They all lift their faces toward the sky, except the three men blind from birth, who continue to gaze down on the ground.*]

*Sixth Man.* I don't know whether we are under the sky.

*First Man.* The voice echoes as if we were in a cavern.

*Oldest Man.* I believe, instead, that it echoes so because it is evening.

*The Blind Girl.* It seems to me that I feel the moonlight on my hands.

*Oldest Woman.* I believe there are stars; I hear them.

*The Blind Girl.* So do I.

*First Man.* I don't hear any noise.

*Second Man.* I hear only the sound of our own breathing!

*Oldest Man.* I believe the women are right.

*First Man.* I have never heard the stars.

*The Two Others born blind.* Neither have we. [*A flock of night-birds alight suddenly in the foliage.*]

*Second Man.* Listen! listen! What is that above us? Do you hear?

*Oldest Man.* Something passed between the sky and us!

*Sixth Man.* There is something stirring above our heads, but we cannot reach up there!

*First Man.* I don't know what kind of a noise that is. I should like to go back to the hospital.

*Second Man.* We ought to know where we are.

*Sixth Man.* I have tried to rise; there is nothing but thorns around me; I dare not stretch out my hands.

*Third Man.* We ought to know where we are !

*Oldest Man.* We cannot know !

*Sixth Man.* We cannot be very far from the house; I do not know what to make of any noise now.

*Third Man.* For a long time I have smelled the odor of dead leaves.

*Sixth Man.* If any one has ever seen the island before, perhaps he can tell us where we are.

*Oldest Man.* We were all blind when we came here.

*First Man.* We have never seen.

(To be continued.)

*Translated by the Editors*

## SHAKESPEARIAN BOOKS OF THE YEAR.*

A LIBERAL literary treatment of Shakespeare seems to be a slow evolution. There has been much editing, cogitation over commas, and narrow treatment of special points, before an epoch in Shakespeare study has been marked by a work that is a unifying testimony to the art-power of the poet, such as Gervinus's

---

* Shakespeare Commentaries, by Dr. G. G. Gervinus. Translated by F. E. Bunnètt. Fifth edition. London: Smith, Elder, & Co. New York: Charles Scribner's Sons, 1892. — Shakespeare as a Dramatic Artist, by R. G. Moulton. Third edition. London and New York: Macmillan & Co., 1893. — Jahrbuch der Deutschen Shakespeare-Gesellschaft, edited by F. A. Leo. Twenty-seventh yearly issue. Weimar: A. Huschke, 1892.

Notes on the Plays. 'Coriolanus.' By T. D. Barnett. London: George Bell & Sons. New York: Macmillan & Co., 1892. — Shakespeare and the Thames. Passages illustrative of the Poet's Observation of the "Silent Highway." With an Introductory Sketch, and Notes on Stream and Strand, by W. H. Harper. London: Published by the Author. — Great Pan lives: Shakespeare's Sonnets, 20–126. With paraphrase, and references by Clelia. London: Luzac & Co., 1892. — The Mortal Meon, or Bacon and his Masks. The Defoe Period unmasked, by J. E. Roe. New York: Burr Printing House, 1892. — The Columbus of Literature; or, Bacon's New World of Sciences. By W. F. C. Wigston. Chicago: F. J. Schulte & Co., 1892.

Commentary was in its day, now reissued in its fifth English edition ; or such as was Dowden's 'Mind and Art of Shakespeare' later. Probably the next literary event in the progress of the Shakespearian afflatus was French and twofold, — M. Stapfer's original work in the comparison of Shakespearian and classic master-pieces, as well as Victor Hugo's powerful synthetic portrait of Shakespeare, clearly marking a new period.*

Perhaps the most notable English production, since Dowden's, was Moulton's 'Shakespeare as a Dramatic Artist,' this year also reissued in a third edition. Its excellence consisted, like that of its predecessors, in its broad handling of the plays as expressions of literary art ; its distinction from these was the new illumination it effected by a fresh use of modern scientific methods.

No high wave of production has signalized this year, but in literary tides, " if it be not now, it is to come, the readiness is all."

The Year-book of the German Shakespeare Society is, as usual, a faithful and valuable contribution. Among its contents are important papers on the Shylock legend, and on analogous plays to 'The Taming of the Shrew,' by Johannes Bolte ; a collection of popular quotations from Shakespeare, and remarks on Sprenger's Shakespearian Emendations, by Dr. F. A. Leo, — *à propos* of Dr. Furness's declaration in POET-LORE that too much stress has been laid upon the difficulties and obscurities of Shakespeare's text. Two esteemed contributors of ours appear also, — Charlotte C. Stopes in a paper embodying her researches as to William Hunnis, Master of Her Majesty's Chapel, in Shakespeare's day, and C. A. Wurtzburg in a German translation of her article on 'The Plot of "As You Like It,"' originally published in POET-LORE.

A second edition of 'Coriolanus' is this year added to Mr. T. D. Barnett's series of notes on the plays, wherein Shakespeare on the grammatical, etymological, and prosodical side is well elucidated. Whoso wants to make his progress to Shakespeare along the rather dry high-road which is guarded by University Examiners can have no more thorough guide.

* M. Stapfer's work has not to our knowledge been translated, but McClurg & Co., of Chicago, have brought out an excellent translation of Hugo's 'William Shakespeare.'

Victor Hugo's words, " I love rivers : they do more than bear merchandise : ideas float along their surface," introduce one happily to ' Shakespeare and the Thames.' Its seventy-five pages are rich in more good clews than one would know where else to get in such small space, to incidents of Shakespeare's sixteenth-century London-by-Thames.

It is the common mistake of commentators to leave genius too little space of its own in which to work its wonders. To transmute doubtless requires some earthy materials, yet — as lately, almost within our day, we were witness to the fact that it did not need the knowledge of a Hellenist to make ' Hyperion,' but only Lemprière's Dictionary plus the marvel, Keats — why should it not be credited that a Shakespeare worked miracles of allusion by means of his acquaintance with one familiar tidal river ? The writer of this noteworthy little book well says : —

" Once admit the justice of the assumption, that on the crowded Thames, with its infinite variety of shipping and shipmen, Shakespeare could learn much, by observation and inquiry, of nautical matters ; and the occasion for a good deal of recondite speculation vanishes. We shall not require Shakespeare to visit the Netherlands before settling down in London; nor, in a plague-stricken year, when the theatres were closed, and commerce paralysed, to visit Venice, — when, too, his means of livelihood were seriously jeopardised. He need not see the world, for on the Thames those who had seen the world came home to him."

Portia's allusion to " the tranect" that " trades to Venice " which cost annotators so much labor in surmising learnedly some obscure local Venetian knowledge is, according to Mr. Harper, " the ' common ferry' of the Thames," in the " Elizabethan age still known by the more classic name it bore in the days of Roman London."

It would be a pleasant idea next time one was in London, to follow the beck of this little book of river-lore, and to let it lead one, in fancy, by means of some allusion in the plays, if not by some vestige of an old fact, to Shakespearian " river-pageants," and " frost-fairs," and to trace out some haunt of the poet in Southwark and along shore.

The evidence that Shakespeare passed that way which is offered in 'Great Pan lives' is the very opposite of antiquarian. The book is of a somewhat esoteric sort, prone to be considered "bosh" by the Bourbon Shakespearian, whose bad opinion may do one a service, and incline one to glean from it, not without advantage, although probably without conviction. Beginning with Sonnet 20, the underlying significance of the six sonnets following is understood to be the avowal of Shakespeare to serve Beauty, to write of her "without hyperbole" (see Sonnet 21), and to show his love to her "more by works than by professions" (Sonnet 26). 'Consolation in Beauty' is held to be the argument of the second section (27–32). Then — since the Ideal or Beauty of the soul, to which the poet is vowed, is understood by him in a much wider sense than that called Beauty by the ancients, and includes Love and Truth as well as fair form — he is involved in trials peculiar to so inclusive an ideal; and the next section, made up of Sonnets 33–42, treats of the 'Impeachment of Beauty by Love.' Thereon follows (43–56) the 'Impeachment by Business,' — such as called him away from London and from his art-producing habits (see 44, 50, and 51); the 'Impeachment by Pleasure' (57–77); and by Criticism (78–86); all these being finally consummated in the 'Eclipse of Beauty' (87–96), and issuing in the 'Re-emergence of the Sun of Beauty' (97–108), the 'Return to the Ideal' (109–122), and the 'Soul's Immortality in Beauty' (123–126).

There are some comments in the 'Impeachment by Pleasure' division which bear upon "the tongs and the bones" phase of Shakespeare's art, or, as Clelia puts it, the "sportive period."

"Under the sanction of the Ideal, Shakespeare's genius at this time when Falstaff begins to tread the stage, becomes 'sportive' not only in his writings, but also in his conduct. For the Muse must be true to nature and itself, and, therefore, must present the comedy as well as the tragedy of Vice. Now to present Vice truly the poet must know it, and to know it he must live with it, and to live with it must do at Rome," etc.

The burden of the poet's song is now, in Sonnet 69, that he is "bringing the Muse into disrepute by the curious phase of sportiveness through which" his "genius is passing."

What difference of opinion there can be in regard to an explanation of the Sonnets recently offered by Mr. J. E. Roe, it would be hard to imagine. The claim made in the preface of his book that the part of the matter therein which refers to the Sonnets is new, and that in this alone the reader will " be rewarded for any labor he may bestow upon the work " will not be questioned when it is understood that this interpretation supposes the opening Sonnets to be addressed by Bacon to Queen Elizabeth, urging the coquette of sixty to marry and bear that Protestant copy of herself which alone against " Time's scythe can make defence." We are perhaps justified in saying that there will scarcely be more than two opinions about this (one of these being the author's), and that any reader ought to consider himself already well rewarded for the attention given to so original a theory. But this theory is not poor in exquisite reasons. For example, it supposes the desponding Sonnets — 88, 89, and 90 — to be written by Bacon when his trial for bribery went against him and his fall was accomplished, in 1621, regardless of the little fact that the Sonnets were published in 1609.

If 1596 be not taken as the earliest date for their composition, at which time Elizabeth would be sixty, certainly their date of publication, 1609, must be taken as the further limit beyond which even a Bacon cannot go, unless, like the Red Queen in Alice's Looking Glass Country, he screams first and cuts his finger afterwards.

Not merely Shakespeare, — whose Puritanism is not to be accounted a very present quantity, — but Burton, Defoe, John Bunyan, Swift, Addison, William Penn, and other lights of English letters and politics are claimed to be Bacon's dummies for the spread of a system of Puritan ideas affecting social life, state matters, and philosophy.

In the ' Columbus of Literature,' which is a more learned cousin of ' Bacon's Masks,' Mr. Wigston holds that Bacon was chief of the secret society of the Rosicrucians, and that what he was after in making Shakespeare write the Plays for him, was " nothing short of an entire Restoration of Heathen Religion." Lest this union of Puritan and Pagan seem ill-assorted, let us hasten to add that both

Mr. Roe and Mr. Wigston agree upon Bacon's strong opposition to Papal supremacy.

The correspondence of mispaging in Bacon's 'Advancement of Learning' with Shakespeare's age when he died (page 52 = age 52) is an example of the grounds of belief which Mr. Wigston finds weighty. As an exemplar of a whole dynasty of the same kin, we choose, at random, a set of the verbal comparisons which seem weighty to Mr. Roe : —

"In 'As You Like It' iii. 2., we have      'I prythee tell me who is it? Quickly, and speak apace.' The word is a distinctive Baconian word, and it will be found in every phase of these writings. Bacon in his Natural History, sub. 374, says: 'We see that if wind bloweth upon a candle it wasteth apace.' Note the use of the word in 'The Pilgrim's Progress' . . . p. 332, 'The lion came on apace, and Mr. Greatheart,' etc. . . . In Addison, vol. III. p. 434, we have: 'From this time the armies      polished apace.'"

*P*

## NOTES AND NEWS.

WHEN the Editor of *The Arena* took the Bacon question up out of its ashes and resuscitated it by dint of some little blowing, we scarcely thought it could pose as any sort of a burning issue ; but *Quidvis fit* (a new phrase we respectfully dedicate to the American Editor of *Symposia*), and it soon appeared that there were yet people who could be stirred by Miss Kitty's query, — "Shikspur! Shikspur! Who wrote it?" To them, both Mr. Reed's briefs and also the pleas of the Shakespearian counsel, Drs. Nicholson, Rolfe, and Furnivall, were as new as they have proved able to veterans of the controversy. Dr. Rolfe's presentation, especially, was admirable as a thorough summary of the whole question.

Yet it probably is not the arguments which tell in either case. With literary taste and insight, with an apprehension of literature on the artistic side, it is impossible to confound the Shakespearian and Baconian style and spirit; with a predisposition to identify learning with genius, it is hard to accept the inferiority of university breeding to untaught native capability. What is really weighty to the Baconian is not his detailed " grounds of belief," but the foundation unlikelihood, upon which all else is superstructure, that an " untaught rustic " could have written the works the world honors. Behind "cipher," " secret society," and " parallel passages," the root of the matter is planted in a pedantic bias which agrees very well, to be sure, with the current exaltation of the pedagogue and the current misconception of the breadth and freedom of real culture. The supposition that " education " can endow a mind with sense, or make one man intrinsically superior to another is responsible for the sophism that only a scholar could have written plays of genius like Shakespeare's, and, therefore, that he did not write them, and the most learned man of his time did.

There are some witnesses, however, to quite another fact, — that it is the inborn gift to teach oneself which does really endow a man above his fellows: Browning, who made his own curriculum, and, universityless, held the spheres of the world between his sensitive finger-tips; Whitman, who penetrated some cycles of literary evolutions by means of a little casual reading; Emerson, who, from translations, nourished his clear soul on the essences of civilized thought; "Defoe, the livery-man, Bunyan, the tinker," — we quote a Baconian, — Molière, the upholsterer, Burns, the ploughman, Keats, the apothecary's clerk, yea, even Christ, the carpenter's son, were all born to their missions in despite of class prejudice. Nor need one wonder at it, until he finds the most learned collegians of his own acquaintance the most gifted, also, in mother-wit, artistic craft, moral aspiration, and the synthetic imagination.

—— The anniversary performances of Shakespeare's plays will take place as usual at the Memorial Theatre, in Stratford-on-Avon, beginning on Monday evening, April 24, with ' The Taming of the Shrew.' Mr. Benson's company will present all the plays, Mr. Benson himself acting the Crook-back in ' Richard III.' on Tuesday evening. On Thursday evening, the Merry Wives will play their perennial jokes on Falstaff; and a revival of ' Coriolanus,' with new and well-studied costumes and scenic effects, is set down for Wednesday and Friday evenings and Saturday afternoon.

# SOCIETIES.

The Browning Society of Boston held its fifty-eighth regular meeting on Tuesday, February 28, President Hornbrooke in the chair. After minutes of the previous meeting had been read, and necessary announcements made, Mrs. Mary Gregory read the following poems: 'Meeting at Night,' 'Parting at Morning,' 'A Pretty Woman,' and the Prologue to 'Two Poets of Croisic.' Dr. W. J. Rolfe read a paper on 'Browning's Mastery of Rhyme,' noting interesting characteristics of the poet's technique. Miss Ethel Davis's paper on 'The Poetic Structure of Browning's Shorter Lyrics' considered these poems chiefly as expressions of moods. She showed the frequent twinship of form and content, and noted the undercurrent in several, as the ocean swell of the movement in 'Home Thoughts from the Sea' and the broken sobbing of 'A Woman's Last Word.' (These papers will appear in POET-LORE.)

Col. T. W. Higginson opened discussion on the question, 'Does the Distinction of Browning's Poetic Art consist in his never sacrificing Sense to Sound?' by speaking first of the limitations of all art. When a man has done his utmost, one fault cannot be corrected without risking something more important. A poet has no right to sacrifice either sense or sound; but there is a point when thought and expression are brought so closely together that to touch the poem again would be to hurt it. In the 'Paracelsus' period Browning reached the closest harmony between the two; and in this connection the changes then made in his finished work are most significant. They were always toward the plainer, more literal, more prosaic rendering of the thought. He wanted to be understood, and his disappointment in this regard took almost inevitably two directions. At first he changed and literalized, sacrificing sound to the sense of the average reader; but as he seemed still unsuccessful, he flung himself away more and more from this effort, becoming, except in rare, delightful hours, a devotee of thought rather than of perfect expression. Colonel Higginson pointed out the changes to which he had referred, mentioning the explanations volunteered by changing the titles of 'Night' and 'Morning' to 'Meeting at Night' and 'Parting at Morning,' and by the introduction of "He says" and "She says" in 'In a Gondola,' but dwelling chiefly on the more serious changes in songs from 'Pippa Passes.'

Dr. Rolfe doubted if the change in 'You'll love me yet' might not rather have been made out of consideration for the completeness of each stanza, which a song requires.

Mr. Nathan Haskell Dole believed that every poet must sacrifice either sense or sound to a certain degree, and the necessity is emphasized by the paucity of rhymes for the words poets must use oftenest. One's first thought, that Browning had sacrificed sound to sense more than almost any other poet, is corrected when one studies his wonderful range of words and mastery over form. Even the two and three syllable rhymes, which seem naturally fitted only for comic verse, Browning manages with dignity.                    *Emma Endicott Marean.*

# POET-LORE

Vol. V.

——wilt thou not haply ſaie,
Truth needs no colluur with his cullour fixt:
Beautie no penſell, beauties truth to lay:
But beſt is beſt if neuer intermixt.
Becauſe he needs no praiſe, wilt thou be dumb?
Excuſe not ſilence ſo, for't lies in thee,
To make him much outliue a gilded tombe:
And to be praiſed of ages yet to be.
Then do thy office ——

No. 5.

## ROBERT BROWNING — THE MAN.

### SOME FURTHER REMINISCENCES.

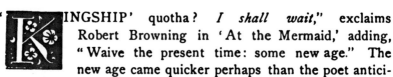

'KINGSHIP' quotha? *I shall wait*," exclaims Robert Browning in 'At the Mermaid,' adding, "Waive the present time: some new age." The new age came quicker perhaps than the poet anticipated; for he stands to-day within measurable distance of acknowledged "poetic chief" of the Victorian era. In dramatic insight as in splendor of conception, he towers above all his compeers, and however tardily conceded, the fact remains that he *was*, in the words of Lowell, "by far the richest nature of his time."

But although the poet well knew that some "new age" would at last do justice to his *work*, he cared very little to be known *himself*, — the man apart from the worker. That he should come to be "catalogued" and "labelled," his likes or dislikes aired for the amusement or edification of the public, was utterly abhorrent to him, — as indeed his own lines suggest: —

" Shall I sonnet-sing you about myself?
　Do I live in a house you would like to see?
Is it scant of gear, has it store of pelf?
　'Unlock my heart with a sonnet key?'

" Invite the world, as my betters have done?
　' Take notice : this building remains on view
Its suites of reception every one,
　Its private apartment and bedroom too ;

" ' For a ticket, apply to the Publisher.'
　No : thanking the public, I must decline.
A peep through my window, if folk prefer ;
　But, please you, no foot over threshold of mine ! "

This feeling may probably account for the destruction of many of his letters written during boyhood and youth. In later years, the numerous reminiscences, etc., which flooded the market must have appalled him, and intensified his conviction that the public had no concern in his life apart from his work. But it may never have occurred to him that danger of another kind awaited his memory, and that he was to be " catalogued " and " labelled " as a " society man," — a hanger-on to the skirts of the aristocracy of wealth. How this notion has obtained vogue is a mystery not easy to fathom ; for of all men in the world he was about the last on whom such a charge could truthfully be laid. The fact is, that during the last few years of his life, when a somewhat sudden wave of popularity overtook him, he was much sought after by a section of "society " ever on the watch for something new; so it came about that he was a frequent guest at "receptions " and kindred gatherings ; and no doubt from this arose the generally received notion that he courted and received the adulation of " society," — according to such only as came under this curious designation the first and possibly only claim on his leisure hours.

Those who knew him, however, knew the cosmopolitan nature of the man, and needed not to be assured that he welcomed any soul who loved him, — be he rich or poor, or hailing from Belgravia or Whitechapel. He had friends, good and true, among the aristocracy of wealth ; he had also friends good and true among the aristocracy of talent, as the aristocracy of labor; and his nature was so eminently sterling, he was so sound and noble at heart, that all who were brought into contact with him loved him at first sight. What he was as a poet the world has long known; what he was as a man it is fitting should be also known. His lovableness, modesty, gentleness, courtesy, — these were but part of his every-day nature. During the last few years of his life, he was no doubt bored considerably by strangers, who sought him from mere curiosity, and under the flimsiest pretexts; but he was very tolerant to such, despite the inroads this made upon his time and strength. But to the earnest spirit, to the man or woman whom his words had helped or healed, he was easily accessible; and he would put himself to endless trouble to gratify or oblige his friends. As an instance of this, let the following letter suffice: —

June, 1889.

MY DEAR KINGSLAND, — Will you be good and kind enough to forgive me under the circumstances which you are to hear. I received a letter from you enclosing one from a friend you wished me to see — as I shall be happy to do. But the letters came just as I was on the point of leaving for Oxford, where I stayed a week — and I had no time to do more than glance at what I was intending to notice particularly on my return, — before which it was useless to do so. Well, on my return, some days ago, I searched everywhere for the letters, and could not find in what safe place I have laid them away: so safe a place that I am sure they will soon turn up — possibly as soon as I make this confession; but meanwhile I am distressed to think you are awaiting an answer so unaccountably delayed. I therefore discontinue a hitherto fruitless search to say that if you will grant me an indulgence I greatly need, and write, in two lines, what you desire, on the part of your friend, I will take care that, this time, you shall not be kept waiting one minute longer than is necessary to say I will (I repeat) be happy to receive your friend — to whom pray make what excuse you can, — and indeed could you know the vexation my apparent carelessness has caused me, your pardon and his also would be cheerfully granted. Ever, my dear Kingsland,

Yours most truly

ROBERT BROWNING.

Another incident occurs to me, which may be of interest, showing, as it does, the kindly nature of the man, and his ready response to all who approached him in a considerate spirit. A teacher in a north-of-England town (and a complete stranger to the poet), feeling the great help he had been to her in many ways, wrote and expressed the debt of gratitude she owed to him. She carefully abstained from giving her address or Christian name, fearing he would think a reply was expected; but by return of post came a few lines from him, addressed to ——, Esq., and bearing merely the name of the town where she lived (which he must have noted from the post-mark on the envelope). " If," he wrote, " my poetry has been useful to you, I am happy indeed ; and whether you see my face or do not see it, you may truly look on it as that of a friend." A year or two later, this same lady, being about to leave England for a time, ventured to call on Mr. Browning; he was unfortunately out, but she received the following note from him, — which speaks volumes for the goodness of heart which prompted it : —

WARWICK CRESCENT, May, 1884.

DEAR FRIEND, — (I shall so venture to style you, in my doubt as to the proper prefix to your name) — I am sorry to have been away from home when you called ; I only got your kind letter on my return from Oxford, and wish to say, while there is yet time, that I duly value all such sympathy as you are pleased to express. Where I may be in three or four years — after which you hope to re-visit England — I cannot tell, nor divine indeed ; but be assured that I am the better for having heard of your care to see me while it was yet possible — and that I am cordially yours

ROBERT BROWNING.

Remembering these kind words, the lady, on her return to England, made another attempt to see the poet. This time he was at home ; and though she called without any introduction, he greeted her with outstretched hand and genial smile of welcome ; and when she feared to intrude more than a very few minutes, he begged her to stay, saying that he was busy in the midst of correcting the proofs of his new book, and glad to rest and have a little chat. As she was leaving, he asked, in his kindly voice, "Would you not like to come into my study ?" and leading the way, he pointed to a little table in the room, and said, " Thereon it was Mrs. Browning wrote 'Aurora Leigh;' and that was her usual seat," pointing to a low folding-chair. On his visitor expressing her love for the poem, he added, in a tone of earnest conviction, " Ah ! she would have given you something finer had she lived." During the whole visit the manner of the poet was full of graciousness, kindliness, and courtesy.

Yet another instance of his kindly feeling may here be mentioned. As I have hinted, he had a perfect horror of being made a show of, and it was no doubt to avoid this sort of thing that he rarely attended the performance of his own plays. On one occasion, when a couple of performances of ' The Blot in the 'Scutcheon' had been arranged for, he had as usual declined to be present. The manager, however, explained to him the trouble the actors had taken in the matter, and how disappointed they would be at his absence. " I felt he was right," said the poet, " so I told him that if I could be put into a private box, and nobody else be told I was present, I would come." This was done, and the sequel is too good to be omitted ; for Mr. Browning, who loved a good joke, told it with considerable hilarity. It appears that at the conclusion of the performance, he at once went behind the curtain, and most heartily thanked the company for the manner in which they had performed his play. He had hardly left, when in came a prominent member of the Browning Society, who, expressing his delight, added that he intended to write to the poet that very evening, and tell him how capitally it had passed off. " *Oh, but we've just seen him !* " was the general exclamation, — to the momentary discomfiture of the prominent member, who had no idea that the poet had been present.

His kindness was indeed proverbial. On more than one occasion within my knowledge, he put himself to considerable trouble to obtain situations for people whom he had come across, and whom he was eager to help. He was, in a very wide sense, the friend of man. As each succeeding volume of verse appeared, he was more than ever grateful for any care exercised by that sorely tried individual, the " printer's reader ; " and he told me that he always made a point of writing and requesting that his heartiest thanks should be forwarded to the "reader" for such help and assistance. Let us hope this intimation was duly forwarded !

His ways with little children were very beautiful, and they were instinctively drawn to him. I can see the old poet now, his face wreathed in smiles, busily explaining various objects of interest in his drawing-room to a little boy (his namesake), whom he carried on his arm ; and the pure delight he afterward exhibited at the little fellow's appreciation of the milk and cake with which he regaled him ! On such occasions as these, he would relate experiences connected with his own childhood, and some note would be sounded in memory of his mother, and of what were apparently happy days in a happy home. This would lead the talk to his early manhood ; and now and again he would speak of his 'Pauline' days, — of W. J. Fox, of Sarah Flower, and her sister ; and one wonders if the author of 'Nearer my God to thee' was not the original of 'Pauline,' — evidently the young poet was much attached to these two accomplished women.

And how modest and unassuming he was ! Lavish in praise of the work of his own contemporaries, you could rarely get him to speak of his own work ; and when he did, and you felt sure some interesting piece of self-revelation was coming, he would pull up suddenly, and glide off on to another topic. I recollect, on one occasion, we were referring to 'Christmas Eve,' and I asked him if he had any special conventicle in view when describing the little chapel. "No," he replied, " it was all imaginary — save the lunar rainbow: *I saw that.*" And as he went on to describe the wonderful apparition, the poem itself was forgotten, or passed over.

It has often been objected that Mr. Browning took little interest in public affairs, — that his poems had no democratic or national ring about them. Be this as it may, it is certain that he was both patriotic and imbued with the democratic spirit. He took a real interest in the people, and was concerned in whatever means were adopted for the amelioration of their condition in life. I remember one evening, stepping into the garden at the back of the house in Warwick Crescent, where, in company with the poet's friend,

M. Milsand, we paced up and down the small square ground. The poet remarked that he rarely went out there, as he was so over-looked; but here, on this quiet summer evening, he entered into some earnest talk touching the condition of the people, and there was a tremulousness in his voice as he spoke of the apparently hopeless condition in which so many of them lived. He alluded to Sunday-schools, among other things, — his interest having been aroused by a request that had come to him to write an ode or sonnet for the Centenary of the Sunday-school movement, then about to be celebrated. This, however, he had to decline, as he made it a rule not to contribute to newspapers or magazines. By and by, he got on to the "drink question," — M. Milsand having waged war against the excessive indulgence in alcohol in his own country. I well remember the indignation of the poet as he spoke of the ruined homes and blighted prospects caused by intemper-ance ; and he related how, but a few evenings since, he had come across a working-man who was so drunk he could scarcely stand. "I helped him along for some distance as best I could," said the poet, "but he was exceedingly unmanageable ; and I was glad when another individual, apparently a fellow-worker, came to my assistance with the remark, 'I think you had better leave him to me, sir.' And as he seemed to understand more about it than I did, I thought that the best thing to do," he added.

I once showed him a little booklet that had come to me from America, containing extracts from his poems arranged under the date of each day of the year. He looked through it with much interest, and as he handed it back to me remarked, "Ah ! how this sort of thing humbles one; and yet it *is* something to have sown seed like this, is n't it ? " How characteristic this was of the man ! He knew the worth of his own achievement, — none knew it better ; but of vain-glory therein no trace was manifest. For long years he had cast his bread upon the waters, and "many days " passed ere it was again found. No "society " petting spoiled his simple and courteous nature ; nor was he intoxicated with the sudden popularity that overtook him as he was nearing old age. So in the fulness of the days he departed from among us, — *a true man*, noble in life as in work, great in achievement as in aspiration, and full of a sublime faith in the ultimate possibilities of humanity.

*William G. Kingsland.*

LONDON, ENGLAND, April, 1893.

## FROM THE PROVENÇAL OF SORDELLO, TROUBADOUR.*

ALAS ! these eyes, how little serves their sight,
That look no longer on my heart's delight.

The breath of spring about the fields is blown,
  The earth with bud and bloom is glad again ;
Therefore that I no longer should make moan
  My Lady, queen of Graces, is full fain,
Praying that song for sighing should atone ;
  Then will I sing, though deadly be my pain,
So much I have of love for her alone,
  So much of longing for her lips in vain.
Alas ! these eyes, how little serves their sight
That look no longer on my heart's delight.

Though Love be cruel even unto death,
  I make not plaint therefore in any wise ;
To think upon my Lady comforteth,
  For I have never looked on gentler eyes ;
Let her but promise, " If Love tarrieth,
  Thou yet shall find him wearing pity's guise, "
So shall my grief be silent, so no breath
  Shall mar her merry days with sad surmise.
Alas ! these eyes, how little serves their sight,
That look no longer on my heart's delight.

Unto my Lady Pitiful I sing
  That life may yet be left me, of her grace,
For, were I dead, the ruth thereof would wring
  Sorrow for sin, and for my cruel case ;

* Raynouard, 'Choix des Poésies des Troubadours,' vol. iii., pp. 441-3.

Nay, surely, but it were a better thing
  To die, than, living still, to lack solace ;
For death, I know, has not so sharp a sting
  As thus to love and miss my Lady's face.
Alas ! these eyes, how little serves their sight,
That look no longer on my heart's delight.

*Owen Seaman.*

# ARISTOPHANES' PHILOSOPHY OF POETRY ACCORDING TO BROWNING.*

FEW poets of ancient or of modern times have a more elusive personality than Aristophanes. So slight, indeed, is the didactic element in his work that a clear or even a concise statement of his views can be obtained only through a careful study of his characterizations. The facts that we possess concerning his external life are few. He was born probably about the year 450 B. C., and it is surmised that he was not of pure Attic descent, as his father may have been from Rhodes or some other colony. However this may be, both father and son were apparently men of culture, mingling in the best society of the Athens of the Age of Pericles, and Aristophanes himself belonged to the order of Knights. Of the forty-five plays produced by Aristophanes between the years 427 and 388, eleven only are extant. Of these, four relate directly to the war, two have as animus his quarrel with Euripides, and the remainder deal with social and literary questions. He lived to be an old man, surviving the conquest of Athens by Sparta, and he worked industriously until the end of his life. Some critics — notable among whom is Grote — believe that Aristophanes in his comedy furnished one of the elements that led to the downfall of Athens. Others, who see

* Read before the Boston Browning Society, Jan. 24, 1893.

31

nothing destructive in his work, find in him no aim loftier than the desire to amuse. Still others, however, probing his meaning, behold in him a would-be-reformer who used the weapons most likely to be effective upon the Athenians, — dramatic poetry in the form of sprightly comedy.

Among these last-named critics stands Browning, who with a poet's insight reaches and brings into full light the deep philosophy underlying the sparkling surface of Aristophanes' comedies. The vehicle through which the English poet communicates the result of his research is peculiarly appropriate, — a monologue within a monologue, — the reply of Aristophanes himself to charges made against his methods by Balaustion. Balaustion, a Rhodian maiden, some time before the fall of Athens, on her voyage toward the Attic capital, had saved her own life and that of her companions by reciting the 'Alkestis' of Euripides. Later she had married Euthukles, an Athenian; and one sad night Euthukles came home to her from the theatre with the news of Euripides' death. Suddenly, as they sat bemoaning their friend, a loud knocking at their door announced Aristophanes, who entered with a host of revellers, the chorus and the actors of his latest comedy. Abashed at the dignified mien of Balaustion, all withdrew except Aristophanes, who, at the challenge of Balaustion, elaborately defended the purpose and methods of his comedy, especially in its contrast with the tragedy of Euripides. In the end he was controverted — if not wholly overthrown — by Balaustion; and the latter recalls the memorable rencontre to Euthukles while the two are on the ship which is bearing them as exiles from fallen Athens to Rhodes. This setting is peculiarly appropriate, for Aristophanes had boasted that the result of his poetic efforts would be the triumph of Athens over Sparta and the allies. From first to last we admire the skill with which the Englishman interprets the Greek. The material which Browning — like any of us — had to use consisted simply of the comedies themselves and the comments of the scholiasts. Of direct statement or definition of Aristophanes' philosophy he had little to draw upon — save in the case of an occasional rhesis or parabasis — and yet his Aristophanes reveals himself to us in a well-rounded individuality.   In this essay I do not propose to follow the argument of Aristophanes in all its intricacy, but rather to show wherein lies his philosophy of poetry.

Browning's Aristophanes clearly states the purpose with which he entered on his career.

> " Do you believe, when I aspired in youth
> I made no estimate of power at all,
> Nor paused long, nor considered much, what class
> Of fighters I might claim to join, beside
> That class wherewith I cast in company?
>
> .   .   .   .   .   .   .
>
> Suppose we minded simply to make verse,
> To fabricate, parade resplendent arms
> Flourish and sparkle out a trilogy, —
> Where was the hindrance?   But my soul bade 'fight'! "

He had been less than a man, indeed, had he failed to use the poetic power with which he was endowed to help his country in her hour of trial.   "One last resource is left us, — poetry!" he cries, and without hesitation makes his choice between comedy and tragedy.   The " exquisite palaistra-tool of polished tragedy " is for other hands than his.   He closed, he says, "with whom you count the Meaner Muse. "

> " Classed me with Comic Poets who should weld
> Dark with bright metal, show their blade may keep
> Its adamantine birthright though ablaze
> With Poetry. "

In making his choice, Aristophanes was not ignorant of the history and scope of comedy.   His own exposition of its development, contained in a parabasis in 'The Knights,' is of the utmost value to students of literature.   Its substance we have in that passage of the 'Apology' wherein the poet tried to prove comedy coeval with the birth of Athenian freedom, and growing with its growth.   Its beginning was at the early feast of Bacchus, when wine unlocked the stiffest lips, when men told truths without fear of punishment.   Gradually the notion came to them to act the fool or knave, so that the crowd might see what they had simply heard of before, and finally as a natural sequence to this rough acting, comedy arose, the invention of Sousarion. In the development of comedy from the crude celebrations of the feast of Bacchus, Aristophanes found his authority for the use of the club as a weapon of attack, — "the old, stout stock," which he would "new tip with steel," and make "an engine proper for rough-chastisement."

For many reasons Greek tragedy was less effective toward reform than comedy. Tragedy not only propounded questions, but answered them; comedy, leaving the question unanswered, stimulated the audience to think for itself and to act. The constant appeal of comedy to the audience was not useless. Comedy to the Athenian was like the newspaper of to-day to the ordinary reader. Presupposing in the audience a complete understanding of the subject of each play, it dispensed almost entirely with plot; for a plot would have diverted the audience from the ultimate end which each play had in view.

"To restore the Marathonian muscle" is the end which Aristophanes keeps constantly before him. Looking about him for the cause of the decadence of political and moral strength in Athens, he is quick to see that the power which the demagogues have gained over the masses is undeniably hurtful. Hence his unsparing attacks on Cleon, and his merciless ridicule of the citizens who uphold Cleon's power. Conservative and aristocratic as he is, he sees but one side of the question. The democracy is always in the wrong; the political innovator is always to be feared.

> "And what's my teaching but — accept the old,
> Contest the strange! acknowledge work that's done,
> Misdoubt men who have still their work to do!"

Almost as hurtful to the State as the professional politician are the professional thinkers, the philosophers, — not one but many, under whose teaching the Athenians are going astray. Detecting, as he says, the vice underlying the superstructure of thought built by the Sophist, "Fancy's sludge and slime," he plainly sees his own duty.

> " To save Sense, poet !  Bang the sophist-brood !
> Would cheat man out of wholesome sustenance
> By swearing wine is water, honey — gall."

Difficult as it is for us to understand fully his general hatred for the Sophists, we must go back to his time, must imagine ourselves in contact with the pedantic youth who professed themselves to be the true product of the Socratic School.  By thus getting the point of view of the average practical and patriotic Athenian, we may understand Aristophanes' hatred of the Sophists.  As to his attitude toward Socrates himself, we are assured that there was no personal ill-will even in his most trenchant ridicule.  The passage in Plato's Symposium representing Aristophanes and Socrates seated side by side in friendly converse probably symbolizes their relation to each other ; and we have no reason to doubt the story that Socrates himself was an amused and interested spectator at the first performance of the 'Clouds.'

To " strike malpractice that affects the state " was certainly a lofty aim, and we have Browning's sanction for this view of Aristophanes' purpose.  To attain this end, his most effective weapon is, as he says himself, —

> " Hate !
> Honest, earnest and directest hate —
> Warfare wherein I close with enemy,
> Call him one name and fifty epithets,
> Remind you his great-grandfather sold bran.
> Describe the new exomion, sleeveless coat
> He knocked me down last night and robbed me of."

Then when he has shown a man's worst points, the audience applauds and cries, " Was he such a sorry scrub as Aristophanes seems to think he is ?  Aristophanes must be right, and we wrong in praising the other man so much."  Thus by improper designation, " scrub," the artist of comedy leads his fickle Athenian audience to the desired conclusion in a way utterly impossible had he used the argument suited to a more intelligent audience.

Closely allied to this extreme personality is exaggeration, Aristophanes' second weapon.  The Aristophanic comedy has

been called " A grave, humorous, impossible great lie related with
an accurate mimicry of the persons introduced." Aristophanes
himself wonders that the keen-witted Balaustion does not detect
the aim of his exaggeration, —

> " Whence, — O the tragic end of comedy ! —
> Balaustion pities Aristophanes
> For who believes him ? "

Those to whom wisdom is not wisdom unless it is clad in sober
and conventional attire, may — like Balaustion — hardly discover
the philosopher behind the comedian's mask. But Browning's
Aristophanes understands himself. " Every word is false," he
acknowledges, —

> " Looked close at ;
> But stand distant and stare through,
> All 's absolute, indubitable truth.
> Behind lies, truth which only lies declare."

Aristophanes was no unworldly recluse. Understanding his
audience, he was willing to use every means likely to move it to
his purpose ; hence his very grossness — for which his warmest
partisan hesitates to apologize — may be regarded as a means of
holding the attention of his countrymen. His grossness, from the
spirit of the times less reprehensible in his day than in ours, might
easily have been effective upon an audience of Athenians, themselves an extraordinary mingling of noble and ignoble qualities.

However lofty Aristophanes' general purpose, at first glance, it
is difficult to see what he expected to gain by his repeated and
bitter attacks on Euripides. Since they were fellow-craftsmen, it
is natural to suspect that literary jealousy may have been at least
a factor in the quarrel between the two. Patriotism, however,
seems to have impelled Aristophanes in his attacks on Euripides as
well as in his attacks on Cleon, or the Sophists. When Euripides
began to write, the Greeks were supreme in Europe, the Athenians
supreme in Greece. If the deterioration of the Athenians kept
pace with the growing popularity of Euripides, what wonder that
Aristophanes should trace cause and effect in these two things
He scoffed openly at Euripides' " Despise the world and reverence
yourself." Proudly he maintained —

> " No such thin fare feeds flesh, and blood like mine,
>   No such seclusion, closet, cave or court suits either."

No, he continues, " I would rather make my country and my countrymen happier and better, by heeding their cries when they shout ' Aristophanes ! '

> " More grist to mill, here 's Kleophon to grind !
> He 's for refusing peace, though Sparté cede
> Even Dekeleia ! Here 's Kleonumos
> Declaring — though he threw away his shield,
> He 'll thrash you till you lay your lyre aside !
>
> .   .   .   .   .   .   .   .   .
> So, bustle !  Pounce on opportunity ! "

The difference between the two is no mere question of the respective merits of idealism and realism, of tragedy and comedy. A deeper ingrain difference of temperament stood in the way of a complete understanding between these men. From the lofty heights of tragedy, Euripides looked calmly down on the poet of comedy. He winced not at the sharp lash of Aristophanes, protested not against the infamous abuse, the malignant censure, of the latter, who cries haughtily,

> " Do you detect in me — in me, I ask,
> The man like to accept this measurement
> Of faculty, contentedly sit classed
> Mere Comic Poet ? "

As to the question which is the more realistic, everything depends on the point of view. Sophocles was wont to say that he painted men as they ought to be, Euripides men as they are. This, if conceded to be true, would place Euripides in the world of realism. Again, Browning makes Euripides advise Aristophanes to relinquish his song and dance and jest — his " wit-fireworks " — and " Rising from all fours, paint man-like actual human life, make veritable men think, say and do." This, if accepted as a true view of Euripides, would put Aristophanes outside of the world of realism. Hence, how decide which is the realist? provided we grant that the difference between these poets turns on this point. Yet it requires no great discernment to see that the world of Aristophanes is remote from the real world. Possibly the true artist is never wholly realistic. To be thoroughly a realist, a man must become a mere machine, reproducing what he sees, but giving to his work little of his own individuality. Aristophanes is always the artist; and although his personality is not thrust upon us, he adapts all his characters to the purpose in hand with a skill that is wholly his own. "Idealism," says a distinguished critic, "is the attempt to imitate things as the mind interprets them;" and accepting this definition, we may call Aristophanes an idealist. The 'Demos' of Aristophanes, for example, is an idealization, — his conception of the democracy; and similar to this are many other of his creations, — types, rather than individuals, yet placed in a real world with which they contrast all the more grotesquely.

Aristophanes well understood the difference between himself and Euripides.

> "'Unworld the world' frowns he, my opposite.
> I cry 'Life!'' Death,' he groans, 'our better Life!'"

The tragic poet, from a "passionless, rational" altitude, looks down upon the writer of comedy, scorning as well the grimly gross ordinary population of Athens. Aristophanes in his turn has a word to say against the writers of tragedy. He calls them "sneaks, whose art is mere desertion of a trust." He is hardly more patient with those critics who make suggestions to him of "comedy built-fresh." He would not change his methods for them. "It is easy," he says, "for you spectators to criticise. Comedy is pleasure and pastime for you; for me it is a duty, a task, and although I am strong enough to go on with my work, I am unwilling to turn art's fixed fabric upside down." Unintelligent criticism was the harder to bear because he had made a deliberate choice of comedy, and because he himself held the highest conception of the poet's mission.

> "Sworn to serve
> Each Grace, the Furies call him minister —
> He, who was born for just that roseate world
> Renounced so madly."

He knows —

> "The enthusiastic mood which marks a man
> Muse-mad, dream-drunken, wrapt around by verse,
> Encircled with poetic atmosphere"

He has renounced all mere dreaming, and is convinced that, in the end, " Strength and utility charm more than grace." " Little and Bad exist," he continues, "are natural: Then let me know them and be twice as great As he who only knows one phase of life." By reporting the whole truth, he believes that he shall prove a better friend to man than Euripides, who shut his eyes to everything but virtue.

Aristophanes' complaints against Euripides are infinite.  Casuistry, hair-splitting, prosiness, meagreness of invention, feebleness of language, monotony, poorness of metres, are among the charges. He is a prig ; he writes bookish odes ; he is immoral, unpractical. But the list is long, and, after all, the justice of charge or defence is not easily determined.

Now, although Euripides and Aristophanes cannot meet on common ground, not all the critics of the latter disparage him.  Into the mouth of Strattis, one of the younger poets of Aristophanes' time, Browning puts a speech full of intelligent appreciation of the Comic Muse, " who evolves superiority, triumph and joy from sorrow, unsuccess, And all that's incomplete in human life."  Out of uncouth body or grotesque soul, fancy, he maintains, uplifted by the Muse, can flit to soul and body, and in the perfect man, thus created, we can see that divergency from type was earth's effect.  By laughter we right man's wrong, reach the fine form, the clear intelligence, and decent law.  Laughter is the attestation of the Muse that the ugly and loathsome are not inevitably man's portion on earth; or if they are, high and fair exist in that ethereal realm where the soul laughs.  The Comic Muse, through Aristophanes, proves that no deformity in man is normal and remediless.  When the deformity is pushed to an extreme, we protest that the opposite somewhere is rule and law.

It is strange, perhaps, that neither young Strattis nor Aristophanes himself makes special reference to the lyrics which, scattered so lavishly through Aristophanes' plays, would of themselves suffice to place him among the great poets of all time.  The choruses of the initiated in 'The Frogs,' the Chorus of the Clouds before they appear upon the stage, the invitation to the

Nightingale, are incomparable in grace and beauty. Nor does Browning dwell as he might on Aristophanes' perfect mastery of his art, shown in his choice of words, in his nice arrangement of rhythms and metres. It is the underlying philosophy, and not the craftsman's skill, to which the Englishman devotes himself in his analysis of Aristophanes. So, too, he has less criticism than might be expected of the coarseness of the Greek, remote as it is from the taste of to-day. His coarseness, like his irreverence, Browning doubtless regards as an accident of the age in which Aristophanes lived, — to be passed over lightly. His strongest condemnation for it he puts into the mouth of Balaustion after she has seen 'Lusistraté.' To her this play was a plague-memory, a pustule to be cured; its bestiality, its loathsomeness, cannot be described ; it seemed all the worse to her because the old comedy was supposed to be acted in the interests of the " Patriot cause, the antique faith, the conservation of true poesy."

In the course of that argument on the night of Euripides' death, Balaustion had challenged Aristophanes. At the end of the discussion, even after the reading of the ' Herakles,' we do not feel that she has wholly proved her case. She has tried to overthrow Aristophanes' claim to prescriptive right in the matter of comedy, and she does not believe with him that comedy is coeval with Hellenic liberty.

> " Why must you comics, one and all, take stand
> On lower ground than truth from first to last."

She plaintively asks, " Have you exchanged brute-blows for human fighting or true god-like force ? Have you tried to attack ignorance and folly by their opposites, knowledge and wisdom ? " and though Aristophanes is driven to answer " no," we still feel that Balaustion, blinded by her admiration for the " tragic para-gon," is unable to comprehend the more subtle philosophy of the high-priest of comedy.

Aristophanes is no pessimist, no cynic ; like Frederick the Great, he towers above his age. His philosophy is not destructive : if he finds fault with worthless citizens, he proposes that the State remedy matters by expelling them. If he blames the Athenians' frivolous love of change, he suggests that new and better leaders might guide them to better things.   At the bottom of his philosophy of poetry lies the notion that the scope of poetry is to make men better.   The other elements of his philosophy are, — his patriotic purpose, his love of truth, his belief that the old is probably better than the new.   Having proposed as his object the restoring of the "Marathonian muscle," having, as his ideal, "work that satisfies," he chooses Comedy, the "Meaner Muse," and crying "Life, Life," avails himself of satire, personalities merciless as witty, of exaggeration, even of grossness and irreverence, to attain his end.   Although Browning is perhaps on the side of Euripides, he is no mere partisan.   His Aristophanes has dignity and force of character, and the philosophy of the witty Greek is wonderfully revealed through the insight of the English poet.

*Helen Leah Reed.*

# IDEALS OF BEAUTY IN KEATS AND BROWNING.*

N treating of ideals of beauty in Keats and Browning, I shall deal less with illustrations from each than with the essential points of difference in the standpoint of idealization occupied by each.

We speak of a poet's "ideals of beauty," but it seems to me that we should express ourselves more accurately to speak of his "ideal of beauties," or, at least, to use the word "ideal" in the singular, seeing that the element of universality is rather in "ideal" than in "beauty."

A poet's ideal of beauty depends upon his standpoint of idealization, or rather upon the power of his intellect to range the various strata of idealization.   The intellectual element in the genius of

• Read before the Browning Society of the New Century Club, Philadelphia, Nov 10, 1892.

poetry, universally considered, is a movable point, capable of describing a mounting and ever-widening spiral, extending upward through the four great strata of the atmosphere of thought; namely, the sensuous, the imaginative, the psychic, the cosmic.

The individual faculty of a Byron is capable of impelling this point to the upper boundary of the sensuous stratum ; of a Keats, to the highest limit of the imaginative ; of a Shelley, to the piercing of the topmost confine of the psychic ; of a Browning, through all of these, out into the sweep of the cosmic verities.

Poetic faculty, individually considered, may be said to exist in three varieties, — the juvenile, the virile, the senile. I need not explain that the rather daring nomenclature I have chosen for these varieties depends not upon the age, the experience, nor the degree of development of the possessor of the faculty, nor upon the times in which he lives, but upon the individual and peculiar character of his powers of mind, — upon what might be called his poetic spirit. Poetic faculty of the juvenile variety manifests itself in the melody of sound and rhythm, in the beautiful as to form, in the portrayal of the softer passions and emotions, in what might be called the picture-making power of the imagination ; the virile variety, in symphonic diapason as to sound and rhythm, in the universal as to form, in the portrayal of the intenser passions and emotions, in the philosophic handling of the imagination ; the senile variety, in the labored monotonies of sound and rhythm, in the stiff-jointed angularities of form, in the portrayal of the petty and drivelling passions and emotions, in that purblind groping as to the imagination in which morbid visions and dreams serve only to mirage eternal truths. The juvenile faculty may exist in all grades, from sentimental mawkishness to exquisite fulness of the joy of life ; the virile, in all grades, from the coarseness of exclusive masculinity of spirit to that delicate balance of masculine and feminine qualities of mind which constitutes the true human ; the senile, in all grades, from the continual mutterings of pettishness and moroseness to that sort of witless babbling that is at best but a ghastly echo of joyousness. That there are poets in whom there is a more or less happy or unhappy mingling of these varieties of faculty, I need not

assert ; nor do I need to add that I would class the faculty of a
Keats under the finest grade of the juvenile, the faculty of a Browning under the finest grade of the virile.

That Keats's poetic faculty manifests itself in the melody of
sound and rhythm, goes without saying ; he revels in onomatopœia
of the most musical sort ; he embodies ideas in melodious sounds.
In every syllable of " The Owl for all his feathers is acold," there is
the gentle rustle of a tiny shiver. Listen to the soundfulness of
" her hollow lute tumultuous." Hear the music in " a voice made
tunable with every sweetest vow." What lullaby could equal that
exquisite apostrophe to sleep, " Bird that broodest o'er the troubled
sea of the mind, till it is hushed and smooth " ! And so might one
quote *ad infinitum.*

That Browning's poetic faculty manifests itself in symphonic
diapason as to sound and rhythm, will probably not go without
saying, — at least not without saying that by symphonic diapason
is meant that basal current of all sound and rhythm which exists
everywhere in nature for him who hath ears to hear, which is not
readily recognizable as musical or rhythmic when considered in itself
alone, which can be fully appreciated only when considered in relation to a whole of which it is a consistent part. This sort of sound
and rhythm cannot be illustrated by a singly quoted line or by a
dozen quoted lines ; it is the swing and harmony of a whole poem ;
it ebbs and flows with the development of the dramatic feeling
which pervades the whole ; it is the Wagnerian principle of musical expression applied to poetic expression. In Browning, therefore, one looks in vain for the onomatopœia which is the adaptation
of sound to isolated sentiment. The informing spirit of Browning's
poetry seems to make its own body as it goes, moulding its sound
and rhythm into conformity to its own soul character. In a word,
Browning's onomatopœia is not the simple adaptation of sound to
sense ; it is the more complex adaptation of sound to soul, — a sort
of adaptation that is coming to be regarded as the highest evolution of genius in poetic composition, as well as in musical
composition.

That Keats's poetic faculty manifests itself in the beautiful as to form, also goes without saying. Keats is the apostle of the gospel of "beauty for beauty's sake." He is the poetic Pygmalion. His poetic form is his Galatea. By virtue of her exquisite perfections the life-blood of poesy flows richly through her veins, but she is without an informing soul.

Browning's gospel is not the gospel of "beauty for beauty's sake;" it does not concern itself with beauty *per se*, either realistic or imaginative. Browning does not build himself an altar to any special cult, and await the descent of the divine fire. The universe is at once his temple and his workshop. His form is universal, because his thought includes macrocosm and microcosm. He is the poetic Prometheus. He appropriates the divine fire to himself for all men, and brings it down to them, so to speak, by assuring them that they as well as he are but tongues of the divine flame, by crying to them, "Behold! the divine fire is within you! Ye are souls! Ye are gods! Makers and forgers of yourselves, co-workers together with the Eternal!"

All poets are, more or less, preachers of the doctrine that "a thing of beauty is a joy forever." The difference in the character of their preaching lies in the difference in their individual power of perception as to what constitutes true beauty. We talk glibly enough about what we call spiritual beauty, and theorize wisely about its standards and proportions; but we are almost as far from that degree of appreciation of spiritual beauty which the Greeks had of physical beauty as the men of the Iron Age were from the point of appreciation to which the Greeks had attained.

The time is coming when beauty, as to the human at least, will mean to us utterly another thing than it does to-day; when the power of individuality shall have so asserted itself over the influences of heredity and of environment that the material — the physical, the outward — shall become, what it is destined to become, the absolute, definite, unmistakable expression of the inward; when we shall be able to see contours of character, over the beauty of which we shall feel a more delightful thrill of admiring joy than the contours of an incarnated Venus or Apollo could give to us to-day; when we shall be able to gaze upon tints of fine emotions which shall be more exquisitely lovely to our entranced vision than any rose of a cheek, or snow of a brow or a throat has ever seemed to us ; when we shall behold the play of moral muscle, the sight of which shall fill us with a greater glow of enthusiasm than the finest feats of physical power have yet been able to rouse in us.

Of the gospel of this sort of beauty Browning, if not the apostle, — seeing that the time is not yet, — is most certainly the prophet, as witness specially in ' James Lee's Wife.' Keats's didacticism, " Beauty is Truth, Truth Beauty," interpreted by this higher conception, Browning would doubtless accept and indorse ; but he would be far from falling in with the added preachment, " This is . . . all ye need to know." He realizes that truth is more than beauty, — taking the latter even in its widest and highest sense, — that truth is even what we call ugliness, since ugliness is only a stage in the evolution of beauty.

The human is divine, and the divine human ; but who would limit the divine to one special phase of the human ? Truth is power, the consistency of continuity, — the beginning, the middle, the end. Truth is the universe, and the universe is truth.

Keats's ' Lamia ' is a sermon consistent with his doctrine. With beauty, that one small current of the life-blood of truth, it teems ; but of that great arterial flow out of the heart of truth which *is* the consistency of continuity, it has but scant supply. Far from being a humanly embodied serpent, ethically or artistically considered, Lamia has all the pleading grace of innocence incarnated. She inspires in Lycius the sort of passion that might be roused by a vestal virgin ; she exercises her powers of sorcery to make earth a fairyland for her beloved. She is the embodiment of innocent sensuousness, and dies a martyr to the cold, death-darting eye of philosophy so called. Compare this picture of the feminine embodiment of the influence of the evils of sense upon masculine humanity with that natural-born woman having the serpent's taint in her blood, — Ottima.

That Keats's poetic faculty manifests itself in the portraying of the softer passions and emotions, needs not to be asserted. His one finished attempt at depicting the intenser and more fervid sort in 'Otho the Great' is almost a travesty. Auranthe is a mario-nette, and Ludolph is a madman from the beginning.

Keats's highest conception of love is limited to the purest passion that can be experienced between two souls of different sex. This passion he deifies. But Browning's mind grasps love as a cosmic essence, and sees individual loves as the various manifestations of this essence only, taking tinge and character from the individualities which are the medium of the manifestation. The variety of these individual manifestations as portrayed by him is almost infinite, ranging all the stages of the evolution of human character, from the merely animal impulse in love to the highest ethical and æsthetical conception of the perfect balance and blending of sex in soul. But Browning does not deify even this highest conception. He worships the cosmic essence ; he is never guilty of the idolatry of bowing down before the manifestation.

That Keats's poetic faculty manifests itself in the picture-making power of the imagination is evidenced in the fact that he enables us to see, almost with the eyes of the sense, that which his imagination reveals to him ; but he is so occupied with demonstrating specially, and almost exclusively, the " truth of beauty," that his life portraitures lack character *chiaro-oscuro.*

Browning's poetic faculty manifests itself in the philosophic handling of the imagination, in that he gives us experiments or demonstrations in the imagination, worked out on the known principles of the inner life, saying to us, " Thus these things are, as you see ; now let us find out how and why they are ; " and though we may not be able to accept his explanations as to how and why they are, we feel, nevertheless, that here is the scientific handling of the imagination ; that here, in a word, is the effort to show us the cosmic verity of the beauty of truth, rather than to demonstrate to us the special verity of the truth of beauty.

Keats uses the imaginative faculty to restore to life that which is dead, and he works the miracle of resuscitating to living beauty a dead myth. Browning concerns himself more with the effort to discover the essential life-current in that which lives ; but when he does touch a dead past, it is not only with resuscitating, but with resurrectionary power, — a power that endues with new life, and other and higher, — as witness specially his handling of the story of Alkestis. In a word, in Keats's hands the gods are seen as ideal human beings ; in Browning's, men are revealed as potential gods.

When we come to compare Keats and Browning as to power of range in the psychic and the cosmic strata of the atmosphere of thought, we find in Keats no traces of even isolated soarings into these rather rarified *Auræ;* while as to Browning, it is here that he seems to be fully at home : he not only soars to these strata, he floats in them as in his native element. From and through them he sees nothing as small, nothing as revolting, nothing as heretical ; all details are intensified to him as such, but they are regarded by him only with reference to universality. Everything that is, has for him the beauty of truth. He, with that prince of rangers through all strata of thought, — Shakespeare, — untrammelled by any Pagan devotion to "beauty for beauty's sake," can revel in the detailed portrayal of a Caliban, — wonderful Caliban, — in whom, as portrayed by Shakespeare, are epitomized all the sufferings and deprivations, the ambitions and aspirations, of the merely animal human ; in whom, as portrayed by Browning, are embodied all the elements of the unconscious evolutionist, feeling, however blindly, that he has the universe to his father, and finding out this universe through the interpretation of his own individuality.

And so is it ever with all that these cosmic thinkers touch. Their thought, starting with a germ of the special, expands inevitably and spontaneously into the universal. Thus a Shakespeare depicts the ardent heart of a Juliet appropriating the heavens and the earth as theatre of her own little drama of love, reveals the brain of a young Lorenzo as lifting the sense reception of sweet sound into the cosmic conception of the harmony of the spheres. Thus a Browning pictures for us the reflection in the limpid soul of a Pippa of the spirit of God moving upon the face of the deep in his moral cosmos, — paints for us, in the creative genius of an Abt Vogler, the mirroring of the creative faculty of the all-creating Eternal Energy.                                             *Alice Groff.*

# GENTLE WILL, OUR FELLOW.

WRIT IN 1626 A. D. BY JOHN HEMINGE, SERVANT OF HIS GRACIOUS
MAJESTY KING CHARLES I. ; EDITED IN 1892 A. D. AS " ALL,
THOUGH FEIGNED, IS TRUE " BY F. G. FLEAY, SERVANT OF ALL
SHAKESPEARIAN STUDENTS IN AMERICA, ENGLAND, GERMANY, OR
ELSEWHERE.

*(Continued.)*

ARLY in 1599 we opened our new theatre on the Bank-side, called the Globe. It was builded out of the stuff of the old Theater, which had been removed by the Burbadges to the new site. There was a sign of Hercules bearing the Globe, with the motto, *Totus mundus agit histrionem ;* or, as Shakespeare hath it, " All the world is a stage, the men and women merely players," to which our poets were fond to allude.

The first plays of Shakespeare that we there acted were ' Henry V.,' in which he ended his Falstaff histories, ' Sir John Falstaff and the Merry Wives of Windsor,' and ' As You Like It.' I mention ' Henry V.' first, because this play was a continuation of the preceding plays on Henry IV., with which they all together form a trilogy after the manner of the ancient Greeks, to which ' Richard II.' serves as an introduction. In ' The Merry Wives ' Falstaff was again revived by the command of the Queen, who gave Shakespeare the difficult task of writing love passages for him. This play was founded on the old ' Jealous Comedy,' which we had played at the Rose eight years before, some parts of which may still be read in the stolen, imperfect copy printed in quarto. Encouraged by Her Majesty's order, which showed plainly that she retained no anger for the late offence in bringing Oldcastle on the stage, Shakespeare introduced one Robert Shallow, justice of the peace, as bearing the Lucy arms, and even had the boldness to recall the memory of the complaint which Lord Cobham had made against us, by making Ford, the jealous man, assume the name of Brooke. This was, however, altered afterward to Broome. ' As You Like It,' founded on the prose story of ' Rosalind, or Euphues' Legacy,' by Dr. Lodge, was, in the opinion of many, the most perfect instance of a Pastoral Comedy that has been seen on any stage.

After this, in the year 1600, Shakespeare, having brought to an end his English Chronicle plays, began to do for Plutarch what he had done for Holinshed, and wrote his ' Julius Cæsar.' This play, which, as lately published, contains both Cæsar's Tragedy and Cæsar's Revenge, is not in all parts the same as at first acted; one line in particular, " Cæsar did never wrong but with just cause," had offended the criticasters, who cried mew at it; and Jonson, last year, in his ' Staple of News,' held it up to ridicule on our own stage, which, methinks, was hardly fair to the dead poet or to us, seeing that we had printed the altered version in accordance with the wishes of Master Jonson himself.

This murder and revenge play offers a striking instance of that fashion, the continual changes whereof are so mischievous to our quality. Master Heywood hath spoken of the decline of rhyming plays. " There was a time," saith he, " strong lines were not looked after, but if rhyme, O, then 't was excellent ! " Dumb shows and Inductions have in like manner had their day ; Prologues and Epilogues have come into fashion, and now there are signs that movable scenes and such machines as they use in masks will be some day looked for on the common stages. I pray that this may never be in my time. When it shall come, if it come at all, the scene-painter and the upholsterer will stand between the poet and his audience, and well-nigh obscure him from view. But fashion is a strange thing, and not easy to understand. Just at this time the town would have revenge plays in couplets. At the Fortune, which had lately been builded for Ned Alleyn and his company, they acted, soon after, two Danish plays on Hoffmann, a tragedy and a revenge ; and at the very same time that we presented ' Cæsar,' the Paul's boys, who had just reopened the Whitefriars playing-place, were acting ' Antonio and Mellida,' by Marston, and the Chapel boys at Blackfriars the old play on 'Jeronymo,' by Kyd ; in both cases alike a tragedy and a revenge play. On every stage "Vindicta" was the cry.

Ben Jonson did not remain long with us at the Globe. One play he wrote for us, ' Every Man out of his Humour;' but this, unlike his earlier play, which was a true Comedy, was the first of his Comical Satires, in which he brought on the stage living men in feigned characters, especially, as he afterward acknowledged, actors and poets, — Marston, Dekker, Daniel, a relation of the Burbadges, and others. This was a thing not to be endured. Shakespeare would not act in it; and as Kempe, Duke, Beeston, and Pallant, who were among our best actors, had left us when we left the Curtain, and had joined my Lord Pembroke's men, who were now travelling, we were hard put to it to act the play at all. The mislike grew to such a hand that Jonson left us and joined the Chapel children at Blackfriars, where, during the two next years, he wrote two more Comical Satires, ' Cynthia's Revels ' and ' The Poetaster.' As we took scarce any share in this three years' stage war, I forbear to say more about it in this place; but I shall have to come at it again hereafter. But although Jonson had left us, we still had some ado with him. In February, 1600, we printed his ' Every Man in his Humour,' according to the copy we had from him ; and in the next year he refashioned this Comedy for the Chapel boys, and they acted it, with a prologue in which Monsieur Mew vented his sarcasms on the Choruses in ' Henry V.,' that " waft you o'er the seas," and on the " long jars of York and Lancaster " in the old plays of the ' Contention,' which we had re-formed and restored as the second and third parts of ' Henry VI.,' these making, with the first part, which had long been ours, one continued history from Richard II. to Richard III.

These ' Henry VI.' plays had been plotted by Marlowe, who had been aided in writing them by Greene, Peele, and Lodge, in the first and second parts, which were originally acted by the Queen's men ; but the third part, which was acted by Lord Pembroke's, was from his hand only. Stolen copies of the ' Contention,' as it was acted when they travelled, had been five years in print, but nothing near so complete as we acted it after it had been corrected by Shakespeare. Nevertheless, directly we brought it on the stage, its then possessor printed it again in its imperfect shape, and until our late Folio it never appeared in print in its full form.

To come back to Jonson's play: in his renovation of 'Every Man in his Humour' he shifted his scene to England, and replaced all his Italianate names by English ones, and made many other improvements, as may be seen in the author's own copy imprinted in Folio, in 1616, in his 'Works.' But the reader must not be misled into supposing that we acted the play in that manner. The list of our actors at the end is that of its first performance in its Italian guise. About the same time that Jonson altered this play he also gave these Chapel boys the play of 'Jeronymo,' of which, having acted in it with us at the Curtain, he had retained a copy. We took our revenge for this some years after.

This year was a great publishing year with us, so much more important than any other in Shakespeare's time that I deem it worth while to set forth the dates particularly. On Nov. 15, 1599, was entered, for Aspley, in the Stationer's Registers, 'A Warning for Fair Women;' on April 8, 1600, for Holme, 'Every Man out of his Humour;' on May 27, for Roberts, 'Cloth Breeches and Velvet Hose;' on May 29, also for Roberts, 'An Alarum for London.' But these two had not our authority, and we procured them to be stayed; the 'Cloth Breeches' was accordingly not printed, and the 'Alarum' came not to the press until it was published by Ferhard in 1602. On Aug. 4, 1600, 'Every Man in his Humour,' 'Much Ado about Nothing,' 'As You Like It,' and 'Henry V.' were also stayed, we not having given authority for them; but on August 14 we consented to the entry of 'Every Man in his Humour,' for Busby and Burre, and to the setting over of 'Henry V.' from Millington and Busby to Pavier. This last copy was very imperfect, being greatly mutilated for the necessities of the stage, and nothing near so full as that in our late Folio. On August 23 'Much Ado' was entered, along with '2 Henry,' for Wise and Aspley; but 'As You Like It' was not then printed; we preferred to retain it in our hands. On October 8, for Fisher, was entered 'A Midsummer Night's Dream,' and on October 23, for Hayes, 'The Merchant of Venice.' Copies of these two had also been printed by Roberts, who had entered the latter one in 1598. But we had stayed it, just as we did the 'Cloth Breeches' and the 'Alarum;' and although when Hayes and Fisher had obtained our authority, we made no demur to their selling the copies already imprinted by Roberts, which differed only slightly from the true copies, still I can but set down my aversion to this man, who in all dealings with our stage was knavish and arrantly deceitful. We never discovered by whom his surreptitious copies were supplied to him ; but he caused us trouble in this way up to the accession of the late King James.

(To be continued.)

*F. G. Fleay.*

## BROWNING'S MASTERY OF RHYME.*

BROWNING is unquestionably a great master of rhyme. Mr. Arthur Symons does not go too far in saying in his comments on the poet's metre and versification : " In one very important matter, that of rhyme, he is perhaps the greatest master in our language; in single and double, in simple and grotesque alike, he succeeds in fitting rhyme to rhyme with a perfection which I have never found in any other poet of any age."

This mastery of rhyme is shown, in the first place, by the fact that he rarely, if ever, violates the law which, as Sidney Lanier puts it, " forbids the least intrusion of the rhyme as rhyme, — that is, as anything less than the best word in the language for the idea in hand." George Gascoigne expressed it more quaintly three centuries and a half ago : " I would exhorte you also to beware of rime without reason : my meaning is hereby that your rime leade you not from your firste Invention, for many wryters when they have laid the platform of their invention, are yet drawen sometimes (by rime) to forget it or at least to alter it, as when they cannot readily finde out a worde which maye rime to the first . . they do then eyther botche it up with a worde that will rime (howe small reason soever it carie with it) or els they alter their first worde and so percase decline or trouble their former Invention : But do you alwayes hold your first determined Invention, and do

---

* Read before the Boston Browning Society, Feb. 28, 1893.

rather searche the bottome of your braynes for apte words, than change good reason for rambling rime." It is seldom, if ever (except in cases of which I shall speak further on, where elaborately fantastic effects in rhyme are purposely introduced to surprise and amuse us), that Browning seems driven to use a word for the rhyme which he would not use for the sense. His words are such as he needs to express his meaning, and no more than he needs : there is no weakening of the sense, and no padding out of the verse. Even so accomplished an artist as Tennyson is not entirely free from this latter fault, though we seldom find so palpable an illustration of it as in ' The Talking Oak,' where the loquacious veteran of the forest says : —

> "I swear by leaf, and wind, and rain
> (*And hear me with thine ears*),
> That tho' I circle in the grain
> Five hundred rings of years " — etc.

That line, " And hear me with thine ears," is the most flagrant instance of padding for the sake of rhyme in all Tennyson's works. It would be difficult to match it in any reputable verse.[*]

---

[*] Poets who thus pad out their verses for the sake of rhyme might well print the superfluous matter in italics, as a humble New Hampshire bard has done. I am the fortunate owner of a little volume entitled ' Farmer's Meditations, or Shepherd's Songs, by Thomas Randall, a Resident of Eaton, N. H.' (Limerick, Me., 1833.) In a poem on the birds, this couplet occurs (the italics are in the original) : —

> "Their language was charming, 't was lovely and true;
> Each sound was delightful, *and plain to the view*."

The following is from an elegy ' On the Sudden Death of John Hern ' : —

> "That voice that so often has thrilled on the ear,
> By the call of his dog, *and the grasp of his gun*,
> Those limbs, not oft weary, nor startled with fear,
> Are cold now in death, and his voice is undone."

This is from ' Jesus Christ, the King of Kings ' : —

> " May Europe (*now in foreign lands*)
> Soon burst *their* heathen, slavish bands."

The italics in *their* are apparently introduced (as in sundry other places in the book) on account of the liberty taken with the grammatical construction.

A stanza in verses ' On the Loss of Parents ' is printed thus : —

> " Their sleep or slumber we deplore —
> If sleep — *why do they never snore !*
> Or turn or stir within their cell,
> And prove to us that all is well ? "

Browning's masterly ease in rhyming is also shown in the remarkable variety of his stanza-forms. He has more of them than any other English poet, early or recent; and in not a few of them the rhyme-structure is more or less complex and difficult. 'Through the Metidja' is an extraordinary *tour de force* in this respect, a single rhyme being carried through the forty lines. The repetition of "As I ride, as I ride," is counterbalanced by the "internal rhymes," so-called, — "Who dares chide my heart's pride," "Do I glide, unespied," etc.,— introduced in ten of the lines. There are thirty-six rhyming words in all, and *ride* is the only one repeated. In the 'Lover's Quarrel' we have twenty-two seven-line stanzas, with but two rhymes in each, one being carried through *five* lines out of the seven. In 'Childe Roland' there are thirty-four six-line stanzas, with two rhymes in each subtly interlaced. Five-line stanzas appear to have been favorites with the poet for about forty years of his career, — from the period of 'Men and Women,' written between 1850 and 1855, to 'Asolando,' the latter volume containing five examples with three variations in metrical form. In 'Dîs Aliter Visum' a peculiar and difficult internal rhyme (a single syllable between the rhyming words) occurs in each of the thirty stanzas: "Is that all true? I *say*, the *day*," "That I have seen her, *walked* and *talked*," "O'er the lone stone fence, *let* me *get*," etc. These rhymes come in so naturally that we should not recognize them as intentional in one case out of seven, unless our attention had been called to the metrical structure.

Again, this mastery of rhyme is shown by the frequency and facility of rhyming in what the recent Shakespeare critics call "run-on lines" in distinction from "end-stopt lines," the former having no natural break or pause at the end as the latter have. In Pope and the poets of his school we may say that the lines are *all* "end-stopt," the exceptions being too few to be worth noting. You may look through page after page of Pope's heroic couplets without finding a line that has not a comma or some larger stop at the end. It is this enforced pause at the end of each line, with the rare variations in the "cæsura," or enforced pause in the middle of the line, that makes these "classic" compositions so tiresome to our modern ears, accustomed to more varied rhythmical effects. We soon weary of the monotonous jog-trot of the "faultily fault-less" iambics and the perpetual recurrence of the obtrusive rhymes, their jingle forced upon our attention by the necessary pause after each. We can endure it for a hundred lines or so, but when it goes on for thousand after thousand, as in Pope's 'Iliad,' — aptly so known in popular parlance, for it is not Homer's 'Iliad,' — we cry with Macbeth : —

> "What, will the *line* stretch out to the crack of doom ?
>  . . . I 'll see no more ! "

Whether rhyme is doomed to disappear from our poetry, as a device suited only to tickle the ear in the childhood of poetical cul-ture, — discarded with growing taste, as the child throws away the baby rattle, — I will not venture to say ; but these heroic rhymes, so popular in an age that reckoned nothing "classical" that was not pedantically formal and artificial, have certainly had their day, — at least for long poems, or until another Browning appears. He has revived and revolutionized the heroic couplet, his amazing command of rhyme and of the more refined harmonies of rhythm enabling him to get exquisite music out of this old-fashioned jingle and jog-trot, and to continue it indefinitely without tiring us. Whatever we may think of 'Sordello' in other respects, we must admit that it is a masterpiece of rhymed measure. The "run-on" lines are so frequent that we hardly notice that they are arranged in heroic couplets. In Pope, as I have said, there is a point and a pause at the end of nearly every line; here not one line in seven is thus marked off. A person not familiar with the poem might lis-ten to long passages read with proper emphasis and expression, and take them for blank verse. The same is true of shorter poems in the same measure. Take, for example, at random a passage from 'My Lost Duchess' · —

> "Sir 't was not
> Her husband's presence only, called that spot
> Of joy into the Duchess' cheek : perhaps
> Frà Pandolf chanced to say 'Her mantle laps

34

> Over my lady's wrist too much,' or ' Paint
> Must never hope to reproduce the faint
> Half-flush that dies along her throat : ' such stuff
> Was courtesy, she thought, and cause enough
> For calling up that spot of joy.  She had
> A heart — how shall I say ? — too soon made glad,
> Too easily impressed ; she liked whate'er
> She looked on, and her looks went everywhere."

In many of the poems in other measures, the rhyme is similarly obscured by the " run-on " lines, though they are much shorter. Take this stanza from ' Count Gismond,' for example : —

> " Till out strode Gismond ; then I knew
>     That I was saved.   I never met
> His face before, but, at first view,
>     I felt quite sure that God had set
> Himself to Satan ; who would spend
> A minute's mistrust on the end ? "

Or this from ' In a Year,' where the lines are shorter yet : —

> " Was it something said,
>     Something done,
> Vexed him ? was it touch of hand,
>     Turn of head?
> Strange I that very way
>     Love begun :
> I as little understand
>     Love's decay."

In the following passage from ' Easter Day,' the octosyllabic couplets of which run so easily into jingle, we have eight successive lines with no pause at the end : —

> " And as I said
> This nonsense, throwing back my head
> With light complacent laugh, I found
> Suddenly all the midnight round
> One fire.   The dome of heaven had stood
> As made up of a multitude
> Of handbreadth cloudlets, one vast rack
> Of ripples infinite and black,
> From sky to sky.   Sudden there went,
> Like horror and astonishment,
> A fierce vindictive scribble of red
> Quick flame across, as if one said
> (The angry scribe of Judgment) ' There —
> Burn it ! ' "

If anybody thinks this kind of rhyming is easy, let him try it. In the average verse of the day you will find the lines almost invariably " end-stopt." The ordinary newspaper rhymer seldom gets beyond that elementary form of his art.

Browning uses the " end-stopt " form only when the effect of the rhyme as rhyme is to be brought out, in addition to that of the metre or rhythm ; as in ' Through the Metidja,' and in that finer because less artificial horse-poem, ' How They Brought the Good News,' also in the ' Cavalier Songs' and other songs, and in many of the humorous poems.

Certain critics have told us that Browning has many faulty rhymes, and a careless reader might easily get this impression ; but the fact is that his percentage of such rhymes is smaller than in the average of our best poets.  Miss Elizabeth M. Clark has furnished mathematical proof of this in her very interesting paper entitled, ' A Study of Browning's Rhymes,' in the second volume of POET-LORE.  She has found, by actual count, that in the 1096 pages of rhymed verse in the " Riverside Edition " (about two fifths of all Browning's poetry, the unrhymed filling 1572 pages), there are 34,746 rhymes, of which only 322 are bad, being either imperfect or forced, or both.  This is less than one per cent, or one in a hundred.  The list does not include " eye-rhymes," so-called, such as all poets — unfortunately, in my humble opinion — admit ; like *dull* and *full, lone* and *gone, saith* and *faith*, etc.  Of these I am inclined to think Browning has fewer than the average in standard poetry.  A recent British writer, Mr. Joseph Jacobs,* puts it in my power to compare the proportion of Browning's bad rhymes with Tennyson's, — at least with those of ' In Memoriam.'  He finds in that poem 168 bad rhymes in 1448, or somewhat more than eleven per cent.  He gives a list of these 168 bad rhymes, as he regards them ; but on examining it I find that it includes many " eye-rhymes " (*move, love ; most, lost ; moods, woods ; hearth, earth*, etc.), and certain others that are used by the poets generally, — even such unexceptionable rhymes as

* ' Tennyson and In Memoriam,' by Joseph Jacobs (London, 1892).

*again, men ; hour, flower ; fair, prayer ; view, do ; fire, higher*, etc.
By striking out such as these the list is reduced to 48, or three per
cent, and might perhaps be cut down to about two per cent. The
worst of those that are left are *mourn, urn ; curse, horse; put,
short ; one, alone ; Lord, guard*, and *I, enjoy*.

Miss Clark does not give a list of the rhymes she reckons bad
(it is a pity that she does not, as it would occupy little space if
printed in compact form), but I presume that most of them are the
fantastic double and triple rhymes which occur in a comparatively
small number of the poems. As a little experiment of my own,
with a view to a fairer comparison with Tennyson, I have examined
about a thousand lines of Browning's serious verse, taking the pieces
as they come in my ' Select Poems of Browning ': 'Hervé Riel,'
' Clive,' ' How They Brought the Good News,' etc., ' The Lost
Leader,' ' Rabbi Ben Ezra,' ' Childe Roland,' ' The Boy and the
Angel,' ' Prospice,' ' A Wall,' and ' My Star,' — the last three short
poems being taken, out of the regular order, to make 1000 lines, —
and, throwing out the unrhymed lines in ' The Lost Leader,' there
are exactly 1000.* In the five hundred rhymes there are only
fifteen (or three per cent) that are in any degree bad, and fully two
thirds of these are "eye-rhymes," like *watch, catch ; mass, pass ;
word, afford ; shone* (sometimes pronounced *shŏn*), *gone*, etc. The
worst are *quiescence, presence ; light, infinite ; comes, glooms ; dunce,
nonce*, — on the whole, not so bad as the worst I have cited from
' In Memoriam.'

Miss Clark considers that all of Browning's imperfect or forced
rhymes occur in these three cases : —

" First, when rough, uneducated characters speak for themselves ; second, when Browning is speaking about or describing
such characters ; third, when he is speaking in his own person,
evidently or apparently for himself." A simpler statement would
be that these rhymes occur in poems or passages that are more or
less sportive, familiar, or free-and-easy in style. As I have said,
they are generally double or triple rhymes, and as Professor Corson

---

* I will not vouch for the absolute accuracy of my counting, not having gone over it a second time ; but
I think it will be found correct, or nearly so.

remarks in his excellent ' Primer of English Verse,' the emphasis of such rhymes is "too pronounced for serious verse." He illustrates this by extracts from Byron's ' Don Juan,' showing "the part played by the double and triple rhymes in indicating the lowering of the poetic key, — the reduction of true poetic seriousness."

Of course, as Professor Corson adds, it must not be inferred that this is the *peculiar* function of such rhymes.   "They may serve to emphasize the serious as well as the jocose; " as in Mrs. Browning's ' Cowper's Grave.'   The triple rhymes in Hood's ' Bridge of Sighs,' he thinks, "serve as a most effective foil to the melancholy theme," and are "not unlike the laughter of frenzied grief." I cannot agree with him here.   To me there is nothing suggestive of laughter, or of frenzied grief, in

> " One more unfortunate
> Weary of breath,
> Rashly importunate,
> Gone to her death ! "

The strain is rather that of tenderest sympathy and pity.* The triple rhymes are in keeping with the dactylic measure, and are not markedly obtrusive. This dactylic measure, seldom used by our poets, is suited to most opposite effects, — as in this poem contrasted with Tennyson's ' Charge of the Light Brigade,' or Longfellow's ' Skeleton in Armor.'

Similarly, double rhymes are used with fine effect by Browning as by other poets in serious poems in *trochaic* measure, especially lyrical poems ; as in the exquisite song in ' The Blot in the 'Scutcheon,' ' There 's a woman like a dewdrop.'   And this measure, like the dactylic, may be vigorous and stirring, or soft and lulling, or meditative and mournful.

In lighter pieces, like ' The Glove ' and ' The Flight of the Duchess,' the effect of the double and triple rhymes is in keeping with the free-and-easy style of the narration.   In ' The Glove,' as Mr. Arthur Symons remarks in his ' Introduction to Browning,'

---

* It will be remembered that the speaker is not supposed to be a parent or near relative of the hapless girl, but a stranger who is interested in her fate only as illustrating one phase of the lot of womanhood in the great city.

"it is worth noticing that in the lines spoken by the lady to Ronsard, and in these alone, the double rhymes are replaced by single ones, thus making a distinct severance between the earnestness of this one passage and the cynical wit of the rest." The critic might have pointed out a similar change to single rhymes in the gypsy's chant in 'The Flight of the Duchess.' The change, indeed, begins some ten lines before the chant, as if to prepare for it, — or rather, as occasionally in other parts of the poem, it indicates the transition to a slightly more serious vein in the old huntsman's talk.

'Pacchiarotto' seems to me little else than an illustration of the poet's mastery of rhyme " run mad." As Mr. Symons says, it is " a whimsical freak of verse, an extravaganza in staccato," and " almost incomparable as a sustained effort in double and triple grotesque rhymes." We may allow ourselves to be amused by it as a piece of boy's play, but, for myself, I must confess that I rather tire of it before it is over. Let us be thankful that our poet only now and then gave way to such rhyming foolery.

*W. F. Rolfe.*

## BROWNING'S MILDRED.

THE erring and unhappy Mildred Tresham is, with the exception of the pale and gracious Pompilia, the most fascinating and interesting of all Browning's women. I am not sure that to us, as English, her sad history is not more touching than even the sorrows of the fair Italian wife. Her story is more direct and homelike in its telling, her surroundings are more familiar.

'The Blot in the 'Scutcheon' is the most actable, if not the only really stage-worthy of Browning's plays. It possesses the elements of all successful plays. It has force, directness, conciseness, abundance of stir and action, a plot that is easily understandable, a motive that can be felt by all. The doom that follows sin, and of which the cloud appears at the outset, hangs over the chief actors like a visible Fate ; and we watch it gathering and increasing in density until it breaks in the final tempest of tragedy. Our interest in the unhappy love-story is excited at once, and never flags. Our emotions, as we follow the reckless, love-blinded course of the young English girl and her lover, are painfully keen; and pity, sorrow, and admiration fight within us for the mastery.

The date and country of the action are well chosen. We have to deal, not with the love and sorrows of remote and shadowy historical personages, nor yet with the manners of Venetian or Florentine nobles and their intrigues. The date is sufficiently modern, yet not too modern, for it is a "costume play," and so gives scope for effective grouping and the pictorial use of color; and the story and the place are English. It is the tale of the ruin of an English noble house, of the shattering of its family honor, cherished above all things, by the fault of an erring and beautiful member of that house. The conservative English mind, proud of the great families of the land, always interested in their fate and history, admiring the worship of family honor, keenly alive to the progress of any struggle between love and duty, ready to understand, even while it regrets, the excesses to which a too quixotic reverence for the purity of birth and lineage leads its devotees, is certain to be profoundly impressed by the tragedy of 'The Blot in the 'Scutcheon.'

It has been my good fortune to see this play acted, — not at that period of ancient history on the first occasion of its being put on the boards, in 1846. It almost causes one a futile regret that one was not born earlier, — even with the penalty of being older now, — when one reads that Macready and Helen Faucit lent their genius to this play on that representation of it. It was upon its last representation that I was present when the honored poet to whom we owe this beautiful play was among the audience, a living man, and not, as now, a memory and a regret. I brought with me to its representation an experience of acting-plays and a knowledge of the requirements of the stage and of play-goers, gathered from a rather close connection, at one time of my life, with side-scenes and *coulisses*, and the "omnibus box" of the front, and the critical stool of an editor's den; and this play more than satisfied me. It seemed to me to be just the tragedy of English life that ought to be the making of a theatre's fortunes, that should command a " run," — a *furore* even. But the modern English play-goer is too much concerned with burlesque and " spectacle, " the absurdities of comic opera, the sparkling ripple of fantastic melodies, and the turning out of feminine toes. However, there are many of us left who can thoroughly relish a pathetic play of the calibre of ' The Blot in the 'Scutcheon,' and it is a pity we do not often get the chance of doing so.

The main interest of the ' Blot' centres in Mildred. Her sorrows and her beauty capture our hearts at once.

> " If to her lot some human errors fall —
> Look in her face — and you 'll forgive them all."

Though as *patres familias* and discreet devotees of the admirable Madame Grundy, we may loudly censure this foolish girl, yet as men — she is secure of a snug corner in our hearts !

There are many persons not professedly Browning students, who would not have patience or courage enough for ' Fifine at the Fair' or ' The Inn Album,' and who would not be able to go through the four volumes of ' The Ring and the Book' even for the sake of the sweet Pompilia-kernel they contain, who yet know and admire this devoted, naughty, delicious Mildred. My friend Bloxham, Q. C., whose experience of law courts is " extensive and peculiar," and who has a profound knowledge of the female human character as exhibited therein, is rather hard upon Mildred. He says that he is not quite misled by that guilty-innocence of hers, and that her constant pathetic reiteration of the half-excuse, " I was so young; I had no mother," does not altogether exculpate her in his eyes. Bloxham, however, is hard.

We may, however, whisper to ourselves, undeterred by the spectacle of this girl's beauty and sorrows, that there really seems something wrong with her moral fibre. She is too much the slave of the impulses of young blood. She is too sensuous, — not to say sensual. There appears to be no restraining force of conscience within her, no sufficient sense of moral obligation, which in a young English gentlewoman is somewhat to be wondered at. May we fairly

set this down to the want of a mother's care and the absence of all
due feminine training just at the time it was most needed? Or
was it a case of heredity? Is it possible that some strain in her
ancestry was bearing fruit in her? The taint may have come
through the Treshams, a hot-blooded and fiery race, no doubt; and
what, as the world judges, is excusable in a man becomes, in a
woman, unpardonable. She seems to lack the innate purity which
most young girls, certainly girls born in her station, seem to possess, and which we should look for in her. Her brother had an
overstrained sense of the family honor; had Nature none to spare
for her? When her remorse comes, and it comes with a flash, we
are reconciled with her; and yet we seem sorry to note that a good
deal of her trouble seems to be that the days of courting and sinning are over! This is, of course, before the full horror of remorse
takes possession of her; and what we like best in her despair
and her hatred of herself, is her disbelief in· any happiness to be,
though her brother has promised that she shall marry the desired
of her heart, — the possessor, alas! of herself. This is a redeeming
point about her. Had she — as a common woman might — ignored
the past sin, and revelled in the fact that it was condoned and that
marriage would heal the wound in her honor, we could not have
loved her; we should have been very near to despising her. It is
a good thing about her that she has moments of yearning, as a pure
girl might, for the innocent courtship which is now impossible; she
feels how soiled her young life is, feels all she has lost and put away
from her forever: —

> " Then, no sweet courtship-days,
> No dawning consciousness of love for us,
> No strange and palpitating births of sense
> From words and looks, no innocent fears and hopes,
> Reserves and confidences: *morning's over!* "

Yet the worst thing about it all is that we are driven to feel that
she would have gone on sinning still had there been no *discovery!*
Her remorse attains its full proportions only when all is found out,
and she and her foolish boy-lover see the terrible mistake they have
made. Does not Fag, in 'The Rivals,' tell the naked truth about

35

a good deal of human repentance? Says he: "I would not scrupl
to tell a lie to serve my master, but — *it hurts one's conscience to b
found out!*" Mildred and her young lover make use of the pl
of youth as an excuse for what, surely, people in their station mus
have known to be shamefully wrong. We hear his excuse: —

> " I was scarce a boy — e'en now
> What am I more? And you were infantine
> When first I met you; why, your hair fell loose
> On either side! My fool's-cheek reddens now
> Only in the recalling how it burned
> That morn to see the shape of many a dream."

Not such a very innocent boy this. He needed a tutor, and Mil
dred a strong duenna-governess, to keep them straight!

The lover makes himself out a much more ignorant boy than lad
of his presumed age usually are, — certainly nowadays. He say
of Mildred, and to her: —

> " If you
> Accorded gifts and knew not they were gifts —
> If I grew mad at last with enterprise
> And must behold my beauty in her bower
> Or perish — *I was ignorant of even
> My own desires.*"

This we can't believe. He had been dreaming of her, we know,
from his own words; but he goes on: —

> "What then were you? If sorrow —
> Sin — if the end came — must I now renounce
> My reason?"

There is a wonderful force and exquisite pathos in poor Mildred's
frenzied inquiry of her lover when her conscience is fully roused,
and the horror of having been utterly base stares her in the face:

> "Or, Henry I'll not wrong you — you believe
> That I was *ignorant.* I scarce grieve o'er
> The past! We'll love on; you will love me still."

We are sorry to hear these words, — so seemingly inconsistent with
repentance, — " I scarce grieve o'er the past." It is of a piece perhaps with the dying man's reflections: —

> " How sad and mad and bad it was
> And yet — how it was sweet!"

These are the little things, anxious as we are to do justice to poor Mildred and to deal very leniently with her, that forbid us to take her entirely to our hearts. Had she no training in feminine ways at all? Girls of her rank, even when losing their mothers, are seldom left without female influence and female warnings. She had friends, though no mother, and, one would think, could hardly, girl as she was, have been utterly ignorant of the distinction between right and wrong!

It is a noteworthy fact, moreover, that actually after she had by conscience been made to understand the shameful folly she had been guilty of, she makes no great struggle to break loose from the bonds of her sin and folly. On the contrary, she sets her signal-light in the purple pane of the window, as usual, in order that her paramour might come to her. It is probable that her infatuation and passion were too strong for her.

It seems rather wonderful that Mildred, closely associated with her brother as she had been, had not caught from him some of that acute sense of family pride, and respect for the family honor, with which he was filled. She must have had many opportunities of learning such a lesson from his bearing and conversation, but brothers' precepts are of small avail when love is kindled, and the lover appears!

Her fault was yet the fault of human nature, in gentle or simple. How terrible are her reflections when she realizes to what she has reduced herself, and to what lying conduct in the presence of friends and equals she is hopelessly pledged thenceforth. Herein is the voice of true tragedy : —

> " Have I received in presence of them all
> The partner of my guilty love — with brow
> Trying to *seem a maiden's brow* — with lips
> Which make believe that when they strive to form
> Replies to you and tremble as they strive, —
> It is the nearest ever they approached
> A stranger — Henry, yours' that stranger's — lip —
> With cheek that looks a virgin's and that is — I "

Here the horror of the whole situation chokes her utterance. Again, how very bitter her agony must have been when she cries : —

> ". . . my spirit yearns to purge
> Her stains off in the fierce renewing fire :
> But do not plunge me into other guilt !
> Oh, guilt enough !  I cannot tell his name."

Here she saves her lover's honor, as she thinks, poor child, in the midst of her own misery.  She was wrong.  It would have been better for her and for all, had she made her confession perfect.

Then comes her wild cry, as from the depths of despair, and in our pity we forget all her foolish ways and her real sins.  Who could see her, young, beautiful, despairing, and steel his heart against her as she says : —

> "I was so young, I loved him so, I had
> No mother, God forgot me, — and I fell.
> No — I cannot weep.
> No more tears from this brain — no sleep — no tears !"

Worthy this of Shakespeare's utterance, of which it seems an echo, — " Sleep no more.  Macbeth hath murdered sleep — the innocent sleep !"

For Mildred there was no possible future ; there was no healing so bruised a young heart: there was her own life soiled and despised, her honor shattered, her lover slain, her brother his slayer and her avenger.  There was for her only death — and death came.

So ends the short life-drama of Mildred Tresham ; and we leave it, if with a profound sadness, yet with a sense of right and of expiation.  Our chief pity should be for the poor brother and for his ruined hopes, who sinks away from life in the cloud of family shame.

It seems to me that ' The Blot in the 'Scutcheon' must be held to be the finest acting-tragedy of modern days.  It equals in force and pathos, and in the sense of cumulative doom, the wonderful ' Broken Heart ' of John Ford.  But the verse of Ford cannot be compared to the fervor and fire of Browning's.

*J. J. Britton.*

# THE SIGHTLESS.

## By Maurice Maeterlinck.

### (Continued.)

*Second Man.* Don't let us trouble ourselves uselessly ; he will soon return. Let us wait, then ; but we shall not go out with him any more in future.

*Oldest Man.* We cannot go out alone !

*First Man.* We shall not go out any more. I like better not to go out.

*Second Man.* We had no desire to go out; nobody asked him to go.

*Oldest Man.* It was a holiday in the island ; we always go out on great occasions.

*Third Man.* He came and struck me on the shoulder while I was still asleep, saying to me, " Get up, get up! it is time; there is sunlight! " Is there any ? I do not perceive it. I have never seen the sun.

*Oldest Man.* I saw the sun when I was very young.

*Oldest Woman.* I also, a long time ago, when I was a child; but I scarcely remember it any longer.

*Third Man.* Why does he wish us to go out every time there is sunlight? Who is there who observes anything? I never know whether I am walking at noon or at midnight.

*Sixth Man.* I prefer to go out at noon. I have a suspicion then of the great brightness, and my eyes make great efforts to open.

*Third Man.* I prefer to remain in the refectory, by the side of the coal-fire ; there was a fine fire this morning.

*Second Man.* He could lead us into the sunlight in the court ; one is under the shelter of the walls, and cannot get out. There is nothing to fear when the gate is shut ; I always shut it. Why do you touch me on the left elbow ?

*First Man.* I did not touch you ; I cannot reach you.

*Second Man.* I tell you that some one touched my elbow !

*First Man.* It wasn't any of us.

*Second Man.* I should like to go away.

*Oldest Woman.* My God! My God! tell us, then, where we are!

*First Man.* We cannot wait forever. [*A clock far off strikes twelve very slowly.*]

*Oldest Woman.* Oh, how far we are from the hospital!

*Oldest Man.* It is midnight!

*Second Man.* It is midday! Does anybody know? Speak!

*Sixth Man.* I do not know, but I think that we are in shadow.

*First Man.* I no longer pretend to know where I am; we have slept too long!

*Second Man.* I am hungry.

*The Others.* We are hungry and thirsty!

*Second Man.* Have we been here a long time?

*Oldest Man.* It seems to me that I have been here for centuries.

*Sixth Man.* I begin to understand where we are.

*Third Man.* We must go in the direction from which we heard it strike midnight. [*All the nocturnal birds suddenly fly about in the shadows*]

*First Man.* Do you hear? Do you hear?

*Second Man.* We are not alone here!

*Third Man.* For a long time I have suspected something; some one is listening to us. Has he come back?

*First Man.* I don't know what it is; it is above us.

*Second Man.* Have the others heard nothing? You are always silent!

*Oldest Man.* We were still listening.

*The Blind Girl.* I hear wings around me!

*Oldest Woman.* My God! my God! Tell us, then, where we are!

*Sixth Man.* I begin to understand where we are. The hospital is on the other side of the great river; we have crossed the old bridge. He has brought us to the north of the island. We are not far from the river, and perhaps we could hear it if we should listen a moment. We must go to the edge of the water if he does not return; big ships are always passing, day and night, and the sailors will notice us on the banks. It is possible that we are in the forest which surrounds the lighthouse; but I do not know the way out. Will any one follow me?

*First Man.* Let us remain seated. Let us wait; let us wait. No one knows the direction of the great river, and there are marshes all around the hospital. Let us wait; let us wait. He will return; he must return!

*Sixth Man.* Does any one know by which road we came here? He explained it to us while we were walking.

*First Man.* I did not pay any attention to it.

*Sixth Man.* Did any one listen to him?

*Third Man.* We must listen to him in future.

*Sixth Man.* Were any of us born in this island?

*Oldest Man.* You know very well that we came from else-where.

*Oldest Woman.* We came from the other side of the sea.

*First Man.* I thought I should die during the passage.

*Second Man.* I also; we came together.

*Third Man.* We are all three from the same parish.

*First Man.* They say it can be seen from here on a clear day, toward the north. It has no steeple.

*Third Man.* We landed by chance.

*Oldest Woman.* I came from another coast.

*Second Man.* Where did you come from?

*Oldest Woman.* I dare not think of it any more. I remember hardly anything about it when I speak of it. It was a long time ago. It was colder there than here.

*The Blind Girl.* I came from far away.

*First Man.* Where did you come from?

*The Blind Girl.* I could not tell you. How could I explain it to you? It is so far away from here; it is beyond the sea. I came from a great country. I could only show you by signs, and we do not see any more. I wandered too far. But I have seen the sun and the water, and fire, mountains, faces, and strange flowers. There are none like them in this island; it is too dark here, and too cold. Since I have not been able to see, I have never recognized their perfume. But I saw my parents and my sisters. I was too young then to know where I was. I used to play on the shore of the sea.

But how I remember having seen it! One day I saw the snow on the crest of a mountain. I was beginning to distinguish those who will be unhappy —

*First Man.* What are you trying to say?

*The Blind Girl.* I know them yet sometimes, by their voices — I remember more clearly when I do not think about it.

*First Man.* As for me, I have no recollections. [*A flight o large birds of passage goes by above the foliage, with a great noise.*]

*Oldest Man.* Something passed by again, under the sky!

*Second Man.* Why did you come here?

*Oldest Man.* Of whom do you ask that?

*Second Man.* Of our young sister.

*The Blind Girl.* They told me that he could cure me. He tol me that I should see some day; then I could leave the island.

*First Man.* We would all like to leave the island.

*Second Man.* We shall always stay here.

*Third Man.* He is too old; he will not have time to cure us.

*The Blind Girl.* My lids are closed; but I feel that my eyes have life in them.

*First Man.* Mine are open.

*Second Man.* I sleep with my eyes open.

*Third Man.* Do not let us talk of our eyes!

*Second Man.* You have not been here long?

*Oldest Man.* I heard, one evening during prayers, by the side of the women, a voice which I did not know; I heard by your voice that you were very young. I should have liked to see you, to hear you.

*First Man.* I never noticed it.

*Second Man.* He never informed us.

*Sixth Man.* They say that you are as beautiful as a woman who comes from afar?

*The Blind Girl.* I have never seen myself.

*Oldest Man.* We have none of us ever seen one another. We question one another and reply to one another; we live together, are always together; but we do not know what we are like. We have in vain touched one another with both hands; eyes know more than hands.

*Sixth Man.* I sometimes see your shadows when you are in the sunlight.

*Oldest Man.* We have never seen the house where we live ; we have, in vain, touched the walls and the windows ; we do not know where we live.

*Oldest Woman.* They say that it is an old château, very gloomy and miserable, where there is never any light unless it be in the tower, where the priest's chamber is.

*First Man.* There is no need of any light for those who can't see.

*Sixth Man.* When I take care of the flock in the neighborhood of the hospital, the sheep return themselves on noticing in the evening this light in the tower. They never stray from me.

*Oldest Man.* We have been together for years and years, and we have never seen one another ! It might be said that we are always alone. One must see to love.

*Oldest Woman.* I dream sometimes that I can see.

*Oldest Man.* I see only when I dream.

*First Man.* I dream, generally, only at midnight.

*Second Man.* Of what can one dream when one's hands are still ?

(To be continued.)

*Translated by the Editors.*

## BROWNING BOOKS OF THE YEAR.*

BROWNING'S obvious riches in elements of theology and philosophy have attracted myriads of busy bees who have sucked to dryness the particular juices they affect, without noticing that this

---

* Browning and Whitman : A Study in Democracy, by Oscar L. Triggs. London : Swan, Sonnenschein, & Co. New York : Macmillan & Co., 1893. — Sermons from Browning, by the Rev. F. Ealand. London : Elliot Stock, 62 Paternoster Row, 1892. — Browning's Criticism of Life, by William F. Revell. London : Swan, Sonnenschein, & Co. New York : Macmillan & Co., 1892. — Selections from Robert Browning's Poems ; Selected Poems of Elizabeth Barrett Browning. Boston : Joseph Knight Co. — Robert Browning's Prose Life of Strafford, with an Introduction by C. H. Firth, M. A. Oxen, and Forewords by F. J. Furnivall, M. A. Boston : Estes and Lauriat, 1892.

poet's flowers of fact and fancy bear also a golden pollen whose fertilizing dust can animate the future and steal new fame from time. Perhaps Professor Triggs saw this potent gold-dust cumbering the unheeding, dusty legs of the metaphysico-commentating bees swarming around and about in the Browning Garden of Speech, and was led to examine more narrowly the nature of the yield they left so unregarded. He has descried, at any rate, the less obvious, because more original and future-tending, traits and incitements of Browning's genius. It is his glory to have been among the first to recognize the bearing of the universal sympathies of Browning's art, in relation with its supreme allegiance, to the evolution of the individual soul. It is his distinction to have been, actually, the first to trace out, with some system, through chapter and verse, the poet's essentially democratic trend as an artist and idealist.

Readers of POET-LORE will remember, doubtless, this sentence in the article by Professor Triggs, in the October number, on 'Browning as the Poet of Democracy,' which now forms a part of his book, — " Browning is the dramatist of the Whitman principle." It packs up in a word much of the outcome of 'Browning and Whitman : A Study in Democracy.' The English genius moving in Browning freely, outside its island fashions, opening to cosmopolitan influences, and assimilating intimately the processes and ideals of world-evolution, approaches naturally the kindred summings up and prophesyings of the American exponent of the same processes and ideals.

Not that Whitman is the only American poet who has taken this path ; as Professor Triggs points out, Emerson and Thoreau also express the principle of the first struggle of the young Western nation in the first crisis for democracy, — the struggle for isolation and independence; as, later, Lowell, with Whitman, express the principle of spiritual unity for which the second crucial war was waged, — the war for union. Whitman's significance, however, is world-wide, not merely national, — his message being, as he sings, " to bestow upon any man or woman the entrance to all the gifts of the universe." That which Whitman states typically, Browning bodies forth in a thousand varied shapes, and shows in action moving toward fulfilment.

The correspondences in inner content between these most modern of poets, which Professor Triggs brings out, should suffice to convince the reader that their points of contact are as striking and characteristic of each as their differences.   Students of either poet, or of contemporaneous literary tendencies, cannot afford to let this suggestive little volume pass by unread or unthought on. It is also to be expected that the old fogy of literary criticism, whose standards are fixed, as his eyes are set, at an old focus, will grope over it, and grumble about it.   It is the best honor he can pay it, and an index of its significance.                        *P*

The most interesting, because least hackneyed in thought, of the Rev. F. Ealand's sermons founded on Browning texts is the third in his series, entitled 'The Next-to-Nothings of Life, and the Romance of the Unromantic.'   His texts for this are 'Pippa Passes' and 'The Boy and the Angel;' and he draws the eminently sound doctrine from them that unconscious influences for good are immeasurably more effective than conscious ones.   "The highest service which we ordinary five-talented people can render to God in ourselves, and through the lives of our fellow-men, is simply but strenuously to live the life which in its main outlines circumstances have prescribed to us . . . without self-consciousness or needless anxieties as to effects. . . . Such a life is effective for the welfare of others. . . . Such a life is effective for our own development." The other sermons are on 'The Life that now is,' 'The Life which is to come,' 'The All-important in Life.'   They were delivered as a course of Advent lectures at St. Anne's, Holloway, and prove how valuable Browning's poetry may be made from the religious point of view.

It is somewhat startling, after reading this little book of 'Sermons from Browning,' to pick up Revell's 'Browning's Criticism of Life,' and find expressly stated in it that when Mr. Robert Buchanan put the question to Browning, "Are you not, then, a Christian?" Browning immediately thundered, "No!"   It has always seemed to us that the statement so frequently made that Browning was essentially a Christian teacher and preacher had little or no foundation ; but that his nature was profoundly religious is not to be doubted for a moment. In the chapter on Browning's religious thought Mr. Revell has given the best exposition of the poet's attitude in regard to religion that we have seen anywhere. His argument might be summed up in the phrase recently become familiar, that his religion was founded on a belief in internal revelation, not in external revelation. " The God in whom Browning believes, he finds, not in the world outside, nor in the Church, but only in his own soul." But he is a man of such wide sympathies that he realizes that others may be so constituted as to see their vision of truth in some other form, only let each have faith in his own vision, leaving others to theirs, for the principal fact is not the why of faith, but faith itself, not belief in any set of dogmas, but belief in goodness and love eternal. Like Dr. Jones in his ' Philosophy of Browning,' Mr. Revell takes exception to Browning's insistence of the paramount worth of love over knowledge. " Say not that we know therefore we love, but rather that we love therefore we know enough." Both these critics say, very justly, that the highest developments of love are impossible without knowledge, as Mr. Revell tartly expresses it, " to browbeat knowledge is to endanger the higher life." We can but say of Mr. Revell as we said of Mr. Jones, that he has not, it seems to us, quite grasped the poet's attitude toward knowledge. Browning, like every great scientist, and like every great religious thinker, realizes that *absolute* knowledge is an utter impossibility to the finite mind; therefore we can never say " We know " without limiting that knowing with some finite conception, — in short, our finite limitations absolutely debar us from saying " We know " at all, but that " We love," we have personal experience of every day, and, loving, can be content to let wait the solution of that mystery which baffles the attainment of knowledge perfect and complete. To say that Browning " throws overboard knowledge " in its human manifestations is utterly absurd; he, quite as much as Mr. Revell or Mr. Jones, believes in the developing power of knowledge such as may be attained in this life ; but in the passage quoted, Browning is speaking of the knowledge which is unattainable in our present phase of existence. The last essay in the volume on 'Sordello' is a most entertaining and appreciative review of this poem.

The 'Pocket Volume of Selections' published just after Browning's death in London, by Smith, Elder, and Co., has just made its appearance in America under the guardianship of the Joseph Knight Co. But its old friends would hardly know it in the handsome binding in which it now appears. It has been further enriched by dainty little photogravure illustrations, and is certainly one of the most attractive editions of selections we have seen. They also publish a companion volume of selections from Mrs. Browning. It is a reissue of the edition, edited by Robert Browning, and contains much of her most interesting work, including such favorites as 'Lady Geraldine's Courtship,' 'The Rhyme of the Duchess May,' 'A Drama of Exile,' and others equally choice. It is also illustrated and bound in the same style as the Robert Browning volume. The student should have these volumes lying on his table to entice laymen into the enchanted realms of Mr. and Mrs. Browning's poetry, while the butterfly reader, who never dips very deeply into anything, may glean from them an excellent idea of the work of these twin geniuses.

One of the most fascinating pastimes to the student of historical dramas is to compare the figures as they appear in history with their semblances after passing through the idealizing medium of the poet's brain ; but it is a rare opportunity which enables one to compare a historic and poetic portrayal of a hero by the same author, yet this is just what has befallen through a happy chance in the case of Robert Browning's 'Life of Strafford.' As Dr. Furnivall explains in his " Forewords " to the edition of the 'Life' just issued by Estes and Lauriat, Forster, who was writing the series of 'Lives of Eminent British Statesmen' for 'Lardner's Cabinet Cyclopædia,' had collected all the materials for the 'Life of Strafford,' when he was taken ill, and feared he would be unable to finish it at the time specified. Happening to tell Browning of his difficulties, the poet said, " I will finish it for you."

Such being the circumstances under which Browning undertook it, just what part of it is to be attributed to him must be determined entirely upon internal evidence. Judging it by the only other prose essay we have of Browning's, the preface to the spurious Shelley letters, one might be driven to the conclusion that very little of it is Browning unalloyed. The style has none of the concise strength which we should expect from the writer of this masterly essay; it rarely rises above a smoothly felicitous but somewhat commonplace level. Had we the space, we could also point out expressions of opinion which hardly seem worthy of Browning, and then, again, there are passages which indicate a deeply penetrative insight into the inner motives of such a man as Strafford. In fine, it is Browning held in a leash, while the drama of ' Strafford' is Browning, free to see in his characters whatsoever he will, untrammelled by the testimony of this or that one.

The parallelisms between this ' Life' and the drama cannot be taken either as a sure index to the parts which should be attributed to Browning, for there are just as marked resemblances, even to the words used, between the drama and some of the other ' Lives ;' for example, those of Pym and Eliot. Since the evidence for his share in the work must be internal, its convincingness must depend largely upon the personal equation. In his scholarly historical introduction, Mr. C. H. Firth accepts without question Browning's authorship, and makes some interesting observations which supply as good an argument as may be, for taking the ground that in its execution it is entirely Browning's. He considers that the treatment of the subject reflects Browning's characteristic concern in the individual ; Strafford interests him as a man rather than as one of a group of actors in great historical events, yet to get Browning's conception of the whole man, it is necessary to read both the ' Life' and the play. Each contains a part of the truth ; it is as if, in the ' Life,' he were presented as he appeared to other people ; in the drama, as he appeared to himself.

As long ago as 1889 POET-LORE pointed out the passages from Forster's ' Lives' upon which Browning had founded his drama of ' Strafford,' and indicated also the changes made by the poet in the process of moulding the facts into artistic unity. In doing this, Poet-Lore builded better than it knew, for in the light of Browning's authorship of ' Strafford's Life,' the study gains greatly in interest.*                                                    C.

## THE CITY OF DREADFUL NIGHT.†

James Thomson's ' The City of Dreadful Night ' is a remarkable example of the beauty of the horrible. There is not a thought in it that calls forth any answering echo from the heart of the normally happy human being, yet the reader cannot fail to be entranced by the power and variety of the imagery which has made out of so dismal a theme as the utter worthlessness of life a really beautiful work of art. Hopelessness, unending and complete, about things human or divine is the pervading spirit of Thomson's work, which nowhere reaches a more doleful climax than in the passage which describes the despair of the being who " reached the portal common spirits fear," and reading the words, " Leave hope behind, all ye who enter here," would have entered, glad to gain " that positive eternity of pain," but he is unable to pay the toll demanded by the snarling porter, of any smallest hope, having lost all hope years before ; and he is turned away. So, bereft of even the qualifications for admittance to hell, he and his wretched companion, who is in a like plight, agree to search for some minute lost hope, which they may divide between them to win entrance to the longed-for certainties of torture.

Most striking, too, is the scene in the cathedral of the ' city of tremendous night,' where all sorts and conditions of men, from the king to the priest, are challenged as they enter the cathedral by a shrouded figure who demands of them whence they came. Each tells a different tale, but all alike conclude with the pessimistic utterance, " I wake from day dreams to this real night."

* Poet-Lore, vol. i., pp. 282, 332, 372, 426, 511, 562.

† The City of Dreadful Night. By James Thomson, with Introduction by E. Cavazza. Portland : Thomas B. Mosher. 1892. ($1.50).

Although it is the melancholy temperament of the poet which breathes forth from every line, he is sufficiently objective in his treatment of his theme to give to his poetry a decidedly dramatic flavor. There are various characters in this dreadful city, though they are all of one mind in their view of life. Even the poem which touches most closely on the great sorrow of Thomson's life — the death of his betrothed, a very young and beautiful girl — is not subjective in form : he does not pour forth his grief directly, as the lyrists from Moschus to Tennyson have done, but he conjures up a weird scene in the dreadful city, at which the poet himself is present, but as an onlooker at another's grief. The impression given by this indirect method is simply wonderful in the extremity of its despair, — it is as if melancholy had so taken possession of the poet that even his grief is a thing apart from himself ; he has not even the small consolation of feeling his sorrow, he only sees it.

Perhaps the most personal of his poems in the form of its expression is the one on Insomnia, the terrors of which could hardly be more graphically painted.

It is to Mr. Mosher of Portland, Maine, that our thanks are due for this first American edition of 'The City of Dreadful Night ;' and he has given it to us in a style well suited to so rare a genius as James Thomson. Only four hundred numbered copies of the small paper edition have been printed, and a similarly limited number of large paper copies. It is printed on hand-made paper, with uncut edges and Japan vellum cover. Mrs. E. Cavazza has written an interesting introduction for it, and a complete bibliography, prepared by Bertram Dobell and J. M. Wheeler, forms a most useful appendix to the volume. It is altogether one of the most acceptable reprints of the year, and will form a choice jewel in the collection of all book-lovers who are fortunate enough to secure a copy.

*C.*

# NOTES AND NEWS.

A FAIRER field for revel in the study of literary origins could scarcely be dreamed of than one may have in Browning's 'The Ring and the Book,' confronted as it will be with the original of the poet's " Book." This original is now in the library of Balliol College, Oxford, and is being edited, we hear from Professor Triggs, by Mr. W. Hall Griffin, a lecturer in University College, London. Dr. Furnivall writes that Browning omitted the most beautiful part of this ' *Romana Homicediorum* ;' namely, the testimony of the priest who shrove Pompilia and was with her during her last days. " We all felt," he says, " that for this man's fervent witness to the purity and beauty of Pompilia's character we would gladly give up the Procurator and Advocate." But perhaps not all Browning lovers will join themselves readily with Dr. Furnivall's " we." It is so very likely that the maker of ' The Ring and the Book ' knew better than most of us how to mingle " gold with gold's alloy, and duly tempering both," effect a " manageable mass " to work in shape of " rondure brave " and " lilied loveliness." But the "prime nature " of the age-stained quarto written in Italian, " interfilleted with streaks of Latin," mostly printed, partly in writing, the sand that dried the ink not rubbed away, — the " prime nature " of this curious book will certainly throw many a light on the "added artistry" that made it into 'The Ring and the Book.' The Franceschini arms, we hear, are painted in the quarto as described by Browning : —

> " Shield, azure on a Triple Mountain, Or,
> A Palm tree, proper whereunto is tied
> A Greyhound, Rampant, striving in the slips."

—— THOUGH the London Browning Society has ceased to hold formal meetings, it continues to meet informally at the houses of its members and friends. At a recent meeting Dr. Moncure D. Conway gave some pleasant recollections of Browning which were reported by Dr. Furnivall in the *Westminster Gazette* as follows:

"Dr. Moncure Conway first knew the poet when he (Dr. Conway) came to England thirty years ago. But ten years before that, in 1852-4, he was one of a set of Unitarian students in the Theological College at Harvard who were great admirers of Browning. Among them were Lowell, who said he'd give his copy of 'Sordello' to anyone who'd lay his hand on his heart and declare that he understood the poem; Wendell Holmes, keenly alive to Browning's humour; John Weiss, a devoted Browningite; Emerson, who called 'Sordello' 'the whale of the nineteenth century;' and W. H. Channing, who asserted that the poem only needed punctuation to be perfectly plain, who put stops in his own copy, and found they coincided with Browning's when the poet brought out the second and revised version of 'Sordello.' All this Browning set maintained that 'Pippa Passes' was the greatest poem since Shakespeare. What attracted them to Browning was that they had become so weary of the passionless idealism preached to them by their teachers that when the full-blooded English poet gave them living men and women, with passions, hopes, fears, love, and strife, they opened their hearts to his creations.

"Carlyle, in early days, liked talking of Browning: how the youth on foot had accosted him while riding slowly on Wimbledon Common, had called him by his name, said how he admired his writings, and had strolled along chatting by the side of his horse. Carlyle would tell, too, of Browning's love and marriage: how, in Sleeping Beauty fashion, his kiss had woke the poor pale lady from her sad sick-bed into life and motherhood and joy; and how all this arose from Elizabeth Barrett likening Browning's poetry to a man cutting open a 'nectarine.' Mrs. Carlyle tried to correct him, as the fruit was a 'pomegranate;' but Carlyle would have nothing to do with the pomegranate; a 'nectarine' it was, whatever the printed poem said. Dr. Conway thought Browning was in some sense a captive of Carlyle: he mistrusted the people, and loved heroes; but he drew a line at Carlyle's defence of slavery, which Browning hated with all his heart, and he was disgusted with Carlyle's ridicule of the United States Civil War in *Macmillan's Magazine*. Though Browning inclined to the South at first, it was because he did not believe the war was against slavery; but when the North developed its policy, and declared for the negro, Browning sided wholly with it. To the fairs for the poor freedmen after the war Browning sent some of his dead wife's manuscripts and his own autographs, and they fetched large prices. The reverence with which he handled her papers and books, and showed her Hebrew Bible with her notes, saying, 'What learning! what learning!' greatly struck Dr. Conway.

" Browning was a happy man, but did n't laugh much ; he had a sweet smile, and dramatic action in his features ; he was not reposeful, but quickly stirred. He was sensitive to criticism. He once read out a stupid review of one of his poems, and added, ' I sometimes actually meet that man in polite society ! ' Dr. Conway reviewed ' Dramatis Personæ ' from advance proofs given him by Browning. His sharp comment on the silly bit about ' Original Sin ' at the end of ' Gold Hair ' hurt Browning ; they had an argument about it, the poet trying to justify his view ; but when hard pressed he gave it up with a laugh. Dr. Conway had many sharp controversies with Browning about religion. Five o'clock was the time for their walks and fights ; and often Browning would stop in the street and argue earnestly. But Dr. Conway felt continually that Browning was zoölogising him, studying the latest Harvard development in religion. He certainly botanised his society friends for use in his poems, noting the specialities of each.

" Browning was not many-sided like Goethe ; but he was many-folded ; in him was the man of the world, the preacher, the artist, the sensuous man, the mystic, the Greek pagan. When Dr. Conway was going to Rome, Browning said : ' Mind you see the picture (or fresco) in the Bocca della Verita church ; that 'll give you the best sermon for South-place. There is Ceres among the corn, Bacchus in the vines ; she is pressing meal, he squeezing grape-juice into a Christian chalice.' But Dr. Conway found that the priests had whitewashed the picture out of sight ; and he had to complain to the art-director, Salvator Rosa's descendant, about it. Orders were given for the restoration of the picture, but in vain.

" Browning seemed to have a Hebrew or Semitic strain, and when talking earnestly looked Jewish. He liked Moslem fables, and held that all evil was good in disguise, and had a dramatic purpose. There was too much sermonising in his later work; he once said of a tempting emotional topic, ' I should like to write about it, if I had n't lost nearly all my lyrical faculty.' He was a hater of commonplace. His early faith was better than his late ; it was not so optimistic. He held to the dramatic idea of a Great Judgment at the Last Day : ' Why should n't God settle up with mankind, as a master does with his workmen here ? ' He had little sympathy with, and no faith in, Italian and French revolutionists. It was always ' poor Mazzini.' He was a representative of the time that saw only failed revolutions. His publisher, George Smith, once told him that he meant to give a lecture on ' How Robert Browning's Works should be Read,' and that the lecture would be shorter than its title. This piqued Browning's curiosity, and he asked so often about it that Smith at last delivered his lecture to Browning: 'Mind your stops!' "

### BROWNING.

A THOUGHT-BOW which the word-string scarce can pull ;
A hand too heavy for the instrument ;
A gold that needs alloy ere it be sent
To mint or graver ; verse of faults as full
As is the gem of facets ; myriad lights
There sparkle, none converge ; gigantic wings,
With feet unfit for homely travellings :
They can but perch on Himalaya-heights.
Ears may be dull or low, he never seeks
To reach them stooping, as another man.
They rise who hear him ; he hath proved he can
Be understanded of the Babel-host :
And who shall blame the poet if he speaks
His own peculiar language more than most?

*C. E. D. Phelps.*

# SOCIETIES.

The Browning Society of Boston held its sixtieth regular meeting on Tuesday, March 28, President Hornbrooke in the chair. Miss Alice Washburn read 'Soliloquy of the Spanish Cloister,' and Rev. George D. Latimer continued the programme of the afternoon with a paper on 'Browning's Dramatic Imagery.' An essay on 'The Monologue, an Evolved Form of the Soliloquy,' was read by Miss Belle Grant Armstrong.

Mrs. A. H. Spaulding discussed at length the question, 'Does Browning's Treatment of his Characters conform to his Doctrine of the Poet's Impersonality?' She illustrated the variety and consistency of his characters by many references and quotations, in order to show that Browning can keep his own individuality out of the way for the sake of letting the individuality of others shine through his words. He clears the stage for the players, and does not appear himself while the play is on. Yet only one who conceives of things in their universal aspects and subtile relations could enter the inner life of others as he did ; and we feel his warm, loving personality in everything he has written.

*Emma Endicott Marean.*

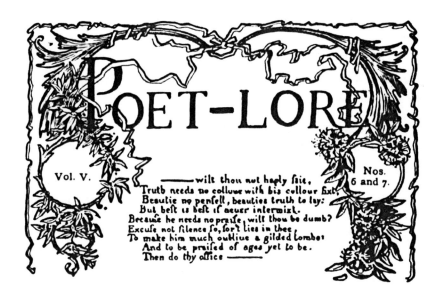

POET-LORE

Vol. V.

————wilt thou not haply saie,
Truth needs no collour with his collour fixt,
Beautie no pensell, beauties truth to lay:
But best is best if neuer intermixt.
Because he needs no praise, wilt thou be dumb?
Excuse not silence so, for't lies in thee
To make him much outliue a gilded tombe
And to be praised of ages yet to be.
Then do thy office ————

Nos.
6 and 7.

## WALT WHITMAN.

NO one can stand to-day at the centre of the World's Fair grounds without being impressed by the strange beauty of the scene: the city so white and wonderful, the lake gleaming beneath the high summer's sun and gently pulsing from afar, the water-birds wheeling above, and the people streaming and endless, thronging street and shore with youthful ardor; all the world is here, — the careless, the curious, the thoughtful; the faces of a few are seen to glow with a newly awakened hope. On many a day before I have watched from this spot the building of the city, and while walls and arch and dome were rising to complete the plan of a perfect deed, I have asked from one and another the meaning of it all, and have received a variable answer. Not until the city was completed did one, who seemed more thoughtful than the rest, say to me as we stood admiring the classic outlines of the noble Art Gallery, — and somewhat sadly did he speak, — "This city is not for us, but for the future. I understand it as a type appearing ere the times are ready, and I look to see it vanish soon as being but a momentary embodiment of an ideal purpose. But while it hovers here upon the shore I

take it as a sign to men of the beauty and the romance, the ideality and the reality, of our life here and now."

After all, — this is what the hopeful faces said, — it is man to
whom exposition is given here, not of materials and products, but
of him toward whose spiritual evolution all things tend; of this
scene the lake alone is contributed by some one other than man.
The rest is man's work, builded by him and for him, and from his
presence is derived the only significance the exhibits possess. The
great roof of the manufacturers' building, which overarches like the
sky, measures the scale of the builder's ideal purpose. The mind
had but to conceive, and the will, helped by the shaping hand,
carried to execution. Who can have doubts of the future when
the soul is thus seen to be supreme amid every environment?
Americanism, in its essence, is a faith, — the faith of Columbus to
discover, the faith of the people to achieve. We did not know
what power a people has of moulding matter to beautiful uses, until
we stood here upon the bridge, and caught this hope from the
passers-by.

" Of the progress of the souls of men and women along the grand roads of the universe,
all other progress is the needed emblem and sustenance."

'Leaves of Grass.'

WALT WHITMAN was born in 1819 in the old homestead of the
family on the Long Island sea-coast. His father was an Englishman, quiet and serious of nature, and with " surly English pluck."
His mother was of Dutch descent, — an ideal woman, practical and
spiritual. One of his grandmothers was a Quakeress, whose face,
" more beautiful than the sky," is lovingly drawn in ' From Noon
to Starry Night.' As a youth, gifted with extraordinary recep-
tivity, Whitman derived from Nature, men, and books a generous
and sincere culture. The influence of Nature is shown in the
record of the child who went forth each day into the world: the
early lilacs, the grass, the morning-glories, the song of the phœbe-
bird, the hurrying, tumbling waves, the strata of colored clouds, the
flying sea-crow, the fragrance of salt-marsh and shore-mud, — these
became part of the life of that child who went forth every day.

On Long Island the child absorbed the incidents of the sea, its rough, ruddy characters, pilots and fishermen. Later, among the turbulent crowds of New York and Brooklyn, mingling freely with artisans and laborers, he made himself familiar with every kind of employment. As printer and journalist, he travelled throughout the Western and Southern States, gathering, with truest poetic insight, men, thoughts, materials, and incidents for his poems. He read from time to time the best books, the great spiritual products of the nations, — the Bible, Homer, Sophocles, Dante, Shakespeare, Ossian, the Nibelungen Lays, and the ancient Hindoo poems. These were read in the open air, — Dante in a gloomy wood, Homer at the shore, with the sea with equal swell rolling in, Shakespeare under the sun amid the far-spreading landscape. After gathering to himself these countless influences, there came to him the "divine power to speak words;" at the age of thirty-six he published 'Leaves of Grass.' It was a strange, audacious, unlooked-for volume, strange even in its outward aspect as in its novel lines and thoughts. No one at the time, except Emerson and Thoreau, comprehended its meaning. They alone were thrilled as we are thrilled by its intimate new seeing of things. For it was absolutely modern, passionately so, teeming with the ideas of the present century. Of reviews and criticisms of life there was nothing; it would rather animate to life itself. It sounded the joys of virile manhood and womanhood. It seemed to reconcile good and evil. One really unique element, which indicated a revolution in modes of thinking, was the attitude it assumed toward the objective universe on the one hand, and to the singer, the self, on the other. And herein was its power; it was the energy of a personality, freely playing forth and revealing itself as to its physical, intellectual, moral, and æsthetical nature. One other formative influence entered succeeding editions. During the Civil War Whitman served in the hospitals. Tender as a mother, he was educated anew in divine compassion. By the ideality, the struggles, the heroisms of the war, the real character of man was disclosed. Emerging from the war, he sings of love and comradeship and eternal hope and joy. 'Leaves of Grass,' complete in 1892, including ' Sands at Seventy ' and ' Good Bye, My Fancy,' is the whole outcome of this man's life.   I take up the book, and it throbs to my touch as if it too had nerves and blood and human heart.   This is no book ; it is a man, — large, calm, superbly formed, eyes clear and penetrating, revealing depths of tenderness, a face full of resolution, radiant, fighting the shadows, like the sunset, to the last.*

In the preface to the ' Neue Gedichte' Heine relates that it seemed to him when writing his poems that he could hear the flutter of a bird's wings above his head, — the pinion-beat of the ideas of his age.   It seems to me that in like manner Whitman must have had some secret communication with the ideas of modern America and times, — not the passing ephemeral ideas, but those battle-thoughts fraught with rich import for the future.   My admiration of ' Leaves of Grass ' is based upon the wealth of its thoughts, the vastness of its conceptions, — there is but one word to express this quality, a vastness like the night and ocean, — and lastly, upon the nobility of its practical philosophy for an era of democracy.   In an age of essential expansion, when an irresistible force, which we term the " modern-spirit," is making its way into every corner of the old world, removing old conditions and imposing new, undermining venerable institutions and establishing new, Whitman, almost alone among poets, has divined the tendencies of the times, and, with a largeness answering to them, has gone on before, singing constructively the ideals of democracy.   He announced to come the great individual, fluid as nature, chaste, affectionate, compassionate, to go fully armed, —

> " Fair, able, beautiful, content and loving,
> Complete in body and dilate in spirit."

For America, well aware of its imperfections, but knowing, too, that it has not yet arrived at its true life, he held up an ideal of its amplitudes, wealths, powers, possibilities, showing with these what the present really means, discovering there beneath the

---

* Of the two heads of Whitman made by the sculptor, Sidney H. Morse, entitled ' Calm, Calm, Calm, and ' Calm, Calm, Alert ' the more characteristic is the countenance of rapidity resting on depth, calmness beneath resolution.

apparent materialism the old cunning genius of poetry which shall save us from our business and commonplaces. There is infinite poetry in this land of ours; it is steeped in poetry; our very life is dædal, dramatic, romantic, — wildly romantic in its faith to achieve things unattempted yet; of themselves these states are the amplest poem. 'Leaves of Grass,' purporting to be the expression of a single individual, is, in truth, in its intention the beginning of a literature which shall be the natural expression of the national life, and which at the same time shall be our spiritual food. The crowning growth of the United States, if it shall have a sufficient literature, is to be spiritual and heroic.

I have tried my stoutest to know what Whitman really signifies. Only those who have endeavored to bring him to book can realize the difficulty of the task. The intellectual often plays no part in perception. He eludes our analyses when we think we are surest. The appeal is to the synthetic imagination, and not to the analytic reason. Undoubtedly the dominant element in his nature is emotional. His sense for science and for art is subdued by that for religion. That "the whole theory of the universe is directed unerringly to one single individual — namely to You" is chiefly true for the moral personality, and it everywhere appears that the artist in him is lost in the rapt, contemplative mystic. "Each moment and whatever happens thrill me with joy." His thoughts thus tend naturally to rapturous utterance. Everything, even the least particle of matter, is regarded with wonder, reverence, and awe. Perhaps no modern writer has so well expressed the religious aspect of Nature. In the presence of the sea and the stars he feels the free and glad expanse of his being. When hearing the lecture of the learned astronomer, he tells us that he rose and went out into the mystical, moist night-air and looked up in perfect silence at the stars. This is the attitude of the worshipper whose soul finds its large and true life in contemplating the infinity of the quiet evening sky. Religion has been defined as the sum of these unfettered expansive impulses of the being, the stretching forth of the hands toward the illimitable. No one therefore will get at 'Leaves of Grass' who does not view its poems from the centre of the author's religious life; yea, he must himself bring to their interpretation an equally natural and noble feeling.

Whitman's religious significance lies in this, that he emphasizes what is of most vital interest to the personality.

> "What are you doing young man?
> Are you so earnest, so given up to literature, science, art, amours?
> These ostensible realities, politics, points?
> Your ambitions or business whatever it may be?
> It is well — against such I say not a word, I am their poet also,
> But behold! such swiftly subside, burnt up for religion's sake.
> For not all matter is fuel to heat, impalpable flame, the essential life of the earth,
> Any more than such are to religion."

The revelation of consciousness is relied upon for knowledge of God. In the dispute of the creeds he is silent. "I have no mockings or arguments but I witness and wait." "Thee, thee at least I know." "No array of terms can say how much I am at peace about God." In the universe without him God is seen in every object, in the stock, in the stone, in the star, and the plant. But pantheism is not held at the expense of the individual; for while God is immanent, he is ethical as well, and to man comes ever the necessity of struggle and infinite expansion.

> "Now understand me well — it is provided in the essence of things that from any
> fruition of success, no matter what, shall come forth something to make a
> greater struggle necessary."

By reason of Whitman's naturalism — that frank avowal of the natural impulses — he is called by a conventional sectarianism Pagan and retrogressive. Really he is neither Pagan nor Christian, but inclusive and eminently human. Too often the creeds have degraded men in their own eyes by fixing their destiny to "darkness, death and long despair." Nature in due time supplies a corrective in the person of such a one as Whitman, who humanizes the dogmas, permitting Nature to assert itself with primitive energy. The truths of Paganism and of Christianity are happily blended when he says: —

> "I give nothing as duties,
> What others give as duties I give as living impulses,
> (Shall I give the heart's action as a duty?)"

Taken all in all, Whitman is, as I think, a great ideal prophet. In the highest sense he is spiritual, and of all poets the most mystic. His theme, so far from being the body in its grossness (a word he would not admit at all), is the spirit in its purity. Every word is symbolical, double. Some one complains: " To think is to discriminate; Whitman blurs." But like all mystics, as Blake and Emerson, he takes the transcendental point of view, reasoning from the whole to the parts. Each line of his poems takes meaning from the whole, and each poem in turn from the final sense of 'Leaves of Grass.' "I will make no poems," he has said, " with reference to parts, but I will make poems, songs, thoughts with reference to ensemble." He aims, in fine, at unity of moral impression, and not by fine phrasing, but by comprehensive conception.

Unity, this is the thought I am coming to, is the explanatory word in his whole philosophy of literature and life. He has parted forever from the dualistic conception of the universe, constructing instead an unibasic system of thought. A vast similitude interlocks all things, matter and spirit, man and nature, the body and soul, and compactly holds them. Matter and mind are differentiated expressions of the same essence, governed by the same laws, part and parcel of the same life. There can be no escape from the conclusion that an intimate relation exists between what we call mental and material action. Being truly correlative, their energy is interchangeable. There is no thrill of the body without a corresponding joy of the mind. There is no change in consciousness without a correlated change in the physical system. If matter and mind are co-extensive, what, then, is the soul?

"See your own shape and countenance, — persons, substances, beasts, the trees, the running rivers, the rocks and sands."

And I am no longer frightened at the thought of being lost in matter. I know that

"My foothold is tenon'd and mortis'd in granite."

What I now fear is that mechanical action will be found to be mere mental action, and that matter will be lost in mind. In truth, both

matter and mind are equally mysterious.   If one is immortal, the
other is also in some form.   Development, continuity, immortality,
are the explanations of all facts of the physical and spiritual world.

> " I swear I think now that everything without exception has an eternal soul !
> The trees have, rooted in the ground ! the weeds of the sea have ! the animals ! "

Thus realizing that man is integral with nature, Whitman has a
heart-felt sympathy with all existence.   The trees drop melodious
thoughts as he passes.   The bird, mourning its mate on the sands
of Paumanok's shore, starts into life within him a thousand similar
songs.   Assigning himself to the sea, he says, —

> " We murmur alike reproachfully, rolling sands and drift and knowing not why."

Then he cries in his joy, "O spirituality of things !"   The great
and inspiring truth is that the earth is being transformed into consciousness.   Personality is not less to-day, but greater.   One's self
is the final substance.

> " I know I am solid and sound.
> To me the converging objects of the universe perpetually flow,
> All are written to me, and I must get what the writing means."

As a scientific commentary upon the truth of ' Leaves of Grass,'
most timely and welcome are the words of Professor Chamberlain
in a recent address upon 'The Immanence of God.'   The eminent
scientist said in closing : —

" The earth has been developing into mentality rather than
into materiality.   If anything has been losing and anything gaining in dominance, it is matter that has been losing and mind that
has been gaining.   A corresponding series of estimates of the
quality we call personality would show in it also an enormous
increase.   If personality in the human form has developed and
flourished so phenomenally, and is now going rapidly forward to
higher qualities and clearer characters and greater dominance,
what ground is there for fear respecting the personality of God ?
God is neither remote nor unknowable, but is immanent in all
things.   That which we know most because it lies right in ourselves will be recognized as only a factor in a universe which is
essentially a unit, *permeated in every part by the essence of what it
contains in the little part ourselves*, and the entirety and sum-
mation of all, with immeasurable super-additions, is the infinite,
omniscient, the omnipotent, the omnipresent."

The contribution of science to 'Leaves of Grass' is indeed everywhere most significant. Discovery has wrought great changes of late in the general materials of literature. The ancient myths have lost their potency and charm, being superseded by truths more wonderful as more real and imaginative. We have often questioned whether there shall not be in the future a poetry of science, though what forms such a poetry may assume is not yet clear. Wordsworth turned away from science because it seemed to regard facts without imaginative coloring, and held firmly to poetry, which he defined as the impassioned expression which is in the countenance of science. Without scientific perceptions, he was content to rest his pantheism upon immediate intuition, embodying in his poetry the vague emotions which he felt — "thanks to the human heart by which we live" — in contemplation of meadows, sunsets, and seas. Tennyson, more modern in spirit, conforms to discovery in that he adopts the nomenclature of science, and shapes his images in accordance with larger knowledge. For an instance, in 'The Epilogue' the poet makes answer to Irene's complaining: —

> " For dare we dally with the sphere
>     As he did half in jest,
> Old Horace? 'I will strike' said be,
>     'The stars with head sublime,'
> But scarce could see, as now we see,
>     The man in Space and Time,
> So drew perchance a *happier lot*
>     Than ours, who rhyme to-day.
> The fires that arch this dusky dot —
>     Yon myriad-worlded way —
> The vast sun-clusters' gathered blaze,
>     World-isles in lonely skies,
> Whole heavens within themselves, amaze
>     Our brief humanities."

In this passage, as also in 'In Memoriam,' where nature is seen in strife with love, Science has given the poet greater knowledge, but has failed in ministering to his faith. The attitude of Whitman in this respect is quite unique. He avails himself of scientific material for certain moral uses. The law of evolution

witnesses to the unity of the universe, furnishing him additional
ground for putting in rapport the mountains, streams, winds, and
forests with the soul of man. The suggestion of an infinite,
rhythmic, singing movement which scientists agree to be the essence
of the atom's life is received by Whitman as the mode of human
action. There is nothing fixed or final. Into a world of pulsing
change, best symbolized by the ever restless sea, the soul is cast
forever; there is no rest, no calm, — "forever alive, forever forward." Research again has shown how all matter is sweet, and in
all its movements almost incomprehensibly refined. The crude
notions of a former age, which conceived matter to be gross and
unlovely, unhappily linger in the popular mind, but, for the most
part, men of science count naught common or unclean. In ultimate analysis matter and spirit are both unknown, and alike
wonderful; they vanish in mystery. A child brought to Whitman
a bunch of grass, asking what it was, and he could not answer any
more than the child, and he accepted the leaves, beautiful, mystical, naming with them his poems; and the Calamus, growing in
close companionship upon the prairies, he took to typify love and
comradeship. Nor can he scorn the body, having learned the
purity of Nature's processes. To loathe life may become a mediæval monk, but Whitman, aware of the sacredness of life, urges
upon his comrades, "Touch me, touch the palm of your hand
to my body as I pass. Be not afraid of my body." What is still
more vital, Whitman has absorbed the scientific influence in his
attitude of trust in the presence of reality. The fruits of the scientific spirit are humility, sincerity, patience, and resolution to face
the world as it is. " I accept Reality," said Whitman, " and dare
not question it." He sought to know what life really means with
that same yearning which his neighbor Thoreau felt at Walden.
Antæus-like, he would touch the earth, and gain power by contact
with the primal energies of Nature.

But while appropriating these and other contributions of
research as materials for his poems, their effect upon the poet is
spiritual and moral. His own report of facts is ever emotional.
If the microscope and telescope have shown the universe to be

infinite in extent, boundless inward to the atom and outward to the stars, Whitman, with an equal range of vision, takes atom and star unto himself, and translates them in terms of himself. As I have said, he claims for matter the spiritual processes of mind. The facts of the physicists which at one time threatened to devour their votaries are made by him vassals to a larger faith in humanity. "Our brief humanities" are of as much account as cosmic laws and spaces. Without man the universe is void.

"All forces have been employed to complete and delight me."

"I open my scuttle at night and see the far-sprinkled systems,
Wider and wider they spread, expanding always expanding,
Outward, outward, and forever outward,
My sun has his sun and around him obediently wheels,
He joins with his partners a group of superior circuits,
And greater sets follow, making specks of the greatest inside them. . . .
See ever so far, there is limitless space outside of that
Count ever so much there is limitless time around that "

And beyond that? What but the human personality projected there into the realms of silence. On reading 'Leaves of Grass,' one feels an enlargement of the self answering to this vastness of vision. I look at myself, as Michael Angelo said on reading Homer, to see if I am not twenty feet in height, — more than this, each of us limitless, greater than the mountains, better than we thought.

It is unfortunate that, when discussing Whitman as an artist, one must endeavor first to prove there is art at all. But remembering the century's experience with reference to Turner's paintings and Wagner's dramas, one may take courage in affirming that Whitman's criticism of life, which all agree is characterized by the excellences of sincerity and strength, is also true to the conditions of poetic beauty. It is only fair that those who find 'Leaves of Grass' poetically uncouth and formless should consider how far thought of such quality admits of the conventional forms of either prose or poetry. Pure speech, I affirm, would not contain the emotion that pulses intensely in every line; pure song could not bear the thought. The poet has created for his purpose a medium that is midway between prose and poetry, not a spurious form of "prose-poetry," which is a pestilential heresy Mr. Saintsbury does well to denounce, but a new harmony, comprehending the real relationship between speech and song, — a relationship which is as intimate as the wedding of music and thought in Wagner's synthetic dramas. And this form will remain as a notable contribution to poetic art, it being suggestive indeed of that ultimate speech which shall be also perfect song.

The justification of Whitman's artistic method will be found in the circumstances of the times. Whitman is the representative in America of the romantic spirit which has informed the best artistic work in Europe for nearly a century. The purpose of the "romantic movement" was to free the personality from its thraldom to formalism. The "return to Nature" was to find a new expression for emotions repressed by existing conventions. Our times are impatient of restraint, whether in the world within or without. We can no longer abide the artificiality of kings or popes in art as in life. It is significant that the peculiar art of the century is music, which is the most free and spiritual and real of all. We long to reach the fountain of being, and drink of reality. It is truth we seek. The Germans, with their passion for music, correspondingly increase their search after knowledge. In obedience to the same yearning for spiritual reality the novel with us has become inner and psychological ; and one great poet of the century has for his single theme the soul of man, its struggles, aspirations, failures, and successes. In such a time of spiritual longing, conventions are readily set aside, and new forms are created by the spirit for its use more akin to its own essential personality.

It is, in brief, from the standpoint of personality that Whitman's art is to be enjoyed. The purely literary in literature is, after all, usually poor stuff for men and women who read not only with their eyes, but also with their hearts. One day I read 'The Song of the Open Road' to a friend who was in trouble of spirit, and my friend went forth light-hearted and joyful. How merely literary canons fell to the ground then !

"Divine instinct, breadth of vision, the law of reason, health, rudeness of body, with-
    drawness,
  Gaiety, sun-tan, air-sweetness, such are some of the words of poems," —

words not rhyming, it is true, but is it nothing that the poet has
faiths and visions and power to illumine life and death, — nothing
that he has the faculty of divining amid our prosaic age the universal genius of romance ?   Do we really care for truth anyhow ?
Do we really long for a fuller life, however given us ?   Or shall
we be content with the poet whose lines jingle properly, careless
whether truth be in them or out of them ?   Whitman endows us at
least with the gift of life.   And is not the problem of art, after all,
the human problem, — that which thought has of reconciling form
and spirit, and of interpreting both from the centre of man's mind ?
"The artist," said Goethe, "must work from within outward, seeing that make what contortions he will he can only bring to light
his own individuality.   I can clearly mark where this influence of
mine has made itself felt; there arises out of it a kind of *poetry of
nature.*"   We recall the remark of Wordsworth about Goethe's
poetry that it was not "inevitable enough," — that is, too little
spontaneous.   The phrases admirably describe Whitman's poetry,
which is at its best as inevitable as Nature itself, — a spontaneous
utterance of an entire personality, egoistic, bombastic, as you will.
Poetry is the means taken to realize the poet's self ; it is the house
of his mind he is building.   The work wants perfection because the
architect has himself in view, and is seeking to express what thought
is generated within rather than to give artistic completeness to what
is without.   He seeks to embody spirit, and not imprison.   The
thought at least is adequate to the life of man.   I seem to see some
faultless versifier putting 'Leaves of Grass' into rhyme : —

> "And indeed the arm is wrong.
> I hardly dare . . . yet, only you to see,
> Give the chalk here — quick, thus the line should go !
> Ay, but the soul ! he 's Rafael ! rub it out !"
>
> ('Andrea del Sarto,' — the faultless painter.)

Better so : 'Leaves of Grass' is true to Nature ; it is an organic
whole whose parts are vitally wedded in a new harmony where

rudeness, discords, enter that we may doubly prize the loveliness
of such lines as these : —

"Smile O voluptuous cool breath'd earth !
Earth of the slumbering and liquid trees !
Earth of departed sunset — earth of the mountains, misty-topt !
Earth of the vitreous pour of the full moon just tinged with blue !
Earth of shine and dark mottling the tide of the river !
Earth of the limpid gray of clouds brighter and clearer for my sake !
Far-swooping elbow'd earth — rich apple-blossom'd earth !
Smile for your lover comes."

Whitman's positive artistic contribution is above all else the
sense of wonder which he applies to the treatment of life. He is
the poet of joy. He has tossed a new gladness among us, wrought
of wonder at the sight of the sky and sea, the body and soul, good
and evil, life and death. What is it to live and to die ? We
know what the ancients thought of death, — to wander, a bodiless
shade, over the joyless meadows thick with asphodel. In the
Middle Ages Death was pictured as a skeleton-archer with inevitable shaft, or as a hideous form summoning every man from his
garden of delights to the tomb, or charactered perchance in the
people's plays as a grim musician, leading a world-procession to
the charnel-house of the grave. The men of the Renaissance
also, rejoicing in the full life of the senses, and still under the
influence of mediæval thought, could but turn with a shudder from
the thought of Eld and Death. Raleigh could write over the
beauty, greatness, ambitions of men only two narrow, melancholy
words, "*Hic jacet.*" This is what Claudio thought was death : —

"To die and go we know not where ;
To lie in cold obstruction and to rot."

Milton for the first time broke with the past, though keeping
in mind the judgment day of the Puritan creed, and expressing his
grief in terms of classical monody, and saw the soul of Lycidas
not as dead, but as risen ; along other groves and streams Lycidas
laves his locks with nectar, and "hears the inexpressive nuptial
song" in the blest kingdom of the saints. Many are the modern
poets who have sung of death attesting to the continued power

of the thought over the soul of man. Death is now robbed of its terrors. Shelley takes a natural view, and sees the spirit of Keats as "awakened from the dream of life" : —

> " He is made one with Nature ; there is heard
> His voice in all her music, from the moan
> Of thunder, to the song of night's sweet bird !"
>
> "Dust to the dust ! but the pure spirit shall flow
> Back to the burning fountain whence it came."

In comparison with the centuries' elegiac songs I do not hesitate in placing the matchless 'Burial Hymn of Lincoln,' which is, as Swinburne notes, the most solemn nocturne ever chanted in the church of the world; it is to other elegies what Beethoven's ninth symphony is to other symphonies. In a chant of wonderful beauty, the divinity of death is sung. Whitman sings the very loveliness of death. It is wonderful to be here, "underfoot the divine soil, over head the sun." It is as wonderful to depart. The soul, equipped at last, its sails all spread, moves out into the loving, Infinite Sea, there to fulfil Time and Space. Death leads toward life, — perhaps the only real life, and we are the spectres. Death is a part of the world-order ; it is plan, happiness ; it is beautiful, mystical, an object of desire, worthy a chant of fullest welcome. And it must not be forgotten that the song issues from the heart of one who has intimate acquaintance with death in its most awful forms, the wounds of battle-fields.

"Long there and then in vigil I stood, dimly around me the battle-field spreading,
  Vigil wondrous and vigil sweet there in the fragrant silent night,
  But not a tear fell, nor even a long-drawn sigh ; long, long I gazed,
  Then on the earth partially reclining sat by your side leaning my chin in my hands,
  Passing sweet hours, immortal and mystical hours, with you dear comrade — not a
    :ear, not a word,
  Vigil of silence, love and death, vigil for you my son and my soldier."

His soldier-comrades are heard to say "good-by" and with the same breath say "hail," —

> " As filled with friendship, love complete, the Elder Brother found,
> The Younger melts in fondness in his arms ; "

and the poet is filled by the very wonder of the process with a sense of the strange and solemn beauty of death.

To conclude, I would that this study were animated more by the spirit of the student than by that of an advocate. How should one who is only anxious to know things as they really are so temper his words of interpretation that he may not offend those who find no justification for 'Leaves of Grass' at all? We gain nothing by being ungenerous, even to a book. It is only when we plunge soul-forward into a book's profound that we get the right good. We have yet to learn that one book does not counterpart another book any more than one eyesight counterparts another eyesight. There may be any number of supremes. Each book makes the growth by which alone it can be appreciated. " Every author," said Wordsworth, " so far as he is great and at the same time original has had the task of creating the taste by which he is to be enjoyed; so has it been, so will it continue to be." 'Leaves of Grass,' as I read and re-read it, is inexhaustible in suggestive thoughts. Those who suppose Whitman to be lacking in ideas should think a moment of the thought, and passion also, stored in these lines : —

" You are not thrown to the winds ; you gather certainly and safely around yourself."
" What do you suppose will satisfy the soul except to walk free and own no superior."
" This then is life, here ; what has come to the surface after so many throes and con-vulsions." " I am myself just as much evil as good and my nation is — and I say there is in fact no evil." " Clear and sweet is my soul and clear and sweet is all that is not my soul."

> " In this broad earth of ours,
>   Amid the measureless grossness and the slag,
>   Enclosed and safe within its central heart,
>   Nestles the seed perfection."

Then who learns these lessons complete is surprised to find it is no lesson at all : it only lets down the bars to a lesson, and that to another, and every one to another still. You are given to form for yourself lessons, poems, religions, politics, behavior, duty, and life. And this is the test of the poet who would assume to sing for America, for whose future is reserved the crowning triumph of history, — countless complete personalities.

" Think of the United States to-day, the facts of these thirty-eight or forty empires solder'd in one — sixty or seventy millions of equals, with their lives, their passions, their future — these incalculable modern American, seething multitudes around us, of which we are inseparable parts. Think in comparison of the petty environage and limited area of the poets of past and present Europe, no matter how great their genius. Think of the absence and ignorance in all cases hitherto of the multitudinousness, vitality, and the unprecedented stimulus of to-day and here. It almost seems as if a poetry with cosmic and dynamic features of magnitude and limitlessness suitable to the human soul, were never possible before. *It is certain that a poetry of absolute faith and equality for the use of the democratic masses never was.*" (Whitman : 'A Backward Glance.')

*Oscar L. Triggs.*

# AT INSPECTION.

## I. *Adagio.*

"HAT girl ought to be court-martialled !" said the colonel's wife, and glared through her lorgnette, with a glare before which the bravest men in her husband's regiment had more than once quailed.

The colonel's spectacled gaze followed his wife's to that corner of the post library where, under a festoon of flags, Peggy Warrington was holding court, surrounded seven deep, or thereabouts, with gentlemen in United States uniform.

"I don't see exactly why, my dear," said the colonel. The colonel had just taken a second glass of champagne ; which explains the temerity of his mild contradiction, where usually he gave unquestioning and unqualified assent.

"Why ?" said she. "Because Peggy Warrington is simply disorganizing the service ; and that 's why !"

"It seems to me, my dear," said the colonel (really that champagne must have been of uncommonly bracing quality !), — "it seems to me, my dear, that just at present Miss Warrington is uniting the service !"

"Stuff and nonsense!" said the colonel's wife.

And yet, judging from appearances, it would seem the colonel was right. For if ever unity of purpose was expressed in a group of faces, — faces grizzled and bronzed, faces mustached and martial, faces beardless and boyish, — such unity was in the score of faces bending eagerly forward to lose no word it might please Miss Peggy Warrington to give to a waiting world. And no less unity of purpose spoke in the attitude of the figures to which the faces belonged, — stalwart figures all, and all with the poise, the firm erectness of bearing, that is the hall-mark of soldierhood ; yet diverse enough in outline, too, from subaltern slenderness to majorly rotundity ; and wearing, on the broad shoulders, insignia of varied rank, from the bar-less straps of little Minnetts, not a year old in service, to the eagles that proudly spread their wings in the neighborhood of the Dundreary-like whiskers of Colonel Caplet, twice widowed, and beginning again to "take notice," his irreverent juniors said. Decidedly, in the matter of attitude Miss Peggy Warrington was uniting the service. From second lieutenant to colonel, the attitudes of her attendant group bespoke but one purpose ; namely, to be the nearest man to Miss Peggy Warrington when it should please her Majesty to change the location of her court, and incidentally to require the arm of an escort.

"But the girl is disorganizing the service, just the same!" said the colonel's wife, implacably, and lowered her lorgnette with every appearance of intense exasperation.

"Does n't a pretty girl's visit to an army post always disorganize the service temporarily, more or less, my dear ?" said the colonel. "I am sure, Cordelia, when you came to Riley, thirty years ago —"

"Don't talk to *me!*" said she, unappeased. "That's just it. The visit of most pretty girls to an army post may upset men and things temporarily, as you say ; but the visit of this pretty girl is going to upset one man, and several things, permanently, or I'm mistaken, — and more shame to her !"

The colonel's glance turned to the tallest of the tall, soldierly group who formed Peggy Warrington's guard of honor. "Yes,

Jack Falconer does seem a bit hard hit," said he, with a cheerfulness that was the last straw to his wife's camel-load of irritation.

" A bit hard hit ? He 's heart-hit, is Jack Falconer ; and for all his heart will ever be in the service again, it might as well have been hit with a Sioux bullet as that girl's eyes. I tell you this is n't the every-day sort of thing. Does the average pretty girl bring to an army post traditions of three millions of money ? That 's where the disorganization of the service comes in. Let one of our boys love the average pretty girl who 'll have none of him, and does he blame it to the service ? Not a bit of it: he realizes he 's not the man of her choice, and that nothing 's at fault but heart's caprice ; and he stands up to his luck with an army boy's pluck, and presently is ready to up again and —"

"And take another ? " finished the colonel, with a twinkle.

" Well, that was n't what I meant to say ; but it 's apt enough," said she. " But what lad, proud with a right man's pride, is ever going to bring himself, and his subaltern's quarters, and his lieutenant's pay, within asking distance of the richest heiress of the season ? And do you suppose such a lad does n't say to himself that if he had n't buried himself in a uniform, he might have stood some chance in the world outside of winning a fortune fit to come a-wooing to hers ? Whereas, once in the service, where 's a man's chance at money-making ? And so the lad who 's been proud, with all his honest heart, to wear the blue, to-day simply damns the service from reveille to taps."

The colonel's wife had seen long and hard service with the regiment; and the use of condensed and fervent English was an army privilege well earned by many army hardships.

" I should have thought," said the colonel, reflectively, " that when a fellow of Falconer's make-up came a woman's way, she 'd be thinking of something else beside check-books."

" You unmassacred innocent! One might know you 'd never been beyond garrison limits except when there was an Indian rampage ! " said the colonel's wife.

The brief recess in the dancing was done ; and from their niche over in one of the deep-sunk casement windows, the regimental band, that was doing itself proud to-night, with so fair a world to hear, began the first swinging and singing chords of the "Sweethearts" waltzes. The group about Peggy Warrington started expectantly astir; and the farthest men shouldered the nearest men, in eagerness to know what would next be the queen's pleasure.

"I think this is our dance, Miss Warrington?" said Captain Forrester; and he flourished triumphantly, before his comrades' envious eyes, the dance-order on which — he being but short, and quite unable to behold Miss Warrington over Jack Falconer's stalwart shoulders — he had kept his eyes fixed, in ecstatic anticipation, for the last ten minutes.

"Oh, but I don't think it is our dance yet, Captain Forrester," said Peggy Warrington; and she moved forward a step or two from where she stood. The light of the low-swinging lamps glinted on her bronze-bright hair. One of the knot of crimson roses loosely fastened in the belt of her soft white Empire gown fell apart, as she moved, in the enervating heat, and fluttered down, petal by velvety bright petal. One, as it floated, brushed fairily against Jack Falconer's strong white wrist. Involuntarily he put out his hand as though to stay its flight; and a swift and sudden color surged up to his frank brown face.

"No, I am quite sure this is not our dance, Captain Forrester," Miss Warrington was saying. "See! They have put up the card that says it is an extra; and I am not to dance one extra this evening, — no!" — in answer to a protesting chorus — "no, not one! You too hospitable people have given me so much merrymaking I am almost tired out. And somehow dancing seems to belong to the winter evenings, and not to the soft first spring — "

"And certainly not to these confounded boxes of casemates!" said Colonel Caplet, and mopped his ruddy and perspiring brow. "A man feels as if he were carrying these stone ceilings on his head, when he's dancing under 'em. You 're very sensible to do as little of it as possible, Miss Warrington. Now, over there in the window there are some such jolly comfortable armchairs — "

"Now, when you 're tired of dancin', Miss Warrington," — thus little Lieutenant Minnetts, breaking eagerly in on the colonel's ponderous and paternal address, — "when you're tired of dancin', there's nothin' so refreshin' as a water-ice, lemon or orange, it does n't matter; and they've got 'em both in Ebbett's quarters, next door, that we're usin' to-night for our supper-room; and if you would n't mind comin'— "

"Oh, I don't believe it is an ice I want," she said. "You've surfeited me with them too, you army people who pretend to such hardships, and are the most famous Sybarites I know. I am so dull to-night that I can't even guess what it is I do want; but I 'm quite sure it's not dancing, nor rest, nor ices — "

"Could it be a breath of fresh air, do you think?" said Jack Falconer. He moved to the nearest deep-set casement window, and lifted it wide. The wet and wooing air of the spring night blew softly in; and mingling with it was a keen and salty tang, and a sound of the voice of the near, unseen sea.

The girl moved forward with a long-drawn breath of sudden pleasure. "Oh, it was just that I wanted," she said; and she leaned her rose-flushed face against the cool stone of the window-side.

"There's so much more of it outside," said Falconer, and paused, questioning her with his smiling eyes. "There's a grand sea-wind on the ramparts to-night; and the moon is just rising, yonder, over the old town. If you cared to come out for just a breath — ?"

"It is good of you to think of it," she said. "If I had my cloak — "

"I saw you'd be wantin' it, and I ran and got it." Thus Lieutenant Minnetts, panting, at her elbow, her hooded white burnous across his uniformed arm. There were moments when the self-abnegation of Lieutenant Minnetts verged on the sublime.

"And you found it, among all those wraps, in just that moment? What a trailsman you would make!" she said. She took a rose from her fading belt-knot. "You deserve a better decoration for such skill; but perhaps you 'll take this, as the best I have to offer?" And while the little lieutenant was trying to force his rapturous thanks past a queer and sudden lump in his throat, she threaded her way lightly, on Falconer's arm, through the merry maze of dancers, and out through the heavy door, on to the silent parade. The wide sky was all a-thrill with the great spring stars. The springing grass of the parade had an oddly restful and friendly feel to the foot after the dance-room's slippery floor. The girl's hood blew back, in the strong, soft wind ; even the faint light of the waning, late-risen moon found the glint in her thick, bright hair.

"There she goes in search of one last scalp!" said the colonel's wife, vengefully. The colonel's wife was eating shrimp salad by the open window of Lieutenant Ebbett's casemate quarters, temporarily turned supper-room. "It's the only one left her to take. There were three up to this time, last night. But she refused Colonel Caplet on the way home from the Repfords' German; and I reckon everybody in the officers' row knew it, for Caplet is so deaf, you know, and he would have her answer loud enough for him to hear. And she finished up little Minnetts at the tennis-court this afternoon. And now it's Jack Falconer, — the best for the last. The girl's a regular Apache!"

"Well, you won't be troubled with her after to-morrow, my dear," said the colonel.

"But Falconer will, — worse luck!" said she. "*Pour dormir bien, il y a certaines rêves qu'il faut n'avoir jamais fait.* Peggy Warrington is one of those dreams. It's never a quiet sleep our boy will know, thanks to her, this many a night, — the heartless minx!" said she. Every unmarried officer in the regiment was "our boy" to the keen-tongued, great-hearted, childless wife of the regiment's colonel; which is why, though the regiment, in the seclusion of quarters, occasionally swore about the colonel's wife, there was not a man in the regiment but swore by her.

They had crossed the parade, and climbed leisurely the narrow, winding stairs, deep-sunk in the stone, which led to the broad ramparts. A little breathless from her climb, the girl moved toward a corner of the low wall, and stood half leaning against the great cannon that, a grim and silent warder, turned its black muzzle seaward. Her ungloved hand, lightly resting on its dark, rough shape, looked curiously small and fragile; its many jewels sparkled drowsily in the faint, soft light. Up here, on this clear, unsheltered height, the freshening wind rioted at its will. Above, the stars flashed and dimmed, through the swift-driven cloud-drift; below, in the channel, the waves of the quick-incoming tide doffed and donned white caps of foam, in·salute to the slow rising moon. The old town across the water was in shadow; here and there a late light twinkled; the quaint towers and gabled roofs made dim, fantastic silhouettes against the sky. From across the parade, through the rush of the wind, came the lilt of the " Sweethearts " waltz.

"Oh, how different it is up here!" the girl said, and drew a deep, soft breath.

" Yes," said Falconer, briefly. " Up here you get the soldierly side of it all, — is n't that what you mean? And down there in the dance-room, only the social side; that 's just like the social side of any other life."

"Oh, so tiresomely like it!" she said, with quick, quaint candor. "That was what was fretting me to-night. I did n't want my last picture of it all to be a picture of lights and waltz-music and folk jigging about just as they do everywhere else; I wanted to remember the dear old place on its soldier side, as you call it, — the quiet, steadfast side, that obeys orders, and keeps long, untired watch — "

The light hand lay against the grim old cannon, as with the comfort of a felt defence. There was something like a wistful weariness in the girl's clear voice.

" And this is the last picture of it you will see?" Falconer said. He stood erect against an angle of the parapet, his back to the sea, looking intently down upon her.

" Almost the last. I go at noon to-morrow, you know; but I shall be here for one more guard-mount and for the inspection. I would n't miss that. Nothing in all soldier-life amuses me like watching an inspection, do you know?" she said, and laughed the low, soft laugh that was music in his ears. "It amuses me just because it seems so unmilitary, — so like something Gilbert might put into one of his operas, instead of a real, serious army function. It is so droll to see those big, broad-shouldered, bearded fellows stand up there to be looked over, to see if they 're properly tidy, for all the world as we children used, in nursery days. When I see them hand over their guns, one by one, I feel as if the next minute I should be down among them, and hold up my pinafore, as I used, to show there were no jam spots on it, and my hands, to show there was nothing in them that should n't be! I should feel so virtuous to have my officer look me over and see nothing to find fault with."

In the uncertain light, she did not catch the odd look that came up into Falconer's eyes. For a long moment he stood looking down at her, — at the lovely outlines of the girlish figure in its wind-blown white draperies ; the brightness of her loosened hair ; the clear, delicate profile, instinct with race and breeding ; the sweet and brave brown eyes ; the pure, young, sensitive mouth. He caught a deep breath. " Well," he said then, lightly enough, " I fancy it 's mighty little to find fault with your officer will see in you, when your impulse gets the better of you, and you go down for inspection some day ! "

There was a quick, military step below them, on the flagged pavement circling the parade. A tall soldier, carrying a bugle, had come out from a casemate door. It was the hour of soldierly good-night.

" And so you go to-morrow," Falconer said again, as if, that being true, there were no more to say.

" To-morrow. You know Hugh, my only brother, — we two are all that are left now, — is on the ocean, and the ' Bothnia ' will make port in a day or two. I would n't for the world fail to be on the wharf. Hugh is all that really belongs to me in the wide world."

" That sounds so strange, — from you, of all people ! " her companion said. " One thinks of you as having all fortune, and all the world belonging to you; a world of friends — "

" Oh, friends ! " she said, and stood erect, facing him with that clear, direct look that had been the despair of Madame de Sucresse in her boarding-school days. " For no demoiselle has such a look: it is a boy's trick of glance, — *un veritable regard de garçon !* "

Madame would protest, almost in tears. "A demoiselle looks meekly, with veiled eyes." But it had never been the way of the Warringtons to look meekly, with veiled eyes. It was with the old, unlost *regard de garçon* that Peggy Warrington faced the young officer beside her, as she said, "Oh, friends!"—and she lifted her hand from the cannon with a curious gesture, as though she were lifting something of light weight and throwing it to the wind and to the sea. "Yes, I suppose I have friends enough; but what is there in friendship of sureness and ownness and belonging?"

It was another moment before he answered. Jack Falconer had never been so dull and taciturn before; and then it was only to echo her words. "No, there is nothing in friendship of ownness or belonging," he said.

The bugler was at his station on the parade. Clear, through the rushing wind, sweet and solemn above the light lilt of the dance-tune, came the call, "Lights out!" Over the grim old fort, over the restless water, over the clover-sown fields, over the white-walled space among them, where slept the soldiers whose warfare is all done, the slow, strenuous, pathetic notes rose and thrilled and faded. "Taps" was sounded; the soldier's day was done.

There were sudden tears in the girl's brown eyes. "There is no cadence in all the world like that," she said. "All soldierhood is in it,—all its simple duty and strait obediences; all its long, stern faithfulness, and sure, safe protection. Ah, how flimsy and superficial other life seems when one has known such a life as this!" said Peggy Warrington. "How one comes to scorn anything that is weak and artificial,—anything that smells of the hot-house, and the life lived away from the open sky!"

She took the Jacqueminot roses from her belt, and leaf by leaf she plucked them apart. The petals strewed the rough stone of the ramparts,—a rich and fragrant rain; and the rioting wind caught at them, and bore them out to sea.

"Miss Warrington," Falconer said, and his voice was not quite steady,—"Miss Warrington, I have done no service, as Minnetts did, to earn it; I shall never have a chance to serve

41

you, but will you give me, just as to a beggar, who asks your charity,—will you give me a rose?"

As if startled at the impetuous words, the girl suddenly opened the hand that held the roses, and the next instant they had dropped, wind-swept, from the parapet, and were tossing in the channel far below.

" I — I am not sorry they fell!" Peggy Warrington said. " Mr. Falconer, I — I did not want you to — I did not want to give you — a rose. Mr. Falconer!"

He had gone deadly white. He caught at the rampart behind him; there was a cloud across his sight.

" Oh, Mr. Falconer, I did not mean —" He put out his hand to stay her words. He was getting himself in hand again, but it was with a stress and strain that left him gray as ashes.

" One moment," he said, "just one moment's patience! I — I am sorry you should have to add to your army pictures the picture of a soldier who is a coward!"

She stood silent, her eyes wide and dark. " I did n't think — I did n't guess — it would hit me like that!" he said. " I forgot a fellow is n't all of a piece, and his heart may hope and dream after his reason has seen it all, and has settled it all for him. You were right and good and womanly not to give me the rose. You knew I was asking — you heard between the words I was asking — for more than the rose."

" I knew," she said. " And that was why —"

" That was why you refused it downright, and did not play with me," he said. " And it was good of you, and brave. Perhaps you heard between the words, too, that I did not mean to speak them. From the hour I knew I loved you, I promised myself I would not speak them. I have known — how well I have known! — that you were here among us for an hour, only as a bird might alight on that old cannon " — he laid his hand where her hand had rested — " for a moment's rest, in its flight between brightness and brightness. If a man's heart wrenches itself out of his breast to follow you when you take flight again, is it your fault, dear?"

There was silence again, but for the voices of wind and sea.

" Don't think I blame you. Don't think I have n't seen it as plain from the first as I see it now. I 've told myself from the first that no woman worth respecting would see a man leave the service he has chosen with heart-choice, and be her pensioner in a world whose ways he 's never learned. You know my father was a soldier, and his father before him. And no man worth respecting would ask a woman who belongs to the world, and the world to her, to leave it all for a subaltern's quarters, and his knock-about life, and dull, quiet routine of duty."

Again silence. For that moment the wind was still.

" And so it 's good-by, and God bless you! " he said. " I shall be on duty to-morrow at inspection, you know ; and — and — so good-by. Forget I was a coward. It was my heart turned coward, and died, when that rose went over the parapet. But my will is alive, and that 's the best part of a fellow, after all ! "

The dance-music had been at pause. Now it suddenly came singing forth again, a new and merrier measure.

" That must be Forrester's dance, I am sure," said Jack Falconer. He crossed to the head of the narrow stair, and held out his hand to her. He stood quite erect, and his voice had its familiar, soldierly ring. As she gave him her hand for a moment, that he might guide her down the rough steps, he held it close.

" I thank you, Peggy. Dear, may I call you that this once ? I thank you for being here with me these good minutes. I thank you for coming into my life. I 'm not going to the devil, — don't think it. And I 'm coming here sometimes, when the wind blows, to remember how you stood here, and how your cloak blew across my shoulder, and you let me call you Peggy, and your eyes did n't scorn me for a coward. God bless you, Peggy ! Now shall we go down ? "

They found Captain Forrester doing "sentry go" before the dance-room door. She passed in, the two men following. Falconer, with a bow, resigned her to his comrade, and turned on his heel toward the still open door. As he turned, the colonel's wife caught a glimpse of his face.

" Take me home ! " said the colonel's wife. And the colonel, much perturbed in spirit, saw her keen eyes clouded with the first tears of twenty years.

## II. *Allegro.*

THE clear, blithe notes of the bugles went ringing over the morning fields. The flag — central glory and chief of army Lares and Penates — flung its broad stripes and splendid stars far skyward at the wind's brave call. The roughened channel ran windily and blue. The soft new grass, the gold-eyed daisies, the sturdy red clover, danced and swayed and nodded till all the earth looked merrily astir and aware. The parade, too, was all astir with ordered lines of blue-coated figures, from whose shining accoutrements the sunlight flashed dazzlingly back. And up and down the ordered lines Jack Falconer went, scanning the accoutrements with a critical eye, handling the polished muskets one by one, and surveying their owners with a glance that no neglected detail was wont to escape. And — "Should I know if anything were wrong, this morning, I wonder, even if it were before my very eyes?" Falconer was saying to himself. "What's wrong with me? What's wrong with me? I've kept night-watch many a time before, and been as fit as a fiddle next morning, when I've had my tub and gotten into my togs. But now —" he swallowed once or twice dry-throatedly ; he looked, curiously and scornfully, at the tremor of the hand held out for a musket. "Will it always be like this? Will there never be sleep in a man's bed any more, nor light in the sun, nor strength in his right hand? Good God! because a fellow's heart has died in him has his head got to turn queer too? I wonder if I seem queer? I wonder if the men notice?"

The men did notice. The privates of the line are wont to stand at attention in more senses than one, as those who know the army have learned long ago. In all possible senses they were standing at attention now, as the most popular officer in the regiment, his face set and very pale, his outstretched hand strangely unsteady, went up and down the line.

"There was junketing a-plenty last night," — thus from one

corner of the mouth, in speech scarcely visible or audible, by the queer trick known to enlisted men in moments of supposed silence, a private, to his neighbor, at the far end of the line. "The young liftenant has the signs of a swelled head this morning!"

"An' it's ahl the signs of a shwelled head you'll exhibit, and it'll be shwelled from an outward an' visible fist, an' not from an inside an' spiritual sensation — if you don't hold yer scandalous whist!" jerked back his next neighbor. Private Michael Mooney's fists had their reputation in the regiment. The conversation dropped.

Was he glad she had not come to the parade-ground? Was he sorry? The question beat itself against his temples as with mailed fingers. He did not know if he were glad or sorry. He knew he was glad from his sick heart that no other of the feminine host of garrison guests had out-rested last night's revel sufficiently to come; and that, inspection once over — would inspection ever be over? would it ever be over? — he could go his way across the unwontedly deserted parade-ground without greeting or stay. Yet he knew that, turn as his duty led him, he saw with the eyes of his heart that sallyport through which, coming from officers' quarters, she must come — if she came — if she came —

She was there. The tumult in his blood told him that, though he could not see her, and the soft grass whispered no secret of footsteps. She had come, not from officers' quarters, but from the sea-path and the meadows. She wore a gown of blue, and her hat had blown back in the sea-wind. Her hands were full of newly gathered daisies, white and gold. She moved slowly across the end of the parade-ground farthest from the line of men; she kept at due and respectful distance from the army function in such evident progress. He mechanically took musket after musket, and turned it end for end, and about and about, but he saw neither musket nor man nor earth nor sea. He saw that she had come to pause, far from the end of the line to whose last man he was approaching, yet exactly in line with the man, and facing as he faced. And Falconer saw, as he took the last man's musket, that she, standing in line far beyond, suddenly, as she felt his glance

wander to her, straightened herself to exact military erectness;
and with exactly the gesture the soldier tendered him his musket
for inspection, Peggy Warrington held out toward him the bunch
of daisies she carried in her hands, and in her brown eyes there
was a smile that shone through a mist, — or was it his eyes that lent
to that smile its mist? It passed in a breath, — in the time of a
beat-beat, — and the next moment the girl was making her idle,
leisurely way toward the staircase to the ramparts, and where she
had stood, the grass was white with fallen daisies.

His soldierhood was instinct of blood and gift of training; and
by grace of his soldierhood he carried through his duty to its end.
But the world danced before his eyes, as if gone mad with joy of
the sweet spring weather; the waves danced on their glad race
seaward; the old flag danced to the joyous wind's wild piping
from the height of its swaying staff; the daisies danced in the
green May meadows; and in his breast the boy's heart, which last
night he had told her was dead within him, danced to the music of
new-awakened hope and a great, mad, dizzying joy, past all believing, past all imagining.   And —

"And, oh, Jack!" she said, as they stood together, well to the
seaward-side of the ramparts, where no prying eyes from the parade-
ground might mark them too clearly, — "and, oh, Jack — for I will
call you Jack, since you called me Peggy last night, without so
much as 'by your leave' — was it so very dreadful for me to bring
my daisies for the inspection of my officer, to see if they did not
please him quite as well as that stupid, glass-grown, sick-sweet
rose — that rose that I would not give him last night because it
was not mine to give — "

"Not yours, my Peggy?"

"Not mine to *give*, I said, you dull, headlong, half-hearing boy!
Not mine to give, because those Jacqueminot roses came to me
yesterday, all the way from New York, and a question came with
them; and I wore them in my belt when I was turning the
question over and over in my heart, — not that it was any use to
turn it, though he isn't a bad sort of man, and he would take me

into a life where we could pick roses every day at ever so many dollars the dozen — Jack!" — for a sudden shadow had crossed his happy eyes — "Jack! Foolish great fellow! Can't you see? In the hour I knew my own heart, dear, his roses slipped away and were lost. It was not his rose I would give you, Jack, — it was not any flower, city-grown, away from the sunlight and the wind and the open truths of things, that I would give you, my soldier; it was a flower grown here, in the shadow of the dear, brave, gray ramparts, — in the wind that floats the old flag — "

"If you had said it, sweetheart! If I had known!"

"And how could I say it, with my officer ordering me off the ramparts, down to the dance-room, and telling me how he had known from the first that this was unfit, and that was impossible — "

"Peggy, my dearest, it is all unfit and impossible, still — only — "

"Only," she said, and it was with no "veiled and meek" demoiselle-glance that her steadfast brown eyes looked straight at the man who loved her, — "only you are not going to insult the woman you love, Lieut. Jack Falconer, by telling her that you reverence and fear her wretched money, where for herself you have neither reverence nor fear!"

"Peggy!"

"I mean it, Jack! What else does a man say when he says: I might dare to ask you for your love, for your womanhood, for all yourself and all that to you is sacredest, — but I dare not ask you to trust me with your fortune!"

"My Peggy, forgive me! I have been coarse and dull and blind! But you will trust me, Peggy, and let me begin all over again, and woo you pluckily, my darling, as a soldier should?"

"Why woo where you have won, my officer?" she said.

The colonel and his wife were crossing the parade as Jack Falconer and Peggy came to the head of the staircase from the ramparts. He stood on the step below her and held out his hand for her hand; and the sunlight was on his face, and the sunlight was in his brave and glad blue eyes.

"My dear!" said the colonel, "does n't it almost look as if —"

"Well, and if — at long and at last and by beneficent miracle — it does look 'as if —'" said she. "Is n't that the best of reasons for not staring them out of countenance with those blessed old binoculars of spectacles of yours ?"

"I — I was curious to see what he was showing her, my dear!" said the colonel, guiltily.

He was showing her a soft, faded something he had found, drifted into a cranny of the rough, gray staircase-wall. It was the petal of a Jacqueminot rose.          *Dorothy Lundt.*

# EMMA LAZARUS: WOMAN; POET; PATRIOT.

## WOMAN.

THE personality of Emma Lazarus is one that has done much to ennoble womanhood. I will first consider Emma Lazarus as a woman, for that is one of the most important things to be regarded in the presentation of her life. By this I mean that many believe that if a woman is to be thoroughly womanly, she is to be nothing else; I therefore intend to show that in the present instance no statement can be more untrue than the one just cited. Her biographer says of her, "She was a true woman, too distinctly feminine to wish to be exceptional, or to stand alone and apart, even by virtue of superiority." This was true; but with genius such as hers, although she was a very woman, it was not possible for her brilliant powers to remain veiled by modesty.

She was one of a large family, parents and children being fondly united. I remember distinctly the vivid picture given me by Col. Thomas Wentworth Higginson, two winters ago, of the beautiful unity of sympathy binding the family together. He said: "I chanced to call at the house, and found every one there in such distress that I thought something terrible must have occurred; my hasty inquiry of the daughters brought out the fact that their father was going away: but, I asked, he will come back? ' *Yes, to-morrow night,*' was the mournful reply." Colonel Higginson said that this little scene was a revelation to him of the wonderful bond of love encircling the family. In conversation, too, with her sister a short time since, it was not difficult to perceive the depth of regard which each held for each, and which death had no power to lessen or change.

The home in which Emma Lazarus grew up was remarkable for its atmosphere of culture and refinement. All the aids to social interchange, all the accomplishments which can give a charm to daily life, softening little anxieties and turning the thoughts to constant aspiration, were present there in a very marked degree. One felt the influence of the fine picture, the choice book, the elegant instrument, not as an outside addition to the furniture, but as an inner factor in determining the elevation of taste, the trend of thought, the entrance of the spirit into pure harmony.

Her life as a woman was comparatively retired. Her quiet, unpretentious manner gave strangers very little indication of the mind contained within that unobtrusive figure. She had many devoted friends, was passionately fond of Nature, and almost equally allured by art. Mr. Emerson corresponded with her for a number of years ; and Miss Lazarus probably drew from this friendship as much benefit in the womanly part of her nature as she derived stimulus from the mental contact with the distinguished author. She was fond of the theatre, and particularly appreciated the splendid impersonations of Salvini. She was much sought after in cultured society in New York.

Although the full consideration of Emma Lazarus' interest in the Russian refugees of 1881 belongs to the department of her poetry, yet we cannot describe her as a woman without dwelling with profound earnestness upon the qualities of noble womanhood which she exhibited at this time. I will quote again from her biographer, who says : " These were busy, fruitful years for Emma Lazarus, who worked, not with the pen alone, but in the field of practical and beneficent activity. For there was an immense task to accomplish. The tide of immigration had set in, and ship after ship came laden with hunted human beings fleeing from their fellowmen, while all the time, like a tocsin, rang the terrible story of cruelty and persecution, — horrors that the pen refuses to dwell upon. By hundreds and thousands they flocked upon our shores, — helpless, innocent victims of injustice and oppression, panic-stricken in the midst of strange and utterly new surroundings. Emma Lazarus came into personal contact with these people, and visited them in their refuge on Ward's Island.

This tragic development in the history of her people drew forth from Emma Lazarus many womanly qualities hitherto unsuspected. Her devotion to the best interests of the refugees was very marked and very consistent. She now felt herself to be not alone a woman, but eminently a Jewish woman. As is said of her, "Her whole being renewed and refreshed itself at its very source. She threw herself into the study of her race, its language, literature and history."

I feel that these extracts from the biographical sketch of our sister in faith do but faint justice to the fine, harmonious outline there portrayed; but it is scarcely possible to represent it as fully here as I should like. Those who will, may seek further in that literary treasure-house, and find many more precious traits than I can possibly have time to depict.

Her first visit abroad was in May, 1883 ; and from a woman she is said to have been almost transformed into a child, so dazed was she with the novelty and beauty of her European visit. She had the pleasure of meeting with great appreciation from many of the most eminent persons of the day, both from leading people of her own race and those of other nations.

Her visit to England impressed her as it does most American women, — with great power and with charm. A day spent with William Morris, the author of that beautiful poem, 'The Earthly Paradise,' appealed to her very especially on the philanthropic side of her nature; the poet himself received her as his guest, took her all over the factory, which he had arranged for his work-people, and showed her how even an old Norman monastery might be converted into a comfortable place of business, where the directing mind had the good-will and kindliness so to order affairs. Her social qualities came very much to the front during this foreign stay, and the whole of this time appears to have been a peaceful, happy period.

Upon the death of her father, the next winter, we find new developments in the character of Emma Lazarus. She was, as has been intimated before, very closely attached to him, and the bereavement seems to have affected her with a sudden failure of composure and energy. Her biographer says, " Truly the silver cord was loosed, and the golden bowl was broken. Life lost its meaning and its charm." Once again she sailed for England, in the hope that the varied life there, with the congenial friends she had made, would restore her to serenity ; and in this she was quite correct. One can imagine when she came to Italy what the superb beauty of that land meant to such a woman as she was, and particularly because Rome and Roman ideas had early fascinated her to a great extent.

She was very soon after this attacked by serious symptoms of disease. She was not conscious that her malady was dangerous, and only by degrees realized that she was too weak to travel about. She herself was now struck with the analogy between herself and Heine on his mattress-grave in Paris. It is said of her that she, too, the last time she went out, dragged herself to the Louvre, to the feet of the Venus, "the goddess without arms, who could not help." Her vitality alone seemed to sustain breath. As she expressed it, she "seemed to have always one little window looking out into life." I do not imagine that she was ever a pessimist ; yet at this time she said, " No such cure for pessimism as a severe illness; the simplest pleasures are enough, — to breathe the air and see the sun."

On July 23 of the same year she came home, returning, however, only to die. Those who saw her in that last phase of her life were amazed at the brilliance of her intellect, which seemed to flame higher and higher as the powers of her body declined. It must have appeared as if her aspiring spirit were preparing itself for a purer and more fitting atmosphere.

I feel that in leaving the part of this essay devoted to the consideration of her womanly qualities, I cannot do better than to repeat what has already been written of her: "It is the privilege of a favored few that every fact and circumstance of their individuality shall add lustre and value to what they achieve."

## POET.

It may be noted as a singular fact that in mental development Emma Lazarus began with the study of Paganism, and passing through many phases of religious thought, arrived finally and forever at Judaism. This was no doubt due to the peculiar education of her earlier years. Her mind does not appear to have been greatly impressed with the ideas belonging to the mental equipment of a young and brilliant Jewess. As no special devotion to Jewish ceremonies was required of her, the forms were not present to array and express the spirit, and her intellect was permitted to lavish itself upon what it would. It was naturally attracted to Greek and Roman ideas, to classic myths, to art as embodied in mythology, to beauty for itself alone. The affinity between her mind and that of Heine has been unmistakably shown ; her translations of some of his songs can probably not be surpassed. As her intellect came to early maturity at fourteen, she wrote then four poems which were marked by a melancholy showing plainly that the young poet was still in that period of life when the imagination takes a leading part, and a bewitching sadness is more coveted than the most glowing joy. It seems as if Nature avenged herself for the free, unchecked buoyancy and careless happiness which really belong to these years, while making the child crave the unrest and "sweet sorrow" which the old would gladly avoid.

At the age of twenty-one, her second book, 'Admetus and Other Poems,' which is a remarkable production, and thought by many to rival the treatment of the same theme by Robert Browning, appeared. It is certainly very beautiful in many respects.

'The Masque of Venice' is supposed to be a dream, and is remarkable for the pictorial quality which marks most of her poems. How wondrously is the word fitted to the idea, proving, too, that our language, in the hands of such a poet as she was, may challenge comparison with the soulful German, or the liquid Italian. One verse of this Venetian dream will explain my meaning.

> " Not a stain,
> In the sun-brimmed sapphire cup that is the sky —
> Not a ripple on the black translucent lane
> Of the palace-walled lagoon.
> Not a cry
> As the gondoliers with velvet oar glide by,
> Through the golden afternoon."

The poems entitled 'Phantasies,' after Robert Schumann, seem to reflect perfectly the poet's understanding of the musician's work. They are beautiful, spiritual, and melodious.

'Epochs' is also a series of poems which show depth of feeling and a wonderful knowledge of the varied phases of life. They begin with 'Youth,' and end with 'Peace.'

'Alide,' published in 1874, was a prose work taken from Goethe's 'Autobiography.' Tourgenieff wrote to Miss Lazarus concerning this romance, "An author who writes as you do is not a pupil in art any more; he is not far from being himself a master."

One of her finest achievements in literature is, I think, her play entitled 'The Spagnoletto.' It is said that Emerson took it up not expecting to read it through, and was not able to lay it down. A careful study of this drama makes one understand just how this could be ; the title gives not the faintest idea of the force and beauty of the production. Not only are we transported into the veritable Italian life, with its devotion to art, its impulsive speech, and its luxuriant Nature, but we are brought face to face with the intense and lovely personality of Maria-Rosa, the heroine. Her father describes her thus : —

> " From this point
> I see her clearly — the auroral face
> A-light with smiles, the imperial head upraised ;
> Her languid hand sways the broad, silken fan,
> Whose wing-like movement stirs above her brow
> The fine, bright curls, as though warm airs of heaven
> Around her breathed."

One does not wonder that even the master-mind of Concord was riveted by words like these. The whole play is harmonious in language, in detail, and in *motif.* It has been criticised as ending inartistically, but in my opinion it would have been impossible to close the drama in any other way.

In 1881 her translation of Heine's poems and ballads was published.

In 1879 the persecution against the Russian Jews had its rise. Almost everywhere in Europe this unholy war was waged. It sometimes happens that out of the most fearful evils a supreme good springs forth. Had it not been for this sudden persecution, it is probable that Emma Lazarus would have passed from her cradle to her grave insensible to her magnificent birthright. Even in 1882 her conception of the modern Jew was scarcely a worthy one. It was the defence, by Madam Ragozin, of Russian barbarity that first roused the poet to the defence of her race. 'The Banner of the Jew' is a poem instinct with enthusiasm and really virile power. 'Rosh Hashanah,' 'Hanuckah,' and the 'New Ezekiel' are splendid testimonials to the poet's faith and devotion. Her biographer says : " She had come upon the secret and the genius of Judaism, — that absolute interpenetration and transfusion of spirit with body and substance which, taken literally, often reduces itself to a question of food and drink, a dietary regulation, and again, in proper splendor, incarnates itself and shines out before humanity in the prophets, teachers, and saviors of mankind."

'The Children of the Ghetto,' which has aroused a widespread interest at the present day, proves the perfect truth of the description just cited.

I come now to the consideration of one of the poet's most important works, 'The Dance to Death.' We are all familiar with the foundation of this drama, which is the oppression of the Jews in the twelfth century, in Thuringia. Emma Lazarus has represented this very interesting subject in the most effective way. Although it is probable that the drama would not be suitable for acting, yet it is, like many of Browning's, an inspiring, intellectual feast when merely read.

It was about this time that her volume of poems entitled 'Songs of a Semite' was published. It was dedicated to George Eliot, in grateful appreciation of what the great author had done to ennoble the idea of Jewish nationality.

Some persons seem to prefer the poem called 'The Choice' to all others by Miss Lazarus. It is certainly very original, very powerful, and with a magnetic quality that fascinates the feelings. Another poem which seems to me one of the most glorious is called 'Gifts.'

Some of her work which appeals to me with the greatest force are the little poems in prose called 'By the Waters of Babylon.' Listen to this, headed 'The Prophet.'

" 1. Moses ben Maimon lifting his perpetual lamp over the path of the perplexed ;

" 2. Ha-levi, the honey-tongued poet, wakening amid the silent ruins of Zion the sleeping lyre of David ;

" 3. Moses, the wise son of Mendel, who made the Ghetto illustrious ;

" 4. Abarbanel, the counsellor of kings ; Alcharisi, the exquisite singer ; Ibn Ezra, the perfect old man ; Gabirol, the tragic seer ;

" 5. Heine, the enchanted magician, the heart-broken jester ;

" 6. Yea, and the century-crowned patriarch whose bounty engirdles the globe ; —

" 7. These need no wreath and no trumpet; like perennial asphodel blossoms, their fame, their glory resounds like the brazen-throated cornet.

" 8. But thou — hast thou faith in the fortune of Israel ? Wouldst thou lighten the anguish of Jacob?

" 9. Then shalt thou take the hand of yonder caftaned wretch with flowing curls and gold-pierced ears ;

" 10. Who crawls blinking forth from the loathsome recesses of the Jewry;

"11. Nerveless his fingers, puny his frame; haunted by the bat-like phantoms of superstition is his brain.

"12. Thou shalt say to the bigot, 'My Brother,' and to the Creature of darkness, 'My Friend.'

"13. And thy heart shall spend itself in fountains of love upon the ignorant, the coarse, and the abject.

"14. Then in the obscurity thou shalt hear a rush of wings, thine eyes shall be bitten with pungent smoke.

"15. And close against thy quivering lips shall be pressed the live coal wherewith the Seraphim brand the Prophets."

The verses just quoted illustrate the power of the poet to be truly poetical even in prose.

The translations from Alfred de Musset are worthy of especial attention. There is a wondrous fascination in the style, and I am tempted to think that her interpretation of the French poet may even surpass the original. Those who are in love with French poetry will possibly smile at this statement; but to my way of thinking, the English language is far richer, more tender and touching, in poetry especially, than the French. Of course we must remember that Emma Lazarus is probably but following the original; yet one is almost persuaded, in these charming translations, that she is the master, not the follower.

Appreciative mention must be made of the lovely translations from the Hebrew poets of mediæval Spain, among the most noteworthy being those from Gabirol and Jehudah Ha-levi. The hymn beginning, 'Almighty, what is man?' is too celebrated to require quotation.

In summing up the qualities which make Emma Lazarus the poet that she was, the most remarkable of all is the atmospheric quality with which she seemed to pervade her work. No matter what mood of Nature she wished to present, her will but ordered, and the scene is instantly before us. We see the crimson dawn with faintly glowing clouds, we feel the pure, fresh air, we rejoice in the approach of the sun. Noon may come with its glorious blue sky, the brilliancy of summer heat, the hum of insects, the delicious languor of an hour of rest. Sunset and night are no more neglected by her than the rising of the day or the noontide.

Our souls float onward in the enchanted air, feeling as she feels, seeing where she points. It is a noble thing to be a woman; it is a proud thing to be a poet. What is it, then, to be at once woman and poet!

## PATRIOT.

ALLUSION has already been made to the patriotism of Emma Lazarus in connection with the Russian persecutions of her people, and it must not be forgotten that she was also a patriotic American. Those who remember her stirring words describing the Bartholdi statue, will feel assured anew that Goldwin Smith was wrong when he asked sarcastically, " Can Jews be patriots ? "

> " Send these, the homeless, tempest-tost to me,
> I lift my lamp beside the golden door ! "

It seems to me that it is far more remarkable that she should have shown what may be called the most patriotic devotion to the welfare of her race than that she should have been zealously attached to the land and the people of her birth ; in fact, there was far more temptation for her to identify herself with purely American interests and American works than to place herself, as she did, beside the unfortunate of her own faith and people, spending herself ceaselessly for them. The attractions of society, the allurements of selfishness, had no power to withdraw her from that complete surrender to duty which crowns her character. It must have been " the still, small voice " that spoke in her soul, which illumined her mind with God-given truth. How singular that here, in a land of glorious freedom, it is true, yet which is marked by a life of tranquillity sometimes almost termed commonplace, that an ardent patriot should have started forth, incarnated as a woman, but transcending the ordinary powers of women by a spiritual force of wonderful extent. Many of her prose writings are expressions of this Jewish patriotism, notably a series of articles entitled ' Epistles to the Hebrews,' written for the *American Hebrew* of New York, published weekly through several months. In these she did not disguise what she considered shortcomings and peculiarities in her race. In closing these ' Epistles,' she explains their object : —

" My chief aim has been to contribute my mite towards arousing that spirit of Jewish enthusiasm which might manifest itself; First, in a return to the varied pursuits and broad systems of physical and intellectual education adopted by our ancestors; Second, in a more fraternal and practical movement towards alleviating the sufferings of oppressed Jews in countries less favored than our own; Third, in a closer and wider study of Hebrew literature and history ; and finally, in a truer recognition of the large principles of religion, liberty, and law upon which Judaism is founded, and which should draw into harmonious unity Jews of every shade of opinion."

The little poems in prose have been mentioned once, but are peculiarly appropriate in the consideration of Emma Lazarus as a patriot. The first one, called 'The Exodus,' and referring to Aug. 3, 1492, unites attachment to her race and to America : —

" O bird of the air, whisper to the despairing exiles, that to-day, to-day, from the many masted, gaily-bannered port of Palos, sails the world-unveiling Genoese, to unlock the golden gates of sunset and bequeath a Continent to Freedom ! "

In presence of the Columbian Exposition now celebrating this " unlocking " by the Genoese, this poem of ' The Exodus ' doubly attracts our sympathies. We feel that had she been spared to us until this season, she would have joined ardently in the sentiments of devotion to this land shown by all women. One who was very closely related to her said, in describing her earnestness, " She was always on fire about something." Hers was truly the spirit of the patriot : a mere spark kindled the sacred fire. But although her form is not with us in this unique period, when the progress of the ages shall pass before our eyes, we are sure that her soul would be in fullest sympathy with the purest aspirations that may fill our minds. And we have always with us, in the literary legacy which she has left, the eternal part of herself. It should be that no one capable of understanding and delighting in the fruits of her study should ever be without the illuminating influence of her stirring thought. I have reason to believe that the poems of Emma Lazarus are not found, as they should be, in every home where character and genius are held dear. When such a mind and such a heart joined to enlighten and stimulate us with radiant thoughts and noble deeds, shall we not stretch out our hands eagerly for these precious possessions ?

A survey of Emma Lazarus in her threefold character of woman, poet, and patriot, brings before us a very striking and beautiful combination. In one person centred all those qualities more frequently divided and often distributed sparingly among many individuals. The example of her womanly worth, of her poetic genius, and of her patriotic fervor may be to us all a proud joy, a constant inspiration. The memory of Emma Lazarus is undying, — as everlasting as the beauty of her thought, the gentleness of her spirit, and the strength of her soul.

*Mary M. Cohen.*

## THE SINGER.

THERE was one who came into the world crippled.

He could not walk nor run nor play as the other children. All day he watched them wistfully. They took no heed of him, and he was very lonely. At first he complained bitterly; but his cries were drowned in the merry echoes of their laughter. And when they saw his frown, they called out that he was ill-humored, and stayed apart from him the more.

As he grew, his heart hardened. He cried out no longer. Dark thoughts were in his mind, and envious evil spirits. He heard their laughter now with impotently clinched hands and muttered curses. They went farther from him, looking askance, and he was very lonely.

\* \* \*

As he neared manhood, there arose within him new, expanding desires. His soul beat against the prison of his maimed body as a bird beats against its cage bruising its wings, ard he suffered.

The world kept its festival, and he sat apart.

One day there was feasting and dancing, and he looked in the face of a young maid who walked, hand in hand, aside with her lover; and by chance her glance fell on him, and something of the hunger in his eyes touched her heart, and there was compassion in her glance. Another instant she had forgotten him, — but he remembered.

"What a beautiful thing is love!" he thought; and his heart was stirred. He looked out upon the dancers; the strains of the music and their floating voices, light and gay, wakened a note before unsounded.

" I too can love ! " he said ; " I too can see the joy of the world. Life is for happiness, and he who persists in gloom casts a shadow against God's sunshine. My feet cannot dance, but surely my heart can."

So he lifted up his voice and sang, and there was love and joy in his song, and it was strangely sweet. The dancers kept time to its rhythm, and the young man pressed his sweetheart's hand more tenderly.

No one heeded the singer as he sat apart.

There were tears in his eyes as he sang, but he was no longer lonely.

*M. A. Worswick.*

# EARLY WOMEN POETS OF AMERICA.

THE early life of New England, narrow as it was, and hemmed in by rugged mountains of religious bigotry, nevertheless furnished many sturdy and some beautiful growths for the early literature of America. Poetry, which, it would seem, could but have died, where it found so little sunshine, grew and flourished there mainly on goodly trees in the form of curious and ungainly or sickly branches which have since been cut away and forgotten. Yet here, too, is found America's first poet, who wrote poetry for itself and not to adorn prose.

Anne Bradstreet, born in England in 1612, came to America in 1629, one year after her marriage to Simon Bradstreet, the son of a non-conformist clergyman. Her early life was spent in the home of the Earl of Lincoln, where she had access to the best literature, and went and came among the noted men of the time. That she was not eager to leave such company and surroundings for the New World, is seen from the following extract from her autobiography : " I changed my condition and was married, and came into this country, where I found a new world and new manners, at which my heart rose. But after I was convinced it was the way of God, I submitted to it." In sympathy with the community in which she lived, who probably denounced Shakespeare and all " play-writers " as followers of the monarch of the realm of eternal darkness, she had little knowledge of or delight in the great literature of the Elizabethan period. Her praises are lavished, instead, on Du Bartas, a French poet of the Euphuistic school, whose popularity was so great that his works had passed through many editions, and had been several times translated into English. Finding him and his school much admired in the new society into which she had come, and shut off from the society and literature in which she had delighted, while still little more than a child, her longest poem — written after being for many years under the new influences — follows her most approved models, and is stilted and tedious. In many of her shorter poems, however, she forgot, so far as habit permitted, to give the polish to thought and form which she had been led to believe was highest art, and sang from herself. During an absence of her husband's, she writes : —

> " Phoebus, make haste — the day 's too long — begone !
> The silent night 's the fittest time for moan.
> But stay, this once — unto my suit give ear
> And tell my griefs in either hemisphere."

Still somewhat stilted, this poem has a note of earnestness one cannot but feel.

That she possessed a very clever satirical vein, and in it wholly forgot her models, is shown in her prologue to her long poem, — ' The Four Elements,' where she says : —

> " I am obnoxious to each carping tongue
> That says my hand a needle better fits ;
> . . . . . . . . .
> If what I do prove well it wont advance
> They 'll say, It 's stolen, or else was by chance."

If she pleads that the Greeks were kinder, and " feigned the Nine of our sex " —

> " This weak knot they will full soon untie
> The Greeks did naught but play the fool and lie."

She grants

> " Pre-eminence in each and all is yours
> Yet grant some small acknowledgement of ours."

And in all meekness adds : —

> " If e'er you deign these lowly lines your eyes,
> Give thyme and parsley wreath : I ask no bays."

Despite this modest request, profusest " bays " were granted.  John Norton of Ipswich says : —

> " Let every laurel, every myrtle bough,
> Be stripped for leaves t' adorn and load her brow."

And many more extravagant enconiums on her genius, by the most noted men of the age, have come down to us.  That her satire was not unjust, however, and that men were prone to doubt a woman's ability to write, or the propriety of her doing it, is evident from the fact that her brother-in-law considered it necessary to preface his edition of her works with a solemn assertion that he bore witness that the following work was, as it purported to be, actually written by a woman.

Mrs. Bradstreet died in 1672, the only woman poet in America in the seventeenth century.

Early in the eighteenth century Jane Colman, afterward Mrs. Turell, was born in Boston.  Her father, Rev. Benjamin Colman, superintended her education.  A clever child and eager to learn, she read much.  Her taste was influenced by her father, and that his influence led her to read mainly the ancient classics and Scripture is shown by her poetry being chiefly imitations of the former and paraphrases of the latter. An ardent hero-worshipper, she chose as the objects of her worship her father's two English favorites, Mr. Blackmore and Miss Singer. Of the former she writes · —

> " Thou for mankind's preceptor Heaven designed,
> To form their manners, and instruct their mind.
> In virtue's cause undaunted you engage,
> To stem the tide of vice, reform the stage,
> And place the present with the golden age."

Of Miss Singer she writes in like strain : —

> " You vie with the famed prophetess of old,
> Burn with her fire, in the same cause grow bold.
> Dauntless you undertake th' unequal strife,
> And raise dead virtue by your verse to life."

In ' An Invitation into the Country, in Imitation of Horace ' a poetic appreciation of gorgeousness and luxury seems to lurk, almost unknown to herself, which fosters the feeling that perhaps she did not despise the things, she informs her prospective guest, she will not have in her country home ; and that, after all,

> "Stately beds . . .
> Of costly purple, by carved panthers borne,"

and

> " Arabia's rich perfumes,
> Diffusing odors through our stately rooms,"

might possess an attraction greater than the more orthodox New England

> "Clean soft pillows . . .
> Filled with the wool from off my tender sheep."

We can judge Mrs. Turell only by imitations. Her father was one of New England's sturdy trees, and growing in his shadow, she died before her genius had caught Heaven's own sunlight and air for itself, unfiltered through another mind.

Mr. Tyler, in his ' History of American Literature,' calls versemaking but a " foible of colonial New England." Either they held this foible under with a strong hand, or kindly time has consigned

it to oblivion, for the works of but few poets of that period have
survived, only two of them women, and these nearly a century
apart.  From the other colonies, the poetry of fewer men and no
women has lived.

When revolutionary times came, the colonies climbed up out
of their separate valleys, and gained wider outlooks and views of
each other; the sun shone on poetry, and she began to grow
stronger and more beautiful.  In these times we find a group of
seven women of note in the literature of America, whose names
and fames overlap each other in the years between 1728 and 1824.

Mercy Warren, born 1728, and died 1814, was first and almost
last of these.  Best known by her prose works, especially her ' History of the American Revolution,' — which is the best contemporaneous history of that event in existence, — her poetry gives an
insight into the spirit of the time, shows her own devotion to and
admiration of her country, and the dauntless earnestness of the men
and women who wrought out America's freedom, by whom it was
received with loud acclaim.  Before the Revolution her poetry was
satirical.  The time was not yet ripe for open defiance, but the
covert defiance that needed but small provocation to declare itself
openly, is constantly shown in her lines, as in her satire on
Governor Hutchinson : —

> " He strikes a bargain with his country's foes,
> And joins to wrap America in flames,
> Yet, with feigned pity and satanic grin,
> As if more deep to fix the keen insult, —
>
> .     .     .     .     .     .     .
>
> He cries, The gathering clouds hang thick about her,
> But laughs within — then sobs, Alas, my country ! "

After the Revolution her poetry was exultant, and prophetic
of future glory for America.  Glorying over the lessening of
Britannia's greatness in the future, and America's growth, she
writes : —

> " No more the lofty ships her marts supply, —
>
> .     .     .     .     .     .
>
> Gray Neptune rises from his oozy bed,
> And shakes the sea-weed from his shaggy head ;
> He bids adieu to fair Britannia's shore, —
>
> .     .     .     .     .     .
>
> In haste to hail the brave Columbia free."

Sister of James Otis and wife of James Warren, she was placed by circumstances right in the heart of the making of American freedom, and the genius of earnest devotion to the cause, evinced in both her poetry and prose, shows her to have been also of the heart of it.

Born in Philadelphia in 1739, and living there until 1801, — with the exception of a few years spent in London in the society of the court, — a part of the most cultured society of America at that time, Elizabeth Graeme Ferguson reflects the culture of her social, rather than the unsettled state of her political world. That she was not wanting in patriotism is shown by the fact that the adherence of her husband to the British party caused their speedy and permanent separation. Probably owing to ill health, she took little active interest in the affairs of the nation, and as far as her poetry was concerned none ; this was written for recreation and to divert her thoughts from the sad events of her life. Her longest work was a translation of Fénélon's 'Telemachus' into English heroic verse. It has never been published, but the manuscript shows it to compare more than favorably with other translations of the same work. A short parody on some lines of Pope's is very clever; and from all her writings we gather that she was a woman of wide culture and much talent.

New York furnishes the next members of the group, — Mrs. Anne Eliza Bleecker and her daughter, Mrs. Margaretta V. Faugères. Mrs. Bleecker was married at seventeen, and in 1771, when but nineteen, went to Tomhanick, a little secluded village eighteen miles above Albany. It was in this year that Mrs. Faugères was born. Mrs. Bleecker's life here for five years was very happy ; she delighted in Nature as she found it in these wilds, and never longed for the gay society of New York, which she had left. During this time most of her poetry was written, and many a dainty woodland note she sings, —

> " From yon grove the woodcock rises,
> Mark her progress by her notes ;
> High in air her wing she poises,
> Then like lightning down she shoots."

44

After this tranquil time came the invasion of Burgoyne's army
and their Indian allies, and with it a time of constant anxiety and
fear, during which she lost some dearly loved members of her
family.  Henceforth her note is one of sorrow which neither can
nor will be comforted.

> " Nor shall the mollifying hand of time,
> Which wipes off common sorrows, cancel mine."

she writes after the death of one of her children.

When Mrs. Faugères was twelve years old her mother died;
she was then taken to New York, and the education begun by
her mother was finished there.  When she entered society, an
heiress of the best connections, unusual natural gifts, and the best
education her time could afford, she was much courted, and suitors
flocked around her.  Against her father's wish, she married Dr.
Peter Faugères, a French adventurer, whose scepticism and infidelity she mistook for brilliant intellectual attainment.  Her father
died soon after this marriage, and her husband squandered her
estate and shamefully maltreated her.  Though relieved of his
company by yellow fever in 1798, her trouble had so undermined
her health that she survived him but three years.  Nursed in the
troublous war times, with a few brief years of happiness in New
York, and so unfortunately married, her poetry seemed to gain
strength and force from her misfortune.  In the drama of
' Belisarius,' there are some fine passages; as when her heroine,
after narrating her plan of vengeance, says, —

> "Then let him try
> If the bright wit that jeered a woman's foibles
> Will light the dungeon where her fury dwells ! "

Many of her descriptions of Nature, notably those in a poem on the
Hudson, are stately and beautiful in their figures.

Of all the women poets of the eighteenth century, Phillis
Wheatley is most easily found and most interesting when found;
this is probably due to her history, which is unique in the history
of literature.  Brought from Africa when a child of seven or eight,
and sold as a slave in the Boston market in 1761, she was pur-

chased by Mrs. Wheatley, who was attracted by her modest demeanor. In sixteen months she had mastered the English language, which she read with remarkable ease, and before long wrote no less easily. After learning English, she studied Latin, with which, also, she soon became familiar. Delighted with the gentleness, modesty, and unusual abilities of the child, her mistress soon considered and treated her more as a daughter than as a slave, and Miss Wheatley gave her what education she had. She attracted much attention in Boston, and was invited to the homes of the most cultured people, despite the prejudice against her race. An amusing little incident is told, — illustrating how fully she had conquered all prejudice in her own case, — about how another slave was severely reprimanded one day, because he had " the impudence to sit upon the same seat with my Phillis!" in the chaise in which he had been sent to bring her home from a dinner party. Her health, always frail, beginning to fail, the physicians recommended a sea voyage, and as Mr. Wheatley's son and his wife were going to England, she accompanied them. While there she was presented to many of the nobility, and many attentions and honors were lavished on her. Just before her presentation at court, however, she was called home by the illness of her mistress, who, with her master, soon after died. This loss happening during the troublous times of the Revolution, her friends of former days had either fled to England, or were so busied with national affairs that she was left alone and poor. Under these circumstances, she consented to marry Mr. Peters, a handsome colored man of some distinction. He failed in business, not long after their marriage, and considered himself too much of a gentleman to turn his hand to any labor to support his family. In poor health, and with three children, she was unable to support herself, and died in abject poverty in 1794. Her manuscripts, which she had entrusted to a friend, were claimed by her husband after her death, and have never been found. Those of her poems which are now in the libraries were published during her stay in London, when she was but nineteen. Never spoiled by flattery, she was always willing to write in answer to any request, and much of her published work is elegiac poetry, written for sorrowing relations. She translated a part of the sixth book of Ovid's 'Metamorphoses,' and there are traces of her Latin reading all through her work. Of a deeply religious nature, passages like the following are also frequent, —

> " Arise my soul ; on wings enraptured, rise,
> To praise the Monarch of the earth and skies,
> Whose goodness and beneficence appear,
> As round its centre moves the rolling year."

Wholly different from any of the preceding women, both in her life and writings, was Mrs. Susannah Haswell Rowson. The daughter of a British navy officer, she was born in England in 1762. While a child she came to America, and spent the remainder of her childhood at Nantasket ; later she returned to England with her father, and there married and went on the stage. Before long she again came to America, and acted in Philadelphia for three years. After leaving the stage she opened a school in New York, which soon became so popular that children were sent there from the most distant parts of the country and from Canada. Wherever she was, and whatever doing, however, she always found time to write ; and her writings are as varied as her life : novels, dramas, biblical dialogues, poems, even the compilation of a dictionary being included in them. Though America was her country only by adoption, she shows her love for it in her writings. One critic says of her poetry that it bears "no mark of feminine genius," and it is true that few women have ever written anything resembling her 'America, Commerce, and Freedom.' There is a note of rollicking gladness in it that certainly America had not sounded before : —

> " Then, under snug sail, we laugh at the gale,
> And though landsmen look pale, never heed 'em ;
> But toss off a glass to a favorite lass,
> To America, commerce, and freedom ! "

This same gladness is constant through all her work, now in a tone of mockery, now, simple lightness of heart, and again in a more solemn joy, as in 'Thanksgiving.'

> ' To solemn temples let us now repair,
> And bow in grateful adoration there ;
> Bid the full strains in hallelujahs rise,
> To waft the sacred incense to the skies."

The last of the group of women poets of America, of the eighteenth century, was Mrs. Sarah Wentworth Morton. She was born in Boston in 1759, and contributed to the newspapers under the assumed name of Philenia. She wrote poems to Washington, Aaron Burr, and other men of note, and a poem on the ' Prospect from Beacon Hill,' but is chiefly interesting as being the first woman to make the Indian a subject for her muse. Insight into his poetic possibilities seems to be more a growth of modern times.

There were, of course, some lesser lights in this period, who sang of virtue, the consolation of religion, the faithlessness of men, and other like topics. I chanced to find, not long ago, a volume of poems written by a Miss Isabella Oliver, and printed in 1809, which was amusing and interesting in its quaintness. That its merit was duly appreciated when it was written, is evident from the list of subscribers, containing over a thousand names of colonial families in Pennsylvania, Delaware, and Maryland. One of the quaintest poems begins, —

> " Mistaken youth in charity forbear ;
> And do not tell young Mila she is fair.
> An altar to her vanity you raise,
> And blast her beauty with the breath of praise,"

and closes, —

> " 'T is strange but true — beauty by beauty 's soil'd,
> And beauty here 's by too much beauty spoil'd."

There is one more poetess, whom I must needs neglect, for to mention her opens a field almost as wide as the Shakespeare-Bacon controversy. Did Mrs. Vergoose of Boston, or M. Charles Perrault of France, write or collect the only — American ? — poetry of that period of which I write which is not forgotten by our own, — the Mother Goose rhymes ?

*Mary Harned.*

## A TALK ON AMERICAN PATRIOTIC POEMS.

" How is it then that our great wars have produced so little poetry ?  Such stirring realities should have borne rich fruit if realities could do it ? "

" Well, have they not ? "

" H'm 1  Some few small apples on very large trees.  Think of the disappointment of Bishop Berkeley's Muse on being presented with the full text of Hopkinson's ' Hail Columbia! Happy Land! ' just as it was sung to the tune of the ' President's March ' at Philadelphia in 1798 l  This it is to be a philosopher's muse !  She was ' disgusted ' you remember, with ' an age and clime barren of every glorious theme,' and rashly awaited

> ' A better time
> Producing subjects worthy fame ;
> In happy climes, where from the genial sun
> And virgin earth such scenes ensue
> The force of Nature seems outdone,
> And fancied beauties by the true.'

She was looking out, like you, you see, for the effects of realism on the Ideal ; and lo! the refrain that floats from that happy shore disturbs her visions with the ' end-stopped ' doggerel of —

> ' Firm united let us be,
> Rallying round our liberty ;
> As a band of brothers *jined*.'

(Don't interrupt, you see it must rhyme ! )

> ' Peace and safety we shall find.'

Even the Autocrat's continuation of this hurdy-gurdy patriotism, written for the Philadelphia celebration of a hundred years later, does not mend matters."

" No, for the pattern was bad.  No piecing could make the garment less of a botch."

" Would the Muse be quite content, then, with Philip Freneau's Fourth of July ode for the year 1799?  Let me see, how did it go? I looked up a choice line or two lately, —

> ' On this returning annual day
> May we to heaven our homage pay,
> Happy that here the time's *began*
> That made Mankind the friend of *man*.'

Or, you don't think she would like Royall Tyler's 'Independence Day' any better?—

> Squeak the fife, and beat the drum,
> Independence day is come ! !
> Let the roasted pig be bled,
> Quick twist off the cockerell's head.
> Quickly rub the pewter platter,
> Heap the nut cakes, fried in butter.
> Set the cups and beaker glass,
> The pumpkin and the apple sauce ;
> Send the keg to shop for brandy ;
> Maple sugar we have handy.
> Sal, put on your russet skirt,
> Jotham, get your *boughten* shirt,
> Today we dance to tiddle diddle,
> — Here comes Sambo with his fiddle ;
> Sambo, take a dram of whiskey,
> And play up Yankee Doodle frisky.' "

" Yes, I venture to say she would. It is rude, but it is free and rollicking. There is more life in such a bucolic satire than in well-intentioned verses like Robert Treat Paine's —

> ' Ye sons of Columbia, who bravely have fought
> For those rights which unstained from your sires had descended,
> May you long taste the blessings your valor has bought,
> And your sons reap the soil which their fathers defended.'

Notice the wary eye of conservatism it casts upon the ' red fool fury of the Celt.' ' While France her huge limbs bathes recumbent in blood, and Society's base threats with wide dissolution,' etc., etc. In the refrain, for ' Sons of Columbia,' you may as well read ' Sons of Britons,' ' And ne'er shall the sons of Columbia be slaves while the earth bears a plant or the sea rolls its waves.' It is all an inherited Briticism, just the sort of thing Berkeley's wise Muse was tired of. She looked for a clime where ' Nature should guide ' afresh, and where man should not ' impose for truth and sense, the pedantry of courts and schools.' The ' great uprising epic rage' was to be 'not such as Europe breeds.' In short, all these illustrations you point against me go to prove the contention that, just in proportion as the realities of the New World actually find an expression that is properly their own, the fruitage of the Ideal is better, and Berkeley's 'Prospect of Planting Arts and Letters in America' not the satire that, I grant you, European imitations make it."

"H'm! I seem to be floored; yet I don't feel that I am. No 1 no! the trouble is that our big realities won't convert into pure poesy; they confront the ideal awkwardly. You might as well put a sewing machine before your heroine of high romance, instead of the picturesque needle and embroidery frame. But I should like to be convinced that Berkeley's last stanza was less a vision than a prophecy, 'Westward the course of empire takes its way, . . . time's noblest offspring is the last.' Now then, to return to phenomena; was there ever a man more imbued with new and altogether American ideals of poetry and progress than he who sang

> ' the mariner who first unfurl'd
> An eastern banner o'er the western world,
> And taught mankind where future empires lay
> In these fair confines of descending day,' —

and yet — "

" No, there was never a *man* more in love with the future than Joel Barlow; but we must yet look for a *poet* as true-hearted to touch with persuasive fire the thoughts of 'The Columbiad.' But I glory in the boldness of that man. Think of his venturing to consider the existence of Homer as 'one of the signal misfortunes of the human mind'!"

"The epic puppy! No wonder his fount of verse is dry! Did he get that off? I confess I never had the patience to read all his dreary ten books."

" Yes, in his preface. Of course, like the first sceptics, he lacked the breadth of wisdom the modern evolutionist has developed, and failed to see the pertinence to the whole scheme of progress of the different ideals of earlier days. Not that he did not admire Homer, mind you, but that he loved his own Bard more, — the prospective bard for whom he said, 'no more beneath their furious gods, old Ocean crimsons,' or 'Olympus nods,' and whose 'clangor' should no more madden up the mind 'to crush, to conquer, and enslave mankind.' The 'new energies' and 'moral charms' he assigns to his poet of the future in lieu of the Homeric 'clangor,' foreshadow Whitman's dream of the 'divine literatus,' and inspire his best lines, I think : —

> ' Soaring with science then he learns to string
> Her highest harp, and trace her broadest wing,
> With her own force to fray the paths untrod,
> With her own glance to ken the total God.' "

"You don't say so ! That pestilent heresy of science in poesy at that early day ! And yet — no poetry ! Why, you hand me over all the arguments ! Why don't these brave dreams flower somewhere ? If the 'course of empire' in literature inspired by the great fact — 'us' — does not begin to march westward in 'Hail Columbia,' nor in this prodigious epic of Barlow's, then does it in 'The Star Spangled Banner' ? 'Oh ! say can you see by the dawn's early light what so proudly we hailed' under the guidance of Bishop Berkeley's fastidious Muse. Or do you, perchance, begin to descry it striding on in Drake's 'American Flag' ?

> ' When Freedom from her mountain height
> Unfurled her standard to the air,
> She tore the azure robe of night,
> And set the stars of glory there.'

And what of the Southern flag song of a later day ? 'Hurrah ! Hurrah ! for the bonnie blue flag that bears a single star.' "

"It is a mere song in comparison. Drake's has some dignity."

"Not a bad idea, that, of enhancing the lofty, not to say skyscraping design of the little flag Washington stepped into the tiny shop at 5th and Arch streets, Philadelphia, to give directions for to the demure Quakeress, who, maybe, helped the General out with more practical suggestions and womanly taste than she will ever get credit for. The closing lines are stirring to a patriot."

"Yes, perhaps we should call that one of the minor way-marks of the patriotic muse stepping westward.   But, after all, it is grandiose and rhetorical.   It would be better, I maintain, with more admixture of the real.   You called up just now a picture of the Father of his Country and the demure gray-gowned dame putting their heads together over the making of the first American flag.   Now that scene carries allusions with it.   Would not that be more tender and responsive to poetic handling than those titanic properties Drake hauls out of the wardrobe of the elements?"

".Dear me, what a venturesome notion!   I tell you the home-spun is risky in poetry.   The poet would have to do it, then, in ballad style, and for fear of being ludicrous, give it a slight humorous touch himself, so that if anybody laughed, it would appear that he meant them to feel a little quizzical.   Dr. Holmes has done that capitally in 'Grandma's Story of Bunker Hill' and 'The Boston Tea Party.'"

" Yes ; but light and happy of touch as they are, they are not the rounded fruit of the new age you and I are hunting for, with Berkeley's Muse to hold the torch."

" Exactly.   You are taking my own argument out of my mouth. And Dr. Holmes's half burlesquing piece of pathos on one of the most stirring initial events of our late war, on the secession of South Carolina, is in point.   Of course you know 'Brother Jonathan to Sister Caroline'?"

" Yes, and there's a fine touch of reconciliation at the close. But there is Mr. Stedman's 'John Brown.'   In that there is no mitigation of the dead earnest, and we do not find its homeliness provoking a smile.   It has a good kind of grimness.

'Then Old Brown,
Osawatomie Brown,
Raised his right hand up to Heaven calling Heaven's vengeance down.
.    .    .    .    .    .    .    .    .    .    .
Mad old Brown,
Osawatomie Brown,
With his eighteen other crazy men, went in and took the town.
.    .    .    .    .    .    .    .    .    .
And each drop from Old Brown's life veins like the red gore of the dragon
May spring up a vengeful fury hissing through your slave worn lands!
And old Brown,
Osawatomie Brown,
May trouble you more than ever when you 've nailed his coffin down!'

And are there any graceful uncertainties in Whittier's 'Barbara Frietchie'? Its homeliness is its loveliness. It's a true note with a long echo."

"I don't know of anything in the patriotic line much better than Boker's 'Black Regiment.' *There's* a crown conserved for the blacks. 'Now,' the flag sergeant cried, —

> '" Let the whole nation see
> If we are fit to be
> Free in this land ; or bound
> Down, like the whining hound —
> Bound with red stripes of pain
> In our cold chains again ! "
> Oh ! what a shout there went
> From the black regiment ! '

And Boker's 'Cumberland' has the fiery touch, too. Long-fellow's poem on the same incident talks about the rebel ship crushing our ribs in her iron grasp 'like a kraken huge and black;' but Boker puts it boldly, 'the cruel tusk of the black sea-boar!' And his 'Manassas' — where else does the day of fear and shame live, in the flesh, before us who never saw it?"

"Yes, I grant you, war stories like that are alive, and like unto them are Lieutenant Brownell's 'River Fight' and 'The Bay Fight.' But how about Berkeley and Barlow? The inspiration is perilously near Homer's — pernicious Homer!"

"And closely allied to an old newspaper, too, you Idealist! Did not Brownell modestly call his poems 'Lyrics of a Day'? But, as a sign of the time, just notice that they are real to the core, and with a moral marrow, moreover, that is peculiarly modern. 'Find me in history, this story's rival or its parallel, — A Nation rising to undo a wrong, Forged by itself and to its mind made strong.' There's your Homer, with a difference."

"But how much better is the poetry for that? Here's a bay leaf for a ballad or two; but where shall we unload our laurel crowns? There's Bret Harte's 'Reveille.' It has breadth of effect as well as directness of aim. Some of the philosophy of fact, I take it you are looking for, is in his question : —

> ' But when won the coming battle
>   What of profit springs therefrom ?
>   What if conquest, subjugation
>   Even greater ills become ?
>       But the drum
>       Answered " Come !
> You must do the sum to prove it," said the Yankee answering drum.' "

" Yes, I acknowledge I am not content with the muscular battle-cry alone ; I want to chord in with that note some of the home-staying, thought-provoking, but not less resolute tones that prolong the echo beyond the battle-field.  Have you noticed how the women's voices enrich the warlike strains?  I don't mean the lyrics of the sweethearts, like Nora Perry's ' Riding Down,' nor the mothers' threnodies, nor the chastened aspiration of the worsted side, as given in ' The South,' by Emma Lazarus, although they are a part of it, but some such stir of contemplation as speaks in Mrs. Dorr's ' The Dead Century,' that shall celebrate events in mass and reconcile their outcome in a wider span of time.  Oh, I don't mean that it comes from women only, but that it is the issue of brain instead of brawn.  Bryant's ' The Battle Field,' for instance, is the sort that looks further than the fight : —

> ' Soon rested those who fought ; but thou
>   Who minglest in the harder strife
>   For truths which men receive not now,
>   Thy warfare only ends with life.' "

" Lanier puts in a long piece of spiritual history very smoothly and cleverly in his ' Centennial Cantata.'  The ' old Shapes and Masks of Things ' who are ' framed like Faiths,' he says, or ' Clothed like Kings,' cry ' No ' to the new life of the Republic, when, —

> ' Hark !
> Huguenots whispering *yea* in the dark !
> Puritans answering *yea* in the dark !
> *Yea* like an arrow shot true to his mark,
> Darts through the tyrannous heart of Denial
> Patience and Labor and solemn-soul'd Trial.' "

" Smoothly and cleverly, you say ?  Have n't you any stronger words for so stanch a stroke ?  Or for this from Woodberry's, ' My Country,' stately and ardent : —

> ' And ever westward leans the God above the joyful steeds ;
> The light in his eyes is prophecy ; on his lips the words are deeds.' "

" All right.   So you don't hold that the deeds should be words. Lowell in his great ' Ode ' seems to look on the question from the soldier side : —

> ' 'T is not the grapes of Canaan that repay,
> But the high faith that failed not by the way ;
> .    .    .    .    .    .    .    .
> And to the saner mind
> We rather seem the dead that stayed behind.'

Now that does not strike what you call the home-staying, thought-provoking tones."

" Yes, I think it is a reflex of them.   It is the lofty strains thrilling behind the deed to the soul of the soldier, the conflux of past purposes pulsing toward the future, that make the modern music, and that constitute the secret charm of Lowell's ode."

" Bayard Taylor's ' National Ode,' I suppose, does not reach that high chorus sound you have in your ears.   Perhaps this full-bodied tone you hanker after is chiefly in your ears, and the unheard melodies that are sweetest are simply beyond our range."

" Not because Taylor did not reach them, though he had the will.   Oh, these conventional occasions for poems !   They make a poet a formal laureated officer, and insidiously steal his unpremeditated fire.   But there is a spiritual way to hail success."

" For example, now, aside from Lowell.   What a pity it cannot be a woman's voice, to round out your theories ! "

" It can be.   I will quote Emma Lazarus on ' Success ' · —

> ' Oft have I brooded on defeat and pain,
> The pathos of the stupid, stumbling throng.
> These I ignore to-day and only long
> To pour my soul forth in one trumpet strain,
> One clear, grief-shattering triumphant song
> For all the victories of man's high endeavor,
> Palm-bearing laureled deeds that live forever,
> The splendor clothing him whose will is strong.
> Hast thou beheld the deep glad eyes of one
> Who has persisted and achieved ?   Rejoice ! '

But that is not purely national, you will say. Have you seen a prose poem of hers called 'Currents,' which celebrates this as the mother-country of all lands? Of course it is so broadly national that there is no war in it."

"No action at all I dare say. Your modern poets all commit suicide with their philosophy, or else they distort themselves with their realism. These national deeds of ours are too foreshortened to look well painted at our present focus. The sage of transcendentalism himself has said it, 'The sea is lovely; but when we bathe in it, the loveliness forsakes all the near water. For the imagination and the senses cannot be gratified at the same time.'"

"Never did Emerson make such an application!"

"Well! and if he did not, how well it excuses the penury of his best phrases in the 'Concord Hymn,' the 'Fourth of July Ode,' and 'Boston,' compared, of course, with the white light he sometimes kindles on subjects that have some vista. Heroism at short range is nothing but biography and anecdote. That is the difference between patriotic green apples and the golden fruitage of the ages."

"Homer, in his day, would have to go down under such a *dictum.* Still, you explain idealism as I would; after all it is nothing but lapsed realism. Why should we not descry the unnamed beauty here and now, and refuse to be cheated with the mere mirage of time. I can match your Emerson quotation with another: —

> '  The lords of life, the lords of life, —
> .   .   .   .   .   .
> They marched from East to West:
> Little man, least of all,
> Among the legs of his guardians tall,
> Walked about with puzzled look.
> Him by the hand dear Nature took,
> Whispered, Darling, never mind!
> To-morrow they will wear another face,
> The founder thou; these are thy race!'"

"To-morrow, didst thou say, to-morrow? We agree again, then, my patriot, though you don't seem to know it."

"And to-morrow has dawned in such a stately heroic ode as

Lowell's, in such a wonderful, mystical, many-folded national flag-song as Whitman's ' The Poet and the Child,' and both the direct fruit of our last war."

" Although not a celebration of it ! "

" ' Time's noblest offspring is the last — ' "

" Or will be as soon as we appreciate it, eh ! Of course we know Lowell, but who knows this poem you call a national flag-song ?   Why is it we don't know it ?   After all, then, it seems to require the brooding quiet of the years to make the thought take root, and it certainly needs the sun of sympathy to spread leaf and petal in the air for all to see.   Why, I wonder, have n't we anything as good as Lowell's ' Commemoration Ode,' to sum up the poetry there was in the first war ? "

" We have Blake's splendid prophecy of America."

" Oh, Blake !   But Blake was an Englishman.   Why is our Revolutionary poetry so scanty that only a crazy Englishman's queer verse is big enough for you ? "

" Blake was not trammelled by any pedantries of mind or phrase."

" Perhaps, living aside from the thick of the fray, he was as good as born later, could get the far effect and look at it, without know-ing too much or aggravating details, through the big end of the poetic telescope."

" I don't know.   I always think a good deal of the trouble lay in the slavishness of our early writers as to the authorized forms of verse.   We rebelled against England's political rule; but how meek and flat we were under her literary dictation those only can conceive whose tired eyes have followed arid imitation after imi-tation of the metres of the orthodox English School of Verse then current."

" And ' Whaur is Wully Shakespeare noo ? ' as the Scotchman said.   To be sure the Puritans did bar him out."

" Yes, but that is not my point.   I would that they barred out no one, in spirit, least of all the giants of the Golden Age, so they did not imitate externally."

" What a pity the poets can't hear us discourse, and take warn-

ing! Read me a bit of this national flag-song nobody knows, and
then good-by; we will wrangle over it some other night."

"'Song of the Banner at Daybreak,' Whitman calls it. The
title is a symbol. I will give you an idea of it, — only a passage or
two. It needs no homage of mine; let it speak for itself! The
Pennant sings : —

'Come up here, bard, bard,
    Come up here, soul, soul,
    Come up here dear little child
    To fly in the clouds and winds with me, and play with the measureless light.

*Child.* Father what is that in the sky beckoning to me with long finger?
    And what does it say to me all the while?

*Father.* Nothing my babe you see in the sky,
    And nothing at all to you it says — but look you, my babe,
    Look at these dazzling things in the houses, and see you the money shops
      opening,
    And see you the vehicles preparing to crawl along the streets with goods;
    These, ah these, how valued and toil'd for these!
    How envied by all the earth.

*Child.* O father it is alive — it is full of people — it has children,
    O now it seems to me it is talking to its children,
    I hear it — it talks to me — O it is wonderful!
    O it stretches — it spreads and runs so fast — O my father,
    It is so broad it covers the whole sky.
      .      .      .      .      .      .

*Poet.* My hearing and tongue are come to me, (a little child taught me,)
    I hear from above, O pennant of war your ironical call and demand,
    Insensate! insensate! (yet I at any rate chant you,) O Banner!
    O Banner, not money so precious are you, not farm produce you nor the
      material good nutriment,
    Nor excellent stores, nor landed on wharves from the ships,
    Not the superb ships with sail-power or steam-power, fetching and carrying
      cargoes,
    Nor machinery, vehicles, trade, nor revenues — but you as henceforth I see
      you,
    Running up out of the night, bringing your cluster of stars, (ever enlarging
      stars,)
    Divider of Daybreak you, cutting the air touch'd by the sun, measuring the
      sky,
    (Passionately seen and yearn'd for by one poor little child,
    While others remain busy or smartly talking, forever teaching thrift, thrift,)
    O you up there! O pennant! where you undulate like a snake hissing so
      curious,
    Out of reach, an idea only, yet furiously fought for, risking bloody death,
      loved by me,

So loved — O you banner leading the day with stars brought from the night !
Valueless, object of eyes, over all and demanding all — absolute owner of
  all — O banner and pennant !
I too leave the rest — great as it is, it is nothing — houses machines are
  nothing — I see them not,
I see but you, O warlike pennant ! O banner so broad, with stripes, I sing
  you only,
Flapping up there in the wind.' "

*Charlotte Porter.*

# EMERSON AS AN EXPONENT OF THE BEAUTIFUL IN POETRY.

How ceaseless has been the war waged between the disciples of beauty as the sole element in poetry, and the defenders of morality, philosophy, and latterly science, as legitimate ores from which poetry may be minted !

Plato, no doubt, thought he had said the last word on the subject over two thousand years ago, when he, in a certain sense, combined the opposing elements by declaring that poetry should deal only with ennobling subjects, in order that the youths should be taught heroism and other Greek virtues. He would have turned Beauty herself into a be-spectacled mistress of ethics, and who would dare to say that in this character she might not bewitch all who gazed upon her ?

Dreary recollections of long-drawn arguments on this or kindred subjects haunt the waking hours of those unnamed brave who have had the courage to explore the Sahara which so conspicuously fills up the greater part of the seventeenth and eighteenth centuries in German literature.

One might have thought that Goethe, combining in his own intellectual personality, as he did, both the poetic and the scientific insight, might like a great Colossus have placed one foot on the head of each faction and crushed them out forever. But not a million Goethes could stamp out this perennially interesting subject of discussion ; the wise and the foolish of all lands still con-

46

tinue to hurl their weapons of wisdom into the thick of the *mêlée*, and from time to time the true poet comes in, like the third dog in the nursery tale, and carries off the bone.

No harmonizing solution of the problem is ever proposed, but there always remains an unexplained residuum which will send men off forever on fresh phases of the discussion ; just as no system of metaphysics ever has or ever will be proposed which will not give man for ages hence opportunities to formulate new theories.

To the on-looker, however, this battle between Beauty and, metaphorically speaking, the " Beast " appears rather as a skirmish of light infantry, than as a foe-annihilating canonnade of heavy artillery; and if only the magic spell which the wicked fairy Prejudice has cast upon the " Beast" could be dispelled, Beauty might recognize him as her own most worthy spouse.

Those, perhaps, come nearest to expressing a fundamental truth who hold that beauty should be the aim of poetry, though they do not, it is to be feared, always see the far-reaching grasp of their own statement; for is not beauty the most inclusive of all abstractions !   Truth, may be foul, body and soul, and goodness is not necessarily beautiful in body, though it must be so in soul; but beauty must be beautiful body and soul, or it is not entirely itself.   But though truth is often relatively ugly, within it lies latent the possibilities of goodness and ultimately of beauty; the exquisite pearly tints of the orchid, the perfect form, are immanent in the unsightly root.

Instead of declaring with Keats that truth is beauty, it would be more in harmony with the conception of a developing Universe to say that truth is everywhere in process of becoming beauty, and finally will merge in its "ultimate prime" into the full noontide splendor of perfect beauty whose soul is love.

Goodness shall also find its completest blossoming in beauty. He is a wise thinker who says that a good action is not perfectly moral until it is perfectly natural, perfectly spontaneous ; and consequently when a purely ideal moral stage is reached, ethics with its rules leading to the production of goodness will disappear. Beauty is indeed like the ' Numpholeptos' of Browning's poem, the white light of the manifestation of the Absolute, in which converge the prismatic rays of all other less complete abstractions.

But since the human mind in its strivings must be debarred from attaining the white light of beauty, how shall the poet decide where lie imbedded the seeds of beauty which he with his individual apportionment of imaginative power is to develop. This is a point round which the forces on both sides rally with renewed vigor.

To refer again to the omnipresent Plato, in the ' Laws ' he commends the Egyptians for establishing laws of beauty which for thousands of years were religiously followed, and suggests that it would be a good thing for the Athenians to do likewise; but who will not be thankful that the Egyptian standards were not accepted for all time, or that Greek standards were not conclusive ? Had the Egyptian standards reigned supreme, we should never have had the wondrous developments in Greek art ; and had the Greeks reigned supreme, where would have been the marvels of the Gothic age ? In short, beauty, to use the words of Guildenstern in George Eliot's ' A College Breakfast Party,' is not a " seedless, rootless flower," it has grown " with human growth, which means the rising sun of human struggle, order, knowledge — sense trained to a fuller record, more exact — to truer guidance of each passionate force."

It would be foolish to declare that there is any subject in which an anointed poet may not find and draw forth into blossom the latent seed of beauty.

The great world artist has put beauty into myriads of forms of inconceivable variety. Here blossoms the modest quaker-lady, making spring fields bright with its delicate hue caught from morning skies. It has no perfume, no use, — only a dainty form and color ; but hard by the violet, with a deeper passion lent it by the purple glow of less cloudless skies, freights the air with its sweet scent. Form, color, perfume,—all lend their aid in the production of this image of beauty. And far above extend the sheltering trees with sturdy trunks and knotty branches, with bark so rough that quaker-ladies and violets well might shudder could they look upon it ; and doubtless they would never realize that the strength and grandeur of the trees would not be possible had they stems as soft and green as theirs. They might even doubt the beauty of the tree ; for with their tiny vision how could they grasp it in its entirety.

The human artist, following the bent of his God-father, and in spite of violet and quaker-lady opinion, also puts beauty into many and varying forms. With his magic wand, he transforms mere words into lyrical blossoms as delicate, as useless,—shall I say ?—as altogether lovely as the quaker-lady.

> "Where the bee sucks, there lurk I ;
> In the cowslip's bell I lie ;
> There I couch when owls do cry.
> On the bat's back I do fly
> After summer merrily.
> Merrily, merrily, shall I live now,
> Under the blossom that hangs on the bough."

Another sweep of the wand, and there appears a sonnet laden with the perfume of the deepest, most sacred passions of the human heart. Another, and, lo ! a mighty tree, a 'Prometheus Unbound,' for example, whose spreading branches are supported on the stout stem of philosophical thought, or a 'Ring and the Book,' where the play of mind on mind, soul on soul, is the sublimated soil from which the blossom of beauty springs.

With none of these manifestations of beauty are we willing to part, nor are disparaging comparisons between them possible. Behold in each and every case a mystery not to be fathomed. Wherever beauty is, there has a spark of Infinity been given visible semblance, — a semblance more or less approaching the " rounded whole."

The real soul of a work of art is not dependent on the thought, the goodness, the truth, the metaphysics, the ethics, or the lack of all these which the poet puts into it, any more than the beauty of a picture or a statue depends upon the raw materials of which it is made. The materials, whatever they are, are but means to an end ; and all materials supplied by Nature, — emotions, intellect, mind, soul, love, philosophy, science, sin and its antipodes, goodness, — all may, nay, must find artistic expression, the end of which is beauty

The only test of whether the poet has succeeded in combining those materials with which he has chosen to body forth his conception into an image of beauty, is the recognition of an intangible something which, when the reader reads, makes his blood flow quickly and the inexplicable sensation which is called pleasure suffuse his being. To some, doubtless, only the quaker-ladies and violets of poetry give pleasure, — that is all of beauty to which they respond; but there are others who feel a strong thrill of delight in the perusal of a consciously philosophical poem like, for example, 'The Sun' in 'Ferishtah's Fancies,' — not because of the beauty of the truth contained, but because out of the materials chosen the poet has moulded images of beauty. As Emerson says: —

"The laws of this translation we do not know, or why one feature or gesture enchants, why one word or syllable intoxicates; but the fact is familiar that the fine touch of the eye, or a grace of manners, or a phrase of poetry, plants wings at our shoulders; as if Divinity, in his approaches, lifts away mountains of obstruction, and deigns to draw a truer line, which the mind knows and owns."

No more interesting example could be found as an illustration of the truth of the foregoing suggestions than the poetry of Ralph Waldo Emerson. He was a passionate lover of beauty, which he called the "most enduring quality and the most ascending quality the pilot of the young soul."

"Whom the Infinite One
Has granted his throne."

Though he attempts no definition of beauty, warned, as he says, by the ill fate of many philosophers who had essayed its definition, his conception of beauty is deep and far-reaching. It must be organic, not external; the form which beauty takes must be the natural result of a beautiful conception, and the measure of beauty depends upon its suggestion of brotherhood with the Universal, for "all beauty points at identity.    . Into every beautiful object there enters somewhat immeasurable and divine, and just as much into form bounded by outlines, like mountains on the horizon, as into tones of music or depths of space."

Upon this view the poet becomes not so much a conscious fashioner as an inspired singer in whose ear "God whispers," and the result is a poem which unfolds itself as naturally as a flower into its appropriate form of beauty.

The office of poet is, in Emerson's opinion, the most exalted among those in the gift of the Muses. "He is the healthy, the wise, the fundamental, the manly man, seer of the secret; against all the appearance, he sees and reports the truth, namely, that the soul generates matter." Not only then must the poet be a philosopher in the vague, general sense in which that term is used, he must be an idealistic philosopher; the "ineffable mysteries of the intellect," wherein is reached the loftiest pinnacle to which beauty may attain, must be his exalted theme.

It must be admitted that this is a lofty conception of the poet's office; yet one cannot but see that it is in a certain sense limited by Emerson's own vision. Poets are no longer members of a struggling humanity who catch occasional glimpses of celestial splendor; indeed, his poet is an image of Divinity itself. There seems to be little room in his mind for the poets whose functions have been to polish but a facet of the rough truth in the infinite gem of beauty; thus he can find it in his heart to complain that "Homer, Milton, Shakespeare do not fully content us. How rarely they offer us the heavenly bread! The most they have done is to intoxicate us again and again with its taste."

The poetry of Emerson naturally reflects his convictions in regard to the poet. His idealistic philosophy is the very body of it. Consciously he sets out to translate "God's whispers" into messages audible to the rest of mankind, and according to the followers of Milton's worn-out saying that poetry should be simple, sensuous, and passionate, one should be prepared to find this philosophical poetry dull stuff. But those who find it otherwise may also claim Milton on their side, for in the most lovely of his own poems, 'Comus,' he declares:

> "How charming is divine philosophy!
> Not harsh and crabbed as dull fools suppose,
> But musical as is Apollo's lute."

If this had been an *a priori* statement of Milton's, awaiting proof, no more convincing proof could have arisen than the poetry of Emerson. It matters not whether his philosophy was intuitional, or the result of slowly acquired knowledge (probably he did not know himself how much of it could be explained by natural processes), the fact remains, and it ought to silence all carpers against philosophy in poetry, that Emerson took it for his main theme, and draped it in such imagery as has fallen to the lot of few themes in poetry.

That a beautiful conception finds its appropriate expression not only in the spontaneity of its imagery, but in that of its rhythm and rhyme is Emerson's belief. He says, speaking of melody, rhyme, and form, "The difference between poetry and stock poetry is this, that in the latter the rhythm is given and the sense adapted to it ; while in the former the sense dictates the rhythm, I might even say that the rhyme is there in the theme, thought, and image themselves. . . . The verse must be alive and inseparable from its contents, as the soul of man inspires and directs the body." Upon this theory Emerson wrote his poetry; and while in many cases the result is entirely satisfactory, there are others where, in spite of poetical figures, the expression is sadly marred through awkward rhyming and clumsy rhythm. Emerson himself would most likely have laid the blame upon the thought ; for with his supreme reliance on intuition, he seems, like most idealists, to be blind to the opposite aspect of things. Doubtless a beautiful conception must be in the mind of a painter before he can produce a beautiful picture, but what would become of his picture if he were not acquainted with the laws of perspective ; and while the soul of a plant is certainly in the seed, it would be a poor plant indeed if it were not fashioned into beauty by sun and air. "God's whispers" may be his supreme marks of favor to his chosen few; but he has given an inheritance of intellect to mankind which even the favored should not overlook in the light of his higher gifts. A poet should surely fashion his intuitions with the sunlight of his knowledge. The Divine gift is given that the Divine inheritance may exert its functions to the uttermost, never as master, but as faithful servant.

Though we may doubt that a fine thought always naturally finds its most appropriate expression without any conscious manipulation on the part of the poet, Emerson certainly possessed the knack, to an uncommon degree, of presenting his thought in wonderfully beautiful and appropriate language.

In the closing passage of 'Woodnotes' is a fine example of the characteristic intensity with which he makes a great thought flash into being. Here he describes the march of evolution, not from the standpoint of the scientist, who sees only the blind inevitable forces of Nature, but from the secret chamber of the idealist, who sees it as the constant, changing aspect of the Eternal mind.

> "From form to form He maketh haste;
> This vault which glows immense with light
> Is the inn where He lodges for a night.
> What recks such Traveller if the bowers
> Which bloom and fade like meadow flowers
> A bunch of fragrant lilies be,
> Or the stars of eternity?
> Alike to him the better, the worse, —
> The glowing angel, the outcast corse.
> Thou metest him by centuries,
> And lo! he passes like the breeze;
> Thou seek'st in globe and galaxy,
> He hides in pure transparency;
> Thou askest in fountains and in fires,
> He is the essence that inquires.
> He is the axis of the star;
> He is the sparkle of the spar;
> He is the heart of every creature;
> He is the meaning of each feature;
> And his mind is the sky
> Than all it holds more deep, more high."

The beauty of this passage is irresistible. We seem to feel the rush of the world spirit through us in his inexorable flight into Eternity. If there is any criticism to be made, we should not pick on any faulty rhymes or halting lines, for any such are lost in the cumulative effect, which is striking; we should rather find some lack of warmth in the conception. After all, the world spirit as represented by Emerson, is strikingly like the scientist's persistent force. It recks not whether stars be stars or flowers, flowers;

alike to him the "glowing angel and the outcast corse." There is no hint that love is the ruling impulse of this mind. Its conditions are but appearances ; in its essence, it is unconditioned, — a being which it makes the mind ache to think of. Just the touch that is lacking in this poem of Emerson's, is added by Browning in the famous closing passages of ' Paracelsus.'

> — "How God tastes an infinite joy
> In infinite ways — one everlasting bliss
> From whom all being emanates, all power
> Proceeds: in whom is life forevermore."

But warmth is not an attribute of Emerson's poetry. It rather sparkles with the beauty of stars on a winter night.

Love is lifted by him into this same rarefied atmosphere ; where though the flame is pure and clear, it has not much tenderness.

> " Higher far into the pure realm
> Over sun and star,
> Over the flickering Dæmon film,
> Thou must mount for love."

If his failures in rhyme, and his sometimes monotonous metre, seem to militate against Emerson's own theory in regard to the organity of rhyme and rhythm, when he essayed blank verse, the organity of the thought with that form of expression receives glorious justification. Then his high, pure thoughts flow forth without let or hindrance, his wondrous tropes are not marred by the exigencies of lines upon which the rhyming axe comes down with its fatal regularity. The ' Sea Shore ' — which I cannot sufficiently admire, so perfect, it seems to me, is its beauty, — is a fine example of the possibilities to which Emerson could attain in blank verse ; and was there ever a more exquisite bit than the little poem called ' Days '? ' Musketaquid ' is another of his perfect poems. What exquisite terms of expression gemmed o 'er with dainty alliteration in the opening lines of this poem. Take these, for instance : —

> " For me, in showers, in sweeping showers, the Spring
> Visits the valley ; — break away the clouds, —

> Sparrows far off, and nearer April's bird,
> Blue-coated, — flying from tree to tree,
> Courageous sing a delicate overture
> To lead the tardy concert of the year."

The simplest commonplaces of Nature were turned by Emerson's heavenly alchemy into beauteous pictures; for let him go where e'er he would he heard "a sky-born music still," like the poet he describes, —

> "The free winds told him what they knew,
> Discoursed of fortune as they blew;
> Omens and signs that fill the air
> To him authentic witness bare."

As hinted before, the very loftiness of Emerson's conception of poetry limits his range. It is the universal, all-embracing truths that the poet is to sing. But to give the most vivid impressions of great universal truths, grand generalizations alone will not suffice ; it is necessary to have clear pictures of innumerable, distinct phases of human existence. Universality is made most apparent through the contrasting of many individualities. Unlike Whitman, who was overmastered by the idea of the equal and exalted importance of every individual manifestation, Emerson was so overmastered by the general universal relations existing among all phenomena of mind and matter, that the particular or special relations between groups of phenomena and the importance of the individual are passed over. He sits on high like the Hindoo Brahma, the tide of the downward flow of Nature from the Godhead, with all its various and intricate manifestations, has turned, and all Nature is again being absorbed into the Divine spirit.

The human struggles and aspirations of men and women do not interest him; all Nature is lovely, —

> " But man crouches and blushes,
>     Absconds and conceals ;
> He creepeth and peepeth,
>     He palters and steals ;
> Infirm, melancholy,
>     Jealous, glancing around,
> An oaf, an accomplice,
>     He poisons the ground."

Though the poet knows that "Deep love lieth under these pictures of time," and that "They fade in the light of their meaning sublime," he is better contented not to dwell upon man in his oaf-like aspect. Though he finds that in the "mud and scum of things there alway, alway something sings," he prefers to contemplate beauty in perfection, rather than the half-tints of beauty he could find among the haunts of men.

He bids farewell to the proud world, with its love and pride of man, the sophist schools, the learned clans, —

> " For what are they all in their high conceit,
> When man in the bush with God may meet."

So he returns ever to Nature. The ineffable mysteries of the intellect he does not seem to find among his fellowmen ; he looks forward to them in the man of whom Nature sings to him in her song, — a man "the sunburnt world" shall breed "Of all the zones and countless days."

Though we find that the realm of beauty over which Emerson holds sway has boundaries, yet within those boundaries is a magic garden where every leaf and twig is instinct with auroral light. He casts such a mystic glamour on sea and land that we feel our-selves touched for brief, sweet moments with the poet's own imagi-native vision ; we, too, can exclaim with him, " My books and chair and candlestick are fairies in disguise, meteors and constellations."

*Helen A. Clarke.*

## AMERICA : A PROPHECY.*

### BY WILLIAM BLAKE.

#### PRELUDIUM.

THE shadowy daughter of Urthona stood before red Orc
When fourteen suns had faintly journey'd o'er his dark abode :

---

* Lambeth. Printed by William Blake in the year 1793. [The text of the reprint here given follows closely the facsimile of Blake's work. It ventures upon no amendment of the mysterious "straig," "anoring" and "glinanering," which our readers will notice and prefer to receive, as we take it, precisely as it fell from Blake's hands, with liberty to conjecture each for himself what the words signify. Blake's system of punctuation consisted of decorative dots and colons, the former of which manifestly did duty for commas as well as periods ; wherefore we have rendered the comma-dots as commas. We have thought it not neces-sary to spell " Pennsylvania " and " oppressors " with one " n " and one " p," considering these and like slips of the artist's drawing pen unimportant. — *The Editors.*]

His food she brought in iron baskets, his drink in cups of iron :
Crown'd with a helmet and dark hair the nameless female stood :
A quiver with its burning stores, a bow like that of night,
When pestilence is shot from heaven, no other arms she needs :
Invulnerable tho' naked save where clouds roll round her loins
Their awful folds in the dark air ; silent she stood as night :
For never from her iron tongue could voice or sound arise.
But dumb till that dread day when Orc assayed his fierce embrace.

Dark Virgin : said the hairy youth, thy father stern abhorr'd :
Rivets my tenfold chains while still on high my spirit soars :
Sometimes an eagle screaming in the sky, sometimes a lion
Stalking upon the mountains, and sometimes a whale I lash
The raging fathomless abyss, anon a serpent folding
Around the pillars of Urthona and round thy dark limbs,
On the Canadian wilds I fold, feeble my spirit folds.
For chain'd beneath I rend these caverns : when thou bringest food
I howl my joy and my red eyes seek to behold thy face.
In vain : these clouds roll to and fro, and hide thee from my sight.

Silent as despairing love and strong as jealousy.
The hairy shoulders rend the links.   Free are the wrists of fire ;
Round the terrific loins he seized the panting struggling womb.
It joy'd : she put aside her clouds and smiled her first born smile :
As when a black cloud shows its lightnings to the silent deep.

Soon as she saw the terrible boy then burst the virgin cry.

I know thee, I have found thee and I will not let thee go :
Thou art the image of God who dwells in darkness of Africa.
And thou art fall'n to give me life in regions of dark death.
On my American plains I feel the struggling afflictions
Endur'd by rods that writhe their arms into the nether deep :
I see a serpent in Canada, who courts me to his love,
In Mexico an Eagle, and a Lion in Peru :
I see a Whale in the South-sea drinking my soul away.
O what limb rending pains I feel.   Thy fire and my frost
Mingle in howling pains, in furrows by thy lightnings rent :
This is eternal death ; and this the torment long foretold.

THE Guardian Prince of Albion burns in his nightly tent,
Sullen fires across the Atlantic glow to America's shore :
Piercing the souls of warlike men, who rise in silent night.
Washington, Franklin, Paine, and Warren, Gates, Hancock, and Green ;
Meet on the coast glowing with blood from Albion's Fiery Prince.

Washington spoke : Friends of America look over the Atlantic sea :
A bended bow is lifted in heaven and a heavy iron chain
Descends link by link from Albion's cliffs across the sea to bind
Brothers and sons of America, till our faces pale and yellow,
Heads deprest, voices weak, eyes downcast, hands work-bruised,
Feet bleeding on the sultry sands and the furrows of the whip
Descend to generations that in future times forget.

The strong voice ceas'd.   For a terrible blast swept over the heaving sea,
The eastern cloud rent : on his cliffs stood Albion's wrathful Prince
A dragon form clashing his scales at midnight he arose,
And flam'd red meteors round the land of Albion beneath.
His voice, his locks, his awful shoulders, and his glowing eyes,
Appear to the Americans upon the cloudy night.

Solemn heave the Atlantic waves between the gloomy nations
Swelling belching from its deeps red clouds and raging fires.
Albion is sick.   America faints ! enrag'd the Zenith grew.
As human blood shooting its veins all round the orbed heaven
Red rose the clouds from the Atlantic in vast wheels of blood
And in the red clouds rose a Wonder o'er the Atlantic's sea ;
Intense ! naked ! a Human fire fierce glowing as the wedge
Of iron heated in the furnace ; his terrible wings were fire
With myriads of cloudy terrors, banners dark and towers
Surrounded ; heat but not light went thro' the murky atmosphere.

The King of England looking westward trembles at the Vision.

Albion's Angel stood beside the Stone of night, and saw
The terror like a comet or more like the planet red
That once inclos'd the terrible wandering camels in its sphere.
Then Mars thou wast our center, and the planets three flew round
Thy crimson disk : so e'er the Sun was rent from thy red sphere :
The Spectre glow'd his horrid length staining the temple long
With beams of blood ; and thus a voice came forth and shook the temple.

The morning comes, the night decays, the watchmen leave their stations;
The grave is burst, the spices shed, the linen wrapped up:
The bones of death, the cov'ring clay, the sinews shrunk and dry'd,
Reviving shake, inspiring move, breathing! awakening.
Spring like redeemed captives when their bonds and bars are burst;
Let the slave grinding at the mill, run out into the field:
Let him look up into the heavens and laugh in the bright air:
Let the inchained soul shut up in darkness and in sighing,
Whose face has never seen a smile in thirty weary years:
Rise and look out, his chains are loose, his dungeon's doors are open
And let his wife and children return from the oppressor's scourge:
They look behind at every step and believe it is a dream,
Singing, the Sun has left his blackness and has found a Fresher
    morning
And the fair Moon rejoices in the clear and cloudless night:
For Empire is no more, and now the Lion and Wolf shall cease.

In thunders ends the voice.   Then Albion's Angel wrathful burnt
Beside the Stone of night: and like the Eternal Lion's howl
In famine and war, replyd art thou not Orc, who serpent-form'd
Stands at the Gate of Enitharmon to devour her children;
Blasphemous Demon, Antichrist hater of Dignities:
Lover of wild rebellion and transgressor of God's Law;
Why dost thou come to Angels eyes in this terrific form?

The terror answer'd: I am Orc wreath'd round the accursed tree;
The times are ended; shadows pass, the morning 'gins to break:
The fiery joy that Urizen perverted to ten commands,
What night he led the starry hosts thro' the wide wilderness:
That stony law I stamp to dust: and scatter religion abroad
To the four winds as a torn book, and none shall gather the leaves
But they shall rot on desert sands and consume in bottomless deeps
To make the deserts blossom, and the deeps shrink to their fountains,
And to renew the fiery joy and burst the stony roof,
That pale religious lechery, seeking Virginity,
May find it in a harlot; and in coarse-clad honesty
The undefil'd tho' ravish'd in her cradle night and morn:
For everything that lives is holy, life delights in life;
Because the soul of sweet delight can never be defil'd.

Fires inwrap the earthly globe, yet man is not consum'd ;
Amidst the lustful fires he walks : his feet become like brass,
His knees and thighs like silver and his breast and head like gold.

Sound ! Sound ! my loud war trumpets and alarm my Thirteen Angels !
Loud howls the eternal Wolf ! the eternal Lion lashes his tail !
America is darken'd ; and my punishing Demons terrified
Crouch howling before their caverns deep like skins dry'd in the wind
They cannot smite the wheat, nor quench the fatness of the earth.
They cannot smite with sorrows, nor subdue the plow and spade.
They cannot wall the city nor moat round the castle of princes.
They cannot bring the stubbed oak to overgrow the hills.
For terrible men stand on the shores, and in their robes I see
Children take shelter from the lightnings, there stands Washington
And Paine and Warren with their Foreheads rear'd toward the east
But clouds obscure my aged sight.　A vision from afar !
Sound ! Sound ! my loud war trumpets and alarm my thirteen Angels :
Ah vision from afar !　Ah rebel form that rent the ancient
Heavens, Eternal Viper self-renew'd, rolling in clouds
I see thee in thick clouds and darkness on America's shore,
Writhing in pangs of abhorred birth ; red flames the crest rebellious.
And eyes of death ; the harlot womb oft opened in vain
Heaves in enormous circles, now the times are return'd upon thee,
Devourer of thy Parent, now thy unutterable torment renews.
Sound ! Sound ! my loud war trumpets and alarm my thirteen Angels :
Ah terrible birth ! A young one bursting ! where is the weeping mouth?
And where the mother's milk ? instead those ever hissing jaws
And parched lips drop with fresh gore ; now roll thou in the clouds,
Thy mother lays her length outstretch'd upon the shore beneath,
Sound ! Sound ! my loud war trumpets and alarm my thirteen Angels !
Loud howls the eternal Wolf : the eternal Lion lashes his tail !

Thus wept the Angel voice and as he wept the terrible blasts
Of trumpets blew a loud alarm across the Atlantic deep.
No trumpets answer ; no reply of clarions or of fifes,
Silent the Colonies remain and refuse the loud alarm.

On those vast shady hills between America and Albion's shore ;
Now barr'd out by the Atlantic sea : call'd Atlantean hills :
Because from their bright summits you may pass to the Golden world

An ancient palace archetype of mighty Emperies
Rears its immortal pinnacles built in the forest of God
By Ariston the King of beauty for his stolen bride.

Here on their magic seats the thirteen angels sat perturb'd
For clouds from the Atlantic hover o'er the solemn roof.

Fiery the Angels rose, and as they rose deep thunder roll'd
Around their shores: indignant burning with the fires of Orc
And Boston's Angel cried aloud as they flew through the dark night.

He cried: Why trembles honesty and like a murderer,
Why seeks he refuge from the frowns of his immortal station,
Must the generous tremble and leave his joy to the idle: to the pesti-
    lence!
That mock him? who commanded this; what God! what Angel!
To keep the gen'rous from experience till the ungenerous
Fire unrestrain'd performers of the energies of nature:
Till pity is become a trade, and generosity a science
That men get rich by, and the sandy desert is giv'n to the straig.
What God is he, writes laws of peace and clothes him in a tempest
What pitying Angel lusts for tears and fans himself with sighs
What crawling villain preaches abstinence and wraps himself
In fat of lambs? No more I follow, no more obedience pay.
So cried he rending off his robes and throwing down his scepter
In sight of Albion's Guardian, and all the thirteen Angels
Rent off their robes to the hungry wind, and threw their golden scepters
Down on the land of America, indignant they descended
Headlong from out their heavenly heights, descending swift as fires
Over the land; naked and flaming are their lineaments seen
In the deep gloom; by Washington and Paine and Warren they stood
And the flame folded roaring fierce within the pitchy night
Before the Demon red, who burnt towards America,
In black smoke thunders and loud winds rejoicing in its terror,
Breaking in smoky wreaths from the wild deep and gathring thick
In flames as of a furnace on the land from North to South.

What time the thirteen Governors that England sent convene
In Bernard's house; the flames cover'd the land they raze they cry
Shaking their mental chains they rush in fury to the sea.
To quench their anguish; at the feet of Washington down fall'n

They grovel on the sand and writhing lie. While all
The British soldiers thro' the thirteen States sent up a howl
Of anguish : threw their swords and muskets to the earth and ran
From their encampment and dark castles seeking where to hide
From the grim flames : and from the visions of Orc ; in sight
Of Albion's angel ; who enrag'd his secret clouds open'd
From North to South, and burnt outstretch'd on wings of wrath cov'ring
The eastern sky, spreading his awful wings across the heavens ;
Beneath him roll'd his numerous hosts, all Albion's Angels camp'd
Darken'd the Atlantic mountains and their trumpets shook the valleys
Arm'd with diseases of the earth to cast upon the Abyss.
Their number forty millions, mustering in the eastern sky.

In the flames stood and view'd the armies drawn out in the sky
Washington, Franklin, Paine, and Warren, Allen, Gates, and Lee :
And heard the voice of Albion's Angel give the thunderous command
His plagues obedient to his voice flew forth out of their clouds
Falling upon America as a storm to cut them off
As a blight cuts the tender corn when it begins to appear.
Dark is the heaven above and cold and hard the earth beneath :
And as a plague wind fill'd with insects cuts off man and beast ;
And as a sea o'erwhelms a land in the day of an earthquake.

Fury ! rage ! madness ! in a wind swept through America
And the red flames of Orc that folded roaring fierce around
The angry shores and the fierce rushing of th' inhabitants together ;
The citizens of New York close their books and lock their chests ;
The mariners of Boston drop their anchors and unlade ;
The scribe of Pennsylvania casts his pen upon the earth,
The builder of Virginia throws his hammer down in fear.

Then had America been lost, o'erwhelm'd by the Atlantic,
And Earth had lost another portion of the infinite.
But all wish together in the night in wrath and raging fire
The red fires rag'd ! the plagues recoil'd ! then roll'd they back with
    fury
On Albion's Angels : then the Pestilence began in streaks of red
Across the limbs of Albion's Guardian, the spotted plague smote Bristol's
And the leprosy London's Spirit sick'ning all their bands :
The millions sent up a howl of anguish and threw off their hammer'd mail,

48

And cast their swords and spears to earth and stood a naked multitude
Albion's Guardian writhed in torment on the eastern sky
Pale anoring toward the brain, his glinanering eyes, teeth chattering,
Howling and shuddering, his legs quivering convuls'd, each muscle and
    sinew,
Sick'ning lay London's Guardian and the ancient miter'd York
Their heads on snowy hills their ensigns sick'ning in the sky.

The plagues creep on the burning winds driven by flames of Orc
And by the fierce Americans rushing together in the night
Driven o'er the Guardians of Ireland and Scotland and Wales
They spotted with plagues forsook the frontiers and their banners sear'd
With fires of hell deform their ancient heavens with shame and woe.
Hid in his caves the Bard of Albion felt the enormous plagues,
And a cowl of flesh grew over his head and scales on his back and ribs;
And rough with black scales all his Angels fright their ancient heavens
The doors of marriage are open, and the Priests in rustling scales
Rush into reptile coverts hiding from the fires of Orc,
That play around the golden roofs in wreaths of fierce desire,
Leaving the females naked and glowing with the lusts of youth.

For the female spirits of the dead pining in bonds of religion
Run from their fetters reddening and in long drawn arches sitting
They feel the nerves of youth renew, and desires of ancient times
Over their pale limbs as a Vine when the tender grape appears.

Over the hills, the vales, the cities, rage the red flames fierce :
The Heavens melted from north to south ; and Urizen who sat
Above all heavens in thunders wrapp'd, emerg'd his leprous head
From out his holy shrine his tears in deluge piteous
Falling into the deep sublime : flag'd with grey-brow'd snow
And thunderous visages, his jealous wings wav'd over the deep :
Weeping in dismal howling woe he dark descended howling
Around the smitten bands, cloth'd in tears and trembling shudd'ring
    cold.
His stored snows he poured forth, and his icy magazines
He open'd on the deep, and on the Atlantic sea white shiv'ring.
Leprous his limbs, all over white, and hoary was his visage
Weeping in dismal howlings before the stern Americans
Hiding the Demon red with clouds and cold mists from the earth :

'Till Angels and weak men twelve years should govern o'er the strong;
And then their end should come when France receiv'd the Demon's
    light.

Stiff shudderings shook the heav'nly thrones! France, Spain and Italy,
In terror view'd the bands of Albion, and the ancient Guardians
Fainting upon the elements smitten with their own plagues
They slow advance to shut the five gates of their law built heaven
Filled with blasting fancies and with mildews of despair
With fierce disease and lust unable to stem the fires of Orc;
But the five Gates were consum'd, and their bolts and hinges melted
And the fierce flames burnt round the heavens and round the abodes of
    men.

---

## DRAMAS OF NEW ENGLAND: 'GILES COREY;' 'SHORE–ACRES.'

FROM THE CORRESPONDENCE OF —— —— AND *

DEAR * * * · I have been to see two dramas of New England
life lately. New England of the past inspires ' Giles Corey,' and
the New England of this morning, so to speak, animates ' Shore-
Acres.' Steeple-crowned hats lord it in one play, and overalls
dominate the other; but the same stern spirit of the steeple-crowns,
which smothers the open expression of native passions, good or
bad, in the earlier play, lives on in the later play in the hardness
of selfish conservatism, much out of sorts with modern sentiment
and with the large free curves and bracing air of Atlantic shore
acres.

While I sat circumspectly in my chair, with my nineteenth century aluminium-mounted lenses at my eyes to aid me in my cool bin-
ocular reflections, my unassisted senses dwelt covertly on a solemn
fact, — my own eight or nine generations of Yankee lineage binding me down into consciousness of my latent kinship with the
intolerant old duffers who make the tragedy of both plays.

Hawthorne's words spoke for me: " Let us thank God for
having given us such ancestors; and let each successive generation thank him not less fervently for being one step further from

them in the march of ages." Bless me! You see, the steeple-crown will never die; it looks a modern opera-glass out of countenance and preaches in a play-house!

The opening of 'Giles Corey' I found sombre, poetic rather than dramatic. Pretty Olive Corey presided at the spinning wheel; the silly old crone, Nancy Fox, hugged the fire-place, chuckling over the witch-pin game she is carrying on surreptitiously with the child Phoebe, when the jealous young woman enters whose spite and hysteria are to instigate the tragedy of the piece. Later appear Giles Corey, to fan the spark of danger with his superstitious, blundering talk; the goodwife Corey, notable housekeeper, pooh-poohing at witch stories; and Olive's lover Paul Bayley. All these important personal elements of the tragic sequel are cleverly introduced in the first act; but, to my mind, they are not made impressive as dramatic factors of the result.

The work was well-designed, low-toned, strictly in keeping with the suppressed passions of New England Puritanism, but it had the effect of narrative.

You would have liked a pretty love-scene there was between Paul and Olive; his face glowing with half-concealed delight over the news he had to tell of the lot he had bought that morning for their future home-building, while he waited for her to finish her stint at the distant spinning-wheel, urging her to come and sit beside him on the settle, and yet approving with all his decorous Puritan heart her seemly reserve and conscientiousness.

The most powerful scene, and decidedly the most applauded, was the trial-scene speech of Martha Corey for her daughter. She stood like a lioness, and her plea had the fire of menace in it. It was Agnes Booth's great acting chance of the piece, and she made the most of it. Mr. Mackey, who played Giles Corey's part with stanch yeomanlike heroism, had his opportunity in the prison scene, where he rudely reasons out his resolve to stand mute and bear the pressing of the weights unto death. The love of the elders seemed to dwarf that of their children with Giles's words: "I will make amends to thee, lass; I swear I will come where thou art by a harder road than the one I bade thee go."

I turned to Longfellow's 'Giles Corey' afterwards for comparison. You remember it? Who can fail to be struck with the
superior skill of Miss Wilkins's more human, more rational way of
rendering the historic story?

Curious how modern this play of hers is in its realism, and yet
how lacking it is in what one is wont to consider the equally
modern note of psychological depth! I amused myself by imagining another mode of treating the same plot. Fancy a new construction of the piece, revealing the very root of action in a strong,
rebellious, double-minded nature, such as a prime mover in the
bewitchment tumult of the day must have had! Would not such
a figure concentrate interest and dramatic force? Would not the
clash of her ill-will against the victims of the public delusion make
the whole piece pulse with fiercer blood?

If you have not seen the pretty little black and white volume
in which Harper & Brothers have brought out ' Giles Corey,' you
must get it. I was twice as interested in reading the play again
after having seen it acted.

I was glad to notice, by the way, that the unjustly abused Theatre of Arts and Letters had done themselves credit in one of their
" cuts." I mean the excision of the needless scene where the child
drags the rheumatic old crone to hide with her under the bed, — a
farcical proceeding dangerous to act. The unkindest cut, I think, is
the belittling of Ann's part. Of course, as I venture to propose
that her part might have been made the vital cause of the tragedy,
I regret the more that the prominence the author herself really did
give it was flattened out, from many an artful speech in the trial
scene, into mere groans and writhings.

Have you noticed how closely Miss Wilkins's subdued style of
writing, bare of imagery, devoid of involution and verbal felicities,
fits her theme? It seems to me to be born of the same conditions
as those that bred the scenes of which she writes with such narrowness of aim. Its felicity is its simplicity; but, I suspect, it would
be poverty in a richer, warmer range of subject-matter. But her
choice of subject is a legitimate part of her art, you will say; and,
certainly, if her New England created her, she has been enabled

thus the fitlier to recreate and set before the world her own New
England.   One may or may not like Hawthorne's way of doing it
better, yet I have a secret notion that Miss Wilkins's is the truer,
the less transmuted into a mystical romance due rather to the indi-
dual vision than to actual life.

Strange to say, ' Shore-Acres,' rough-hewn and homespun as it
is, struck me as idyllic.   It is full of pathetic effects, rich in the
homely comic and in sentiment; but it is picturesque rather than
robustly dramatic.    The children's parts are charmingly real; the
universal heart is captured from the first by the " cute " prattle of
these country children.    Surely never did play-wright make so
much capital out of this natural well-spring of pleasure; it was a
successful graft on the melodrama of the plot, which consisted in
the father's orthodox bitterness against his daughter's lover.   This
young physician has the impertinence, forsooth, to believe in evolution ; while he, Farmer Berry, believes as his father did, and is
ready — as his way of progressing — to sell out every particle of
" sentiment " along with the old farm.    His gentle-hearted brother
Nathaniel has a prominent part to play as the champion of warm heart
and free brain against his brother's narrow mind and selfish soul;
and the irresistible acting — where all the acting was clever — of
Mr. James A. Herne made it a doubly important part.   The large,
quizzical, loving humor he put into it was like nothing but Joe
Jefferson's Rip, and fully the mate of it along a different and original
line of character interpretation.

Have you heard of the stage-trick of the light-house scene?   It
was the dramatic climax of the piece.  While the schooner carrying
the eloping lovers is driven in by the " Sou'easter," inside the light-
house, a grim tussle is going on between the two brothers, — the
father is trying to keep Nathaniel from replenishing the light.   It
grows dimmer and dimmer in the theatre in the conventional way
the audience is used to, when, at the same instant, as Nathaniel
breaks from the churl and makes for the light-house stairs, the
audience gets a genuine surprise, — out goes all light, and the house
is black for full three minutes before the light streams out again
from the tower and the " Liddy Ann " is saved.   I can fancy you

commenting wisely: " A scenic effect impossible before the day of electric lighting, and directly due, therefore, to scientific mechanism." And so it is, and why not ?   Only one half hopes that the intricacy of stage effects, made possible by these new material resources, may out-do itself, at last, and lead to the unalloyed impress of dramatic genius.   The ethical climax reached in the last scene by quite human means is an example.   The sweet-natured Nathaniel, having yielded to his brother even his chance to win the woman both love, having reconciled the family and brought about the happiness of all who knew him, is represented in this final scene in the nightly acts of care-taker for the household, — setting to rights, bolting doors, attending to the kitchen fire; then turning bedward, candle in hand, alone and silent in the happy house, he contemplates with a face wholesome to look upon the fruit of a beneficent life-time.   This good genius of the house of Berry sees his work that it is good, and the audience watch his slow clumping boots and rustic figure up the kitchen-stairs to his bedroom with a democratic and moral emotion quite new to the theatre.

Yours,            —— ——.

## SOME RECENT AMERICAN VERSE.*

SOME one has recently calculated that there are at the present time about one hundred thousand poets in America.   Fortunately

---

* A Book of Day Dreams, Charles Leonard Moore.   New York : Henry Holt and Co., 1892. — Songs and Sonnets, by Maurice Francis Egan.   Chicago: A. C. McClurg and Co., 1892. — Eleusis and Lesser Poems, by William Rufus Perkins.   Chicago: A. C. McClurg and Co., 1892. — Red Leaves and Roses, by Madison Cawein.   New York : G. P. Putnam's Sons, 1893. — Francis Drake ; A Tragedy of the Sea, The Mother and Other Poems, by S. Weir Mitchell.   Boston and New York : Houghton, Mifflin, and Co., 1893. —*El Nuovo Mundo,* by Louis James Block.   Chicago: Chas. H. Kerr and Co., 1893. — Some Rhymes of Ironquil of Kansas.   Chicago: A. C. McClurg and Co., 1892. — Ideälä, A Romance of Idealism, by Charles Grissen.   Portland, Oregon : J. K. Gill Co., 1893. — Thought Throbs, by Creedmore Fleenor.   Louisville : John P. Morton and Co., 1892. — By the Atlantic, by I. D. Van Duzee.

for the reviewer they have not all put forth their powers during the past year; but still enough of them have done so, and have produced work of sufficiently good quality, to make it impossible in the limited pages of a magazine review to do them the justice they deserve. If we have not yet sighted the long expected great American poet, we have a goodly array of minor poets who at their best may easily put to flight much of the work of those poets of the last generation whom we are accustomed to call "great."

All lovers of poetry will derive intense satisfaction from the "Century" of sonnets by Mr. Leonard Moore, which, though written some time ago, appear now in a second edition revised.

They reflect that mellow quality which somehow genius seems to be born with. Throughout the whole series of a hundred sonnets the poet wings his imaginative flight through the mysterious realms of his own thought; and so closely do the links in the development follow each other that the reader is led onward as if by enchantment. The atmosphere of this poet's thought is full of life's dark shadows, but occasionally there bursts forth a gleam of sunshine, and finally, in the last sonnet 'To My Mother,' this modern Faust casts off his dark and embittered thought, — shamed by her sweet content, — and the reader comes back to earth, conscious that his artistic soul has had a rare treat. A hundred sonnets do not make a great poet, but among them there are so many evincing unusual power and beauty of expression that we nurture hope that Mr. Leonard Moore may have something great in store for us.

There is a whiff of spontaneous originality about the songs and sonnets of Maurice Egan that is very refreshing, and proclaims

---

Boston : Lee and Shepard, 1892. — The Loves of Paul Fenly, by Anna M. Fitch. New York : G. P. Putnam's Sons, 1893. — Fleeting Thoughts, by Caroline Edwards Prentiss. New York : G. P. Putnam's Sons, 1893. — Songs, by Neith Boyce. Original Drawings by Ethelwyn Wells Conrey. Boston : Arena Publishing Co., 1892. — From Heart's Content, by Clara Doty Bates. Chicago : Morrill, Higgins, and Co., 1892. — Fair Shadow Land, by Edith M. Thomas. Boston and New York : Houghton, Mifflin, and Co., 1893.

him one of Nature's poets. His sonnets sometimes lack that con-
centred complexity which is the mark of the perfect sonnet; but
among them one will find some lovely fancies, — for example, in
his ' Legends of the Flowers,' — while his lyrics " sing themselves "
quite in the fashion of those of the good old days of Elizabeth.

There can be but one ' In Memoriam,' and a poet of the ability
of Mr. William Perkins does himself an injustice by choosing to
model his work on the same plan. ' Eleusis' is written in exactly
the same philosophizing vein and the same stanza form as ' In
Memoriam,' and if it were the first of its kind would be worthy of
all praise ; but as it is so palpably imitative, it calls for only such
share of admiration as falls to the lot of a good copy of a celebrated
painting.

Mr. Madison Cawein still continues to pour forth his flood
of song from the South. In his last volume there are hardly any
of the verbal monstrosities which marred his first work; but there
also seems to be lacking the wild exhilaration, like that of a mock-
ing-bird untamed, which was to us the main charm and promise
of his budding powers. It is to be hoped that his critics have not
caged him; but, after all, his main difficulty, like that of many
another American poet, is lack of inventive power. Facility of
expression will soon be exhausted if it has not variety of thought
or incident upon which to expend itself.

Dr. Mitchell has an assured place among our latter day poets,
and fresh volumes from him are always welcome. Within the
year he has published two, — one of miscellaneous poems, and the
other a drama founded on that strange tale of history, the con-
demning for treason of Thomas Doughty by Francis Drake.
Though not the hero, Doughty's is the most interesting character, in its curious mixture of lovableness and criminal weakness,
strongly indicated in Dr. Mitchell's portraiture. The scene where
he makes choice of his sentence, particularly, shows a subtile grasp
of the inner currents of this man's being; and the striking scene
at the close, when the man about to be beheaded is the host and
the most joyous of the party, is most skilfully drawn. The miscellaneous poems of the other volume, ' The Mother and Other

49

Poems,' do not show the sustained power of his last volume; but
there are some charming pieces in it, especially the reflective
poems written in Italy, chief among which we should place the
beautiful poem written by the grave of Keats, 'In the Protestant
Cemetery at Rome,' the closing lines of which we quote: —

> " Never more in life
> May I, companioned by the friendly dead,
> Walk in this sacred fellowship again;
> Therefore, thou silent singer 'neath the grass,
> Sing to me still those sweeter songs unsung,
> ' Pipe to the spirit ditties of no tone,'
> Caressing thought with wonderments of phrase
> Such as thy springtide rapture knew to win.
> Ay, sing to me thy unborn summer songs,
> And the ripe autumn lays that might have been,
> Strong wine of fruit mature, whose flowers alone we know."

Mr. Louis James Block has celebrated the Columbian year with
a long poem entitled ' *El Nuovo Mundo.*' Mr. Block is a writer of
thoroughly serious aims, and has thoughtfully considered the theme
of the development of the principle of liberty, which, like Shelley,
he conceives to have been the primal thought of God. The poem
is in four parts: 'The Old World,' ' The Man' (Columbus), ' The
Deed' (The Discovery), and 'The New World.' The stanza-form
chosen is, in our opinion, of too marked a character not to become
monotonous in so long a poem. Perhaps the alternate shortening
and lengthening of the lines is intended to represent the rhythmic
flow of the mounting waves of time; but however legitimate such
effects may be in short poems, they are a mistake in poems of any
great length. The regularity of the irregularities counteracts the
effect of variety aimed at. Though we miss the imaginative touch
which so illuminated much of the work in Mr. Block's former
volume, he has on the whole expressed his thought in smooth and
flowing language.

There is a beautiful confidence in themselves of the poets of the
far West, which, failing other signs, betokens the consciousness of
genius. Ironquil prefaces his rhymes by the clever lines: —

" When back into the alphabet,
    The critic's satires shall have crumbled,
    When into dust his hand is humbled,
    One verse of mine may linger yet."

It would not be surprising as things go if Time were to send Ironquil to keep company with the critics ; but we hope better things may be in store for him, since he brings a new territory into the republic of verse. One catches glimpses of life as it is in the Kansas Wilds, — a life sadly lacking in richness or fullness, but with touches of pathos and nobleness. 'The Washerwoman's Song' and the 'Tobacco Stemmers' are among the best things in the volume.

From the outermost confines of our land is heard the piping of Apollo. Charles Grissen, of Portland, Oregon, has written a Romance of Idealism in twelve cantos called 'Ideälä.' He claims in his introduction that it is an entirely original production ; and truth to say, it shows more inventive faculty than American versifiers are in the habit of displaying. Poetry is with him, he says, an acquired language ; and considering this fact, there are many creditable lines in it.

Kentucky also furnishes a book of poems which the author informs us in the preface is paid for. It is perhaps a good thing that the precaution was taken of paying for it in advance, for the public might be discouraged if it happened to open at a poem on the life of a cat, called 'Despicable Tom,' containing ninety-four stanzas.

It would not be fair, however, to judge Mr. Fleenor by this somewhat dreary poem ; 'On the Street,' for instance, has a breath of life in it, and there are many others of the shorter pieces which show considerable talent.

'By the Atlantic' contains the collected poems of I. D. Van Duzee, many of which have appeared in various newspapers. His poems are thoughful and well put together, a number of them being addressed to various great names. One of the best is a dainty fancy called 'Psyche and the Winds.'

'The Loves of Paul Fenly,' by Anna M. Fitch, is a cleverly told story in verse of the shortcomings of a man of the Don Juan type. It contains many shrewd and cynical observations on society, but is too long drawn out to become very absorbing. It would seem to attempt something in the direction of Browning's 'Red Cotton Night Cap Country,' but is completely lacking in the dramatic intensity which illuminates that poem.

'Fleeting Thoughts,' by Caroline Edwards Prentiss, strew themselves in from one to three verses a page through a volume of one hundred and twenty-eight pages. Though there is nothing in the least striking, the general quality of the verse is good.

Quite dainty, too, are the songs by Neith Boyce which have been printed in a tasteful booklet with illustrations by Ethelwyn Wells Conrey as dainty as the poems.

In 'From Heart's Content,' Clara Doty Bates joins pretty fancies out of her head to many of the common flowers and birds. Her rhythms and rhymes are often faulty ; but she has a certain appreciative observation of every-day phases of Nature, and a simple way of telling her tales about the birds or flowers, which gives a real charm to her verses.

Edith M. Thomas is fast winning a distinguished place among our minor poets. She possesses a certain reticence and concentration of expression which shows her to have her art well in hand, — the right word is used, the thought is well rounded, — but there is that same lack of imagination which we have such reason to deplore in most of our American poets. We read and admire the skill, but, alas ! we are not stirred except in rare instances.

*C.*

## NOTES AND NEWS.

At a recent meeting of the Browning Society of Philadelphia, the subject of ethics versus beauty in poetry was discussed, with several defenders on either side. The middle ground was concisely summed up by Miss Alice Groff, as follows : —

"I have come to the conclusion that purely artistic expression is not possible to pure ethics. I find that the beautiful expresses itself in the artistic, the true in the scientific, the good in the ethical; but I also find that what we call *art* is never the whole of painting, of music, of poetry, of anything; that there is to neither painting, nor music, nor poetry any fullness of life except in combination of the artistic, the scientific, and the ethical.

"We hear on all sides unsparing denunciations of the artist, the poet, who subordinates the beautiful, — or rather its legitimate expression the artistic, — to either the scientific or the ethical. How is it that we never hear complaints of the subordination of the scientific or the ethical to the artistic; surely we have only too often just cause for such complaint.

"Beauty to my mind is therefore not the sufficient end of poetry, of any creation, — seeing that beauty is but one element of the ideal, and that the grosser element. Nor is pleasure — which is the highest form of emotion that mere beauty is capable of inspiring in us — the loftiest form of appreciation of the ideal; for of such appreciation pleasure is only the body, while delight may be called its mind, and joy its soul. Pleasure may be felt over the recognition of the beautiful, delight over the realization of the true; but joy — that all-pervading life-principle of blissful emotion which the waters of grief even cannot drown, and which mere beauty is utterly insufficient to inspire, much less sustain forever — is experienced only over the recognition of the unity of the beautiful, the true, and the good in truth.

"Truth, then, is the only sufficient end of poetry, of any creation. Truth is one, but it is also a trinity, — in its essential essence, a trinity of the beautiful, the true, and the good; in its manifestation, a trinity of the artistic, the scientific, the ethical.

"Poetry which aims simply at the beautiful in essence, the artistic in manifestation, has but a reflected semblance of life; poetry which aims only at the true in essence, the scientific in manifestation, has but a mechanical semblance of life; poetry which aims only at the good in essence, the ethical in manifestation, has but the protoplasmic energy without the quickening principles of life; poetry which aims at no one of these singly, but all three of them in unity, is life — is Truth."

## A DREAM OF FREEDOM.

WHITTIER.
The airs of heaven blow o'er me;
A glory shines before me, —
. . . . . .
A dream of man and woman
Diviner but still human,
The love of God and neighbor;
An equal handed labor;
I feel the earth move sunward,
I join the great march onward,
And take by faith, while living,
My freehold of thanksgiving.     ('My Triumph.')

LOWELL.
So charmed, with undeluded eye we see
In history's fragmentary tale
Bright clews of continuity,
Learn that high natures over Time prevail,
And feel ourselves a link in that entail
That binds all ages past with all that are to be.
('Under the Old Elm.')

WHITTIER.
On then, my brothers! every blow
Ye deal is felt the wide earth through;
Whatever here uplifts the low
Or humbles Freedom's hateful foe
Blesses the Old World through the New.
('Lines for the Anniversary of the 1st August.')

LOWELL.
For soul inherits all that Soul could dare:
Yea, Manhood hath a wider span
And larger privilege of life than man.
('Commemoration Ode.')

WHITTIER.
O East and West! O morn and sunset, twain
No more forever! Has he lived in vain
Who, priest of Freedom, made ye one and told
Your bridal service from his lips of gold?     ('To T. S. King.')

LOWELL.
The single deed, the private sacrifice,
. . . . . . .
Is covered up erelong from mortal eyes

With thoughtless drift of the deciduous years ;
But that high privilege that makes all men peers —
That leap of heart whereby a people rise.—

. . . . . . . . .

These are imperishable gains,

. . . . . . . .

These hold great futures in their lusty reins
And certify to earth a new imperial race.

('Commemoration Ode.')

## AMERICA.

LANIER.     Now fall the chill reactionary snows
Of man's defect, and every wind that blows
Keeps back the spring of Freedom's perfect rose.

('Psalm of the West.')

WHITMAN.   Be not disheartened — Affection shall solve
the problem of Freedom yet ;
Those who love each other shall become
invincible — they shall yet make Columbia victorious.

('Drum Taps.')

LANIER.                     How if this contrarious West
That me by turns hath starved, by turns hath fed,
Embraced, disgraced, beat back, solicited,
Have no fixed heart of Law within his breast?

('Psalm of the West.')

WHITMAN.        I see Freedom, completely armed and
victorious, and very haughty, with Law
by her side, both issuing against caste.

('Drum Taps.')

LANIER.   And the Time in that ultimate Prime shall forget
old regretting and scorn ;
Yea, the stream of the light shall give off in a shimmer
the dream of the night forlorn.   ('Psalm of the West.')

WHITMAN.     — Then turn and be not alarmed
To where the future, greater than all the past,
Is swiftly, surely, preparing for you.   ('Drum Taps.')

*From the MS. of ' Poets' Parleys ' by the Editors.*

# SOCIETIES.

The **Browning Society of Boston** held its sixty-first regular meeting on Tuesday, April 25, at Hotel Brunswick, and was called to order by the president, Rev. Francis B. Hornbrooke. After reading of the minutes, and necessary business, Rev. Philip S. Moxom read 'The Grammarian's Funeral,' prefacing it by a few lines from Tennyson. Rev. Julius H. Ward read a paper on 'The Characterization of Lord Strafford,' sketching briefly the condition of England in the beginning of the seventeenth century and a few of the leading men, before proceeding to an analysis of Strafford's character and aims. An essay on 'The Dramatic Motive in "Strafford"' was read by Miss Charlotte Porter. (This paper will appear in full in POET-LORE).

In discussion Mr. Charles H. Ames sought the grounds for believing that Browning had correctly motivated the play of 'Strafford.' After his own first reading of the drama, he had found himself entirely "a Strafford man," and he had doubted if this pivotal man, around whom the history of the period turned, ought to be so represented. As poetry is the highest form of art, so dramatic art is the highest form of poetry, since it is the most concrete. Considering Browning the greatest dramatic poet since Shakespeare, it is right to ask if he gave us what Shakespeare did, remembering that poetry may be truer than history, art truer than fact. Shakespeare's supreme power as dramatist lay in his ethical insight. Conceiving man as a responsible being, he worked out logical conclusions. Tragedy is where great principles collide, and Strafford's " adhesion to right principles at the wrong time " could have resulted in nothing less. He was committed to belief in the supremacy of the king at a time when the nation was demanding room for development. The plays of 'Julius Cæsar' and 'Strafford' can be brought together only for contrast. Rome had passed the republican period and there was nothing left of it. It was right that imperialism should come at that time. In Browning's play the conditions were reversed; Strafford was the logical victim of his time, and the play was rightly named.

*E. E. Marean.*

POET-LORE

Vol. V.

———— wilt thou not haply see,
Truth needs no collour with his collour fixt
Beautie no pensell, beauties truth to lay:
But best is best if neuer intermixt.
Because he needs no praise, wilt thou be dumb?
Excuse not silence so, for't lies in thee,
To make him much outliue a gilded tombe
And to be praised of ages yet to be.
Then do thy office ————

Nos.
8 and 9.

# A PESSIMIST POET.

GIACOMO LEOPARDI was born on the 29th of June, 1798, at Recanati, a small town in the March of Ancona. His father, Count Monaldo, was of an old family, but not wealthy. He was a scholar and an author, but full of aristocratic prejudice, and opposed to reform, either political or religious. His wife seems not to have had much influence over her children ; at least, they write to her and of her with respect, but with little affection.

Giacomo was the eldest of the family. Brought up in the solitude of a provincial Italian city, he buried himself in books, which alone offered him access to the world. The account of his youthful studies is prodigious. When fifteen years old, he set himself to learn Greek without a teacher, and succeeded so well that the following year he was able to write a commentary on Porphyry's ' Life of Plotinus.' He also made himself familiar with Hebrew and the modern languages, except German.

These studies soon gained him a name. One of the first results of them was a friendship with Pietro Giordani, which lasted during Leopardi's life. His letters to Giordani form a large portion of his correspondence; and they give us a good idea of his early years, — of the various difficulties he had to contend with in his literary pursuits, and of the formation of that peculiar philosophy which is always associated with his name. In the first place, his enthusiastic study had broken his health. " I often endure for many hours," he writes, " the horrible torment of sitting with my hands folded." And again: "Ah, my dear Giordani, what do you think I do nowadays? Get up in the morning — late, because now — a diabolical state of things — I prefer sleeping to waking. Then get immediately to walking and walk without ever opening my mouth or seeing a book till dinner. After dinner walk likewise till supper: unless by making a great effort, often stopping and sometimes giving up altogether, I manage to read for an hour."

Ill-health was not the only cause of Leopardi's melancholy. He found himself condemned to pass the best years of his life in a small provincial town. He was not naturally inclined to see good in everything, — rather, he spoiled every possibility of present pleasure by dwelling on an imaginary future; and his abuse of his native place is extremely violent. " What is there beautiful in Recanati? What is there that a man would take pains to see or learn? Nothing. Now, God has made this world of ours so beautiful, men have made so many beautiful things in it, there are so many men in it, that any one in his senses burns to see and know; the earth is full of wonders, and I, at eighteen, must say; 'In this den shall I live and die where I was born?' Do you think these desires can be bridled, that they are unjust, tyrannous, extravagant, that it is folly to be dissatisfied with seeing nothing, to be discontented with Recanati?" In this passage we see Leopardi's weakness: he was always talking about love, he was gentle and affectionate to his friends; yet he was haughty, too forgetful of sympathy and human kindness. In the same way he talked about philosophy and studied it; but he never possessed that supreme philosophy of life which teaches us to take the world as we find it, and respect facts.

There was yet another source of unhappiness for our poet. If the boy — for at this time he was hardly more — had found comfort at home, Recanati might have seemed tolerable. But his mother was nothing to him; Count Monaldo approved his son's taste for philology, but they differed on philosophy and on politics. Their relations were altogether unfortunate, owing to misunderstandings and to general incompatibility. Biographers at first sided with Giacomo. Of late years some things have come up to excuse the old Count; yet the following sketch of him, taken from his own autobiography, will show what his character was : —

"The experience of my whole life has taught me the truth of the saying — Seneca's, I believe — that there is no great intelligence without its dose of madness, and I have been surprised to see that in some corner of the loftiest mind there lurk incredible puerilities. I have made some examination of myself in order to learn the weak point of my reason, and not having found any, I am tempted to believe my mind superior to many, not indeed in loftiness, but in balance." Poverty obliged Monaldo to deny his son many things, and Giacomo was but too ready to assume a harsher motive.

A close affection bound the young scholar to his brother Carlo and to his sister Paolina, who seem, nevertheless, to have been greatly his inferiors. One person only in his family might have been really helpful to him, — his aunt, Ferdinanda Melchiorri, who, unfortunately, died when he was twenty-four years old. The few letters of hers which Signor Piergili has collected show a mind of great clearness, a sensibility equal to Leopardi's, and a calmness and resignation he was never able to attain. "Little by little we learn to forget our miseries by slighting them or by not keeping the image of them forever before us ; reason must persuade us of this, and we must use reason for our happiness, not for the contrary." You see Leopardi lost much when he lost her.

The life at Recanati, — living death he would have called it, — with its tedium, its fierce protest against the tyranny of circumstances, its idealization of the outside world, continued till the man's nature was thoroughly confirmed in a philosophy of defiance. The influence of Giordani had separated him from the Catholic

Church, and filled him with liberal ideas; yet he never adopted these ideas with great enthusiasm, — they were sweet illusions, but illusions.

In 1822 he finally succeeded in getting away and going to Rome. It is pitiful, even if a little amusing, to see his disappointment. Rome is no better than Recanati, after all. "Speaking seriously," he writes to his sister, "you may take it as certain that the most stolid Recanatese has a greater dose of good sense than the wisest and gravest Roman. Believe me, when I say that the frivolity of these idiots is beyond anything. If I tried to narrate all the absurd stuff which serves as matter for their talk, and which they revel in, a folio would not suffice." Truly, *cœlum mutat, non animum.*

Leopardi went to Rome to get recognition and encouragement in his studies, and also to seek some sort of public employment that would enable him to live away from detested Recanati. Reputation as a scholar soon came to him, though such work as his was better appreciated by foreigners than by his fellow-countrymen. Bunsen, then Prussian ambassador at Rome, treated him kindly, and Niebuhr expressed great admiration for him. We read in 'A Memoir of Baron Bunsen' that Niebuhr, "returning from his visit to the wretched lodging of Leopardi, entered the office-room at Palazzo Savelli, where Bunsen was at work, exclaiming with an unwonted burst of satisfaction, that he had at last seen an Italian worthy of the old Italians and of the ancient Romans." But admiration came more readily than preferment. The ecclesiastical authorities at Rome were ready to do what they could, but only on condition that Leopardi should enter the church. In order to bring this about, they deferred giving him even an insignificant lay office, hoping literally to starve him into obedience to their wishes. But his so-called "philosophical conversion" had taken hold of him too deeply for honest acquiescence in Catholic doctrine; and the inflexible uprightness which marked him, as it has some other unbelievers, made him scorn a hypocritical compliance. Therefore, after lingering on at Rome through the winter, he was obliged to return to his father's house.

Recanati did not seem any more agreeable than formerly. His ill-health continued to make study impossible, and he was driven back upon his own thoughts ; which fills his letters of this time — chiefly to Giordani and to Brighenti, a Bolognese friend — with an endless monotony of wretchedness. In the year 1824 he published at Bologna a collection of poems, most of which were new. He also published the first of his philosophical prose works, — ' A Comparison of the Opinions of the Younger Brutus and of Theophrastus, on the Approach of Death.'

In the spring of 1825 he once more left Recanati, — this time intending to proceed by way of Bologna to Milan, where he had engaged to do various kinds of literary work for the publisher Stella. He found Bologna very attractive. His reputation had preceded him thither, and the literary circle received him cordially. In Milan it was different. He had no friends, no connections. Stella's work was disagreeable to him, — editing, with little or no prospect of either freedom or great profit. After a stay of two months he returned to Bologna, having arranged to carry out his agreement with Stella at that place.

The next year was perhaps the happiest, or the least miserable, of his life. His health was, as always, bad ; he had little money, and was obliged to give lessons, like many another unfortunate man of letters. But he was in the company of people who made much of him, and he found the social diversion lacking in Recanati. " These lessons," he writes to his brother Carlo, " which eat out the heart of my day, bore me horribly. Except for that, I have nothing to complain of. The literary men, who in the beginning, as I have been told, looked upon me with envy and mistrust, expecting to find me haughty and disposed to put on airs, are now well-pleased with my affability and readiness to give way to every one ; in short, they speak very well of me, and I feel that they consider my presence an acquisition to Bologna." At this time, also, we find the trace of one of his few love affairs, — that with the Countess Malvezzi. The bodily weakness, amounting almost to deformity, which resulted from his early studies, made him painfully sensitive in his relations with women ; but in this particular case literary sympathy seems to have been added to merely social attractions. "When I first knew her," he writes, " I lived in a sort of delirium and fever. We have never spoken of love, unless in jest, but we keep up a tender and sympathetic friendship, with mutual interest, and a freedom that is like love without love's disquietude." Alas, such "sympathetic friendships" hasten so quickly to their end !

In the autumn of 1826 Leopardi returned to Recanati. From this time on his life was a losing struggle with ill-health. His hatred of his native place grew more and more bitter : " It seems a thousand years till I can escape from this hoggish city, where I know not whether the men are more fools or knaves ; I know well that they are both one and the other." Harsh notes like this occur too often in Leopardi ; yet his situation was undoubtedly a trying one.

In 1827–28 we find him at Pisa, the climate there suiting him better than at Florence or Bologna. The death of his younger brother Luigi at this time called forth a few words which it is well to quote, in contrast with the passage just given : " I have lost a brother in the flower of his years : my family in their grief looks for no other consolation than that of my return. I should be ashamed to live, if anything but a perfect and utter impossibility prevented me from going to shed my tears with those I love."

He did, indeed, return to Recanati for another winter ; but in May, 1830, he left there for the last time. For the next three years he lived in Florence and Rome, his health getting steadily worse and worse. Finally, in the autumn of 1853, he went to Naples with Antonio Ranieri, whose name is inseparably connected with Leopardi's later years. After this the letters gathered in the correspondence become few and brief, being chiefly pitiful requests for money to make him less dependent on his friends. Extreme weakness rendered any continuous work impossible ; and it was probably only the constant and affectionate care of Ranieri and his sister that prolonged the poet's life. They were successful in doing this till the spring of 1837. Then, quite suddenly,

death came on the 14th of June, caused by dropsy affecting the
heart. The cholera was in the city at the time, and Ranieri was
only able to secure private burial for his friend by bribing the
priest of the little church of San Vitale with a present of fish.

## II.

Leopardi's prose is either philological or philosophical. The
philological work belongs chiefly to his younger days. It is now,
of course, much out of date; Leopardi had no idea of the discoveries that have been made in this century as to the relationship
of the different European languages. Yet he was undoubtedly a
thorough scholar, and probably had that delicate insight which
goes so much farther than erudition, and which so many great
scholars have been without. Perhaps his most permanent work of
this kind is his translation of various classical authors, executed
with the care and patient search for accurate expression that marks
all his work. The excellence of his scholarship appears in his imitations of Greek and old Italian writers, which long deceived some
very learned men. The chief original product of his early years
was a book on the ' Popular Errors of the Ancients,' written when
he was seventeen years old, and showing certainly extraordinary
learning for a boy of that age. Outside of the curious citations,
the reader will find little to interest him here, — nothing of the
large Renaissance curiosity that informs the fascinating work of
Sir Thomas Browne. In treating the superstitions of Greece and
Rome, Leopardi manifests the same dogmatic spirit that appears
in his later writings ; only he had not yet hit upon his extreme
pessimism, nor even left the fold of the Catholic Church. The
book closes with this apostrophe: " Religion, loveliest of things, it
is indeed sweet to be able to end with speech of thee that which
has been undertaken to do some good to those whom every day
thou benefitest; it is indeed sweet to conclude in security and
confidence of heart that he is no philosopher who does not follow
and respect thee, nor is there any one who follows and respects
thee who is not a philosopher." We are in the full vein of the
' Imitation.'

In a few years the tone changes.  Acquaintance with Giordani and others brought about the " philosophical conversion ; " and after that Leopardi's letters are full of attacks upon the system of nature which creates man for useless, purposeless misery.  All his remaining prose works not strictly philological develop these views in one form or another.  The list is not extensive, — some two dozen dialogues, and about a hundred ' Thoughts ' varying from two to thirty or forty lines.  Any one who goes to these writings expecting to find in them the formal and logical exposition of the great German metaphysicians will be disappointed. Leopardi was anxious to teach what he considered to be the true doctrines of philosophy ; but his first instinct as an author was literary.  The models he had before him were Plato, or, still more, Lucian ; and he aimed to convey his teaching by illustration, even allegory, rather than by a system of laborious deduction.  Whatever may be thought of his conclusions, his methods have the great merit of simplicity and literary charm.

As to the matter of his philosophy, the general character of it is well known : it consists in an ever-renewed proclamation that the sole certainty of man's life is misery, that the universe exists for no apparent purpose, that if there are gods at all, they only augment the wretchedness of man ; though on this last point Leopardi is always reticent, leaving it to the reader to infer the complete incompatibility of any divine love or goodness with such a system as he insists on finding out in Nature.  It is not necessary to look far for passages illustrating these things.  Here is one from a letter written when he was twenty-one years old : " This is the wretched condition of humanity and the barbarous teaching of reason, that, human joys and griefs being mere illusions, work that is based on the certainty of the nothingness of things is the only work that is just and true.  And if it be argued that by regulating all our lives on the feeling of this nothingness, we should end the world and should justly be called mad, it is nevertheless logically certain that this would be a madness rational in every respect, and even that compared with it all wisdom would be madness ; since this world goes on only by the simple and continual forgetfulness of this universal truth that everything is nothing."

This instantly recalls an eloquent passage from a more celebrated philosopher than Leopardi : " Rather do we freely acknowledge that what remains after the entire abolition of Will is for all those who are still full of Will certainly nothing ; but, conversely, to those in whom the Will has turned and has denied itself, this our world, with all its suns and milky ways — is nothing." Indeed, the names of Schopenhauer and Leopardi are often associated together more closely than is justified by the circumstances of the case. Schopenhauer's philosophy consists of two parts, which, though skilfully and intimately blended, may yet be separated, and have not, I venture to think, so vital a connection as is generally assumed. The metaphysical part is the theory of Will as Thing-in-Itself constituting the absolute basis of the floating world of phenomena, manifesting itself momentarily in consciousness, then dissolving and vanishing again into the unknown from whence it came. The practical part is the unwearied assertion of the utter misery of man's mortal life, — misery alleviated only by the encouragement of false and foolish illusions, which make him believe he is ever approaching nearer to what it is impossible he should attain. Whether Schopenhauer deduces his practical doctrine from his abstract theory, or whether, as seems more probable, his empirical view at least colored his metaphysics, I cannot say ; at any rate, the two components fit together very neatly.

Of these two elements of Schopenhauer's 'World as Will and Idea,' only one appears in Leopardi. Schopenhauer found him a most satisfactory exponent of his doctrine as to the evil of existence. " No one," he says, " has so thoroughly and exhaustively handled this subject as in our own day Leopardi. He is entirely filled and penetrated by it ; his theme is everywhere the mockery and wretchedness of this life ; he presents it upon every page of his works, yet in such a multiplicity of forms and applications, with such a wealth of imagery, that he never wearies us, but, on the contrary, is throughout entertaining and exciting." Indeed, the Italian poet's proclamation of pessimism is so thorough and consistent that it could not but be gratifying to his German follower. Of metaphysics proper, however, Leopardi has little or nothing. He has a great deal to say about philosophy, and about the importance of giving it a place in Italian literature ; but in his works he never does more than reiterate a few phrases about the misery of life and the inanity of all human pursuits. Such theory as he has would seem to be derived from the English empirical school of Locke, Hume, and their followers. He was not a German scholar, and evidently knew nothing even of Kant, much less of Kant's successors. Except for a few coincidences of expression, he has no trace of the elaborate system of Schopenhauer, and would probably have found talk about the Will as Thing-in-Itself simply unintelligible.

Nevertheless, Schopenhauer is right in saying that Leopardi presents the mockery and wretchedness of this life upon every page of his works, and with a multiplicity of forms and illustrations. I think the philosopher is mistaken when he declares that this is always entertaining and exciting ; but it is done with such skill that, considering the narrowness of the subject, there is wonderfully little monotony. Every dialogue ends with the same refrain : it were better not to have been born ; having been born, it is best to die as soon as convenient ; but this theme is constantly varied. Sometimes, as in the ' Hercules and Atlas,' or ' The Earth and the Moon,' superhuman beings satirize the unhappy lot of mortals. Sometimes philosophers discuss it, as in the ' Dialogue between a Physicist and a Metaphysician,' or in the ' Plotinus and Porphyry.' Sometimes a forlorn creature addresses a higher power with reproach or prayer, as in the ' Dialogue between Nature and a Soul,' or in that ' Between Nature and an Icelander.' Sometimes the misery of man receives illustration or comment from beings lower in the natural world, as in the ' Dialogue between a Will-o'-the-Wisp and a Gnome,' or in the ' Eulogy of Birds.'

The very titles show how much there is of literary art in all these. Some of them are playful, — at least, on the surface. Hercules persuades Atlas to use the earth for a game of ball, in the midst of which they drop it, greatly to their dismay. Fashion points out to Death the immense services she renders her by leading mankind into infinite pernicious follies. A passer-by questions an almanac-vender as to the coming year, and tries to prove to him that there is no reason why that should be happy, if none of the past have been. Some are poetical, almost lyrical, like the ' Song of the Wild Cock,' and the exquisite ' Eulogy of Birds.' The latter, especially, is an Aristophanic piece of musical grace. " Other animals appear commonly grave and solemn ; if they take pleasure in the green fields, in broad and pleasant prospects, in splendid sunshine, in a crystalline and gentle air, they make no sign. . . . But birds show their joy by their movements and their very look."

Most of the dialogues are, however, of a gray and melancholy cast. The 'History of the Human Race,' the first in the collection, gives anything but a cheerful account of the gradual degradation of humanity down to the nineteenth century, which Leopardi detested with all his soul. The 'Wager of Prometheus' recounts Prometheus' efforts to prove the excellence of his invention of man, and his complete failure to do so. 'Copernicus' ridicules the fluctuations of science. The 'Dialogue between Frederick Ruysch and his Mummies' represents the latter as reviving for a short space, and enlightening their owner about the other world, as well as about the departure from this.

Perhaps as complete an exposition as any of Leopardi's pessimism is to be found in the ' Dialogue between Nature and an Icelander.' The native of the northern island, after seeking everywhere the author of the miseries of life, finds in the centre of Africa a vast image of a woman, who condescends to discuss the matter with him. She points out that the universe exists only by a continual process of production and destruction. " That is what all the philosophers argue," says the Icelander, " but inasmuch as that which is destroyed suffers, and that which destroys receives no pleasure and is soon destroyed in its turn, tell me what no philosopher can tell me : who is pleased or benefited by this most miserable existence of the universe sus-

tained by the suffering and death of all things that compose it?"
The interesting response to this question is interrupted by the
arrival of two hungry lions, who proceed at once to make away
with the curious Icelander.

The 'Memorable Sayings of Filippo Ottonieri' gives a sort of
idealized sketch of Leopardi himself, embodying the curious combination of defiant nihilism with high moral principle which was
peculiar to him. The piece ends with an epitaph of singular and
melancholy dignity : " The bones of Filippo Ottonieri, born for
virtuous deeds and for glory, lived indolent and useless, and died
without fame, not ignorant of his own nature nor of his own
fortune."

Besides the ' Dialogues,' or ' Operette Morali,' Leopardi wrote,
shortly before his death, about a hundred 'Thoughts,' much the
same in tone as his longer pieces. They are, however, colder
and more gloomy. Now and then there is a touch of calm insight,
as : " There is no greater mark of feeble philosophy and little
wisdom than to demand that the whole of life should be philosophical and wise." But the majority are quite as cynical as
La Rochefoucauld, without his brilliancy and point.

The thing that strikes one most about Leopardi's mental
attitude is the absoluteness of it. Happiness is a dream, he
says ; because we no sooner obtain what we wish for than it
becomes repugnant to us, and we begin to long for something
else. No situation is so delightful but that we can imagine
another more so ; and desire for that other makes the actual one
wretched by comparison. But does it? Is it not possible to
recognize that one might be happier, and yet to be very happy
at the same time?

With such beliefs as these, the natural course to take would
be suicide. If life is so utterly worthless and miserable, why
not get out of it? On this point Leopardi is not satisfactory.
Schopenhauer treats it logically by explaining that life is, indeed,
miserable, since it is the indulgence of the tyrannous Will ; but
to take one's life is an even more violent act of will, which, instead
of freeing us, involves us only more deeply. We must emancipate

ourselves by becoming indifferent to life, death, or anything else. Leopardi has not this resource. He is constantly dwelling on the superior charms of death, and charging mankind with cowardice for not seeking it; but he does not state clearly whether he is himself deterred by this consideration, or by some other. The ' Dialogue between Plotinus and Porphyry ' turns on this subject ; but the arguments are neither very clear nor very strong.

The truth is that, like every one with a dogma to defend, Leopardi was blind to any consideration that did not support his position. He was not contented with being unhappy himself, he was determined that every one else should be unhappy as well. Not, of course, that he was anxious to make them so; but he wished them to understand that they were necessarily so, and that nothing but their own folly prevented them from seeing it. Thus it was natural that he should be irritated when told that he looked at life through dark glasses, and was misled by his own physical weakness and suffering. He solemnly denies this, not seeing, apparently, that no denial of his could possibly affect the argument; unless, indeed, he had brought forward as the greatest proof that Nature was malign, her having made him to call her so. This he neglects to do ; and the healthy part of mankind will, therefore, forever regard him as a melancholy hypochondriac.

Independent of his health, it is, however, clear that many circumstances combined to give him a peculiar view of things. His family relations were trying. He had constantly before him the degradation of Italy, brought home more keenly by his familiarity with the history of her past. Above all, as we have seen, he was long isolated in a provincial town, removed from the stir of modern life, which produces scepticism, but teaches toleration, comprehension of varying conditions. The results of this are everywhere seen in Leopardi, and make him seem, in spite of all his scholarship and all his literary ability, like a fretful and irritated child, who cries, as I heard one the other day : " I 'm not happy, and I have n't got anything to make me happy." This is the whole philosophy of Leopardi.

### III.

Leopardi was not a philosopher, but a man of letters. His work does not embody a consistent system of reasoning; but it offers us a study of human life, — not, indeed, broad in its scope, yet subtle, above all, passionate, and carried on with an exquisite feeling for certain kinds of beauty in style. The models that he set before himself were the Greeks and the early Italians: he sought purity and simplicity rather than the richness and variety of color that belongs to a great deal of modern writing; but such means as he used were perfectly within his control, and his care and patience are shown by the great number of varying readings in his works, which have been published of late years. This devotion to the technical part of style recalls Flaubert, with whom Leopardi has something in common; though the great French novelist had a far wider and stronger hold on human life in general.*

The love of simplicity, of a pure yet energetic form, is undoubtedly what gives Leopardi his popularity in Italy, as to which Signor Piergili says: "Does not this person know that Leopardi is one of the authors most studied among us, — that he is studied and learned by heart, not only by the pupils in the schools, in the technological institutes, and in the universities, but even by young girls who cannot pretend to more than a moderate education?" 'Amore e Morte' seems a curious study for young girls; but then, so is Shelley's 'Revolt of Islam.'

This simplicity of form also separates Leopardi from the romantic school of his own generation in Italy, France, England, and Germany. His quiet and isolated life, his constant preoccupation with the classics, made him prize a severe and statuesque restraint much more than they did. Yet in spirit, in feeling, he was profoundly romantic; and it is just this combination that

---

* An Italian critic gives some statistics as to Leopardi's style, stating, among other things, that the number of adjectives in a thousand words averages 62, taking all his poems but one, — ' La Ginestra.' This is also the case with Dante's ' Divina Commedia.' Such figures have not much value, yet they are suggestive. I give some computations that I have had the curiosity to make on the English poets. In ten thousand words taken from different poems of Keats, the proportion of adjectives to the thousand is 126; in Milton, 113; in Spenser, 108. In Shakespeare it is only 63; and this is not wholly owing to Shakespeare's work being dramatic, since I find the proportion in Fletcher to be 79.

makes him interesting. His classicism was not the tawdry frip-
pery of the eighteenth century, which injures Byron when he does
not shake himself free from it: it was the same passion for clear,
perfect lines that possessed Goethe; and Leopardi, with Italian to
work in, was able to satisfy it better than Goethe ever succeeded
in doing. But underneath the polished form lurks a fire none the
less fierce for being hidden: all the restlessness, the questioning,
the defiance, which Byron wore upon his sleeve for daws to peck
at, Leopardi carried in his heart, wove it subtly into the fibre of
his verses, to be plucked out readily enough by a sympathetic
hand. I say his verses, because the personal element comes in
there more clearly than in his prose. In spite of all his skill, the
dialogues are tedious. They have an air of pretension which is
unjustified. We look for philosophy, and get nothing but railing;
not cynical, indeed, — there is too much earnestness for that, —
but cold. The writer evidently makes an effort to keep in the
background. But Leopardi's poetry is personal, lyrical. It is less
vehement, less incoherent, than Byron or Shelley or Obermann,
but not less passionate, less sincere. Sincerity, genuineness, are,
indeed, stamped on every line Leopardi wrote. His thinking may
have been neither clear nor logical; but his feeling is at once
subtle, thoroughly modern, and of a kind not quite to be paralleled
in any contemporary literature.

Leopardi's poetry consists, besides some boyish work, of translations done in his youth, when he was busy with philology, of
forty-one short pieces published in his lifetime, and of the 'Para-
lipomena to the Batrachomyomachia,' formerly attributed to Homer.
The latter poem, which is of considerable length, is a mock heroic,
composed in Leopardi's last years to satirize contemporary political events. It is difficult for a foreigner to follow, and, moreover,
attempts humor, which with Leopardi always results in a sort of
skull and crossbones effect. The execution is skilful, and reminds
one constantly of Ariosto, — but only to bring out the difference
between his joyous license and the contracted grimaces of his
modern imitator.

Of the 'Canti,' or 'Odes,' the first four or five, written before their author had learned his strength, are full of patriotic rhetoric about Italy. Leopardi ostensibly kept his moral enthusiasms quite independent of his philosophical doctrines; but, nevertheless, these poems ring a little hollow. The imitation of the classics is too apparent; and it is hard to associate passion with such a frequent appeal to " numi," in the plural, or with such frigid encouragement as : "But for thine own sake set thy heart upon the goal. What is life for? For nothing but that we should contemn it: it is happy only when, absorbed in perils, it forgets itself, takes no note of the filthy, tedious hours, hears not the flowing of them, happy only when, with foot treading the Lethean shore, it begins at last to smile." Yet these Odes, like the later ones, have traces of the grand style about them : one is reminded everywhere of Petrarch, often of a greater than Petrarch, — of the greatest of all the poets of Italy.

Such poems as those addressed to Count Carlo Pepoli or ' La Ginestra ' have a general philosophical tendency resembling that of the ' Dialogues.' ' La Ginestra ' is one of Leopardi's latest and longest works, written with all his simplicity, and with such Dantesque touches as, —

> " Come star può quel ch' ha in error la sede."

It is the most complete exposition of his more mature philosophical views, and shows a certain abandonment of the attitude of fierce scorn for that of love and tenderness ; as in the celebrated line, " I know not which prevails, laughter or pity." But I am inclined to think Leopardi's most devoted readers generally prefer the shorter and more lyrical pieces.

These are of two kinds : those which depict the feelings of some other person than the poet himself, or are at least general ; and those which are strictly personal, and express his own experience and opinions directly. Among those of the first class we have ' The Last Song of Sappho,' ' Calm after Storm,' ' The Nocturnal Song of a Wandering Shepherd of Asia,' ' The Setting of the Moon,' ' Love and Death.' The descriptive pieces usually begin with a sketch of some scene or event, and conclude with a moral, —

a melancholy moral, of course. Thus, in 'Calm after Storm,' we have first the picture of peace returning to the landscape, and then the comment, quite in Leopardi's vein : —

"O, courteous Nature, these are thy gifts, these the delights thou bestowest upon men. To escape from grief is a delight to us. Sorrows thou scatterest with an open hand; woe springs unsummoned; and such joy as is born rarely, a wonder and miracle, from ill, is a precious gain. The human race dear to the Gods! Happy enough are we, if we are allowed to breathe exempt from misery, blessed if death frees us from all pain."

The quality of natural description that appears in all these poems is that of Greek and Latin poetry ; it is clear, direct, simple, — as, for instance, in 'The Village Saturday': "A maiden comes from the fields at sunset with a sheaf of grain, bearing in her hand a bunch of roses and violets." Color, the rich warmth of feeling for Nature which belongs to the northern nations, Leopardi has not. His passion is all for the interests and sufferings of man. And in these semi-dramatic poems it makes itself felt with wonderful intensity. Still it is the same refrain : " All is mystery save our grief. Neglected offspring, we are born to tears, and the cause is hidden in the bosom of the Gods." " This I know and feel," sings the Shepherd of Asia, " that from the endless flow of things, that from my frail being, some good or joy may come to others; but life is misery to me." 'The Setting of the Moon' ends thus : —

"But mortal life, when once fair youth has vanished, shines with a lovely color never more, knows no new dawn. Widowed is it till the end ; and on the night which sheds its shadow over all past years the Gods have set the sepulchre for sign and seal."

More impressive still becomes this cry of revolt and pain in the pieces where the poet speaks himself. The most common subject of lyrical outbursts, love, is not very prominent in Leopardi. Yet a number of poems touch upon it vaguely. 'Silvia' and 'The Recollection' refer to passions of his youth, "when the harsh, unworthy mystery of things comes to us full of sweetness." 'Aspasia' recounts a later affair, which resulted in disappointment

and bitterness.  He was no more fortunate in love than in other
things.  Here, too, he was, perhaps, led astray by the worship of
an impossible ideal.  The verses 'To His Lady' would form rather
a perilous standard for earthly love-making: "Naught on earth
resembles thee ; and if anything should seem to resemble thee in
feature, in act, in speech, it would be, even so like, less beautiful
than thou."

The most interesting of these personal lyrics are those in which
the poet strikes slight chords in his own remembered life, the echo
of which shudders into a vague harmony of grief.  Such is the
poem 'To the Moon,' grand and clear as Petrarch, with its —

> "Il rimembrar delle passate cose."

Such is 'The Infinite,' which I give in verse, reflecting, alas ! but
feebly the solemn beauty of the original : —

> "This tender slope was always dear to me,
> And this enclosure, which shuts off my gaze
> From half the circle of the far horizon.
> And sitting here, in thought I have devised
> Interminable vastness out beyond,
> And superhuman silence, and some rest
> Profoundest, gazing, where a little while
> The heart frets not itself.  And as I hear
> The night-wind howling idly through the woods,
> I can compare its turbulence with that
> Infinity of silence, and remember
> The eternal and the years past, and those present
> And passing, and their murmur.  So in this
> Immensity my thought has lost itself,
> Nor am I loath to wreck in such a sea."

Such is the longer 'Evening after a Festival,' describing the poet's
agony at parting from his mistress, and comparing it to the fretful
sorrow of a child, who, after his holiday has fled, lies oppressed
with the utter blank monotony of life : —

> "In my first childish years,
> When some bright longed-for, happy day had come
> And passed and gone, I grieving on my couch
> Lay, watched ; and in the stillness of the night
> A song far-heard in dark and quiet ways,
> Which swelled upon the silence and died off,
> Even then, as now, passionately wrung my heart."

He to whom this does not recall a thousand things will find
nothing to please him in Leopardi.

It will be sufficiently clear that Leopardi, in spite of his great
originality, has a good deal in common with the Sénancours and
Chateaubriands of France, the Byrons and Shelleys of England.
He was an idealist, as they were.   The realities of life disgusted
him.   His heart was fixed on a new heaven and a new earth.
Only he had no sort of confidence that the ideal would ever
become real.   He shows not one trace of interest in the great
democratic movement that began with the French Revolution.
He is full of scorn for the nineteenth century, with its printing-
press, its philanthropy, its calm assumption of superiority over
the past : " The wise heads of my time found out a new and
almost divine plan : not being able to make any one on earth
happy, forgetting individuals, they set themselves to work to seek
a common happiness ;  and this being found easily, these people
make of a race each wretched and miserable, a joyous and happy
nation."   Leopardi is irreligious, as were many of his French
and English fellows.   But his irreligion is cold and indifferent, not
defiant.   The gods are not to him great blighting shadows, to be
combated ;  they are vague personifications, too insignificant to be
treated even with contempt.   Yet neither Shelley nor Byron nor
Heine has surpassed the blank, tremendous blasphemy of Leopardi,
sterner and more overwhelming because it is so cold : " Bitter and
gray is life ;  there is naught else but grayness and bitterness ;
mere slough is this world.   Rest forever.   Despair now for the
last time.   To me fate gave nothing but to die.   Nature ever
spurns thee, — Nature, the ugly power, which rules in secret to the
common ill, and the infinite vanity of things."   Yet even here one
sees that the poet is led astray by the very excess of idealism in
him.   It was said that he was led to think all men knaves, because
he was ready to trust all men.   The same childish absoluteness is
manifest in his writings.   Every one must notice his extreme fond-
ness for personification.   This poor deity, Nature, is maltreated
by him because he conceives her, not formally, but constantly, as
a remote human being animated with the most anthropomorphic
spite.   Scherer, the French critic, notices this in his essay on

Amiel: "'I know Nature is deaf,' cries Leopardi, 'that she thinks not of happiness, but of being only.' Passion of a fretful child! Nature is neither deaf, nor preoccupied, nor cruel — she is what she is." Taken by itself, this sounds rather oracular; but it offers just the correction Leopardi requires.

But it is this very absoluteness that makes him lovable. It is because his heart beats so warm with human affection that he revolts against the necessary conventionality of life; it is because he conceives so high a destiny for man that he proclaims the utter vileness of all that man has done or does. He is no sceptic, no cynic, no Epicurean. He is hopeless, but not loveless; and by that tenderness and breadth of love he has a close kinship with the great English poet who lived near him without knowing him, who sung the woes of life as clearly as Leopardi, but far more clearly the regeneration love might work, if only love would take heart and face its task.

The net result we get from Leopardi is certainly disappointing, and to most people irritating. We rebel against this positive assertion of our misery on grounds of sentiment, but still more on grounds of fact. Tell us life is wretched, if you will, — perhaps even more wretched than happy; but tell us that life contains no happiness at all, and most of us answer, "Please speak for yourself." Life is not made on such an absolute plan. Mysterious it certainly is; but there are bright spots in it, — yes, for all of us! Sainte-Beuve says, speaking of Chateaubriand, "I know the race of René: they have their moments of unhappiness, when they cry from the housetops and pour out their miseries to the universe; they have days of joy which they bury in silence." The insinuation of rhetoric and posing here implied does not affect Leopardi; but he has his notes of quietness and peace, though rare. With one of these, an appeal to Nature not as an "ugly power," but as the sweetest, gentlest of comforters, let me end: "For even if life is shorn of love and all sweet dreams, even if starless night shuts round me in the midst of spring, yet have I my comfort and revenge lying here idle, quiet on the grass, smiling at earth and sky and sea."

*Gamaliel Bradford, Jr.*

# RUSKIN AS ART TEACHER.

## SOME FURTHER UNPUBLISHED LETTERS.

WITH greater eagerness than even Shelley, did Walter Savage Landor, the large-hearted Roman, anticipate the dethronement of kings as a first step in the ultimate emancipation of man. To him, as to so many others of whom the world was not worthy, the very name of king or priest symbolized the fetters that bound the world to the tyranny of custom or the invidiousness of class. He, too, with prescient vision, saw the day at hand when their power would surely wane, — for lo! in the dim distance was the dawn of the reign of the people, when Democracy, far-sounding as the seas that swept the shores of his native land, would crush under its all-conquering heel the prejudices and tyrannies wherewith whole generations of Englishmen had been enslaved. Landor had yet nine years of eventful life to be lived, when in 1854 a movement was inaugurated symbolic of the new democratic spirit. It was the founding by Frederick Denison Maurice of the Workingmen's College at No. 31 Red Lion Street, Bloomsbury; and it may be said that thus were laid the foundations of an edifice whereby the gulf of class might be bridged, and the intellectual emancipation of the worker assured. The day of the Lord had indeed dawned, as Kingsley sang; and Maurice soon gathered about him a band of workers whose hearts were in their work, the outcome of which is surely beginning to be seen in our custom-ridden England, for the democracy has at last evolved a full and complete measure of free education.

Of those early workers who so nobly seconded Maurice in the formidable task he set himself, some few are still living among us, — Thomas Hughes (of "Tom Brown's School-days" fame), Dr. Furnivall, etc.; but chief among them all is John Ruskin, who, with the enthusiasm born of the truest sympathy, early threw in his lot with the workers. A circular on the founding of the proposed college had been sent to him, presumably with the object of obtaining a monetary subscription; his response, however, suggested something far more valuable, — he proposed taking the oversight of a drawing-class for working-men. With his usual impetuosity Mr. Ruskin at once set about his self-imposed task, and at the beginning of the second year he had a large and enthusiastic class. His assistants were Dante G. Rossetti and Lowes Dickenson. The former did not long occupy his post, but Mr. Dickenson went on teaching for many years. Among the students were Mr. George Allen (now well known as Mr. Ruskin's publisher) and Mr. William Ward, a gentleman favored with the more personal tuition of the master, whom indeed Mr. Ruskin took specially in hand, discovering in his work the draughtsman to the manner born, and who, under the wise and judicious guidance of the professor, rose from the ranks of the "workers" ultimately to take his place as a successful and accomplished art teacher. Thus early in his career did Mr. Ruskin become the " Friend of Man," and take rank in the forefront of those who inaugurated the new democratic movement, which has led, not, indeed, as Landor fondly hoped, to the abolition of kings, but to the spiritual and mental emancipation of a whole generation of Englishmen.

As readers of Mr. Ruskin's works may imagine, it was exceedingly interesting to watch him as he made the round of the easels, and hear him talk to the students about their work. One of these students, who has kindly given me some particulars concerning these old days, writes: —

"I remember being much impressed, young as I was (I am talking of thirty-seven years ago), by one incident. He was speaking to a student in whose work he believed he saw a want of steadiness of purpose, and he recommended him to read 'Bleak House,' and study the character of Richard Carstone. The next class night Mr. Ruskin brought the book, and lent it to the student. I cannot tell if it steadied the man at all, for I have lost sight of him for many years. I mention this as an instance of the way in which our teacher tried to make the men's characters and work serve each other."

At this period of his life Mr. Ruskin is described as being fair, and somewhat slightly built, with deep, penetrating eyes, and an inexpressible charm of manner. His plan of teaching would seem to have been peculiar, and was evidently all his own. He would first set his students to copy a white leather ball suspended by a string. They were to draw exactly what they saw, making no outline, but merely shading the paper where they saw shade. After the ball came plaster casts of leaves, fruit, and other natural objects. On one occasion a tree, cut down by Mr. Ruskin's directions, was sent from Denmark Hill, and fixed in a corner of the class-room for light and shade studies. The professor would often bring his students treasures from his own collections, — minerals, shells, Rembrandt etchings, Albert Dürer and Turner engravings, etc., — his delightful way of talking about these things affording the most valuable lessons. Mr. Ward writes: —

"On one occasion he took for his subject a cap, and with pen and ink showed how Rembrandt would have etched it and Dürer engraved it. Another evening he would take a subject from Turner's 'Liber Studiorum,' and with a large sheet of paper and some charcoal, gradually block in the subject, explaining at the same time the value and effect of the lines and masses. Now and again he would take his students for a ramble through Dulwich wood. On these occasions sketching-materials were taken, and the professor would criticise the work done, winding up with tea and talk at the Greyhound."

If there was one thing about Mr. Ruskin, it was his thoroughness, and he certainly carried this out in his dealings with the students. When he found a man with real talent, he spared neither money nor time, but helped him in a right royal manner. It is gratifying to have the assurance of Dr. Furnivall that, so far as is known, only one man in any way abused his kindness. One of the pupils in whom Mr. Ruskin took a special interest was, as I have stated, Mr. William Ward, whom he helped in many ways, and to whom — from 1855 to 1886 — he addressed numerous letters on the subject of drawing, copying, etc. A selection from these letters (all of them hitherto unpublished) has now been privately printed,* under the

* "Letters from John Ruskin to William Ward." Edited by Thomas J. Wise. London: Privately printed (not for sale), 1893.

editorial supervision of Mr. Thomas J. Wise; and the readers of
POET-LORE will no doubt be glad to make acquaintance with them.
If these letters reveal the idiosyncrasies of the writer, they also
reveal his nobility of mind, as his sensitiveness to the feelings of
others. Take this, for instance : —

MY DEAR WARD, — I was just going to write to you about your
drawing, which is very good, though I can't give you much for it,
or I should unjustifiably raise the hopes of the other men. We must
finish a little more before we can command price. I am only going
to give you ten shillings for this. It is *worth* that to me, though
more to you; but as you get on you will put more value on your
work, in less time. I will send you a prettier model; and then, I
think, you will make a very lovely drawing.

Don't allow yourself to dwell on the evil, or you will fall into
despair ; and you will come across veins of good some day. There
are beautiful people — beautiful in sense of all goodness — in the
world here and there ; the worst of it is, most of them are apt to
be foolish.

I am more oppressed and wonder-struck by people's *absurdity*
than anything else in the world ; and then, what wonderful power
a single fool has — the wrong way!

But you know all your annoyance, as well as mine, comes of
their disbelief. If you really suppose there is a master to the
household, you have nothing to do but to attend to his business
and be quiet and comfortable.

Truly yours,

J. RUSKIN.

Always write to me when it does you good, as it does *me*
good too.

Sometime in 1855 Mr. Ruskin had in mind to formulate a community of art workers, whose main business should consist in their
employment by the public in copying illuminated manuscripts and
other descriptions of art work. Nothing, however, seems to have
come of this scheme, to which reference is made in the following
letter, dated "Denmark Hill, 1855 " : —

MY DEAR WARD, — I should be glad indeed if I thought that so
many of the workmen were of your mind as to admit of your using
that large " *we* would relieve ourselves." At all events I am truly
glad to know whom I can count upon to help themselves in such

a spirit. But as I said to you, I do not count upon such a temper as an available practical element. All I hope for is to be able to show, and to make men understand, how they may live more comfortably — get better wages — and be happier and wiser than they are at present. If, after that, they are led on to better things — well! But at present, it seems to me, that good friendship — reciprocal help — exercise of brains with the hands — and such other matters, may be got out of (or into) thousands who would not listen for a moment if one were to begin talking to them of the influences of the Holy Spirit. All these things *are* His influences ; but I think we have to advise and preach them just as simply as one would advise children, who were fighting in a ditch, to get out of it, wash their faces, and be friends, — without endeavouring, at that moment, to instil into them any very high principles of religion.

I am glad you are thinking of the Protestant Convent plan. I have *no doubt* we shall carry it out, and that all over the country ; but just because it is so important a scheme, we must not attempt it 'till we are sure of succeeding. Let us all work, but still the main word for us all must be *patience.*

Truly yours always,      J. RUSKIN.

Occasional snatches of teaching, too, come to light in many of these letters, — witness the following, under date Aug. 9, 1870:

*I* don't want *any* of these leaves painted. You are to work on them for practice, doing one or two over and over again — fifty times, if needful.

Of course, *all* painting — oil — water — fresco — and everything, is done at *one* coup, when it is right. But certain processes of colour require laying of two or three different colours over each other; *then* the under one must dry first, &c., &c. All this mechanism you have to learn, but the French know hardly anything about it.

*Of course* Meissonier paints at a blow; and his work is like a plasterer's, as all French work is. Titian also paints at a blow — but *his* work is not like a plasterer's. Titian paints with a sense of mystery, and Meissonier with none; and Titian with a sense of true hue, and Meissonier with no more sense of colour than a common stainer of photographs.

But learn of *anybody* how to do what *they* do, — it will always be useful.

Ever truly yours,      J. RUSKIN.

53

Mr. Ruskin had very much at heart the copying of pictures by Turner, hoping by this means to spread the knowledge of the master's work. This copying in itself was no light work, for nothing less than absolute faithfulness would suit the professor, who minutely examined all copies produced with lens and compasses. Here are some three letters bearing on this subject, written sometime in 1867, each of them possessing a separate and distinct interest of its own : —

" I think you ought to fix your mind on this Turner work quite as the thing you *have to do.* You know me well enough to trust me that I do not say this to keep you captive for my own purposes. If I thought you could be a successful artist, I would not let you copy. But I think your art gifts are very like mine ; *perfect* sense of colour, great fineness of general perception, and hardly any invention. You *might* succeed in catching the public with some mean fineness of imitation, and live a useless, though pecuniarily successful life ; but even that would be little likely. Whereas in rendering Turner you will live a useful life."

" The reason copying has been (justly) despised is that people have never done it but for money only, and have never therefore given their hearts to it. To copy Turner, and any one else rightly, you must always know what he means ; and this requires constant looking at nature from *his* point of view. There is no degradation in doing this any more than in letting him, if he were alive, teach you. For instance, your own point of view or De Wint's, or Constable's of a tree might relate only to the green of its leaves, their quantity. Turner might disregard the colour, and imagine half the leaves gone from the branches in autumn in order to express the grace and anatomy of the limbs. All these views are *natural,* — but in looking at nature with a view to illustrate the work of any given Master, you must look at her not ' *with his eyes* ' (which you cannot, and should not) but from his *place,* and *to* his purpose. It will do you great good to see more clearly what Turner *means* by those odd touches and scratches of French towns and fortresses, and to see the character of the scenes he tried to render. . . . Luxemburg I believe you can *do* nothing at, the sentinels would stop you instantly. Turner could draw with his hands in his coat-tails, or while the sentinel walked the other way ; but you cannot. . . .

"If I had to make my own bread, I should at once endeavour to get employment in copying the great Italian frescoes — while at least half my time would be spent in anatomical and other studies from nature; and I should feel myself quite usefully and rightly employed putting my whole energy into the business. I should do so, even now, with far more satisfaction to myself than my present desultory work, of teaching in various ways, gives me; but I do not feel justified in abandoning intellectual labour altogether, or giving up the rudder which is in my hand."

"You cannot enjoy Turner's 'fairy' work too much. *That* is divine to the very day of his death. But haste — weariness — *Death*, in its widest sense, as it begins to seize on what is called old age — all the effects of solitude, of absence of all human sympathy and understanding; and finally sensuality proceeding clearly from physical disease of the brain, are manifest to me in those later works in a degree which is proportionate to my increasing reverence and worship of the divine fact of them."

Very thoughtful, yet peremptory in his "orders," was the master. Here is an "instruction," delightful in its way, for the benefit of his pupil : —

"I want you to begin Drawing Master on Monday. I consider you at present worth about five shillings a lesson, which therefore you are to ask; but not including therein any omnibus fare, which I shall tell the people I send you to, to pay. On Monday, I want you to go to Miss ——, and to show her how to draw leaves like this of yours. I have told her that she is to expect nothing more from you than mere instruction in drawing from nature."

Here again is a letter referring to some drawings, but which branches out into a perfectly ingenuous expression of his own feelings : —

MY DEAR —— : Try for a little more definiteness in outline: they are a little too vague. Don't be afraid of a falsely-strong line or two to express *form*, as long as they are *lines* only. The eye always *forgives* a well-meant outline, but not a false colour, or a *careless* form. Keep such outlines in colour harmonious with their place.

You may write me whatever you like to talk about, provided you write large and clear. You may trust to the *truth* of my sympathy; but you must remember that I am engaged in the investigation of enormous religious and moral questions, in the history of nations; and that your feelings, or my own, or anybody else's, at any particular moment, are of very little interest to me, — not from want of sympathy, but from the small proportion the individuality bears to the whole subject of my inquiry.

I have *no* affections, having had them, three times over, torn out of me by the roots, — most fatally the last time, within the last year [1867]. I hope to be kind and just to all persons, and of course I *like* and *dislike;* but my word "affectionately" means only — that I *should* have loved people, if I were not dead.

As a matter of practical fact, you may always trust to my kindness in a *due* proportion, as you stand among other people who require it; and to my understanding sympathy in proportion also. But I have no *pleasure* myself, now, in any human relation. Knowing this, you will be able to understand a good deal in my ways of going on, otherwise inexplicable.

Faithfully yours,

J. RUSKIN.

Scattered through these one hundred and seven letters are many lines and phrases characteristic of the writer, and many words which reveal his exceeding kindness of heart, as the deep tenderness of his nature. As, for instance, —

"You may take holiday immediately, if you can leave your wife; any little extra expense I will meet. Is there any place you have a fancy to go to? You can cut teaching for a while and learn to walk. .

"I hope you will be able to live in the way you enjoy; indeed I have no doubt of it. But all enjoyments become mixed with pain eventually, however our life may be occupied; and there is a certain enjoyment resulting from escape from what is irksome to us, which is itself worth much.

"You may comfort the young lady whose hand runs away with her by telling her that when once she has bridled it, properly, she will find many places where she can give it a pleasant canter — or even put it to speed — in sketching from nature. But it must be well bitted (braceletted, perhaps, would be a better word) at first."

In the course of an interesting preface appended to these letters, Mr. Ward says: —

"Ruskin was a rare presence among us, teaching us to see and feel beauty in things, not how to draw them prettily. He made everything living and vital, and disliked servile copying and 'niggling.' Excessive care he admired, but not work for work's sake. To show this, he would make a rapid drawing by the side of a student's work that he might see how, with all his elaboration, he had missed the 'go' of the thing. He never cared to find fault with your method, unless it were mechanical; what he did find fault with was want of perception. I recollect that a student once came with his copy of a Liber Studiorum etching, in which he had so entirely missed the feeling of Turner that Mr. Ruskin, looking at him searchingly, asked him if he had been ill."

Even a slight perusal of these letters will show how "rare a presence" among these working-men John Ruskin was; and how, having taken up this work, he threw himself heart and soul into it. They reveal, too, the manner of man he was, — courteous, kindly, considerate, while always giving utterance, with no uncertain voice, to the conviction that was in him. In those early days he must have been as Ariel-like as Shelley, but having a stronger and true moral ballast, — a right-royal companion for all lovers of the beautiful. Then his vision was clear and unclouded, and he had supreme faith in man. But with the heat and burden of the day the vision would seem to have become dim, and the glory to have departed therefrom; he appears to have lost touch with the democracy, while an inexpressible sadness has permeated the later years of his life. The ways of the world are not his ways, neither are the desires of men his desires. He has shut himself up within himself; the burden of life for this man had to be borne alone; and to-day he sits in solitary silence amid the plenitude streaming from the wide bosom of the All. Few know or realize the sorrows of his budding manhood, when, day by day, he worked on in conscious strength, albeit his soul must have been seared with the agony of the great tragedy of his life. To the many this episode, full of a pathos and a heroism as strange as it is rare, is but dimly known — and well that it is so. For this man's affections were founded upon a rock, yet tender in their womanly strength; but they were, as he himself expresses it, "torn out by the roots." When the foibles and eccentricities of the last few years of his career are urged against him, men will do well to turn to the splendid achievement of his meridian; to note his bearing when the great sorrow struck at the core of his being, the noble self-sacrifice of his nature, the splendor and purity of his life and faith. And in these various letters we have seen the man himself revealed to us, with all his inconsistencies and eccentricities, yet as true and brave and good a human soul as ever trod God's earth. Doubtless there are other, and equally wise and beautiful, letters in existence which will one day see the light, and which we may yet have the honor of transferring to the pages of POET-LORE; but for the present we take affectionate and kindly farewell of Mr. Ruskin as writer of letters.

*William G. Kingsland.*

LONDON, August, 1893.

## GENTLE WILL, OUR FELLOW.

WRIT IN 1626 A. D. BY JOHN HEMINGE, SERVANT OF HIS GRACIOUS MAJESTY KING CHARLES I.; EDITED IN 1892 A. D. AS "ALL, THOUGH FEIGNED, IS TRUE" BY F. G. FLEAY, SERVANT OF ALL SHAKESPEARIAN STUDENTS IN AMERICA, ENGLAND, GERMANY, OR ELSEWHERE.

*(Continued.)*

THE next year, 1601, was in many ways an eventful one for us. After acting 'All's Well that Ends Well,'— a play which was partly founded on an older one, in which Shakespeare had told the story of Giletta of Narbonne, taken from one of his favorite books, Painter's 'Palace of Pleasure,' but now enlarged with the humor of Parolles, — we, to our misfortune, mixed ourselves in the Essex troubles.

In February, Sir Gilly Meyrick, on the seventh day, being Saturday, the day before the insurrection, gave our fellow Phillips forty shillings to play at the Globe the play of 'Richard II.,' which had become obsolete and outdated, on condition that it should contain the "tragic abdication," as Master Camden calls it. Now, this was the scene which had been inhibited and omitted in our

published copies ; so that by performing it at all we grievously
offended Her Majesty. But she also knew, as she told Master
Lombard in the August of the same year, that we had acted it
"forty times in open streets and houses," and that she was intended by Richard II. "I am Richard II. ; know ye not that ?"
were Her Majesty's very words. Yet how could we help it ?
The Earl of Southampton, who was the especial patron of our
chief poet and of our theatre, to which he came wellnigh every
day when he was in London, Sir Gilly Meyrick, who liked us,
and other of our best friends were of the Essex faction ; while
Brooke, Lord Cobham, who had given us so much trouble about
the Oldcastle business, was of the Cecil faction, and grievously
suspected of intending to murder my Lord of Essex in his bed.
There were many things in these examinations which showed my
Lord Cobham's private spite against us ; and any one who desires
to know how matters of state at this time (when the companies
played in the names of the great lords, and not, as now, in the
names of the King and his family) were handled on the stage,
may do worse than study the trials of Essex and his fellows. In
the trials, historical parallels were brought forward with 'Richard
II.,' 'Edward II.,' 'The Duke of Guise,' and the 'prentice riots under
Henry VII. ; and all of these had been presented on the stage in
Shakespeare's or Marlowe's plays, or in the play of Sir T. More,
which last, like Marlowe's 'Massacre of Paris,' had been grossly
mutilated, as I have already told.

When these trials were over in March, we thought it the better
part to withdraw from London till the Queen's displeasure should
overpass; and accordingly we travelled this year, contrary to our
custom, visiting the Universities of Cambridge and Oxford, and passing even into Scotland. At Cambridge we presented ' Troilus and
Cressida.' Shakespeare had long before written the love scenes in
this play, in which the faithless Cressid is opposed, as I may say, to
his faithful Juliet; but the parts in which the proud myrmidon,
Achilles, enters were now for the first time presented. In these he
followed the ' Iliads ' of Homer, so far as the seven parts of Master
Chapman's translation then published would enable him ; in the

earlier play he had used only Chaucer and the old ' Destruction of Troy.' The new part contained many allusions to the quarrel between Jonson and Marston, some of which I may set down here, because, the play never having been acted on the public stage, they may not be understood rightly by the reader. Jonson, in his ' Poetaster,' at the beginning of the year, had brought in an " armed Prologue," who speaks in " well erected confidence." Shakespeare has " a prologue armed but not in confidence." Jonson has also an anti-prologue spoken by Envy ; this was imitated from the Envy prologue to our ' Mucedorus,' at the end of which play Envy, along with the spectators, says Amen to a prayer for the Queen. In the ' Troilus ' this is thus alluded to : " Devil Envy say Amen." Jonson, in his ' Comical Satires,' had represented himself as Asper, Critic to Horace, and described himself as of a perfect and divine temper in whom the humors and elements are peaceably met ; in ' Troilus,' Ajax is described as one into whom all the humors have been crowded by nature. It is well known that Jonson beat Marston, and took his pistol from him : so does Ajax beat Thersites in ' Troilus ; ' and that Thersites is meant by Marston, witness the line " Rank Thersites with his Mastic tooth," which can only refer to the titles of ' Histrio-mastix ' and ' Therio-mastix ' used by Marston. It does not, as some have thought, mean Dekker's ' Satiro-mastix,' for we ourselves acted that play.

The ' Troilus' was so well liked at Cambridge that in a witty play acted at St. John's College the next year, the author thus speaks of it : " Here's our fellow Shakespeare puts them all down, ay, and Ben Jonson too. Oh that Ben Jonson is a pestilent fellow : he brought up Horace giving the poets a pill but our fellow Shakespeare hath given him a purge that made him bewray his credit." This author, methinks, remembered imperfectly the line in ' Troilus,' " Physic the great Myrmidon," for by that line was meant Achilles, and not Jonson, who is Ajax. Nevertheless, on our return to London we did not think fit to act this play, for the quarrel between Jonson and Marston was then made up, and it was not for us to fan the smoking embers.

In February, 1603, Roberts, who had by some privy means got

a copy thereof, tried to get it allowed for the press, but we procured it to be staged at that time. Six years thereafter it was licensed for Bonyon and Whalley, who issued it as " acted by the King's Servants of the Globe." It was enough that a stolen play of ours should be printed against our consent without the addition of this impudent falsehood ; and we required its retractation, which we obtained; and they added a preface in which they acknowledged that it had " never been staled with the stage," but added an inso-lent statement implicating that we, " the grand possessors," were opposed to the publication of any of Shakespeare's plays, but in this case were compelled to allow it. What ! May we not do as we will with our own ? This was our last trouble with these pirati-cal land-sharks. Pity that the meshes of the law are too large for them !

We also acted ' Julius Cæsar ' before the heads of the colleges. Another play that we acted at the Universities was ' Hamlet.' The plot was taken from the old play by Kyd, which we had performed for seven years past. We had been acting in a re-formation thereof about the city at the same time that we acted ' Richard II.,' but the version we presented at the Universities was entirely new, being altogether made by Shakespeare. The old play never came to the press, but some parts of it may be seen in the first edition, which was printed from a mangled and stolen copy, by rogue Roberts, who, after our return in July, 1602, got it licensed without our privity, and disposed of the copyright to Ling and Treadwell. As these seemed to be honest men, we did not think good to deprive them of their interest, as we might have done ; but we stayed the issuing of imperfect copies, and gave them, to print from, a copy in the form in which we acted the play in London, after our return. This they sent forth in 1604, the year after Roberts had printed his stolen copy ; but this shifty companion had bound them to have the print-ing done by him. This form differs somewhat from that in our late Folio, which, in the main part, has the play as we acted it during our travel. This Shakespeare has cunningly told us in the play itself, when he makes Rosencrantz say that the tragedians of the city — meaning us — are travelling after an inhibition caused by the late innovation (or rather by Essex's attempt to produce one), not being so much followed as they were wont, because of the fashion of the children actors, who were then berattling the London stages. For, indeed, the chapel boys at Blackfriars and the Paul's boys at White-friars, with their two rival poets, Jonson and Marston, had for two years drawn all the gallants away from the common or public thea-tres to their private houses, as they then began to be called. More-over, we had lost many of the commoner sort in our audience when Kempe left us; for he, like his master, Tarleton, before him, was wont to introduce his extempore merriments in the midst of a scene, flout-ing at any things or persons that might be in the public view, — somewhiles, even at church and state. Now Shakespeare would not have his clowns say more than was set down for them ; he looked only to the question necessary to the play, and so it was, that, when after Kempe left, he reformed this matter altogether, many of those " barren spectators," who had been wont to laugh at these villa-nous merriments, came to us no more. In this matter the better sort of authors were at one with Shakespeare, — such were Jonson, Beaumont, Fletcher; but the others, Marston, Dekker, Heywood, and all the meaner men were fain, if so they might set up a laugh at their comedies, to mark the places where the Fool might graft in jests of his own ; and even in the printed copies you may find such places ofttimes marked, now by an " etc.," now by a marginal direction.

This play, at first called ' Hamlet's Revenge,' was much scoffed at by the envious on other stages ; but it was in truth the very acme of our author's productions, and, as finally corrected by him, the be-ginning of a new stage in his career. It was the first of those great tragedies of his in which he entirely held the mirror up to man's inner nature ; for his only tragedy (among the tragedies I do not here include his histories) before this time was ' Romeo and Juliet,' which, being only a tale of lovers whose path of love did not run smooth, is not to be named with those deeper passions in which he showed " the age and body of the time his form and pres-sure." Moreover, the scenes in which the players enter might well be named a school for actors, for nowhere else is there so briefly and yet so completely laid down a body of pithy aphorisms for the guidance of those who make up our little world, the stage.

From Cambridge we went northward and across the border into Scotland, even as far as Aberdeen. We were there most kindly received; our fellow Lawrence Fletcher, under whom we travelled, was in October made a burgess of guild of the borough. We were honored with the title of the King's Servants; and Shakespeare received a letter from the King written in his own hand. We acted before His Majesty among other plays one on 'Macbeth;' but as this was nothing near so complete as Shakespeare made it five years after, I defer further mention of it to that place. This was in October, and just after we heard that John Shakespeare, William's father, had died in the month before, which was a great sorrow to him.

Immediately after this we returned to London, and in November we acted 'Satiro-mastix,' written by Dekker, against Jonson. This play was also acted by the Paul's boys at their private house. Dekker got it entered for printing as soon as it was acted; but it was not printed till after Jonson published his 'Poetaster' in the next year. In both these plays Jonson, Marston, and Dekker were brought on the stage under the names of Horace, Crispinus, and Demetrius. Shakespeare was ill-pleased that after the quarrel, now of three years' standing, had been brought to an end, it should be fanned again by the ill-advised printing of those two plays. But Jonson was always self-determined, and averse to own himself wrong even "with just cause." As to the ending of the quarrel, it had been in this way: Jonson, Shakespeare, Chapman, and Marston had, nigh the close of the year 1601 [that is, in March, 1602, in modern reckoning], been induced to club together their verses on the 'Phœnix and the Turtle' for Chester's 'Lover's Complaint;' and, as they could not well do this while at open enmity, advantage was taken of the occasion by their well-wishers and friends to patch up a truce between them; but the untimely publication of these plays wellnigh spoiled all. This book of Chester's was writ for Sir John Salisbury, who married Ursula, half-sister to Ferdinando, Earl of Derby, who for six years before his death had graciously bestowed on us his patronage.

In the last year of the Queen's reign, what with the trouble we
had had in the Essex innovation, what with his private trouble of
his father's death, Shakespeare did little but furbish up some old
plays. It was a dull year for all of us. For the first time for ten years
we had presented no plays at court during the Christmas festivities,
and men were too much disturbed about the imminent changes
that must ensue at the Queen's death to care greatly about coming
to plays. She was sick and failing at her last meeting with her
Parliament in the bygone October. Moreover, we greatly missed
my Lord of Southampton, who, with his friends, until this sad business of my Lord of Essex, had been of late years a spectator at
our house wellnigh every day. On the 2d of February, at the
Reader's Feast at the Hall of the Middle Temple, we acted 'Twelfth
Night,' otherwise called, 'Malvolio ; or, What you Will.' This was
founded on an older play by Shakespeare begun many years before,
but the satirical part was now all being aimed at the Marston quarrel
with Jonson. The title, 'What you Will,' is taken from Marston's
play of that name, then in action by the children at their private
house. The serious part of the play is from the story of 'Apollonius
and Sylla,' which Barnaby Rich had translated from the Italian in
his 'Farewell to the Military Profession.' Shakespeare had already
used this plot in part in his 'Two Gentlemen of Verona ;' but that
play was mostly built on the groundwork of a very old play of
'Felix and Felismana,' which had been made for the Queen's men,
in 1585, out of Montmayor's 'Diana,' and had come into our hands
with other of their plays when we first went to the Rose. The
likeness of the twins in this play seems to have tickled the Inns of
Court men, just as it did in the Errors play which we acted at
Gray's Inn.

Besides the necessary alteration of 'Hamlet' by the omission
of those parts which speak of us as travelling, etc., of which I have
already made mention, the play of 'Richard II.' was at this time
smoothened out into the shape in which we printed it in our Folio,
many words being changed, and many lines, unduly lengthened in the
old quartos, being pressed into a seemly shape. Thus the work of
re-formation of the series of the York and Lancaster plays, origi-

nally plotted by Marlowe and written by several hands, he being the chief, was brought to a timely end. We had, about two years before, acted the other of these plays in their perfect shape ; and now that we had finished this work, Master Pavier (another such a rogue as Roberts) purchases the old, imperfect, stolen copies of the 'Contention of York and Lancaster' from Master Millington, and enters them in the stationers' books under our new title of 'Henry VI.' But the stationers smelled a rat, and would only admit them *salvo jure cujuscunque;* belike the blundering title of "First and Second," instead of Second and Third parts, gave them an inkling of what this pirate intended. We put our right in force, and made him keep his true title on his frontispiece, except that, when he again printed these plays seventeen years after, he called them ' The *Whole* Contention of York and Lancaster,' which they were not, the first part of 'Henry VI.' being left out, but this we could not help.

Another play we acted early in the year was 'The Life and Death of Lord Cromwell,' in which we sailed very near the wind, and might have been brought before the council for representing matters of state; for in the rise and fall of this Earl of Essex the career of the late favorite was somewhat too plainly shadowed. This play was printed for Jones by Cotton in August, and again, on Dec. 16, 1611, Jones assigned it to Browne, who put in his title, " By W. S.," meaning, doubtless, to pass the play for Shakespeare's, who certainly had no hand in it. Jones, in his assignment, had deceived Browne in this matter, for his stationer's entry had the lying statement, " By W. S. ; " and Snodham, who printed for Browne in 1613, was innocent in this deceit. By that time Shakespeare had left the stage altogether, and we did not think it worth while to move in the matter, nor could we without his concurrence ; but surely the many attempts, of which this was one, to pass other men's work under his name, was a mighty testimony to the excellence of his craft. Of the true author of the play I shall not here give the name, as he is yet alive, and does not wish it to be known that he ever strove for the laurel " with those the thronged theatres that pass ; " but I may remind the reader that of the men who wrote

for us Drayton alone never set his name to any printed play, and
that a play in which he had a main finger, ' Sir John Oldcastle,' was
published as " by William Shakespeare."

*F. G. Fleay.*

(To be continued.)

———— • - • ————

## WALT WHITMAN.

WHENCE is the voice that I hear, so full, so sincere, so free?
      Hark! how it fills the air
With its mighty resonant tones and its cadences novel and full!
      The singing awakens the land
      With its power and joyance and hope,
      With its call to labor and light;
Whence does it come, a wonderful fountain of silvery sound,
      Taking the sun in all its crystalline drops?


Upward unto the skies, thou leapst in very delight,
      Higher and higher thy reach,
O marvellous fountain of song, upward unto the stars;
      And the fair manifold fires
      Studding the night of Time,
      Scattering the beaten dark,
Births from the soul of all things, growing more numerous and bright,
      Bicker and burn and flash reflected in thee.


O singer, whence do the visions come, whence does thy soul
      Fill all its longings deep?
Whence does the might of the rush of thy wide-winged, world-sweeping
        song
      Gather its splendor of flight?
      What are the sources clear,
      What are the fathomless springs,
Where thy high passion lingers and dwells and loftily dreams,
      And drains in great draughts the cup of the soul of the all?

Not from the scrolls that the strongest and best of the fame-crowned
      dead
      Wrote with their lives for the world,
Not from the records of eld where the heart of mankind is revealed
      In stories varied and sad,
      Not from the woods and the winds,
      Nor the mountains peaked with old snows,
Not from the toil and the tempest of moaning and restless seas,
      Drankst thou the fluctuant fervor that glows in thy song.


Simple manhood wert thou, and thy heart confronted in strength
      The shows of the vanishing years,
Feeling them all to be pageants and mutable forms of thyself.
      Thou knewest Poesy and Thought,
      Best births from the Life of Man,
      To be pictures and metaphors vast
Of the ultimate Truth that, gazing within, thy penetrant eyes
      Saw flowing beneath and around the magical maze.

God, who is Man at highest, and Nature, that toils up to Man,
      Dwelt in thy song and in thee, —
Not as involved in the garb of the dim and mouldering Past,
      Not as in tomes and in tombs,
      But truth, alive and afresh,
      Flowing again in the mind
That gave up its life to be cleansed and refilled with its essences pure,
      Bubbling anew in this late year of the world !

Presage of strength yet to be, voice of the youngest of Time,
      Singer of the golden dawn,
From thy great message must come light for the bettering days,
      Joy to the hands that toil,
      Might to the hopes that droop,
      Power to the Nation reborn,
Poet and master and seer, helper and friend unto men,
      Truth that shall pass into the life of us all !

                          *Louis James Block.*

## SHAKESPEARE'S 'JULIUS CÆSAR.'

### II.

BRUTUS. — Brutus has been called "the most perfect character in Shakespeare but for one great error in his life ; " and perhaps this is not going too far. He is clearly one of those creations of the dramatist's genius for whom his author felt a peculiar affection ; and he is determined that we shall admire and love the man as he does. And yet Brutus, even more than Cæsar, has been in some respects a puzzle to the critics. They are perplexed by certain apparent inconsistencies in his character ; but these are really consistent with the character, and Shakespeare intended that we should recognize them as inconsistencies. Brutus has allowed himself to be drawn into a position where it is impossible that he should be entirely true to himself, and these inconsistencies are the inevitable result. He is one of the noblest and purest of men, but he is implicated in a conspiracy which, though nominally patriotic in its purpose, is utterly base and execrable in the means it proposes for carrying out that purpose, and in which his companionship has been sought by the unscrupulous leaders mainly to give a color of honesty and right to the enterprise, and win for it the popular approval. " O Cassius," says Cinna, " if you could but win the noble Brutus to our party ! " and a moment afterwards Casca exclaims · —

> " O, he sits high in all the people's hearts ;
> And that which would appear offence in us,
> His countenance, like richest alchemy,
> Will change to virtue and to worthiness."

The figure is an expressive one. The endorsement of the plan by Brutus, in whose pure patriotism the people had full confidence, would, as it were, transmute the base and worthless metal of that plan to golden virtue and worthiness, — that is, in the people's eyes. There is to be no actual transformation. The name of Brutus is to be used to gull the people, — to *gild* the base metal, that it may *seem* to be gold, though worthless as before.

Once committed to the conspiracy, Brutus is inevitably one of the leaders in it. He takes that position from the first by the natural right of the ablest, — that divine right of a real king among men, — and also in part by his very nobility of character, which his companions cannot but respect in spite of themselves. Again and again he sets himself in frank opposition to the suggestions of Cassius and the rest, and always carries his point, though always in the wrong, so far as the interests of the conspiracy are concerned, and often failing to convince the others that he is right.

But Brutus cannot in all cases have his own way in the management of the enterprise ; and hence he sometimes finds himself in a position where inconsistency is inevitable. Moreover, he is lacking in practical wisdom. He is a scholar, a philosopher, a man of books, an idealist. He is more at home in the world of books — of theories and ideals —than in that of real life. He seems to me the perfect type of a certain class of reformers, — men of the noblest sentiments and the most patriotic and philanthropic intentions, but incapable of carrying these out wisely in action. Such men are easily made tools of by the unscrupulous ; as Brutus was by Cassius. They are often inconsistent in argument, influenced by one-sided views of a question, deciding it hastily and foolishly.

Coleridge was particularly perplexed by the soliloquy of Brutus in i. 2. 10–34 ; but nothing could be more natural when we understand the man. It is perfectly consistent with his character as I have imperfectly sketched it. Shakespeare, moreover, intended that we should see in it the fundamental mistake which Brutus makes, in order that later we may recognize the poetic justice of his fate.

"It must be by his death," Brutus says ; but why ? Again and again he admits that it is not for anything that Cæsar has done or shown any disposition to do. But

> " He would be crown'd :
> How that *might change* his nature, that 's the question."

Ambitious men, when they attain the height to which they have aspired, are apt to abuse their greatness and become tyrants.

> " So Cæsar *may* :
> Then, lest he *may*, prevent. And, since the quarrel
> *Will bear no colour for the thing he is,*
> Fashion it thus : that what he is, *augmented,*
> *Would run to these and these extremities ;*
> And therefore think him as a serpent's *egg,*
> Which, hatch'd, would, as his kind, grow mischievous,
> And *kill him in the shell."*

That is, he resolves to kill his friend and benefactor, not for what he has been or what he is, but for what he may become. This is his mistake, his crime; and for this the vengeance of the gods, whose prerogatives he has rashly assumed, falls upon him.

Shakespeare has emphasized the error and the inconsistency of Brutus by making him, not long after, reprove Cassius for suggesting in regard to Antony the very same course, and on the same grounds, which he (Brutus) here justifies in the case of Cæsar ·

> " *Decius.* Shall no man else be touch'd but only Cæsar ?
> *Cassius.* Decius, well urg'd. — I think it is not meet,
> Mark Antony, so well belov'd of Cæsar,
> Should outlive Cæsar. We *shall find of him*
> *A shrewd contriver, and you know his means,*
> *If he improve them, may well stretch so far*
> *As to annoy us all ;* which to *prevent,*
> Let Antony and Cæsar fall together.
> *Brutus.* Our course will seem too bloody, Caius Cassius,
> To cut the head off and then hack the limbs,
> Like wrath in death, and envy afterwards ;
> For Antony is but a limb of Cæsar.
> Let us be sacrificers, but not butchers, Caius.
> We all stand up against the spirit of Cæsar,
> And in the spirit of men there is no blood ;
> O that we then could come by Cæsar's spirit,
> And not dismember Cæsar ! But, alas,
> Cæsar must bleed for it ! " —

*must,* solely for what he *may* become, — the very reason which the shrewd Cassius has just given for killing Antony.

In the famous tent-scene (iv. 3) we learn that Brutus has sent to Cassius for gold to pay his legions : " for," he says, —

> " For I can raise no money by vile means :
> By heaven, I had rather coin my heart,

> And drop my blood for drachmas, than to wring
> From the hard hands of peasants their vile trash
> By any indirection."

Admirable sentiments, and worthy of the man who utters them! But the legions must be paid, and Brutus must get the money somehow. *He* can raise no money by vile means, and sends to Cassius for it ; but he knows how Cassius raises it. He has just been reading him a moral lecture on the meanness of bribery, and having an itching palm, and selling offices to undeservers, and the like. He did not accept the excuse made by Cassius, —

> " In such a time as this, it is not meet
> That every nice offence should bear his comment ; "

that is, situated as we are, we cannot afford to be over-scrupulous ; it is no time for punishing petty offences as in strict justice they might deserve. And from his point of view Cassius was unquestionably right.

In that most pathetic scene (v. 1) where Brutus and Cassius, both despondent, are anticipating the worst that may befall, and saying the farewells that may prove to be the last they can exchange, there is an illustration of this inconsistency of Brutus, — the philosopher brought face to face with the stern realities of life, — which has been a stumbling-block to the critics, and which some of them have explained as probably due to a misapprehension of a passage in North's ' Plutarch.' I believe that Shakespeare knew what he was writing, and that he inserted it as an illustration of this characteristic of Brutus : —

> " *Cassius.*          Now, most noble Brutus,
> The gods to-day stand friendly, that we may,
> Lovers in peace, lead on our days to age !
> But, since the affairs of men rest still incertain,
> Let 's reason with the worst that may befall.
> If we do lose this battle, then is this
> The very last time we shall speak together :
> What are you, then, determined to do?
> *Brutus.* Even by the rule of that philosophy
> By which I did blame Cato for the death
> Which he did give himself. I know not how,
> But *I do find it cowardly and vile,*

> *For fear of what might fall, so to prevent*
> *The time of life,* — arming myself with patience
> To stay the providence of some high powers
> That govern us below.
>     *Cassius.*                 Then, if we lose this battle,
> You are contented to be led in triumph
> Thorough the streets of Rome ?
>     *Brutus.*   No, Cassius, no ! think not, thou noble Roman,
> That ever Brutus will go bound to Rome ;
> He bears too great a mind.   But this same day
> Must end that work the ides of March begun ;
> And whether we shall meet again I know not.
> Therefore our everlasting farewell take :
> For ever, and for ever, farewell, Cassius !
> If we do meet again, why, we shall smile ;
> If not, why, then this parting was well made.
>     *Cassius.*  For ever, and for ever, farewell, Brutus !
> If we do meet again, we 'll smile indeed ;
> If not, 't is true, this parting was well made."

It will be noticed here that Brutus again condemns himself out of his own mouth for the assassination of Cæsar. It is cowardly and vile, as his philosophy teaches him, to commit suicide for fear of what *may* happen. One should patiently "stay the providence" of the gods, — trust their foresight and guardianship, not rashly and arrogantly usurp their high functions. If the argument is good against killing one's self, it is equally good, or better, against killing another. Brutus forgot his philosophy when he decided that Cæsar "must bleed for it ;" and now he cannot live up to it. Suicide is cowardly and vile, but he cannot arm himself with patience to be led in triumph through the streets of Rome. We are reminded of Leonato's passionate repudiation of "counsel" and "philosophy" in 'Much Ado' (v. 1. 3 fol.) : —

> " *Antonio.* If you go on thus, you will kill yourself ;
> And 't is not wisdom thus to second grief
> Against yourself.
>     *Leonato.*           I pray thee, cease thy counsel,
> Which falls into mine ears as profitless
> As water in a sieve ; give not me counsel ;
> Nor let no comforter delight mine ear
> But such a one whose wrongs do suit with mine.
> Bring me a father that so lov'd his child,

Whose joy of her is overwhelm'd like mine,
And bid him speak of patience;
Measure his woe the length and breadth of mine,
And let it answer every strain for strain :
As thus for thus, and such a grief for such,
In every lineament, branch, shape, and form : —
If such a one will smile, and stroke his beard
Bid sorrow wag, cry ' hem ' when he should groan,
Patch grief with proverbs, make misfortune drunk
With candle-wasters : bring him yet to me,
And I of him will gather patience.
But there is no such man : for, brother, *men*
*Can counsel, and speak comfort to that grief*
*Which they themselves not feel ; but, tasting it,*
*Their counsel turns to passion,* which before
Would give preceptial medicine to rage,
Fetter strong madness in a silken thread,
Charm ache with air, and agony with words.
No, no ; 't is all men's office to speak patience
To those that wring under the load of sorrow,
But no man's virtue nor sufficiency
To be so moral when he shall endure
The like himself.   Therefore give me no counsel :
My griefs cry louder than advertisement.
   *Antonio.* Therein do men from children nothing differ.
   *Leonato.* I pray thee, peace ! I will be flesh and blood ;
*For there was never yet philosopher*
*That could endure the tooth-ache patiently,*
*However they have writ the style of gods,*
*And made a push at chance and sufferance."*

Portia, one of the noblest of Shakespeare's women, is a worthy
mate for her noble husband; and the poet has given us no more
impressive and beautiful picture of conjugal love and fidelity than
theirs.   Portia's conception of her rights as a wife might satisfy
the most " advanced " views of our own day, while at the same time
it is associated with the tenderest and most devoted affection.

" No, my Brutus," she says, when he tries to evade her appeal
for his confidence by telling her that he is not well (ii. 1. 267), —

    " You have some sick offence within your mind,
    Which by the right and virtue of my place
    I ought to know of; and, upon my knees,
    I charm you, by my once commended beauty,

> By all your vows of love and that great vow
> Which did incorporate and make us one,
> That you unfold to me, yourself, your half,
> Why are you heavy."

And again : —

> " Within the bond of marriage, tell me, Brutus,
> Is it excepted I should know no secrets
> That appertain to you ?  Am I yourself
> But, as it were, in sort or limitation,
> To keep with you at meals, comfort your bed,
> And talk to you sometimes ?  Dwell I but in the suburbs
> Of your good pleasure ?  If it be no more,
> Portia is Brutus' harlot, not his wife."

No wonder that he exclaims · —

> " You are my true and honourable wife,
> As dear to me as are the ruddy drops
> That visit my sad heart."

Portia knows her rights as a wife, and can claim them no less eloquently than lovingly ; but she also has a delicate perception of the
wisdom of occasionally refraining to urge them.  In the dialogue
preceding what I have just quoted, she tells how she has noted her
husband's disturbance of mind ; and she adds : —

> " And when I ask'd you what the matter was,
> You star'd upon me with ungentle looks :
> I urg'd you further ; then you scratch'd your head,
> And too impatiently stamp'd with your foot ;
> Yet I insisted, yet you answer'd not,
> But, with an angry wafture of your hand,
> Gave sign for me to leave you : *so I did;*
> *Fearing to strengthen that impatience*
> *Which seem'd too much enkindled, and, withal,*
> *Hoping it was but an effect of humour,*
> Which sometime hath his hour with every man.
> It will not let you eat, nor talk, nor sleep ;
> And, could it work so much upon your shape
> As it hath much prevail'd on your condition,
> I should not know you, Brutus.  Dear my lord,
> Make me acquainted with your cause of grief."

What womanly, wifely wisdom there ! To see that to persist in her appeal, loving though it was, could only strengthen the impatience she was striving to overcome ; and withal to make allowance for the effect of " humour," — the transient mood, due to causes within or without, which for the time makes the man other than himself, changing him sometimes so completely that, as Portia says, if his personal appearance were proportionally transformed, his own wife would not know him.

The married relations of Brutus and Portia are ideally beautiful ; but equally beautiful, and in some respects more remarkable, — at least in a Roman, — is the almost affectionate regard of Brutus for the slave-boy Lucius. It is Shakespeare's way of adding a new grace to a character otherwise singularly gracious as well as grand. It is to me of peculiar interest as giving us a glimpse of " Shakespeare the Man." It is a fine touch that could never have occurred to one who was not himself like the person to whom he ascribes it. Shakespeare must have had that delicate consideration for others, even those in humblest condition. It is one of many indications that he was a man of peculiar refinement, — a *gentleman*, in the truest and best sense of the word.

*W. J. Rolfe.*

(To be concluded.)

## " IN GREAT ELIZA'S GOLDEN TIME."

SOME men in ruffs are drinking round a table in an arbor.

The morning light filters through the clear green leaves. Within, it is like an emerald turned to air. Stray sunbeams find their way through chinks of foliage, and flash on the gay silks and velvets and the golden Rhenish in the tall glasses.

The men are handsome, with pointed beards and large eyes. They call to one another by their Christian names, and pledge healths.

Two men are disputing eagerly. The rest listen. One is a rough-hewn Silenus with a harsh, fighting face. The good wine has sent the blood flushing to the roots of his hair. He is soon angry, and they call him Ben.

His opponent is a man of middle size, with auburn beard and hair. His eyes are hazel, and his cheeks are fresh-colored. His high forehead is bald. He waits till the other is out of breath, then says something with a quiet smile, at which the rest laugh. In their applause, they name him Will.

They are talking of one Peter Ronsard, a French poet, and his tale of the lady who flung her glove among the lions for her lover to fetch.

Ben vehemently denounces the lady. Will parries the fierce charges deftly, and urges many reasons in her defence.

In the heat of the debate, a tall girl of sixteen, in ruff and farthingale, enters the arbor, with two fresh bottles.

Her hair is auburn, and her cheek is like a rose-leaf. She looks like the man they call Will.

The men clamor, " Leave the question to Mistress Judith." " Let us hear Mistress Judith's censure of the matter."

And they ask her if the woman did wrong or right to send her lover into peril. " Would you have flung your glove ? " they say.

The girl draws herself up. " Can I tell ? " she says. " This little hand is a free English hand. It never knew the straitness of a glove."

Her answer has all the inconsequence of an answer in a dream ; but the men laugh, and Ben brings his fist down on the table so that the Rhenish flies from his beaker.

" Spoken like a right English lass ! " he cries. " Will, thou must make a sonnet on this."

Judith's father never did. But I know that this is true, for I, the Dreamer, was standing by and heard it all.

*Archibald MacMechan.*

## SONNET CXXVIII.

An antique room with rich hangings, and carved windows of vermilion-tinted glass with armorial devices wrought upon them in dull gold; sombre panels and curious chairs, and an inlaid table with a pair of little leather gloves, pearl-embroidered, lying upon it; an embroidery frame in a recess, with its square of satin, and fruit and flowers sketched upon it, just begun.

A small dark lady sat before an ebony harpsichord, light and graceful as herself. Her gown of silvery brocade, with tiny yellow moons upon it, twinkled in the dim, soft light, as she played and sang.

A grand-looking man tossed aside the hangings and stood within the room. His brown cheek glowed; he had been riding fast, fast, through wind and weather. Hair and beard were tawny and grizzled, — youth was past; but the eyes glowed as if immortal. Was the lady illumined then and for all time by the splendor of their gaze? She sparkled and shone like a jewel. He bowed low, yet bore himself like a king as he said, —

"I have been listening to thy music — my music — without. Hearing, I could for a space forbear seeing. Yet I could not forbear envying the 'saucy jacks, that had leave to kiss thy fingers.'"

The lady, swaying like a flower in her silver-satin sheath, threw back her little head, and with crimson cheeks, tiptoeing as she came, lisped, —

"But my lips are for thee, even as thou didst ask so prettily, my Will."

I open my eyes. The trees stand bare against a gray winter-sky; the snow falls softly to a low sighing wind.

My finger keeps its place at sonnet one hundred and twenty-eight; on its music I had slipped back into the three hundred years ago.

Landscape, be wintry, fall snow, sigh wind, the sonnets bloom in one long Hesperean summer! * My heart glows yet with the thought of them, but my eyes weep.

False lady of the sonnets, is it because of you, or in spite of you, that they live and glow forever, — blood-red roses upon the wintry breast of all-conquering time?

*Gabrielle Lee.*

---

## THE PEARL.

### ll. 157–223.

[The Early English alliterative poem known as ‘The Pearl’ is the dream of a sorrowing father by the grave of his child.  He sees her on the opposite bank of a shining stream, clothed in glory, and adorned with pearls.]

“ MORE marvels did my purpose daunt:
I saw beyond that merry mere
A crystal cliff full glitt:ring ;
Many royal rays did from it spring.
At the foot thereof there sat a child,
A maiden of honor, full debonair.
Glistening white was her linen robe,
(I knew her well, I had seen her ere)
As gleaming gold that man did purify,
So shone that shining one upon the other shore.
Long I looked towards her there,
The longer I knew her, more and more.

“The more I gazed in her fair face,
Her figure fine, when I had found,
Such gladdening glory glanced to me,
As little before thereto was wont.
To call her, wish did me enchase,
But shyness gave my heart a brunt ;
I saw her in so strange a place,
Such a blow might make my heart faint.

---

* For “ Summers in the Hesperides are long ” — EMILY DICKINSON.

Then raised she up her fair front,
Her visage white as ivory clear,
That stung my heart, a blow full stray,
And ever the longer, more and more.

"More than me liked, my dread arose :
I stood full still, and durst not call ;
With open eyes, and mouth full close,
I stood as hendy as hawk in hall.
I hoped that right was that purpose —
I dreaded what might at last befall —
Lest she should escape me that there I chose,
Ere I at steven her might stall.*
The gay and gracious, without stain,
So smooth, so small, so seemly slight,
Rose up in her array royal,
A precious thing in pearls bedight.

" In pearls bedight of royal worth ;
There might one by grace have seen
How she, fresh as the fleur-de-lis,
Adown the bank came speedily.
All glistening white was her vesture fair,
Open each side, and bound full well
With the merriest margarites at my devise,
That ever I saw yet with mine eyes.
With borders deep, I wot and ween,
Dubbed with double pearls and dight ; —
Her kirtle of very sute so bright
With precious pearls all edged and pight.

" A pight crown also wore the girl
Of margarites, and none other stone,
High pinnacled, of clear white pearl,
With figured flowers embossed thereon.
Her hair, too, all about her gone ;
Her semblance sad, for duke or earl ;

---

* Ere I could get her within ear-shot.

Her hue more white than whale's bone.
As pure bright gold her hair then shone,
That over her shoulders lay lightly unlapped.
Her deep 'colour' yet wanted none
Of precious pearls in purfile pight.

    " And decked and trimmed was every hem
At wrist, at side, at opening,
With white pearls, and none other gem ;
And burnished white was her vesture.
And a wondrous pearl without a flaw
Upon her breast was set so sure."

*Translated by Anna Robertson Brown.*

## THE POETIC STRUCTURE OF BROWNING'S SHORTER LYRICS.*

WHEN I was a young girl just beginning the study of artistic anatomy, I entered the lecture-room and looked with much awe at the man about to begin his lecture to the class before him. He startled me by saying quietly, "I have been chosen to give this course because I know so much less of anatomy than your other professors that it is less likely that I shall confuse you by trying to tell you too much."

It must be for the same reason that I have been requested to speak of the structure of Browning's shorter lyrics. Did the idea conveyed to me by the word "structure" mean just the same that I fancy it may to you, I should not attempt to analyze these poems before you who know them so much better than I do; but it so happens that the lyrics are adapted to a method of studying Browning in his capacity of poet that has given great pleasure to the pupil who has followed it.

Perhaps I am placing myself quite out of sympathy with those about me by finding it necessary to confess my belief that poetry should never be studied. It seems to me to be intended to picture

* Read before the Boston Browning Society, Feb. 28, 1893

a mood, and to rouse that mood in the hearts of those who have felt its truth, but not to present that truth for the first time to the mind. It may enlighten knowledge already acquired, but not yet comprehended, and deepen and broaden emotions already felt; but Holmes has said, "If there is anything that gives one a title to that name (of poet) it is that his inner nature is naked, and he is not ashamed." But when a soul is to be bared, it surely should be to those who can find within themselves already the sympathy and experience that teaches them to understand. There is something repellent in the thought of the spirit of the poet waiting, pained and anxious, before his reader, while the meaning of his deeper nature is being dug from between his lines.

It is because of this feeling about poetry that until last winter I never held a volume of Browning's poetry in my hand; and it is also from this cause that I have laid many of his poems aside after a glance at them here and there. It may be that with many re-readings they will fail to be conveyed to my mind, and yet it may be that even now, if I should pick some of them up again, I should find that they have already become a part of myself.

Although the lyrics are, like Browning's other poems, new to my sight, they have for some years been familiar to my ears. Almost all of them have been recited to me many times by one who loves them, and, with the rhythm of the verse, pictures fill my mind which I can hardly tell whether are most formed from the words and thoughts themselves, or if the purr of the ocean and the whispering of the pine-trees by which they were first heard, painted their larger part. It is these pictures that seem to my fancy to be the structure of the poem, — that untold half the story that is conveyed by something in the sound; and each of the lyrics has this second story of its own.

On the first reading of 'Through the Metidja' the twinship of form and matter is perhaps the most strongly marked. One hears in the opening verse no word to picture the horse that carries the speaker, but at once he becomes the central figure of the poem. His beating hoofs exhilarate, and the fresh, clear air animates in spite of lines which in themselves would surround the rider with dust and heat. The man himself would be forgotten but for the added length of the sixth line. In that the motion of the steed is gone, and one is brought back to the fact that the thought dominates the gallop.

The bracing, reckless courage that comes to a man with his conscious power over a horse is wonderfully expressed in the metre of three of Browning's poems. His physical dominion is triumphant in the ride in 'Through the Metidja,' and in the gallop in 'From Ghent to Aix;' and in a third poem,' The Last Ride Together,' one feels that the man's steadfast look into a future holding only such hope as he can evolve from within his own soul, would only be possible to him at just that time, while he held the control over a creature stronger physically than himself. These closing lines give this feeling with especial emphasis.

> "And yet — She has not spoke so long !
> What if heaven be that, fair and strong
> At life's best, with our eyes upturned
> Whither life's flower is first discerned,
> We fixed so, ever should so abide ?
> What if we still ride on, we two,
> With life forever old yet new,
> Changed not in kind but in degree,
> The instant made eternity. —
> And heaven just prove that I and she
> Ride, ride together, forever ride ?"

There is nothing in these cadences that brings the horses too prominently before our imaginations. The even, steady trot is a sing-song in the ears of the silent riders, making an association that will haunt the man for all his life.

I know that properly this poem does not belong with the group of lyrics under consideration to-day, but its affinity to the two referred to, and with one point in 'My Star,' has led me to include it. In each of these the humanity of the poem is expressed in a lengthened metre, and the motion in short, broken phrases. In the last-mentioned lyric is this especially marked. It seems to hurt the opening verse to read it naturally, so clearly do those brief, interrupted lines suggest the twinkle of that half-visible star. The form would grow tiresome if held to, but, too soon for that, is altered for the light cadences of the tender, closing lines.

In contrast with this poem, but in common with it, having boundless space for its setting, is the song in ' Paracelsus,' sung by that host of undone shades which represent man's neglected powers. The movement here curiously suggests the short strokes of the beating wings bearing a long line of spirits in an endless spiral, which brings them one by one close to the listener, and allows each spirit in turn to dominate the receding chorus for a few lines.

Two other lyrics show Browning's masterly expression of movement in his rhythm, by giving different motions of the sea in their lines. One would feel by reading slowly the opening of ' Meeting at Night,' that the water was falling against sheltered sands.

> "The gray sea and the long black land;
> And the yellow half-moon large and low "

In the sing-song words it is easy to fancy the two lapping waves we hear before the third wave drops with its decided break upon the shore; and in turning from this to ' Home Thoughts from the Sea,' one instantly feels the long, slow swell of a rolling ocean below a large vessel.

> " Nobly, nobly Cape Saint Vincent to the North-West died away;
> Sunset ran, one glorious blood-red, reeking into Cadiz Bay;
> Bluish 'mid the burning water, full in face Trafalgar lay."

So prominent is the suggestion of sweeping water in these lines that until preparing this paper I never attended to what the words that composed them signified, the last three lines embodying the sentiment of the poem to me, and the other four merely expressing the ocean that called forth the mood in the poet.

Among the purely emotional lyrics two express in their form the under-current of repressed sobs with which a woman tells her heartache when a lull in the storm permits her to speak with partly controlled voice. In the first and in the last two verses of ' A Woman's Last Word,' one instinctively holds the breath as if about to sob.

> "Let's contend no more, Love,
>  Strive nor weep:
> All be as before, Love,
>  — Only sleep!
>
> "That shall be to-morrow,
>  Not to-night:
> I must bury sorrow
>  Out of sight:
>
> "—Must a little weep, Love,
>  (Foolish me!)
> And so fall asleep, Love,
>  Loved by thee."

And in the two following verses of 'In a Year' one feels the quality of the broken voice still more: —

> "Was it wrong to own,
>  Being truth?
> Why should all the giving prove
>  His alone?
> I had wealth and ease,
>  Beauty, youth:
> Since my lover gave me love,
>  I gave these.
>
> "That was all I meant,
>  — To be just,
> And the passion that I raised,
>  To content.
> Since he chose to change
>  Gold for dust,
> If I gave him what he praised
>  Was it strange?"

In contrast to these, which show the woman in their form, is 'A Lover's Quarrel,' which with all its tenderness indicates in its structure the hardness that almost always characterizes the speech of a pained man. The key-note is in this verse, —

> "Woman, and will you cast
>  For a word, quite off at last
>   Me, your own your You,
>   Since, as truth is true,
>  I was You all the happy past —
>   Me do you leave aghast
>  With the memories We amassed?"

As examples of the lyric in the first and derivative meaning of the word, the song of the Page to Queen Catherine is a nearly perfect example, the refrain of the maiden delightfully suggesting the accompaniment of a lyre. This quality is still more marked in the lyric which is only titled, ' A Song,' one verse of which I would like to give.

> " Because, you spend your life in praising :
>     To praise, you search the whole world over :
>     Then why not witness, calmly gazing,
>         If earth holds aught — speak truth — above her ?
>     Above this tress, and this, I touch
>     But cannot praise, I love so much ! "

In the poems in which Browning has directly addressed his audience, the form is so straightforward that it gives the feeling of a conversation in a delightful manner. But for a few words not usually chosen in personal intercourse one would entirely forget the form of many of the stanzas in such verses as those of ' Old Pictures in Florence.' For instance, this bit : —

> " Yet I hardly know. When a soul has seen
>     By the means of Evil that Good is best,
>     And, through earth and its noise, what is heaven's serene, —
>         When our faith in the same has stood the test —
>     Why, the child grown man, you burn the rod,
>         The uses of labor are surely done ;
>     There remains a rest for the people of God :
>         And I have had troubles enough, for one."

It does not seem a lack of metrical emphasis that makes the reader ignore the rhythm in the reading, but a fitness that leaves the mind free to grasp the sense. The same fitness is a part of ' The Flower's Name,' although in that the versification is more marked. But after hearing this, what man would wish to use different words to give his confidence to a friend ?

> " This flower she stopped at, finger on lip,
>     Stooped over, in doubt, as settling its claim ;
>     Till she gave me, with pride to make no slip,
>         Its soft meandering Spanish name :
>     What a name ! Was it love or praise ?
>     Speech half asleep or song half awake ?

In quoting these lyrics in this rambling way, it is a puzzle at which to stop. A line catches the memory here, a sentiment there. In my first acquaintance I had the advantage of hearing them bit by bit, because they fitted some already present mood. There was no danger of quoting too many or too few; and now when I let myself weigh the circumstances in which I am presenting my thoughts about them, — thoughts perhaps of no interest to any one but myself, — I am surprised at my boldness. I am going to ask you to find a justification for me in the familiar lines which I have already referred to, and am now about to quote as a close to my paper.

> " All that I know
>     Of a certain star
>   Is, it can throw
>     (Like an angled spar)
>   Now a dart of red,
>     Now a dart of blue ;
>   Till my friends have said
>     They would fain see, too,
> My star that dartles the red and the blue !
> Then it stops like a bird ; like a flower, hangs furled !
>   They must solace themselves with the Saturn above it.
> What matter to me if their star is a world ?
>   Mine has opened its soul to me : therefore I love it."

*Ethel Davis.*

---

## THE SIGHTLESS.

### By MAURICE MAETERLINCK.

#### (*Concluded.*)

[*A gust disturbs the forest, and the leaves fall in heavy masses.*]
*Fifth Man.* Who touched my hands ?
*First Man.* Something is falling around us !
*Oldest Man.* It comes from above ; I do not know what it is.
*Fifth Man.* Who was it that touched my hands ? I was asleep; let me sleep on !
*Oldest Man.* Nobody touched your hands.

*Fifth Man.* Who took my hands? Speak loud; I am a little deaf.

*Oldest Man.* We ourselves do not know.

*Fifth Man.* Has some one come to aid us?

*First Man.* It is useless to reply; he hears nothing.

*Third Man.* It must be confessed that deaf people are very unfortunate!

*Oldest Man.* I am tired of sitting down!

*Sixth Man.* I am tired of being here!

*Second Man.* It seems to me that we are very far from one another. Let us try to draw a little closer together; it begins to be cold.

*Third Man.* I dare not get up! It is better to stay in your place.

*Oldest Man.* One does n't know what may be between us.

*Sixth Man.* I believe both my hands are bleeding; I was trying to stand up.

*Third Man.* I hear that you are bending over toward me. [*The idiot blind girl rubs her eyes violently, moaning and turning persistently toward the motionless priest.*]

*First Man.* I hear still another noise.

*Oldest Woman.* I think it is our poor sister, who is rubbing her eyes.

*Second Man.* She never does anything else; I hear her doing it every night.

*Third Man.* She is foolish; she never says anything.

*Oldest Woman.* She has never spoken since she had her child. She seems always to be afraid.

*Oldest Man.* Are you not afraid here, then?

*First Man.* Who?

*Oldest Man.* All of us!

*Oldest Woman.* Yes, yes, we are all afraid!

*The Blind Girl.* We have been afraid for a long time!

*First Man.* Why do you ask us that?

*Oldest Man.* I do not know why I ask! There are some things I do not understand. It seems to me that I hear weeping all at once among us.

*First Man.* We must not be afraid. I think it is the idiot.

*Oldest Man.* It is something else; I am sure there is something else. It is not *that* I am afraid of.

*Oldest Woman.* She always weeps when she is nursing her baby.

*First Man.* No one weeps as she does!

*Oldest Woman.* They say she sees still at times.

*First Man.* No one hears the others weep.

*Oldest Man.* One must see to weep.

*The Blind Girl.* I smell flowers around us.

*First Man.* I smell nothing but the odor of the earth!

*The Blind Girl.* There are flowers, there are flowers around us!

*Second Man.* I smell nothing but the odor of the earth!

*Oldest Woman.* I smelled flowers in the breeze.

*Third Man.* I smell nothing but the smell of the earth!

*Oldest Man.* I believe they are right.

*Sixth Man.* Where are they? I will go and pick them.

*The Blind Girl.* At your right. Arise. [*The sixth man rises slowly and advances, gropingly, knocking against the bushes and trees, towards the asphodels, which on his way he overthrows and crushes.*] I hear you breaking the green stalks! Stop! Stop!

*First Man.* Don't bother about the flowers; think of our return!

*Sixth Man.* I dare not return upon my steps!

*The Blind Girl.* He must not return! Wait. [*She rises.*] Oh, how cold the ground is! It is going to freeze. [*She advances hesitatingly toward the strange, pale asphodels, but is stopped by the fallen tree and the bowlders, near the flowers.*] They are here! I cannot reach them; they are on your side.

*Sixth Man.* I believe I can pick them. [*He gathers, gropingly, the flowers that had been spared, and gives them to her; the night-birds fly about.*]

*The Blind Girl.* It seems to me that I have seen these flowers before. I do not remember their name. But how sickly they are, and how soft their stems are! I scarcely recognize them; I believe it is the flower of death. [*She twines the asphodels in her hair.*]

*Oldest Man.* I hear the sound of your hair.

*The Blind Girl.* It is the flowers.

*Oldest Man.* We cannot see you.

*The Blind Girl.* Neither can I see myself. I am cold. [*At this moment the wind rises in the woods, and the sea roars all at once with violence against the closely neighboring cliffs.*]

*First Man.* It thunders!

*Second Man.* I think a storm is rising.

*Oldest Woman.* I think it is the sea.

*Third Man.* The sea? Is it the sea? But it is not two steps away from us! It is beside us! I hear it all around me! It must be something else!

*The Blind Girl.* I hear the noise of the waves at my feet.

*First Man.* I think that is the wind in the dead leaves.

*Oldest Man.* I think the women are right.

*Third Man.* It is going to come here!

*First Man.* Where does the wind come from?

*Second Man.* It comes from the sea-shore.

*Oldest Man.* It always comes from the sea-shore; it surrounds us. It cannot come from anywhere else.

*First Man.* Don't let us think of the sea any more!

*Second Man.* But we must think of it if it is going to reach us!

*First Man.* You do not know if it is that.

*Second Man.* I hear the waves as close as if I were going to dip my hands in them! We cannot stay here. Perhaps they are all around us!

*Oldest Man.* Where will you go?

*Second Man.* No matter where! No matter where! I will not hear that noise of the water any longer! Let us go away! Let us go away!

*Third Man.* It seems to me that I hear something else. Listen! [*A noise of steps is heard, hurried and far away in the dead leaves.*]

*First Man.* It is something coming!

*Second Man.* He is coming! He is coming! He has come back!

*Third Man.* He comes by little steps, like a little child.

*Second Man.* Don't let us reproach him to-day!

*Oldest Woman.* I believe it is not the step of a man! [*A big dog comes into the forest, and passes in front of the blind people. Silence.*]

*First Man.* Who is there? Who are you? Have pity on us, we have waited for such a long time! [*The dog stops and comes and puts his front paws on the blind man's knees.*] Ah, ah! what have you put on my knees? What is it? Is it a beast? I believe it is a dog! Oh, oh! It is the dog! It is the hospital dog! Come here! Come here! He comes to save us! Come here! Come here!

*The Others.* Come here! Come here!

*First Man.* He is coming to save us! He has followed our track here! He licks my hands as if he had found me again after centuries! He howls for joy! He is ready to die for joy! Listen! Listen!

*The Others.* Come here! Come here!

*The Oldest Man.* Maybe he preceded some one!

*First Man.* No, no; he is alone. I hear nothing coming. We need no other guide; there is none better. He will lead us wherever we wish to go; he will obey us.

*Oldest Woman.* I dare not follow him.

*The Blind Girl.* Nor I.

*First Man.* Why not? He sees better than we can.

*Second Man.* Do not let us listen to the women!

*Third Man.* I believe the sky has changed; I breathe freely; the air is pure now.

*Oldest Man.* It is the sea-breeze blowing around us.

*Sixth Man.* It seems to me that it is clearing up; I believe the sun is rising.

*Oldest Woman.* I think it is going to be cold.

*First Man.* We are going to find our way. He drags me away! He drags me away! He is drunk with joy! I can no longer hold him! Follow me! Follow me! We shall return to the house! [*He rises, dragged by the dog, who leads him toward the motionless priest, and stops.*]

*The Others.* Where are you? Where are you? Where are you going? Take care!

*First Man.* Wait! Wait! Don't follow yet; I will come back. He stops. What is it? Ah, ah! I have touched something very cold!

*Second Man.* What do you say? We scarcely hear your voice any more.

*First Man.* I have touched — I believe I touch a face!

*Third Man.* What do you say? We do not understand you any more. What is the matter with you? Where are you? Are you already so far away from us?

*First Man.* Oh, oh, oh! I don't know yet what it is. — There is a dead man in the midst of us!

*The Others.* A dead man in the midst of us? Where are you? Where are you?

*First Man.* There is a dead man among us, I tell you. Oh, oh! I touched the face of a dead man! You are sitting beside a dead man! One of us must have died suddenly! But speak, so that I may know who is alive! Where are you? Answer! Answer, all of you! [*The blind men and women all reply one after the other, except the idiot and the deaf blind man; the three old women stop praying.*]

*First Man.* I no longer distinguish your voices! You all speak alike! Your voices all tremble!

*Third Man.* There are two of us who have not answered. Where are they? [*He touches with his stick the fifth blind man.*]

*Fifth Man.* Oh, oh! I was asleep; let me sleep!

*Sixth Man.* It is not he. Is it the idiot?

*Oldest Woman.* She is sitting beside me; I hear that she is alive.

*First Man.* I think — I think it is the priest! He is standing! Come! Come!

*Second Man.* He is standing?

*Third Man.* He is not dead, then !

*Oldest Man.* Where is he ?

*Sixth Man.* Let us go see! [*They all rise, except the idiot and the fifth blind man, and advance, groping, toward the corpse.*]

*Second Man.* Is he here? Is this he ?

*Third Man.* Yes, yes ! I recognize him !

*First Man.* My God ! My God ! What is going to become of us ?

*Oldest Woman.* Father! My father! Is it you ? My father, what has happened to you ? What is the matter ? Answer us! We are all around you. Oh, oh, oh !

*Oldest Man.* Bring some water; maybe he is still alive.

*Second Man.* Let us try. Maybe he can guide us back to the hospital.

*Third Man.* It is useless; I don't hear his heart. He is cold.

*First Man.* He is dead without a word.

*Third Man.* He ought to have warned us !

*Second Man.* Oh, how old he was ! This is the first time I ever felt his face.

*Third Man* [*feeling the body*]. He was larger than we are !

*Second Man.* His eyes are wide open ; he died with his hands clasped.

*First Man.* He is dead, thus, without any cause.

*Second Man.* He is not standing; he is sitting on a stone.

*Oldest Woman.* My God ! My God ! I did not know all this ! all this ! He was ill for such a long time. How he must have suffered to-day ! Oh, oh, oh ! He never complained. He only showed his pity for himself by clasping his hands. One does not always understand. One never understands ! Let us go pray around him ; kneel down, all of you ! [*The women kneel, moaning.*]

*First Man.* I dare not kneel down.

*Second Man.* One don't know what one may kneel on here.

*Third Man.* Was he ill ? He never told us so.

*Second Man.* I heard him speak in a subdued voice when he went away. I believe he spoke to our young sister ; what did he say ?

*First Man.* She will not reply.

*Second Man.* Will you not reply to us any more? Where are you, then? Speak!

*Oldest Woman.* You made him suffer too much; you made him die. You would not go on any farther; you would sit down on the stones by the way to eat; you murmured all day. I heard him sigh. He lost courage.

*First Man.* Was he ill? Did you know it?

*Oldest Man.* We knew nothing about it. We never saw him. When did we ever know of anything under our poor dead eyes? He did not complain. Now it is too late. I have seen three persons die — but never so! Now it is our turn!

*First Man.* It was not I who made him suffer. I never said anything.

*Second Man.* Nor I; we followed him without a word.

*Third Man.* He died going to fetch water for the idiot.

*First Man.* What are we going to do now? Where shall we go?

*Third Man.* Where is the dog?

*First Man.* Here; he will not leave the dead.

*Third Man.* Drag him away! Drive him away! Drive him off!

*First Man.* He will not go away from the corpse!

*Second Man.* We cannot wait here beside a corpse! We cannot die here in the darkness!

*Third Man.* Let us stay together; don't let us go away from each other; let us hold each other's hands; let us all sit down on this stone. Where are the others? Come here! Come! Come!

*Oldest Man.* Where are you?

*Third Man.* Here; here I am. Are we all together? Come closer to me. Where are your hands? It is very cold.

*The Blind Girl.* Oh, how cold your hands are!

*Third Man.* What are you doing?

*The Blind Girl.* I am putting my hands on my eyes; I thought all at once I was going to see.

*First Man.* Who is it who is weeping so?

*Oldest Woman.* It is the idiot, who is sobbing.

*First Man.* And yet she does not know the truth !

*Oldest Man.* I believe we are going to die here.

*Oldest Woman.* Perhaps some one will come.

*Oldest Man.* Who is there to come ?

*Oldest Woman.* I don't know.

*First Man.* I think that the nuns will come out of the hospital.

*Oldest Woman.* They don't go out in the evening.

*The Blind Girl.* They never go out at all.

*Second Man.* I think that the men at the lighthouse will see us.

*Oldest Man.* They don't go down from their tower.

*Third Man.* But perhaps they will see us.

*Oldest Woman.* They always look out toward the sea.

*Third Man.* It is cold !

*Oldest Man.* Hear the dead leaves; I believe it is freezing.

*The Blind Girl.* Oh, how hard the ground is !

*Third Man.* I hear, on my left, a noise that I do not understand.

*Oldest Man.* It is the sea moaning against the rocks.

*Third Man.* I thought it was the women.

*Oldest Woman.* I hear the ice breaking under the waves.

*First Man.* Who is shivering so ? It makes us all shake on the stone.

*Second Man.* I cannot open my hands any more.

*Oldest Man.* Again I hear a noise that I cannot explain.

*First Man.* Who is it among us who shivers so ? It makes the stone tremble !

*Oldest Man.* I think it is a woman.

*Oldest Woman.* I think it is the idiot who shivers the most.

*Third Man.* We do not hear her child.

*Oldest Woman.* I think he is still nursing.

*Oldest Man.* He is the only one who can see where we are !

*First Man.* I hear the north wind.

*Sixth Man.* I think there are no more stars; it is going to snow.

*Second Man.* We are lost, then!

*Third Man.* If one of us goes to sleep, he must be waked up.

*Oldest Man.* I am sleepy! [*A gust makes the dead leaves whirl about.*]

*The Blind Girl.* Do you hear the dead leaves? I believe some one is coming toward us!

*Second Man.* It is the wind; listen!

*Third Man.* No one will come any more!

*Oldest Man.* The great frosts are going to come.

*The Blind Girl.* I hear walking in the distance!

*First Man.* I hear nothing but dead leaves!

*The Blind Girl.* I hear walking a long way off from us!

*Second Man.* I hear nothing but the north wind!

*The Blind Girl.* I tell you some one is coming toward us!

*Oldest Woman.* I hear the sound of very slow steps.

*Oldest Man.* I believe the women are right! [*It begins to snow in great flakes.*]

*First Man.* Oh, oh! What is it falling so cold on my hands?

*Sixth Man.* It is snowing!

*First Man.* Let us crowd close together!

*The Blind Girl.* Listen to the sound of the steps!

*Oldest Woman.* For God's sake! Be still a moment!

*The Blind Girl.* They approach us! they approach us! Listen! [*The child of the idiot blind girl suddenly begins to scream in the darkness.*]

*Oldest Man.* The child is crying!

*The Blind Girl.* He can see! He can see! He must see something, since he is crying! [*She seizes the child in her arms, and advances in the direction from which the sound of the steps seems to come; the other women follow her anxiously and surround her.*] I am going to meet it!

*Oldest Man.* Take care!

*The Blind Girl.* Oh, how he cries! What is it? Don't cry. Don't be afraid: there is nothing to fear; we are here; we are all around you. What do you see? Fear nothing. Don't cry so! What do you see? Tell me, what do you see?

*Oldest Woman.* The sound of steps comes close ; listen ! listen !

*Oldest Man.* I hear the rustling of a robe over the dead leaves.

*Sixth Man.* Is it a woman ?

*Oldest Man.* Is it a sound of steps ?

*First Man.* Maybe it is the sea in the dead leaves ?

*The Blind Girl.* No, no ! They are steps ! They are steps ! They are steps !

*Oldest Woman.* We are going to find out ; listen now to the dead leaves !

*The Blind Girl.* I hear them ! I hear them close beside us ! Listen ! Listen ! What do you see ? What do you see ?

*Oldest Woman.* On which side does he look ?

*The Blind Girl.* He follows the sound of the steps always ! Look ! Look ! When I turn him away, he turns back again to see. He sees ! He sees ! He sees ! He must see something strange !

*Oldest Woman.* [*Coming forward.*] Lift him above us so he can see.

*The Blind Girl.* Stand aside ! Stand aside ! [*She lifts the child above the group of blind people.*] The steps have stopped in our midst !

*Oldest Woman.* They are here ! They are in the midst of us !

*The Blind Girl.* Who are you ? [*Silence.*]

*Oldest Woman.* Have pity on us ! [*Silence. The child cries desperately.*]

(THE END.)

*Translated by the Editors.*

## BROWNING STUDY HINTS: THREE POEMS RELATING TO MARRIED LIFE.

'A WOMAN'S LAST WORD.'—This poem, Mrs. Orr says, "is one of moral and intellectual self-surrender." The speaker has been "contending with her husband, and been silenced by the feeling, not that the truth is on his side, but that it is not worth the pain of such a contention. What, she seems to ask herself, is the value of truth when it is false to her Divinity or Knowledge, when it costs her her Eden? She begs him whom she worships as well as loves, to mould her to himself, but she begs also the privilege of a few tears,—a last tribute, perhaps, to her sacrificed conscience and her lost liberty." If this is a true interpretation, do you think such an attitude on the part of a wife would be conducive to the best development of both? Can any indication of the nature of the quarrel be gathered from the poem? What does she mean in stanza ii. by saying, —

> " I and thou
> In debate, as birds are,
> Hawk on bough."

Does the simile suggest the idea that while they contend, their love is in danger of being swallowed up in hate?

What does she mean in stanza iv.? —

> " What so false as truth is,
> False to thee ?
> Where the serpent's tooth is
> Shun the tree — "

Is it that her love for her husband is so great that her own convictions of truth become false if they in any way endanger the bond of love between them? Or does she mean that the nature of the truth about which they are contending is some falseness to him of which she was or he thinks she was guilty, and the exact nature of which she refuses to tell, —

> " Where the apple reddens
> Never pry —
> Lest we lose our Edens,
> Eve and I "

Notice the peculiar form of the rhythm (see the article in the present number of POET-LORE, 'The Artistic Structure of Browning's Shorter Lyrics').

'A FORGIVENESS.'— *Subject-matter:* What do you think of the motives of this husband and wife? Was either of them at all justified in the action taken? For which of them can the most excuse be made? Compare the characters and the situations with those in 'The Flight of the Duchess.' Did the husband recognize the lover from the first? Note the lines, —

> "or his who wraps
> — Still plain I seem to see! — about his head
> The idle cloak."

What others are there to the same effect?

Do you suppose the lover became a monk to elude the husband's vengeance, as he says, or do you think he may have gone into the monastery because his life was completely broken through the incident with the wife? Can any justification for the monk be made, and did he deserve his fate of death at the hands of the husband? Mrs. Orr says, "'A Forgiveness' might serve equally as a study for jealousy, self-reproach, contempt and revenge, the love which is made to underlie these feelings and the forgiveness with which it will be crowned." Can that be said to be forgiveness which ends only in the death of the person forgiven? Is there any hint in the poem to show that the husband regretted his action? Can this poem be said to have any moral import?

*Form:* Is the title of the poem satiric? Is it purely narrative? How many speakers are there in it? How many characters? Study the mode — the monologue form — Browning uses with a view to exhibiting the poet's skill in letting hints fall all through which show at whom the speaker is aiming his confession; in revealing the natures of the husband, the wife, and the lover, and what befell wife and priest because they came in contact with the will of the husband. In what metre is the poem written? Examine the images used, and show their pertinence, — *e. g.*, "the athlete" running "life's race;" the "actors" before the "curtain;" the "arms of Eastern workmanship," — as a symbol of the plot.

QUERY FOR DEBATE: Are our sympathies aroused for any of the three actors in this tragedy; and if so, for whom do we feel the most, — the deceived priest, the deceived husband, or the deceiving wife?

'JAMES LEE'S WIFE.' — *The Story and the Characters of the Poem:* Was James Lee's wife plain of person? Is one to credit what she lets fall as to her appearance or as to James Lee's handsomeness? Is there any trace of justification for his *ennui?* Compare the hero of 'Another Way of Love.' Is it the truer notion of love that it is a "lust of the blood and a permission of the will" ('Othello,' I., iii.), or that it is "an ever-fixèd mark" (Sonnet CXVI.)?

*An Outline of the Idea and its Artistic Development:* Where is the scene of the whole poem laid? Show how the *mise-en-scène* and the externals peculiar to each part of the poem occasion the images used, and denote the leading thought of each division. Which should be accounted the main interest, and which the accessories of the poem, — the aspects of nature described, the incidents of the love and estrangement, or the effects of all these on James Lee's wife? Trace the poetic working out, through these incidents and descriptions, of the processes of her experience. Show, in particular, the meaning of the lesson she gets from the "poor coarse hand" she is learning to draw.

QUERIES FOR DEBATE: "The only fault we find in her," says Miss Burt of the heroine, "is that she clings to the faithless husband and cannot at once resign herself to the loss of the love which had sought hers." Is this a fault, or an indication of high development?

If in the end she concludes that change is inevitable and good, that the Ideal in life is impossible and of less value than the unlovelier truth, is James Lee to be applauded for doing her a psychological service?

In contrast with the women in the two previous poems, is James Lee's wife a higher type intellectually and emotionally? Why?

*P. A. C.*

## THE CENTURY'S ST. MARTIN'S SUMMER.

FROM THE CORRESPONDENCE OF —— —— AND * - -

DEAR —— ——: Has it ever seemed to you that in this latter end of the nineteenth century we are living in a sort of St. Martin's Summer? In whatever direction one may turn for fresh inspiration, little is to be found but old, way-worn thoughts grown thin to emaciation, and bolstered up by dull heaps of words. Occasionally an idea will seem to startle by its strangeness. Here, for example, is an earnest mind who has set up a new god whom he calls "Biologos." Gaze at him steadily a moment or two, and his lineaments melt into a misty form as old as the Greek philosophers. He is found to be in his essence but that inconceivable conception, the self-moved thing, with a touch of the Persian Ormuzd, for he is not so omnipotent but that he must continually struggle against evil. It looks very much as if a few men such as Carlyle, Emerson, Spencer, Browning, Whitman, and others whom the century ushered in had between them monopolized all the thought of the century, and all that the later-born pilgrims up the shining slopes of Parnassus can do is to beg a leaf from the script of one or other of their divinely endowed brethren, and pad it out to the size of a volume with which a problematical entrance to the society of the immortals is gained.

You will say, I know, that the constant reiteration in more and more popular forms of the great thought of the age is the process necessary for spreading it to the utmost confines of a heterogeneous humanity; and no doubt you may be right, but what an unconscionable amount of inertia the greater part of humanity exhibits! Books multiply, planned upon evolutionary principles; idealism flourishes; democracy is rampant; but all, alas! in print. Few of us apply any of these great fundamental principles to our daily lives. We stick to the old-time shibboleths with a tenacity that would shame a barnacle. Perhaps, owing to the dilution of thought going on, it is administered in such homœopathic doses as to have lost all power of vital action.

If only the all-embracing tenets of evolution could escape from the fetters of print and get into our daily lives, not only would our ideals of life improve, but the new dispensation might bring about conditions favorable for the engendering of fresh thought.

The only philosophical maxim which has got into current use is the doctrine of the pursuit of happiness ; but how is it shorn of all nobleness, for the pursuit of happiness which philosophy preaches is reached through the exercise of the highest human faculties. The peace of mind which comes through the attainment of universal sympathy, — that is the happiness in store for those who love philosophy, not the isolated sprinklings of that inferior sort of happiness which comes through the amusement of the moment. What man or woman is there among us who reads with any desire but for the pleasure of the moment ? Who listens to music with any deeper intention than having his senses tickled ? Does not every artist one meets declare, " I cannot sing good songs; they would not *please* the audience " ? Does not every lecturer watch with anxious heart to see the smiles of his audience catch at the anecdotical bait which he throws to them ? Each knows that his bread and butter depends upon his appeal to the senses and not to the intellect of his audience. Life appears at bottom to be such a miserable affair for most of us that we bless the individual who will make us smile ; our god is " Brightness " (merely a quality), not " Light " (an essence).

But once let us receive into our inmost being the glorious doctrines which the young century gave birth to, and no longer would people, nor poems, nor paintings, nor musical compositions be regarded as detached phenomena which we like or don't like as they appeal or not directly to our senses. All would fall into their places as avatars of an ever-changing but ever-permanent spirit of existence. Perhaps we should realize that the *new* does not give place to the old, only is it another arc in the circle of existence, borrowing and giving glory to that which is past and to that which is to come. Our concert programmes would give us everything from an old-fashioned gigue to a modern fantasia, so that we might hear and compare for ourselves the wondrous forms in which the divine spirit of music has become manifest.  Our clubs and societies would not worship at the shrine of one poet, but open their hearts to Euripides as to George Meredith, so that we might see and know how curious and marvellous are the shapes through which the divine spirit of poetry has shone out.

The much-despised critic may help in this broadening of the sympathies if he will.  He, if he possess the true sympathetic insight, may render the greatest of services to humanity.  His high office it is to point out the complex and far-reaching relations which bind together the eternal procession of the creations of the human mind, just as it is the poet's office to present every subtilest analogy discernible in the creations of Nature.  There are those who declare that it is of no use to read criticism ; but this is as short-sighted as it would be to say, " Do not look at pictures ; better go straight to Nature yourself, and look at the men and women and scenery all around you, than get your knowledge through the painter's art."  But we should all laugh at the idea that we look at pictures in order to gain a knowledge of Nature.  It is the comparison of the artist's impressions of Nature with our own which constitutes his value to us, for, as Fra Lippo Lippi says, —

> " We 're made so that we love
> First when we see them painted things we have passed
> Perhaps a hundred times, nor cared to see."

Or, again, why read Shakespeare ?  Would it not be better to study human character direct from the friends about you ?  But to adapt Lippo, —

> " We 're made so that we love
> First when we see them *portrayed, beings* we have passed
> Perhaps a hundred times, nor cared to see."

Then why should not the critic's art be the subtilest of all arts? — the art which holds up for our inspection, in all the intricacies of their artistic and moral relations, the thronging crowds of mindborn beings who people a mind-born world ; the art which makes us love first the " things " of genius we may have passed a hundred times.

Indeed, what we need is a modern Renaissance, not one which will take us to the past for models, but one which will show us its beauties, so that we may the better appreciate the true beauties of our own age. We must not be satisfied with the ephemeral pleasures of a diluted literature, the second-rate pleasures of a St. Martin's Summer, we must go to the fountain-heads of thought; and through our increase of wisdom who knows but we may help to form the soil out of which the future great-thoughted ones must spring. But I will not weary you longer with this rambling talk.

Yours,

## SOME RECENT BRITISH VERSE.*

THE quizzical way Nature and Fact have of satirizing exactness almost convicts those grave impersonalities of enjoying a joke at the expense of the defining animal, — man. I have heard that Professor Gray once replied to a correspondent who complained that the colors of the flowers she found were not in accord with their description in his 'Manual,' that he had been trying all his

* A Country Muse, by Norman R. Gale. New York: G. P. Putnam's Sons, 1893. — Amenophis and Other Poems, Sacred and Secular, by Francis T. Palgrave. London and New York: Macmillan and Co., 1892. — Valete. Tennyson, and Other Memorial Poems, by H. D. Rawnsley. Glasgow: James MacLehose and Sons (New York: Macmillan and Co.), 1893. — Old John and Other Poems, by T. E. Brown. London and New York: Macmillan and Co., 1893. — Fortunatus the Pessimist, by Alfred Austin. London and New York: Macmillan and Co., 1892. — The Poems of William Watson. New York and London: Macmillan and Co., 1893. — The Eloping Angels. A Caprice, by William Watson. New York and London: Macmillan and Co., 1893. — Modern Love. With an Introduction, by E. Cavazza. Portland: Thomas W. Mosher. — Jump to Glory Jane, by George Meredith. Edited and Arranged by Harry Quilter, with 44 designs invented, drawn, and written by Laurence Hausman. London: Swan, Sonnenschein, and Co., Paternoster Square. New York: Macmillan and Co., 1892. — Poems. The Empty Purse. Odes to the Comic Spirit, To Youth in Memory, and Verses, by George Meredith. London: Macmillan and Co., 1892.

life to make the flowers grow according to his descriptions, but had not as yet quite succeeded.

Literary phenomena slip the noose of ascertained formula in the same playful manner, and only that critic can keep even with them who takes these aberrations into his calculation,— yes, even although they multiply fast enough to swamp his dearest definitions. The work of most latter-day poets shows their allegiance to the approved dictum that poetic form is what constitutes poetry; and they seem to lavish their academic trust on the plausible labors of the file only to remind the reader that the inevitable beauty of the handicraft of genius differs from ordinary verse rather in the indefinable poetic spirit than in metrical externalities. If they had set out to prove that poetry is more than its form, — which it includes as an incident of its being, and not as a proxy for it, — they hardly could have demonstrated it more clearly. It is a case of facts overruling precision.

So, too, one of the prettiest growths of recent poetic seasons Mr. Norman Gale's 'Country Muse' — thrusts its old-fashioned fragrance under one's nose in saucy disregard of the statement in a good and useful Handbook of Versification just published, that the loves of shepherd swains and village maids are not attempted by modern poets, "because much of the charm and simplicity of country life has disappeared before the manifold invasions of commercial enterprise." Yet here are Strephon and Chloris disporting themselves with true archaic meagreness of thought, although in a way up to date and not unsuited to the market ; and here are Corin and Jane sidling up the stage with an air of gayety as genuine as if Clarinda's " garter-knot," and Laura's " necklace of tan," were pastoral properties as modish as an Intimation of Immortality.

The simple grace of Mr. Gale's modern bucolics appears characteristically in 'The Shaded Pool,' describing how a laughing knot of village maids mean to be water nymphs, wreaking much easy rhyme on the unlacing of the country shoe, the loosening of " the cheated stockings lean and long," and yet concentring all the tiptoe phrases of the little idyll on Laura's praise, for

> " though each maid is pure and fair
> For one alone my heart I bring
> And Laura's is the shape I love,
> And Laura's is the snow I sing."

The refinement and quietude of ' Amenophis and Other Poems,' whose every felicity is meditative, seem sophisticated in comparison; yet, after all, the Egyptian poem which gives its title to Professor Palgrave's volume, the hymns of which it is half composed, and the various poems, rich in scholarly allusions, with which it concludes, are all marked by simplicity. No exceptional fervor or splendor of invention appears, but the good taste of a gentle and cultured nature breathes throughout, and speaks gracefully enough, for example, in this ' Invocation ': —

> " Come, Love, as in the golden days
>   When I was child and thou wast king;
> Come, poet-wreathed with Lesbian bays,
>   And touch each common thing
> To heaven by the waving of thy wing.
>
> " And crown the crimson wine of life
>   With roses of celestial birth,
> And bid the banquet-hall be rife
>   With strains unheard on earth,
> And sadness sweeter than the songs of mirth."

The homage of poets to poets is noticeable in recent books of poetry. Was so wide a range of appreciation ever acknowledged in song before ? In so far as these poems to poets, now in fashion, are catholic, and not confined to expressions of discipleship to a master, to the exclusion of all other bards, are they not a sign of the fit appreciation and increasing influence of the poetic priesthood ? Here and there this kingdom of the spirit is prophesied, although scarcely anywhere is it perceived as yet; so we may note with the more interest the fact that Professor Palgrave's verses include two or three such poems of praise, and that Mr. Brown's volume adds others, while Mr. Watson's and Mr. Rawnsley's collections are thick-sown with garlands of honor, selected with nice taste, to suit the traits celebrated. It is more a matter of criticism, however,

in Mr. Watson's case, and is chiefly rosemary and rue in Mr.
Rawnsley's 'Valete,' one whole section of his book being a series
of Memorials to Tennyson; and famous "Shepherds of men,"
"Leaders of men," and "Thinkers among men," as well as "The
Royal Dead," and "Friends and Neighbors," dividing laurels with
the "Singers among men" whom the world has lately mourned,
— Rossetti, Arnold, Browning, Lowell, Whitman, Whittier. It is
practised versification, sometimes happy in allusion, but never
imagination-compelling. The idea of making its whole theme
the heroes of art and deed gives it, however, the interest yielded
to the exploitation of a new vein of book-making.

The author of 'Old John and Other Poems' is neither so conventional nor so unexceptionable in his style. He loves unequal
lines, now of one foot, two, or three, and an occasional long line;
and he has a knack of ungovernable rhyming which seems to race
him off on a hot, broken trot and gallop, as if by nailing rhymes
enough at hazard he would finally pull up abreast of his idea. His
subject-matter is often a homely dialect tale, sometimes told in
monologue fashion, as the series of half-dramatic yarns entitled
'In the Coach,' of which the following citation, from a mother's
replies to her fellow-travellers anent "Joe," will show the fashion:

> "Yes, ma'am, no, ma'am;
> We called him Joe, ma'am;
> Eighteen —
> My name's Cregeen —
> Yes, ma'am, no, ma'am;
> Had to go, ma'am.
> *Faver?* aye;
> Young to die;
> Eighteen for spring.
> *(Chorus of Sympathisers.)* 'Poor thing! Poor thing!'
>
> . . . .
>
> But I'm makin' very bould.
> Yes, ma'am, no, ma'am
> Rather slow, ma'am,
> In this coach;
> But I hope I don't encroach
> In my head the pain's
> *(Chorus as before.)* 'In her heart she manes.'"

The metrical mannerisms are notable, and seldom get lost in the sense; if they were more subordinate to it, one would be forced to descry an unusual gift; as it is, only here and there am I able to derive much but oddity from Mr. Brown's muse. But its attempts as well as its occasional hits have the advantage of less monotony than accompanies many sleeker verses. The stanzas called 'The Bristol Channel,' at any rate, have some striking and unworn images: —

> " The sulky old gray brute !
> But when the sunset strokes him,
> Or twilight shadows coax him,
> He gets so silver-milky,
> He turns so soft and silky,
> He 'd make a water-spaniel for King Knut.
>
> " This sea was Lazarus, all day
> At Dives' gate he lay,
> And lapped the crumbs :
> Night comes ;
> The beggar dies —
> Forthwith the Channel, coast to coast,
> Is Abraham's bosom ; and the beggar lies
> A lovely ghost."

The bent in the direction of what Mr. Gosse calls naturalism in modern poetry, and which has taken such an archaic turn toward the pastoral in Mr. Gale's 'Country Muse,' finds in Mr. Austin's 'Fortunatus the Pessimist' a pastoral expression, curiously intermixed with the conventional as it is in Great British society. The main figure is a Duke Fortunatus, apparently one of the one hundred and fifty who own half of England's acreage, for he is waited on of a morning by the vicar, who wants a new belfry and a new lectern ; by the schoolmaster, who petitions for another wing to the school ; by the hands of the mine, on the one side, and the leasers of the mine, on the other, to settle their labor snarls ; by office-seekers who crave the shire vacancy; and so on in endless bounty-beseeching for what the nobleman is privileged to give, and in this case, does give, right and left, but with a hopeless hand, his one reply being —

> " Answer yes to all,
> And leave all thereby discontented still,
> With satisfaction surfeited."

This joyless benefactor, himself most surfeited with satisfaction,
is then, by the casting of his horse's shoe and the cunning of one
Abaddon, — a mischievous modern species of devil, compounded
of Autolycus and Mephisto, — introduced into the household of
a wonderful yeoman, who boasts of a daughter as good and almost
as wise as she is beautiful, and of a library of sages and poets, and
who proves himself able both to shoe the Pessimist's horse and
mend the Pessimist's philosophy.  Fortunatus blames fate for
stimulating the mind "to invent the arts that undermine the
body," while man, " the dupe and victim of his faculties," takes pride
in this enervation of himself and christens with the "name of
Progress each new link Enslaving him to matter."   The gist of
the franklin's reply is this bit of moral sense : —

> " We feed not on the poisons we discover
> Nor fall upon the sword our wit hath sharpened.
> Why then should man to matter fall a slave,
> Being first so much its master that it yields
> Its secrets to his seeking, nor reject
> Its less ennobling aid and services?
> Let man do all things, but remain himself,
> And 'mid progressive splendour, still maintain
> The lordly rule of simple appetite.
>
>          .      .                    .      .
>
> Life is as large as we ourselves do make it.
> But little room is needed for the scope
> Of individual faculty, desire,
> And practicable duty.   If we fill
> More space than nature hath allotted us,
> We waste ourselves in tenuous expansion,
> And all our force but drifts to feebleness."

If the implications of this speech were followed out consistently, one suspects there would be no room for the pessimistic
occupiers of privilege who "fill more space than nature hath
allotted;" but it is one of the curious inconsequences of Mr.
Austin's allegorical dramas — in ' Prince Lucifer' as in ' Fortunatus'
— that the latter part of his story always proceeds to blunt the

point of the philosophic lance he has earlier worked to sharpen. The wise franklin is made spurious as a franklin. He turns out to be, not one of Nature's own noblemen, after all, but the elder Duke and rightful incumbent of the Pessimist's prerogatives. This present-day Prospero, 'mid tribute of song from his shepherds and ploughers and mowers, and applause from his vicar, schoolmaster, and cottagers, thereupon resumes the load of privilege beneath which Fortunatus staggered, leaving the elderly Ferdinand free to assume "the lowlier tasks that mate with understanding and wise happiness ;" in other words, to shoe horses, and farm in his stead, and — lure in chief ! — to marry his daughter Urania, a book-sophisticated Miranda, whose purity has been unwittingly devoted all these years, moreover, to mothering an unknown child, fruit of her future husband's world-weary dissipations in the "counterfeit" of love. This poor little waif dies conveniently, when marriage consoles her father. Are not the graceful songs, the pastoral scenes, the ingenuity and artifice of the poet thrown away on a conclusion so crippled by conformity with the desires and customs of Philistia? The whole is yet a characteristic product of Great Britain.

In the collected poems of Mr. William Watson there is an affluence of poetic expression, here and there unsupported by inspiration. In 'Mensis Lacrimarum,' for example, the "Month of Tears" is described as " March that comes roaring, maned, with rampant paws, and bleatingly withdraws," and in spite of the apter phrases that follow, the straightforward metaphor of the old proverb that "March comes in like a lion and goes out like a lamb," seems to have the advantage over its versified elaboration. This is a trifling sign, perhaps, of the natural facility which will require the poet to seek an inner wealth to match his outer equipment. Throughout the whole book, within a purely lyric vein, there is no poor range of feeling. A light touch and go of pretty fancy attracts one in ' The Keyboard,' a deeper impress of melancholy is felt in 'World Strangeness,' and a breath of a wilfully wise and human philosophy, reminiscent, unconsciously perhaps, of Browning's ' Rephan,' allures in ' The Dream of Man,' and lurks

at the bottom of a later work, the whimsical 'Eloping Angels,'—a
bit of thistle-down in poetry, suggestive enough if lightly understood, and too impalpable to be stumbled over in dead earnest as
it has been by the captious.

The mellowed craft of Mr. Watson's verse appears advanta-
geously in this sonnet, called 'Vanishings' : —

> "As one whose eyes have watched the stricken day
> Swoon to its crimson death adown the sea,
> Turning his face to eastward suddenly
> Sees a lack-lustre world all chill and gray, —
> Then, wandering sunless whither-so he may,
> Feels the first dubious dumb obscurity,
> And vague fore-gloomings of the Dark to be,
> Close like a sadness round his glimmering way ;
> So I, from drifting dream-bound on and on
> About strange isles of utter bliss, in seas
> Whose waves are unimagined melodies,
> Rose and beheld the dreamless world anew :
> Sad were the fields, and dim with splendours gone
> The strait sky-glimpses fugitive and few."

Others of the poems are the offshoot of criticism of poets,
and in these a too-fondly conservative spirit is plain. It is no less
perceptible, be it understood, that his own poetic gift is a genuine
and native endowment. No man's predilections should determine
his praise as an artist; but inasmuch as they may come to narrow
his power through limiting the growth of his thought-faculty, they
may show the bounds the poet sets to his own future. It is
from this point of view that one may recognize with pleasure
Mr. Watson's instinctive art, and regret the bias that shuts out
his mind from catholicity, — fit pasturage of the greatest poets.
His true appreciation of Tennyson in 'Lachrymæ Musarum,' and
of the Laureate's great predecessor, in 'Wordsworth's Grave,' are
wrought with a magical smoothness which has earned him his early
fame; but his boyish talk of "the froth and flotsom of the Seine,"
of "the Hugo flare against the night and Weimar's proud elaborate
calm" being outweighed by "one flash of Byron's lightning, Wordsworth's light," does not fitly praise either Byron or Wordsworth;
it only exhibits in a silly light the young poet's own mental limita-

tions. It would be a calamity to the growth of mind and pleasure if, instead of enjoying all true characteristics of poetic utterance, one set pattern and polish should be prescribed as supreme. England should stand in no fear of any Renaissance, — that is, of any influx of foreign thought and art-impulse. She has drunk in its heady wine before now with no imitative feebleness, but with reconstructing strength. Æsthetic liberty would serve her now in better stead than insularity. Her present symptoms of poetic sameness and thinness are most apparent in the well-nigh universal re-echoing by her latter-day poets of Tennyson and Wordsworth. It is, in fact, the most hopeful sign of life in English poetry that it has differentiated from these all-on-one-note songsters a Meredith who pours forth a strange, new song to speak for England, alongside of the smooth, idyllic, but less compact strain of a Watson.

Let both speak for England; and the English-speaking world, finding delight in the picturesque and pensive loveliness of ' Vanishings,' may find it no less in the passion-mastery that in ' Modern Love' mirrors mind and heart at the most intimate moment of their interplay. The satire of the materialism and pietism of his countrymen, which leaps out in an odd but ingeniously suitable fashion in Meredith's 'Jump to Glory Jane,' will be least understood by those who most need the tonic of this whim, caught crudely in its own doggerel chains before it could escape a more careful art. Too much should not be made of this caprice ; but it is worth a " wee cantie " smile to hear this woman, whose body " was a harp With winds along the strings," imploring squire and vicar to " up and o'er the flesh with me "!

The sermon George Meredith preaches to " our later Prodigal Son " is, as he says, a "furious Yea of a speech " in the cause he " would have prevail For seed of a nourishing wheat." Whoever goes on to ask, with him —

> " *Is it accepted of song* —
> Does it sound to the mind through the ear
> Right sober, pure sane ? " —

will be likely to find it, as he says, "a test severe." Yet let him

understand the poet's aim, the lofty humanity of his sudden metaphors, the sheer "spirit in verse" which animates his passionless
measures, — let him "drink of faith in the brains a full draught,"
— and he will find it can ring "for Reason a melody clear."

Meredith's poetics are tersely expounded in these lines from
'The Empty Purse' · —

> "No singer is needed to serve
> The musical God, my friend.
> Needs only his law on a sensible nerve :
> A law that to measure invites,
> Forbidding the passions contend."

This is "lean fare, but it carries a sparkle," and offers not
husks to the Prodigal Sons of this earth, but instead —

> "for sustainment supreme,
> The cry of the conscience of Life :
> *Keep the young generations in hail,*
> *And bequeath them no tumbled house !*
> There hast thou the sacred theme,
> Therein the inveterate spur,
> Of the Innermost.  See her one blink
> In vision past eyeballs.  Not thee
> She cares for, but us.  Follow her.
> Follow her, and thou shalt not sink.
> With thy Soul the Life espouse :
> This Life of the visible, audible, ring
> With thy love tight about, and no death will be ;
> The name but an empty thing,
> And woe a forgotten old trick :
> And battle will come as a challenge to drink ;
> As a warrior's wound each transient sting.
> She leads to the Uppermost link by link ;
> Exacts but vision, desires not vows."

In 'Youth in Memory' also, a rare and splendid fire allures
the thought to dwell on the pleasures sacred from sensation,
although they are the fruit of it, for —

> "by the final Bacchic of the lusts
> Propelled, the Bacchic of the spirit trusts."

'Night of Frost in May' and 'Tardy Spring' witness the lighter
response of Meredith's originality to the touch of natural out-
door beauty.  'Tardy Spring,' in particular, sounds a lyric note,

the more persuasive to charm that its sweetness is not artfully prolonged and played upon, but strikes home very simply, its tropes
sounding sententious, its phrases wearing the air of apothegms of
a graceful staccato variety.

> " Now the North wind ceases,
> The warm South-west awakes ;
> Swift fly the fleeces,
> Thick the blossom flakes.

> " Now hill to hill has made the stride,
> And distance waves the without end :
> Now in the breast a door flings wide ;
> Our farthest smiles, our next is friend.
> And song of England's rush of flowers
> Is this full breeze with mellow stops.

> .    .    .    .    .    .

> The stir in memory seem these things,
> Which out of moistened turf and clay,
> Astrain for light push patient rings,
> Or leap to find the water way.
> 'T is equal to a wonder done,
> Whatever simple lives renew
> Their tricks beneath the father sun
> As though they caught a broken clue.

> .    .    .    .    .    .

> But now the North wind ceases,
> The warm South-west awakes,
> The heavens are out in fleeces,
> And earth's green banner shakes."

*P.*

## BOOKS OF CRITICISM.*

ANOTHER volume of the interesting series of poetical criticisms
edited by Prof. Albert S. Cook has recently been issued.
Leigh Hunt's answer to 'What is Poetry?' — being the initial

* Leigh Hunt's ' What is Poetry?' including Remarks on Versifica-
tion, Edited by Albert S. Cook; Analytics of Literature, by L. A.
Sherman. Boston: Ginn & Co. 1893. — Orthometry, a Treatise on
the Art of Versification, with a New and Complete Rhyming Diction-
ary, by R. F. Brewer. New York: G. P. Putnam's Sons. London: C.
W. Deacon & Co. 1893. — Popular Studies of Nineteenth Century
Poets, by J. Marshall Mather. London and New York: Frederick
Warne & Co. 1892.

essay in his volume on 'Imagination and Fancy'—is the choice for the present reprint. The essay is marked by that innate good sense and charm of style for which Leigh Hunt's prose is conspicuous. At a time when the incumbents of the critical office felt it their sacred duty to treat all new poets as so many obstreperous school-boys in need of stern castigation from their masters, the penetrative vision of Leigh Hunt recognized prophets where others saw only drivellers. His sweet wide soul could open to the influences of new beauty, but without losing any of its sensitiveness to that of the past. Speaking of Sir Walter Raleigh's verses on 'The Faery Queene,' in which he said that Petrarch was thenceforward to be no more heard of, and that in all English poetry there was nothing he counted of any price but the effusions of the new author, Hunt laconically remarks, "Yet Petrarch is still living; Chaucer was not abolished by Sir Walter; and Shakespeare is thought somewhat valuable."

The definition of poetry given in this essay is perhaps the most inclusive and satisfactory answer that has been proposed to the stubborn question of "What is poetry?" but a still more interesting topic is the discussion upon the distinction between imagination and fancy. Professor Cook has had the happy thought of printing at the end of the volume extracts from Richter, Coleridge, and Wordsworth, giving their contributions toward the settlement of this difficult question, so that the student may see for himself what a dance imagination and fancy have been led at their hands. Unfortunately, what the English writers call imagination, Richter calls *phantasie;* and after one has firmly grasped the notion that *phantasie* is the "World-soul of the soul" and the "elementary spirit of all other forces," it is confusing to have it in its form *fancy* relegated to a secondary place. The usefulness of this book to students is made complete by the addition of line-numberings, of foot-notes giving the whereabouts of the copious quotations found both in Leigh Hunt's essay and the extracts from the three other writers, and an index of proper names.

The method of the professor of biology who began his instructions to his pupils by placing a basket of clams before them with the directions that they should observe them, and note everything they saw, is fast coming to be the one used in the acquisition of all branches of knowledge. Until recently literature, the supposed spontaneous efflorescence of the mature mind, has flourished apart in a soil where the intrusion of the methods of the analyst or the synthesist were regarded as a pure impertinence. Posnett and then Symonds have been among the few who have ventured to approach the study of literature in a scientific spirit; their methods, however, have been almost entirely of a synthetic character, and therefore somewhat hypothetical, the necessary complementary analyses not having been made. To this side of the subject Professor Sherman has made an important contribution in his 'Analytics of Literature.' The literary critic of the old school who rests upon his intuitive perception of the various qualities of style and so forth, in those authors whom he elects to study, will take fright at the word "analytics;" but Professor Sherman has so broadened the field of investigation that the dry-as-dust terrors with which that word has been associated in the past are completely dissipated. Freed from its scholastic fogs, it merely stands for the common-sense method of the professor of biology before mentioned. Look into your centuries of authors, and note what you find! But the undeveloped mind, having eyes, may yet not see all, nor perhaps even a small part of what is to be seen. To help such minds first to see the facts, then to compare them, then to make deductions from them, is the aim of Professor Sherman.

The book is divided into two parts, — the first treating of poetry, its elements and their development, and the second of prose. The general law in both cases is found to be gradual condensation of style and concentration of thought; and the means by which such results have been accomplished are pointed out at great length. The elements which go to the formation of the art of poetry are severally considered; for example, words are regarded in relation to their suggestive quality, and comparisons are made of the use of such words in the English poets. Upon this one point Professor

Sherman is inclined to lay rather too much stress, for the intrinsic suggestiveness of words depends so largely upon the experience of the individual that a definite conclusion as to which are naturally poetical words is practically impossible.

On the other hand, the poetical quality of words depending upon their allusional and figurative use is much more definite ; and the chapters dealing with this subject, and pointing out the trend of development in their use throughout English poetry, are especially interesting. Other elements considered are Tone Coloring, Rhythm, Metre, and the Theme, which last Professor Sherman wisely considers of paramount importance. " The student's first and perhaps principal task is to determine the significance and importance of the theme. He must identify the inherent ideals to which the poem appeals, and analyze the method and expedients of the author's plan. . . . He will note that the paramount types must be contained, not incidentally in the illustrations, but in the theme itself." The most appreciative piece of special criticism in the book is the chapter on the art of Browning, in which are defined very clearly the underlying causes of the peculiar strength and force of the monologue form as developed by Browning. The principles of dramatic art which he deduces from both Shakespeare and Browning are not altogether self-evident; but if not accepted as conclusive, they are interesting and instructive as individual expressions of opinion.

Though the aim of the book is objective, there is woven in a thread of subjective reasoning, which refers all manifestations of literary art, critical or creative, back to an unknown reality which he calls the *Ego.* The dethronement of *Phantasie* from the high seat upon which Richter placed it is complete. Not only is it no longer the elementary spirit, it is but a mode of that spirit; not only is it a little lower than imagination, where Coleridge, Wordsworth, and Leigh Hunt placed fancy, but it is almost the exact opposite of imagination. Phantasy, as he defines it, is the faculty of the mind which reproduces what it has seen or heard, by aid of the memory alone. "What we put in as essential for truth's sake is of the phantasy, what for our pleasure is of the imagination." Many readers will find it hard to divest their minds of associations, decidedly imaginative, which have gathered about the word "phantasy;" and it may be questioned whether it would not have been better to choose some other word to designate the simple processes of perception and memory. The main point to be noted in connection with his æsthetical theories is his insistence upon the moral uses of art and poetry, — "the end of culture is the spiritual life." "Poets do not fulfil their mission in raising all men to the accomplishment of knowing and admiring their work. They are only models by whom all may learn how to be their own interpreters and see the open secrets at first hand for themselves. . . . Every man his own seer and poet is the end of culture and the consummation of society."

The sections devoted to the consideration of prose will be found no less interesting and suggestive than those on poetry.

Professor Sherman claims for his book that it is a guide to students and teachers. If it were only that, there is more than one excursus which we should think might serve to confuse an immature student; it is, however, much more than a mere text-book, for while there is much in the working out of the principles enunciated which will in many quarters not meet with immediate acceptance, the principles themselves are sound, founded upon a definite yet broad basis, and it is to be hoped that Professor Sherman's setting forth of them will have a beneficial effect upon the at present much-abused art of criticism.

The would-be poet will find no lack of aids in these latter days for the sharpening of his blunt faculties. One of the most complete hand-books upon the art of versification is R. F. Brewer's 'Orthometry.' The book may safely be placed in the hands of the most innocent young poet, for there are no new theories in it to upset the time-honored rules of the rhetoricians. The clumsy terms, survivals from the classic days of quantitative rhythm, are retained. English poetry is still described as going upon feet shod in trochees, iambuses, dactyls, and anapests, when it might better be said to wing its flight through airy spaces. The consequences of holding to the old-fashioned feet, instead of regarding accent

only, as the more advanced critics of versification do, is that a
large proportion of the best poetry has to be explained under the
head of poetical licenses.  However, poets must learn to walk before they can fly, and a better book for initiating them in the first
steps could hardly be found.  The descriptions of the different
kinds of poetry, and of the various stanza forms, are concise and
instructive.  There is an interesting chapter upon the development
of versification, and one on imitative harmony, which sensibly
points out the limitations of the *Onomatopoetic* or " Bow-wow "
theory of language.  An account of the English works upon versification and a dictionary of rhymes complete this well-edited
volume.

Very pleasant reading one will find in the ' Popular Studies of
Nineteenth Century Poets,' by J. Marshall Mather.  They were
originally a series of lectures delivered to a class of working-men.
Without being very profound, they all show a just appreciation of
the poets considered, and are calculated to inspire an interest in
poetry, not as a pastime for idle moments, but as a very present
help in living a more ideal life.

*C.*

## BOOK INKLINGS.

Mrs. Dall's ' Barbara Fritchie ' is as truly a memorial of Whittier
as if it had been altogether from the first so planned.  His death
came before his friend could have the pleasure she intended of showing him her valiant vindication of a poem so verily begotten of the
genius of the Civil War that it aroused in its early readers the same
loyal but contending sectional feelings.  The piece itself, ' Barbara
Frietchie,' was clearly a poetic stroke which turned the force of a
casual picturesque incident to internal and spiritual effect.  Without
the verse the deed would have been lost, frittered away in a newspaper paragraph, or else mislaid in a dry foot-note to some tiresome
county history, to meet there only the blear eyes of an annalist,
with all its "ifs" upon its head so heavy that no one would ever be
stirred to strike out of it its latent fire.  The poet, whose soul was
like a flame within some meek gray dove, discovered the human
value of the deed when he made it into a poem.  The "ifs" that

ventured to attack its efficacy Mrs. Dall has shown are all the sum of nothing, since the vitality of it is real; and if the occurrence the verses sing happened not in the morning, if Stonewall Jackson was not at that time " riding ahead " of his troops, and if the " banner " was not " rent " by the " rifle-blast," — none of which small matters so befell, and over which there has been much pother, — what matter ? How many of the facts of the story were real, provable, or probable, Mrs. Dall has taken much pains to ascertain. Many readers will wish to follow her clear guidance for themselves, and many more, in the future, will be grateful to her for pushing her inquiries while yet it was possible ; for we cannot but believe that the contact of creative literature and the well of life from which it draws its sustenance is an increasingly interesting and profitable point of study. (Barbara Fritchie : A Study, by Caroline H. Dall. With portrait of Barbara, and picture of her house, from photographs. Boston: Roberts Brothers, 1892. $1.00.) —— GINN & Co. will increase their already enviable reputation as publishers of works of genuine worth by the issue of ' Old English Ballads,' selected and edited by Prof. F. B. Gummere, of Haverford College, author of the valuable little Handbook of Poetics, etc. This volume is now in press, and will make available, in condensed and popularized yet scholarly shape, a much larger body of literature than could be otherwise given ; for the aim is to present the best of the traditional English and Scottish ballads and also to make the collection representative. The publishers announce that the texts have been taken by permission from Professor Child's monumental edition, with no " improvements " whatsoever, and but few changes in arrangement. The *Gest* of Robin Hood is given entire, not only for its intrinsic merits, but to assist in the study of epic development. The glossary will be found full ; but simple philological details have been given only when the explanation of the passage rendered them necessary. The introduction presents a detailed study of popular poetry and the views of its chief critics, with notes on metre and style. —— THE name of Mr. Beeching's anthology suits its nature and tells its story perfectly. It is most truly a ' Paradise of English Poetry,' from whose " Garden of the Dead " one misses almost none of the choicest flowers of our earlier English stock. Here are charming naïveties of unknown parentage selected from old Tudor collections, and the most odorous buds of pretty rhythm due to Raleigh, Campion, Daniel, Brooke, Breton, or quaint Dr. Donne, as well as the better-known blooms of Chaucer, Shakespeare, or Milton. Besides these, there are many posies from the modern flowerage of Coleridge, Wordsworth, Shelley, Keats, and

Blake, and Beddoes, but further down in time Mr. Beeching's cullings do not go. These two volumes, however, will be the more desirable books for many shelves, because the goodly space of their luxurious wide-margined pages is chiefly taken up with the older and rarer poems. The classifications, — Love, Patriotism, Nature, Death, etc., — under which the compiler has exercised his good taste, add further to the value of the collection. This, with the little volume Mr. Watson has gathered and entitled happily from Browning, 'Lyric Love,' would suffice to equip one with an admirable library of the best of poetry. For although poems of love make up an important first division of Mr. Beeching's, and all of Mr. Watson's anthology, there are barely twenty duplicates, the two editors having proceeded on different principles in making their selections; and Mr. Beeching having given much larger space to Elizabethan pens, where Mr. Watson has preferred the Cavalier circle, and has included much work of modern, and also of many living writers on whom Mr. Beeching has not drawn at all. The disadvantage of Mr. Watson's principle of selection, which seems to have been the choice of such poems and ballads as by the genuineness of their love or the beauty of their art stood the test of modern ideas of love and art, is that the characteristic differences of each literary epoch do not appear so markedly. This disadvantage will be a merit to many persons who are of Mr. Watson's mind; but these differences being in themselves interesting, and the art of any past period being open to the very heart only through æsthetic sympathy, there are many early poems which are both beautiful and true to their time if judged by their own measures, whose truth and beauty the editor, picking with an eye to modern standards, would fail to perceive. Here the 'Paradise' unconsciously supplements 'Lyric Love;' while the latter, too, adds greatly to the former through its wealth of examples of what love means to such moderns as Elizabeth Barrett Browning, the two Rossettis, Coventry Patmore, and Robert Bridges; although one misses from these any word of Robert Browning's, and but one — and that 'Love within the Lover's Breast' — of George Meredith. An ideal anthology would be one that gave full representation to the most intimate utterances of all epochs on the main subjects that have exercised the best art of English poets; and this these collections taken together almost supply. (A Paradise of English Poetry. Arranged by H. C. Beeching. Vols. I. and II. New York: Macmillan and Co., 1893. $6.00. Lyric Love: An Anthology. Edited by William Watson. Golden Treasury Series. London and New York, 1892. $1.25.) —— ALPHONSE DAUDET has arranged with Messrs. Ginn and Co. for a volume of selections from his works, and has written a piece specially for this volume. The book is designed for use in high school and college classes, and will be specially annotated for this use by Prof. Frank W. Freeborn, of the Boston Latin School. —— ALL students of Cowper will be eager to possess themselves of Mr. Thomas Wright's biography of the poet. Mr. Wright has a great deal to say concerning the habitual depression of mind so characteristic of the author of 'The Task,' and while admitting inherited melancholia, suggests the possibility of other things co-operating to derange or impair his mind. The influence of Newton, it appears, counts for something; but a singular dream Cowper had in the winter of 1773 seems to have told most injuriously on his vivid imagination. However, for full discussion of these theories we await Mr. Wright's book. —— WORD reaches us from Mesnil-Dramard & Co. of a new volume by Mr. Theodore Tilton, entitled 'The Chameleon's Dish, a Book of Lyrics and Ballads, founded on the Hopes and Illusions of Mankind.' The book consists of about thirty different pieces, — in various keys, grave and gay, — written during Mr. Tilton's residence in Paris, and now published for the first time.

## NOTES AND NEWS.

DOROTHY WORDSWORTH'S journal often yields a witness that she was a latent poet; and one of the happiest of these glimpses of a nature open to poetic impression is given in this passing word about a birch-tree : —

"As we went along we were stopped, at once, at a distance of perhaps fifty yards from our favorite birch tree. It was yielding to a gust of wind, with all its tender twigs ; the sun shone upon it and it glanced in the wind like a flying sunshiny shower. It was a tree in shape, with stem and branches, but it was like a spirit of water."

—— THE Browning Courtship story which Mrs. Louise Chandler Moulton told as she had it from Browning's own lips, in the

March POET-LORE, has been appreciated so thoroughly by some English newspapers that they have forgotten it was not a tale of their own. Mrs. Moulton writes, —

" Looking over some back numbers of the *Sunday Sun* (London), I find this cool appropriation of our story, with no credit either to POET-LORE or to me. I saw another London paper (I forget what, now) where it was stolen in the *same* way, as very likely it was by many I did not see. The *New York Tribune* did give us both credit."

The clipping from the *Sun* which Mrs. Moulton enclosed gave the story itself precisely as it appeared in this magazine, but considerately ignored all sources, including the poet himself, the original authority, — perhaps in order to show that literary piracy, even in small matters, is not an exclusively American faculty.

—— MR. DOLE's verses, in the March POET-LORE, ' To a Beautiful Nun,' have called out the following lines from Miss Ray : —

### THE NUN'S REPLY.

I thank you kindly, gallant scribe,
    For penning lines to one
Who, though her mind 's on higher things,
    Is woman more than nun.

Your words are sweet unto my ear,
    Your incense to my nose ;
Perchance the violet 's as vain
    As is the flaunting rose.

Though living in the cloistered shade,
    We read the daily news ;
And now I take my pen in hand,
    To rectify your views.

My many talents 't is a sin
    Within a cloth to hide ;
And yet I do assure you, sir,
    The napkin 's not too wide.

My voice, you say, is rich and strong,
  Yet few men would admire;
Its upper tones are far too shrill
  For aught but angel choir.

My face would grace society
  And call forth thoughts of love;
But yet, beneath my hood, my hair
  Is growing thin above.

But chief of all the reasons, sir,
  Why I the world do shun,
Lies in the deeds of sordid greed
  My dressmaker has done.

For years I bore her tyrant rule,
  Nor dared I to rebel;
But e'en the worm will turn, in time,
  And so I broke her spell.

Here, far from fashion's wilful course
  And Mrs. Grundy's whims,
I live in peace, and only mourn
  In thinking of her sins.

And, sitting in the cloister dim,
  Above all thoughts of pelf,
By one unchanging pattern now,
  I make my gowns myself.

*Anna Chapin Ray.*

# SOCIETIES.

The L. L. C. Shakespearian Group of Grand Rapids held a memorial meeting, Jan. 12, 1893, in honor of the three great poets who have died within the last year, — Whitman, Whittier, and Tennyson. The afternoon's programme, presided over by Mrs. Loraine Immen, chairman for the occasion, was as follows : —

> " For words like nature half reveal
> And half conceal the soul within."
> — *Members of the L. L. C. S. G.*

> " And for love, sweet love, but praise! praise! praise!"
> — *Whitman.*

> " Forgive me if too close I lean
> My human heart on Thee."
> — *Whittier.*

> " I have not lacked thy mild reproof
> Nor golden largess of thy praise."
> — *Tennyson.*

READINGS : — 'The Miracles of Nature,' 'The Miller's Daughter,' 'Snow Bound.'

In response to the several sentiments the lives and works of the three poets were admirably considered. Over fifty members were present, and all expressed great pleasure in the afternoon's programme.

Woodland Shakespeare Club. — The study of 'Henry VI.,' 'Richard III.,' 'Merry Wives of Windsor,' 'Merchant of Venice,' and 'Hamlet' has been shared with that of 'The Jew of Malta' and 'The Duchess of Malfi' by the Woodland Shakespeare Club during the year ending May, '93. A new feature of its analytical work has proved most successful. This is the propounding of a stated number of questions, by every member of the Club instead of the President alone, at the finished reading of each play. This gives to all the analysis of many minds of varied cast, and promotes individual research into every line of thought. It intensifies and maintains interest, and vitalizes a body of students much more strongly than impromptu criticism (which is still carried on in each weekly reading) or by any other method hitherto adopted by the Club.

*Mrs. S. E. Peart, Pres.*

Vol. V.

No. 10.

——— wilt thou not haply ſaie,
Truth needs no colloue with his cullour fixt,
Beautie no penſell, beauties truth to lay:
But beſt is beſt if neuer intermixt.
Becauſe he needs no praiſe, wilt thou be dumb?
Excuſe not ſilence ſo, for't lies in thee,
To make him much outliue a gilded tombe:
And to be praiſed of ages yet to be.
Then do thy office ———

# A PHASE OF WILLIAM BLAKE'S
# ROMANTICISM.

R. WALTER PATER has described the romantic temper in its technical sense as one that possesses, in
addition to the love of beauty, which is an integral part
of every artistic nature, the element of curiosity. By
virtue of this element, there exists a longing for fresh impressions,
a sense of satiety of the old, and a seeking after a departure from
precedent into untried regions and untrodden fields. This, which
Mr. Pater calls the element of curiosity, may be said to exist in all
romanticists, but in the higher types of the school it deserves the
name of originality. In them the mere spirit of inquiry into the
novel leads to creation. The classic temperament, on the contrary,
clings to the models established by the artists of the past, and sees
in these alone the basis for all canons of true art. Its outcome is
an adherence to form, unbalanced by an intuitive discernment of
the prompting spirit. It is when the two are united in one man
that the product of highest genius is given. Dante claims Virgil
as his guide, and the five noble poets to whom he awards the

meed of admiration are classic authors of greater or less repute; yet Dante can feel the charm of the "sweet new style," and can throw the light of romantic beauty around Francesca da Rimini and Ugolino. Shakespeare and Milton are by no means free from a debt to the past, but whatever their fancy touches —

> "Doth suffer a sea-change
> Into something rich and strange."

Such a blending, however, of the classic and romantic elements is as rare as genius, and in any age the preponderance of the one over the other is to be detected. It is as men's minds have been stirred with creative enthusiasm and a craving for true self-expression, or as conventionalism has satisfied them, and a subservience to the most minute of established details, that the romantic temper or its opposite has colored the age in which they have lived. The conditions of the present day with its gloomy dearth of romantic writers are closely akin to those prevailing in England during the latter part of the eighteenth and early in the nineteenth centuries. This was the age of classicism. The creative imagination must work strictly under the stern control of Reason. As in the pulpit the divines held out to their hearers no sweet high realms

> "Above the smoke and stir of this dim spot
> Which men call earth,"

but treated them instead to maxims of wise morality, so in the poetic world imagination must give way to the expression of sage truths and sententious utterances to which the prim couplet was essentially adapted.

In such a period as this, William Blake is a figure of peculiar individuality. He was a romanticist by nature, and no surrounding influences of classicism could completely control him. He rebelled against the very form of verse then in vogue, which was too confining a channel for his turbid imagination. He knew what it was

> "To see a world in a grain of sand,
> And a heaven in a wild flower;
> Hold infinity in the palm of your hand,
> And eternity in an hour;"

and to the rush and melody of his thoughts he forced the verse to conform. The workings of his inner nature were far from normal, and in proportion as they were complicated, it was necessary that the substance in which his thoughts were clothed should be pliant material in his imagination's hands.

In no feature of Blake's style is this fact so strongly indicated as in his use of figures. They serve him in their proper province, as tools for the clear delineation of the pictures with which his fancy is teeming. He never forces them irrelevantly; with the tact of a writer in harmony with his theme, he omits them entirely where the simple narrative pictures the scene or object with sufficient vividness. Perhaps the poem of " Holy Thursday " furnishes as apt an illustration as any of his moderation. The description there is absolutely direct, yet the figures are so suggestive that their boldness does not in the least mar the simplicity of the whole —

> " The hum of multitudes was there, but multitudes of lambs,
> Thousands of little boys and girls raising their innocent hands.
> Now like a mighty wind they raise to heaven the voice of song,
> Or like harmonious thunderings the seats of heaven among;
> Beneath them sit the aged men, wise guardians of the poor,
> Then cherish pity, lest you drive an angel from your door."

This use of a figure to suggest an entire scene is frequent in Blake's poems, and serves to connect him strikingly with the romantic movement. Where a classicist revels in a minute and detailed description, Blake with a word strikes the correct cord of association. He finds an adequate descriptive power in such expressions as, —

> " Tiger, Tiger, burning bright
> In the forests of the night; "
>> (' The Tiger.' )

and, —

> " Every tear from every eye
> Becomes a babe in eternity ;
> The bleat, the bark, bellow and roar
> Are waves that beat on heaven's shore ; "
>> (' Auguries of Innocence.')

or again, —

> " When the silent sleep
> Waves o'er heaven deep."
>
> ('A Little Girl Lost.')

In the poem of ' London,' too, there is a forcible expression of the
same type : —

> " In every cry of every man,
> In every infant's cry of fear,
> In every voice, in every brain,
> The mind-forged manacles I hear."

The last verse in its simplicity presents, as no detailed description
could, the picture of a world " groaning and travailing together."
In ' Broken Love,' also, whatever the poem may mean, there is
no question that this characteristic pervades the figures of the
lines : —

> " A dark winter deep and cold
> Within my heart thou dost unfold ;
> Iron tears and groans of lead
> Thou bindest round my aching head."

In Blake's personifications this suggestive power of which I am
speaking, manifests itself very clearly.  Personification was a pet
figure with the classicists ; they had found Fortuna, Pax, Con-
cordia scattered through the pages of their Ovids and Horaces,
and they flattered themselves that if only they gave an abstract
quality a capital letter at the beginning of its name, they were
classical.  That the old mythology was a growth, that the existence of these gods was ever believed in, did not come within their
mental ken, and as if the ancient models in cold blood had created
a Pantheon, so these disciples sought to follow in the footsteps
of their masters by simply turning out divinities by the line ; the
more capital letters the better poet.  " Sweet Memory," sings
Rogers,

> " From Thee gay Hope her airy coloring draws ;
> And Fancy's flights are subject to thy laws.
> From Thee that bosom-spring of rapture flows,
> Which only Virtue, tranquil Virtue, knows."

But Blake does not let Conscience speak, without allowing us to hear seraphic melodies and listen to angelic choirs singing in harmony with her tones.

> " When neither warbling voice
> Nor trilling pipe is heard, nor pleasure sits
> With trembling age, the voice of Conscience then,
> Sweeter than music in a summer's eve
> Shall warble round the snowy head, and keep
> Sweet symphony to feathered angels, sitting
> As guardians round your chair ; then shall the pulse
> Beat slow, and taste and touch and sight and sound and smell
> That sing and dance round Reason's fine-wrought throne,
> Shall flee away, and leave him all forlorn ;
> Yet not forlorn if Conscience is his friend. "
>
> (' King Edward III.')

Particularly noticeable, too, in contrast with the ponderous movement of classicism is the light, airy grace of his fancy in ' Memory, hither come,' and the peculiarly characteristic personification that occurs in the 'Cradle Song ' : —

> "Sleep, sleep; in thy sleep
> Little sorrows sit and weep."

Not only abstractions, however, did Blake personify ; but seeing as he did, with double vision, he could discern in all the objects of Nature a twofold essence : —

> " With my inward eye 't is an old man gray,
> With my outward a thistle across my way."

The universe had for him a slender reality in comparison with the spiritual truths that, to his mind, it bodied forth; and just because it existed for him as an allegory, he was peculiarly apt in endowing abstractions and objects of Nature with a personal existence. Her every phase has a fantastic meaning of its own. She is a thesaurus from which he draws at pleasure : —

> " I walked abroad on a snowy day,
> I asked the soft Snow with me to play;
> She played and she melted in all her prime ;
> And the Winter called it a dreadful crime."
>
> (' Couplets and Fragments,' I.)

In the 'Mad Song,' for example, not a single natural object nor an element is mentioned that is not endowed with a strange,

wild life. If a man sees spirits, fiends, and angels lurking in
the objects about him, a personification of Nature is absolutely
essential to the expression of his imagination.

> " With a blue sky spread over with wings,
>   And a mild sun that mounts and sings ;
>   With trees and fields full of fairy elves,
>   And little devils who fight for themselves,
>
> .    .    .    .    .    .    .    .
>
>   With angels planted in hawthorn bowers,
>   And God himself in the passing hours."

Such a treatment of Nature as this stands in strong relief to that
employed by the eighteenth century poets.   They regarded her as
a series of phenomena, so judiciously ordered as to be worthy of
deep admiration and respect.   Thomson, though undoubtedly a
more intense lover of Nature than most of his contemporaries,
handles her formally.

> " These roving mists that constant now begin
>   To smoke along the hilly country,"

serves as an opportunity to discourse on theories of the sages in
physical geography ; nevertheless, he impresses us with his own
careful observation of Nature, and shows plainly that he had
watched the "father of the tempest" come forth " wrapped in
black glooms," so that he is able to describe his actions with
greater accuracy and feeling than the majority of his fellow-poets
could have manifested.   With Blake, however, the case is entirely
different.   With an imagination capable of seeing spiritual truths
in the world about him, he does not surprise us when we find
even in his figures that truest indication of a love of Nature, a
susceptibility to her sympathy with human feeling.   The ' Laughing Song,' for instance, fairly ripples with the sound of laughter ·

> " When the green woods laugh with the voice of joy,
>   And the dimpling stream runs laughing by.
>   When the air does laugh with our merry wit,
>   And the green hill laughs with the noise of it."

But his imagination increased Blake's sympathy also, and gave
him the power of understanding the aspirations of man for the
ideal world.   However complex and elusive his theory of Nature

may be, this is plainly a moral truth that he finds her setting forth. To this theme he devotes, with a curious union of mystery and power, the 'Daughter of Thel,' and the shorter lyric, 'Ah! Sunflower,' which is so characteristic that it serves as its own apology for quotation.

> "Ah! Sunflower! weary of time,
> Who countest the steps of the sun;
> Seeking after that sweet golden prime
> When the traveller's journey is done;
>
> "Where the youth pined away with desire,
> And the pale virgin shrouded in snow,
> Arise from their graves and aspire
> Where my sunflower wishes to go."

In another and less subjective feature do Blake's figures indicate the extent to which he belonged to romanticism. Men were tired of cut and dried phrases in letters, bereft of meaning by incessant use; and when Macpherson's 'Ossian' appeared, they welcomed with keen delight its sonorous turns and rolling lines, vigorous with the sound of war and strife. Blake, with his sense of harmony and his need for the free expression of his boisterous imagination, readily imbibed the spirit of these poems, and in more than one place do we detect him using Ossianic figures. The thistle, that we have already found he saw as an old man, had appeared in the poems 'Carthon' and 'Lathmon' in the same guise; and just as in 'Gwin, King of Norway,' the hosts of men dash down the hillsides "like rushing mighty floods," or move along "like tempests black," so in 'Cath-Loda' and 'Temora' we have this same murmuring of waters and rolling of seas. There is, moreover, a general resemblance of thought which, perhaps, predominates over verbal similarity.

Thus, finally, by his literary taste as well as by his power in picturesque suggestion, in ideal delineation of a scene, and in spiritualizing Nature, — by his appreciation, also, of Nature's beauties, — Blake shows himself distinctly a romantic poet. The sense that his poems awaken, Rossetti's words describing that which Blake had attained best express: "Tenderness, the constant unison of wonder and familiarity, so mysteriously allied in nature; the sense of fulness and abundance, such as we feel in a field, not because we pry into it all, but because it is all there." He comes with the sunlight of poetic feeling through the heavy air of classicism, and while he eludes us with his imagery he fascinates us with an imagination of the most mystical type : —

> " For double the vision my eyes do see,
> And double the vision always with me."

*Lucy Allen Paton.*

# THE MISTRESS OF THE RED LAMP

C(arlotta) R(egina).

> " *But take it — earnest wed to sport*
> *And either sacred unto you.*"

IN a city of the South there is a long high room, in which a red lamp burns continually. By day and night in the rich, darkened room its flame never goes out; and by its side sits the mistress of the lamp. Her eyes and hair are the color of night, and her ways are the ways of a queen-witch, who knows that her subjects cannot but obey her. Many are the slaves of the lamp and of its mistress. Even I, who am of the North and not of the South, have known her power and done homage to her queenship. I can bear witness that she is no tyrant, but of infinite condescension. She will unbend even to the meanest of her vassals. She has gone a-hunting in the forest, with a single Page like Schön-Rohtraut. But no Page was ever so daring as was Schön-Rohtraut's; nor did all the leaves on the trees ever lisp and whisper the pretty secret that he had looked longingly at her and had kissed her on the lips.

The red lamp was a centre of light in that city, and many were drawn by it into the presence-chamber of its mistress. Whether it was the lamp Aladdin found in the wonderful garden, and by merely touching it, the slaves came, I cannot tell. There was some white witchcraft about it, some sweet compulsion, which, after all, may have lain not in the lamp, but in the lady. Just without the circle of its red rays, between the light and the mysterious shadow, sat the mistress of the lamp enthroned; and it is in that pose that her liegemen best remember her. It was there that she received votive offerings of flowers; there she held her audiences; there was much incense burned, as before a shrine. Very often this audience-chamber would be thronged with levees of young men and maidens; and in place of courtly silence or decorous murmurs, there was the sound of many light voices talking, of clear laughter, and of tinkling music. A hush would fall upon the gay assembly, when some one in a corner swept the plectrum over the strings of a mandolin, or when a singer stood up to sing. The songs were quite unfashionable songs; for they had pith and mean-ing, and they wavered between smiles and tears. They were old ballads about hard-hearted Barbara Allan, or lays of Green Bushes, or tender, gallant, little preachments on the text, "Love is not love Which alters when it alteration finds." Their memory cannot wither.

The Mistress of the Lamp was the soul and centre of it all; but she did not sing nor deal with any instrument of music. The harmonies which she created were the visible and unheard rhythms of color. With a deftness that had something of magic in it (I have called her a witch) she would change a blank square of canvas or white paper into a mirror of stream and sky, of wood and field; and excursions into the surrounding champaign were often needful to find nooks worthy the honor of her highness' portrayal. One Spring day with a single attendant she visited for this purpose the old fortress which once defended the city. That was a borrowed day, a day to be marked in the calendar with white chalk. The May sun shone bright and warm on the earthen mounds and wide embrasures, through which huge guns looked out on the broad, rippling water. The long grass waved high over the grim engines of destruction, and the spirit of gladness was in the air. You sat in the deep-arched doorway of the inner citadel, and with your swift pencil caught and fixed some of the beauty of the day. Children of some soldier, black-eyed and foreign-looking, strayed from the deserted barracks, and came to you shyly when you spoke. The moving picture of which you were the centre was even better worth looking at than the one which grew so fast under your skilful fingers.

When we came back to the city, we became aware that we had been living, for some hours, far away from the work-a-day world and its briers. We promised ourselves many more such escapes. But the other days to be marked with white never came.

*Archibald MacMechan.*

# THE SUPERNATURAL IN SHAKESPEARE:

## I. 'MACBETH'; 'A MIDSUMMER NIGHT'S DREAM.'

IN considering the place occupied by the supernatural in Shakespeare's dramas the student must bear in mind that he lived in an age when the belief in such things was universal; when the presence of beings of another race and another world, their subjection to magic acts and their influence upon human life, made a part of the environment in which men lived. Supernatural agencies were looked for on every hand; the realms of nature and of mind were alike held to be controlled by spirits, good or bad as might be, but always potent. In every wood and stream, in the depths of the seas, and in the encircling air, dwelt nymphs and naiads; fairies hid in the cups of flowers; the homely brownie lurked beside the hearth-stone, and the mermaiden's strains floated over the moonlit ocean.

The gods of heathenesse still survived as malevolent demons; Woden rode upon the storm-blast, not as its cloud-compelling master, but as the Wild Huntsman, pursued by demon-hounds; Frau Venus lured Tannhäuser to perdition in her subterranean palace ; and the fair Moon-Goddess, as Hecate, ruled a band of midnight hags.

Enchanters there were, who, strong and mighty, claimed to constrain spirits to do their will, since they had mastered some of the laws by which the universe was fashioned and maintained ; who comprehended the motion of the constellations, and could read the destinies of men written upon the starry skies, or penetrate to the chemic forces of nature in their mysterious lurking-places.

There were witches, who had snatched by hellish arts at some scraps of knowledge, who could destroy cattle and blight the standing corn ; raise tempests, and foretell the future ; but their art was imperfect, devilish, —

> " It leads to bewilder,
> And dazzles to blind ! "

That Shakespeare should have believed much of what all others of his day believed is probable ; that he believed with his imagination, with his heart if not with his head, is certain, and he addressed himself to a public who did believe entirely. His fairies and witches, his Calibans and Ariels, have a reality in their ideality, are types and individuals both, to as great a degree as any of his mortal heroes and heroines ; but to comprehend and enjoy we too must believe.

The scene of ‘ Macbeth ’ is laid in a land which is the chosen abode of wild and fantastic romance. In the Highland lakes, monsters, " the relics of an earlier world," were believed to exist yet ; the ourisk haunted the hidden cave ; around " the wind-swept Orcades " still rang the cries of demon-worshippers, who sought with ghastly rites the gift of " second sight." Among the heather-clad Lowlands Thomas the Rhymer had heard " the horns of Elf-land faintly blowing," and bell-fringed bridles ringing clear, as the Queen of the Fairies, robed in mantle of green, rode with her train out of the grassy hillside, and led him away with her to a home of wonder and delight. There had the spae-wife vainly warned the first James of the death that awaited him at Perth, and the spirit of the Rhymer prophesied the repeated risings of Castle Dangerous from its ruins; and there, by Tweedside, slept in fair Melrose the wizard, Michael Scott, with his mighty book upon his breast, and the ever-burning lamp by his side. Who now could tread the soil of Scotland and not yield to magic spells, not see the witches rush past upon the blasted heath, nor fancy Roslyn Castle blazing with presageful fires, nor hear the holly-bush rustle as it bends beneath the airy coming of the White Lady of Avenel?

In such a land and in such an age we should expect the super-natural, and we find it awaiting us at the threshold of the drama. The play opens in a desert place, a lonely heath, and we see three strange creatures, the witches, on their way from some horrible *Sabbat*, and planning another meeting. As Coleridge has said, their appearance strikes the key-note of the whole play, and prepares us for something extraordinary and awful.

Again we meet them, and hear their "Hail Macbeth," as the conquering chieftain enters, exultant from the field of victory, with Banquo by his side. They speak the things that are theirs to tell, and vanish into air. "The earth has bubbles as the water hath, And these are of them;" but into the mind of one man they have looked, and seen the germs of evil which are one day to grow into outward and visible deeds of crime, while in the pure soul of the other blooms already the noble whiteness of honor and of truth. Once more we see the sisters, when their mistress, Hecate, rebukes their daring in trafficking with Macbeth without her sanction, who could have shown "the glories of their art;" and again, when with proper infernal rites they display to the arrogant tyrant the full resources of their skill, lead him, by juggling with the truth, to his doom, and blast his vision with the sight of the long line of mon-archs that claim descent from his murdered comrade, that "silent father of the kings to be."

What are these beings that make treason and murder more awful by their presence, and show us evil incarnate in their direful forms? Are they witches, or fates, or Norns, or all in one? Whence did Shakespeare learn their nature, and what is their purpose in the drama?

It has been clearly shown that they include every attribute of the witch : they are akin to the Thessalian sorceresses, who could call down the moon from heaven, and who predicted to Pompeius the fate that awaited him at Pharsalia ; to Medæa, with her honey-cakes and poisons and her rejuvenating caldron ; to Canidia, in the alley of Horatian Rome, as well as to the witches of the sixteenth century. A witch, like the enchantresses of the Arabian Nights, could change her form at will ; but whatever animal shape she might assume, she was betrayed by the lack of the tail, as was the ghastly were-wolf of the German forests.

> " And like a rat without a tail,
> I 'll do, I 'll do, I 'll do 1 "

sings one of the witches. They could raise storms, and overthrow tower and castle, though the consecrated bells protected the church's spire ; they could stir up the sea to its depths, and bury ship and crew beneath the whelming waves. James VI. of Scotland, returning from Denmark with his bride, narrowly escaped destruction from their spells, and instituted a series of witch-trials that brought about the deaths of hundreds, and of which the records yet remain for our instruction in such matters. Strangest of all, there were found many who not only confessed their guilt, but accused themselves, describing the fell arts by which they had put the waters in a roar, and purchasing a brief notoriety by a fearful doom. These sorceresses, notably those of Lapland, kept winds for sale, and disposed of them carefully knotted together, or wrapped in napkins ; and many a sailor, more lucky than Odysseus, secured a speedy voyage and safe return by paying money down, and taking good heed to his easily scattered purchase. So in the play the second witch says to the first, " I 'll give thee a wind." " And I another," adds the third sister. These " posters over sea and land " travel in sieves, as did the witches of Hellas ; they melt into the air and vanish from sight; they prepare a loathsome brew in their hellish caldron out of all noisome things ; they can look into the future, and " say which grain shall grow, and which shall not," and can destroy human life by melting a waxen image, which, like the brand of Meleager, causes life to waste slowly away. — " He shall dwindle, peak and pine."

So far these strange beings bear the witches' mark beyond a doubt; but they are more than this. They are the Weird Sisters, as Holinshed tells us, when he relates the story, as they name themselves. The word is of old English origin, and means the thing spoken, the fate. The force of the word has unhappily become somewhat weakened in our day, when it is applied to anything odd or unusual, from a spider to a bonnet; but in the happier time of " Shakespeare's language," it had a solemn meaning. "A man must dree his weird," says the Scottish proverb; he must work out his own destiny, bear his own fate. And these dread beings recall the Parcæ, the Fatal Sisters, who spin, and direct, and cut the thread of life, twisting " the mingled threads of joy and woe." Are they also the Norns of Scandinavian myth, the Past, the Present, and the Future, the fates of the austere North? They are each of these, combined into something that is quite like none, yet bears the stamp of all. They typify the belief of all ages and of all climes, and yet are individual, dread servants and prophets of doom, who tempt and warn at once, by showing what is possible to each human soul. No common witches they, to frighten old women and be haled before a judge, but the dread handmaidens of Satan himself, yet capable of becoming to the upright in heart the warning messengers of the Almighty. Such they are to Banquo, who sees that he should guard more closely yet " the bird in his bosom," the priceless treasure of an honorable soul ; but to Macbeth, in whose heart evil thoughts are already lurking, they awaken all secret aspirations, and embody them, born suddenly into the light. Or they are the outward opportunity, touching into flame the hidden spark, when the thought, that might have been crushed in the darkness, becomes a deed, and blazes in all its horror before the eyes of men.

From the wind-swept moors and misty hills of Scotland, we pass to a summer night in a wood near Athens, — Athens, the home of all sweet and gracious ideals, where the divinest gods of the Hellenic heaven bore sway ; and we are ushered into a world of faëry, the most exquisite and fantastically charming that was ever depicted for the delight of man.

Here we may know the life and character of these airy creatures, the children of the twilight and the soft, fragrant darkness, of the home where judgment sleeps, and dreamy fancy rules. " Such stuff as dreams are made on " are these delicate beings, and they fade in the clear, hard light of common day and of common-sense, although they are immortal in that realm which is illumined by " the light that never was on land or sea, the consecration and the poet's dream." In his fairies, as in his witches, Shakespeare has combined many traits, forming thus a whole which embodies all the popular ideals, and yet gives us something more complete than any.

He has joined the fays of old romance with the elves of his own day. The Fata Morgana, whose airy palace may still be seen from the Sicilian shores, rising and falling in magic beauty, the Lady of the Lake and her companion queens, who led King Arthur into the island valley of Avillion, lend some traits to the portrait of Titania, and Oberon is a lineal descendant of the dwarf Alberich of the Niebelungen Lied and the Auberon of the old French romance of Huon of Bordeaux.

The fairy state is ruled by a king and queen, whose powers seem nearly equal, and whose court is modelled upon those of earthly sovereigns ; they have ladies-in-waiting, knights and pages, and trains of attendants, while the offices of court-jester and prime minister are combined very prettily in the bewitching little rascal Puck. One can imagine nothing daintier than these tiny creatures, so delicate and fine, loving all things neat and sweet and beautiful ; punishing the lazy and the slattern, helping the industrious. They dance upon the margin of the sea, or the soft, green turf, where the rings tell of the pressure of their circling feet ; and they love music, and pretty garments of butterfly-wings and the petals of flowers. Their courts and pageants are splendid beyond conception ; their steeds and hawks and hounds far surpass those of earthly lineage, and their halls echo to ravishing music, as we are told by Sir Walter Scott, who knew more of their ways than any other man save Shakespeare.

Ever fair and young, endowed with immortality and versed in magic, the fairies, mischievous often, are rarely malevolent, although they sometimes steal away human children, to fill their places with their own babies, in the hope to acquire for them a human soul and a chance of heaven, while the adopted mortal is bathed in the dews of fairy-land and enters into the joys of the fairy kingdom. So, too, we find now and then a neglected fairy who is uninvited to a christening-feast and comes unbidden, to counteract, if possible, the gifts of her kindly sisters. But the representative of classic discord is in the minority ; and although her evil predictions are always fulfilled to the letter, they are finally counteracted by the activity of the beneficent godmothers whose type is found in the story of Cinderella.

Out of the dream-land of the mysterious East the fairies have come treading in the footsteps of the summer night, and they hold their revels in a wood near Athens, as full of melody and sweetness as were the nightingale-haunted bowers of Colonnos. But, alas! discord has entered into the fairy realm ; its royal master and mistress have fallen out upon the question of a pretty changeling, whom the king would have for a knight in his train, and whom the queen refuses to part with. All the court takes up the quarrel, and queen's followers and king's followers are as bitter as Guelfs and Ghibellines, and the times are out of joint indeed, with no immediate prospect of being set right again. But a grand festivity attendant upon the marriage of Theseus, Duke of Athens, with the Amazonian queen Hippolyta, and the fortunes of two pairs of Athenian lovers, afford opportunities for fairy interference, and the reconciliation of the many difficulties and cross-purposes that beset the paths of the mortals effects at last the union of the fairy sovereigns.

All the traits noted of fairies are exemplified in this play. How tiny the elves must be to "creep into acorn-cups and hide them there!" and a third of a minute is a good space of time for them to rob the rere-mice of their wings. They steal the honey-bags from the bees, and "crop his waxen thighs for tapers." How swift they fly!

> " We the globe can compass soon,
> Swifter than the wandering moon! "

> " I do wander every where,
> Swifter than the moon's sphere."

> " I 'll put a girdle round about the earth
> In forty minutes! "

They love the flowers, and slay the canker in the musk-rose buds ; they can render themselves invisible; and Puck relates how he has assumed at will all sorts of strange and perplexing shapes. But Puck, the Lob of spirits, the tricksy Brownie, is yet a lover of order and tidiness : —

> " I am sent with broom before,
> To sweep the dust behind the door," —

while his special office would seem to be " to jest to Oberon, and make him smile," with merry frolics, or to carry out his lord's commands. The last duty is somewhat blunderingly performed now and then, and the mistakes do not always seem wholly accidental, as he rejoices in the mishaps he has caused, and laughs merrily at the expense of poor humanity.

> " Lord, what fools these mortals be! "

Titania, like Queen Mab, is a bringer of dreams, and all the sweet, incongruous fancies that may come in sleep, characterize the story. Why should all things go so strangely, so out of all order and reason? Nay, why should they not, when the dainty queen herself loves that most earthly of creatures, Bottom the Weaver, with his ass's head, and lavishes upon him such poetic fancies, such sweet cares? Who wonders that Puck squeezes the potent flower-juice into the wrong man's eyes, and then chuckles over the consequences of his error? It is a world upside down, a land of dreams, but for all that, real in itself and beautiful; for we ourselves are but "such stuff as dreams are made on, and our little life is rounded with a sleep."

As the dawning approaches and the fairies must depart, things change, Oberon making everything as it should be for the daylight ; he reconciles the lovers, and straightens out his own

64

domestic tangle, while Titania, awakened from her delusion, joins with him in blessing the house and life of the Athenian sovereigns. The dream is past, the sun rises; and Theseus, unaware of what a tremendous anachronism he himself is, declares that all the mysterious doings of the night were idle fancy. He speaks the language of plain common-sense; but Hippolyta, woman-like, with her love of the marvellous, accepts his theory with some reservation.

*Annie Russell Wall.*

(To be concluded.)

## WALT WHITMAN'S "ARTISTIC ATHEISM."

TRUTH resents no challenge. It throws off all poisons, all thrusts, all enmities fair and foul, as good blood repels disease. It rather invites the test of heat and cold, of curse and question. In whatever form crossed or halted, its lip wears the same smile and its eye fires the same confidence.

I know that Walt Whitman never accused any opponent of anything but a necessary repugnance. "I have been aware from the start," he said to me, in discussing this fact, "that all that has come was sure to come and should have come and was bound to be met. Never a day but found me prepared for what uprose. I knew, too, that with enemies would come friends, and with, or after, controversy, would come truth. If I had a cause that deserved success, opposition would not harm it. If I had a cause that deserved to be defeated, these antagonists were instruments of truth. Either way you put it, the end was certain to be a good one. Therefore, the decision was to be respected — and I, first of all, should meet it with extended hands." I mean to speak in that spirit.

At every doorway the stranger must expect challenge. Has he a pass-word? Are there purposes he may initiate, or new meanings he may introduce? The host, the eternally human, waits; the lord is not yet come. Many the messengers, many the travellers, many the disappointments. The feast is spread;

the guests are collected.    The head of the house, unnamed, unheralded, must at last assume his place.

Greatly has the world discussed Walt Whitman.    Whether he means much or little, or is braggart merely, or flaunts a democracy as impossible as undesirable, or outrages tradition, or travesties progress, or brings a richer message of comradeship and cheer, — these are features which excite wide interest, and must, in some way or other, be as frankly dealt with by friends as by foes.

My purpose now and here is to examine and destroy one indictment only.    The item may be thus set down :

*Walt Whitman is without art.    He discards the past, he laughs at the old heritage, he barbarously mis-interprets and misapplies.* As one eminent critic employs it, he is guilty of *artistic atheism.*

Let us see.    Let us report out of long study and contact the impressions left and grouped.    The phenomena are not to be reviewed in passion.    Things are not true or false according to our wish, but according to their own evidence.

Art is medium only : it is not an end ; it is not an agent self-explicable ; it is not vital by inheritance.    If it have pulse, it gains that pulse out of something beyond itself.    It is not in its nature dynamic ; it lifts a weight because it is first invested with the potencies of the master's arm.

Religions die.    They come, they rival the sun and stars, they grow old, and in their enfeeblement are put to rest.    Men may struggle against the burial of the dead, but duly and inevitably the last act must be and is performed.    Governments come and go; sciences flourish and wane, or are replaced; social forms rise and fall.    Into all the institutions of men pour the streams of success, and empty the poisons of dissolution.    Man only is immortal.

Art cannot evade the decree.    The sentence is read in experience.    It is the first item of prophecy.    We will use this weapon till it grow dull; when it no longer serves our purposes, we will lay it away.    The historic museum gets its own.    No disrespect accompanies the process.    Man must never surrender to the instruments of his safety.    He holds them for their uses, subject always to recall.

It is all one if we make a machine or write a poem. When the old vehicle ceases to give us the peculiar aids to expression which a time or an individual requires, it must be retired. The alphabet yields perennial and infinite combinations. It is arbitrary and contrary to reason to suppose that our fathers discovered the last word of art or of religion. Development takes everything into its universal arms. It dictates entrances and exits; it fills the cup; it medicines pale culture, and it births the pioneer and iconoclast. At its lip civilization listens, and upon its doorsteps the beggar arts linger and supplicate.

Walt Whitman compels acceptance on grounds native and healthy. The soil clings to him. He enters, newly expositing nature. The old order is done. Though scholarship lament at the door of the tomb, no attitude of effacement can avail to withhold the departed. Whitman has not said a word against the outgrown weapons, as fitting their sphere and stage. He has in fact accorded them his respect. But he realizes that for his needs, and the vital announcements of democracy, a freer measure and type have become necessary. He was not less bold in his acts than in his promises. Holmes shakes his head at the new declaration of independence. So did King George at the old, and so must the under-world at all times doubt the stars. But movement is not distressed with stagnancy or reaction.

To say that Whitman is without the old art is not, in spite of the critics, to say that he is without art and emptied of the majesties and graces. It is true, he shrinks from that art to which the average writer attains. Prettinesses, merely verbal music or correctness, the polish of the pedagogue, contain no charm and effect no end. Art is discredited and grows mean if it be narrowed to a set of rules, or be confined to the discoveries and mental appetites of ancient writers. If we are really to respect and revere it, we must inhabit it with a power to enrich and make free its own nature and office. To call *atheist* after one who disputes literary finality, is to borrow a weapon of priesthoods and autocracies.

Whitman's ' Leaves of Grass ' is in fact an enfranchisement.

He puts art on a fresh basis; he gives it liberty. Rather than an absence of art, we here find art globed in sublimest manifestation. Creature tallies with creator. No burden but it easily carries. In the variegation of Whitman's book the method is tried by every test. No touch of pathos, or delicacy, or power, or philosophic or satiric emotion but demands to be shouldered and delivered. Played upon by all the intimacies of feeling and thought, any less ductile style than that adopted, or grown to, by Whitman would have broken down.

It is absurd to accuse a writer writing as he did with a disregard for art. Never a classic which more unmistakably contributed the vouchers of its own right to judgment. From earliest poem to last, from the voyage entered upon to the voyage closed, from sunrise to sunset, there prevails an atmosphere of radiant coherency and life. The one book, charged with the electric colors of a multiform experience, graded up and down and in and out deftly as by any potter at his wheel, proves the existence in its intention and triumphs of as wholesome a sympathy with art as anywhere, among ancients or moderns, discloses itself.

Whitman took his art from Nature; lesser men take their art from artists. At every remove color is lost. By and by the best reflection fades beyond recognition, its parentage becomes of dubious record. Vocalism lapses to echo, and echo to silence. It is not exceptional that Whitman should have been encountered on the highway and subjected by gray-beards to a catechism more properly belonging to a retrospective school-curriculum than to a symposia of seers and philosophers. Another man, in our own day, inaugurating an era in another sphere, has known a like experience. I shall quote from Schumann, who wrote to Mendelssohn, in 1845, of Wagner: —

" The aristocracy is still in raptures over him on account of his ' Rienzi,' but in reality he cannot conceive or write four consecutive bars of good, or even correct, music. What all these composers lack is the art of writing pure harmonies and four-part clauses."

The trouble with Schumann was, that his standpoint and measure were not nature, but interpretation, — not what he saw, but

what others had said they had seen.  I quote him further, as uttering the judgment of a later year : —

" Wagner's music, apart from the performance, is simply amateurish, void of contents, and disagreeable ; and it is a sad proof
of corrupt taste that, in the face of the many dramatic master-
works which Germany has produced, some persons have the presumption to belittle these in favor of Wagner's."

It is obvious that the critics of Wagner and Whitman tread the
same ground.  They tie art, music, down to a peg, and recreantly
allow it only a little rope in whose stingy pleasure to stretch and
breathe and contract.  Growth makes no truce with conditions so
mean.  The verdure dies ; life becomes sterile.  If rebellion had
never raised its head against a limitation so harmful and fatal, the
classics and their golden scales would not themselves have existed.
The logic of the condemnation of Whitman wipes out the whole
literary list.  Art sings its heroics.  It must from time to time
go back to the seas again, and to the skies — back to human nature
and its intuitions — to be reminded of its origin and to consult
anew the melody of birth.

The issue is not, *our art or no art*.  The priests insist upon, *our
religion or no religion*.  We make a broader statement : *our art or
yours, our religion or yours*.

Whitman went sufficiently to school with the old order.  He
knew its underlying virtues and defects.  He even tells us how he
had to struggle that they should not maim him, as they had others.
But he clearly saw beyond their utmost reach, into pastures and
over hills which to them were impossible.  There were reasons why
he should wander beyond the settlements.  However tempting the
galleries, and libraries, and churches, and parlors, their garniture
ceased to give out for nature the assurances which his constitution
and dreams demanded.  From what was stuffy and crowded he went
to what was free and isolated.  Men had originally sought their
houses for shelter.  Now these houses had become hiding-places,
the spirit the hardest inhabitant to find.  This would not do.  The
call of health was to the inspirational, the primal.  Writing had
become an exercise ; it was devoid of the human.  Poets were

inspired of dictionary and grammar. Nature, deserted, her singers strayed and lost, hung her head and wept.

The lusty swing of Whitman's lines appeals to the sense of the cosmic. You are never reminded of its art. Through whatever difficulties, it threads its way with an easy grace. It is foolish for Mr. Stoddard to argue with himself that Whitman, failing in the traditional forms, adopted his own gait and manner because in its formlessness and caricature it indulged his lazy and lethargic nature and may have promised him some temporary success in literature. It is the rule-maker, not the rule-worshipper, to whom difficulties and problems arise. Whitman welcomed, and defied, and defeated the outlawry that his heterodox initiative entailed. His style is the most difficult of styles. Its appearance of simplicity is the best guarantee of its good birth. Mr. Stoddard is no skilful reader of pedigrees that reach quickly back to Nature. The lazy clouds that float across the heavens, the lazy streams that cut a waving line down a continent, the lazy sea that pushes and works its will with the plastic shores, the lazy emotions that stir men to sympathy and action, the lazy mental processes which arrive in unintended harbors, — if we may fairly comprehend and sneer at these, we may with equal fairness put Whitman in the dock as a false claimant.

'Leaves of Grass' is a complete book. I see it full-circle. The first poem meets the last, the fulfilment comes back to the intention. Its message could not have been fitted to the old forms. Nor should any message be forced into any mould. The mould is second, and must acquit its shape of any rebellion. Whitman had supreme gifts, by whose powers a new light shone out of what men call creation. He introduced art upon unexpected, even unexplored, principalities. He brought rhythm new accessions of melody, and carried its conquests to every field and shore. Once the poetic was described by its limitations; hereafter it may be known by its universality. Rhyme goes unto permanent eclipse. Regret may write its epitaph but cannot renew its purple.

They mistake Whitman's compass who think to describe him as an artist, or a writer, or a literary itinerant. Beyond all that

could be limned by the best word in the vocabulary he is the seer
through whose insight and fervor and heroism an epoch is
ushered to its inheritance. Verbalism grows faint in its efforts to
label such a man. So, too, must the children of Verbalism fail in
an endeavor to ticket his art. That it bears the insignia of the
subtlest art any student may comprehend who has ear for its
rhythmic splendor or soul to absorb the interlacing threads and
laws. Like the orbs, this book has gravitation. Like man it has
organs, continuity, mystery, measureless reach. It is subtle as the
individual : it reflects all shades of personal demeanor, latency,
success, failure, development. It participates in the curious
certainty and directness — we may say, the art — with which Nature
makes her combinations. Great souls, endeavoring to reflect Nature
in speech, strive to penetrate and share it. They become her progeny.
This is not denial, — it is affirmation. Whitman himself craved
from the sea a taste of its mystery. Had he the undulations of one
wave explained, its sacred trick unveiled, all were possessed ! For
that revelation he would consent to infinite sacrifice ; against it,
not Shakespeare's power or prestige would tempt or prevail. This
intense absorption in reality and genesis was seminal. It led out
to what he has effected, as surely as life to life. As to the exact
degree of his success, men may differ ; but that he has caught the
flavor of evolution, and immortality, and of that eternal music which
stirs the soul from resident torpors to spring-tide, making it reliant
and holy in self, will day by day add evidence to conviction. He
was wont to tell me : "I do not pretend to have achieved an
ultimate. I have done what I have done, — opened up a few hints,
indirections, pathways into the infinite. I was not so particular to
prove what I could do as to prove what might be done. The
cramped borderlands we will push farther and farther away ; we
will not halt, stumble, apologize, more than we must. Nor will we
even volunteer to select any agents of life which cramp us or make
us mean. My work has tendencies, voices ; it is evolution, *en
semble*, democracy ; it leads to the sea, it sets men free in spaces.
What it has done or can do is at best but small compared with
what will be done by others to come. At the most, I seem to be
only preparing a way, or helping to it."

It would seem as if nothing more could be said. Any writer who doubted Whitman's choice in what is professionally called a "style" has only to try to dress Whitman's peculiar message, manner, and amplitude in scholastic verse, to see how wisely he selected. It was not a wild guess. It is not a chance which diversifies the careless nonchalance of seas and clouds, — an inherent law makes for the results we see. Nor does the same law of integrity and beauty refuse its genius to this book. Poetic order rescues literature from pedagogic chaos, creative art succeeds institutional artifice, the solar rays shame reflection. The old reign, continued beyond its natural life, becomes a usurpation. Thus it is art for art, with this difference, — the artist sets art at the pinnacle, acknowledging its supremacy; the seer makes it his interpreter, his subject, giving and withdrawing rights at will. With Whitman is restoration. He demonstrates for art that it may be more than the schools make of it. He demonstrates for himself that he is art's august master, not its slave.                 *Horace L. Tranbel.*

## GENTLE WILL, OUR FELLOW.

Writ in 1626 a. d. by John Heminge, Servant of His Gracious Majesty King Charles I.; edited in 1892 a. d. as " All, though feigned, is true " by F. G. Fleay, Servant of all Shakespearian Students in America, England, Germany, or elsewhere.

*(Continued.)*

In September Shakespeare was busied with his private matters as to property at Stratford. He had in May bought from the Combes no less than 107 acres of land for £320; and now he purchased of Walter Getley a house and garden in Chapel Lane, covering a quarter of an acre. But on neither occasion did he visit Stratford; his brother Gilbert had received the first conveyance for him; and now he did not attend the Manorial Court at Remington, but left the property in the hands of the Lady of the Manor until he could complete the purchase in person, which he accordingly did in the next year.

At the next Christmas we performed twice before the Queen, and after that the only other play that we acted before her death was 'The Taming of the Shrew.' In this play the only part by Shakespeare was the scenes between Katharine and Petruchio, in one of which there is a sly allusion to Heywood's ' Woman killed with Kindness,' which was then being acted in March 1603 by my Lord Worcester's men at the Rose. This play was based on the old play acted by Pembroke's men fourteen years before; we bought it, with others, of them in 1596, and had acted it in several shapes after that with reformations, which took in wellnigh the whole play; but the copy printed by us is that of Shakespeare's final recast, as already stated.

### SHAKESPEARE IN THE SERVICE OF KING JAMES.

At the accession to the throne of his late Majesty, James I., our expectations were greatly excited on account of the favor which he had so lately shown to us by making us his especial servants, and by the singular commendation which he had bestowed on our fellow Shakespeare. Nor were we disappointed. Within a fortnight of his coming to London we received his license to act as his servants in England, as well as in Scotland, where only we had been by him licensed in the late Queen's time. At the same time Queen Anne took to her the Earl of Worcester's men, and Prince Henry the Lord Admiral's; so that all the public theatres were now filled by companies who from lords' servants had become servants to the Royal Family. The new Queen's men moved to the Curtain (the Rose being allowed to fall into ruin), so that henceforth we had no rival theatre on the Bankside. The Prince's men continued at the Fortune, Allen's theatre, which he had built for his company three years before.

Neither were the children's companies left long in the cold, deprived of the sun of the Royal favor; for in the next January the Queen was pleased to take the Children of the Chapel, as reconstituted under Samuel Daniel, to be the children of His Majesty's Revels. True it is that they did not retain this favor long for their misconduct; but after regaining it, they growing to be men actors came to be the servants of the Princess Elizabeth; while the other boys' company of Paul's, which four years after the King's coming were adopted as the Children of His Majesty's Revels, came three years after that into the service of the Duke of York, now his gracious Majesty Charles I.; and from that time till this present there hath been no company of players of note in the service of any lord, but only straggling wanderers in the countries, for whom no poet will write, being fit rather for a Christmas mumming than for such a stage as ours hath grown to be.

I have been thus particular in setting down these alterations, because of the influence they had on us, not merely at that time but ever since. We being in royal service have been more looked to by the multitude, and in many other ways the change hath conduced to our profit. But one thing hath, methinks, not been profitable: by always writing for the same patrons our poets have of late got to look to them only; and a sameness hath arisen in their plots and characters, as if they had been all coined at one mint. And for this same reason the quality of acting seems to me to be nothing like what it was in the time of Shakespeare, Burbadge, Alleyn, Field, and others who then adorned our stage. No one can be more grateful for the many favors bestowed on me and my company by three successive sovereigns; and yet, if it were possible, I should be curious to know what the stage would be like, if it were free to conduct itself without any patrons at all. I fancy it would not thrive so well under King Mob as under King Charles; that painted scenes and jigs, and parts to tear a cat in, would mostly tickle the groundlings; and that the great poets, nearly all of whom now write to be acted on the stage, would then prefer to be read in the study.

About a fortnight before the Queen's death all the theatres were shut, and the poorer companies, who could not afford to be idle, went into the country. The plague had become hot in London; and although an attempt was made to reopen some of the play places in May after the King's coming, they did not remain open more than a week. In our own license we were expressly forbidden to act till the infection should decrease; nor could we do so until just before Christmas. Again in the next February we were prevented in the same way; but the King graciously gave us £30 for our maintenance at that time. Nevertheless, in the December of his Majesty's first year, we had acted at Wilton before our most kind patron the Earl of Pembroke, who both then and thereafter was prodigal of his favor to us; and at Christmas we presented at Court no less than nine plays.

In the next year we, naturally, after such a pause in our action, produced more plays than we had been accustomed. Shakespeare wrote for us 'Measure for Measure,' one of his least pleasing plays, the plot being taken from Cinthio, or from 'Promos and Cassandra,' an old play by Whetstone never acted. This was the last of his comedies until, at the very close of his career, he wrote 'The Tempest,' and 'Winter's Tale,' which savor rather of tragi-comedy than comedy pure and simple. In all his work about this time there is a gloom, a depression as of a foggy darkness, which suits his following Tragedies; but this play of 'Measure for Measure' is not grateful to look upon; the stage of his inner man seems hung with black. How else could it be in such a time of pestilence and conspiracy and innovation in religion? He also gave us 'Othello,' which, like 'Measure for Measure,' was plotted on a novel in the 'Hecatommithi' of Giraldi Cinthio. I know not who translated these novels for him, but sure I am that he had not enough Italian to read the originals. In this last play he has succeeded in a tragic handling of the passion of jealousy, a feat of such difficulty that most poets have been content to make a comedy thereof, as indeed he himself had already done. But that was at the Queen's command; and he showed afterwards in his scarcely less perfect 'Cymbeline,' how tragically this theme naturally presented itself to him.

Besides these plays of Shakespeare's, we this year staged some of other authors. One of these, the earliest, was 'The London Prodigal,' in which Armin played the part of Flowerdale. Armin was now for us what Kempe had been during many years under the Queen, — our chief comedian of clowns and fools. This play was written for us in 1603 by the same author as 'Lord Cromwell;' but, on Jonson's rejoining us at the end of that year, he left us, and, I believe, never wrote for the stage again. In 1605 he gave it to one Butter, a bigger rogue than the generality of publishers, who had it printed as "by William Shakespeare." Only one poet had been so impudent as to utter such a forged title, and he was the principal author of 'Sir John Oldcastle,' as I have already noted; yet I will not set his name here; he has repented of his evil ways, and written a worthy eulogium on Shakespeare in his epistle to Henry Reynolds. Another play, acted almost at the same time, was 'Sejanus,' by Ben Jonson. For this he was accused of being a Papist (which indeed at that time he was), and seditious (which he was not) by my Lord of Northampton, who had him called before the Council in the next year. It was to have been published in November; but this was interrupted by Jonson's imprisonment for another matter, and when it did pass the press was nothing like as we played it; for Jonson had replaced with weaker lines of his own the work of a second pen who had loathed his usurpation of them. Who this second pen was I must not say; some men say it was Chapman, who was imprisoned with him in the other trouble. But Master Chapman never wrote for our company. It certainly was not Shakespeare; and, if the reader finds so many poets writing for us at this time that he cannot choose among them, I am sorry that I can help him no further. Another play of this year, or rather of Christmas in the year before, was 'The Fair Maid of Bristow,' which we played before the King at Hampton, and afterwards published.

'The Malcontent' by Marston, which we also acted in this year, was not a play of ours; we came by it in this way. When Jonson left us to go to the Chapel Children, he took with him the old 'Jeronymo' play, and reformed it for them, and they acted it. This had been our play for eight years, and they had no right to it whatever; so we waited an opportunity to retaliate. In July of this year, 1604, 'The Malcontent' was published as these children had acted it three years since, and we, having obtained a perfect copy from the author (for they had made many omissions), got him to write us a new epilogue, and acted their play "with reformations," as they had acted our 'Jeronymo.' In the epilogue Marston alludes to the comedy which Jonson had promised us, and which he afterwards wrote, — 'The Fox.' Besides this we got Master Webster to write us an Induction, telling how we had got the play, and now named it 'One for Another,' because we had thus paid them for their ill-dealing by 'Jeronymo.' It might seem that all these additions would make the play too long; but in those days we used not to have music between the acts, as they did at the private houses, and it was for the sake of lengthening the music that the play had been abridged. In this Induction Webster brought on the stage divers of our fellows in their customary dress; to wit, Burbadge, Conditt, Lowin, Sinklo, and Sly. When we had acted this play we gave the "additions" to Aspley the publisher, who inserted them in his second edition before the end of the year.

In December we performed a tragedy on Gowrie twice, with exceeding concourse of all sorts of people; but some great councillors were much displeased thereat, thinking it unfit that princes should be played on the stage in their lifetime, and the play was therefore inhibited.

At Christmas we played many times at Court; and in order to make clearly known how we were dependent upon Shakespeare during his abode with us more than on all other poets together I will here set down in particular the names of all the plays we presented at this season. These were: 1. At Whitehall in the Banqueting house, on Nov. 1, 'The Moor of Venice;' 2. on Nov. 4, 'The Merry Wives of Windsor;' 3. on Dec. 26, 'Measure for Measure.' These three were, two of them, new plays of this year, and one, 'The Merry Wives,' was reformed for this time as we printed it in our late Folio. 4. on Dec. 28, 'Errors;' 5. at my Lord of Southampton's house before the Queen at the beginning of the year, 'Love's Labor's Lost;' 6. at Whitehall again on Jan. 7, 'Henry V.;' 7. on Jan. 8, 'Every Man out of his Humour'; 8. on Feb. 2, 'Every

Man in his Humour ;' 9. on Feb. 10, and again on Feb. 12, to the King's command, 'The Merchant of Venice ;' and 10. on Feb. 11, 'The Spanish Maz,' — seven of these ten being by Shakespeare and two by Jonson.

Just before Christmas Jonson went to the Chapel Boys, who had now become the Children of the Queen's Revels, and with Chapman and Marston (who had dedicated 'The Malcontent' to him) wrote a comedy called 'Eastward Ho,' in which there was much against the Scots. This misliked the King, and the authors were imprisoned. When they were released, Jonson, in the autumn of the next year, brought us his comedy, which we acted both publicly and at Court. It offended the King, and we made our submission at once; and in the new additions to 'Mucedorus,' which we presented before the King on the Shrove Sunday following, we took care to apologize for having been entrapped by an author who had already got the Queen's Revels Boys inhibited by his factions and dark sentences, we always eschewing such malicious jests. His Majesty having extended his grace to us, Jonson left us, nor did he return to write for us till after Shakespeare had left playing and writing too. This play of 'The Fox' was the last play of Jonson's making in which Shakespeare acted, and he as well as the rest of us was grievously vexed at being unwittingly led to take part in a presentation so obnoxious to the King. Jonson could not get authority to publish this play forthwith, and when Thorpe, his publisher, did issue it, in 1607, with one of Jonson's Jesuitical dedications, it was, as his manner was, much changed from the form in which he had led us to act it. He and Chapman were the chief offenders in this way during the time that he remained a Papist ; and it was not till after his recantation in 1610 that he came to us again. Notwithstanding that 'The Fox' had been well received at the Universities, Jonson did not write the mask for the next year, being displaced by Dr. Thomas Campion ; and it was not till after he had appeased the King by his "judicious" compliments in the entertainment at Theobalds, in which he was employed by the Earl of Salisbury, his constant patron, that he recovered his position as chief writer of masks for the Court.

I have here somewhat deviated from my course, which mainly follows the exact time of our action, in order to have done with these flytings of Master Jonson. I now come back to 1605. In this year Shakespeare wrote, and we acted, his great tragedy of 'Lear,' taken somewhat from a miserable old play of the Queen's men's, but far more from the same chronicle of Holingshed, which he had used for his Histories. The old play was a comedy, but directly after we had acted our new tragedy one Stafford entered it as a "tragical history as it was lately acted;" although it had not been staged for a dozen years. We suffered greatly, and still suffer, at the hands of these nefarious pirates; pity 't is that some better order cannot be taken with such landsharks. We played the tragedy before the King in the Christmas of the next year, with many reformations, Shakespeare expunging such matters as might be unpleasing to his Majesty, and inserting many new lines. A copy of this Court version having strayed into the hands of Butter, another of these rogues, he published it two years after. It was most vilely printed, with such arrant nonsense as "cartericks and hiscanios; analher might ensove; awrynted flesh," and the like. The stolen copy of 'Hamlet' wandered terribly, but it was nothing to this. Our copy in the Folio is the true copy as we acted it on the public stage, and, although it be deficient of some few insertions used for the Court, is the only one to which we have given any authority. Yet there be men who still hold to this old imperfect copy as the better of the two!

In July, two months after the first acting of the play, Shakespeare was busy in purchasing a lease of tithes at Stratford; he had this matter under consideration seven years; and now, at last, he invested £440 in this way. In October we were at Oxford, where we performed before the mayor and corporation, as well as before the University. It was then that we acted in 'The Fox,' as I have already noted. The Crown inn there was kept by John Davenant, who had taken out his license in the year before; and to this house Shakespeare made great resort. He was a grave man, much given to plays and playmakers, with a passing fair wife, concerning whom and our fellow Shakespeare idle tongues thereafter raised a passing scandal, which was void of all likelihood. The son of these worthy people, William Davenant, was born four months after our visit. He was much favored by Shakespeare, and now, being grown up, is beginning to write for our company ; but I scarce dare to hope that he will be for us what his godfather was in days gone by. Not long before (in August) the King and Queen had visited Oxford, and among other university shows there had been presented to them three boys dressed as sibyls, nymphs, or Weirds, who celebrated the fulfilment of the old prophecies made to Banquo in his illustrious descendant, now monarch of the three kingdoms of England, Scotland, and Ireland. This set Shakespeare, when he heard of it, to work on the reformation of his ' Macbeth.' But before I say anything of that I must note some plays by other men.

In April of this same year a most unnatural murder was practised upon his wife and children by Mr. Walter Calverly, for the which he was pressed to death at York Castle on the fifth of August. This man's wife was Philippa Brooke, daughter of Sir John Brooke, son of our old enemy, my Lord Cobham. As this murder made great stir in London, we hired George Wilkins to make a play thereon, which he accordingly did. The name Calverly he changed to Scarborough ; but, not finding enough matter to make a play by, he brought in the story of Scarborough's sister, which with the tragedy of Clare Hascop and that of Scarborough's subsequent prodigality made up, as one of us said in jest, ' Three plays in One.' Wilkins, however, would only make one comedy of it, and called it ' The Miseries of Enforced Marriage.' When the murder trial came on, and Calverly was found guilty, we having had the story of the murder itself written by another hand, acted it at the end of the other play, and called the whole performance ' The Four Plays in One.' When Wilkins left us two years afterwards he reclaimed his share of this piece and brought it to press, and in less than a year after that we published the other portion, with the title of ' All's One ; or One of the Four Plays in One called A Yorkshire Tragedy ; ' and more fully to mark the connection with the other play, we printed as the first scene one which had no concern with what came after, being, indeed, a scene written for Wilkins and belonging to the first of the four plays, that on Clare Hascop. The author of this 'Yorkshire Tragedy' was, as far as we know, William Shakespeare. The play was entered with his name in the Stationers' Books, and imprinted with his name on the frontispiece. It was so printed through his life, and again three years after his death; and yet, although he always took the responsibility for this play on his own shoulders, we still thought that another wrote it, and he only corrected it. It is more like what he might have written in his nonage, or what some younger playmaker who took him for a model would indite, than what we looked for from the author of 'Hamlet' and 'Lear.' My own guess is that it was written by his brother Edmund, who had joined us in play-acting, but did not wish to be known as a playwriter; and that William, after his brother's death, printed it, as not willing that so good a play should be entirely lost. Edmund was at this time four-and-twenty years of age.

Another play which we acted at this time was 'The Revenger's Tragedy.' It was published two years after. But, like the play of 'The Usurping Tyrant,' which we acted six years later, it had no author's name on the copy, neither did we place any to the printed book. Of all the plays not his that we published during the time that Shakespeare was with us, two dozen in all, only six had author's names to them; four of these six were Jonson's, who would have his name set forth, and in the other two ('Satiro-Mastix' and 'The Malcontent'), other companies were also concerned, so that we could not help it. We had no wish to set forth any name in rivalry with Shakespeare, who was our mainstay through all that time and since; and the authors for the most part (except Barnes, whom I shall mention presently), did not care to have their names made public in things which they esteemed as beneath them, being but, as Lodge called them, "penny knaves' delight," or as Drayton says, less depreciatingly, the glory of "those that press the thronged theatres."

This same year, in May, we lost our dear fellow, Augustine

Phillips, under whose management òur stage had prospered so well in the time of the late Queen.   In his will he appointed me, with Burbadge and Sly, his executors, and left to each of us along with Shakespeare and Condell, a thirty shillings in gold; nor did he forget to mention others his fellows — Fletcher, Armin, Cowley, Cooke, Tooley — to whom he bequeathed a twenty shillings each; moreover he gave legacies of remembrance to Beeston his servant, now of her Majesty's company, and to Gilburne and Sands his apprentices.   This may serve to show our chief actors at that time, but Beeston had left us half a dozen years before.

*F. G. Fleay.*

(To be continued.)

## DRAMATIC MOTIVE IN BROWNING'S "STRAFFORD."*

Is there a more potential moment in the life of England than that which poises, in even scales, the struggle between the King's prerogative and the people's will?   Is there another man than Strafford who so perfectly incarnates the fated issue of that portentous clash of the old with the new?   It is this moment that Browning selects for the opening of his first stage-play; it is this man he makes its protagonist.

The subject he chose has been called difficult.   Its great difficulty consists, I think, in the peculiarly modern quality of its motive, and in the fact that an original path for it had to be struck out.   Fate steers the action of the Greek tragedies through the personal adventures of the heroes of famous houses.   Revenge, reconciliation, pride, ambition, passion, dominate the later European drama, or that punctilio of " honor " which Spanish playwrights introduced and which has been cunningly appropriated no less in the romantic drama of Victor Hugo than in the classic drama of Corneille.   What road in common have such plays of family or personal interest with the play whose attempt must be to

* Read before the Boston Browning Society, April 25, 1893.

show personal interests and abilities in the huge grasp of an un-honored, unrecognized, — until then an almost unexistent, — impersonal power?

"The main interest of Strafford's career," says the able historian of this period, Mr. Gardiner, "is political, and to write a political play '*non dî, non homines, non concessere columnæ.*' The interest of politics is mainly indirect. Strafford is impeached not merely because he is hated, or because he has done evil things, but because he is expected to do more evil things. Such possibilities of future evil which the historian is bound to consider, are, however, essentially undramatic."

This is the verdict usually pronounced, and 'Strafford' rests under this adverse cloud of pre-conceived opinion as to the capabilities of art. Yet, in the light which Browning's genius has shed upon these "possibilities of future evil," I believe a new fact in the development of dramatic craft may be descried which promises to show that they are not necessarily undramatic.

The Nemesis that brooded over and foreshadowed the outcome of the Greek tragedies shapes forth a dramatic effect most moving and intense. The Nemesis of Conscience that Shakespeare adopted tended to like resistless and predestinate effect. Both find a sister of their own gigantic disembodied kind where, but in the obscure shape met at the very threshold of 'Strafford,' whose undescried presence fills the structure and the onset of the piece with omens of her energy, and closes the tragedy, at last, in pity and in terror, but in exultation, too, with the clear perception of her power? Her name is "England's fate," her champion is Pym, her half-unwitting enemy is Strafford, her manifestation is the growing potency of the people exerted against the councillor and the king who oppose her future possibilities of good. Her shape is new, her relationship with her well-known lordly sisters of Hellenic and Shakespearian drama is not yet all traced out; but are not the marks of her dramatic kinship sure?

The antique fate that animates events in Æschylus, that breathes submission in Sophocles, that, in Euripides, knows how to reconcile itself with revolt and change, for "the gods bring to pass many divine things in an unexpected manner ; both what has been expected has been accomplished, and God has found out a means for doing things unthought for," — is in Shakespeare modernized to work, subjectively, within the actions and history of the individual character. Thus in the dramatic evolution fate becomes moral choice. In this play of Browning's it is modernized still more. It becomes human will: the will for the Ideal. But it is remarkable that in the guise it wears in such a play as ' Strafford ' it tends both to old and new dramatic effects. For it is expressed no less in the actions and history of the individual character than in the larger processes of a great social movement. Such movements, to a poet like Browning, are after all not impersonal but personal. They are the complex issue of many human wills. Personality, then, really holds sway over the " possibilities of the future" as it does over the private course of every single action in the struggle. The poet's use, therefore, in this play, of these " possibilities of the future" is not abstract and historical, but living and dramatic.

Browning uses ideas to differentiate them. He is never a direct borrower, yet one can sometimes detect or suspect the influence upon him of two great English poets, — Shakespeare and Shelley.

It is of interest to remember that Shelley had once chosen Charles I. as the subject of a drama he never completed, and Browning's early devotion to the ardent young poet leaves one room to suppose that he did not pass that fragment by unnoticed. But the centre of action in Shelley's unfinished draft is the opposite of that Browning chooses. King Charles himself as lover — Henrietta Maria's luckless influence over him, that is, is to be the dramatic motive, so far as one may judge from the fragment left us ; the tragedy is to be pivoted within the court circle, not motived conspicuously outside it in the hidden power of the people. In fine, the poet of spiritual revolt seems to be preparing to treat this moment, big with the destiny of democracy, in a manner that belongs to the elder way of writing, suited to feudal customs and those classic fashions Aristotle prescribes when he shows how the subjects of tragedy should not be ignoble or unknown, but selected from the familiar legends of mighty houses.

Strong as Shelley's sympathies were with the new order — and were planned to be shown, no doubt, in the whole of this interrupted piece — his art was not yet free to wing its flight as its dreams willed. It is necessarily a later day of the world when Browning chooses the master-force of his play from a mighty house, indeed, O Aristotle! although its legends and adventures are even yet more unfamiliar than those of royalty, — from the rising house of the people. And in shaping his art in consonance with his motive-force the poet makes his craft as fresh and new a source of interest as the issue of the events he tells.

Shakespeare himself, in the only play dealing with a political interest at all comparable to that which holds sway in ' Strafford,' has alone indicated the way whose general direction Browning has followed independently and often divergently, as his need was.

' Julius Cæsar ' opens on a scene with the Roman Rabble, as ' Strafford ' does on a scene with the English Faction. The rabble is ignorant and unstable, the faction is intelligent and capable of self-control; yet the rabble is designated in Shakespeare, no less than the faction in Browning, as the background of power, — the Court of Appeal, in whose hands the future rests uncertain. Before the people the decision is placed, later, in both plays : in ' Cæsar' after the death of Julius ; in ' Strafford ' at the time of the earl's trial. Each play makes its close refer to a political future which has hung from the first upon the tragic fate of the man against whom the action proceeds. The sympathies implied are not the same. The comparison, in many respects, results in contrast. What is similar, to some degree, is the general dramatic structure ; what is dissimilar is the material, and the moral issue of the story. Both Brutus and Pym are friends of the men they resolve to sacrifice for love of country. Brutus is the hero of ' Julius Cæsar,' much as Pym is the hero of ' Strafford ' ; but Brutus, presently, divides this honor with Antony, as champion and representative of the dead Cæsar, and the whole play takes a turn whose direction is grounded on the fickle purpose of the people. The ghost of Cæsar then grows powerful. That royal spirit holds the lordship of the future, and therefore is impressive. With the imperial ghost is the final victory, and the principle is maintained against which Brutus fought. The result of the whole is not to ennoble Cæsar's personality, but to assert Cæsar's principle.

In 'Strafford' Browning works similarly just far enough to make the difference more striking. Pym's leadership continues unshaken because it is grounded on the steadfast purpose of the Parliamentarians, instead of on the fickle nature of the Rabble as Brutus's is ; not even Strafford's great ability, therefore, and the pity his misfortunes and his nobleness justly excites, can swerve Pym's stroke aside. The weak and inefficient *rôle* of the people, in 'Cæsar,' is, in 'Strafford,' the weak and inefficient *rôle* of the king ; and Charles's champion, Strafford, is made personally interesting and luckless throughout, as the noble exponent of a mistaken policy, just as Brutus, champion of the people, is in 'Cæsar.' Pym stands for much the same sort of sacrifice as Brutus, — he makes the same choice between the good of his country and the ill-fate of his friend ; but, as the play goes on, and in the consummation of his sacrifices of his friendship and his friend for England's sake, Pym grows less strong personally, and more and more identified with the principle he asserts.

Cæsar and Cæsar's principle conquer in 'Julius Cæsar.' Pym and Pym's principle conquer in 'Strafford.'

Shakespeare, one may suppose, felt the mockery of Brutus's struggle since he showed him thus as one who —

> " From desperate fighting, with a little band,
> Against the powerful tyrant of the land,
> To free his brethren in their own despite,
> Awoke from day dreams to this real night."

Browning, on the contrary, one may suppose, feels nothing of the futile or unwise in Pym's battle to free his brethren, since he shows them as impelling and sustaining his course, and paints him as one whose ideal was not a vain one while unflinchingly he obeyed its lofty beckoning, although his heart was rent and emptied and made marble.

It is not alone historic truth that makes these two plays end as they do, — Shakespeare's with Cæsar's impersonal triumph, Browning's with Pym's equally impersonal triumph. With events as they are, in each case, they might have been construed differently. Shakespeare shows his dramatic design in turning his weak and peevish Cæsar into an almost contradictory mighty Cæsar who speaks through Antony's golden mouth and ranges as an angry ghost in the remorseful ill-foreboding heart of Brutus, to the end that Cæsar's political principle shall survive and lay its impress on the future; Browning shows his design dramatically, no less, I think, in making Pym embody England's will and crush himself as well as Strafford under the footsteps of her mightier fate.

An able writer on Shakespeare's dramatic art, Mr. Denton Snider, considers that Shakespeare's sympathies were decidedly conservative; and he adds, moreover, that they had to be so "to make him a great dramatic poet." Certainly Shakespeare did not have the same open sympathies with the promise of popular power that Browning's construal of the events of ' Strafford ' exhibits ; but one scarcely can forget that no one had, — that the whole range of ideas which Browning loves to dwell upon were yet to be evolved; and the fact remains that Shakespeare chose so unique a subject as ' Julius Cæsar ' presents for a drama; that he did not make a hero of Julius Cæsar, but rather made heroic the principle he represented ; and, furthermore, that the principle is one — as the philosophic historian, Mommsen, has demonstrated — which was really more closely identified with the welfare and freedom of the people of the Roman Empire at large than the rule of the urban aristocracy whom Brutus represented. Shakespeare did, then, express the most liberal tendencies, the most enlightened view possible in his day. That his mode of procedure has somewhat of importance in common with Browning's I have pointed out in order to demonstrate how far the shining glance of the poet outruns the careful pace of historical and critical wisdom. Study of the development of literary ideals proves how unsafe it is to decide off-hand what genius cannot do.

In the first act of ' Strafford,' the *protasis* as the rhetoricians of the drama call it, the exposition of its motive-forces is unerringly given. Not a trait is too much or too meagre for the plan. The curtain rises on a "stealthy gathering of great-hearted men" in "an obscure small room" where broods the motive of all the future conflict, — the hidden evolving power of the people embodied in this gathering of patriots, and rising to a head in Pym, just as in Wentworth is summed up the opposed ability alone capable of "so heartening Charles," as Vane puts it, that " England shall crouch, or catch at us and rise."

The first note of the conflict Vane strikes sharply. What is it? It is fear of Wentworth's will and skill. " I say if he be here," Vane bursts out; " And he *is* here," grumbles Rudyard. The king at this moment, indeed, calls to his side the able President of the North to counsel him in the larger concerns of his troubled kingdom. This news sets the future brewing. It is a scene almost of mutiny against the caution of Hollis, the forbearance of Hampden, and Pym's unwillingness to disbelieve in Wentworth. The disorder, and the apprehension of Wentworth's power against England, which master the hour, is suppressed only by the conviction that "One rash conclusion may decide our cause, and with it *England's fate.*"

At these first words Browning cleaves to the heart of the action. The large outlines prefiguring England's fate are coextensive, however, with subtler, more narrowly and warmly human interests.

Vane, who breaks the word to the audience of the wary watch England is keeping on Wentworth, tells, also, the story of Pym's and Wentworth's ancient friendship. His account of the meeting of these two men at Greenwich prefigures the tragedy, and identifies Pym with the oncoming opposition to Strafford. It points, too, to Pym's own heart as the field of a conflict between love and conscience, — between the yearning of a mighty friendship and his soul's best fealty to a lofty vision of England's future good.

This is one of the strokes of the poet which show how infinitely closer is his touch on life than the colder groping of the historian.

Mr. Gardiner feels bound to warn us that Pym never had such a friendship for Strafford as he is represented as having; and he tells us this because he cannot find it set forth weightily in the records as it is in the play. The personal motive is always rightly the poet's affair of the imagination, not the historian's matter of fact. But, besides the story of the early intimacy and the anecdote of the Greenwich meeting told by Dr. Welwood in his Memoirs, and from which Browning, or Browning and Foster, took it, there are passages in Strafford's last speeches which imply the reality of the old friendship, in a way that need not cause one to scruple about yielding the poet this cherished rich red thread of human feeling to weave in with the larger pattern of his wide web. Mr. Gardiner, indeed, though he gives it no certificate, does not grudge it to him; he wisely adds that, rather than point it out as erroneous, we will do better to ask the end it serves, and what higher truth of character results.

If this conflict within Pym's heart is not true it ought to be ; if we have not a historian's warrant for it we have what's better, — a poet's need of it to signify a higher guarantee of its probable truth than annalists are able to sign and seal us with their doubtful facts. And is it not true, then, true to the life, that in large actions which the world remembers long the pulse of personal love once beat devotedly? In the thick of the ferment what attractions and repulsions, what impervious hearts, what loyal souls! Word of not half this spiritual energy reaches the ready misquoting ear of rumor, yet the most unknown of such potencies plays its part and is registered silently in the result.

This inner human truth underlies the events Browning dramatizes. Pym's true-hearted yearning over Wentworth ; Lady Carlisle's admiring self-ignoring devotion to the earl; the earl's fascinated loyalty to the king ; the king's slavery to the slightest displeasure of his wilful queen, — these close-linked springs of inward action are revealed one after the other in the first act of the play, and warn us of the presence of forces of the heart whose interplay is to humanize and enrich the huge march onward of the master-motive.

The second act presents the *epitasis*, or tightening, of the plot. Precedence is yielded here, as in the first act, to the larger social motive, the first scene depicting the exasperation of the leaders against Strafford's skilful ministry on the king's behalf, and preparing the way for their meeting, face to face, with the earl in the second scene. From the violence of his reproaches of the faithless king, the interruption of Pym and his companions recalls Strafford's loyal service to the king forever, and the same instant fixes Pym's eye upon him, henceforth, as foe not friend to England. No hesitation is henceforth possible; and now, in the third act, comes the clash.

Strafford goes to his fate flushed with the certainty of triumph. " Pym shall not ward the blow," he plans, " nor Savile creep aside from it ! The Crew And the Cabal—I crush them." What quite other thing occurs the audience learns from a scene whose arrangement fits in strikingly with Browning's dramatic scheme. The proceedings are witnessed not from inside the House, but outside, with the waiting mob in the ante-chamber, as if the populace — always represented in ' Strafford ' as the main power, whose bidding Pym and Hampden but interpret — were the supreme factor of the event. The stormy sea of the two parties is shown in ceaseless commotion. Puritan and Cavalier ride to victory with exultation, and each tastes the triumph but one side may enjoy, when, at last, with the rage of the righteous comes the text of the Puritans, — one of the most effective of the scriptural outbursts used to such picturesque purpose throughout the play · —

> " The Lord hath broken the staff of the wicked !
> The sceptre of the rulers ! He who smote
> The people in wrath with a continual stroke,
> That ruled the nations in his anger — he
> Is persecuted and none hindereth ! "

and Strafford issues, with the scorn of men behind him, impeached and insulted.

Most plays drag a little after such a climax is reached, but the usual downward movement of fourth acts is in this fourth act rather onward than downward. The action halts splendidly in the trial scene, only to gather head again for the next steps of attainder on the side of attack, of respite or rescue on the side of the defence.

I have heard the trial-scene censured for what seems to me, in view of Browning's main motive, a token of its great originality and most appropriate art. The censure was that this scene should have been laid in the court itself, and that the chance should not have been lost of giving Pym's speech and Strafford's defence. It would have been a more panoramic spectacle; it would have been more oratorical; it would have given greater prominence to the single figures of the strife, ignoring what would ordinarily be considered the unimportant supernumerary bystanders. The effect would have been more in accord with dramatic precedent. But Browning chose rather, I believe, to give the broken talk about the trial as it fell from the lips of the people whom it so deeply concerned, and who so substantially sustained it both in its inception and its issue. He framed his craft in this scene in order to bring it in close harmony with his larger motive. It suits new conditions of social life and an original purpose in art.

The last act gathers to a focus all the sunny threads of human interest that irradiate the play. Lady Carlisle's affection plans Strafford's escape from the Tower, while he sits in prison with his children about him, for a breathing-space, at peace, in an island of childish song and prattle, till Hollis brings him word that the king has failed him utterly and the scaffold waits. Strafford's last act of loyalty is then consummated, — to yield assent to his own death and forgiveness to the king. He did this by letter in the records; in the play it is shown more forcibly. A masked attendant enters with Hollis. It is the king. Every word of Strafford stings him, most of all his loyal-hearted excuses for him. Lady Carlisle's love is stanch enough to dare to save Strafford, and her plan of rescue is ready to be carried out; but Pym's love stays fast and last. His prophecy holds good.

> " *Strafford.* Not this way!
> This gate — I dreamed of it, this very gate.
> *Lady Carlisle.* It opens on the river: our good boat
> Is moored below; our friends are there.

*Straf.*            The same:
Only with something ominous and dark,

.      .      .      .      .      .

Not by this gate !   I feel what will be there !
I dreamed of it, I tell you ; touch it not !
*Lady Car.*   To save the King, — Strafford, to save the King !
[*As* STRAFFORD *opens the door,* PYM *is discovered with* HAMPDEN,
VANE, *etc.* STRAFFORD *falls back ;* PYM *follows slowly and
confronts him.*]
*Pym.*   Have I done well ?   Speak, England, whose sole sake
I still have labored for, with disregard
To my own heart, — for whom my youth was made
Barren, my manhood waste, to offer up
Her sacrifice — this friend, this Wentworth here
Who walked in youth with me, loved me, it may be,
And whom for his forsaking England's Cause,
I hunted by all means (trusting that she
Would sanctify all means) even to the block
Which waits for him.

.      .      .      .      .      .      .

I never loved but one man — David not
More Jonathan !   Even thus, I love him now :
And look for my chief portion in that world
Where great hearts led astray are turned again.

.      .      .      .      .      .      .

This is no meeting, Wentworth !   Tears increase
Too hot.   A thin mist — is it blood ? — enwraps
The face I loved once.   Then, the meeting be ! "

But the end is not yet rounded out. Strafford's personal devotion to the king in which Browning embodies the great feudal virtue — loyalty to the liege — fights yet to the last gasp against the
new political virtue, — belief in the people, — and most against the
horror of the last obstacle Pym shall remove from the path of England's future.

" Oh, my fate is nothing —
Nothing !   But not that awful head — not that ! "

pleads Strafford. Pym replies — " If England shall declare such
will to me " ——

" Pym, you help England ! " falters Strafford, vanquished ; yet
only for an instant. He breaks out again consistently into a last
agony of prayer for Charles : —

> " No, not for England now, not for Heaven now, —
> See, Pym, for my sake, mine who kneel to you !
> There, I will thank you for the death, my friend !
> This is the meeting : let me love you well !
> *Pym.* England, — I am thine own ! Dost thou exact
> That service ? I obey thee to the end.
> *Straf.* O God, I shall die first — I shall die first ! "

" Possibilities of future evil," against which Pym guards England, thus destroy Strafford and with grim certainty shadow forth his royal master's doom. Stubborn political impersonalities are made plastic by the poet's incarnation of them in loving souls.

Is it, indeed, impossible for the dramatist to depict liberal tendencies ? No. He puts them not into words but into struggling hearts, conflicting wills, and lo ! the drama is wrought.

*Charlotte Porter.*

## " AH! HAPPY BOUGHS THAT CANNOT LOSE YOUR LEAVES.

FROM THE CORRESPONDENCE OF —— —— AND * - -

YOUR last letter, full of penetrating thought, dear * * *, finds me packing the fag end and fribble of my summer in trunks and boxes. I am a little doleful and reminiscent, and while I pack and corner-cram I am asking myself more or less unnecessary questions.

Is all of the brier-rose I can carry away with me this rough touch of it on my clothes; all that I can call my own of the breezy joy of rock-rambling this sad shabbiness along the hems of duds I have been happy in; all that even the white sea-sprite of the laughing foam has dowered my eyes with, actually mine merely by token of these dirty little dots capriciously spotted over my garments, constellations that daylight discovers? Do I wear on my retina yet one guise of Nature I enjoyed? Already I try to conjure up a scene, and know too well I am trying. How then can I flash the picture on my inward eye when I am pent in next winter between Belgian blocks and trolley wires? Why am I not so blest as to store up and check on to town my choice of sunsets, or that still afternoon on the glowing downs, that living look of the bayberry tangle, that crescent moon-path on the bay, or the sudden sun-spill of wide-flowing silver after the rainy day, instead of these ignoble cloth-written hieroglyphs of dead delight?

But no! The glory is fading from me, and the only tangible fruit of it all is the necessity to repair and newly furnish forth my shattered outside.

A sigh or two scarcely escapes me before my reflections revolt at their own issue. Unnatural parents! And I refuse to consider my old clothes — the archæology, truly, of past enjoyment — as fit witnesses to the life that was; the poetry and drama, that tell the truer and more vital story of mankind's past age than its potsherds can, should find a corresponding record in the unseen and interior effects of my summer.

Sunburn is not enough for me, you see, nor will a pound of flesh quite answer my desire to bear good testimony of my long crop of beauty. Like the ardent souls whom neither a halo and a gold harp, nor yet the Comtist eternity of good deeds, will satisfy in lieu of an immortality of conscious intelligence, I crave some continuous embodiment of my summer's æsthetics which shall make the joy persist.

If the immediate sensuous pleasure of one phase of a day by the sea must suffer a town change, nor can be satisfactorily perpetuated in its material effects either in the water-color I tried to make of the view, the poem about it I never finished to my mind, or the clothes I brought home worn in the service of beating about the burning bush, am I not fairly driven to conclude very much as Professor Weismann does about his germ plasm, that its essential feature resides, so to speak, not in the cell, but in the nucleus, — not in the outer shape or shaping of it, but in its withinward, self-developing potencies? Which reminds me of an anecdote a wise old professor of mine once told me to illustrate the similar internal workings of the education that leadeth to culture. An auld Scotch wifie praising the Dominie's sermon was cross-questioned a little severely as to what in particular it was, when she answered,

imperturbably: "An' what if I ken nae mair the verra words?
They gaed frae me as the water frae the claise I am bleaching 'oot
i' the sun, but that gars naught if the clout's the whiter for it."
That property of cloth to receive the opposed wetting and drying
processes to its own peculiar advantage, why should not the human
being imitate to like profit, saturating sense in the natural beauty
the summer pours forth and the winter work-a-day world as thoroughly absorbs, to the end that his very fibre is the purer?

I lead myself thus to the cheering conclusion that the summer
may be never so present as when the winter effaces its image and
fastens within one its force; and thereupon proceed calmly to pack
my last box of books, and acquaint you, according to custom, with
my every thought.

That petty amusement of the moment you wax impatient over
in your last letter could not create any such dynasties of gladness;
and only persuasion to such superior happiness can vanquish the
current tendency you deplore to a spurious pleasure incapable of
living out the next breath. Pleasure that is vital must be capable
of transmutation, and reduction to human terms.

As for "true religion and undefiled," is it not just the same?
The essential joy and beauty of it consists not in keeping it sacred
for the Sabbath, but in secularizing it during such whole weeks of
Sundays as shall end by giving the holy day no exclusive and
superior sanctity.

May the time come when mankind shall more and more secu-
larize its religion, and appropriate its happiness in beauty! Con-
cluding with this revolutionary moral prayer, you will have no
doubt about believing me quite in accord with your last letter,
and                              Yours,         —— ——.

## THE 'ANALYTICS OF LITERATURE' AGAIN.

WE have received from Professor Sherman the following communication : —

In the review of the Analytics of Literature in the last issue of POET-LORE, you allude (p. 470) to the principles of dramatic art deduced from Shakespeare and Browning, etc. May I ask what principles are referred to, — the doctrine of ' effects ' in general, or ' negative effects,' or ' association ' ? I have watched with no little interest for criticism of the chapters on Browning and Shakespeare, and am anxious to identify exactly the points had in mind by yourself in writing the paragraph in question. Yours is the first notice that has at all taken up the attempt there made to explain the modes of imagination. An answer to the above question, and any fuller statement of the way the positions taken impress you, will be esteemed a great favor. I am very glad to have read a review so conscientious and deliberate as you were so good as to give the volume. Yours very truly,

*L. A. Sherman.*

We make this note of Professor Sherman's the occasion to say a few more words upon the chapters in his ' Analytics of Literature ' dealing especially with the art of Shakespeare and Browning. The art of Shakespeare is so universal that to bring it within the limits of any fixed set of principles would tax the strength of a critical Titan. It is with his characters as with the real men and women about us, — one can never count upon the exact impression they may make upon their fellow beings outside the play. It needs only to point to the varying interpretations of Shakespeare's characters to prove this. If the impression they are to make could be measured by any artistic rule of three, we should perforce echo Browning's sentiment, " The less Shakespeare he ! " It is the non-appreciation of this fact which weakens, in our opinion, Professor Sherman's analyses of Shakespeare's plays. He argues as if the workings of the imagination of a whole audience, which may be taken to mean the whole reading world, could be considered as being absolutely in unison, that its sympathies as if of one man could be confidently reckoned upon. For example, according to

68

Professor Sherman, the very bone and sinew of the artistic form of
' Macbeth ' depends upon the poet's rousing the sympathies of the
" audience " for Macbeth. It (the audience) is represented by Professor Sherman as desiring above all things that Macbeth should
become king. It throws in its lot with Macbeth because it is
shown how inadequate the present rule is by the contrasting of the
prowess of Macbeth with the pusillanimity of Duncan and Malcolm.
Certainly the contrast is there, and Professor Sherman is right in
instancing the use of contrast as one of Shakespeare's artistic
weapons; but when he undertakes to show the exact effect produced by such contrasts, he is deviating from the path of the
purely objective critic into that of the subjective critic, whose sensations must always carry with them the limitations of the personal
equation. Personally, we never experienced that sort of sympathy
for Macbeth which hopes he will succeed, and therefore an analysis
of the play based upon such sympathy as a starting point, and
followed finally by the undermining of it, is unsatisfactory as the
formulation of the art principle upon which that play is constructed.
In fact, may not the true artistic sympathy be less a partisan feeling for this or that character or action than a universal sympathy
for all phases of human character, as portrayed by the poet? The
dramatist who makes each character consistent with itself, regardless of the partisan feelings of his audience, has reached the pinnacle of his art. Such a dramatist is Shakespeare. Thus we can
admire the portraiture of a Falstaff, though not many of us would
care to have him for a friend.

The characters, themselves, are of course often partisans, as in
the case of the conspirators in ' Julius Cæsar '; but the prerogative
of the reader is to see that, and realize that all their remarks about
Cæsar are colored by their party spirit, — not to accept without
question everything they say of Cæsar, as Professor Sherman contends when he declares that sympathy is with the conspirators.

Again, the general principle deduced in the chapter which speaks
of Browning's ' Colombe's Birthday' is as follows : " The author
simply presents traits or elements that please, keeping the rest
from sight until the mind has inferred a whole character spiritually

proportional to, or consonant with, the features shown. Then, within certain limits, the worser side, if need be, may be shown with safety." Such a principle does not, it seems to us, apply to a character such as Colombe, who is not presented to us as a static character, but as one suddenly developing under new and unforeseen conditions. That we are made cognizant of only lovely characteristics at first, is because her life has been such that no others have been brought into play; but there come into her life conditions which will be a crucial test of her nobleness. There is a struggle between those lower dormant instincts, which have never been tried before, and the higher ones, which all her past life has tended to preserve. The poet's art consists, to our mind, in presenting truly such a development of character, rather than in arbitrarily showing us the good side first and the bad side later on. Enough has been said to show upon what grounds we distrust the infallibility of a principle of art-analysis which depends upon rousing the partisan sympathy of the reader either for an individual character or a course of action ; it only remains to be said that we are entirely in accord with Professor Sherman's remarks upon what he calls "inferential art." The "indirections by which we find directions out" are among the most powerful weapons of the modern poet, and it is good that students should have this quality pointed out to them, instead of being left to grow up to the consciousness of it through years of reading.                               *C.*

# NOTES AND NEWS.

—— APROPOS of Mother Goose's claim to Yankee blood comes the following letter : —

DEAR EDITORS : In the June–July number of POET-LORE, to which Miss Harned contributes an article on the ' Early Women Poets of America,' — she makes reference to the authorship of the melodies of Mother Goose. It so happened that a friend from Boston was visiting me, and when I read to her the article, she told me the following tradition which had always been cherished as of interest and value in a branch of her own family.

Elizabeth Foster of Charlestown, a member of the Old South Church, married in 1692 Isaac Goose of Boston who was a widower with several children. The second wife (Elizabeth Foster) became the mother of six children, the eldest of whom, Elizabeth (named for her mother), married Thomas Fleet, a printer. When children came to the Fleets, the Grandmother Goose delighted to care for them and sung to the babies numerous songs and ditties which she knew, and, although her son-in-law tired of the baby nonsense, he appreciated their value sufficiently to write them out and make a book for the benefit of other babies than his own. This he did in 1719. No one claims that Mrs. Goose originated these songs, but *recalled* them as she had learned them in her own babyhood. Mrs. Goose died in 1757, and was buried in the Granary burying ground on Tremont Street. The said Thomas Fleet was the grandfather of Mr. Samuel Eliot who married a cousin of the mother of my friend. And the Eliot family possess a pair of ear-rings belonging to Mrs. Goose, also the watch which belonged to her husband. It seems that the family did not think it important to preserve a copy of the rhymes, although some years after it was known that a Fleet copy was in the Library of the Antiquarian Society of Worcester, Mass. It has since disappeared ; and, although Mr. Whitman who has published several articles *denying* this origin of the book, corresponded twenty years ago with a Mr. Wheeler who upheld the Fleet origin, and who, with Mr. Crowningshield and Mr. Eliot, *saw the book* in the Worcester Library, it cannot be proved to the satisfaction of the public, because the three named gentlemen are dead. Still the story has come down through the Eliots and other descendants of the Fleet family, and the Eliots *believe* it to be true, and that Mother Goose was Mr. Eliot's great-great-grandfather.

I do not know that this story will seem to you of value; but you will perhaps agree with me that the songs are really of foreign invention, but collected, arranged, and adapted for American use, by one who had caught their jingle, as wafted from over the sea more than three hundred years ago.

Yours very truly,

*E. F. R. Stitt.*

NEWPORT, June 16, '93.

—— An interesting Russian view of Hamlet is given in the essays of Prof. V. D. Spasovitch. He does not consider Hamlet as reflective, but rather as a man who acts under inspiration. In his conversations with the players he displays the deepest familiarity with æsthetics, together with a strong distaste for any prolonged systematic labor. "'T is e'en so," he says, "the hand of little employment hath the daintier sense." He is capable of great deeds requiring great courage or dexterity, but only under the condition of an immediately preceding nervous excitement due to a received impression, — that is, as long as the excitation has not passed and the deed can be accomplished during the same state as a reflex ; in other words, if it flashes as lightning, blending itself with the cause which has produced it, and not separated from it by intervals of reflection. As soon as a hindrance is met, a feeling of constraint, instantly there are born iridescent thoughts, with the imprint of either burning melancholy or irony, and the prince is unable to combine them and master them ; not he guides them, but they draw him in their own direction. Vainly does he reiterate to himself that time is precious, that there is need of haste, that a man's life is short, "no more than to say, one." In vain does he, with a special effort, cry, "O, from this time forth, my thoughts be bloody, or be nothing worth ! " In spite of all efforts, he still cannot count that "one," and either revolves upon the same spot, or is carried by the wind without sails, helm, or oars, on the tempestuous waves of events. He is too keen and penetrating to permit anybody, and not only such awkward pariahs as Rosencrantz and Guildenstern, to play upon him as upon a flute; yet he involuntarily plays the part of a pipe, from which events extract uncertain sounds.

Hamlet is a poet, and therefore capable of much to which the feeling of duty will not constrain him, but solely from *art-ism*, from love of art, from the interest which the process itself excites in him, independently of its purposes and meaning. To this love of art the prince sacrifices everything ; for its sake hearts are trampled, and thousands of wounds inflicted upon souls ; the trace of Hamletian plots and fantasies is marked with death and disaster.

" For though I am not splenetive and rash," he says, " yet have
I in me something dangerous," — namely, a small portion of that
sentiment which animated Nero when he uttered, *Qualis artifex
pereo !*

For this summary of Mr. Spasovitch's theory of Hamlet we are
indebted to an old number of a periodical no longer extant, —
*The Transatlantic.*

---

## LONDON LITERARIA.

MANY years have elapsed since lovers of poetry were attracted
to a dramatic poem entitled 'Within and Without,' — a poem full
of spiritual insight, and charged with many poetic gems.   Other
poems followed ; but the author apparently found the writing of
fiction more to his taste, — or rather shall we say, more to the
taste of the reading public.   So to-day the fact that George Mac-
Donald has produced sufficient verse to fill a couple of goodly
volumes will come as a surprise to many readers.   But George
MacDonald is a poet, — albeit more widely known as a novelist.
Many of the poems in the collected edition now issued by Messrs.
Chatto & Windus are not only very beautiful, but are full of suggestion and aphorism, and are all more or less charged with that
distinctive quality which emphasizes the work of the true poet.

Some interesting autograph letters were brought to the hammer not long ago at Messrs. Sotheby's, — the prices fetched being
somewhat remarkable.   A couple of folio pages of MS. verses by
Burns, and including the following unpublished stanza, were sold
for £10 : —

> " Were it in the poet's power,
>    Strong as he shares the grief
>    That pierces Isabella's heart
>    To give that heart relief."

The verses were entitled ' On reading in a Newspaper the Death of
John M'Leod, Esq., Brother to Miss Isabella M'Leod, a Particular
Friend of the Author's.'   Four autograph letters of Burns were also
on sale, — £27 being paid for one addressed to Cunningham in 1794,
and containing the song, ' Wilt thou be my Dearie ? '   An epistle
from George Eliot to Mrs. Trollope fetched £4 17s. 6d. ; while

four letters from Emerson to Thomas Carlyle realized £12 15*s.* Of course there was the inevitable letter from John Keats to Fanny Brawne, — which sold for £26. One wonders what the sensitive soul of Keats would say to this hawking about of words written to one who was the light of his life, and who was involved to so large an extent in the tragedy of its close. These letters should have been buried with him — or consigned to the flames. Eight letters of the "gentle Elia" were sold for £54; one from Edgar Allan Poe for £5 5*s.* ; and sixteen from Ruskin (addressed to M. Ernest Chesneau) for £17. The MS. of forty-seven sonnets, and of the titlepage of Rossetti's 'House of Life,' fetched £27 ; and a MS. of Shelley's ' A Proposal for putting Reform to the Vote throughout the Kingdom, by the Hermit of Marlow,' realized £135 ! The MS. of Thackeray's lecture on Swift brought £19; of Thackeray's two ballads of ' John Hayes ' and ' Catherine Hayes,' £11 11*s.* ; and an autograph letter of George Washington to James Mercer, Mount Vernon, December, 1774, concerning the purchase of cattle and land, £15 15*s.*

From a literary point of view, however, perhaps the most interesting of the recent events at Sotheby's was the sale of a series of autograph letters of George Eliot. The letters number four-and-twenty, and date from August, 1871, to December, 1877. Early in the course of this correspondence, we find an interesting piece of self-revelation : —

" I may tell you that my worship for Scott is peculiar. I began to read him when I was seven years old, and afterwards, when I was grown up and living alone with my father, I was able to make the evenings cheerful for him during the last five or six years of his life by reading aloud to him Scott's novels."

In the course of a letter dated Sept. 11, 1871, we find her writing as follows : —

" Perhaps you do not imagine me as a writer who suffers much from self-distrust and despondency. If I had not had a husband who is not only sympathetic, but so sagacious in criticism, that I can rely on his pleasure in my writing as a satisfactory test, it would be difficult for me to bring myself into print. Especially as I have the conviction that excessive literary production is a social offence ! "

Elsewhere in this correspondence she writes : —

" Every one who contributes to the ' too much ' of literature is doing grave social injury, and that thought naturally makes me anxious."

Referring to a review of her book, she says : —

" If it were my habit to read stuff of this kind, the effect would be very injurious to me, and I shall not taste of that cup again for a long while." . . . " I can't help wondering at the high estimate made of ' Middlemarch ' in proportion to my other books.  I suppose the depressed state of my health makes my writing seem more than usually below the mark of my desires." . . . " My dear husband, I am thankful to say, is in better case, and does everything for me that can be done by proxy.  I think you can divine something of his — not superhuman, but — exquisitely human goodness."      " You understand that I necessarily care most about the impression my books make on the young.  Mr. Lewes has been wont to say that neither the very young nor the ignorant could care about my writing."

It seems that the little book ' Renunciations,' by Mr. Frederick Wedmore, has been so successful that a second edition is shortly to be issued.   Unlike most second editions, however, it is to be considerably enlarged by the addition of a series of stories, which appeared originally in 1877 under the title of ' Pastorals of France,' — ' A Lost Love at Pornic,' ' Yvonne of Croisic,' and the ' Four Bells of Chartres.'  Mr. J. Fulleylove has designed a special titlepage for the book, which will be limited to six hundred copies, and published at 4*s*. 6*d*. net.

At last we are within measurable distance of a Life of Dean Stanley, which Mr. John Murray is about to issue in a couple of volumes.   The author is Mr. R. E. Prothero, and his task has been accomplished, we are told, with the sanction and co-operation of the Rev. G. G. Bradley, Dean of Westminster.

A new volume of verse, entitled ' A Fellowship in Song,' has for its authors Mr. Le Gallienne, Mr. Norman Gale, and Mr. Alfred Hayes.   The first of this poetic triune has already achieved much success in song; and a notable addition to modern poetic literature may be anticipated.                          *William G. Kingsland.*

Vol. V.    No. II.

# THE FIRST ENGLISH ESSAYIST
# WALTER MAP.

INCE the publications of the Camden Society in 1850 and 1851, the name of Walter Map has been tolerably familiar to students of literature, and the 'De Nugis Curialium' has taken a certain rank among historical documents. The Reports of the German Imperial Academy for 1853 contained a paper by Phillips in which Map's life and relations to Henry, Becket, Gilbert Foliot, the Cistercians, and other men and affairs of his time were thoroughly worked out: his birth between 1133 and 1138; the services of his family to Henry in the recent civil wars, and Henry's gratitude; his studies in Paris, where he saw a town-and-gown riot; his ecclesiastical advancement and presence at the Lateran Council of 1179; with other intermediate items, — altogether a passably satisfactory biography as biographies of that period go. In 1210 Gerald Cambrensis wrote "May God be gracious to his soul!" and Phillips estimates that he died near the beginning of the century.

It is a strange comment on fortunes and shifting opinions that

while three hundred years later English writers still trembled to
intrust their immortality to a language which they felt was destined to decay or death, and some, like Moore and Bacon, put
capital into Latin securities as a safer investment, the brightest man
in England in the twelfth century found in this immortal Latin
language, if not a tomb for his name and fame, at least a narrow
room, a "quiet limit of the world," that gave him but a Tithonian
shadow of immortality.  Even that shadow is partly a mistake;
but whether he wrote any of the Latin satires that have come
down to us, or merely the strength of his name gathered them
around it, he wrote himself in the book which he called 'De
Nugis Curialium,' — 'Court Gossip,' or more literally, 'Trifles of the
Court.'  My present endeavor is to represent briefly what sort of a
book this clever man wrote, and through the book what sort of a
man he was who wrote it.

In the first place, he was an essayist; the 'De Nugis Curialium' is not primarily an historical document, but a collection
of the essays and miscellaneous papers of Walter Map, which
collection he made and arranged himself, and divided into books, or
*Distinctiones*, as he called them, with an Introduction to each book.
The papers often consist of a mere paragraph containing an
anecdote or squib, not what we should be justified in calling an
essay; but it is the air of immediate contact with the reader which
distinguishes the essayist, though it may take other matters to
furnish forth the essay, and on the other hand many of Map's
subjects are all that a Lamb or Leigh Hunt would require.  The
essay in Map's time had no precedents, and consequently no recognized literary form; but all the essential qualities of it are found
in the 'De Nugis Curialium,' and Map will be better understood
under this name and view of him than any other.

The Introduction to the first book begins as follows : —

"'I am in time and I speak concerning time,' said Augustine,
but adds, 'I do not know what time is.'  In a similar astonishment I may say, that I am in the court, and I speak concerning
the court, but I do not know, God knows, what the court is.  Only
I know the court is not time.  It is temporal certainly, mutable

and various, local and erratic and never stays in the same place. When I go away from it, I see it as a whole, but when I come back I find nothing or little that I left. The court is the same but the parts have changed."

It seems that some friend by the name of Galfrid was distressed that Map's literary talents should rust so long in idleness, and entreated him to write a didactic poem on the court; this, on account of the distracting nature of his life, Map found himself unable to do, and started to write an apology for his inability. He proceeded to show why the court was like Infernus, and discovered such startling parallels that the wonder is, not that he did write poetry there, but that he did anything there except to get out of it immediately. His objection to this was probably that he did not like any other place as well. He concludes:—

"Of the court we testify what we have seen. Moreover, the envelopment of flame, the density of the darkness, stench of rivers and great grinding of demons' teeth, wandering exiles and miserable with anxious hearts, the dreadful creeping of all vipers, snakes and every reptile, impious roaring, evil smells, lamentation and horrors, if I wished to make an allegory of each of these, there would be no lack of symbols but it would take more time than I care to spend. . . . Nevertheless I do not say that the court is Infernus, which does not follow, but it is as like it as a horse's shoe is like a mare's. . . This is not the king's fault [he adds, fearful that it may reflect something on his friend and sovereign], since there is no man wise enough to so dispose his house that there be no trouble in it. For I am ruler of a small household and yet am unable to hold the reins of that little family of mine. It is my study that, as far as I am able, all shall be provided for and none lack food or drink or raiment, and yet they try in every way to cut off my substance and increase their own. If I reprove any one justly, he denies the fault and his fellows back him up. If any one of my household speaks well of me, they call him a flatterer. 'You stand well with the master. You lie to please him and get paid for it but we will be honest if we are turned off inside of an hour.' . . . I have asked advice of them, to whom I should entrust the care and ministration of the priory, not that I might choose the one they wanted but the one they did not; for I knew what counsel the dogs would give me. There is an old and well-known story of a

man who quarrelled with his wife about which part of the pig they
should put in the pot. The wife said the side and the husband
the back and the dog said ' Put the back in, man, because then the
best part will be left for me.' And I knew their advice would be
for their benefit, not mine. . . . So I dare not find fault with the
king that in so great a court there are many mistakes and much
tumult. . . . You ask me, my dear Galfrid, to write a poem about
the court. I am a child at such things; besides I tell you I am tied
to this court that I have so veraciously described, banished to it,
and you command me to philosophize about it, who protest that *I*
am the Tantalus of this Infernus. How can I pledge your health
if I cannot get anything to drink? Poetry comes of a quiet mind
and devoted to one thing. Poets want a residence entire and safe.
Good health and property are of no avail unless there is a mind
tranquil with inward peace. So you might as well tell the young
men in Nebuchadnezzar's furnace to sing as ask this miracle of
me, a foolish man, in writing inexperienced."

Follows shortly a story of the King of Portugal, — how he was
wickedly persuaded to kill his friend and his queen, his repentance
therefor, and how such things are liable to happen in courts.

" And you would have me in this court, — the mother of affliction and the nurse of wrath, — write poetry ! and urge me with
words as Balaam urged his ass with spurs. But I am afraid that
I in my folly, unlike the ass, shall yield, and you unlike Balaam,
who caused his ass to speak instead of bray, will cause me to bray
instead of speak and make an ass of a man instead of a poet. However I will be an ass if you like."

The only manner of satisfying his friend Galfrid which his distractions allowed, was to write these little papers or essays whenever he found time, " raptim," he says, — by snatches. Phillips
estimates that they were written between 1180 and 1193; and,
naturally enough, they were not arranged in the order of composition, but with a general view to the subject, although this purpose
is not strictly maintained. The first two books are largely about
monks and military orders, ghosts and various supernatural matters, " fantastic apparitions," he calls them, and " prodigies."

" Concerning the Origin of the Carthusians. The bishop of
Grenoble saw in sleep seven suns come together from different

directions to the mountain which is called Cartusia in the valley of Grisevold, and stop there. The next day, when he had considered much with himself but found no explanation, lo, six clerics, men magnificent and with them a seventh, their master Bruno, who straightway asked for a location that they might build an oratory there. Glad then was the bishop that his vision had so happy an outcome and built them cells and a church, according to their plans, and bestowed them therein with his benediction. It is, moreover, a lofty mountain, in the midst of its summit a deep valley, barren and uncultivated, although abounding in springs. They have thirteen cells; the prior lives in one and each brother in one. The prior on the Sabbath distributes bread for the whole week and pulse and oil, but three days in the week they content themselves with bread and water. They eat no flesh except they are sick, purchase no fish or eat it, unless it is given them and may be divided among them all. They are always clad in goathair cloth, always girded and always praying or reading. No one besides the prior is allowed to put more than one foot outside his cell ; the prior may for the purpose of visiting the brethren. On feast days they assemble in the church. They hear mass not daily, but on certain days."

Hermits are very unusual people, but this is the only case on record of a sect that was able to "assemble in the church," and each leave a foot behind in his cell, without exciting remark.

Map gives a pathetic little anecdote of a certain monk of Cluny who was forced to leave his monastery and take up arms, and being mortally wounded, said to the boy who was with him : —

" ' Conjure me by the mercy of God, dear son, that in the name of Jesus Christ my soul be penitent on the day of Judgment, that the Lord may pity me and I see not with the impious the face of fury and wrath.' Then said the boy, with tears : ' Sir, I conjure thee that thou divide thy lips with penitence in the presence of the Lord,' and he, nodding his head devoutly, promised to do so and died."

The poor old monk thought if he made a solemn promise on the brink of death, he might perhaps remember it when he had become a reckless, irresponsible spirit.

' Concerning a Certain Hermit ' and an extraordinary lizard. — This animal entered his cell and humbly manifested a desire for

something to eat. The hermit was a charitable man, " having," in
Map's favorite phrase, " the zeal of the Lord, though not according
to wisdom," by which, I take it, he means to reflect here on the
evils of indiscriminate charity. He fed the lizard so well that it
grew too large for the cell and eventually swallowed him, at least
he disappeared. It is an allegory of gratitude, a not uncommon
one, and the lizard's is a besetting sin.

The archdeacon had a private grudge against the Cistercian
monks, and his account of them is evidently bitter and prejudiced;
but the corruption of the church in all places was a sore point
with him as a conscientious churchman, and the essay that follows
the account of the Cistercians, on monks in general, is a piece of
fiery invective that must have made some of the cowled brethren's
blood run hot. In the paper on the Sect of the Assassins, his
position toward the papacy is clearly brought out.

" Jocelin, bishop of Salsbury, once said to his son who had been
elected by violence to the bishopric of Bath, and was bewailing
that Canterbury refused to consecrate him, ' You idiot, run to the
pope, hesitate not, hit him a good slap with a large purse and he
will stagger any way you like.' So he went, gave the blow, the
pope staggered and fell, the pontifex rose and forthwith wrote a lie
at the beginning of all his letters, for when he should have said
' by the grace of the purse ' he said ' by the grace of God,' and did
in fact whatever the bishop desired. Nevertheless be our mistress
and mother Rome as a staff broken in the water and let us not
believe what we see."

I find Map's " fantastic apparitions " more interesting than his
monks and hermits, and suspect he was secretly of the same opinion. He is quite sarcastic on occasion with regard to some of the
reputed saints and their spectacular miracles, but to his " apparitions " he is uniformly respectful. " I do not know the reason," he
remarks of one, — which he calls a " prodigy," however, — " but I
know it is true." Among them appears our old friend, the Undine,
in a water-maiden who comes out of the lake called Lenem and marries a dweller in dry places. And although she warns her husband
against thrashing her with his bridle-rein, he incautiously insists
upon it. Consequently his wife goes back to the water again, and

leaves him only one of their children, whose name is Triunnes Nagelauc; whereafter Triunnes Nagelauc has certain adventures. Another version of the same myth, apparently, tells of a company of beautiful women,—ghosts, to be sure,—in a house in the woods, one especially, "*forma facieque præstantem,*" whom a hunter carries off, not without being liberally scratched. But her son turned out to be eminently pious, gave all his money to the Church in gratitude for restored health, and went on a pilgrimage, —"a thing which," Map remarks very seriously, "is quite unparalleled in the ancient histories of the children of nightmares."

"A passing apparition is called a phantom from phantasia. These are the visible forms that demons take upon themselves from time to time, licensed by God, and in their passage harmful or not according to his desire or permission. But what must be said of those phantoms that remain and perpetuate themselves in their children, like this Alnodus or the Briton, spoken of before, who had actually buried his dead wife and recovered her and afterward had sons and grandsons from her, who remain to this day, who trace their origin thither, multitudes of them, and are all called 'children of the dead woman'!"

A certain William Laudun, a reckless kind of a man, came to Gilbert Foliot, then Archbishop of Hertford, in a quandary. He said a Welshman had died near him recently. This Welshman was an infidel, and took to walking about in the night and calling people by name; and these people all died. It was very unpleasant, because there were not many left in the neighborhood. The bishop thought likely an evil spirit had got into the corpse, and the best plan was to pour holy water on the grave, which William did, without any perceptible effect. Finally, one night, after there were very few left indeed, the ghost called William himself; and the reckless man rushed out with his sword, chased him into a ditch, and cut off his head. After that there was no more trouble, and the best of it was William did not die.

'Concerning King Herla' of the ancient Britons, who made a compact with the king of the pygmies that each should attend the wedding of the other, — how the king of the pygmies came to Herla's wedding with a great retinue and rich presents; how a year thereafter Herla was taken through a dark cave to a place where was no sun or moon, but lit by many lamps, and witnessed the wedding of the king; how on his return he found that his few days with the pygmies had been many years on earth, and the Saxons ruled the land; how ever since he has wandered, seen by many, unquietly and without resting-place, until in the first year of the coronation of King Henry he disappeared in the river Wye and wanders no more.

But whatever delight the archdeacon took in his prodigies and apparitions, popular superstition had to run the gauntlet of his sarcasm along with its betters, as in the following instance, that deathbed advice is better than any other kind of advice.

"A certain soldier, hereditary seneschal of France, said to his son before he died, ' My son, you are very popular and the favor of the Lord is manifest in you. Now keep these my precepts for your own safety and prosperity. Do not set free any man justly condemned, do not drink stale water, not fresh from the brook, do not advance a servant, do not marry the daughter of an adulteress, do not trust a low born man who has red hair.' After his father was buried the son came into his hereditary office, was very acceptable to the king and all France, very gentle and wise and good-mannered. He quite neglected his father's precepts, married a woman of questionable parentage, had a redhaired servant, who looked like a hungry jackdaw and turned out to be very active and useful. . . . He prospered in family, wealth and all other respects."

Map was a Welshman, born on the border, but he speaks as disrespectfully of his countrymen almost as Heine does of Alma Mater of Göttingen, chiefly complaining that they were such conscienceless cutthroats and given to interminable feuds. He recollects a conversation with Thomas à Becket in connection with this, when the latter was chancellor. Becket asked him if the Welsh could be trusted; and Map told him a story about a soldier who found King Louis, the son of Charlemagne, in the forest of Behere, sitting on a stone, and did not know him. Louis was much interested in the soldier's sword, and while he was examining it forgot his incognito and said in a royal kind of way, " Bring me a stone to sit on!" The soldier was afraid of the sword, and brought the stone; but when he got the sword back, he told the king to put the stone in its place again, and the king did. "That is the way with Welsh good faith," said Map to Becket, — "when you hold the sword they beg, but when they hold it, they begin to give orders."

One paper is headed, ' Concerning the Undiscriminating Piety of Welshmen.'

"In every tribe, it is said, the fear of God is acceptable to him, but among our Welsh people the fear of the Lord is seldom according to wisdom. My lord, William of Braose, who was a practiced warrior, told me himself that he had a Welshman with him once, of noble family and very strict in his honesty, who every night, at first cock crow, would rise from his bed and kneel naked on the bare floor, praying till dawn and fasting, as was proper. He kept such stringent guard over himself that you would have thought him little short of an angel, but if you saw how stupid he was in society, how quick at blood, how negligent of his own safety and eager for another man's death, how he delighted in the perpetration of any crime or homicide, you would not have doubted that he was inwardly given over to iniquity."

The assumption that the fact that the man was a bore, "*infrunitus in congressibus,*" was an associate evidence of his inward iniquity, is characteristic of Map, for in spite of his disrespectful comments on the Welsh, he was a thorough Celt. His bright, lively manner and epigrammatic turn are the ear-marks of the race ; and I suspect this was a secret reason for his discontent at court, possibly somewhat exaggerated, however. "This unhappy and curious court," as he calls it, where "I languish and renounce my tastes to please other people." "In the court," he observes, "the man that laughs is laughed at, and he who sits in sadness is considered wise. So our judges punish gladness and reward melancholy, although the good may properly rejoice in a good conscience and the bad from a bad conscience be deservedly melancholy." His student life at Paris had left him in spite of himself with an un-English love for the bright and pleasant people of France.

"It happened that when I sojourned awhile with king (Louis) at Paris, he talked with me about the wealth of kings, and among other things he said, ' The wealth of kings is diverse and of great variety. In precious stones, lions, leopards and elephants are the riches of the kings of Ind, the emperor of Byzantium and the king of Sicily glory in gold and silken garments. . . . The emperor of Rome, whom they call Alemannorus, had men-at-arms and war horses, but no gold or silk or any opulence. . . . Your lord, the king of England, lacks nothing and possesses all things, men, horses, gold and silk, gems and fruits and wild game. We in France have nothing except bread and wine and happiness.' I noted these words, because they were both polite and true."

In another paper, after referring again to the legend of Herla and his ghostly army, a kind of Cambrian Wild Huntsman, he repeats that he disappeared about the beginning of Henry's reign, and bequeathed his general foolishness to the land; and then follows a curious passage which recalls the saying that " The English take their pleasures sadly."

"We generally seek among other nations the causes of grief, because with us people seldom grieve, the causes of happiness because we seldom rejoice. We have indeed comfort for grief, but we know nothing of happiness. We are supported by our consolations but we are not happy in our joys."

Whatever else may be said of this, it is not only a keen but a French or Celtic analysis of the English character. It is the same as saying that Teutonic happiness is equivalent to Celtic consolation.

Next to the Cistercians, Map's particular detestation was the king's illegitimate son Geoffrey. The feeling was cordially returned. Geoffrey was elected Bishop of Lincoln, but was not ordained. The Pope insisted that he should either be ordained or retire. " He retired," Map remarks, " to Marlborough. There is a fountain there, of which if any one drinks, they say he spoils his French, and consequently, when any one speaks that language very badly, he is said to speak the French of Marlborough." When Geoffrey announced his resignation to the Archbishop of Canterbury in Map's hearing, the archbishop asked, " *Quid loqueris ?* " (What were you saying?), wishing him to repeat what he had said, that all might hear ; when he was silent, the archbishop asked again, " *Quid loqueris ?* " and Map answered for him, " *Gallicum Merleburgæ* " (The French of Marlborough), " thereupon the rest laughed, but he was angry and went out." Map had too sharp a tongue to be a comfortable enemy.

The literary opinions of so thorough a man of letters would naturally be interesting. In the ' Prologus ' to the Fifth Book he writes : —

" The result of the industry of the ancients is in our hands. The deeds of their times, now past, they make present to ours, but we are silent, and so, while their memories live in us, we are forgetful of our own. O miraculum illustre ! the dead live, and the living are buried before them. And yet we have in our times something of Sophocles, are not lacking in dramatic talent. . . The Cæsar of Lucanus, the Æneas of Maro, live in great honor, much through their own merits, but not less through the vigilance of the poets. But with us the divine nobility of Charlemagne and Pepin are celebrated only in vulgar rhythms."

Which one of the miracle playwrights possessed this " something of Sophocles " and was " not lacking in dramatic talent," if that is what " *non indigens cothurno* " means, is not mentioned. The mantle of Sophocles has never been recognized among them since with any startling certainty. At the end of the ' Prologus ' he instances a fish of the Danube called the " usula," which in its last gasp listens eagerly to strains of music, and calls it a symbol of the scholar and man of letters, whom no disease or difficulty can keep from his labors. It is either an unconscious or remorseful stab at himself, because he had already offered much the same excuse for his lack of literary activity, — that a poet at court was like a fish out of water.

He is rather hypocritically modest about his own literary talents, though touchy on the score of his honesty.

" I see that I have been compared by the monks in an uncomplimentary way to the Cluvian poet (of Juvenal) accustomed to ' the chalk and coal, (as Horace says,) an insipid idiot of a scribbler.' Without doubt I am, but while my satires may be worthy of ' the chalk and coal ' and admitting that I am an idiot, I do not lie, I do not flatter. . . . . An unskilful poet I confess myself, but not a writer of falsities."

We may say for his prose, however, that it is frequently bad Latin, but always good sense. His meaning is clear out on the finger-points of his language; and his style passes from easy narrative to the clean-cut antithesis and epigram, like the snap of a whip, with uncommon grace and effect. Without searching for a more exact illustration, I translate from a paper called 'Conclusio Prædictæ Epistolæ,' for the sake of the antitheses : —

"Hard is the hand of the surgeon, but healthful; hard is this sermon but healthful, and I would it might be as useful as devoted to you. Narrow, you say, is the rule of living I inflict upon you. Be it so. Narrow is the way which leads to life and the path is not plain that goes to the plenitude of joys."

There is a pun in the last lines between "plana" and "plena," which the translation barely hints at; but the archdeacon's puns, I suspect, were his particular pride, and the attempt to chase them into the English language is quite hopeless. To pepper a page with puns in a guileless, unconscious way, as if it were nothing but high spirits, is a prerogative that belongs strictly to mediæval Latin. The 'Prædictæ Epistolæ' is that written "ad philosophum Rufinum" whose real name was John, in which Valerius, or Walter, attempts to dissuade him from getting married. It is to be hoped he utterly failed, because his logic is quite exasperating. A classic example was always a powerful argument to the mediæval mind, and is still looked on as rather a majestic affair ; but after all, if Rufinus had an opportunity to get married, it was not charity to throw Hercules and Deijanira in his face, or construe the paternal wrath of Apollo, which resulted in his becoming the shepherd of Admetus, as a concretely terrible warning. Just how seriously Map meant it to be taken is a question, but certainly not altogether.

This Epistle to Rufinus seems to have been written and widely circulated before it was included in the collection. After a solemn appeal, — "Friend, the omnipotent God grant that you be not deceived by the wiles of the omnipotent female, and illuminate your heart that you go not with deluded eyes whither I fear," — in the section entitled 'Finis Epistolæ Præmissæ,' he declares that "this letter has pleased many people, been widely seized upon, copied carefully and read with great delight. Nevertheless, some people say it is not mine, but written by some ordinary person. For they are envious of the epistle and would violently take away its glory and its author," — which seems to imply that its "glory" and its "author" were synonymous in its author's mind.

The essays of the Fifth Book·are more strictly historical in subject, on Earl Godwin, Cnut, William Rufus, Henry I., and Louis of France. But in these, too, Map is the discursive essayist rather than the historian. An anecdote satisfies his mind better than a sober statement, and he delights to wander off in personal reminiscence and reflection. The men of the past were real men to him, not historical characters, or political agencies, or the nucleuses of a certain number of facts. He talks of Cnut as he talks of Becket, and the sense of actuality never drifts away from him. Lowell has said that the best motto for Chaucer are the words he dreamed were written over a gate : —

> "Through me men go into that blissful place
> Of heartès heal and deadly woundès cure."

Map writes his own motto, too, and prescribes the way in which his writing should be read. "When from the palace," he says to Galfrid, "descend the officials, wearied with the immensity of royal business, they are pleased to incline to more humble occupations, and to lighten the weight of their gravity with jokes. Perhaps when you have breathed in solemn senate with the pages of philosophy and divinity, you may be pleased to read the ignoble and weak of this volume for your recreation and pastime." But as a motto this is not altogether successful. Map was no sunny, tranquil spirit like Chaucer. His wit is stinging, not infrequently spiteful, and often bitterly in earnest. However it was with his friend Galfrid, there must have been many in the court who read him with emotions scarcely consistent with "recreation and pastime." "This little book on the court of king Henry, . . . written by snatches and on stray leaves" did not always seem to him such a trivial affair. " I have drawn it with violence from my heart, compelled to follow my lord's command, for I trembled at what I did, I struggled to accomplish what I could not."

He closes the book — this man who once went under the strange misnomer of "the jovial archdeacon" — with a return to the gloomy picture that he drew in the beginning : —

"Augustine said, 'I am in time, and I speak concerning time, but I do not know what time is.' In a similar astonishment I may say, that I am in the court and speak concerning the court, but I do not know what it is. Only I know it is not time. It is temporal certainly, mutable and various, local and erratic. . . . We leave it frequently and return as the exigencies of the affairs of each dictate. When we are away from it we recognize it as a whole; if we remain outside a year, it meets us with a new face on our return and we ourselves are new. . . . It is like Infernus, having its fiery rivers, the Styx which is hatred, Phlegethon, passion, and Lethe, forgetfulness, Cocytus, remorse, and Acheron, melancholy. Charon is there, the court usher, who admits none without his stipend, — in his mouth and not in his hand, because an usher is obsequious enough in view of a promised bribe, but the bribe once given does not influence him at all. Tantalus is there with his desire ever at the ends of his fingers, Ixion bound to the wheel of Fortune, and Sisyphus rolling his slippery stone up the mountain of wealth till his own heart becomes the stone he rolls. There is the dissolute Tityus and the children of Belus, who strive to fill the vase that has no bottom."

Very much a place of shadows it seemed to Map, unreal and vain, as to another humorist of the nineteenth century seemed the social world he lived in, who wrote at the end of his book, "Vanity of vanities! which of us has his desire in the world, or having it is satisfied?"

A keen and versatile man was Map, sensitive to many influences, of varied culture and marked Celtic character, a conscientious churchman, a polished courtier, an acknowledged wit, and a man who, it is at least highly probable, originated a great school of satire. In the 'De Nugis Curialium,' under its cowled and curious garb of mediæval Latin, lies a real element of literature, for in it "the dead live" and "the deeds of their time, now past," it makes "present to ours."        *Arthur W. Colton.*

# JEAN PAUL RICHTER.

EAN PAUL, though not occupying the highest pedestal amidst the group of great writers that have dazzled the modern world with their genius, has yet a place secured and satisfactory in the hearts of his countrymen, and wins his way also to the inner nature of all sympathetic readers. After wandering with Goethe through labyrinths of deepest intellectual doubt, morbid miseries, dissatisfied aspirations, and pessimistic philosophy, we turn to Richter's hopeful mind with a sense of relief from the alternating exaltation and depression of the (perhaps) greater mind. It is like the descent into a peaceful vale, where limpid streams flow through flowering meads, where sunshine and birds make warmth and melody, with only the shadows of far-off clouds dimming for a moment the bright serenity of the landscape, after having been on lonely mountain-tops during a storm, when the forces of Nature met in mighty conflict. Our natures were uplifted by the grandeur of the contest; the deeps of our souls were stirred; we obtained glimpses of the Infinite; the power and majesty of creation penetrated into our very being; the earth below us, with its small experiences, seemed too remote to disturb us. We revelled on the heights of great undefined thoughts, dissatisfied with the narrowness of human life, and impatient at its trivialities, while we soared into realms of the unknown.

But we are mortal. The environments of Time and Space draw us down earthward ; and we return, wearied with the turmoil of a struggle with the Limitless, and yield our souls to the sweet influences of Nature made manifest in more peaceful guise. It seems to be the impulse of Richter's genius to present to us the universe in this manner. His mind turns toward light and warmth. These are the elements of growth, and certainly the genius which basks in them must develop something of perfection. He is an apostle of hope and joy. He says, " Nations and men are only the best when they are the gladdest, and deserve heaven when they enjoy it. The tear of Grief is but a diamond of the second water ; but the tear of Joy of the first. And therefore, oh, Fatherly Fate, Thou spreadest the flowers of joy, as nurses do lilies, in the nursery of life, that the awakening children may sleep the sounder."

While Byron seems to revel in the magnificent misery of his dream of darkness, Jean Paul recoils with unspeakable horror from the unfathomable abyss of chaos his imagination pictures. We admire the one ; we yield ourselves to melancholy and romance, and allow our deepest sympathy to be stirred by his pictures of woe. By the other, our hearts are uplifted. We become cheerful, and are buoyed up with patience and hope in our pilgrimage through life. We are ready to grasp all that is bright and cheery, rather than sink into apathy and despair. He says : —

"Of ways for becoming happier (not happy) I could never inquire out more than three. The first, (rather an elevated road) is this : to soar away so far above the clouds of life, that you see the whole external world, with its wolf-dens, charnel-houses and thunder-rods, lying far down beneath you shrunk into a little child's garden. This skyward track, however, is fit only for the winged portion of the human species, for the smallest. The second is simply to sink down into this little garden, and there to nestle yourself so snugly, so homewise in some furrow, that in looking out from your warm lark-nest, you likewise can discern no wolf-dens, charnel-houses, or thunder-rods, but only blades and ears, every one of which for the nest-bird is a tree, and a sun-screen, and a rain-screen. The third, finally, which I look upon as the hardest and cunningest, is that of alternating between the two. The foregoing second way is not good enough for man, who here on earth, should take into his hand, not the sickle only, but the plow. But even by walking a man rests and recovers himself for climbing, by little joys and duties for great. The victorious Dictator must contrive to plow down his battle Mars-field into a flax and carrot-field, to transform his theater of war into a parlor theater, on which his children may enact some good pieces from the 'Children's Friend.' . . . Can he accomplish this, can he turn so softly from the path of poetical happiness into household happiness? then is he little different from myself, who even now, (though modesty might forbid me to disclose it) who, even now, I say, amid the creation of this letter, have been enabled to reflect, that when it is done, so also will the roses and elder-berries of pastry be done, which a sure hand is seething in butter for the author of this work."

How Richter as a writer is to be considered, depends upon the decision of the literary world as to the scope of novelist. If it be simply to present us with a narrative of human life enclosed within its web of sentiments, aspirations, and acts, then Jean Paul cannot be considered a novelist. If the author present the realism of nature to view endowed with color and life and soul, the ideal side of it is portrayed; and he becomes a poet. If he reason from his portrayal of human life, its fancies and passions, its loves and hates, its temptations and triumphs, and if he evolve from a contemplation of the beauties and mysteries of creation a conception of the Author of Creation, and of duty in its creatures, then he becomes a philosopher. Jean Paul unites these faculties in his writings in a remarkable degree. His books, considered simply as novels, are not artistic. There is no well-conceived plot, smoothly and completely worked out to a pleasing *dénouement*, with due regard paid to received rules of critics. There is an unusual admixture of elements in them which produces an incongruous whole. The man possessed the most far-reaching imagination, the most acute poetical sensibility, a keenest sense of humor, a philosophical mind, the most penetrating intellect, the softest, kindest heart, the simplest faith in God and good, the most enthusiastic love of Nature, and a thousand other traits, which are all shining in his writings.

The main incidents of the stories could be told in a hundred sentences, but the world of feeling and thought portrayed repay the reader for travelling through his voluminous works. He is never satisfied with one perusal. He will read them over and over again, finding new riches each time, and end by loving the man who wrote them. Richter is called " Jean Paul the Unique," for he stands alone as to the peculiarities of his genius. He writes according to no received standards of taste. Just as the great thoughts come surging from his brain he gives utterance to them. If a stray fancy seize him, he gives expression to it (in an aside or a parenthesis), not caring if it be irrelevant to the subject. His intellect seems to me like a hidden torrent of pure crystal water which must burst its bounds and come to the light. It overcomes all impediments, rushing in an impetuous, headlong course, perhaps destroying the barriers which have restrained it, bearing in its current débris which mar its purity; but it is a life-giving element, which will leave its impress as it goes on the freshened earth, in tender herbage and blossoming plants, and which at last will become calm and broad as it nears the ocean of eternity. The distinguishing traits of his genius are imagination and humor; I know of no author who excels him in either. His imagination knows no bounds. Creation is its playground; suns and worlds its balls; the Milky Way its footpath; the heights of Infinity or the depths of chaos its goal. His humor is like the misty radiance which envelops the earth when the sun shines upon its wet bosom, after it has been deluged with rain tears, — a mixture of pathos and merriment. So while laughing at human frailties, his great heart is sorrowing over them. He paints the homeliest details of a poor meagre life, and philosophizes over them in the same paragraph, and makes you feel that as a human life there is something of divinity in it, and that it is grand in spite of its triviality. Carlyle says of him, "There was a bold deep joyful spirit looking through those young eyes, and to such a spirit, the world has nothing poor, but all is rich and full of loveliness and wonder." His style is called difficult; it may be so. There are parentheses within parentheses, digressions, notes, allusions to obscure facts and unknown minutiæ; but we are willing to endure all this, for the truth and beauty which we are sure to find underlying them. The pearl-diver goes to the bottom of the ocean for his gems. The miner delves within the dark bosom of the earth for his precious stones. Why shall we not search for gems of thought and feeling which are surely to be found, though the half obscure labyrinths through which we wander may sometimes discourage us. Some of these word pearls and diamonds might well be strung into an amulet to be worn upon the soul as a charm against hopelessness and scepticism. For example : —

" More than one Savior has already died for the earth and for man, and I am convinced that CHRIST will one day take many pious human beings by the hand and say to them ' Ye too have suffered.' " " The human spirit could not take on the infinite stream of knowledge, which flows through the infinite duration of time, unless it were imbibed by degrees and after intervals. The eternal day which would else blind our spirits, was divided into diurnal periods by midsummer nights, which at one time we call sleep, at another death, and the midday of these periods was thus set between morning and evening." " He who finds a GOD in the physical world, will also find one in the moral which is History. Nature forces on our hearts a Creator, History a Providence." " The crystal light.reflecting grotto of an August night, spread its illuminated vault over the dark green earth, and the ocean calm of nature rebuked the storm of the human heart." " There aloft the fogs of our days must one day be resolved into stars, even as the mist of the milky way parts into suns." " The source of the best and holiest, from the universe up to GOD, is hidden behind a night full of too distant stars."

The ' Campaner Thal,' Richter's last writing, is perhaps the most interesting and important of his works. The characters in it stand out clearly, — real persons, without any minute pencilling of traits. Besides Jean Paul himself we have the sceptical, disputatious would-be philosopher, the poetical, melancholy lover, the happy, genial, successful man of the world, the pure, cold, meditative maiden, and the bright, tender, sparkling, sympathetic girl plainly before our mind's eye with very few words of description. Karlson, the disappointed lover of Gione, and Jean Paul, his chosen friend, join the wedding party in the Pyrenees on the eve of the marriage of Wilhelm and Gione, and journey with them through the beautiful valley of which Jean Paul says, " I know none other in which I would rather awake or die, or love, than in this one." His descriptions of the beauty of Nature in this book are the most exquisite I have ever met with. He not only sees them with an artist's eye, and describes them with a poet's tongue, but his spirit seems to have penetrated to the very heart of Nature, and beats responsive to her throbs; for instance, the wedding morn of Wilhelm and Gione : —

"Through the whole night a half lost thundering was heard, as though it murmured in its sleep. In the morning Karlson and myself stepped out into the wide cloud tapestried bridal chamber of nature. The moon approached the double moment of its waning and its fullness. The Sun standing on America as on a burning altar drove the cloudy incense of its *feu de joie*, high and red into the air, but a morning tempest boiled angrily above it, and darted its fierce lightnings to meet his ascending rays. The oppressive heat of nature drew longer and louder plaints from the Nightingale and evanescent aroma from the long flower meads. Heavy warm drops were pressed from the clouds and beat loudly on the stream and on the foliage. Only the Mittagshorn, the pinnacle of the Pyrenees, stood brightly and clearly, in the heavenly blue. Now a gust of wind from the waning moon dispersed the raging storm, and the sun stood victoriously, under a triumphal arch of lightnings. The winds restored the heaven's blue, and dashed the rain behind the earth, and around the dazzling sun diamond there lay only the silvered fringes of the once threatening clouds."

After the marriage, at which neither Karlson nor Jean Paul was present, the whole party proceed on a day's jaunt through the valley, at the extremity of which Karlson has had prepared a luxurious home for his bride, of which she knows nothing. It is during this day's journeying that the dissertation on the immortality of the soul is given, which I believe to be the most satisfying ever given by any philosopher. There is a charm in the picture presented to the mind's eye by the author, in his description of this day in the beautiful valley. The sunshine, the birds, the flowers, the streams, the mountains, the happy companionship, the grave discourses, the merry jests, the softening shadows of sorrow, the mellowing influence of love, the strengthening tonic of irony, while over all, in Carlyle's words, lay "a deep genial humor like warm sunshine, softening the whole, blending the whole into light sportful harmony," — everything is there to create harmony of tone in the mind of the reader. And then comes the picture of the evening, which is a perfect completion of a perfect day : —

"Around us in their majesty, reposed the Pyrenees half robed in night, and half in day, not stooping like man beneath the load of years, but erect forever. On the mountain heads hung wreaths of roses, cloud woven, but each time that a star appeared upon the clear deep sea of ether, and sparkled upon its azure waves, a rose from the mountain chaplet faded and dropped away. The Mittags-horn alone, like a higher spirit, gazed long after the sinking lonely sun, and glowed with ecstasy. Down beneath us an amphitheatre of lemon trees by its perfumes brought us back to the veiled earth, and made a dusky paradise of it. The Nightingale in the rose hedges by the lake awoke, and the plaintive tones from its tiny heart, pierced into the great heart of man, and shining glow worms flew from rose bush to rose bush, but in the mirror of the lake, they were but as golden sparks floating over pale yellow flowers. But when we looked again towards the heavens lo! all its stars were gleaming, and in place of rose woven wreaths, the mountains were clad in extinguished rainbows, and the giant of the Pyrenees was crowned with stars, instead of roses. . . . In this moment it was with each of our enraptured souls, as if from its oppressed heart Earth's load had dropped away : as if from her mother's arms, the earth were giving us matured, into the Father arms of the Infinite Creator."

Carlyle says, " Report also we regret to say is all that we know of the Campaner Thal, one of Richter's beloved topics, or rather the life of his whole Philosophy, glimpses of which look forth on us from almost every one of his writings." He died while engaged, under recent and almost total blindness, in enlarging and remod-elling this 'Campaner Thal.' The unfinished manuscript was borne upon his coffin to the burial-vault, and Klopstock's hymn, " Aufer-stehn Wirst Du " (Thou shalt arise, my soul) can seldom have been sung with more appropriate application than over the grave of Richter.                                        *J. F. Wallace.*

# THE SUPERNATURAL IN SHAKESPEARE:

## II. 'THE TEMPEST.'

SHAKESPEARE's fairies love secluded, romantic spots,—

> " A bank where the wild thyme blows,
> Where oxlips and the nodding violet grows ; "

and in the 'Tempest' we behold those that

> " On the sands, with printless foot,
> Do chase the ebbing Neptune ; "

for a yet remoter fairy-land is open to our entrance in that magic island, ruled by the wisest and kindliest of enchanters, Prospero, — an isle " full of noises, sounds and sweet airs, that give delight and hurt not."

And in this enchanted spot, which since its lord broke his magic wand has vanished from the world, or has been transformed into common earth and rock, we find that most exquisite, elemental creature, Ariel, — the incarnate air, which should be " the most pellucid air " of Athens ; the type of all that is light and graceful, changeful and poetic ; his master's docile, if sometimes impatient, servant ; desiring his lord's affection, yet longing for freedom ; full of humane and gracious inclinations, but not wishing to be too strictly bound by ideas of duty, or kept too closely to the dull round of labor.    Frolicsome as Puck, he is more delicate in his fancies ; so full of music that he gives forth strains of melody, like an Æolian harp, whenever he moves ; bringing out, like the witches, the hidden thoughts of men, but moving them always to finer issues ; comforting sorrow, arousing remorse, awakening love, and now and then punishing evil-doers with mischievous delight.    He can take every form, from the fire blazing on the yard-arms of the ship to that of a sea-nymph ; but he refuses to obey the commands of the hideous Sycorax, and so is imprisoned by her spells in the cloven pine, from which Prospero frees him, winning thereby his eager service.    To him he " comes with a thought " : —

> " I drink the air before me, and return
> Or ere your pulse twice beat ! "

he cries.    He masters the other spirits and exacts their service; he invents and brings before Ferdinand and Miranda the lovely masque for their delight ; in him are embodied " sweetness and light," music, art, and poetry.    Who could wonder if, even when restored to place and power and friends, his master should miss the dainty Ariel who has done his spriting so gently ?

But what is this other strange creature, this man-monster, Caliban? As Ariel is all of air, light and beautiful, he is of the earth, earthy; coarse and brutish, but yet interesting, and even with something to be said for his side of the story.

Ere Prospero came into the island, a witch had dwelt there, Sycorax by name, of most malignant temper, and so potent that she

"Could control the moon, make flows and ebbs,"

and even overmaster Ariel and fix him in torment, although not strong enough to force him to obey. Here she abode for years; and when she died, Caliban, her son, was left, the only human creature, if such we may call him, upon the spirit-haunted island.

Then comes the banished Duke, and takes possession; frees Ariel, and controls him; subjects the other spirits to his will, and makes the monster his servant. Kindly at first, but forced to severity, Prospero is the master, and Caliban the slave, bound to unwilling service where once he reigned.

"For I am all the subjects that you have,
Which first was mine own king,"

he exclaims. Something nobler than he had ever known was offered to him, could he have had the soul to recognize it. Prospero gave him much; he developed his intellectual faculties a little; he taught him language, "and the profit is that he knows how to curse;" but with it all he has deprived him of his birth-right, or Caliban thinks he has, as civilized man always has done, and still is doing, by the savage everywhere. So it must be, no doubt, if the lower comes in conflict with the higher, and so humanity moves onward; but the reverse of the shield will present itself to the being crushed beneath it.

Caliban's service is all unwilling, not that, like Ariel, he pines for the airy joys of freedom, but because he hates both work and master; and while the fairy serves in the hope of liberty as his prize, and from grateful love of Prospero, Caliban toils grudgingly for fear of punishment, and in every accident that befalls him, in the apes that mock and bite, in the hedge-hogs that prick his feet, he fancies his master's agents are avenging neglected duty.   He takes the rascally sailors for gods, and exalted by the wine they give him, offers them his service if they will help him to his revenge ; he tells the tale of his dispossession, and bids his new masters burn the tyrant's books, since without them he is powerless to control the elemental spirits, who hate the new-come lord, even as he does ; then they may slay him, shorn of his power, and reign joyously.   He bursts forth into what has been called " the Marseillaise of the Island," and sings of liberty, —

> " 'Ban, 'Ban, Ca-Caliban,
> Has a new master.   Get a new man !
> Freedom, heyday ! "

His gods, however, prove themselves very wretched specimens of humanity, — drunken, pleased with petty toys, and, like many another conspirator, letting their great enterprise slip, by turning aside to trivial issues.   Beside such as they, even Caliban assumes a certain dignity, as one of more single purpose, aiming at grander crime.

Those who seek an allegoric significance in this marvellous drama have invented many meanings for Caliban.   He is the understanding, the primitive man, the missing-link, brute matter, coarse, but serviceable if controlled by mind.   All these, and more, no doubt, he may be ; he certainly seems a halfway creature between man and brute, capable of some odd, rudimentary feeling of gratitude, and with a strange reverence, or rather fear, for what is mightier than himself.   In these days, when heredity is so much regarded, we must remember that his father was a demon, which would render any attempts at his moral development more difficult than if he were merely the human struggling to emerge from the brute existence, since he has as an inheritance an active love of evil.   It were easier to

> " Let the ape and tiger die,"

than to escape from the acquired nature of a line of devils.   But Browning accredits him with theological speculations ; and those who would investigate one of the aspects in which a sense of something superhuman first works in the soul of primitive humanity may pass profitable hours in the study of 'Caliban upon Setebos.' But although Prospero failed in his teaching to implant the germs of morality, he appears to have brought out a poetic faculty, which is certainly remarkable; or is that possibly a trait of the natural man, which Caliban was able to manifest when he had acquired the gift of articulate speech?   He says to Trinculo:

> "I prithee, let me bring thee where crabs grow;
> And I with my long nails will dig thee pig-nuts;
> Show thee a jay's nest, and instruct thee how
> To snare the nimble marmozet; I 'll bring thee
> To clustering filberts, and sometimes I 'll get thee
> Young scamels from the rock."

And again, —

> "The isle is full of noises,
> Sounds and sweet airs, that give delight and hurt not.
> Sometimes a thousand twangling instruments
> Will hum about mine ears, and sometimes voices
> That, if I then had waked, after long sleep,
> Will make me sleep again : and then, in dreaming,
> The clouds, methought would open, and show riches
> Ready to drop upon me, that, when I waked,
> I cried to dream again."

Is it possible that there may have come to poor Caliban in his dreams a vision of some better things?   When the plot has failed, when the ignoble nature of his gods has plainly manifested itself, and the master orders Caliban into his cell, with the command to trim it handsomely if he look for pardon, the ruined conspirator exclaims, —

> "Ay that I will ; and I 'll be wise hereafter
> And seek for grace.   What a thrice-double ass
> Was I, to take this drunkard for a god,
> And worship this dull fool !"

Does Caliban at last " know the greatest when he sees it," and amend his life?   For his sake we may hope it ; for our own, perhaps, we should prefer not to see him in his changed condition, if such things should be.   He will have become commonplace.

*Annie Russell Wall.*

# AN OBJECTION TO BROWNING'S CALIBAN CONSIDERED.

IN dealing with the criticism that Browning has endowed Caliban with more intelligence than has Shakespeare, two points should be discussed. First, Is the criticism a true one? Must we regard Browning's Caliban as mentally superior to Shakespeare's? Second, If Browning has taken the liberty of thus modifying one of Shakespeare's creations, has he, by so doing, violated any law of literary propriety?

In the first place, Is Browning's Caliban superior to Shakespeare's in mental power? Shakespeare gives us, with a few powerful strokes, a picture of Caliban as he would impress an observer, — a degraded creature, half man, half brute, without moral sense, and without intellectual aspiration. He has, however, a sufficient degree of understanding to master a language, learn something of astronomy, acquire a practical knowledge of the resources of the island, and to *plot* a murder. Yet, in spite of all this, we feel that he is a stupid creature, for he makes no remark throughout the play that proves even an ordinary degree of intelligence.

Browning adopts his own method of presenting Caliban to us. He does not, like Shakespeare, take the point of view of an outside observer. He gives us Caliban's most secret thoughts, his inner life. Yet we find that Browning's Caliban is, in the main, a faithful reproduction of Shakespeare's, — the same grovelling and cowardly brute. Browning has, however, brought out a side of Caliban's nature that Shakespeare has not dwelt upon. Shakespeare has represented Caliban's actions and behavior among men; Browning has given us Caliban's inner life. The question then is, Is the inner life of Caliban, as presented by Browning, inconsistent with his outer life, as described by Shakespeare?

Poetical license, I am sure all will agree, allows Browning to make Caliban think in verse, in somewhat poetical language, and to think rather more connectedly than would be natural in reality for a person to think who had no intention either of following up his thought by action, or of communicating his thought to others. If we concede this privilege to the poet, the question then becomes, are Caliban's thoughts, as conceived by Browning, thoughts which we must suppose it would be impossible for Shakespeare's Caliban to have entertained? It is to this question that our answer is no.

We arrive at our conclusion in this way. Suppose that Browning's 'Caliban' had been written first, Shakespeare's 'Tempest' afterward. Would it then seem to us that the stupidity of Shakespeare's Caliban was inconsistent with the train of thought followed out by Browning's Caliban? No; we should fully expect that the creature who thought like Browning's Caliban would act like Shakespeare's Caliban. I believe it is true that a reputation for stupidity generally results not from being without ideas that might be interesting or even bright if expressed well and opportunely, but from not knowing that one's ideas are worth expressing, or from not having the poise of character and the presence of mind to choose for their expression an appropriate occasion and a sympathetic audience. Although nowhere in 'The Tempest' has Caliban shown the power of thought that Browning has bestowed upon him, yet there is nothing in 'The Tempest' to prove that he did not have it. If he had all the mental power that Browning credits him with, his craven nature would have prevented him from expressing himself before others. If Browning had made Caliban, instead of soliloquize, talk his ideas to some person, he would have doubled, or even tripled, his apparent intelligence.

We now come to our second point. For the sake of argument, let us grant that Browning has endowed Caliban with more mental capacity than has Shakespeare. Has he, by so doing, been guilty of literary impropriety? We think not. Shakespeare's Caliban may be regarded as representing man in a degraded savage state. Now, Browning wished to depict the thoughts concerning God which a savage of degraded nature might naturally be supposed to entertain. To have invented a new story would simply have been to make a tool with which to accomplish his purpose. This would have been a waste of time. Shakespeare's Caliban was already familiar to readers. Browning chose to adopt Shakespeare's Caliban as the representative of a degraded savage. If Browning's conception of a degraded savage was somewhat different from Shakespeare's, that is of little consequence. Inasmuch as Browning used Caliban for the same purpose for which Shakespeare invented him, — to represent savage man, — he committed no impropriety, even if his conception of savage man differed from Shakespeare's.

I am willing even to go farther than this. Suppose that Shakespeare's Caliban could not possibly have thought like Browning's Caliban, and suppose, moreover, that no savage man in his savage state could possibly have had the train of thoughts that Browning has put into the mind of Caliban, yet is there any one thought in the poem beyond the capacity of the average mind of a low savage race? Might not, then, a savage race, as a whole, in the course of time, have had all the thoughts ascribed to the individual, Caliban? And rather than deny the poem a place in the literature of the world, should we not allow the poet the privilege, for the sake of the picturesque effect necessary to make the composition a poem, of centring the thoughts of a race in one man, — the type of that race?

*Maude Wilkinson.*

## GENTLE WILL, OUR FELLOW.

WRIT IN 1626 A. D. BY JOHN HEMINGE, SERVANT OF HIS GRACIOUS MAJESTY KING CHARLES I.; EDITED IN 1892 A. D. AS "ALL, THOUGH FEIGNED, IS TRUE" BY F. G. FLEAY, SERVANT OF ALL SHAKESPEARIAN STUDENTS IN AMERICA, ENGLAND, GERMANY, OR ELSEWHERE.

(*Continued.*)

WE acted ten plays this Christmas at Court.

Shakespeare now reformed his great tragedy founded on Scotch chronicle, 'Macbeth,' and introduced passages touching on the miraculous power of cure of the King's Evil possessed by the late King.

It was made almost a new play, and was left by him in a perfect shape, but the growth of a liking for music, songs and dances, compelled us, after his death and just before we published our Folio, to give the play to Master Middleton for further alteration, contrary to our former practice of eschewing these adornments of our plays. He put in two songs from his play of ' The Witch,' and a dance of six witches, there being only three in the scene as it first stood, and to this end added the character of Hecate. This making the presentment too long for the patience of the auditors, we made more omissions in other parts than to most of us seemed desirable; but we nevertheless thought it best to print the play as it was then acted. It hath in this new shape been well received; and belike it will, as Master Davenant now desires, at some time be again reformed and be enriched (so he thinks) with more music and dancing — which Heaven forfend! It is a strange chance that these changes should have been lately made by the same poet who, now twenty years ago, directly after the play was first acted on the London stage, scoffed at " the ghost in the white sheet who sat at the upper end of the table instead of a jester," in his ' Puritan,' which was acted by the Paul's boys and published the year following as by W. S., meaning concerning W. Shakespeare, just as ' Sir John Oldcastle ' had been seven years before.

This play, otherwise called ' The Widow of Watling Street,' was filled with allusions " by " William Shakespeare's plays, at least half a dozen being girded at, one of which, ' Pericles,' was, like ' Macbeth,' even then on the stage. But ' Pericles ' was not all Shakespeare's ; it was at first intrusted to Wilkins, who wrote the first two acts, Shakespeare afterward contributing the story of ' Marina,' just as he had added ' The Yorkshire Tragedy ' to this same man's ' Miseries of Enforced Marriage.' Shakespeare's part is a play in itself; neither could he be induced to enter on the abomination of the accursed story of King Antiochus, as old Chaucer called it. The fitting of this Marina story into the play was not made by him. But this was two years after, when Wilkins had left us. The play as at first acted was all his and very displeasing ; he took offence, and went to the Queen's men in the next year, 1607. We acted the play as it now stands in 1608; and then, out of the old ' Pattern of Painful Adventures,' by Twine, and his own play as presented by Gower, this Wilkins cobbled up a prose story of what he called the "true history of the play as it was lately presented by the poet Gower." This was printed privately without authority by Pavier for Butter, rogues both of them; and at the same time an attempt was made by Blount to print the play itself along with another play of Shakespeare's, ' Antony and Cleopatra,' which we had then also acted; but these we procured to be stayed, and in the next year put forth the play with Shakespeare's ' Marina ' in it by the hands of Gosson.

This has carried me beyond my career; I must come back to 1606. Besides ' Macbeth,' Shakespeare wrote a play on ' Timon of Athens,' which, being too short to make up full five acts, we, after his death, placed in the hands of a second author, who enlarged it into the form in which we have published it in our Folio. Why it was not acted at the time of its writing will be clear to those who will examine the Bills of Mortality of these years, for now began a succession of plague years, which lasted all the time that Shakespeare remained with us; and although the infection was nothing near so hot as in the coronation years of His late Majesty, and of our present Gracious Sovereign, still for many months together we were deterred from exercising our quality.

In this year, 1606, the theatres closed in the middle of July and remained so till December. But before their closing we had performed twice at Greenwich and once at Hampton Court before their Majesties the Kings of Great Britain and of Denmark; likewise at Christmas we presented nine plays at Court. One of them was ' King Lear,' as I have before stated; another was ' The Devil's Charter, or the Tragedy of Pope Alexander the Sixth,' by Barnaby Barnes, which was modelled somewhat in the same way as ' Pericles.' Barnes made Paul's work of it, because it had been set before the King, and a dainty dish it was.

Then Shakespeare wrote his 'Antony and Cleopatra,' returning to that great fountain of noble histories, the 'Lives' of Plutarch. He had, in his ' Julius Cæsar,' already eight years since, begun the story of Mark Antony, which he now continued to its tragical end.

This year the theatres were again closed from July to November. Before their closing Shakespeare left us to go to Stratford for his daughter Susanna's marriage to Dr. John Hall, the eminent physician of that place. This match caused him great delight; but when the theatres had reopened, and he had returned to London, this was dashed by the death of his youngest brother, Edmund, who had followed his fortunes on the stage. He had been with us too short a time to attain to eminence in his profession; but we had hoped, though he was as yet scarce heard of, that he would hereafter be a Shake-scene only second to his brother. He died, aged twenty-eight, and was buried in the church of St. Saviour's, Southwark (in which parish his brother and he lived when they were in London), with a forenoon knell of the great bell on the last day of the year.

This Christmas we presented thirteen plays at Court.

On the 21st of February, Elizabeth Hall, the only child of Dr. Hall and Susanna Shakespeare, was baptized at Stratford. After this Shakespeare wrote for us his ' Coriolanus,' and brought to a close his Roman tragedies from Plutarch. These plays — ' Cæsar,' 'Antony,' ' Timon,' and ' Coriolanus '—are, by the most part, though well liked, thought to be inferior to the other great tragedies of ' Hamlet,' ' Othello,' ' Lear,' ' Macbeth,' and ' Cymbeline,' which last three are taken from the English Chronicles; but for my part, and there are some who think with me, though the passions in them be more vivid and from their very nature more eloquent in their appeal to the feeling of the spectators, yet the perfect workmanship of the Roman plays and the deep knowledge of the natures of women, in which last matter Shakespeare was sans peer, will always keep Portia, Cleopatra, and Volumnia side by side with Ophelia, Imogen, and Desdemona in the memories and the hearts of those who love the stage and venerate the powers of its mightiest tragedian.

In September our Coriolanus lost his Volumnia ; she was buried at Stratford. We had been, on account of the plague, travelling along the South Coast. It was an ill time for us, for from the end of July till the end of November the next year all the play places were closed in London; and this plague, though by no means so severe as the three great ones that I have known, was far harder to us, on account of its long continuance. Nevertheless, we acted at Court as usual, presenting at Christmas no fewer than twelve plays. During our travels Shakespeare was for the most part not living at Stratford, but accompanying us; and although he was of course present at his mother's death and burial, his suit against Addenbrooke, which lasted from August, 1608, to June, 1609, was conducted by his solicitor, Thomas Greene, without his personal attendance. This was a small matter of a debt of six pounds, but I mention it to show how he always set his duty to us before his personal interests; for he might easily have absented himself from us in our travels when we did not need a full company, and have saved expense by staying at Stratford and seeing to these matters himself. In October, however, he was at Stratford, where he stood godfather to William Walker. This was a month after his mother's death.

In May, 1609, Shakespeare's sonnets were published, but not by him or with his assent, but by ' Mr. W. H.,' to whom Thorpe the publisher dedicated them. As to who this 'W. H.' was, I have already offered my conjecture ; but this matter will likely never be made clear.

A very great change was made by us at the end of the year, by our taking over the private house at Blackfriars, so that we had then, and have retained ever since, a public playing place, — the Globe, on the Bankside, for the generality, — and a private one at Blackfriars, on the other side of the Thames, for the better sort, a thing which no other company ever attained unto. It came about in this way. The Burbadges had, as I have already set forth, as early as in 1597, let out the Blackfriars room to N. Gyles as a playhouse for the Chapel boys. Three years after they leased it to one Evans, who was then at the head of these boys. In April of the year after that, Evans got into trouble for irregular proceedings in taking up boy players, and the house was inhibited. After the great plague, when the late King came, there was some talk of Evans surrendering his lease to Burbadge ; but nought came of it, the

Queen's Revels boys being set up there in January, 1604. When they got into disgrace about the play of 'Eastward Ho,' and the Queen withdrew her countenance from them, then they, acting as their own masters, again offended in the matter of the play of 'Byron,' written by Master Chapman. This was in April, 1608. These continual troubles, and the irregular payment of the rent which followed thereon, made it inexpedient for Burbadge to allow of a continuance thereof; and he procured a surrender of the lease in August of the same year. The plague thereafter kept the house shut until the December of 1609, and then we took it to our own use. At the same time we received into our company many of these boy actors, some of whom had grown up to man's estate. Of these were Ostler, Underwood, Ecclestone, Robinson, and others; but Field, their chief actor, who also came to us at that time, left us in the next January. The chief sharers in this to us new theatre were Burbadge, Shakespeare, Condell, and myself, we four being all that remained of the original shareholders, or housekeepers, as we prefer to call them, of the Globe, — Phillips, Kempe, Bryan, and Pope, who had at former times been housekeepers, having all died before this time. At first we thought of keeping the boys as a separate company, and we had one play acted, 'The Scornful Lady,' by Fletcher, in their name, having obtained permission from the Queen to call them by their old title, — the children of Her Majesty's Revels; but we found it now feasible to include them with ourselves, all in one company.

One play by Shakespeare we acted in 1609, before Christmas, — the play of 'Cymbeline.' He had begun to write this play in 1606, and all that part of it taken from the English Chronicles was then made just after he had been using them for 'Macbeth' and 'Lear;' but all the jealous story of Iachimo and Posthumus was now newly added. It was the breaking out of the plague, in July, 1606, that had interrupted its completion, when so happily begun. The jealous story will be found in Boccaccio. I have in this and other instances set down the founts and origins of these plays, that the curious may compare the rude outlines with the finished pictures, and see how everything touched by our Midas, or rather our Apollo, turned to gold. Later on, the ever-growing liking for singing and music caused us to allow the rhymes, in the scene where Posthumus hath a vision of his ancestors, to be inserted; but for my own part, I could never away with such addition. I am old, and perhaps peevish, and like the old ways best.

As I shall not need to mention again any travelling on account of the infection or otherwise, I may here briefly note such places as I remember to have visited with our company since the coming of His late Majesty. They may serve to show how our poet became known all over the realm, even to many who had never seen the lordly theatres of our chief and capital city. In 1603 we visited Bath and Shrewsbury; in 1604, Oxford; in 1605, Oxford and Barnstable; in 1606, Safron Walden, Oxford, Dover, and Leicester; in 1607, Oxford; in 1609, Shrewsbury and New Romney; in 1610, Oxford and Shrewsbury. All these were in plague times, as far as I can remember, except the two early visits to Oxford, which were in our summer vacations. But I am not quite certain of my memory in this matter.

There were no performances at Court this Christmas. Early in the next year, in January, a new company of boys began to play under Rossiter, at the Whitefriars. These were called the children of the Queen's Revels; and then we gave up the use of that name for our boys at Blackfriars, and made them part of the King's men. Field was the chief actor of Rossiter's new company. In March another new company — that of the Duke of York, now His Most Gracious Majesty King Charles — was set up at the Curtain, under Taylor, now one of our own best actors. This succeeded to the King's Revels boys who had acted at Whitefriars. So that there were now, with the Queen's and Prince Henry's, five companies in all, at which number they have stayed from that time till now; but there were six theatres, for we had, and have retained, two for our own use.

In the early part of this year 1610, Shakespeare wrote for us 'The Winter's Tale,' the plot being from an old story of Greene's, 'Dorastus and Fawnia.' In this play he brought in a dance of twelve satyrs, and claimed for Nature a precedency over Art; for,

as he says, Art itself is a part of Nature, and all means that better
Nature are made by her, which Jonson took as if meant for him,
and in the Preface to the Reader, in his next play, resented
accordingly.

From July to November the theatres were again closed on
account of the plague, for the last time until the coming of the
present King. At this time, in August, as Jonson has been careful to tell us in the play itself, he wrote his 'Alchemist,' and finding
the disease so hot that it was unlikely to be played, would have it
published in October; but before it came to press, about the end
of November (for he was always slow in such things, though quick
enough in making when the fit was on him), the number of deaths
falling below forty, he stayed it, and would have it acted. Now
just at that time Shakespeare was minded to leave play-making
and play-acting; and we had his last play in our hands for reading
before presentment. So we, casting about for some one to succeed
him, and finding that Beaumont and Fletcher were busied for the
Queen's Revels boys, and Webster for the Queen's men (though in
the next year or two all these men came over to us), could find no
one so fitting as Jonson to stop the gap. We accordingly treated
for the play, and acted it in December. But Shakespeare would
by no means take part in the action; and when Jonson published it
two years after, he retained the Address to the Reader, in which
he inveighed against dances and antics, and those who contemn art
but, to gain opinion of being copious, utter all they can, — all which
being manifestly meant for our poet, — of whom, when alluding to
what we said, that " we had received scarce a blot in his papers,"
he malevolently wished that he had blotted out a thousand lines, —
might have been, methinks, as well omitted. But in the play itself
there was not a line concerning Shakespeare. It was not till he had
again left us and was writing for the rebuilt Bear Garden that he
scoffed on the stage at Tales and Tempests, servant monsters, and
nests of antics and drolleries, where one man's head was mixed with
other men's heels. Nor was it till Shakespeare had been many years
dead that he said he had loved him to idolatry. We knew both
men; and though we admired Ben's rare learning, and thought his

plays held the second place of all in our time brought on the stage, we ever preferred our true gentleman to the envious courtier ; and yet some men say that we got Jonson to write our Preface to our Folio. What! Has he not jeered at it himself ?

Just before this, Shakespeare, who had in June been making a further purchase of twenty acres of arable land at Stratford, gave us his last play, 'The Tempest.' It was about the first week in November that the deaths fell below forty, — namely, on the eighth; and on that very day was issued from the press a tract called 'The True Declaration of the Colony of Virginia.' In this the tempest of 1609, in which Sir F. Gates and others were nigh wrecked on the Bermudas, was described as a 'Tragical Comedy.' Now this is the true designation of Shakespeare's later plays, although we, having used but three heads for all, were fain to rate 'The Winter's Tale' and 'The Tempest' comedies, and 'Cymbeline' a tragedy. And it was on this very storm that Shakespeare plotted his play. Some things in it he took from Eden's 'History of Travel,' somewhat from Montaigne's Essays; but the finest touches were from Jourdain's 'Discovery of the Bermudas,' published about a month before we acted the play. It was greatly liked at Court; and two years after we presented it, not only to the Palatine and his bride, the Princess Elizabeth, but also to the King. On the occasion of the royal marriage we got Master Beaumont to insert a masque (with music and songs suiting the festivity of the time, and much like unto the masque by him then presented by the gentlemen of the Inner Temple) in place of the dumb show, as Shakespeare had left it. This made the whole performance too long ; and we were perforce compelled to omit some of the scenes, especially the character of the Duke of Milan's son, of whom there is now left but a bare mention. Some men may blame us for not giving, in all these plays as published in our Folio, the full text thereof, as written by the poet; but they can only do so in ignorance of the great losses we had at the burning of our theatre, when many copies of our plays were destroyed; only those in the hands of the bookholder, as then in action, having been saved from the fire. And yet I do not think that in more than three plays — that is to say, in 'Macbeth,' which was pieced out afterward by Middleton ; this present one; and 'Henry VIII.,' of which I have yet to speak — have any of the lines of Shakespeare been lost in this way. For it was not until the liking for music and show had grown up at Court, being fostered by the continual production of masques, as presented by the lords and ladies themselves, that these abbreviations became necessary, to keep the time occupied in the performance within reasonable bounds. In earlier times we had never shortened our plays but for performances in the country on our travels.

We performed fifteen plays at Court this Christmas. Thereafter Shakespeare left us and went to live at Stratford as a country gentleman. In the next year we were hard put to it to replace him. Jonson, Beaumont, Fletcher, and Webster, all wrote for us, and their best plays too; but the loss was not to be so made up. At Christmas we presented two and twenty plays at Court, and the next Christmas, eight and twenty. In order to show how we were still depending on revivals of Shakespeare, I will here set down a list of twenty plays, as we presented them in the Christmas of 1612. To the Lady Elizabeth and the Palatine Elector, these by Shakespeare: 'Much Ado About Nothing,' 'The Tempest,' 'The Winter's Tale,' 'Sir John Falstaff and the Merry Wives of Windsor,' 'The Moor of Venice,' and ' Cæsar's Tragedy,' six in all ; by Beaumont and Fletcher: 'Philaster,' 'The Maid's Tragedy,' 'A King and no King,' and ' Philaster,' once again, under its new name of 'Love lies a-bleeding,' three in all ; by Drayton, 'The Merry Devil of Edmonton;' by Turner, 'The Nobleman;' by Nicols, ' The Twins' Tragedy;' and by I know not whom, ' The Knot of Fools.' Then to the King these by Shakespeare: ' The Hotspur ; or, Henry IV.;' ' Benedick and Bettris ; or, Much Ado About Nothing;' by Jonson, ' The Alchemist;' by Beaumont and Fletcher, ' The Captain and Cardenas ; or, Love's Pilgrimage;' and by the concealed author, 'The London Prodigal,' under the name of ' A Bad Beginning makes a Good Ending.' So that wellnigh half our performances were still from Shakespeare.

*F. G. Fleay.*

(To be concluded.)

## HOW TO STUDY TENNYSON'S 'IN MEMORIAM.'

In his recent volume, 'Tennyson and "In Memoriam,"'*
Mr. Joseph Jacobs has given a most interesting example in his
study of 'In Memoriam' of the objective method of studying a
poem. He has, however, overlooked one very important line of
investigation, which, as I shall attempt to show, is the principal
*raison d'être* of objective study, and one which puts the critic in a
position to exercise to the best advantage his subjective faculties
of criticism. Mr. Jacobs' plan of procedure is much like that followed by POET-LORE in its outline studies of poetry; but as every
poem demands some variation in its treatment, it will not be out
of place to give here an outline of his method. He divides the
study of the poem into two main heads, Analytical and Comparative. The main subdivisions under the first head are Form and
Matter. In studying the form, there are, of course, a number of
things to be observed, — the metre used, the rhymes, whether
good, bad, or indifferent, how frequently alliteration is employed,
the philological value of the vocabulary, the changes made by the
poet in various editions, then the general style and beauty, including the choice of words, the figures, and finally the effect produced
in the artistic combining of all these elements, found by Mr.
Jacobs to be grace and power. The author has given very fully
the results of his studies of the form of 'In Memoriam,' pointing
out the bad rhymes, of which he finds one in every nine, and also
giving lists of the metaphors, personifications, and so on, used.
Under the division, Matter, are considered the object, the development, and the matter analysis of the poem, besides the philosophy,
which includes psychology, ethics, sociology, metaphysics, and
theology, with an appendix on the dates when the various portions
of the poem were written. Under the second main head, Comparative, are considered the resemblances of the form and matter with
Tennyson elsewhere, and the influences which are to be observed

---

* Tennyson and 'In Memoriam,' by Joseph Jacobs. London : David
Nutt. 1892.

in him from the English, Classic, and Italian poets, and then the relation of his thought to that of Kant through Coleridge, of Darwin and various other thinkers, and finally, the influence of 'In Memoriam' on poetry and thought. It is under this second main division that something is lacking. Mr. Jacobs' only aim in the comparison with other poets is to trace their influence on Tennyson both as to matter (not motive, be it observed) and as to form; but this sort of comparison deals only with resemblances, and while a very interesting branch of comparative study, is, to my mind, by no means the chief one. It is like studying the environment and the inheritance of an individual, without giving any attention whatever to the individual, or to the central fact upon which these factors work. In the case of 'In Memoriam' the central fact, the main motive, underlying even the "subject-matter,"— which is, after all, a part of the form,— is the emotion of grief in the human heart; and the chief end in a comparative study of this poem should be to investigate how the emotion of grief has manifested itself in other poetry which treats of the same theme,— whether there has been a growth or a deterioration in the intensity of the emotion, whether the differences in the expression are merely external, the result of the individuality of the poet himself, or of peculiar circumstances, or whether they result from the inevitable relations of the poet to his world environment.

It happens in the present instance that there is a remarkable series of poems based upon the emotion of grief, ranging from the Idyllic age of Greek poetry to the present. The first of these is the exquisite 'Lament for Adonis' by Bion. The emotion of grief in this idyl is perfectly simple, and besides there shines through it plainly a cosmic element. The grief for the death of Adonis is renewed every year; thus it is not a lasting grief, but a grief which alternates with joy. The origin of the myth of Venus and Adonis in a worship of Nature should here be looked into, as it will explain the strange idea that Cytherea is to lament anew each year. It should be noted that the figures used in the idyl are everywhere suggestive of the death of Nature. The blood-drops of Adonis bring forth the rose, the tears of Venus the wind-flower. Every one knows how the wind-flower springs up in the damp ground of early spring where the tears of Nature have fallen ; and those who have seen the autumn-crimsoned downs of a New England landscape, with tardy wild roses blooming here and there among the brilliant tangle, will understand how the blood of Adonis brings forth the rose. It is also to be noted that this idyl belongs to the period of Greek poetry, which came under the influence of Alexandrian civilization. The cult of Adonis was not Greek, but was borrowed from the Egyptians, and traces of Alexandrian influence are to be found in the language, which, as Andrew Lang points out, is frequently borrowed, not from Nature herself, but from Nature as she was represented in Alexandrian paintings. To sum up, we have in this idyl of Bion's a lament for dying Nature personified as a god, expressed in the language of human grief ; but the human quality of the grief is reacted upon and limited in its humanness by the inevitable processes of an ever growing and fading Nature, which everywhere reveals itself through the personifications as the body through a garment.

Almost contemporary with this poem is 'The Lament for Bion,' by Moschus. Here is still simplicity of grief and now entirely human ; but it follows the model of Bion's 'Lament for Adonis' by giving expression to this grief in symbols drawn from Nature direct and from Nature personified : thus as the wells weep for Adonis, and the flowers flush red for anguish, and all things perish in his death, so Moschus makes the rivers weep and the roses redden, and the flowers in sad clusters breathe themselves away. As Cypris mourned for Adonis, so she does for Bion ; but Moschus enlarges on Bion. Many more are the mourners recounted by him, and there is no alternating joy indicated in this poem, the grief is hopeless ; and we find the first step taken in that philosophizing which has since become the chief feature in the poetry of grief. It is the philosophy of the Greek with no hope in a future.

"Ah me, when the mallows wither in the garden, and the green parsley and the curled tendrils of the anise, on a later day they live again, and spring in another year; but we men, we, the great and mighty or wise, when once we have died, in hollow earth we sleep, gone down into silence, a right long, and endless and unawakening sleep."

Spenser's 'Astrophel,' the next poem of the series, impresses one as being in some respects farther back in time than Moschus' 'Lament for Bion.' There is no real depth to the grief over the death of Sir Philip Sidney; and it might be supposed that the emotion of grief had less intensity in the time of Spenser than in the time of Bion and Moschus. A mark of its lateness in time as compared with Moschus lies in the fact that the spontaneity of the idyllic atmosphere of Moschus has become in Spenser an artificial pastoralness. Astrophel is a shepherd, and Stella is a nymph who bemoans the fate of her swain. There are direct imitations from the 'Lament for Adonis;' for example, Astrophel is killed while hunting, by a thrust in his thigh from a wild beast. Venus fades away and loses her beauty on the death of Adonis; and grief for the loss of Astrophel kills Stella. But Spenser makes the flower transformation much more elaborate; for lying together on the field, Astrophel and Stella are both transformed into one flower, that first grows red and then into blue doth fade, and in the midst is a star like Stella's eyes, and all day long it is full of dew, which are the tears from Stella's eyes. In short, the nature language of the Greeks is imitated; but it has lost its inevitableness. There is not the same underlying reason why Astrophel and Stella should turn into a flower as there is for the blood of Adonis becoming a wild rose; one is a genuine, transparent nature myth, the other is a manufactured one. Now, what is the cause of the inferiority of this poem as compared with the Greek poems? Is it the fault of the poet, of peculiar circumstances, or the time in which he wrote? To answer these questions satisfactorily, the poem must be compared with other work of the poet (it is one of his least successful poems); we must look into the special circumstances under which it was written, and we must investigate the channels through which the writing of pastoral poetry was introduced into England (through the Latin and French).

Though Milton's 'Lycidas' still shows the influence of classic models, he commands rather than is commanded by them, as Spenser is. To be sure, Lycidas is a shepherd (his name is borrowed either from an Eclogue of Virgil or an Idyl of Theocritus),

and is bemoaned by all the wood nymphs and satyrs in the truly
pastoral manner, but mingled with the imitative artificiality are
outbursts of a real appreciation of Nature herself, undraped in any
mythologic disguises. Besides, not only Greek and Latin but
Christian and Druidic lore are called upon to adorn his grief.
The poet has brought all his marvellous book knowledge, and
his regardful observations of Nature, and formed a beautiful
mosaic on a Greek pattern, and this he lays on the bier of his
friend. But is there nothing more in this poem? There are
two elements which have not before appeared in the poems we
have been considering. The death of Lycidas leads the poet
to consider how much better he could have spared some other
people, — namely, the corrupt clergy, — and he takes occasion to
scathe them in highly metaphoric language. So here is a marked
sign of the addition of an intellectual quality to the emotion of
grief. It is no longer so simple as to preclude thought; it is
rather itself the instigator of thought, not exalted, it is true, for
it has that partisan quality of a Puritan who scorns the Established
Church. This is also the first in the series of poems under consideration in which a belief in immortality comes out. From the
ever-renewed grief of Bion's ' Lament ' and the never-ending grief
of Moschus for Bion, through the unthinking grief of the present
moment in Spenser's 'Astrophel,' we come to the grief that is
quenched in the thought that the beloved one is living in the

> "blest kingdom meek of joy and love,
> There entertain him all the Saints above
> In solemn troops and sweet societies,
> That sing and singing in their glory move
> And wipe the tears forever from his eyes."

It is worth while to notice that in one of the elegiac poems on
Sir Philip Sidney, written by an unknown hand, he is referred to
as a happy sprite in heaven ; but the thought of his happiness does
not assuage the grief of the weeping shepherds.

Shelley's 'Adonais' is the next in the series to claim attention, and in this the emotion of grief will be found surrounded by
an entirely new atmosphere. We no longer touch the earth with

our feet, but glide through the air as in dreams. Adonais is not a shepherd for whom the woodland nymphs weep; he is the child of time personified as Urania, who bemoans the fate of her youngest-born, and other mourners are human qualities and emotions and

> "All he had loved and moulded into thought
> From shape and hue and odor and sweet sound
> Lamented Adonais."

We are given imaginative pictures of the mystical forms — "astral" personifications, they might be called — of these abstract qualities, vague but suggestive, who weep at the bier of Adonais. Urania struggles with death for her son as Apollo once struggled with death for Alkestis. Poets come to weep, — Byron, a frail form, his head

> "bound with pansies over-blown
> And faded violets, white and pied and blue."

But while Shelley illuminates his theme with the glorious light of his own wonderfully imaginative faculty, he has not quite escaped Greek influence in form. And there are other echoes from the Greek poems. The Morning and Lost Echo mourn; the Spring goes wild with grief; like Moschus he wonders why it is that Nature renews herself year by year.

> "Nought we know dies. Shall that alone which knows
> Be as a sword consumed before the sheath
> By sightless lightnings? the intense atom glows
> A moment, then is quenched in a most cold repose."

But while in Moschus there is a Pagan certainty of nothing, and in Milton the Puritan certainty of everything, — an anthropomorphic immortality including body and soul, — in Shelley there is a pantheistic strain. His grief is overcome in the contemplation of the freed spirit of Keats flowing

> "Back to the burning fountain whence it came,
> A portion of the Eternal.
> .   .   .   .   .   .   .
> He is made one with Nature: there is heard

He is a portion of the loveliness
Which once he made more lovely : he doth bear
His part, while the one Spirit's plastic stress
Sweeps through the dull dense world, compelling there
All new successions to the forms they wear."

He also seems to have Moschus in mind in the passage —

" Our Adonais has drunk poison.  Oh,
What deaf and viperous murderer could crown
Life's early cup with such a draft of woe ? "

Bion was literally murdered by poison ; and Keats is said to
have been killed by the review of 'Endymion' in the *Quarterly*.
Moschus to his own question, " What mortal was so cruel that could
mix poison for thee?" declares only, " Surely he had no music
in his soul," and " Justice has overtaken them all;" but for the
murderer, metaphorically speaking, of Keats Shelley launches out
into the bitterest sarcasm.   Milton's grief was mingled with indignation that his friend should be taken while his enemies continued to flourish ;  Shelley's grief is mingled with indignation
that his friend should have enemies.   Milton brings in Saint Peter
to smite his enemies; Shelley considers the worst chastisement
for his friend's enemies, and others like them who are the enemies
of truth and beauty, is that they shall live and be free to spill their
venom, but that remorse and self-contempt shall cling to them.
These differences are indicative of the moral fibre of the two poets,
and the influences that formed both of them might profitably be
discussed.

Such are some of the points which a student of this series of
poems will notice ; and after such a study he will be prepared to
see just what fresh elements have been introduced by Tennyson
in the treatment of the same theme.

In the first place, Tennyson's is the first of the poems in which
the expression of grief is through the direct utterance of the poet's
own feelings.   In all the other poems, the poet's grief is almost or
entirely shown as reflected in the grief of others, — either Nature,
rural deities, allegorical shepherds and shepherdesses, or with, in
the case of Shelley, the addition of the dead poet's own mind-born
offspring.   Thus it is a complete break from the classic models.

It is the first of the English poems which calls the dead friend by
his own name, and not by some name borrowed from the pastoral
world. And furthermore, the grief of Tennyson, besides being
expressed directly, is introspective. It is not a simple expression of feeling, but a complex analysis of those feelings. Where
Milton's grief leads him to attacks on his enemies, Shelley's to
attacks on the enemies of his friend, and of those of the noble and
beautiful, Tennyson's leads him to a minute study of his own
sensations and moods. He watches with the interest of an outside observer the progress of his grief through many fluctuating
phases from despair to hope. He is not writing the poem for the
glory of his friend, but to give his own heart relief; and first he
can only compare his grief with that of others who have suffered
a similar loss. His intellect is hardly active, but with the passage
of time thought begins to awaken. Through his great desire that
he may again sometime hold communion with his friend, he is led
to ponder on the hard problems of life and death. The spirit of
the Pagan and the spirit of the Puritan meet in conflict on the
battle-ground of his mind. The Pagan " certainty of nothing "
cannot win, nor the Puritan "certainty of everything," only in this
case the individual certainty of Love. Upon the human emotion
of Love the poet founds neither a negative nor a positive certainty,
but a hope that " good will fall at last to all." Having been led to
the irresistible conclusion that Love is eternal, he breaks forth into
a mystic utterance resembling Shelley's in ' Adonais,' with this
difference, that the mysticism of Shelley is not the result of a long
course of introspective reasoning, nor does the consciousness of
his friend's spiritual immanence in Nature soothe his earthly lot
as it does Tennyson's. Shelley exclaims, —

> " Why linger, why turn back, why shrink, my Heart?
> Thy hopes are gone before : from all things here
> They have departed; thou shouldst now depart.
> . . . . . .
> No more let Life divide what Death can join together."

But Tennyson, —

> " Far off thou art, but ever nigh;
> I have thee still and I rejoice.
> I prosper circled with thy voice,
> I shall not lose thee though I die."

Taking another glance over the road just travelled, we are surprised to note that the intellectual development indicated from the time of Bion and Moschus to Shelley is very slight as compared with that from Shelley to Tennyson. As before hinted, this may be due to local causes, such as the individuality of the poet or the special occasion producing the poem rather than to any universal law of development; but possibly one of the chief causes is not so much an increase in intellectual power as a recognition that the emotions are no longer to be regarded as qualities existing in isolation from the qualities of intellect, but that they may be enriched by all the tributary streams of knowledge and thought which intellect can pour into them. And with the broadening of the emotions comes naturally the enlargement of the materials of poetry; for the more the emotions are fed by knowledge and thought, the more must knowledge and thought enter into the expression of these emotions. May it not follow, then, that the subjective critic — the *appreciator*, as he loves to call himself nowadays — who judges largely by the poet's appeal to his emotions, by some such study as the preceding, will sharpen what I venture to call his emotional perceptions, and should he feel and say, in the artistic phrases of an *appreciator*, that 'In Memoriam' is the finest poem upon such a theme in literature, his "appreciation" will have added to it the only legitimate kind of human authority, — that which comes from patient investigation of facts?

*Helen A. Clarke.*

## 'THE PURSUIT OF HAPPINESS.'*

THAT childhood is not the happiest time in life, old age not the period of wisdom; that wealth is to be measured not by the surplusage of money over wants, but by the satisfaction of many and varied desires; that appreciation of poetry does not diminish with

---

* 'The Pursuit of Happiness,' a Book of Studies and Strowings, by Daniel G. Brinton, A.M., M.D., LL.D. Philadelphia: David McKay. 1893 ($1.00).

maturity; that for women especially the pleasures of the intellect are most desirable ; that religions tend to obscure Religion; that the sweetest joys are consoled sorrows, — these are some of the more striking contentions upheld by Dr. Brinton in his last book, a volume full of wit and pith, which is generally sensible as well as epigrammatic, and always thought-provoking.

The yearning for happiness, says Dr. Brinton, is the secret of evolution : biologists have found the avoidance of painful, and search for pleasurable, sensations to be the first principle of growth in the lower forms of life ; and since in man it is the motive of action and development, it should be his study to regulate and increase that consciousness of all the powers of self which make both for individual happiness and the future advance in felicity of the race.

The pleasures of sense, of course, have a part in this conception of happiness, but no undue place if they awaken and strengthen the faculties of heart and brain, and exalt the consciousness of self. It follows that pains of sense, when under special conditions they effect the same result, — individual development, — can be just as valuable. An important under-study in the pursuit of the main subject is, indeed, the extent to which misfortunes of all kinds can be turned to profit, — that is, to happiness, — and this in the final division of Dr. Brinton's book concerning the consolations of affliction is healthfully and helpfully handled ; but for any compensating advantage to be derived from such occasionally necessary and voluntary conditions as a straitened income and limitations in dining and smoking, one would best seek other guides, since here, as it would seem, the circumstances and predilections of our author make him comparatively unsympathetic. It is true, however, that this set of obstacles to happiness pertains, like affliction, to the obverse of the theorem in hand, and that the principles laid down are broad enough to deal effectively with more of the converse side than the author has included.

His chapter on morality, too, good as it is in its clear assertion that there is no such thing as a universal or even a general code of morality, that there is no act which may not sometimes be right and sometimes be wrong, that morality and the sense of morality are never the same, and must be opposed, yet does not carry on consistently, with relation to self-development, his own distinction between morality and the moral sense. That distinction should lead, as we think, to the recognition that the growth of the individual moral sense supplies a source of self-development, and consequently of happiness, just as does the development of any other individual faculty, and that the satisfaction of that sense leads to such happiness as, Epictetus says, is "an equivalent for all troublesome things." If Dr. Brinton is right, as we think he is, in distinguishing Religion from religions, and in finding in any of the conventionalized creeds that claim the possession of all necessary or of supreme truth a source of unhappiness and self-restriction, while in Religion, on the contrary, — that is, in the vital principle which tends to the Ideal of Humanity, — he perceives a source of growing happiness and self-fulfilment, he should, we think, make a corresponding acknowledgment for the vital principle in the moral sense, whose culture and evolution through its satisfaction in the individual life tends also to the Ideal of Humanity, and supplies a complex source of growing personal and public happiness.

In making these two criticisms against the perfect balance of the subject, we believe we are trying the work by itself, and accepting its main dicta that "the mission of the species is the perfecting of the individual," and that "there is no 'order of excellence' in the faculties of man." One being as excellent as another, play should be given "to all according to their strength."

The manner in which the author applies these principles is practical and interesting. After considering what happiness is, the relative value of pleasures, the distribution of happiness, — in which he contends, by the way, that women have less happiness than men, — and laying down some principles of self-education for the promotion of happiness, he divides his work into discussions of, How far our Happiness depends on Nature and Fate, in which he treats of physical and mental traits, of dress and home-surroundings, and of luck and its laws; of How far our Happiness depends on Ourselves, when enter questions of work, money-making, pleasures of sense, intellect, religion, and the individuality; of How far our Happiness depends on Others, which involves, of course, inquiries as to education, duty, society, friendship, love, and marriage, and leads to the final division of the work, — the education of suffering through the loss of friends.

It will be seen that the aim which Dr. Brinton would pursue issues from a much livelier sense of man's possible control of the very fountain-heads of happiness than is shown in the famous fragment of Cleanthes, — " Conduct me, Zeus, and thou, O destiny ! wherever thy decrees have fixed my lot, I follow cheerfully, and did I not, wicked and wretched I must follow still." Its spirit is to proceed actively, and not follow perforce; yet it asks, in much the same way as Epictetus, what things depend on ourselves and what not, to the end that we may consider that only to be ours which truly is so. So also in the maxim already noticed, that there is no order of excellence in the faculties of man, there is agreement with the statement of Epicurus that " no kind of pleasure deserves in itself to be rejected," yet there is an appreciable new and modern note, for where the Greek would weigh one kind of pleasure over the other and make his choice of the one he considered most agreeable, our American philosopher would unify them all by striving " to render the pleasures of the senses and emotions as intellectual as possible, and to keep the pleasures of the intellect in touch with the emotions and the senses."

Whitman's rhythmic voice is tuned to the same effect; and Browning's ideal of the continuous evolution possible to such concordant human consciousness rises to rapture with the thought of its possession of what he calls " the secret of the world," — to know

" what we are,
What life is — how God tastes an infinite joy
In infinite ways —
. . . in whom is life forever more,
Yet whom existence in its lowest form
Includes ; where dwells enjoyment there is he :
With still a flying point of bliss remote,
A happiness in store afar, a sphere
Of distant glory in full view ; thus climbs
Pleasure its heights forever and forever."

75                                              *P.*

## BOOK INKLINGS.

ONE of the limitations of the Rev. Mr. Burridge's desultory homily on ' Robert Browning as an Exponent of a Philosophy of Life ' is indicated by the fact that his illustrations of his subject are drawn from Browning's earlier work. Except for a few strains from the much beharped Epilogue to ' Asolando,' there is scarcely any reference to an important body of the poet's later work which necessarily reflects his developed ideas. No treatment of the religious and philosophical inferences to be gathered from Browning's poetry can lay any strong claim to attention which shows a reading acquaintance with but a part of the field of investigation, still less when neither new word or fresh method marshal the way along that already crowded thoroughfare whose end is Browning's philosophy.

Having, confessedly, almost no appreciation of Browning's quality as an artist, Mr. Burridge is handicapped in his task of philosophical elucidation, and is apparently unable to distinguish creator from creature,—speaking, for example, of Bishop Blougram's " Why not, the Way, the Truth, the Life," as practically Browning's own.

The pamphlet is very attractively printed, although unfortunately blemished by printers' errors, and is prefaced by a laudatory letter from Dr. Berdoe, whose few words on Browning's reconciliation of science and religion lend some coherence and purpose to the writer's intentions. ('Robert Browning as an Exponent of a Philosophy of Life,' by Brainerd Marc Burridge. Pamph. The Book Shop: Cleveland, O. 1893.)

—— AMONG the summer novels Mr. Nathan Haskell Dole's ' Not Angels Quite ' is entertaining reading. The plot is slight, turning upon the discovery of two sets of engaged couples that they are severally not intended for each other, and ending with a transposition of lovers. Such a turn of events seems probable enough; but we feel a little provoked at the author for not making all four of the young lovers equally attractive. The interest centres round the charming Miss Doubleday and Harry Carburn, who certainly possess a great magnetic affinity for each other; and in order to justify each of them in breaking their engagements, Miss Doubleday's *fiancé* behaves in a really ungentlemanly way, although it must be confessed he has some provocation, — thus giving her the opportunity she is longing for; and Harry Carburn's *fiancée*, Beatrice Ware, is represented as growing faded through her long confinement as a school-teacher, so that while we have no doubt of the fitness for each other of Alma Doubleday and Harry, we can't help experiencing the sensation that the other two are left to Hobson's choice. There are many glimpses, throughout the book, into Boston life as it exists at present, one of the cleverest being the scene at the Parliament Club, which is drawn with a thorough appreciation of the humorous side of such gatherings.

The book also abounds in sprightly dialogues, in which many of the current topics of the day are touched upon with some wisdom and not a little wit. ('Not Angels Quite.' Nathan Haskell Dole. Boston: Lee & Shepard. 1893. Cloth. Issued also in "Good Company Series." 50 cts.)

# NOTES AND NEWS.

ZOLA's proposal that political articles should not, and literary and artistic criticism should, be signed, the *Athenæum* does not find reasonable, and not unnaturally, since the *Athenæum* is one of the older-school journals whose authority has been much enlarged by mystery. One can only guess at Zola's reason for making fish of politics and flesh of art and literature. The inconsistency may be due to an acknowledgment that the treatment of politics is not yet on as high a moral plane as that of letters and art, and that questions of governmental policy are questions of party and partisanship, and hence of an organ's authority, whereas considerations of art and literature are not so much so, and should not be so at all. They rest, for each expression of opinion, on individual fairness or bias, on critical ability and literary sympathy or the lack of it, and cannot honestly be referred in bulk to the name and credit of a devouring incognito.

## LONDON LITERARIA.

CHIEF among topics of varied interest dealt with of late in the German press, we find Paracelsus — the hero of Browning's first acknowledged poem — occupying a foremost place. Several accounts have appeared of late concerning the house where the great pioneer of modern medicine first saw the light; and unwary travellers are, it appears, often misled in this matter. I have just seen an interesting photograph, recently taken, of the undoubted "birth-house" of the great Doctor, — accompanied by a letter from a recent traveller thereto, the following extract from which will be of interest to Browning students : —

"The house in which Paracelsus was born is the oldest in the whole Mount Etzel, and which wears quite a different stamp from the others, and betrays the Suabian origin outside and inside. Wherever Suabians came to dwell in our mountains, they brought their own style of building, as it is everywhere discernible in the Alps. Characteristic remains the ' Laube ' on the side, where there is only one window scarcely visible, and where a blanket is hanging over the entrance. A part of the house has been rebuilt (1811). It is easily discernible. In the new part, the covering consists of planks; in the old everything is covered with *schindeln* (shingles ?). Stones were on the roof, but, as on all the other houses, they had to be removed some twenty years ago. This is what I found out by dint of inquiry among the oldest people of the place. The date 1811 is given in a little book on Paracelsus which was published in Zurich in 1851 by a Dr. Locher. Documents about Aureolus there are none in the Kloster of Einsiedeln, — only some papers about the relations of Paracelsus' father with the Kloster."

Dr. Edward Berdoe, author of 'The Browning Cyclopædia,' ' Browning's Message to his Time,' etc., is certainly an indefatigable worker. A London physician, with an extensive practice, he yet finds time to produce not only voluminous works in his own special line of study, but also to indite Browning treatises which are of real and permanent value to the student. The Doctor has for some time past been engaged on a work dealing with the attitude of Browning to Christian theism ; but I understand he has put this aside for the present in order to prepare for Messrs. Smith and Elder a Browning Glossary, to accompany the ' Asolando ' poems, as the last volume of the completed works. The Glossary will embrace the principal characters and places in the " works," and will certainly be of value to all readers of Browning. Dr. Berdoe has also written an Introduction to a work just published by the Rev. B. M. Burridge of Ohio, entitled, 'Robert Browning as an Exponent of a Philosophy of Life,' — of which only one hundred and fifty copies are issued as an *édition de luxe*.

A collection of manuscripts relating to Shelley and Mary Godwin has been presented to the Bodleian Library by Lady Shelley. The chief conditions to be observed are that all these documents — excepting, of course, such as have already been printed in whole or part — shall until the year 1922 (the centenary of the poet's death) be kept apart, and seen by no person save the curators and librarian of the Bodleian, and that no one shall be allowed to copy any portion of them. The collection consists of letters written by Shelley and Mary Godwin, and also original manuscripts of Shelley's poems.

In the ensuing autumn is to be published 'Early Editions,' by Mr. J. H. Slater, — a work which will assuredly be of great interest, not alone to " collectors," but to readers in general. The book describes, values, and collates the works of the chief of the modern poets and prose writers, gives " certain rules for detecting reprints," and affords a fund of information to all seekers after " first editions."

An interesting work is announced by Messrs. Isbister, 'In the Footsteps of the Poets,' — a collection of biographical, critical, and topographical sketches. The poets dealt with are, — Milton, by Professor Dr. David Masson ; Herbert, by Dr. John Brown, of Bedford ; Cowper, by Canon Benham ; Thomas, by " Hugh Haliburton ; " Wordsworth, by " Henry C. Ewart ; " Walter Scott, by Mr. John Dennis ; Browning, by Mr. R. H. Hutton ; Mrs. Browning, by the Lord Bishop of Ripon ; and Tennyson, by Mr. William Canton. *William G. Kingsland.*

LONDON, September, 1893.

## THE ACTOR IN SHAKESPEARE.

ANOTHER word at this time about the Shakespeare-Bacon controversy, in spite of *The Arena's* recent revival of the issue, is certainly suggestive of Falstaff's damnable iteration ; but there is one point of internal evidence bearing upon the Shakespearian authorship of the plays that is, as it seems to me, not uninteresting to note. This is the frequent allusion in season and out of season to stage representation, showing that the plays were written either by an actor, or by one incessantly familiar with dramatic performances. When Cassius says, after the murder of Cæsar,—

> " How many ages hence,
> Shall this our lofty scene be acted over
> In states unborn, and accents yet unknown ! "

and Brutus replies,—

> " How many times shall Cæsar bleed in sport," —

we are instantly struck by the impossibility of such an idea occurring to the minds of either of these noble Romans at that supreme moment. I venture to say that it would not have suggested itself to any author who was not part and parcel of the stage for which the play was written. It is also unhistorical from the fact that actors were held in extreme scorn by the Romans, so that the thought of their " lofty scene " being represented by actors would have been intolerable to both Brutus and Cassius.

Cleopatra, when enumerating the horrors of her captivity, speaks of the " quick comedians " who

> " Extemporally will stage us, and present
> Our Alexandrian revels ; Antony
> Shall be brought drunken forth, and I shall see
> Some squeaking Cleopatra boy my greatness."

This does not seem so incongruous, as Cleopatra had acted all her life on the stage of Egypt ; but it is nevertheless suggestive of the actor in the author as well as in the queen.

Again, in 'Cymbeline,' it seems hardly probable that it would occur to Posthumus in the last act, when the unknown Imogen speaks to him in his anguish of remorse, to exclaim —

> " Shall 's have a play of this ? Thou scornful page,
> There lie thy part."

His wrath with the supposed page is a fine dramatic touch ; but the expression of it comes from the thought of an actor of the Elizabethan age, rather than from that of a prehistoric British nobleman.

There are many little touches in the clown's burlesque of 'The Midsummer Night's Dream' that come from behind the scenes; and it seems to me that the constant trifling allusions to the drama, and the similes drawn from the stage, would be only likely to occur to the mind of one who was in continual and intimate relation with acting and actors. It is true that the whole air at that time was surcharged with the dramatic spirit; but that does not sufficiently account for the number and nature of these allusions.

I am convinced that any student of Shakespeare who finds this idea interesting will be struck by the unconscious evidence given in lines all through the plays, that transcendant as was the genius that produced them, they were written not by an outsider and visitor to the playhouse, however familiar he might be, but were poured from the wise head and mellow heart of him who had made himself " a motley to the view," and who left to his " fellowes, John Hemynge, Richard Burbage, and Henry Condell, twenty-six shillings eightpence apiece to buy them rings."

*Isabel Francis Bellows.*

# SOCIETIES.

The " Starr King Fraternity " of Oakland, Cal. was organized several years ago, for self-culture among its members, philanthropy, and usefulness to the general community. The work is done mainly in sections, though general meetings are held often.

The program for the session 1892–93 included a section for the study of English literature. The Fraternity was fortunate enough to secure as its leader Mrs. Katherine B. Fisher, who has kindly given much of her time, and the benefit of her ripe experience, to the work. To her is due the great success and interest in the section.

The meetings are held every Monday evening in the reading-room of the Fraternity; they are very informal. There are no officers, other than the leader, and no dues.

The section was opened to all members of the Fraternity; but soon it was deemed wise to restrict the membership to thirty active workers.

The time, so far, has been spent upon the study of Shakespeare. The following plays have been taken, ' Macbeth,' ' The Winter's Tale,' and ' The Tempest.' This latter is to be followed by ' King John.'

We, as members, feel that we have studied in the true spirit, trying to interpret our poet in his highest purposes, and to feel the beauty of his thoughts and language. No time has been spent in analyses of mere words and form.

The parts are assigned, and papers arranged for, several weeks ahead. Generally two acts and two papers are given for the evening's work. This leaves time for questions and discussion later. The readings are spirited, and papers show study and enthusiasm.

By way of review, the play is always read in its entirety, with some effort at characterization. These evenings are very enjoyable, for there is an unusual number of fine readers connected with the section.

We look back with great pleasure to an evening spent with us by Hon. Horace Davis, the former President of the University of California, and for many years the leader of a large Shakespeare Club in San Francisco. He spoke to us on 'The Classic and the Romantic.'

We are fully in sympathy with the aims and object of POET-LORE, and wish to express our indebtedness to it for its great help. We followed closely its outlines on 'The Winter's Tale,' and found them very suggestive and broadening.

Our session closed in May, but we trust that September may find us ready for further study.                              *Elizabeth Sherman.*

The **Baltimore Shakespere Club** held eleven meetings during the season of 1892 and 1893. During the winter the plays of 'Hamlet,' 'Richard II.,' and 'Love's Labour 's Lost' were read and studied. Original papers were read by Dr. Edward Renouf on 'Ophelia contrasted with the Margaret of Goethe;' by Wm. L. Marbury, W. Woolsey Johnson, and Col. Richard Malcolm Johnston on 'Polonius' (a discussion of his character); by Henry P. Goddard on 'Horatio;' by Miss Lizette W. Reese on 'The Poetry of the Elizabethan Era;' by Doctors Wyatt, W. Randall, and J. W. Bright on 'Richard II.;' by H. B. Hodges on 'Stage Versions of Shakespere;' by W. Woolsey Johnson on 'Midsummer Night's Dream.' Original poems were read by Mrs. Julia Valentine Bond on 'Fair Mistress Anne,' by Miss Essie Jackson on 'Horatio,' and Miss Ruth Johnston on 'Love's Labour Won.' At the meeting on St. Valentine's Day, February 14, valentines composed entirely of Shakespearian quotations were presented each guest by the hostess, Miss Jackson. On February 8 the Club gave a reception to Miss Julia Marlowe at the house of Mrs. Delano Ames, where the fair young actress captured the hearts of all the members present, regardless of their sex. On April 11 Mrs. Wm. Winter's essay on 'Love's Labour 's Lost' was read to the Club by the President, H. P. Goddard. On the night of Tuesday, May 2, the Club, as usual, at its last meeting, took a "Field Night." On this occasion the Club met at the Hotel Shirley, and carried out a program prepared by Mr. H. B. Hodges, which consisted of the reading of 'Midsummer Night's Dream' (condensed into two hours' action) to the accompaniment of Mendelssohn's music written for the play. Assisted by a single non-member, the entire program was most successfully carried out. The Club closes its eighth season with forty members on its rolls.                              *H. P. Goddard.*

Vol. V.

No. 12.

──wilt thou not haply faie,
Truth needs no collour with his collour fixt;
Beautie no penfell, beauties truth to lay;
But beft is beft if neuer intermixt.
Because he needs no praife, wilt thou be dumb?
Excufe not filence fo, for't lies in thee,
To make him much outliue a gilded tombe
And to be praifed of ages yet to be.
Then do thy office ──

# LESSING'S 'DRAMATURGIE.'

HE autumn of Lessing's thirty-eighth year finds him in Berlin, "standing idle in the market-place because no man hath hired him." He has been a rolling stone now eighteen years ; has been hack-writer, journalist, play-wright, tutor, private secretary, major-domo, translator, and is still sorely put to it sometimes for bread. He has written some half-dozen dramas, one of which posterity will call the greatest German comedy, and has published a treatise on æsthetics which is to revolutionize poetry and art. And yet he has just been suing, through his friends, for the vacant post of librarian in Berlin, which would bring him a thousand *thalers* a year, and has seen an insignificant Frenchman appointed over his head; for the Great Frederick, in all matters literary, prefers the French. Perhaps, too, his dislike for Lessing comes from his remembrance of that quarrel fifteen years ago between the latter and Voltaire ; or, more likely, Gottsched's friends have been slandering Lessing. And so this best brain in Germany still has to wait in the market-place. At one time he seriously considers the project of managing at his own risk a troup of itinerant players, but gives it up

because of the bad moral repute of the stage. To increase his
worriment, urgent letters keep coming from home, asking for help,
as the village pastor's family is in straits for money. At last, in
December, a godsend arrives in the form of an offer from
Hamburg.

In this wealthy city, some dozen merchants and literary men
had formed a company to manage a theatre and elevate the German drama. Loewen, the first promoter of it, himself a poet, had
published a paper to air his complaints that "art in the theatre
was debased to money-making; that the actors and play-wrights
lacked proper encouragement; that not enough heed was paid to
morality." * His motives were purer than those of another of the
promoters, the merchant Seyler, who was an admirer of the actress
Frau Hensel (whom he afterward married), and was now wanting
to give her a good position above her rivals.

Whatever may have been the motives of the other partners,
the new enterprise had some noble aims. The director was to be
relieved of all financial care, and should look after the morals and
the training of the actors, especially developing the younger ones
in a "Theatrical Academy." Respectable provision for the actors
should be made against their old age. Prizes of fifty ducats should
be offered every year for the best tragedy and the best comedy.
To secure the sympathy of the public, benefit exhibitions should
be given for the institutions of charity. Great actors were engaged,
such as Eckhof, Frau Hensel, and others. Lessing was to be the
counsellor and critic, publish a semi-weekly journal in the interest
of the enterprise, and receive eight hundred *thalers* a year.

To such fine theories, of course, there could be no lack of opposition and ridicule. Then, no sooner had the theatre opened than
each one of the twelve partners wanted to have his say in the
direction of it. This led to differences. And Lessing soon
offended the actors by his criticisms, especially Frau Hensel, by
intimating that she was a little stout in figure for the part she was
playing. He had, therefore, to cease speaking of anything but the
plays themselves. And worst of all, the enterprise found itself

---

* See W. Cosack, ' Materialien zu Lessing's Ham. Dram.'

gradually losing its public. The wherewithal was failing, and in a year and a half the theatre had to be closed. "The sweet dream of founding a national theatre in Hamburg had vanished all too soon."

Bitter was Lessing's disappointment, and equally bitter his failure soon after in the publishing business, which he had been carrying on simultaneously with the other. Loaded with debts, he left Hamburg to take a position as librarian at a small salary in Wolfenbüttel. He no doubt looked back all the rest of his life on these experiences as humiliating failures. But out of these trying fires came the pure metal of the 'Dramaturgie ; ' "out of a mere theatre journal came a world's classic."

Like all great productions of the mind, the 'Dramaturgie' was a growth of many years. It was germinating in its author's head as he was eagerly absorbing Plautus and Terence, Shakespeare and Corneille, in his boyhood. It was growing rapidly in his student years, when he spent his days and nights in the theatre. A little later it leafed out into ' Beiträge ' and 'Literaturbriefe.' Then it received a new graft from Diderot, which in eight years more bore the perfect fruit.

The author's aim, as he expressly stated,[*] was not to produce a system of dramatic principles, but only " to scatter some *fermenta cogitationis.*" Any discussion of these, therefore, must needs be rather unjointed. Indeed, there has been made up from them a good book of dramatic maxims ; and as these form so prominent a part of the whole work, it may be permissible to quote a few of them here. We have selected them almost at random : —

" A man's character in a drama must be shown by himself. We will not believe any character given him by the others in their words " (Piece 9).

" The less the title of a drama reveals of its contents the better " (21).

" Nothing is more offensive than that for which we can give no cause " (23).

" It is even essential to pride that it express itself less through words than through actions " (25).

" A comedy must make us laugh at vices, not at bodily or mental defects which are incurable.   And the vices must not be those
of a good-for-nothing character, but rather of one who has admirable qualities " (26).

" Out of fifty women in history who have deposed or murdered
their husbands, there is hardly one whose motives cannot be
shown to have been injured love " (30).

" A poet has no right to change the characters he takes from
history.   He may change the facts, but the facts must be the
result of the characters " (32).

" A drama must have harmony and purpose.   Each character
must be consistent with itself throughout " (34).

" In comedy the characters are the chief thing ; in tragedy, the
events.   In comedy the events are only to bring out the characters ; in tragedy the characters are there only to bring out the
events.   The events are to arouse sympathy and fear " (52).

" If kings and queens dare not use the simple language of
nature, so much the worse for them.   The poet must make them
use unstilted language in his dramas, as Euripides did in his
' Hecuba ' " (59).

" Whenever we perceive a plan, our curiosity is aroused " (79).

" The universal is the final cause of poetry, even when it
assigns particular names.   How does it aim at universality by
assigning proper names?   By assigning names that by their
etymology, or history, or association, already indicated the character of the one bearing them " (90).

And many more suggestive apothegms are found in this work.

One of the most striking and oft-repeated features of the
' Dramaturgie ' is its relentless criticism and ridicule of Voltaire.
Even a reader who might be ignorant of Lessing's unpleasant
episode with Voltaire would naturally seek some personal cause
for his prejudice ; and lest this word applied to so just a character should offend any one, let us see what his biographers have
said about it.

Adolf Stahr, though more of a panegyrist than a biographer,
admits that it was the Richier affair * which led to his hero's
severe attacks on the French poet.   James Russell Lowell, on the
other hand, in his admirable essay on Lessing, tries to refute this

---

* See Carlyle's Essay on Voltaire.

opinion by showing that only a year after the affair, Lessing called Voltaire "a great man." But this is hardly sufficient proof. For K. G. Lessing, in his frank biography * of his brother, says the latter "really had the whim of seeing nothing good in Voltaire." We have not read the monograph on this point by Boxberger, but we believe that a placing together of the various sharp things said by Lessing against Voltaire, taken in connection with the Richier episode, must produce a strong impression of prejudice. We quote from the ' Dramaturgie ' : —

"What is there that Voltaire will not write? How he is always trying to show his erudition, and how badly he generally fails in it" (Piece 55).

" It is one of the weaknesses of Voltaire that he wishes to be a very profound historian."

He then shows how the French poet, in criticising Corneille's ' Count Essex,' took Dudley and Leicester for two different persons. We can imagine Lessing's delight over catching his enemy so.

In another place he severely rebukes the vanity of Voltaire in allowing himself, after a performance of his ' Mérope,' to be called before the curtain by the Paris *parterre*, thus establishing a foolish custom. And he adds, " I should rather have done away so bad a custom by my example than to have occasioned it with ten ' Méropes ' " (Piece 36). Again, he accuses Voltaire of writing under his own name a flattering critique on the Italian dramatist Mattei, and writing a scathing criticism of the same person under the false name of Lindella (Piece 41). Farther on it is remarked : " Voltaire's ' Semiramis ' was equipped with all that the furnishers could supply of imposing scenery, and yet there is nothing colder than this play. . . . Voltaire has nothing of the really tragical in him."

In many other places ridicule or censure is heaped upon the French poet until the unbiassed reader feels moved to take his part. Lessing himself felt the excessiveness of these attacks, and in one place (70) tries to apologize for it by citing Aristotle's example of seeking controversy in order the better to discuss his subject. If

*

more proof be needed of our great critic's vindictiveness, witness
the personal bitterness of the ' Autigötze,' written in Wolfenbüttel
some time after.  The fair-minded reader must confess that the
spirit of it is too pugnacious to be scientific.  To be sure, the chief
purpose of the Hamburg writings was to weaken the French influence over the German drama.  It was good strategy, therefore, to
attack relentlessly the greatest representative of that influence.
Though this may justify in large measure the attack, it can
hardly justify the acrimonious spirit of it.  So much to show that
Lessing was " a man of like passions with ourselves."

Let us now move on to some of the higher planes of the
' Dramaturgie.'  It might be interesting to tarry a while on
some minor points, — such as the non-adaptation of the Christian character to the use of the tragic poets ; the value of the
harlequin whom Gottsched had banished from the stage ; the
relative importance of the plot and the characters in tragedy ;
and the necessity of making the characters in both tragedy
and comedy typical.  These are deep questions, and the writer
has gone to the bottom of them.  But we pass on to the two
weightiest subjects in the work ; namely, the meaning of the
famous three unities and of the tragic sympathy and fear in
Aristotle's ' Poetics.'

This is not the place to discuss whether the ' Poetics ' is only a
fragment.  Many good scholars — as A. W. von Schlegel * and
J. H. Newman † — say it is.  Lessing, however, affirms that it
is not a fragment, but rather as infallible as Euclid.  We will
leave the classical scholars to settle this point, — if it ever can be
settled,— while we return to the three unities.

Their fidelity to the unity of time, of place, and of action had
been the chief boast of the French classical poets; and their
zeal in this was shared by the whole nation.  " Every Frenchman," says Schlegel, " who has sucked in Boileau with his
mother's milk, considers himself a born champion of the Dramatic Unities." ‡  As Aristotle was the originator of these, let

* Essay on Aristotle's ' Poetics.'            † Dramatic Lit., Lect. xvii.
‡ Dramatic Lit., Lect. xvii.

us hear what he has to say about them.   Of the unity of action
he says : —

"We affirm that Tragedy is the imitation of a perfect and
entire action which has a certain magnitude: for there may be
a whole without any magnitude whatever.   Now a whole is what
has a beginning, middle, and end.   A beginning is that which is
not necessarily after some other thing, but that which from its
nature has something after it, or arising out of it.   An end, on
the other hand, is that which from its nature is after something
else, either necessarily, or usually, but after which there is nothing.
A middle is what is itself after some other thing, and after which
also there is something.   Hence poems which are properly composed must neither begin nor end accidentally, but according
to the principles above laid down " (' Poetics,' chap. viii.).

With respect to the unity of time we find only the following :

"Moreover, the Epos is distinguished from  the tragedy by
its length : for the latter seeks as far as possible to circum-
scribe itself within one revolution of the sun, or to exceed it but
little ; the Epos is unlimited in point of time, and in that respect
differs from tragedy.   At first, however, the case was in this
respect alike in tragedies and epic poems " (' Poetics,' v.).

On the unity of place Aristotle does not say a syllable.   But
Corneille, Racine, Voltaire, and all the French Classical school,
taking their stand on these rules, and on the exemplification of
them in Æschylus, Sophocles, and Euripides, considered any
violation of them sacrilege.   They overlooked the fact, pointed
out by Lessing,* and after him by Schlegel,† that the constant
presence of the Chorus necessitated unity of time in the ancient
drama, and that the modern division of plays into separate acts
does away with this necessity.   Moreover, they failed to notice
that the Greek poets themselves sometimes violated the unity of
time and place.   For Æschylus violates the unity of time in his
' Agamemnon ' by making the signal fires over the fall of Troy
begin his piece, then has Talthybius tell shortly after, as an eye-
witness, the shipwreck of the Greeks on their way home.   The
piece lasts from the fall of Troy to Agamemnon's arrival at
Mycenæ, which must have been a considerable number of days.

---

* ' Dramaturgie,' Piece 45                † ' Dramatic Lit ,' Piece 247.

Again, in the 'Supplices' of Euripides during a single choral song the entire march of an army from Athens to Thebes is supposed to take place, a battle to be fought, and the General to return victorious.* Similar liberties with time and place can be found in Sophocles.

Rigidly trying to confine themselves within the narrow limits marked out for them by their understanding of the three rules, it is no wonder that Corneille and the rest felt obliged to stretch out the "single revolution of the sun" to thirty hours, and to widen the place of action to a whole city. No wonder that Voltaire, while striving to uphold the rules, still overstepped them in his plays. To the notorious three Unities we must lay the blame for most of the stiffness, monotony, artificiality, the frequent dulness of the French classic drama. Only the genius of a Corneille could make it tolerable, and even that not very long.

Lessing was quite right, then, in seeing no hope for a German national drama as long as it was modelled after the French. In recommending Shakespeare as the best pattern, he produced within his nation a literary revolution, and anticipated by fifty years the overthrow of the classic school in France. A. W. von Schlegel, though failing to give him due credit in the proper place, declares that "Shortly after the publication of the 'Dramaturgie,' translations of French tragedies, and German ones modelled after them, disappeared altogether from the stage." †

We now come to the part of our subject which has been a bone of contention to the scholars ever since Lessing gave it to the public; we refer to the interpretation of Aristotle's famous definition of tragedy. A literal translation of this definition might be given thus: "Tragedy, therefore, is an imitation of a worthy or illustrious and perfect action, possessing magnitude, in pleasing language, using separately the separate species of imitation in its parts, by men acting, and not through narration, through pity and fear affecting a purification of such like passions." ‡ The great point of controversy has been the last line: "Through

---

* Schlegel, Dram Lit, Lect. xviii † Dram Lit., Lect xxx.
‡ Poetics, vi.

sympathy and fear affecting the purification of such like passions." — What did Aristotle mean by this ? Ever since Lessing
broke a new path through the difficulty to show that the French·
had been going the wrong way, scores of others, from Goethe
himself down to the obscurest Gymnasium Rector, have been
trying either to widen his road or to make new ones. Let us
glance a moment at his interpretation.

"Tragedy must awaken sympathy and fear. Aristotle did
not mean terror, in the sense that his interpreters have explained,
for the old Greek poets tried to soften the terror in their plays by
laying it to fate or a god. . . . Sympathy requires a man who
suffers undeservedly, and we fear for one of our own kind. . . .
Aristotle must be interpreted by comparing him with himself.
His ' Poetics' must be read in connection with his ' Rhetoric.'
In the latter is explained what is meant by sympathy and fear.
The fear is because we feel liable to suffer the same evils.
Neither the hopeless man nor the perfectly happy man can feel
sympathy with others. Fear includes sympathy ; each includes
the other. One cannot exist properly in the drama without the
other. . . . The sympathy and fear which tragedy awakens shall
purify our sympathy and fear, but no other passions. Comedy
and epics may do this for other passions. . . . How does tragic
fear purify our sympathy ? — According to the philosophers, every
virtue possesses two extremes between which it stands midway.
Therefore tragedy, if it is to transform our sympathy into a
virtue, must be able to free it from both extremes ; that is, it
must purify the soul of him who has too little, and of him who
has too much sympathy. Fear, likewise, through tragedy, must
purify the soul of him who fears nothing, as well as of him who
fears everything. All poetry may teach virtues, but tragedy is
distinguished from the other kinds by this effect of fear and sympathy " (Pieces 74–78).

So much for Lessing's dictum. Goethe, on the other hand,
speaking always as poet and artist, expressly declares himself
against this, and holds that neither poetry nor any other art
can work on morality. With him, the *Katharsis*, or purifying,
is only a reconciliation, or adjustment of the passions of fear
and sympathy, at the end of the tragedy. But unfortunately

for him, grammar and philology do not bear him out in such an interpretation.

Herder seems to refer the *Katharsis* to the characters in the play, and not to the spectators.

The next most notable interpreter was Jacob Bernays. With great ability and learning he goes back to the pathological meaning of *Katharsis* in Aristotle's ' Politics ; ' namely, " the removal, or alleviation of disease by proper medicinal means." Applying this idea, then, metaphorically, his definition reads, " Tragedy brings about, by exciting sympathy and fear, the alleviating discharge of such affections of the mind." * This is an application of the old medical maxim, " Similia similibus," and sounds quite materialistic.

Passing over more than a score of other expositors of the famous passage, we will only stop to cite an excellent translator of Aristotle's ' Poetics,' — Ueberweg. His translation reads : " Tragedy is . . . imitation which, by exciting sympathy and fear, has as a final result the temporary setting free from such feelings." In explanation of this he refers, as Bernays did, to the ' Politics,' according to which the cathartic effect of music and art in general is to set the person free from certain emotions by means of stimulating in him certain other emotions. " As the stimulated feeling runs its natural course to the end, it dies out for a time, and thus the inclination to cherish feelings of a similar kind is, for a time, taken away. Fear and sympathy are the feelings to be called up by tragedy, and the *Katharsis* is the doing away with these, or the freeing from these." This explanation seems to us the most satisfactory of all.

Thus, after " a whole Iliad of critical combats has been fought out over the question," we can see that Lessing was not only the first to make a new path, but his path was in the right direction. His best successors have only straightened his road a little, and given it a deeper foundation. The historians of German literature have good reason to say that but for Lessing and his ' Dramaturgie,' Schiller and Goethe and the rest would have been impossible. *J. W. Thomas.*

* ' Politics,' viii 7

## DURING THE RIOT:

### NOTES OF AN OPERA-GOER.

FRIDAY, June 11, 1870.

IT is a quarter after nine. They are playing 'Faust.' House full and brilliant; all the shoulders and all the diamonds of a Friday, which is the great day. Madame Carvalho is singing, —

> " Ah ! within the mirror there
> I smile to see myself so fair ! "

     \*     \*     \*

I go out from the house into the flies. Here and there among the machinists and firemen the little peasant maidens are wandering about who are soon to dance Gounod's waltz in the Kermesse. Mademoiselle G. comes up to me ; very pretty with her coiffure of gold· brocade, her blue woollen skirt, her little apron of white muslin with its bands of cherry, and underneath, her ankles, which are charming.

" You are here," she says to me, " when you might go and see the riot ! "

" I came away from it. I like ' Faust ' better."

" Oh, ' Faust'! They play 'Faust' three times a week, while a riot — I saw it yesterday from a window at Menilmontant. Oh, how amused I was ! "

At this moment up rushed Mademoiselle M.

" Oh, come, Marie ; come quick ! I have found a little window in the second story, in the property-room ; no one is there, and one can see very well. Come quickly — you too ! "

They take flight gayly, and I follow them, threading the labyrinth of the stairways of the Opéra. The window was indeed very well situated, on the Rue Drouot, equally distant from the Boulevard des Italiens and the Mayoralty house of the ninth district.

The boulevard black as ink, a forest of heads, carriages at a foot-pace, hosts of white blouses, not one policeman. Suddenly a great surging in this immense throng : it is a regiment of cavalry coming up slowly from the Madeleine. They pass, and one hears on the macadam the heavy tramp of five hundred horse. Helmets and breast-plates shine like silver. The regiment withdraws ; and behind the soldiers the flood of people and carriages falls in again.

The two little dancing-girls prattle on in the gayest manner.

" Hark ! They are going to sing the ' Marseillaise ' soon, — ' Aux armes, Citoyens ! ' Only they don't know it very well. The other evening, after dinner, papa, mamma, and my brother, sang it, — the ' Marseillaise.' Oh, they know it ; that was much better."

" The cavalrymen, — they were cavalry ? " rejoins the other, who seems to care very little about the ' Marseillaise.'

" Yes ; they were cavalry."

" But then La R—— was there among them ? "

" No ; he is no longer in the cavalry. He has entered the Empress's dragoons."

Great outcry on the boulevard side, — " The ' Marseillaise ' ! " They sing the ' Marseillaise.' We listen. Then silence.

" How droll everything is ! " says G. Then, turning toward me, " Ah ! do you know, on the 17th, — Thursday the 17th —"

" What is Thursday, the 17th ? What is there to be on Thursday, the 17th ? "

" Oh, my appearance, — my first appearance at the École Lyrique. I play ! "

" What is it you are going to play ? "

" The rôle of Madame de Bryas."

" In what piece ? "

" How ! in what piece ! "

" Well, yes, the title of the piece ? "

" The title of the piece ! Ah ! that I don't know. All that I know is that I play Madame de Bryas, and that I shall have a blue gown. You are going to take a box for me ; it will cost only twenty francs."

I take the box and give the twenty francs.

On the boulevard the crowd increases, increases still, ever increases. Cries, shouts, songs, and hisses have full vent.

I hear at the same time what goes on in the street and on the stage. They have just recalled Madame Carvalho and Faure after the cathedral scene. In the theatre, applause ; behind the scenes, cries of the call-boys, " Clear the stage ! clear the stage ! "

At the same time, great hubbub in the Rue Drouot. The door of the Mayoralty opens, and we see a whole little army holding itself jammed in, infantry and cavalry, within the court of the old Hôtel Aguado. Clarion calls, rolling of drums, orders. A squad of policemen come out of the Mayoralty and try to clear the Rue Drouot. The crowd gives way slowly, slowly, when all at once, out of the great door of the Mayoralty darts on the trot, suddenly throwing itself on the boulevard, a squadron of city guards. The big horses of the municipal guard are admirable in this evolution. Not a slip, not a fault, in passing out thus at a great pace, under these heavy cavalry-men, from the court pavement to the asphalt of the street.

And, during all this evolution, from the open windows of the Opéra the soldiers' chorus soars out at full height : —

> " Honor undying
>   Of our great sires
> Feed we, supplying
>   Life through death's fires."

Two companies of foot, sword-bayonets at the ends of their guns, follow the horsemen on a run ; then after the foot comes a squadron of blue hussars. Ah, the poor little Arab horses ! They are not, like the good, patient steeds of the city guards, wonted to crowds and uproar. They understand nothing of what is going on. They come out leaping and curvetting, furious, frightened, startled, prancing, pawing, kicking, running against and over each other. The hussars disappear in a vortex of enormous manes and long tails flying in the wind.

" Ah, how pretty it is, — how amusing ! " cry my little comrades. They were right. It was charming.

* * *

In the Court of the Mayoralty, on the pavement, the little Arabs hold good, and leap like madmen without losing their equilibrium. But out on the asphalt, they slip, slide ; four horses fall, — one drags another down ; all roll in a heap with their riders

pell-mell. The crowd utters a great cry. The policemen precipi-
tate themselves in the midst. The poor hussars must be crushed,
pulverized. Not at all. The four little Arabs are already on their
legs, and the four riders in the saddle. For the moment one can
hold no more. One forgets everything, — the riot, Rochefort, and
the 'Marseillaise ;' one sees nothing but the spectacle, and applauds it.

After the hussars, a squad of policemen, then again horse
guards, foot guards, again a squadron of hussars, and again and all
the time, policemen. It all passes like a hurricane, and launches
on the boulevard in two columns, — one taking the right toward
the Madeleine, the other the left toward the Bastille. When all
have disappeared, chasing the crowd and leaving emptiness behind
them, like a piston in a pump, the Rue Drouot is deserted, the
boulevard deserted ; and Monsieur Perrin's soldiers finish Gounod's
Chorus : —

> · "And under thy wing,
> Soldiers victorious,
> Lead thou our steps ; our hearts feel thee over us ! "

The doors of the Mayoralty close. Prolonged, confused murmurs come to us from the boulevard. It is the crowd scattering
and fleeing away before the troops. Little by little the noises die
away, die out. A great stillness follows ; and little G. cries out, —
"On my word, we shall never be ready for the fifth act."

They go off on a run, and after five minutes I have stared
long enough at the street, now absolutely empty and silent.

＊        ＊        ＊

I descend to the theatre. In the flies I stop near two of the
chorus : one, helmet on head, cuirass upon his shoulders, leans
back against a door ; the other, with battlemented cap, coat of
mail, and slashed doublet, rests upon a ponderous sword for two
hands.

"For all that," says one, "it is not going to be very convenient
to get out to Belleville to-night. I hope that will cure you of
voting for Rochefort."

"Me, not at all. I will vote for him again."

"And why so?"

"Because that will worry the Government, and because it would be amusing to see him in the Chamber of Deputies."

"And then we shall have riots and revolutions."

"Oh, as to that, there is no danger."

"How! no danger!"

"No, no. I vote for Rochefort. I hope he will come back. But if, once returned, he tries to play the rogue too far, the Government will soon bring him to reason. Oh, it is solid, the Government; that is why you can worry it."

Upon this profound reasoning the man in the coat of mail went away, after shouldering his two-handed sword.

I went away also. I entered the dancing-hall. Scarcely anybody. Monsieur Auber slept in a corner, seated on a red bench before the great mirror which has reflected so many pirouettes, so many salutes, sallies, cuts ; Mademoiselle Baratte, with one foot on the floor, and the other planted on the hand-rail, talked with Monsieur L. Mademoiselle Beaugrand made little wheels on one leg gravely in the middle of the room. A few black coats wandered among the fair Trojans and Nubians.

\* \* \*

I return to my little window. The look of street and boulevard is changed. In the street, before the Mayoralty, a hundred policemen. Among them two drummers of the Paris guard and a police commissioner, sash crossed. On the boulevard a considerable gathering of people. At the entrance of the Rue Drouot, the policemen look at the mob, and the mob look at the policemen. From time to time a cat-call or a cheer for Rochefort.

At a command the policemen put themselves in motion, and preceded by the commissioner and the two drummers go up to the boulevard. Three rolls of the drums. The groups, without dispersing, draw farther off, and keep at a distance. After the third roll, the policemen advance, and five minutes afterward begin the filing off of the arrested people, — rioters or the inquisitive, but without doubt more of them inquisitive than rioters. Those of the policemen who had followed a losing hunt and returned empty-handed wear a sheepish and confused look as they defile before the commissioner on their return.

Many prisoners, many curious scenes, distressing or ludicrous: "But I did nothing at all, Monsieur, I did nothing: I went back home." "My God! my poor wife, who is waiting for me! I went to the Rue Vivienne on an errand," etc. One brave fellow, who bore a great packet under his right arm and a little white dog under his left, cried out in a lamentable voice, "But I would not have carried all this to make a riot!" Five minutes later he was put at liberty, himself, his packet, and his dog. A young man in an overcoat and a waiter try to resist, and immediately are thrown violently into the court of the hotel. A band of thirty prisoners defile thus before me, and are all shut within the door of the Mayoralty. I light a cigar, and hear behind me Valentine's curse falling upon Margaret. The fourth act is ended.

*     *     *

My two little dancers return, — G. dressed as a Nubian, M. as a Trojan. Behold them ready for the ballet.

"We have ten minutes yet before the dance," says G. to me. "Do they still sing the 'Marseillaise'?"

"No; they sing no more."

We are all three at the window, — I black-coated, with white cravat, M. the Trojan, with her little Phrygian bonnet and blue silk tights under a skirt of white crape; and G. the Nubian, with her sphinx coiffure of red and gold, and her long white tunic and scarlet trousers.

Up comes my friend Z. He has come across the boulevard. A saying of a bourgeois has delighted him. This bourgeois went very respectfully to find the police commissioner.

"Pardon, Monsieur the Commissary, at which summons to disperse are you?"

"At the first, sir."

Whereupon the bourgeois returns to say to his wife, —

"He is only at the first summons. We can remain a little while longer."

On the boulevard and in the street all is ready for a new sally.

One by one the policemen, disembarrassed of their prisoners, leave the Mayoralty. Then at the corner of the street, on the boulevard, groups form again quietly, and, one must say, very stupidly. They begin again to gaze at the policemen. The fish returning in crowds to the same spot where the filet had just been caught! I guessed well enough what would soon come, and I had — I, between my Nubian and my Trojan — a foolish wish to go and ask these idiots what pleasure they found in contemplating that squad of policemen. The riot of curiosity, in all its imprudence and silliness, was revealed to me.

Things followed a perfectly regular course. By the time the hundred police, the two drummers, and the commissioner with his scarf were all together again in front of the Mayoralty door a fine mob was collected on the boulevard, which asked nothing more than to be dispersed and pursued.

It was done, after the three regulation drum-rolls.

The Trojan and the Nubian were charmed at first with this little spectacle: the drums, the crowd in flight, the policemen launched on a grand trot down the boulevard, — all that was very delightful to them. But the military piece suddenly turned into huge melodrama. The second batch of prisoners was infinitely less peaceable and resigned than the first. Resistance as well as submission is contagious. The fray began in front of a wine merchant's shop, which alone remained open between the boulevard and the Rue Rossini. A very young man, bareheaded, his gray coat torn, fell on the side-walk, and when the police would have picked him up, he made a fierce defence with hands and feet. Wrath soon reached the little troop of prisoners, and for some instants it was a violent brawl. Hats, caps, and cocked hats rolling to earth, swords wrenched from their scabbards, clothes in tatters, cries, oaths, curses; one woman above them all, with piercing clamor, threw herself full into the fight, catching hold of the policemen and trying to tear from their hold a man in a blouse who, for his part, fought with all his force, and gave as many blows as he received. The police held him by the blouse, and his shirt, pulled out from his trousers, showed the bare abdomen and hairy chest. A vague remembrance of the barricades and the Morgue! Around this rabid struggle the crowd cries, hoots, howls, and hisses the police.

\*       •       \*

"Let us go away! Let us go away!" said M. and G. at the same time. "Come quickly; come with us! Don't stay there, — it is frightful!"

I let myself be dragged away, my heart leaping in my breast a little.

In the lobby we meet the second manager of the dance.

"Ah! What are you doing, young ladies? Everybody is on the boards for the ballet. You are late."

They escape, running. I cross the side-scenes mechanically; passing out by the door of communication from the stage to the audience-room, I go and sit down in the orchestra stalls, — my usual seat.

I think I was never seized by a stranger or more violent contrast. I find myself in that magnificent, ostentatious hall of the Opéra. My neighbors of every evening are there, my friends M. and V. at my right and left. "Why do you come so late?" asks M. I do not reply. Madame de S. from the depth of her box smiles upon me in the most charming way. On the stage, in the clouds, witches gallop by on broomsticks. Mephistopheles invites Faust to come

> "At the feast of dames of race
> And of courtesans take place."

And the mountain opening reveals a resplendent palace; floods of light deluge the hall; sixty beautiful girls descend from the back of the stage and begin to dance to the most delicate and voluptuous strains.

After the most brutal and disgusting spectacle, after those cries and howls, after those blouses and tatters, without transition, twenty steps away, at the same minute, the most delicate and sensuous of sights, this sparkling hall, all full of elegance and harmony, — which was the dream? which the reality?

\*       \*       \*

And at the same moment I see again distinctly, as if it were before my eyes, Delacroix's picture, — ' Liberty on the barricades of 1830.' This woman, standing on a mound of stones and corpses, a gun in one hand and the tricolor in the other ; beside her, crying " Long live the Republic ! " the heroic boy, gray with powder, pistol in hand, the long shoulder-belt of the national guard flying at his heels ; and this workman with the blue blouse and the red cap who, lying flat on the ground, lifts himself with great difficulty, and dies gazing at Liberty ; in the background Paris in the smoke of powder and under the lowering July sun of 1830.

Ah, well ! I am awaiting something like that, with less of its grandeur and more of its horror. At every instant it seems to me that I shall see it appear among these amiable silk-clad people, with their flowers and diamonds, coming to claim its place at the feast of dames and courtesans, — the pallid man of the streets, torn, bruised, dirty, clothed in a blouse of white and holding in his hand, instead of the tricolor, a singular red flag made of a broomstick and a petticoat.

\* \* \*

A quarter of an hour afterward, while the drumming and summoning continues in the Rue Drouot, the exit of the audience from the Opéra was made with all its wonted elegance and splendor. The grand Parisian dames slowly descended the steps of the hall stairways, and the footmen made the carriages draw up in file beneath the great awning of the theatre.

I meet the Director of the Opéra, Monsieur Émile Perrin.

" Bad receipts," I say to him, " with this rioting."

" Better than ever ! " he replies.

*Translated from the French of Ludovic Halévy.*

## GENTLE WILL, OUR FELLOW.

WRIT IN 1626 A. D. BY JOHN HEMINGE, SERVANT OF HIS GRACIOUS
MAJESTY KING CHARLES I. ; EDITED IN 1892 A. D. AS "ALL,
THOUGH FEIGNED, IS TRUE" BY F. G. FLEAY, SERVANT OF ALL
SHAKESPEARIAN STUDENTS IN AMERICA, ENGLAND, GERMANY, OR
ELSEWHERE.

*(Concluded.)*

JUST before this a small matter arose, which I must not omit,
because it argues the honesty of our quondam fellow. A dozen years
before, Jaggard the printer had sent forth a book which he called
'The Passionate Pilgrim,' " by William Shakespeare." Now, all
that was by him was a couple of Sonnets, how obtained I know not,
and a few pieces stolen from out the new Quarto copy of ' Love's
Labour's Lost.' Shakespeare made no complaint, but when the book
in 1612 reached a third edition, this Jaggard impudently added
thereto two love epistles by Master Heywood, who forthwith, in
his ' Apology for Actors,' acknowledged that his lines were not
worthy Shakespeare's patronage, and said that he knew that
Shakespeare was much offended with Jaggard's presumption in
thus making bold with his name. The upshot was that Shakespeare made him withdraw his name from the title.

While Shakespeare was thus attending to another man's interest he was not inattentive to his own ; for at this same time he was
concerned in the Chancery suit of Lane, Greene, and Shakespeare
*vs.* Combe and others, who would not pay their valuable portions
of the reserved rent for the tithes of which he had purchased a
moiety of the lease seven years before. And he was not free from
domestic trouble; for in the preceding February his brother
Gilbert died, and in the February after, Richard the only brother
he had now left him.

Immediately after this we saw him once more in London. On
March 10, 1613, he purchased a house, yard, and shop in Blackfriars
for £140, and let it to one John Robinson, a haberdasher. I myself
was, with William Johnson and John Jackson, a co-trustee in the

legal estate thereof; and although the other trustees only signed the duplicate conveyance of this property and the mortgage deed for £60 left unpaid of the purchase-money, it not being convenient for me to be present at the delivery thereof, yet two years after Shakespeare's death, when, following the directions of his will, we transferred this estate to the trustees of Susanna Hall, his daughter, I duly signed, sealed, and delivered the deed of transfer.

When Shakespeare came to London on this matter we were grievously distressed for new plays. During the two years that he had been away, we had been abundantly provided; but in this winter Beaumont married and left play-writing; Webster also ceased to write; Jonson was going abroad with young Raleigh; and Fletcher alone, of any great note, remained with us. We, therefore, urgently requested Shakespeare that he would provide us with a play; but he was not fain to return to his old quality, and all that we could obtain of him was a part of a play, which he had plotted on 'Henry VIII.' This we put into the hands of Fletcher, who completed it with scenes of his own; and on the day of Saints Peter and Paul, June 29, we played it at the Globe under the name of 'All is True.' This name we gave it because there were no "irregular humorists" in it, as there had been in Shakespeare's other histories. It was staged with great magnificence, the dresses being very costly. While some chambers were being let off behind the scenes, the thatched roof took fire and the theatre was burned. We lost many of our properties and some play-books: among them that of the play then acted; but some of us having saved our parts, Fletcher having another copy of such part as was written by him, we, by the hand of Massinger, reformed the whole play some years after and acted it as it is now in print. This may serve as an excuse for us and as a warning to some men who have unjustly blamed us for not printing every play as we received it from our author. We have done the best we could, but when the first copy had been burned, what else could we do but print such as we had? Fortunately for us, the most part of our play-books were stored at our other house at Blackfriars; and we were careful thereafter to keep our copies more safely. Another warning we had from this fire was the dangerous condition of thatched roofs ; and when we rebuilded the Globe the next Christmas we had the roof covered with tiles.

This is the last note of Shakespeare in connection with the stage ; but one other play he left with us unfinished in the same way as he did that of ' Henry the Eighth.' This was the play of 'Timon of Athens,' which, however, was written, as far as Shakespeare's part was concerned, much earlier, it having been, like ' Cymbeline,' interrupted by the breaking out of the plague in 1606. The play as he left it was complete but very short ; and to make it fit for the stage we had it enlarged by another hand. The reformer, whose work was far inferior and nothing near that of Massinger in ' Henry VIII.,' — which is to many indistinguishable from Shakespeare's own, — could not make it into a full play ; and in spite of the excellence of the part that is not his, this tragedy as presented has had so little effect that I do not remember one instance of its being mentioned by any poet or critic of my time. Now that it is published, the judicious reader, who can separate the gold from the dross, will most like see reason to think better of it than those who saw it in its seldom presentment. It was written just after ' Antony and Cleopatra,' while Shakespeare was at work on Plutarch's great men, but the additions not till some half-score years after.

In the July of this year, 1613, he was troubled by the scandalous reports about his daughter, Mrs. Hall, and one Ralph Smith ; but after the excommunication of John Lane, the author thereof, at the suit of Dr. Hall, no more was heard of them. In November the next year, he was again in London, while Jonson, who had returned from abroad, was scoffing at his latest plays in ' Bartholomew Fair.' Among these I do not reckon 'Henry VIII. ; ' for Fletcher having had a hand in that, and he and Jonson being now writing for ·Henslow's new Bear-Garden, the Hope, of course Jonson said not a word thereof. It was his way only to vilify the theatres and authors with which he was not at the moment connected. But Shakespeare gave no heed to such matters now. He was only concerned in supporting the enclosure of certain common lands at Welcombe, near Stratford, in which matter the Corporation, who misliked the same, got the better at last. Thenceforth I saw him no more after he returned to Stratford, in the beginning of the next year, 1615.

Yet one year more and all in this earthly globe was ended for the Hercules who so long bore the weight of our lesser stage. On Jan. 25, 1616, his will was drawn up. On February 10, his daughter Judith was married to T. Quincy, vintner at Stratford, without a license, for which they were summoned to the Ecclesiastical Court at Worcester. On March 25, the will was executed ; on April 23, Shakespeare died, and was buried at Stratford two days afterward.

In his will he left his real estate to his daughter, Mrs. Hall ; £300 and a bowl to Mrs. Quincy ; £20, with a life interest in her dwelling-house in Henley Street, and clothing, to his sister, Joan Hart, now a widow ; his plate to his niece, Elizabeth Hall ; two marks, each for rings, to each of his fellow housekeepers, Burbadge, Condell, and myself ; some legacies to his executors, the poor, etc. ; and to his wife his second-best bed. It was noticed that although sufficient provision for her was provided by the law, by the way of free-bench and dower, he did not leave any other token of affectionate remembrance to her, not even a kindly word, but named her quite curtly as " my wife."

And here, having done the task imposed on me, I might draw to a conclusion ; but seeing that I, having relations at Stratford, and having known the Hathaway family before I knew Shakespeare, am perforce acquainted with some matters concerning him, which are only matter of hearsay to men in London, I think it well to set down here what I have learned, — somewhat of my own knowledge, somewhat from public report in Stratford, for the truth of which latter I will not be bound to answer — concerning his private affairs there.

### SHAKESPEARE'S PRIVATE LIFE.

First, then, as to his birth and family. His father, by degrees, between 1557, when he was admitted as a burgess of Stratford, and 1572, had been successively member of the court leet, ale-taster, constable, affeeror, chamberlain, alderman, high bailiff, and chief alderman. He was, I think, a glover by trade. His mother inherited landed property called Asbies at Wilmecote. These two, John Shakespeare and Mary Arden, were married about the year 1557, and had eight children, of whom only five survived their infancy, — William, Gilbert, Joan, Richard, and Edmond ; Joan is still living ; the deaths of the sons I have already set down in their places. The prosperity of the family was interrupted about the year 1578, and they gradually fell into great straits in a few years' time.

Next, as to his education. He never attained a high place at the Stratford Free School, having been taken therefrom to help (as I have been told) in his father's business, who dealt in wool, besides his glove-making. Jonson truly said of him that he had little Latin and less Greek. Lilly's Grammar, The Accidence, the Sententiæ Pueriles and Mantuanus were wellnigh all that he mastered in Latin ; and for Greek, it is most unlike that he ever construed it at all. Of the modern languages he learned some French from Dr. Lodge, while they were both writing for our company ; of others he knew only some scraps gathered in his reading. For he read much, not as Jonson did, who was an absolute *helluo librorum*, as I have ofttimes heard him boast, but as a man should do who allows himself time to digest his reading. His favorite books were Plutarch's 'Lives,' Holinshed's 'Chronicle,' Montaigne's ' Essays,' Painter's 'Palace of Pleasure,' some of the tracts of Greene, Rich, and Lodge, which have narratives therein, the poems and plays of Chaucer, Marlowe, Jonson, Drayton, and others. But his reading was never, as some men's is, for a pastime merely ; when it was not for the plotting or illustrating of his own plays, as it most times was, it was for the acquiring of knowledge in matters which he thought he ought to be acquainted with. In this way he would read such books as Raleigh's ' Discovery of Guyana,' ' The Book of Honor and Arms,' Scot's ' Discovery of Witchcraft,' and the like. But all that he read he absorbed. It so sunk into him that he needed not to quote other men, which, indeed, he scarce ever did ; he gave forth all that he had learned so naturally, and so, as it were, grown into his own thought, that all alike seemed to be of his own nature. Whence it came that some maligned him and said he wanted art.

Then, as to his marriage. Richard Hathaway, *alias* Gardiner, was a substantial yeoman of Shottery near Stratford, who had eight children living at the time of his decease in July, 1582 : three sons and one daughter were then under twenty years of age; one son and three daughters were over twenty. Every one of these except one was mentioned in his will, made Sept. 1, 1581, to which will my cousin, John Heminge, was one of the witnesses. It is from him that I have learned these particulars. The one exception was his daughter Anne, with whom her father is said to have had grave reason for displeasure at the time. Immediately after his death this Anne Hathaway, *alias* Gardiner, and William Shakespeare came together in a manner which I may best describe in the poet's own words in ' Measure for Measure,' when Claudio says : —

> " upon a true contract
> I got possession of Julietta's bed :
> You know the lady ; she is fast my wife,
> Save that we do the denunciation lack
> Of outward order : this we came not to,
> Only for propagation of a dower,
> Remaining in the coffer of her friends,
> From whom we thought it meet to hide our loves
> Till Time had made them for us. But it chances
> The stealth of our most mutual entertainment
> With character too gross is writ on Juliet."

Immediate marriage thus became necessary ; and November 27, a license for marriage was obtained at Worcester between William Shakespeare and Anne Whately of Temple Grafton (which is about four miles from Shottery) with once asking of the banns. These had been asked the Sunday before, and the marriage was to take place on Wednesday, the 28th ; but it was then found that the name of the bride did not agree with the license. But Fulk Sandells and John Richardson, both friends of the late Richard Hathaway, — one being a supervisor, and the other a witness, to his will, — were not minded that their neighbor's daughter should be blurred in reputation by any delay in the marriage, and bound

themselves for £40 that there was then no action pending, ecclesiastical or temporal, concerning any impediment to matrimony,
that Anne Hathaway's friends had given their consent, and that
William Shakespeare (who, being a minor, could not be bound
himself) should save harmless the Bishop of Worcester (John
Whitgift, afterward Archbishop of Canterbury) for licensing the
marriage.  In which bond there are things worthy of note : first,
that the consent of the bride's friends should be required, she being
then at least six-and-twenty years of age; secondly, that no note
is taken of the bridegroom's friends' assent, although he was only
nineteen; thirdly, that all expense that might arise from any
future difficulty about this marriage is thrown on Shakespeare,—a
responsibility which he, being under age, could not undertake.  If
my cousin has made no mistake, I cannot doubt that Shakespeare
must have presented himself as of full age to give his consent;
and that Sandells and the others were acting as if they were guardians to Anne is evident from their using, not their own seals
below the deed, but the seal with the impress R. H., which had
belonged to Richard Hathaway.  I cannot believe that Shakespeare's family or friends knew anything of this marriage before-
hand ; nor that such a marriage with one so much older than he,
and forced on him as a retribution for an act of youthful folly,
could ever have proved happy, though beyond doubt he strove
hard to make it so.  Those who think otherwise should read his
own words in ' Twelfth Night ' [ii. 4 30–40] ; 'The Tempest ' [iv.
1. 12–22] ; ' Winter's Tale ' [iv. 4. 405–420].*  The first offspring of
this marriage was Susanna, Shakespeare's favorite daughter, baptized
May 26, 1583, six months after the marriage.  The twins Hamnet
and Judith were baptized Feb. 2, 1585.  Shakespeare became of
age in the following April, and some say that he then went to London
and joined the Lord Leicester's men ; others say that he accompanied
them for the first time after they played at Stratford in 1587.  For
my part, I only know that I first met with him in the latter year ;
for Phillips and I were not with these men when they went abroad
the year before.

* The references in brackets are of my insertion, from Elze's ' William Shakespeare,' p. 82, etc.
F. G. F.

Now, as to the real estate which Shakespeare had at Stratford. In 1597, Easter, he purchased New Place for £60; and for an addition to this property in 1602, Michaelmas, he gave another £60 ; in September, 1601, he inhabited a house in Henley Street which had been his father's ; in May, 1602, he purchased 107 acres of land for £320, which in May, 1610, he increased by 20 acres, for which he gave another £100 ; in September, 1602, he bought the copyhold of Getley's cottage in Chapel Lane ; in July, 1605, he acquired the moiety of the tithes at Stratford, etc., for £440; and in March, 1613, his house in Blackfriars, for which he gave £140 subject to a mortgage for £80. He must have died worth £1200 at the least. His purchases had cost him £1060; but during his later years, after he left us, he spent the whole of his annual incomings, for he had not enough moneys at his death to take up the Blackfriars mortgage; nor was it taken up till February, 1618. Some have alleged that he made great gain by the sale of his shares in the Globe and the Blackfriars theatres ; but this is bruited abroad merely to make it appear that we who are now housekeepers make far greater profit than in truth we do. True it is that when he left the stage he was owner of four out of sixteen shares in the Globe and two out of eight shares in the Blackfriars ; it is also true that, according to the convention made between him, Burbadge, Condell and myself, then the only house-keepers, his shares were sold to Cuthbert Burbadge, the brother of Richard, our fellow, who was no play-actor, — which thing had never theretofore been allowed, not even to Phillips, Pope, Bryan, or Sly. But how small the sum was that this Cuthbert gave him may appear from his only having £60 to spare when he bought his house in Blackfriars, and leaving no money to redeem the mortgage thereon when he died. Yet compared with the generality of his fellows he was a wealthy man, though far less so than charitable Master Alleyn, who founded his College of God's Gift at Dulwich.

In person he was handsome and well made ; his hazel eyes could sparkle with wit or flash with spirit ; in manner he was open and free and always gentle, but had withal a native dignity, which made him the best personator of royalty whom our stage possessed ;

his nature honest and sociable; his fancy excellent in expression
and facile even to overflowing; his thought full and rapid. But
this is best seen in his works, of which it may seem presumptuous
in me to speak, but this much I will say. Of the men, and many of
them are great ones, who have written for our stage, many there
be who in some single point have excelled him. Jonson is more
learned; Webster can excite a greater horror in the spectator;
Massinger is a better plotter; Marlowe, had he lived, might have
equalled him in tragedy, for he came to maturity earlier; Beaumont,
who came,nearest him in general power, could, like Jonson, do one
thing which he could not, — namely, write a mask; Fletcher and
Dekker could equal him in song-writing, and Heywood in industry; while Chapman when at his best has a terse masculine power
which is especially his own. But if the best excellences of all these
men were given to one of them, he would still be far below Shakespeare in one quality, the greatest of all, — a head that can understand
and a heart that can sympathize with the feelings of all that are
human, from Falstaff to Othello, from Gobbo to Coriolanus. Such
an all-embracing soul has never been known till now; and it will
be centuries ere the world will look upon his like again.

*Frederick Gard Fleay.*

THE END.

---

## THE SUPERNATURAL IN SHAKESPEARE:

### III. 'HAMLET,' 'JULIUS CÆSAR.'

ALTHOUGH Shakespeare holds up to scorn the vulgar terror of
a mob of demons and evil spirits, yet he has not failed to depict
them for us, and there is scarcely an imp named in the calendar of
hell that he has not pressed into his service, with all the attributes
ascribed to him. For in those days nothing was more natural than
a belief in the supernatural; and all the ills that flesh is heir to,
and all the misfortunes that befell luckless men, were held to come

from evil spirits, as God and the saints were blessed as the sources of happiness and peace.

It was a common article of faith that demons might manifest themselves in any form, although they generally chose the human, to beguile men to sin, offering them the desire of their hearts in exchange for their souls. As the familiars of witches and enchanters, they often appeared in animal form, preferably as flies or cats, and sometimes put on the likeness of dead friends to lure the living to their doom; hence Hamlet questions whether what seems his father's spirit may not be a fiend, who would plunge him headlong from the steep, and leave him to die in his sins without absolution. Often these demons entered into men, who became raving mad, and could be cured only by holy arts or spells, strong enough to exorcise the evil spirit, and send it back to its own abode.

As States in the classic and modern world were under the protection of tutelary deities or patron saints, so individuals were guarded and guided by genii, who sought to keep them safe from harm, and who admonished or advised in dreams ; but evil angels lurked about man's path, to deceive with lying visions, to urge to crime. "You follow the young prince up and down, like his ill angel," says the Chief-Justice in ' Henry IV.' " For Brutus, as you know, was Cæsar's angel," — the one whom he loved and in whom he trusted. But the protecting spirit was sometimes compelled to bow before another, mightier than himself, when he came into his presence ; and so Macbeth says of Banquo : —

> "There is none but he,
> Whose being I do fear: and, under him,
> My Genius is rebuked ; as, it is said,
> Mark Antony's was by Cæsar."

In ' Antony and Cleopatra ' the soothsayer utters these words of warning : —

> " O Antony, stay not by his side :
> Thy demon, that 's thy spirit which keeps thee, is
> Noble, courageous, high, unmatchable,
> Where Cæsar's is not ; but, near him, thy angel
> Becomes a fear, as being o'erpower'd."

From time immemorial men have believed in ghosts, and have had a fearful pleasure in so doing. Tales of them have been told by many a winter fireside to audiences spell-bound in terror and delight; and their history and customs have been subjects of careful study. No ancient homestead is complete without its ghost, who flits around its tower, or paces up and down the secluded garden path ; who wanders sadly through the gloomy corridors, and puts aside the arras of the haunted chamber. Usually they were believed to come in the form and garb which they had worn in life, that they might be known at a glance, although the sheeted dead sometimes manifested himself in the garments of the grave. They were to be evoked by magic spells ; and in the other life they seem to have won the power of forecasting the future. Hence we have *necromancy*, or prophecy of the dead ; and we are all familiar with the stories of the evocation of Tiresias by Odysseus, and of Samuel by the Witch of Endor. Learning was needful for the ghost-raiser, for unless suitable spells were employed the spirit refused to come when men did call for them, or to answer if they did appear; they seem, moreover, to have been impatient of questioning and eager to escape, whether interrogated as to things in their own past or in the future of others. In ancient Greece, we are told, there were sorcerers who could summon the ghost in the perfect likeness of the form he wore on earth, from out the hidden precincts of the world of shades, and show him, visible to all men's eyes.

But spirits often manifested themselves voluntarily, in which cases they would answer none except those to whom they had specially come ; and they seem to have been unable to speak at all unless first addressed. In many instances they were doomed, like Hamlet's father, to walk the earth in penance for sins committed in the flesh; or they return because proper funeral rites have not been performed, or to set right something which they have neglected in this earthly existence ; or to warn, protect, or punish those who are dear or hostile. Their coming was often announced before they became visible, by a change in the color of the lights, which burned faintly, by a cold wind, by a footfall, or an eerie feeling in the mortal to whom they presented themselves. On the eve of Bosworth Field King Richard cries: —

> " The lights burn blue. It is now dread midnight.
> Cold, fearful drops stand on my trembling flesh.
>
> . . . . . . . . . .
>
> Methought the souls of all that I had murder'd
> Came to my tent."

So, too, as Balaam's ass recognized the angel when his master did not, animals were held to be capable of detecting spirits imperceptible to human senses. The ghost of Banquo, which rises, blood-stained, at Macbeth's board, is unseen, save by the guilty man, whose conscience makes a coward of him in his victim's presence. Here the spectre bears all the cruel tokens of his fate, speechless and grim. The courtiers see him not; the queen, whose soul is also stained with blood, suspects him, but seeking with all her energy to protect her husband, professes to consider him a figment of her lord's distempered fancy. In a painting of this subject by Maclise, a fine touch is added by the figure of a dog, which crouches, trembling, beneath a chair, with its eyes fixed upon the spectre, thus asserting its reality.

The ghost in ' Hamlet ' we have no hesitation in accepting as an objective apparition; it shows itself to others besides the prince, but will speak to none but him. He for the moment hesitates; is it his father, or a fiend luring him to death? And when the spirit declares himself, and confesses that, dying unshriven and unabsolved, he must purge himself of his earthly misdeeds by nightly wanderings, Hamlet can yet hardly bring himself to believe the tale, although some suspicion of the crime has long been lurking in his mind.

And as the soul of Agamemnon, in visions of the night, calls for vengeance upon his slayers, so the dead majesty of Denmark bids his son avenge his " foul and most unnatural murder." Unlike Agamemnon, however, he does not demand the death of his wife. No son's hand shall commit that awful deed ; she shall be left to Heaven and to her own soul ; and it may be that here we find a reason for believing that although Gertrude had ceased to love her husband, she was innocent of his death.

His purpose achieved and Hamlet advised of the truth, the ghost vanishes with the dawning day, which sends all uneasy spirits back to their own abode ; nor does he again appear, either to aid the wavering counsels of his distracted son, or to triumph when his death has been avenged.

The ghost of Banquo may have been purely subjective, non-existent save in the alarmed conscience of Macbeth ; but the spirit of the Danish king is a necessary part of the machinery of the play. It is his office to reveal to Hamlet the tragic story of his father's murder and his uncle's guilt, and yet the prince does not put implicit faith in the ghost's story ; he will at least make assurance doubly sure by the device of the play, before executing righteous vengeance upon the guilty. A recent writer says that people in Shakespeare's time believed in ghosts because they saw them ; that we do not, because we see too many of them, and know that they are only hallucination or optical delusions ; that Hamlet sees the ghost because the story that he hears has already been suspected, and that the spectre's appearance to the others is to put us into Hamlet's frame of mind ; and he also adduces Hamlet's trick of the play as a proof that he did not wholly believe in the reality of the apparition. I do not think Shakespeare meant us to think so ; Hamlet doubts not the reality, but the character of the spectre. Is it his father, or " some goblin damned " who lures him to ruin by intensifying what may be the false, unworthy thoughts which he has suffered to take up their abode in his heart, and drawing him onward, plunge him headlong into death and hell ? That is the question which tries his very soul.

Ghosts are not common in Roman story. The Lar cares for family fortunes, but he does not appear in bodily guise; we are told that the spirit of Romulus manifested himself to a shepherd, and bade him tell the Romans that their vanished king had been taken up among the gods. The spirits of the dead manifested themselves often in visions of the night ; the soul of Julius Cæsar was thought to have been seen, ascending into heaven, but it was in the likeness of " a great star," " trailing clouds of glory " behind it, as it moved across the sky ; portents are many and various, but genuine ghosts are not.

On the night before the murder of Cæsar, which was to plunge the Roman world once more into war and misery, the story tells us that a fierce tempest raged over Rome, and, by the flashing lightning, the forms of men in white garments, "the sheeted dead" of Shakespeare, walked about the streets. "The graves did ope," and their tenants revisited the upper air as if to betoken the coming of misery and death.

Plutarch, describing the scene in the tent of Brutus, when years of bloodshed are soon to bring the day of Philippi, tells us that a spirit appeared to the republican leader as he pondered over his book, but he does not say that it was the ghost of the murdered Dictator; it was his evil genius. Sir Walter Scott, speaking of Plutarch's story, but with evident reminiscence of Shakespeare's drama, says that it was most natural that Brutus, on the eve of decisive battle, should have allowed his thoughts to revert to the past, and that he should realize the consequences of his own act; that doing so his imagination and his remorse would readily combine to present before him the vision of the man whom he had slain; that the spirit of Plutarch's story was a subjective one. That this, except that the historian does not speak of Cæsar, is the truth of the actual scene, I have no doubt; the evil spirit that Brutus thought he saw, was the projection of his excited brain, let us hope of his awakened conscience. Does Shakespeare also mean us to accept that theory? It may be so; and it is a wonderful touch of art that transforms the nameless "evil spirit" of history into the ghost of the murdered man.

Brutus is sitting in his tent at Sardis, alone with his book and his memory, albeit a page sleeps softly near at hand. He cries, —

> "How ill this taper burns! Ha! who comes here?
> I think it is the weakness of mine eyes
> That shapes this monstrous apparition.
> It comes upon me. Art thou anything?
> Art thou some god, some angel, or some devil,
> That mak'st my blood cold and my hair to stare?
> Speak to me, what thou art.
> *Ghost.* Thine evil spirit, Brutus.
> *Bru.* Why comest thou?
> *Ghost.* To tell thee thou shalt see me at Philippi!"

When he takes heart, the spirit vanishes. Was it Cæsar, or did
his conscience make him see in his evil genius the spirit of his
murdered friend? Or has the evil angel put on the shape and
garb of the dead?

Cæsar was so magnanimous in life that we can hardly fancy
him becoming after death the evil spirit of one he once had loved,
whom perhaps he loved and pitied still; and whatever Shakespeare
said, we may be permitted to believe that it was remorse and an
insight that came too late that made him see his victim in bodily
guise before him, and wrung from him later the despairing cry, —

> "Oh Julius Cæsar, thou art mighty yet !
> Thy spirit walks abroad."

*Annie Russell Wall.*

## AN INTERPRETATION OF BROWNING'S 'IXION.'

BROWNING has so seldom drawn from the great storehouse
of Greek legend for poetic themes that when he does do so his
handling of them is of peculiar interest. In his treatment of the
myth of Ixion he proves himself a true child of the Greeks, not that
he makes any slavish attempt to reproduce a Greek atmosphere
as it existed in the lifetime of Greek poetry, but he exercises that
prerogative which the Greek poets always claimed, of interpreting
a myth to suit their own ends.

It has become a sort of critical axiom to compare Browning's
'Ixion' with the 'Prometheus' of literature. This is one of those
catching analogies which lay hold upon the mind, and cannot be
shaken off again without considerable difficulty. Mr. Arthur
Symons first spoke of the resemblance; and almost every other
critic with the exception of Mr. Nettleship has dwelt mainly upon
that aspect of the poem which bears out the comparison. But
why, it might very well be asked, did Browning, if he intended to
make another Prometheus, choose Ixion for his theme? And the
answer is evident, because in the story of Ixion he found some

quality different from any which existed in the story of Prometheus, and which was especially suited to the end he had in view.

The kernel of the myth of Prometheus as developed by Æschylus is proud, unflinching suffering of punishment, inflicted, not by a god justly angry for sin against himself, but by a god sternly mindful of his own prerogatives, whose only right is might, and jealous of any interference in behalf of the race which he detested, — the race of man. Thus Prometheus stands out as a hero in Greek mythology, a mediator between man and the blind anger of a god of unconditional power; and Prometheus, with an equally blind belief in fate, accepts while he defies the punishment inflicted by Zeus. He tacitly acknowledges the right of Zeus to punish him, since he confesses his deeds to be sins, but nevertheless, he would do exactly the same thing over again.

> " By my choice, my choice
> I freely sinned — I will confess my sin —
> And helping mortals found mine own despair."

On the other hand, Ixion never appears in classic lore as a hero. He has been called the " Cain " of Greece, because he was the first, as Pindar says,[*] " to introduce to mortal men the murder of kin not unaccompanied by cunning." Zeus appears, however, to have shown more leniency to him for the crime of killing his father-in-law than he ever did to Prometheus, as he not only purified him from the murder, but invited him to a seat among the gods. But to quote Pindar again, " he found his prosperity too great to bear, when with infatuate mind he became enamoured of Hera. . . . Thus his conceit drave him to an act of enormous folly, but the man soon suffered his deserts, and received an exquisite torture." Ixion, then, in direct contrast to Prometheus, stands forth an embodiment of the most detestable of sins, perpetrated simply for personal ends. To depict such a man as this in an attitude of defiance, and yet to justify his defiance, is a far more difficult problem than to justify the already admired heroism of Prometheus. It is entirely characteristic of Browning that he should choose perhaps the most unprincipled character in the

* Second Pythian Ode.

whole range of Greek mythology as his hero. He is not content, like Emerson, with simply telling us that " in the mud and scum of things there alway, alway something sings;" his aim is ever to bring us face to face with reality, and to open our ears that we may hear for ourselves this universal song. In fine, Browning chose Ixion and not another, because he wanted above all things an unquestioned sinner; and the task he set himself was to show the use of sin and at the same time exonerate the sinner from the eternal consequences of his act.

So mystical is the language of the poem that it is extremely difficult to trace behind it the subtile reasoning. Mr. Nettleship has given by far the best exposition of the poem, though even he does not seize all its suggestiveness; and it is a realization of this fact which causes the present writer to rush in where angels may well fear to tread.

Ixion, the sinner, suffering eternal torment, questions the justice of such torment. The first very important conclusion to which he comes, and it is one entirely in accord with science, is that sin is an aberration of sense, merely the result of external conditions in which the soul of man has no active part. The soul simply dreams; but once fully awakened, it would free itself from this bondage of sense if it were allowed to do so. Ixion argues that it is Zeus that hath made him and not he himself, and if he has sinned it is through the bodily senses which Zeus has conferred upon him, and if he were the friendly and all-powerful god which he claimed himself to be and which Ixion believed he was, why did he allow these distractions of sense to lead him (Ixion) into sin which could only be expiated by eternal punishment? Without body there would have been nothing to obstruct his soul's rush upon the real; and with one touch of pitying power Zeus might have dispersed " this film-work, eye's and ear's." It is entirely the fault of Zeus that he had sinned; and having done so will eternal torture make him repent any more who has repented already? This is the old, old problem, that has taxed the brains of many a philosopher and the faith of many a theologian,— the reconcilement of the existence of evil with an omnipotent God. Then follows a comparison between the actions of Zeus, a god, and of Ixion, the human king; and Ixion declares could he have known all, as Zeus does, he would have warded off evil from his subjects, would have seen that they were trained aright from the first, — in fact, would not have allowed evil to exist, or failing this, could he have seen the heart of the criminals and realized how they repented he would have given them a chance to retrieve their past. Ixion now realizes that his human ideal is higher than that of Zeus. He had imagined him possessed of human qualities, and finds his qualities are less than human. What must be the inevitable result of arriving at such a conclusion? It means the dethronement of the god, and either a lapse into hopeless atheism or the recognition that the conception formed of the god was that of the human mind at an earlier stage of understanding. This conception becomes crystallized into an anthropomorphic god; but the mind of man goes onward on its way to higher heights, and lo! there comes a day when the god-ideal of the past is lower than the human ideal of the present. It is such a crisis as this that Ixion has arrived at, and his faith is equal to the strain. Since Zeus is man's own mind-made god, Ixion's tortures must be the natural consequences of his sin, and not the arbitrary punishment of a god; and what is Ixion's sin as Browning has interpreted the myth?

The sin is that of arrogance. Ixion, a mere man, strives to be on an equality with gods. In Lucian's dialogue between Hera and Zeus, the stress is laid upon the arrogance of Ixion. Jupiter declares that Ixion shall pay the " penalty not of his love — for that surely is not so dreadful a crime — but of his loud boasting." Browning raises the sin into a rarer atmosphere than that of the Greek or Latin. Zeus and Hera may be taken to represent the attributes of power and love as conceived by man in Divinity; and Ixion, symbolic of man, arrogantly supposes that he is capable of putting himself on an equality with Divinity by conceiving the entire nature of Divinity, that out of his finite mind he can construct the absolute god, and this is the sin, or better, the aberration of sense, which results in the crystallization of his former inadequate conceptions into an anthropomorphic god, and causes his own downfall. Ixion, now fully aroused to the fact that the god he has been defying is but his own miserable conception of God, realizes that the suffering caused by this conception of God is the very means through which man struggles toward higher ideals : through evil he is brought to a recognition of the good ; from his agony is bred the rainbow of hope, which ever shines above him glorified by the light from a Purity far beyond, all-unobstructed. Successive conceptions of God must sink; but man, however misled by them, must finally burst through the obstructions of sense, freeing his spirit to aspire forever toward the light.

'Ixion,' then, is not merely an argument against eternal punishment, nor a picture of heroic suffering, though he who will may draw these lessons from it, but it is a tremendous symbol of the spiritual development of man. Pure in its essence, the spirit learns through the obstructions of sense to yearn forever for higher attainment, and this constitutes the especial blessedness of man as contrasted with Zeus. He, like the Pythagorean Father of Number, is the conditioned one ; but man is privileged through all æons of time to break through conditions, and thus Ixion, triumphant, exclaims : —

> " Where light, where light is, aspiring
> Thither I rise, whilst thou — Zeus, keep the godship and sink."

*Helen A. Clarke.*

## RECENT BOOKS ON TENNYSON.*

THE most original in thought as well as the most exquisite in expression of recent criticisms upon Tennyson is the essay on 'Tennyson as Prophet' in Mr. Frederic W. H. Myers' just pub-

* Science and the Future Life, with Other Essays, by Frederic W. H. Myers. London and New York : Macmillan & Co. 1893. Tennyson and ' In Memoriam,' An Appreciation and a Study, by Joseph Jacobs. London : David Nutt. 1892. Essays on Lord Tennyson's ' Idylls of the King,' by Harold Littledale, M. A. London and New York : Macmillan & Co. 1893. Alfred Lord Tennyson, A Study of his Life and Work, by Arthur Waugh. London : William Heinemann. 1892.

lished volume of essays. Such a passage as the following is proof that the art of writing fine prose is not yet lost: —

"The true poet comes nearer to inspiration than any prophet to whom we can hope to listen now. Let his intuitions come to us dissolved in that fusion of thought and melody which makes the highest art we know: let flashes of a strange delight — 'like sparkles in the stone Aventurine' — reveal at once the beauty and the darkness of the meditations whence the song has sprung. Give us, if so it may be, the exaltation which lifts into a high community; the words which stir the pulse like passion, and wet the eyes like joy, and with the impalpable breath of an inward murmur can make a sudden glory in the deep of the heart. Give us — but who shall give it? or how in days like these shall not the oracles be dumb?"

The first essay in the volume 'Science and the Future Life' gives the keynote upon which Mr. Myers frames all his criticism. His is a mind that finds in the great discoveries of science the means of the total disillusionment of the spiritual aspects of life, unless science itself can apply the remedy; and science, he thinks, can apply the remedy, and is even now going about its merciful errand. In fine, he places his hope in the investigations of psychological science, and looks for the absolute proof at no distant date of the existence of disembodied spirits. This spiritualistic attitude will no doubt prejudice many readers against him at the outset; but Mr. Myers is a man of such wide culture, and his attitude is so entirely that of an investigator only too conscious of the enormous difficulties in the way of success, that all he says upon the subject should be listened to with respect though agreement may not be possible.

Whether the certainty of spiritual existence is to prove the salvation of France, as Mr. Myers declares in his fine essay on the 'Disenchantment of France,' is, to say the least, doubtful. We have heard from those who know, of Protestant revivals in the byways of France; and it is quite possible that a revived Christianity might prove a stronger element in the salvation of France than any of the certainties which psychologic science may have to offer, to say nothing of the new social ideals which are fast honey-combing

France. In the course of tracing Tennyson's spiritual development in his poetry, Mr. Myers finds in Tennyson many hints of an agreement with his doctrines. He is one of the first, as far as we know, to give proper prominence to that magnificent passage in 'Sea Dreams' where the wife describes her dream. In this, he holds, the first word of Tennyson's true message is presented; its import is that "the truth of things is good," that all good and all evil conform to an underlying principle of harmony. He goes on to point out how Tennyson draws from "the standing mystery of a child's birth the conception of a double, a synchronous evolution" of the spirit as well as of the body; how he describes a state of ecstasy, which he had himself experienced; how he leans to a belief that soul may communicate with soul, — from all of which he concludes that "Tennyson is the prophet simply of a Spiritual Universe : the proclaimer of man's spirit as part and parcel of that Universe, and indestructible as the very root of things." But he does not accept as final the intuitions of the Poet-Seer; the final answer "must depend on the discoveries of science herself."

In the essay on 'Modern Poets and Cosmic Law,' keen comparisons are made between the attitude toward the Unseen of such poets as Swinburne and Morris with that of Tennyson. It seems strange that in this essay he does not dwell more upon Browning, who is, if anything, a stancher believer in the spiritual universe than Tennyson. The reason for his great partiality for Tennyson as a prophet is to be sought in the fact that Browning never passed through the phase of disillusionment; an optimist without visions, he needs no extra-mundane proof that the "truth of things is good," while Tennyson if it were not for occasional visions (or subjective illuminations) would be a melancholy pessimist. He stands, in fact, if not for the whole tendency of his age, for at least a marked characteristic of it, — for the disillusioned who have yet found hope, — and with this class Mr. Myers' mind vibrates in sympathy.

Of the other two essays in the volume, 'Charles Darwin and Agnosticism,' and 'Leopold, Duke of Albany' (a memorial of the late duke), the first is especially worth reading.

The 'Appreciation' of Tennyson by Mr. Joseph Jacobs is

marked by that careful balancing of praise and blame which should impress the reader with the extreme judiciousness of the critic, and gain his immediate assent, but which too .often leaves in his mind only a lively recollection of the clever dialectic of the critic at the expense of his views upon the qualities of the poet.   The praise and the blame are each so negatived that any abiding force which the criticism might otherwise have is dissipated, and the poet emerges from the Aslaksen-like cloud of " discreet moderation " more brilliant than ever.

But with all his discretion, there are to be discerned here and there signs of critical bias in Mr. Jacobs.   The comparison of Tennyson with Pope, on the ground that they each represent the perfection of artistic workmanship of their respective ages, is founded on a resemblance totally external.   Tennyson has broadened and deepened the harmonies of poetry; to the clear vision of the Romanticist he has added a peculiar sensibility to form, and may be said to have created a Classicism of Romanticism ; but the genius of Pope was not directed to the enlargement of poetical boundaries.   His polish has the imitative refinement of a backward-looking mind.   And why should Tennyson be criticised for not writing an epic in the ' Idylls of the King,' when he does not claim them to be an epic ?   If an epic must be, as Mr. Jacobs says, "the presentation of a national myth regarded as sacred," then the ' Idylls of the King ' are certainly not epical ; but we should hardly think ' Paradise Lost ' was, on this definition, though Mr. Jacobs cites it as answering to the description.   The heroes of ' Paradise Lost ' could scarcely be called national heroes.   With a preconceived notion of what an epic must be, and a conviction that Tennyson was attempting an epic in the ' Idylls of the King,' Mr. Jacobs' appreciation of them is decidedly lacking in sympathy. What if Tennyson did conceive the character of Guinevere in the spirit of a nineteenth-century gentleman ?   She is not less interesting as a literary creation than if he had conceived her in the spirit of a twelfth-century knight.   In fact, it is just what Tennyson has put of himself and his own age into the ' Idylls of the King ' that makes their great interest.   He has taken the ancient ideal of

chivalry and its subsequent failure as a symbol of life's development; and with the pictures of Arthur's court the poet has interwoven much beautiful and characteristic philosophy. This may
not square with Mr. Jacobs' preconceptions, but the result is a
very beautiful series of poems. Where Mr. Myers finds Tennyson
a prophet Mr. Jacobs finds that " it cannot be said of Tennyson
that he has been a great spiritual force in the national development
of the last half century." Probably he is the resultant rather than
the leader of the rich thought of the century; but there is this to
be said in favor of Mr. Myers' opinion, he traces a development in
Tennyson's philosophy of which ' In Memoriam ' is only the first
step, while Mr. Jacobs, like many others, seems to consider ' In
Memoriam ' the poet's complete confession of faith. There is,
however, something like a burst of appreciative enthusiasm near
the close of the essay, where in speaking of Tennyson's later works
he declares : —

" It is in the Tennyson of these later days that we recognize the
Master — the great poet-soul looming behind the poem, and greater
than it."

Mr. Harold Littledale's essays on the ' Idylls of the King ' form
a very useful as well as entertaining volume. He gives an account
of the Arthurian Legends taken from Malory's ' Morte Darthur,'
upon which Tennyson founded his Idylls, and points out the
changes made by Tennyson. At the end of each chapter are
instructive notes on the text; and the critical remarks scattered
throughout are thoughtful and suggestive. The book justifies its
claim to be a summary of information for the general reader not
easily accessible at first hand, while the earnest student will find it
of real value as a guide-post to further studies.

Very readable is Mr. Arthur Waugh's study of Tennyson's life
and work. In his pages one may follow the steps in the development of the great poet's genius, from prize-poem days, when the
Cambridge Board of Examiners waived their time-honored predilections in favor of the heroic couplet and awarded the prize to
' Timbuctoo,' blank verse and all, to the full noontide of his powers,
which were scarcely dimmed at the time of his death. There one

may find recorded many varying shades of criticism, from the sorrow of Fitzgerald that Tennyson should spend his energies upon such slight stuff as ' The Princess' to the equally undiscriminating eulogiums of those who never see a flaw. Mr. Waugh himself has too much the attitude of a disciple to be entirely reliable as a critic. His decision that ' Harold ' is a " play as rich in character as in action " will hardly be borne out by the facts ; on the other hand, what he has to say of the ' Idylls of the King ' is in the main good. All through will be found agreement with popularly received opinions as to the poet's master-pieces, and a vein of special pleading where opinion says he failed; for example, Mr. Waugh softens the failure of ' Queen Mary ' on the plea that " History rarely lends itself to Drama. Had he to stand or fall by the reputation of ' Richard II.' or ' Henry VIII.,' Shakespeare himself would fare little better than Tennyson with ' Queen Mary.' " We should say it depended very largely on the period of history chosen, and the way in which it is managéd, whether it lends itself to drama or not. We think Shakespeare might venture his reputation on ' Julius Cæsar,' or the ' First and Second Henries,' or ' King John,' or even 'Richard II.' It is such lapses as these which discount the value of the book as a critical study of Tennyson's work.

*C.*

---

## BOOK INKLINGS.

—— It is quite true, as Mr. Wilder says in a prefatory note to his ' Life of Shakespeare,' that " no brief and accurate biography of Shakespeare is now before the public." Even the short lives prefixed to most editions of the complete works of William Shakespeare are unsatisfactory, either through the addition of flattering probabilities or the defect of some ascertained facts of legal or contemporary record, perhaps not in themselves important, and yet not to be omitted from the biography of a man concerning whom every genuine stray scrap of fact attracts interest.

We were once asked what biography would be best prefixed to an eclectic *édition de luxe* of Shakespeare in which the Cambridge Text, the fullest glossary, and the Boydell Illustrations were set off

by hand-made paper, vellum binding, and a new type cut for this
edition.* Our advice was against the employment of any of the
usual "lives" if it were not feasible to reprint the only authoritative biography, cut off from the cumbersome notes upon notes in
the two thick volumes in folio in which it is embedded, — that of
Halliwell-Phillipps. The edition was issued, accordingly, without
the customary more or less fanciful 'Life of the Poet.' Mr. Wilder
has now compiled a trustworthy 'Life' based upon the authoritative biography by Halliwell-Phillipps. He has released a clear and
continuous narrative from its perplexing, sometimes exasperating,
tangle of notes, illustrations, qualifying statements, and added ves-
tiges of information, providing the public thus with a biographical
manual that may be depended upon and commended. It is a pity
that its value is not enhanced by a careful Index. We notice, also,
in glancing through this serviceable little book that its citations of
the lines bearing on Shakespeare from 'The Returne from Parnassus' has not been enriched by the additional allusions from, or by
any mention of, the two preceding parts of the trilogy, — 'The
Pilgrimage to Parnassus,' first discovered by the Rev. W. D.
Macray among the Hearne manuscripts in the Bodleïan Library,
and printed by him in the winter of 1886. This omission comes
of following Halliwell-Phillipps too exclusively. The antiquarian
himself possessed the rare manuscript of 'The Returne,' printed
copies of which were well known, but in common with the rest of
the world he did not know that the two preceding parts of 'The
Pilgrimage' were still extant until Macray discovered and published them. It must be remembered that the strongest authority
does not stay best in all respects for any length of time, and must
be brought up to date with such discoveries as Mr. Macray's or
such investigations as Mr. F. G. Fleay is continuously making. It
happens that these additional allusions are peculiarly interesting,
intimating as they do that Shakespeare was the "fad" with the man
about town in 1600, but that he had not yet gained the unqualified
approval of the critics; that is, of the scholars who had their own
classic preconceptions of literary form, and who considered Shakespeare's popularity to be with a special class, and not of a sort to
be desired. As it may interest some of our readers to know, the
dialogue of Gullio with Ingenioso, who draws him out for the
benefit of Studioso, Philomusus, and Luxurio, thus witnesses: —

"*Ingenioso.* Nowe, gentlemen, youe may laughe if you will,
for here comes a Gull. . . . (We shall have nothinge but pure

Shakspeare and shreds of poetrie that he hath gathered at the theators!)

"*Gullio.* Pardon mee, moy mittressa, ast am a gentleman, the moone in comparison of thy bright hue a meere slutt, Anthonie's Cleopatra a blacke browde milkmaide, Hellen a dowdie.

"*Ingen.* (Marke, Romeo and Juliet! O monstrous theft!) . . . Sweete Mr. Shakspeare! . . . Faith, gentleman! youre reading is wonderfull in our English poetts! . . .

"*Gull.* But stay! . . . I had almoste forgotten the chiefe pointe. I cal'd thee out for New Year's day approcheth, and wheras other gallants bestowe jewells upon there mistresses . . . I will bestowe upon them the precious stons of my witt . . .; therefore, I will have thee, Ingenioso, to make them, and when thou hast done I will peruse, pollish, and correcte them.

"*Ingen.* . . . What vayne woulde it please you to have them in?

"*Gull.* Not in a vaine veine (prettie, i' faith!) : make mee them in two or three divers vayns, in Chaucer's, Gower's, and Spencer's and Mr. Shakspeare's. Marry, I thinke I shall entertaine those verses which run like these, — ' Even as the sunn with purple coloured face Had tane his laste leave on the Weeping morne,' — O, sweet Mr. Shakspeare! I'll have his picture in my study at the Courte."

Whereupon, we may be sure, such conceit of superiority and mirth arose in the minds of Gullio's hearers as is wont to arise now in the minds of certain Shakespearians over the foolish enthusiasm of a Browning lover. Times change, indeed, but not all of us change with them. Some of us will still be a little blunt of perception in matters of literary appreciation only, of course. It may be well to add to our commendation of Mr. Wilder's excellent and needed work that the publisher has given it clear type and a plain, durable cloth binding, and put it at a price ($1.00) which should insure its entrance on many public and private book-shelves. ('The Life of Shakespeare,' by Daniel W. Wilder. Boston : Little, Brown, & Co. 1893.)

—— THE account of the English Religious Drama which has come to the public this autumn from the hand of Katharine Lee Bates of Wellesley College is more than a useful manual, much as that is to the student, when it compacts in one volume, as this does, an amount of information not elsewhere to be found so conveniently. It adds to utility the grace and allurement to knowledge of a fluent and picturesque style. Within its scope is gathered such an outline of Latin passion-plays and saint-plays, miracle-plays and moralities, together with well-selected quotations from them, as makes the reader catch a glimpse of their simple-minded audience and of the life of the time, and reflects light, also, upon the scarcely less simple-minded makers of these early plays and on the dramatic value rightly to be assigned to them in the critical history of literary art.

It is these qualities which make this book interesting to read as well as good for reference, for which latter purpose its value is augmented by an appendix giving titles of reference-books on the subject, and classified lists of extant English miracle-plays and moralities. ('The English Religious Drama,' by Katharine Lee Bates. New York and London : Macmillan & Co. 1893. $1.50.)

—— OF special interest to the student of literature are the following volumes, published this autumn by Ginn & Co., — 'The Beginnings of the English Romantic Movement,' by William Lyon Phelps, Instructor in English Literature at Yale University, which confines its investigation to the period, 1725–1765, germinal of English romanticism, and discusses, with references and illustrations, the various causes that brought about the transition of taste from classicism to romanticism; 'The Classic Myths in English Literature,' edited by Charles Mills Gayley, Professor of Literature in the University of California; and 'A Plot-Book of Some Elizabethan Plays,' by George Pierce Baker, Instructor in English in Harvard University, giving the sources of plots of plays by Greene, Peele, Marlowe, Beaumont and Fletcher and others. The material for this book existing, for the most part, only in rare and costly editions, or unique pamphlets, the work promises to be of uncommon value. 'A First Book in Old English'— by Albert S. Cook, Professor of the English Language and Literature in Yale University, and author of 'Cook's Sievers' Grammar of Old English, The Phonological Investigation of Old English'— is published this autumn by the same firm. This book is intended to be at once simple and scientific. It will contain an outline of grammar, selections for reading, notes, and a glossary, — in a single volume all that the beginner needs. The grammatical sketch will include only essentials, but under all the main heads,— phonology, inflection, word-formation, syntax, and prosody. The selections will be as easy and interesting as practicable, and the texts, with the exception of the poetry, will be normalized carefully to an Early West Saxon basis. The notes will consist of grammatical references and brief explanations, and the glossary will be wrought out with care. The elementary yet comprehensive character of the book will be a recommendation to those who have found existing works on the subject too difficult or too superficial.

—— THE little book of ' Old World Lyrics ' and its twin in size and daintiness, ' Songs of Adieu,' are rare issues in contents and form, made up as they are of choice bits of old-world poesy set off in odd type and binding irresistible to the holiday purse, and yet considerate of the many demands upon it, for the price of each is $1.00 only. (The Bibelot Series. Portland : Thos. B. Mosher.)

—— THE pleasure the writer of ' The Trial of Sir John Falstaff' has taken in the Fat Knight will not increase in any way, we believe, the pleasure of any one else therein. The few earlier pages of the book, taken up with various opinions of Falstaff, are mainly repetitions of passages more conveniently found, for example, in Dr. Rolfe's edition of the plays, which is, in fact, a Variorum of the best character-criticism. The many remaining pages — made up of diluted Shakespeare and irrelevant slang stirred into a very tedious yarn of a descendant of Sir Robert Shallow whose death by a cyclone in Kansas is supposed to have put the world in possession of a manuscript describing a free and easy trial of Falstaff by Justices Shallow and Silence — constitute somewhat more of an affront than a tribute to Shakespeare's own temperate and artistic use of the " trunk of humors " whom he, like Prince Hal, did only for "a while uphold." ('The Trial of Sir John Falstaff,' by A. M. F. Randolph. New York and London : G. P. Putnam's Sons. 1893.)

# NOTES AND NEWS.

HAMLIN GARLAND wields a vigorous pen in defence of the " Literary West " in the October *Forum*. He is quite right in saying that no one city should lay claim in this great land to be the sole purveyor of taste in literary matters ; but he is unnecessarily fierce in his strictures on culture, and the ordinary helps to knowledge in the way of libraries and colleges. The latter are, too often, it is true, hot beds of conservatism, and may hamper more than aid the genius ; but what great poet ever lacked a library? It is all very well to say, " Go like Shakespeare to your fellow-beings, observe them, and then write ;" but if ever a writer

owed a debt to books, that writer was Shakespeare, with hardly
a character for which he did not get a hint, and sometimes much
more than a hint, in some old history, play, or chronicle, with
such various and special knowledge freighting every page that no
human being could have known it except at second-hand.   His
art resulted from his omnivorous digestion of other people's
knowledge combined with keen observation of his neighbors.
If the "Literary West" would ape Shakespeare, let it not in its
studies from life forget that the life of the past — without which
the full portent of the life of the present may not be grasped — is
to be found only in books, — histories, plays, and poems, romances,
and even philosophies.

——— THE "pound of flesh" story, which Shakespeare got perhaps from the Italian and used in his 'Merchant of Venice,' seems
to have been almost as popular a folk-tale as the "I love thee as
well as salt" story apotheosized in 'Lear.'  Our readers will
remember a Persian version of the Shylock story which we gave in
'Notes and News' of January, 1890, and they may be interested
in the following German variant called 'The Judgment of Schem-
jaka,' taken from the old German of the Villingen State paper in
Freiburg University and given in the *Zeitschrift für Vergleichende
Litteratur Geschichte.*   The Villingen version is derived from
'Der Meistergesang' of 1493.  We avail ourselves of the translation of *The Literary Digest:* —

"A poor fellow was once reduced to such absolute poverty
that he knew not how he should, could, or might pay his way,
either in body or in soul.  He took counsel with himself as to
what were best to be done, and then went to a Jew and prayed
him to make him a loan, which he promised to refund after a
reasonably short time.  The Jew said: 'Good friend, thou art
welcome' (that is, 'here comes the Devil').  'You know very
well, if you want to borrow, that we Jews never lend without
security.'  The poor fellow had no security, and could offer
nothing but his honor, his piety, and his faith.  The Jew said:
'I don't want that sort of security, but I will lend you forty
gulden on the security of one pound of fat from your body, to be
cut out by me, if you fail to make repayment at the appointed

time.' The poor fellow agreed, and promised to abide by the terms of the contract. The day at length arrived, but he was not ready, and the Jew cited him to appear before the Court. The poor, good fellow was troubled, and thought: there is no denying the Jew's claims. So, in the morning, he loaded up a cord of wood, and went to the city to plead his case in Court. On entering the city he drove over a young child. The child's father came out, cursed and swore. ' May the Devil take you! ' he said. ' Thou hast killed my child, my flesh, my blood ; thou must make the loss good or die according to the law.' ' My dear sir,' said the poor man, ' I am even now on my way to the Court, and was thinking of what answer I should give, and being troubled, I drove along without looking where I was going. I pray thee let me go and thou shall have justice.' So the father of the child went with him to the Court and demanded justice ; and the poor fellow was at a loss how he should rightly answer the demands of the Jew and of the father. When the Judge saw the poor fellow he took very little notice of him, as often happens ; he had little to ask of him, so let him sit still. The poor fellow, finding that no notice was taken of him, left the Court, went out, and mounted a flight of steps, and before there was any inquiry after him, he fell asleep. While he was sleeping, he rolled over the side of the steps and fell to the ground. In falling, he struck an old man and killed him. The old man's son came out, and said: ' Now, may the Devil take thee ! ' ' Thou shalt make good the loss of my father, according to the law.' So he took the poor fellow back again to the Court, and lodged his complaint. By this time the Judge had already forgotten all about the two previous complaints; but when this last charge was filed he proceeded to pass judgment on all three charges. And now think what the judgment was in the three cases, all of which were thought worthy of death! The Judge decided on behalf of the Jew that he was entitled to cut a pound of fat from the poor fellow, but if he cut either more or less he should be prosecuted. Rather than do that, the Jew withdrew his complaint and paid the costs. The judgment in respect of the child was given on the same principle of justice: the father was ordered to take the accused to his wife and give him an opportunity of repairing the loss he had occasioned. The result must, of course, be left to Providence; but the bereaved father was entitled to the effort as a matter of law and justice. Rather than agree to this form of restitution, he, also, withdrew his complaint. In the third case, the Court gave judgment as follows : The accused must go and sit down under the steps, on the spot where the old man was killed, and the son may mount the steps and fall down upon him. Whether he killed him or not, was in the hands of Providence; but he was entitled to the opportunity in law and justice. Rather than make the jump, he, too, withdrew his claim; and so the poor fellow got off on all three charges, and left the Court without incurring the death-penalty."

—— On the question, roused recently by M. Zola, " Should Criticism be signed or unsigned ? " there has been no fairer summing up of the arguments on both sides than that excellent and well-tempered journal, *The Dial* of Chicago, gives in its issue of November 1. This judicious balance of reasons by the Editor of *The Dial* does not proceed, however, from neutrality of opinion ; and when Mr. Browne shows how the scales incline toward signed criticism his conclusion carries the greater weight because of its deliberation. The usual argument for anonymity as the most expedient because it permits the authority of a journal to have sway is met thus : —

" The criticism which is published in a review of high character and recognized authority does receive added weight from that very fact, if signed no less than if unsigned. We do not believe that the addition of a signature detracts from the authority of the criticism, and we are sure that it adds to the reader's confidence in the sincerity of the writer. If the name of the writer is well-known, his opinion comes with the added authority of the review in which it appears ; if the name is not well-known, the importance to be attached to the opinion will be measured, not by the obscurity of the writer, but by the confidence which the editorial conduct of the review inspires. In a word, when critical articles are signed, there is at least no loss of weight, and there may be a distinct increment of gain."

" If the name is not well-known," there is, apparently, no distinction possible for the writer, although he were a Stendhal in bud, except that which the " authority " of the organ would lend him to cloak the indecorum of his necessary first appearances. This is a curious witness to the prevailing disrespect for the reading public in which, it seems, even the Editor of *The Dial* shares, in some degree, with his brothers of the autocratic class.

Yet it ought to be evident to any attentive reader, from the review itself, that its writer is fair or competent or penetrating or thorough, or if, perchance, he show peculiar qualifications for analyzing and grasping his subject; and the reading public ought to know enough to perceive such qualities when it gets them, and to understand perfectly well that a careless or unfair or even an incompetent review may flow from a celebrated pen, and its opposite, marked by good critical traits, issue from a hand unknown.

We believe the public is not altogether a fool, although so often fooled to the top of its bent; and the publisher, and the author criticised too, are sure to gather opinions certified to by the true authority of merit instead of name. The review's "the thing," not the signature, or the organ. The public or the editor should care for nothing in a review but competence; and all concerned, including its writer, should wish that its author, known or unknown, be named.

—— THE Contributors' Club is rarely least, though last in *The Atlantic*, because it deals with matters of literary and artistic perception more often than is the wont of periodicals in general. In the November number, the urban quality, cleverness, is lightly arraigned, as the *Boston Transcript* trenchantly remarks, "in a manner itself bordering dangerously upon the clever."

Who has not felt the emptiness of metropolitan social sparkle, the tiresomeness of brilliancy without earnestness or wisdom in conversation and in literature, against which the "Contributor" proposes a co-operative tilt of the "plodding fellows"? We felt "called" to the crusade at once, but were deterred by a suspicious mixing up of friend with foe which, added to the "manner itself bordering dangerously upon the clever," made us fear that our Peter the Hermit was himself little better than the enemy. In short, we felt the necessity of extricating a true believer or so, in the very act of visiting the Holy Place with homage, from being confused with the Turks and Infidels on whom we were righteously stirred to fire. We insist, therefore, on making a needed discrimination or two. The cleverness that requires a crusade to correct it is that, as the "Contributor" declares, which is destitute of purpose and barren of thought, however it sparkle and jingle verbally. Neither George

Meredith's, Browning's, nor Ibsen's cleverness, fruit of complex civilization as it is, has the baneful, bubbly glitter of the merely metropolitan "cleverness" from whose specious wit and spurious thought the world and its progress suffers. The traits to be rightly charged against these authors are clearly not a lack of either thought, insight, or seriousness. Yet the "Contributor" ingeniously smuggles these three names into his indictment! It is wily, but, as we said, suspicious.

—— POLISHED poetic workmanship distinguishes Mr. Francis Howard Williams's lines on 'An Ionian Frieze' in the last *Atlantic*. It is hard to choose one bit more perfectly elaborated than another, yet there is a peculiar happiness of phrase in this : —

> "Her carmine lips wed to a silver flute,
> As though their budding beauty to transmute
> To music dying off along the air."

## LONDON LITERARIA.

IF "daintiness" in books is a thing to be desired, then are Messrs. J. M. Dent & Co. to be congratulated on the success they have achieved in this direction, the works of Maria Edgeworth, Fielding, Jane Austen, and the Brontés being issued in such dainty and "taking" volumes that they are a positive delight to look upon, as well as joy to read; while the illustrations are, as a rule, of quite exceptional merit. It might not be inappropriate to suggest to Messrs. Dent that there is still one unique genius apparently forgotten amid the present resuscitation of eighteenth-century writers, and who, when the present century was but young, issued a complete edition of his works in eight volumes octavo : I refer to Henry Mackenzie, the "Man of Feeling." This work, together with 'The Man of the World,' 'Julia de Roubigne,' and the tales from the *Mirror* and *Lounger*, well deserve to be enshrined in the clear type of these charming volumes, — for however "out of fashion" their old-world tone may now be, they are indisputably among those writings fitly named "of genius."

I learn from the *Bookman* that Mr. Edmund Gosse has in preparation the 'Letters of Thomas Lovell Beddoes.' This will assuredly be a work of absorbing interest to all lovers of literature, for the author of 'Death's Jest Book' had a wide circle of friends and admirers. It seems that the Beddoes papers were at one time handed to Mr. Robert Browning, — who was a very hearty admirer of his poetry. On being opened by Mr. Browning, in the presence of Mr. Gosse, there was found among them the painful particulars of Beddoes's suicide, and this appeared to render Browning unwilling to go on with the work; which was thereupon taken up by Mr. Gosse, who has issued the poems, and will now complete his task by the publication of the prose.

Messrs. Elkin Matthews and Lane will shortly publish a collection of poems by Mr. Grant Allen, the larger portion of which have been as yet unpublished, many of them being of comparatively early date. The volume is to be called ' The Lower Slopes : Reminiscences of Excursions round the Base of Helicon, undertaken for the most part in Early Manhood.' The longest poem is, for the most part, of a philosophical cast, and is entitled, ' On Magdalen Tower.' Other of the verses are political and revolutionary in character, while some of the shorter lyrics deal with social questions "from a somewhat advanced standpoint." Another work shortly to be issued by the same publishers are three plays by Mr. Oscar Wilde, — who, by the bye, is " stated " to be writing a new book of maxims, to be entitled ' Oscariana ' ! If every day " begins with a new thought, or fresh idea " to Oscar, — as he says it should do, — a truly wonderful ' Oscariana ' should be the issue. We shall see !

Another work of much interest to be issued by Messrs. Matthews and Lane is a series of papers dealing principally with fiction, and collected by Mr. W. P. James. The book will be called after the opening paper, ' Romantic Professions;' but the volume will be of wide scope, as the following chapters will indicate : ' The Nemesis of Sentimentalism,' ' Romance and Youth,' ' On the Naming of Novels,' ' Names in Novels,' ' The Historical Novel,' ' The Poet as Historian,' and ' The Great Work.'

Mr. Heinemann is preparing for publication, under the title of 'A Friend of the Queen,' the correspondence between Marie Antoinette and Count Axel Fersen. The story of the life of the disguised coachman of the ill-fated queen is both romantic and exciting, and this correspondence will doubtless prove of exceptional interest. The same publisher also announces a translation of M. R. Waliszewski's book, 'The Romance of an Empress, Catherine II. of Russia.' The work is founded upon unpublished documents in the State archives, and upon the memoirs and correspondence of the Empress, and will be of special value to students of European history.

*William G. Kingsland.*

LONDON, ENGLAND, October, 1893.

## SOCIETIES.

**The Browning Society of the New Century Club** of Philadelphia adopts the following programme for the season of 1893–94, based upon a comparative study of American and English writers. It has been the effort of the Committee to bring into juxtaposition writers who, either in motive, manner, or form, or in all of these, have characteristics in common.

### EMERSON-CLOUGH.

FIRST GENERAL MEETING, Nov. 9, 1893.

READINGS: 'The World-Soul,' — Emerson. Selection from Canto III.: 'The Bothie of Tober-na-Vuolich,' — Clough. 'Mithridates,' 'Uriel,' — Emerson.

PAPER: The Transcendental Element in the Emersonian Philosophy, — Prof. Henry N. Hoxie.

DEBATE: Does the Philosophic Temperament consist with the highest Poetic Achievement? Affirmative, Dr. Daniel G. Brinton. Negative, Miss Agnes Repplier.

FIRST STUDY MEETING, Nov. 22, 1893.

READINGS: 'Qua Cursum Ventus,' 'Duty,' — Clough. Selection from 'May Day,' — Emerson. 'Dipsychus' (Part I., Scene 2, and Part II., Scenes 3 and 5), — Clough. 'The Initial Love,' — Emerson.

DISCUSSION: On the Metaphysical Significance of 'Dipsychus' and 'The World-Soul.' Question stated by Mr. Francis Howard Williams.

## LOWELL-ARNOLD.

### Second General Meeting, Dec. 14, 1893.

Readings : ' Harvard Commemoration Ode,' — Lowell. ' Thyrsis,' — Matthew Arnold.

Paper : The Interdependence of the Poetic and Critical Faculties, — Miss Louise Stockton.

Debate : The Commemoration Ode has been held to be the greatest poem written by an American. Can this claim be sustained? Affirmative, Miss Anna Robertson Brown. Negative, Prof. H. H. Hay.

### Second Study Meeting, Dec. 28, 1893.

Readings : ' The Strayed Reveller,' — Matthew Arnold. ' Rhœcus,' — Lowell. ' Dover Beach,' — Matthew Arnold. Selection from ' The Vision of Sir Launfal,' — Lowell.

Discussion : On Poetry as a "Criticism of Life." Question stated by Mr. Harrison S. Morris.

## POE-COLERIDGE.

### Third General Meeting, Jan. 11, 1894.

Readings : ' Lenore,' ' Ulalume,' ' Annabel Lee.' — Poe. ' Christabel.' Selection from Part II., — Coleridge. ' To Helen,' ' The Bells ' (two stanzas), — Poe.

Paper : The Poetry of the Supernatural as exemplified in Coleridge and Poe, — Miss Mary M. Cohen.

Debate : Have Poe and Coleridge made a Legitimate Use of Sound as an Artistic Device ? Affirmative, Mrs. Seth B. Stitt. Negative, Miss Harriet Boyer.

### Third Study Meeting, Jan. 25, 1894.

Readings : ' Kubla Khan,' Coleridge. Selection from ' Tamerlane,' Poe. Selection from ' The Ancient Mariner,' — Coleridge. ' The Raven,' — Poe.

Discussion : On the Symbolism of the Raven and the Albatross. Question stated by Dr. Edward Brooks.

## HAWTHORNE-RUSKIN.

### Fourth General Meeting, Feb. 8, 1894.

Readings : Selection from ' The Dolliver Romance,' — Hawthorne. Selection from Lecture II., ' The Ethics of the Dust,' — Ruskin. Selection from ' Our Old Home,' — Hawthorne.

Paper: Prose Poets as Stylists, — Mr. Charles Leonard Moore.

Debate : Should the term *Poetry* be used to cover Compositions in Prose Form ? Affirmative, Miss Alice Groff. Negative, Mr. Harrison S. Morris.

FOURTH STUDY MEETING, Feb. 21, 1894.

READINGS : Selection from 'The Stones of Venice,' — Ruskin. 'The Scarlet Letter' (Chapter 12th), — Hawthorne. Selection from 'Queen's Gardens' ('Sesame and Lilies '), — Ruskin. 'David Swan ' (from 'Twice-told Tales '), — Hawthorne.

DISCUSSION : On the Natural and Acquired Styles of Hawthorne and Ruskin. Question stated by Miss Elizabeth Carpenter.

## LANIER-WATSON.

FIFTH GENERAL MEETING, March 8, 1894.

READINGS : Selection from 'Sunrise,' — Sidney Lanier. 'Lachrymæ Musarum,' — William Watson. 'Clover,' — Sidney Lanier.

PAPER : Present Poetic Conditions in America and England, — Prof. Felix E. Schelling.

DEBATE : Can a Science of Verse be based upon the Musical Notation? Affirmative, Mrs. Edward Wetherill. Negative, Miss Laura H. Earle.

FIFTH STUDY MEETING, March 22, 1894.

READINGS : 'The Lute Player,' Dedication to 'The Dream of Man,' — William Watson. 'The Stirrup Cup,' 'A Ballad of Trees and the Master,'— Sidney Lanier. Selection from 'Wordsworth's Grave,' William Watson. Selection from 'The Marshes of Glynn,' — Sidney Lanier.

DISCUSSION : On the Enduring Elements in the Work of Lanier and Watson. Question stated by Prof. Henry Willis.

## WHITMAN-BROWNING.

SIXTH GENERAL MEETING, April 12, 1894.

READINGS : Sixth section of the 'Song of Myself,' — Whitman. 'My Last Duchess,' — Browning. 'Old Salt Kossabone,' — Whitman.

PAPER : The Rebellion against Fixed Forms in Modern English Poetry, — Miss Constance Mackenzie.

DEBATE : Does the Presence of Rhythm justify the Absence of Metre in Verse-forms? Affirmative, Miss Harriet T. Babb. Negative, Prof. D. Batchellor.

SIXTH STUDY MEETING, April 26, 1894.

READINGS : 'James Lee's Wife ' (I., III., V.), — Browning. 'With husky-haughty lips, O Sea !' 'A Farm Picture,' — Whitman. Selection from ' By the Fireside,' — Browning. 'Spirit that form'd this Scene,' 'A Clear Midnight,' —Whitman.

DISCUSSION : On Picturesqueness *versus* Thought as the qualification for Poetry. Question stated by Hon. Robert N. Willson.

*F. H. W.*

CPSIA information can be obtained at www.ICGtesting.com
Printed in the USA
BVOW02s1035260416

445642BV00028B/401/P